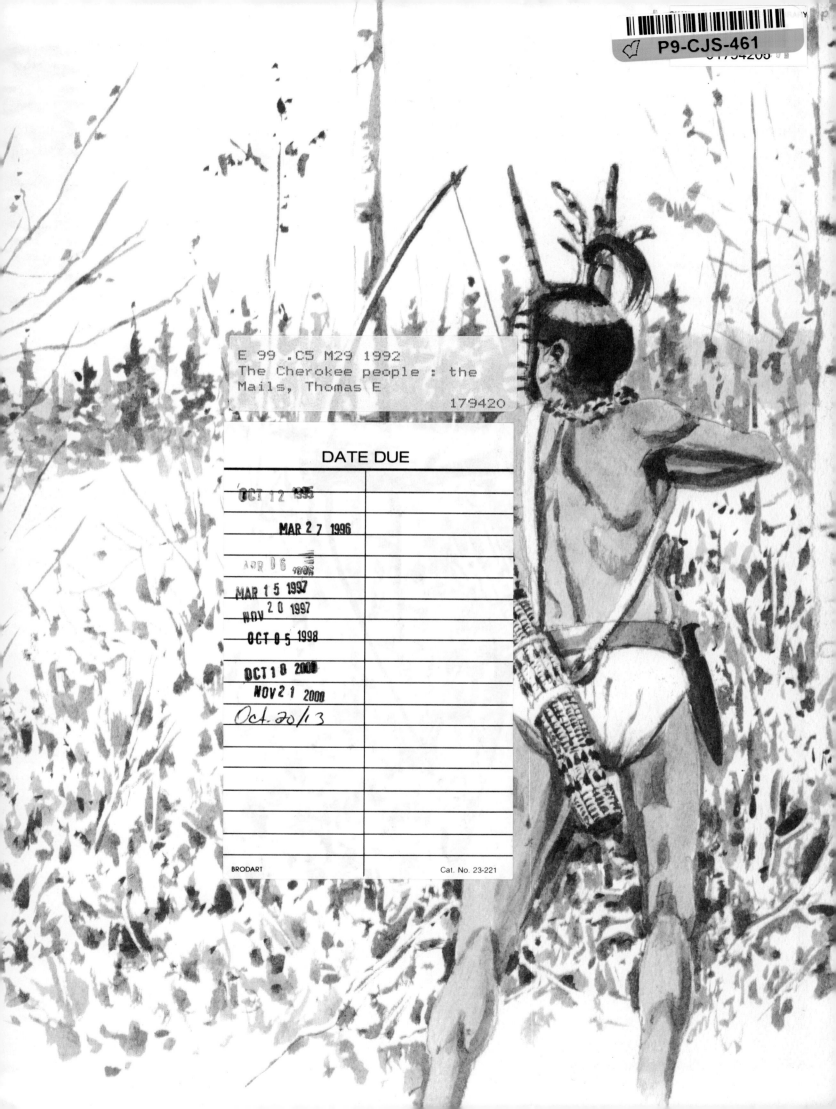

THE

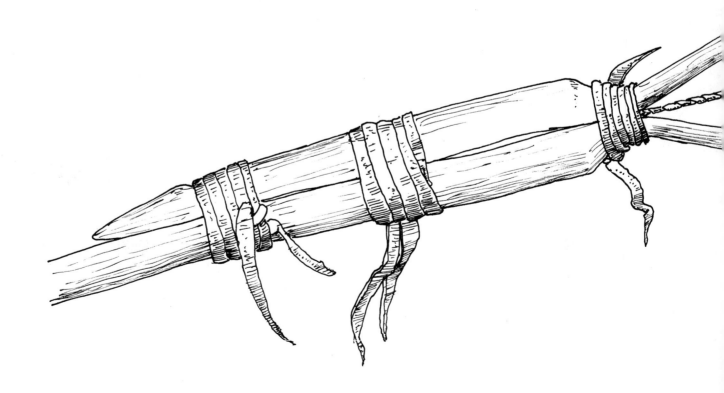

CHEROKEE PEOPLE

The Story of the Cherokees
from Earliest Origins to Contemporary Times

THOMAS E. MAILS

COUNCIL OAK BOOKS · TULSA, OKLAHOMA

© 1992 Thomas E. Mails

All rights reserved.

96 95 94 93 92   5 4 3 2 1

ISBN 0-933031-45-9 (regular edition)
ISBN 0-933031-46-7 (limited edition)
Library of Congress Card Catalog Number 91-73541

PUBLISHED AND DISTRIBUTED BY
COUNCIL OAK BOOKS
1350 East Fifteenth Street
Tulsa, Oklahoma 74120
1 800 247.8850 In Oklahoma, 918 587.6454
FAX 918 583.4995

DESIGNED BY CAROL HARALSON

To Joyce Johnson; my sister, Joy Motts;
my wife, Lisa; my sons, Ryan and Andrew;
and to the memory of Archie Sam,
this volume is devotedly dedicated

· C O N T E N T S ·

Preface

The Cherokee Indians of Oklahoma and North Carolina are at once the best known and the least known of the Indian tribes of North America, and they are perhaps the largest of the Indian tribes, numbering somewhere between 125,000 and 150,000 members.

To say both the "best" and the "least" may seem a contradiction, but it is true. They are the best known due to their amazingly rapid transformation from the ancient culture to white ways between 1700 and 1825 and for their becoming the first "civilized" tribe. And they are the least known precisely because of this rapid transformation. So quickly and completely was the old religious and material culture modified and then discarded that evidence of it passed into near oblivion. In much of the literature concerning them it seems as though the Cherokees suddenly appeared out of nowhere. Once their transformation was complete and their removal from the ancestral lands in the Southeast to present-day Oklahoma was accomplished, interest in them subsided, as though nothing in their continuing culture warranted further investigation.

Until recently, if one searched for information about the prehistoric Cherokees, it was as though he approached a blackboard upon which the entire history of the people had once been written, yet all but the period from 1700 to 1840 had been wiped away, leaving behind only pale traces of the time periods before and after that. He knew something was there but could only wonder what it was. I suppose we could let go at that, were it not for the fact that what is so amply described about the Cherokees during the years 1700 to 1840 assures us they were originally, and must be today, an extraordinary people, whose full history should be made known.

My goal then is to penetrate the mysteries, to restore what has been wiped away, and to trace, so far as it possible with the limited materials available, in words and pictures the history of the Cherokee Nation from the earliest known reminiscences of the natives themselves down to the present. As the extensive bibliography indicates, I have for this purpose drawn upon a multitude of sources, both literary and personal. The major portion of the material dealing with ancient Cherokees has come from one remarkable but unpublished manuscript, the John Howard Payne Papers, and from three published books: *The Eastern Cherokees*, by William Harlen Gilbert, Jr.; *History of the American Indians*, by James Adair; and *Myths of the Cherokee and Sacred Formulas of the Cherokees*, by James Mooney. Please bear in mind that what I reconstruct deals primarily with those areas not already adequately treated by other authors.

The Payne Papers are unique and of considerable length, and they are known to all who research Cherokee history. Virtually every published book on the tribe mentions the manuscript in one way or another and in particular refers to its material on the ancient festivals as the most voluminous and worthwhile extant. This being so, I wondered why more use had not been made of the papers, and I decided to find out. They reside in the Ayer Collection of Americana, Newberry Library of the University of Chicago, Illinois, where they are listed as the John Howard Payne Papers, Ayer MS 689, fourteen volumes, and after seeing a sample I knew the principal reason. The papers are handwritten, in what is for the most part a minuscule and extremely difficult-to-decipher script. Photocopying them only compounds the problem, and prior to the blessed day of microfilm, it would have taken a genuine hero to read and extract information from them. But with the aid of magnification in microfilm, they can be battled through — a task which my wife, Lisa, undertook for me over a period of several months.

Even then we used only the four volumes that contain ethnological data of importance — some 715 manuscript pages contained in Volumes 1, 3, 4, and 6. But the battle, as William H. Gilbert found when he read them the hard way, was worth the effort, for the papers are a treasury of information about the aboriginal culture.

About 1835, and just prior to the removal of the tribe to Indian Territory, Payne (1791-1852), a poet by trade who had a deep sympathy for the Cherokees, went to stay with them and became involved in their political controversies with the state of Georgia and the federal government. His inquiries into the subject of Cherokee history, antiquities, and rights resulted in a collection of data, principally with the aid of Daniel Sabin Butrick, missionary to the Cherokees from 1817 to 1847. Although colored slightly by doctrinal views, the papers nevertheless provide the best available sketch of Cherokee life ever garnered from Cherokees who had been told and remembered how it had been, and were, in the face of sweeping secular and religious changes, doing their best to carry on the traditional life.

What was obtained was in part witnessed and in part oral tradition, and yet it is corroborated substantially by other authors such as Haywood, 1823, Washburn, 1869, and Adair, who in 1736 was a trader to the Cherokees.

Volume 1 of the Payne Papers is entitled "Traditions of the Cherokee Indians," and it contains an organized summary by Payne himself, in 170 manuscript pages, of parts of the other manuscripts dealing with origin legends, lore of the moon and corn, uses of divining crystals, conjuring practices, annual moon festivals, and vegetation rites.

Volume 3 of the papers is entitled "Notes on Cherokee Customs and Antiquities" and consists of 128 manuscript pages of field notes made by Butrick concerning many different topics, including divisions of time; social organization of villages; clan names; priest training; mourning customs; divining crystals; hunter training; sacred things; dreams and "signs," or omens; beliefs concerning future life, hairstyles, war

customs, uncleanness, treatment of snakebite and other wounds and illnesses; women's dress; and the annual calender of festivals.

Volume 4 is entitled "An Account of the Customs of Traditions of the Cherokees," by Butrick, in 378 pages of manuscript. It deals with traditions of origin, ceremonies and rites, government and social organization, priests, variations in dress and ornament, the different types of food, war and weapons, economic matters, musical instruments, crime and punishment, ball play, etiquette and manners, death and burial, the town council house, marriage and the family, training of hunters, religious beliefs, houses and household organization, furniture, birth and education, uncleanness, omens, taboos, making of glue and soap, and the similarities between the ancient Hebrews and the Cherokees.

Volume 6 contains a short paper entitled "Sketches of Cherokee Characteristics," by J. P. Evans, in thirty-nine manuscript pages. Evans sums up the life-style as it existed about 1825-1835 in sketches on social organization of towns, clans, superstitions, and ceremonies; the dress of men and women; the dwellings; and a few observations on appearance, diet, ball play, and dances.

References have already been made to the condition of the manuscript, and in particular, Volume 4 has been badly scratched and has passages crossed out — as though it had been recopied at a later date and then discarded. Beyond this, there are the problems of information which pose numerous questions that a researcher would dearly like answers to, and there are more than a few seeming contradictions.

As for questions, they must go unanswered. There are no more complete documents than Payne's. What I conclude here is what there is. The little more that can be offered comes from other publications, and is often less clear and always less complete. As for the seeming contradictions in the offerings of the informants, we know that convictions and memory are selective things. They filter out unwanted or disagreed-with ideas. Yet alternative stories are not always contradictory; they are often just different views of the same thing, and in the loose soil of Cherokee logic they actually contribute priceless insights into the Cherokee past and present.

Butrick called upon numerous informants for his information, some of whom were 100 years old or more. Their names are listed in the footnotes.

Readers should know some of the thoughts of Butrick and Payne as they compiled the material.

In one letter to Payne, Butrick complains that "It is hard to get information from the Indians. Lack of knowledge among the people, belief among the old who have information that it is a sacred trust, dislike of whites, and freedom to lie to whites." Still, Butrick, during the thirty years he lived among the Cherokees, obtained letters of introduction from John Ross and Charles Hicks, both of whom were beloved and esteemed men, and this, he felt, "enabled him to obtain information that others might never have received."

In a choice letter to Payne, dated April 5, 1837, (Vol. 4, pp. 166-167), Butrick writes as follows:

Dear Sir,

If I have burdened you with trash, not worthy of your notice, yet you will bear with me, as a desire to please and gratify you, sir, as far as practicable, has been, with me, one important object. What I have communicated, is what I have received from the Cherokees, and what, I believe, they communicated sincerely. Yet should we examine the whole again, we should doubtless find many errors and imperfections. Having had no written language, it may well be supposed that many of their antiquities are lost, and many are handed down connected with some degree of error. *Some* of the old men remember *some* things, and *others* again delight to retain, and ruminate on other *parts* of their history. It is, therefore, with much difficulty that we can collect anything like a connected history of their antiquities. . . .

But in the United States, with regard to Indians, and Indian affairs, the public mind is inexorable. Let a work therefore, be ever so correct, and complete, yet if it is impartial, treating the Indians with strict justice, it will not be popular. How then could we hope for forgiveness in publishing what must of necessity be more or less incorrect. On learning lately from a press in New York City that the Indians 'are characterized by war revenge and blood, without natural affection,' etc. I at once concluded that all farther attempts to give an impartial view of the Indians to citizens of the United States, would be vain. . . . When the Indian character is held up impartially for a moment, they will instantly dip their arrows in gall, and pierce the hand which holds it, and blacken the picture with the venom of asps, and then present it as exactly representing the *blood thirsty savages.* . . .

Permit me here to make one request, that is viz. that if a part, or the whole of what I have written you, should not be of service, you will please burn it, and not let it go from your hands; but if anything I have said should be of service, you are at liberty to make such use of it as you may see fit, mentioning my name as seldom as possible, only as one, among many, from whom you have derived information. And should I be favored with a copy of your work, I should know what information I have transmitted to you, and should feel responsible for its correctness; or if discovered to be incorrect or deficient in any important particulars, I should feel under obligation to correct, or enlarge as the case might be, and forward all such information to you as soon as possible for the benefit of a second edition. . . .

Respectfully yours,
D. S. Butrick

Unfortunately for us, not even Butrick knew what was about to happen to the Cherokees, and the further enquiries never materialized. After "the Trail of Tears," the Cherokees were not talking to anyone.

Since there are so many informants represented herein, it is helpful to know something about them, and Butrick understood this. In Volume 4, p. 12, he describes a man named Thomas Nut sa wi, who was a full-blooded Cherokee, born and brought up among the unenlightened Indians of his country.

He had an uncle who was a priest to offer the sacrifices of the town, and perform the various duties of the priestly office, as attended to in his day. While Nut sa wi was young his uncle selected him, set him apart, and instructed him as his right hand man. He of course became learned in the ancient religious customs and principles of their fathers. He continued second or assistant priest till he was probably about fifty years old.

Having occasion to purchase some articles at a mission station, he paid for them in labour, and thus came under the influence of set Christian instruction. In his youth he was married and had two children, but as his wife died during the boyhood of her youngest son, he never married again, but remained single to honour the wife of his youth, and to mourn for her. His general appearance was that of a mourner.

As he became acquainted with the doctrines and duties of the Bible, and the great salvation of the gospel, his attention was immediately enlisted, and in the course of a few months he became a firm believer in Christ. When he made this known to his aged uncle, his grief and mortification was so great, that he left the place where he had long resided, and went back into the mountains, to avoid the sight of those objects and places which would remind him of his loss.

Nut sa wi also left his residence and made his home at the mission station, where he laboured for his support. At length he was seized with an old family complaint, viz., bleeding at the lungs, with which a number of his connexions had died. At first he thought of applying to the same means for relief that his predecessors had, that is, a certain root, and the charms of the Indian doctor. But on second thought he determined to have no conjuring about him, and therefore resolved to apply to no doctor, but get the roots, and prepare them as usual.

Having his medicine prepared he took it, and retired alone, and fell down on a certain rock, and prayed to that Savior who was able, as he had heard, to cure diseases. Sometimes he devoted whole days to fasting and prayer for this purpose, and shortly found himself in usual health.

As parts of the Bible began to appear printed in the Cherokee language, he became exceedingly anxious to read, but being advanced in age, he found it difficult to learn. By continued perseverance, however, he ascended the first height, and became master of the alphabet. He then engaged the gospel of Matthew in Cherokee. . . .

The political changes and troubles of the nation never appeared to affect him, till a short time before they were taken prisoners, by the United States troops. He then called me into a private room, and told me he thought the people were about to be exposed to great sufferings, and danger, that he and his nephew Johnson, had spent much time in prayer, but he wanted *all to pray,* he wanted the *whole* church to meet and spend a day in fasting and prayer for the people; and at his request a public fast was appointed.

When the Cherokee were taken captives I obtained permission for him to remain in the mission family till called to leave the country. From this time he was almost wholly devoted to reading and conversing with his poor, distressed countrymen. He seemed cheerful and happy in going from one camp to another to comfort his friends. When he was taken sick, his pious sister was providentially with him. We requested him to take medicine, but he thought his sister could get some herbs, etc., which would relieve him; and therefore we left him mostly to her care. On evening, however, as he lay in the shade, and his sister sat by him, I perceived a change in his countenance. I took him by the hand and requested him to go to the house. By my assistance, he arose and walked onto the porch. Soon after he lay down I saw he was going. I enquired if he had thought of being so near his end. He replied calmly that he had thought he might live till the next morning. We immediately got him into a chair, and as I leaned it back against me and stooped over him he calmly resigned his breath, with no apparent pain, that I recollect. He was never able to talk or understand English. The name, Thomas was given him at his baptism.

In his personal introduction to the manuscript, Payne writes, "It has cost us no brief study to discover what their first creed was, and when and how they came to diverge from it; branching off afterwards to innumerable varieties. We will now offer the result of our researches, divided with the carefulness which, upon a subject so entangled as we found it, seems indispensable to perspicuity."

When I asked permission of Mary P. Wyly, director of library services at the Newberry Library, and Emily Miller, permissions officer, to make liberal use of the Payne Papers, they most generously granted me the right to quote and to paraphrase what I wished. And they have my profuse thanks for this. In consequence, at least a portion of the superb papers is not "unpublished" anymore.

Where it is possible, I have sought to eliminate confusion in the material, but my efforts in this wise are only guesses. Where it seems that Payne or Butrick should have cited an informant and no informant is listed, then there is no citation, and we can assume it is Payne or Butrick drawing his own conclusions about what he has been told. To those who are wary of the Payne materials being colored by religious views, you will find that Payne is most fair, stating in one instance that "the ceremonies must have been confounded at a very remote date" and suggesting that some of what he received he knew was intermixed information. In another place he states that "the old people seem to know the difference between ideas being ancient or modern, and say so" (this note in the "occasional festivals" section of the manuscript).

William Harlen Gilbert, Jr., author of "The

Eastern Cherokees" (Washington, D.C.: *Bureau of American Ethnology*, Bulletin No. 133, 1943), is one of the "heroes" I referred to in regard to the deciphering of the Payne Papers. While delving into Cherokee lore in 1931 and 1932, with fieldwork limited to two visits to the Eastern Cherokee Reservation from September to December 1932, he centered his investigations in the community of Big Cove, North Carolina, where he obtained a fairly complete description of the society as it existed at that time. Living at the home of the chief informant, who was also the headman of the village, enabled him to follow the daily round of activities and participate frequently in the native dances and games. But since his goal was to outline the past and present social organization of the Cherokees in its formal and integrative aspect and to portray the historical changes in this social organization insofar as they could be gleaned from past records of Cherokee culture, he too turned to John Howard Payne, and made extensive use of Volumes 1, 3, 4, and 6, finding them to be of incomparable worth; however, he chose to summarize and abbreviate their parts, and mainly the material on annual festivals and political organization. Hence the personal charm and attention to detail of the Payne Papers is missing from the Gilbert book.

Gilbert also draws heavily on Mooney's work concerning Cherokee myths and formulas, and he summarizes and quotes a considerable amount of this material too.

The appendix of *The Eastern Cherokees* is an astonishingly complete twenty-eight-page breakdown and listing of the facets of Cherokee culture as described by scholars — particularly Payne and Mooney — and including most others whose material is of major importance.

In its totality, Gilbert's contribution comprises some of the finest work on the Cherokees, and I make frequent reference to it.

James Adair, on the title page of *The History of American Indians*, published in London in 1775, refers to himself as "a trader with the Indians, and resident in their country for forty years," and by "their country" refers to those nations adjoining to the Mississippi, east and west Florida, Georgia, South and North Carolina, and Virginia.

Adair migrated from Scotland to South Carolina in 1735 and went to be with the Cherokees in 1736. From this year through 1768, when he left Chickasaw country, he was a careful observer and recorder of Indian life, and as a rule his efforts receive high praise from early and present scholars. It is certainly most useful, and for antiquities it is hard, if not impossible, to surpass. And yet, it suffers from two unfortunate flaws. The first is that he overwhelms the Indian material by his powerful conviction that the southeastern Indians were in some way descended from or linked to the Hebrews, and thus perpetuated Jewish customs. The second is that he lumps, often without making distinctions, the tribes into a single mold, so that in reading one cannot tell which tribe exactly he is talking about. It must, of course, have seemed to Adair that the lifeways were so close to identical as to make distinctions superfluous, but later scholars do cite divergences that are of considerable importance and which help to render tribal identities possible.

James Mooney cannot be ignored when someone wishes to write accurately about the Cherokees. His *Myths of the Cherokee*, first published in 1900, and *Sacred Formulas of the Cherokees*, first published in 1891, are classics. He is recognized as the foremost student of Cherokee lore, and his works remain the most comprehensive and authoritative in the field.

Collected in successive field studies from 1887 to 1890, and primarily in the Big Cove area of the Eastern Cherokee Reservation, his 126 myths about origins, animal stories, legends, and historical traditions are part of a large body of material comprising extensive notes, together with original Cherokee manuscripts relating to the history, archaeology, geographic nomenclature, personal names, botany, medicine, art, home life, religion, songs, ceremonies, and language. The sacred formulas, gathered in 1887 and 1888, cover virtually every subject pertaining to the daily life and thought of the Cherokees, including medicine, love, hunting, fishing, war, self-protection, destruction of enemies,

witchcraft, crops, council meetings, ball play, and more. The original manuscripts for these were written by the conjurers of the tribe for their own use in the Cherokee characters invented by Sequoyah in the 1820s. Many of the manuscripts date back to 1858, and some are probably older. The collection now resides in the Bureau of Ethnology archives in Washington, D.C. I have copies of the original Bureau of Ethnology publications of Mooney's work, but because of their age and unwieldy size, I have used the Charles Elder reprint of 1972, and most of the page numbers I cite in quoting or referring to Mooney are from the Elder edition.

As for current sources, I have many to thank, but for the greatest assistance I am indebted to Joyce Gatlin Johnson, Ray Johnson, and Archie Sam.

I first met Joyce and Ray in 1975, while I was on a book tour and gave a talk at Central Library in Tulsa, Oklahoma. Something I said about the value of preserving the traditional Indian life stirred a responsive chord in Joyce, for while she was of Cherokee and Choctaw descent, was very active in Indian affairs in Tulsa, and had learned a considerable amount about her heritage from her father, mother, and other elders, she was neither living nor pursuing a traditional life. Ray is white and had only a mild interest in tradition at that time.

They invited me to their home, where we explored the idea of traditional values further, and the result has been an amazing transformation in both of their lives. Since that day, she, with Ray's devoted help and unflagging interest, has given herself entirely to gathering written information and to searching out Cherokees, particularly in communities of full bloods in Oklahoma and North Carolina, who remember the old days and the stories and who have been part of the continuing traditional life. She has also become a staunch traditionalist, belongs to a ceremonial dance ground, and in basket making ranks as one of the finest craft workers in North America. It was Joyce and Ray who became my guides and escorts into the full bloods' country, who introduced me to the informants and rituals cited and described herein, and whom I count among my dearest friends.

Joyce was born September 4, 1928, and is the mother of three children and the grandmother of six. Her Choctaw mother and her Cherokee father passed on to her the tales and lore of herbology and spiritual life that had come down to them from grandfathers and grandmothers. As a rejuvenated Cherokee, Joyce is now passing on this culture, first through her contributions to this book, and second through presentations in public school systems and to groups and museums in many states. She is much sought as an authority on Cherokee basketry and culture. She has served as secretary and councilman of the United Keetoowah Band of Cherokees in Oklahoma, which is a rare privilege for a woman, and is a member of the Redbird Smith ceremonial dance ground. She also has rendered voluntary service on numerous advisory boards concerning Indian affairs and rights, including the board of Claremore Indian Hospital and the Tulsa Mayor's Indian Advisory Board.

Joyce introduced me to Archie Sam, who was chief of the Medicine Spring dance ground and a noted authority on Cherokee history and ritual.

Archie was born on June 30, 1914, in the Greenleaf Mountain community near Braggs, Oklahoma, the youngest son of White Tobacco Sam of the Bear Clan, a Natchez-Creek, and Aggie Cumsey Sam, a Cherokee of the Long Hair, or Wind, Clan. Both parents were members of the Sulphur Springs, later called the *Nu wo ti*, or Medicine Spring, tribal town. Archie's paternal grandfather, Creek Sam, held a prominent position in the origin and development of the Redbird Smith nativistic movement that is highly significant in traditional Cherokee culture. A seer and conjurer who was considered expert on the tribal lore of the Cherokee, Natchez, and Creek tribes, Creek Sam was chosen by Pig Redbird Smith to instruct his son, Redbird, in the old Cherokee traditions, and Creek Sam continued to serve in this capacity throughout the famous Redbird's lifetime.

Archie's childhood training was received within the cultural authority of the Four Mothers' Society, an intertribal organization of the civilized tribes. He received his elementary and high school education at Sequoyah Indian School, Tahlequah, Oklahoma. After spending one year at Bacone College in Muskogee, Oklahoma, he graduated from Connors State College, Warner, Oklahoma, in 1940. He served in World War II with the 45th Infantry Division and the U. S. Air Force. After the war, Archie was stationed in Germany and then was assigned to a logistic-support group for scientific study sites in northern Greenland at Thule Air Base. After serving twenty years in the military service and ten years in civil service, he retired from the U. S. Postal Service in 1972 and settled down in Oklahoma City, Oklahoma.

Archie married Maudie Louise Quinton, a Cherokee of the *Ani godige*, or Savannah Clan, from the Brushy community in Sequoyah County, Oklahoma. They are the parents of Roy Wayne Sam and Adeline Naeher, both residents of Oklahoma City, and grandparents of Gregory Wayne Sam, Kristin Fawn Naeher, and John Raymond Naeher III. To our lasting sadness, Archie did not live to see, as he so wished to do, this book completed and published. He died on May 23, 1986, and is by his special wish buried in the small military cemetery at Fort Gibson, Oklahoma, which served as the destination point for the Cherokees at the time of removal and is a place that is seared into Cherokee memory. From the time he became hereditary chief of the Medicine Spring tribal town, Archie was engaged in the preservation of all aspects of the traditional culture of the southeastern Indians. The Medicine Spring tribal town has been studied by a number of eminent scholars. In anticipation of the extinction of the Natchez language, the renowned ethnologists and linguists John R. Swanton, Dr. Mary R. Haas, and Victor Riste visited the area periodically from 1907 to 1940 to collect linguistic material, myths, songs, and dances from these Natchez-Cherokees for deposition in the archives of the Bureau of American Ethnology. Watt Sam and Nancy Raven, both relatives of Archie's, were documented as the last two Natchez speakers in Oklahoma and worked with Riste in 1931. As a result, sociological, philological, and mythological data collected from the Medicine Spring locality can be found in the archives of the Smithsonian Institution and the Library of Congress in Washington, D.C.; the Museum of Natural History, the Museum of the American Indian, and the New York Public Library in New York City; the University of Pennsylvania in Philadelphia; and the University of Indiana in Bloomington.

More recently, as part of the U.S. bicentennial celebration in 1976, a collection of the traditional songs and dances from the Medicine Spring ground was recorded by the Rockefeller Foundation of New York City to exemplify the southeastern Indian culture of the United States in a series of records representing 200 years of American music. They were distributed to educational institutions, libraries, and other facilities throughout the nation.

The discussions with Archie were many and extremely fruitful. Since he was concerned to not ever say anything that might hurt the feelings of another and to not reveal medicine information of a certain nature, we often turned off the tape while we talked of such things, and that part finished, turned it back on. This procedure was also followed during our talks with other informants, for the same reasons.

My profound thanks go also to others for their contributions: to former Cherokee Principal Chief W. W. Keeler and to Joyce Sequichie Hifler for providing the original impetus to do the book, and to Reba and Clarence Olson, Victor Gatlin, Lydia Sam McLure, Maudie Sam, Eli Sam, Albert Carter, Jim Carter, Celia Carter, Jim Wolf, Maudie Wolf, William Smith, Charley Tee Hee, Eliza Sumpka, Robert Sumpka, John Mulley, William Glory, Sig Vann, Barker Dry, Sam Hider, Karen and Don West, Almoneeta Sequoyah, Robert Toineita, Pauline Bennett, James Parris, Nancy Coheen, Maggie Wachacha, Netche Gray, Howard Tyner, John Hair, Betty Jumper, Willie Jumper, Jasper Smith, Charlotte Rogers, Don Morton, Tom Bunch, Viola Glass, Eliza England, Joe Duck, Charley Watts, Walter Fargo, Robert Bush, Rufus Smith, John Holt, Z. B. Conley, Jr., Earl Boyd Pierce, and Martin Hagerstrand.

My thanks go also to the directors and staffs of the Thomas Rivera Library at the University of California, Riverside; the Thomas Gilcrease Institute of American History and Art, Tulsa, Oklahoma; Oklahoma Historical Society, Oklahoma City; Woolaroc Museum, Bartlesville, Oklahoma; the Union Catalog archives, Emory University Library, Atlanta, Georgia; the Robert W. Woodruff Library for Advanced Studies and Emory Museum, Emory University; Georgia State Museum and Archives, Atlanta; and the South Carolina Department of Archives and History, Columbia. I further thank Milo B. Howard, Jr., at the State of Alabama Department of Archives and History, Montgomery, and Ilene J. Cornwell, public services, Tennessee Historical Commission, Nashville.

Beyond these, heartfelt thanks go to my longtime friends, Mr. and Mrs. Paul M. Daniell, for their encouragement and special help, and to Deborah J. Marks, who was retained by Daniell to provide what proved to be exceptional research assistance in the southeastern states.

In the realm of thanks for transcending efforts, I thank my wife, Lisa, for her continuous assistance in and enthusiasm for the project, and who, along with our sons Ryan and Andrew, has again endured the often lonely existence of an author's spouse.

Some final notes regarding method: Among its wondrous collections, the Oklahoma Historical Society has an abundance of documents that are not cataloged. Therefore, these can only be cited as coming from their general collection. Several of them are used herein, and if there is no citation for a document other than the name of the society, it is because there is none. And, while I include, so that readers can get the feel of the native language, some Cherokee words, I do not, following the lead of such outstanding and reputable authors as Grace Steele Woodward, retain the accent marks. Other authors who follow this custom would probably agree that the accent marks only tend to confuse in a book intended for general readers, and are not germane to the goal at hand. Payne inserts occasional aids to pronunciation. I retain these, and in the appendix there is also a simplified guide to pronunciation.

THOMAS E. MAILS
ELSINORE, CALIFORNIA

PLATE ONE. Ancient Cherokee man

PLATE THREE. Installation of the new War Chief

PLATE FOUR. The Great War Chief in war regalia

PLATE FIVE. The middle Cherokee Warrior

PLATE SIX. The Little People

PLATE SEVEN. First New Moon of Spring Festival

PLATE EIGHT. Driving
away the storm gods

PLATE NINE. Cementation Festival

PLATE TEN. Cementation Festival

PLATE ELEVEN. Bounding Bush Festival

PLATE TWELVE. The Trail of Tears

PLATE THIRTEEN. Booger dancer and mask

PLATE FOURTEEN. W. W. Keeler, former principal chief of the Cherokee Nation of Oklahoma

PLATE FIFTEEN. Present-day Cherokee children

Origin and Settlement

Well known as the Cherokee Indians are today, enthralling veils of mystery surround important questions concerning the great nation and its individual citizens:

Where did they originate, and when did they first establish their home in southeastern North America?

What were this southeastern home and the ancient culture truly like? What were the physical characteristics of the Cherokees? How did they dress? Were they warlike? Were they religious? Were they creative?

Was the ancient culture dynamic and impressive, and if so, why did so many of the people exchange it for white ways?

Did the transformed Cherokees of the eighteenth and nineteenth centuries leave all of the ancient culture behind, or were some essential parts retained and practiced? If something was retained, why was it, what was it, and what of this is still being observed today?

What qualities and special powers enabled the Cherokees to endure and to triumph over a series of trials and tribulations so devastating they should have been crushed by them?

MAJOR INDIAN TRIBES IN THE SOUTHEAST

Parting the Veils

Can these questions be answered today? Not conslusively, but we can answer them sufficiently well to tell an absorbing story.

For instance, the veil shielding the question of origin is no longer as dense as it once was, although there are two distinctly different views regarding it – the view of the Cherokees themselves, and the view of archaeologists, anthropologists, and ethnologists.

Except for the information collected by Payne, Butrick, and Adair, material dealing with mythical creation accounts is exceedingly sparse and tells us next to nothing about geographic places of origin. In 1888, James Mooney, one of whose Cherokee informants was born in 1800 and the other in 1835, was unable to reconstruct any origin material dealing expressly with the Cherokee people — although he did gather a number of fascinating accounts describing the origin of creatures and celestial bodies. Adair's origin material links all of the southeastern tribes he traded with to an ancestry and development that associates them with the Hebrew people. Payne, whose extensive collection of origin material deals expressly with the Cherokees, also associates them with the Hebrews. In most of its parts, it comes close to duplicating what is written in the first five books of the Bible. The exception is that the Cherokee informants — who described events such as the creation story, flood, expulsion from Eden, Tower of Babel, Abraham, crossing of the Red Sea, Moses, the wandering in the wilderness, and the construction of the tent of worship and the sacred ark — shaded them with words and meanings unique to the Cherokees, and by this tactic made them their own. The Payne origin account is interesting to read, but there is little to be gained by recounting it here in its entirety. The exceptions are those portions that relate to certain things and ideas that were observed by white traders when the historic period began at the dawn of the eighteenth century. Since these portions are a necessary prelude to the description of the annual cycle of festivals that were celebrated by the ancient Cherokees, I describe them in Chapter Six.

As for the other view of origins, all professional scholars presently in the field of Cherokee studies reject outright the idea of a Cherokee ancestry and development that parallels that of the Hebrews. They believe instead that such versions are the merged result of Cherokee and Christian thought — the latter being learned from the earliest Europeans to visit Cherokee country. Whether or not this opinion is entirely defensible I cannot say. Payne is careful to point out that his information came from Cherokee sources who had little or no contact with one another, and who had no common education in European ideas. It is also worth observing that some of Payne's informants were born as early as 1735, and thus gathered knowledge about their ancestry at a time when contact with outsiders had barely begun. There were no missionaries present then, and the remembrances included tales orally handed down by Cherokees who had lived prior to historic times. Payne also points out a valid truth — that most native Americans did not easily give up or exchange their ancient traditions for European ideas and ways. However, the Cherokees had an adaptable nature, and may have been an exception to this pattern of reluctance.

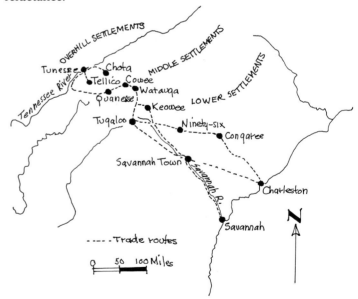

CHEROKEE TRADE ROUTES 1670 - 1750

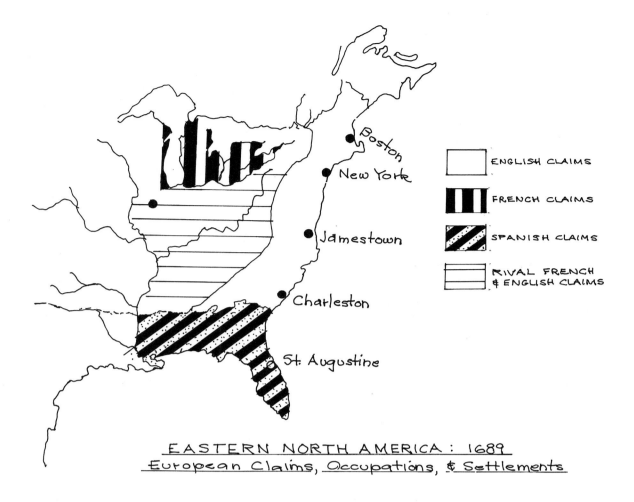

ENGLISH CLAIMS

FRENCH CLAIMS

SPANISH CLAIMS

RIVAL FRENCH & ENGLISH CLAIMS

EASTERN NORTH AMERICA : 1689
European Claims, Occupations, & Settlements

The view of the current scholars began its evolution in 1823, when John Haywood made the first serious study of Cherokee origins and concluded that two nations with diverse cultures had, in the distant past, merged to form the Cherokee tribe. The first of these two groups built mounds, erected fortifications, constructed wells with adobe-brick walls, worshiped idols, performed human sacrifices, used seven as their most sacred number, and ruled themselves by autocratic princes. Their place of origin was southern Asia, and their culture was linked to that of the ancient Hebrews and Hindus. When they migrated to North America, they settled in the southeastern area dominated by the Natchez tribe, who at that time ruled most of the lower Mississippi and Gulf Coast regions. Later, a second culture that was democratic in organization and had a strong military arm came from northern Asia, took control of eastern Tennessee, and gradually merged with the first group to form the Cherokee tribe that existed when the first whites arrived in A.D. 1540.[1]

The Cherokee Place, Its Climate and Natural Resources

Haywood's idea has been rejected, and the currently accepted view is that similarities of language, warlike spirit, common traditions, and the use of the Iroquois unnotched arrow point and grooveless ax head indicate that the Cherokees were once part of the Great Lakes Iroquoian family. Then at an unknown and distant point in time, some form of discord caused the Cherokees to separate themselves from the other Iroquoians, and to migrate slowly southward through what are today known as Ohio, Pennsylvania, and Virginia. Finally, the Cherokees found a suitable new home and quickly laid claim to a vast wilderness empire. The limits of this domain can be established by drawing a line that begins fifty miles north of present Charleston, South Carolina, and then runs northward along the Kanawha River to the Ohio River. From there it follows the Ohio to the Tennessee River, turns southward for a hundred miles into northern

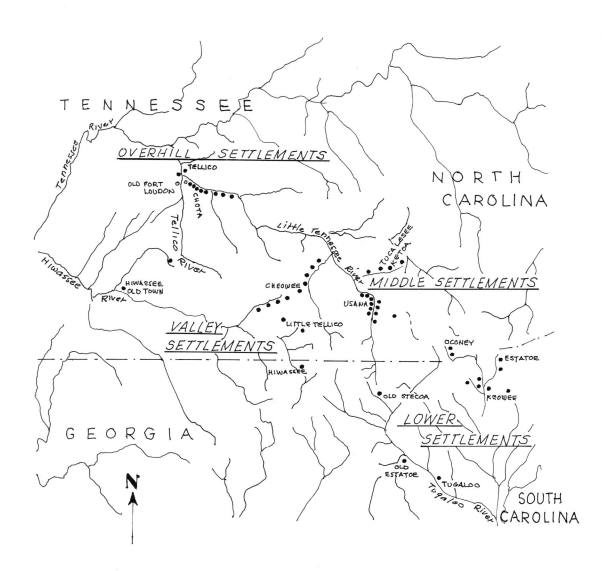

TENNESSEE

Tennessee River

OVERHILL SETTLEMENTS

TELLICO

OLD FORT LOUDON

CHOTA

Tellico River

Hiwassee River

HIWASSEE OLD TOWN

NORTH CAROLINA

Little Tennessee River

TOCALESEE

KETOA

MIDDLE SETTLEMENTS

CHEOWEE

USANA

VALLEY SETTLEMENTS

LITTLE TELLICO

OCONEY

ESTATOE

HIWASSEE

OLD STECOA

KEOWEE

GEORGIA

LOWER SETTLEMENTS

OLD ESTATOE

TUGALOO

Tugaloo River

SOUTH CAROLINA

N

THE CHEROKEE SETTLEMENTS, 1762-1776

Alabama, and finally goes eastward to the starting point, passing slightly north of Atlanta, Georgia. In terms of present states, this sprawling area includes western North Carolina, South Carolina, Virginia, West Virginia, northern Georgia and Alabama, all but the western parts of Tennessee, and those parts of Kentucky that adjoin Tennessee. The Cherokees divided it into four regional settlements. The eastern, Lower Settlements lay in what is now called the Southern Piedmont Province — a gently rolling plateau crisscrossed by streams and deep valleys and surrounded by isolated mountain peaks. The central area was the heartland of the tribe and was comprised of the Kituhwa (Middle) and Valley settle-

ments. It sat within the Blue Ridge Province and included the Great Smoky Mountains, flat-bottomed valleys, and numerous coves. The Overhill, or Tennessee, settlements were to the north and west in the Appalachian Great Valley Province and were situated on gently rolling land that was carved by deep river valleys. The Cherokee domain was marked by a mild, temperate climate. In winter, even though the temperature might drop to fifteen or twenty degrees Fahrenheit at night, the sun would heat the surface of the mountain slopes to fifty or sixty degrees at midday. Winter winds were prevailingly north to south, and winds in the summer blew southwest to northeast. On the high slopes there were few winds save during storms, and when these high winds did come, they went away in a remarkably short time.

Winter precipitation amounted to forty or more inches on the highest peaks, thirty to forty inches in the semihigh areas, and twenty to thirty inches in the valleys. During this season, the billowing masses of clouds pressed like huge cotton balls against the heavily wooded mountain slopes and appeared strange to chance, outside observers. White travelers in the high mountain country were seized with uncanny foreboding when they came upon the dark shadows, glens, and the steep and twisted gorges; similar encounters by the Cherokees gave rise to numerous legends and fears.[2] The first white traders found the eastern parts of the region to be sharp and cold, yet not disagreeable, but life in the towns and villages that lay among the Appalachian Mountains was a different matter, for it was bitterly cold there. The Cherokees wisely fortified themselves against the cold by the use of hothouses, by constant bathing in the rivers, by anointing their bodies and faces with grease and paint, and by a regimen of outdoor life and hunting that was carried on in all manner of weather. The sum of these acts transcended the climate, and made the natives almost as impenetrable to cold as a bar of steel.[3] Spring was a joyous time of new birth for the Cherokees, but it did have its perils. Thick ice and snow clung tenaciously to the north sides of the slopes until late in this season, when rain began to fall. Then, if the rain was heavy enough, huge pieces of ice mixed with prodigious torrents of water rolled down the slopes and over steep craggy rocks with such speed and force that nothing could resist them. Rivers would overflow their banks, and at times whole settlements or portions of them would in a frightful moment be washed away. But once this danger was past, the rivers quietly filled their courses in running no more than thirty miles and were as clear as glass. In summer, the region took on its most genial aspect. High mountain rainfall was thirty to forty inches, and the rest of the country received twenty to twenty-five inches. The moon and stars shone brilliantly at night, and the hot but invigorating sun

beat down during the day. Storms were fewer and of shorter duration.

Cherokee mythology dealing with this season gives some attention to the problem of thunderstorms and lightning, but such things as landslides, earthquakes, and floods were so infrequent they were ignored. The climate factor of Cherokee country had a rhythmic or cyclical nature that was a strong influence on Cherokee culture and led to a complex mythology and ritual performance. While these things are explored in detail in the chapters ahead, examples are the alternation of moon and no moon as occasions for special monthly rites, winter and summer for ceremonial and nonceremonial seasons, and of planting, plant sprouting, plant ripening, and harvesting as occasions for lesser rites and major festivals of thanksgiving and celebration. Even the menstruation of women was accompanied by strict taboos and in the minds of the Cherokees was related to the phases of the moon. The responses of the Cherokees to the cycle of seasons are found in their uses of fire, smoke signaling, divination with crystals, sun gazing as an aspect of priest training, imitation of nature's sounds while on hunting expeditions, rites to control the weather, cosmogonic tales, and in the intimate connection the priests made between the celestial phenomena and health or disease, between waterfalls and thunder, and between snakes and lightning.[4]

The seasons also combined with the rich soil to nourish an abundance of hemp and wine grapes, hops, hickory nuts, acorns, and chestnuts. There was a variety of herbs for food and healing, and tobacco for ritual use. Reeds flourished along the level edges of the rivers, and also great brakes of winter canes, the foliage of which made excellent food for the horses and cattle that were obtained from white traders during historic times.[5] The flora of the southern Appalachians divided itself naturally into three plant worlds, and we easily learn where the Cherokees went to obtain the things they needed for the various aspects of daily and religious life. In the Appalachian Mountain district there were vast deciduous forests with a predominance of hardwoods such as poplar, pine, spruce, balsam or fir, hemlock,

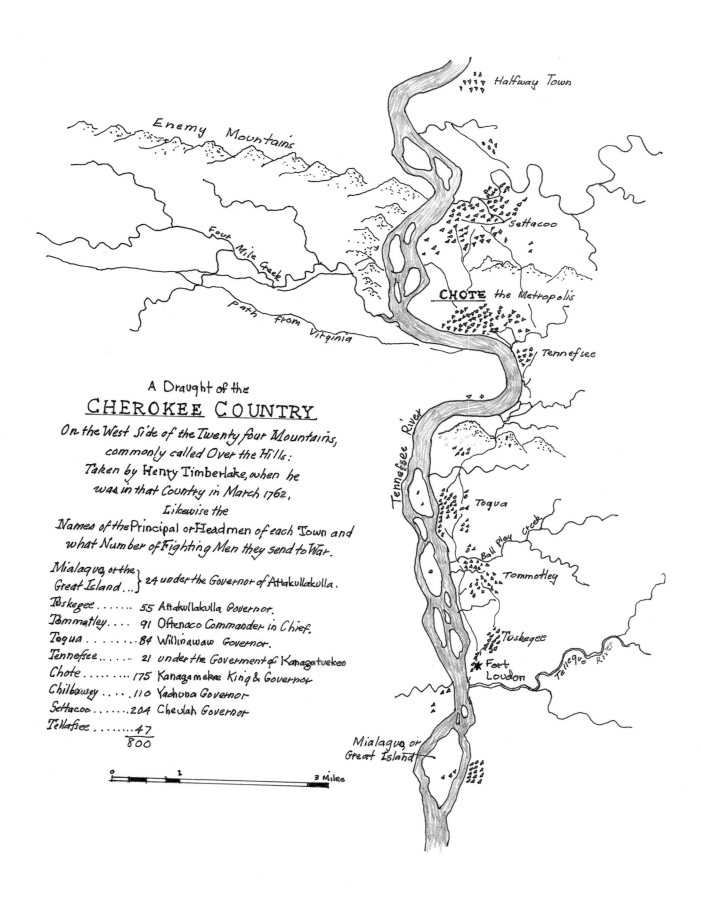

buckeye, tulip tree, chestnut, and bird's-eye maple, along with many species of herbaceous plants and cryptogams. The Piedmont district vegetation was quite different and consisted largely of undergrowth and herbaceous species. The Alleghanian-Ozark district was marked by broad-leaved trees of some 700 species and a scarcity of evergreens.[6]

Plants and wildlife were essential to the Cherokees and played a central role in mythology and lore. Both were associated with the causation and cure of disease. Animals and birds were associated with clan names, education, and mimetic or "imitational" dances to guarantee success in hunting. Despite the disappearance of perishable artifacts, it can safely be assumed that all mammals, reptiles, amphibians, fish, and insects became design elements in the weaving of mats and garments, and subjects for ritual ceramics, carvings, and paintings. Animals were thought of in human terms and as being organized into clans and tribes with their own council houses and village settlements. And, since some animals embodied malevolent spirits, these spirits must be fought against. The relationship between the people and these animals even duplicated the character of intertribal confrontations. Through vivid imagination and ritual, spiritual wars were waged, spiritual blood revenge was demanded and secured, spiritual alliances were contracted and dissolved, and spiritual peace was declared.[7]

As the lore of the ancient Cherokee culture evolved, plants were spiritually connected with food, shelter, clothing, and medicine. Compared to animals in general, plants were believed to be friendly agents to man and helpers through their curative powers in the struggle against spiritual enemies that existed in the animal world. Typical plants used for healing and for dealing with these enemies were sassafras, cinnamon, wild horehound, seneca snakeroot, St. Andrew's Cross, and wild plantain. Weeds that grew in streams were burned for lye to be used as a salt substitute and in soapmaking. Wood was used for many purposes, and especially for house construction. Bark and herb fibers were twisted into twine and used for weaving certain types of garments.[8] Over a period of time, the list of

cultivated plant staples was broadened from corn and beans to include potatoes, pumpkins, peas, squash, strawberries, tobacco, and gourds.

The native mammals of the Cherokee domain included most that were common to North America — bats, moles, shrews, raccoons, skunks, weasels, otters, bears, wolves, foxes, wildcats, mountain lions, rabbits, porcupines, groundhogs, beavers, rats and mice, squirrels, bison, elk, deer, opossum, and native dogs. It was the same with birds, of which the most important to the Cherokees were eagles, hawks, ravens, crows, turkeys, wild ducks, and geese. It was taboo to kill some species of birds, but the rest could either be snared by nets or traps, or shot with blowguns or arrows. Reptiles and amphibians consisted of rattlesnakes, copperheads, other snakes, lizards, skinks, iguanas, turtles, frogs, toads, and salamanders. Rivers and streams abounded with perch, croakers, bass, pike, catfish, garfish, salmon, trout, sturgeon, and shellfish. Mollusks were gathered for food and for shellworking and decoration. Insects included ants, butterflies, beetles, crickets, flies, bugs, dragonflies, bees, and wasps. Worms were thought to be an important cause of disease in man. As for domesticated animals, the native, barkless dogs were tamed, and probably the bee. Turkeys were kept captive only while they were young. Members of the Wolf Clan trained wolf pups as they would dogs, the Deer Clan members kept deer for religious purposes, and the Bird Clan kept crows and chicken hawks.

The Cherokee Language

The Cherokee language was soft and beautiful, with the charming melody of the tongues of southern Europe. It has a phenomenal richness of vowel sounds and was filled with artful figures that led to an enduring treasury of musical names for landmarks, rivers, mountains, and to a wondrous imagery of earth and sky . . . names such as Chatooga-Tugaloo, Keowee, Coosa, Oostanaula, Etowah, Chatahoochee, Little Tennessee, Tuckaseegee, Nantahala, Iliwasee, Hiwassee, Swannonoa, Tellico, and Sequichie. Most of their neighbor nations called the Cherokees "Uplanders" or "Mountaineers," but

Top: Early Cherokee man. *Bottom:* Conception of Pisgah village at an early stage of its development.

the Iroquois called them "Cave Dwellers," and the Cherokees referred to themselves as "the Real People," or "the Principal People," which in their language is "Tsalagi." This was rendered phonetically by the Portugese as "Chalaque," by the French as "Cheraqui," and by the English as "Cherokee."[9]

No one knows how large the Cherokee tribe was when it migrated, but it was large compared with most other tribes. Guesses are that in 1650 the population was 22,000. A trader's report in 1715 listed 2,100 in eleven Lower Towns, 6,350 in thirty Middle Towns, and 2,760 in nineteen Upper Towns, for a total of 11,210. In 1720, estimates ranged from 10,000 to 11,500. In 1729, the population was 20,000, including 6,000 warriors who were distributed throughout sixty-four towns and villages. Warfare and epidemics during the next twenty-five years brought about a rapid decline in population, and in 1755 there remained only 2,300 warriors. But by 1809, the population had risen again to 12,395, and in 1819, it was 15,000. Despite the tragic loss of one-fourth of the nation's population during the removal to Indian Territory (present Oklahoma) in 1838-1839, the government census of 1910 reported there were 31,489 Cherokees, and in 1930 there were 45,238.[10] The number on the tribal rolls today is more than 137,000, of which not more than 8,300 can properly be called "full bloods."

Earliest Settlements

As for the question of determining precisely when the Cherokees first settled in southeastern North America, efforts to do this have been and are being made. It appears to have been somewhere between A.D. 1000 and 1500, most probably around 1300. The 240-year period from then until the explorer de Soto made contact with the tribe in 1540 might best be described as a formative one, during which the Cherokees established themselves in their new home and began to shape their civilization. It is certain that they had not yet risen to their full heights, for de Soto describes them as living in a province of Chalaque that was inhabited by a poverty-stricken tribe subsisting on roots, herbs, serviceberries, and such game as deer and turkey,

which they shot with bows and arrows. The people were clothed in only a few skin garments, made usually of deer hide, and they wore feather head-dresses. Their villages were palisaded, and they had a barkless kind of dog. But as time went on, the Cherokees progressed and in many ways came to resemble in culture the more established tribes of the Southeast, for they adopted many of the traits common to their Indian neighbors. Along with other practices, they used the pottery techniques of the Catawba Indians and the Missippian-style double-weave basketry. Moreover, it is probable that some of the Indians who were displaced by the Cherokees merged with them to make an amalgam of cultures.

Natchez warrior in summer dress armed with bow and arrows and a war club. Based on etching by Le Page Du Pratz, *Histoire de la Louisiane,* Paris, 1758, vol. 2, p. 308, Negative no. 1168-b-4. Smithsonian Institution, National Anthropological Archives. It can be assumed that Cherokee male dress was somewhat similar to this, being enough different for the tribes to differentiate between the two.

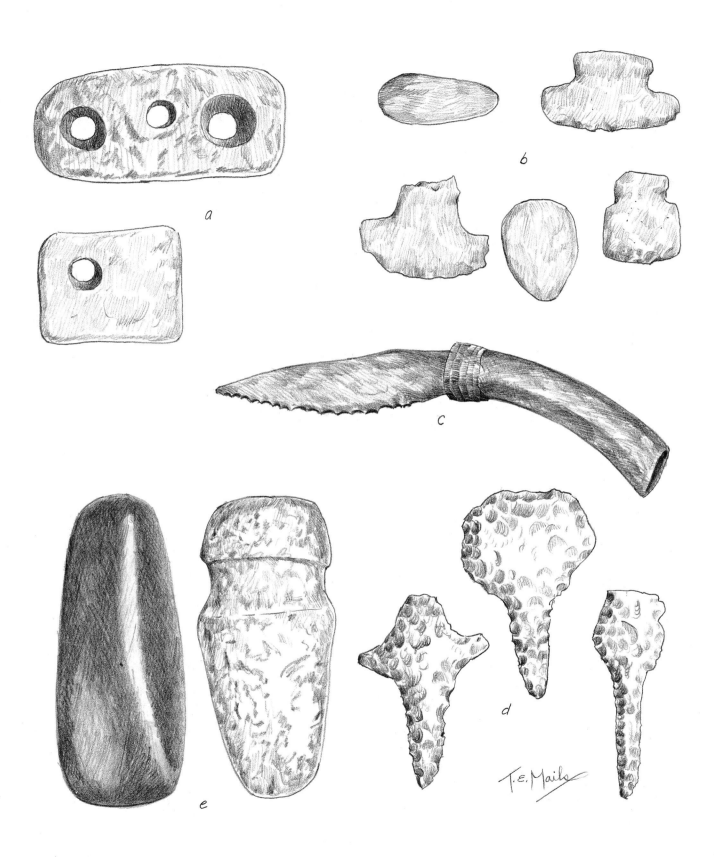

Types of tools: **a.** hearth boards for fire drills, Emory University Museum. **b.** stone scrapers for hides, Emory University Museum. **c.** typical hafted stone knife. **d.** stone drills, Museum of the Cherokee Indian. **e.** typical stone ax heads.

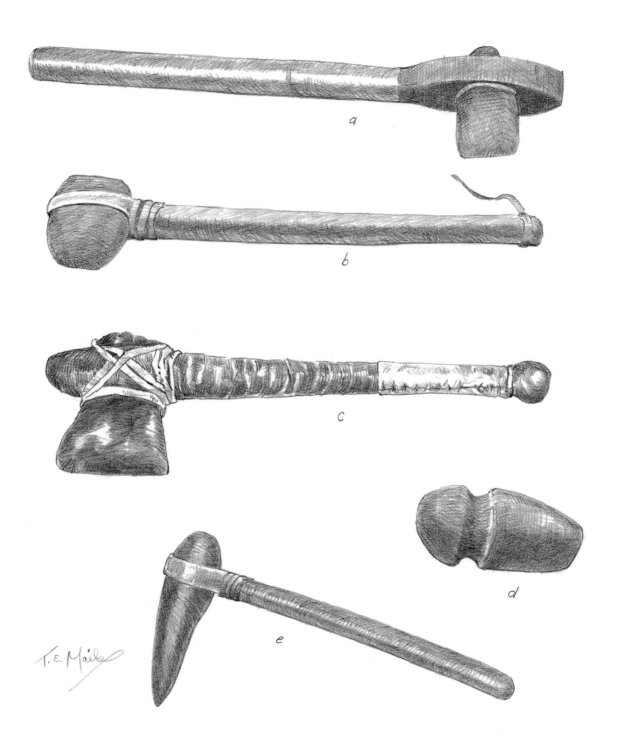

Types of tools: **a.** typical grooveless ax used for cutting wood and trees, Georgia State Museum. **b.** full-grooved ax, hafted with sinew; vine, gut, and hide were also used to attach ax heads to wooden handles, Georgia State Museum. **c.** ax made by inserting the stone head into a slit in a limb of a cedar tree and allowing the limb to grow around it, bound with sinew, rattlesnake skin, and buckskin, Museum of the Cherokee Indian. **d.** typical full-grooved stone ax head. **e.** adze used for woodworking, such as peeling logs and hollowing out log canoes, Museum of the Cherokee Indian.

Pottery: Top, carved paddles used to stamp outer surface of pots, Museum of the Cherokee Indian. *Middle,* pottery shard, simple check stamp, Georgia State Museum. *Bottom,* Cherokee method of forming clay coils, and at left, various instruments for shaping and polishing.

Pottery: **a., b., c.** hanging pots, Georgia State Museum. **d., e.** cooking pots, Smithsonian Institution. **f.** chestnut burr pot, Museum of the Cherokee Indian.

Pottery: all from Georgia State Museum — **a.** late Mississippian clay food bowl with simple stamped decoration covering entire surface. **b.** food bowl with complicated incised decoration confined to vessel neck. **c.** negative incised bottle. **d.** complicated incised decoration confined to vessel neck. **e.** food bowl. **f.** Emory University Museum, stone grinding bowl.

Basketry, Eastern Cherokee: **a.** breadbasket of native split cane. **b.** pack basket of white oak splints. **c.** fish basket of oak splints. **d.** hominy sifter basket made of oak splints. **e.** carrying basket made of split cane, with hole used for carrying basket on the back. Cherokees used only three construction techniques: **f.** twilling. **g.** wickerwork. **h.** checkerwork. Designs shown with heavy lines are typical.

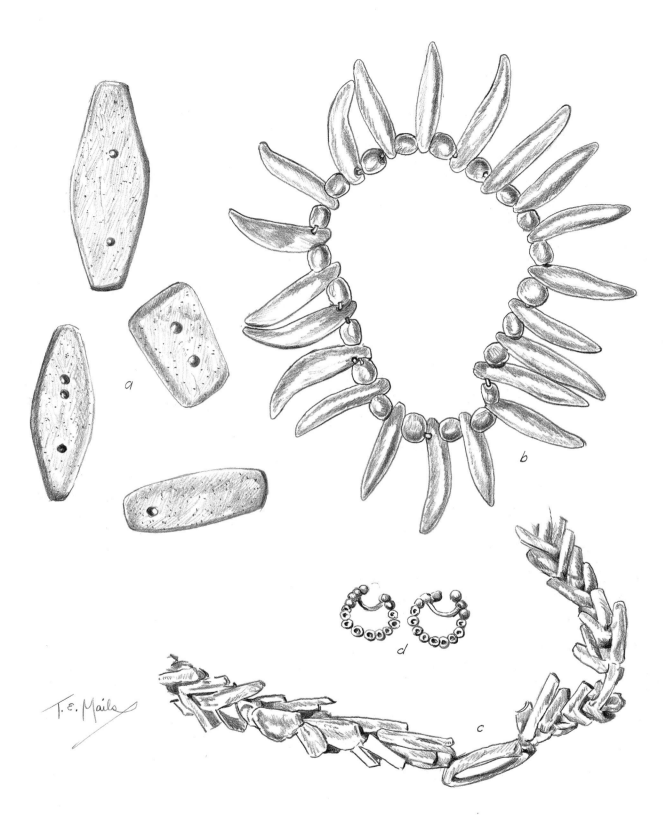

Jewelry: **a.** stone gorgets, Emory University Museum. **b.** bear-tooth necklace, Museum of the Cherokee Indian. **c.** turtle-bone necklace, Museum of the Cherokee Indian. **d.** shell earrings, Smithsonian Institution.

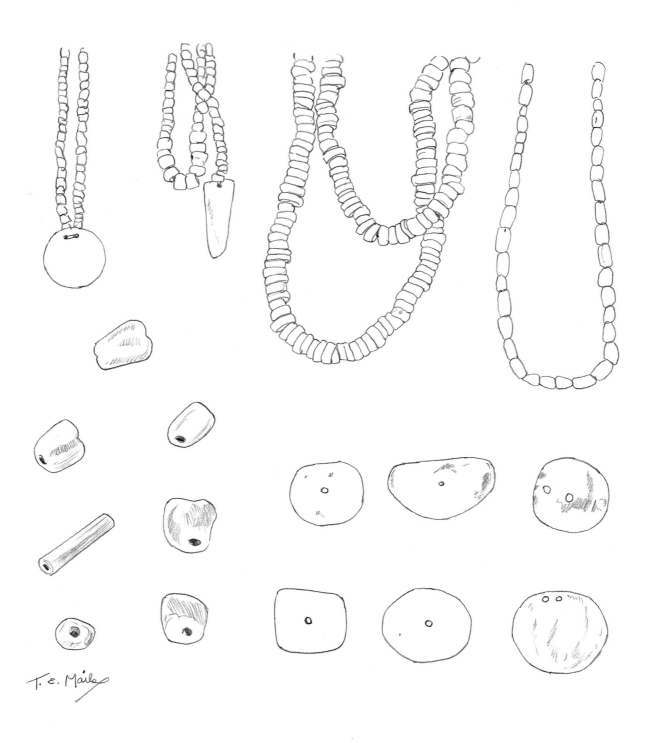

T. E. Mails

Top, shell necklaces, Museum of the Cherokee Indian. *Lower left,* stone and bone beads, Emory University Museum. *Lower right,* shell gorgets, Museum of the Cherokee Indian. Shells were acquired through trade with coastal tribes, and were engraved with sharp flint stones. Many shell gorgets have been found in Tennessee burial sites dating from A. D. 1400-1500.

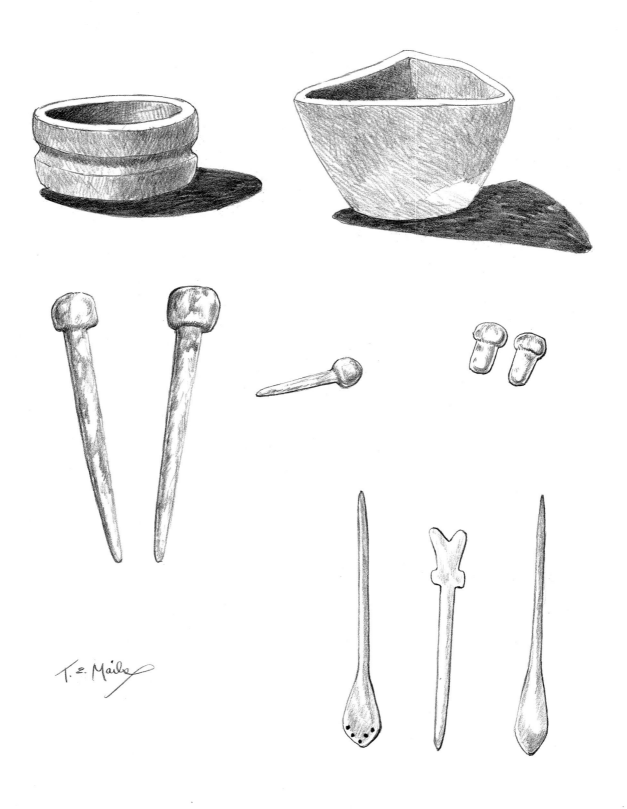

Top, hand-held paint pots. *Middle,* bone ear pins and plugs. *Bottom,* bone hairpins. All items from Museum of the Cherokee Indian.

Major Culture Phases

In researching Appalachian summit archaeology from the earliest times of habitation to the twentieth century, contemporary archaeologists have compiled a list of seven distinctive phases wherein aboriginal remains can be identified and placed on a time scale on the basis of content and stratigraphy, or superimposed layers of remains. They begin with the Qualla Phase, ca. A.D. 1500 to historic times, and move backwards in time to the Pisgah Phase, ca. A.D. 1000 to 1500; Connestee Phase, ca. A.D. 100 or 200 to 1000; Pigeon Phase, ca. 200 B.C. to A.D. 100; Swannanoa Phase, ca. 750 to 150 B.C.; Savannah River Phase, ca. 2500 to 750 B.C.; Morrow Mountain Phase, ca. 4300 to 2500 B.C.; and conclude with earlier occupations that range from 7500 to 4300 B.C.[11] Of these eight periods, only two are associated with the Cherokees — the Pisgah and the Qualla — in other words, only with time periods after A.D. 1000, and even then with only a portion of the Pisgah Phase. What remains have survived from these two periods allow us to imagine quite vividly what the formative years of Cherokee life in the Southeast were like. We can pin down the settlement locations, determine something of the people's appearance and dress, and make useful judgments about their material and spiritual practices — enough that we can depict them in words and illustrations with a conjectural, yet reasonable degree of accuracy.

Life in the Pisgah Phase

Pisgah Phase sites of the A.D. 1000-1500 period have been found throughout an area of about 14,000 square miles in the South Appalachian Province. In its earliest years, many of these sites were occupied for relatively short periods of time, but in the interior of the region, sites were occupied throughout the phase. Settlement sites varied in size from a quarter of an acre to six acres, and the more spacious portions of alluvial valleys were the favored locations.[12] Houses of this phase bore some resemblance to the primitive pit houses of the Arizona and New Mexico Anasazi. They were constructed of upright posts and had a twenty-foot-square or slightly rectangular plan.

They had a depressed floor, a central platform hearth, and a vestibule entrance. They were probably walled with bark or woven mats, and were roofed with bark or straw thatch. House floors and the areas immediately surrounding the houses contained burials and clay deposits used to make storage pits and fire basins. From what is known about the early life-style, it is probable that the villages had sweat houses, storage cribs, and other small structures. Everything was arranged around a central plaza that fronted the town council house, and the entire complex was enclosed by a defensive palisade, whose entrance, at least in its early stages, was formed by an offset in the wall that was located at the point of easiest access to a nearby river. Excavations in two villages at the Garden Creek site have revealed platform mounds. In the smaller of these villages, the original had been erected in the Connestee Phase and was reused by the Pisgah Phase occupants. The second and slightly larger village had, in an early stage, been surrounded by a palisade with several projecting and rectangular bastions, and there is evidence of an elaborate sequence of combined ceremonial and civic structures placed on an ever-enlarging mound top. Initially, there were two joined earth lodges that were adjacent to a large and probably arborlike structure. Eventually, this arbor was torn down and covered by a course of river boulders. Later still, the boulders and the earth lodges were overlaid with earth fill and a clay cap to form a large, flat-topped mound that was enlarged several times, with a new structure that was similar in shape to the typical village house being placed on each new surface.

The mound's final use was in the Qualla Phase. Burials were made both in the house floors and adjacent to the houses, suggesting either that it was prudent to inter quickly, that the family wished to have the deceased close by for spiritual reasons, that the general climate of warfare made it dangerous to venture far without adequate protection, or that desecration by enemies was feared. Perhaps a combination of the reasons was involved. In some instances the home's central hearth had been removed to accommodate a burial, after which a new hearth was constructed on top of the filled-in burial pit. At Garden Creek, there were also burials in the mound floors. All burials of the Pisgah Phase were made either in simple pits, side-chamber pits, or central-chamber pits. It seems that the side-chamber form was reserved for infants and for male adults of high rank. Bodies were usually placed in pits in a loosely flexed position, with the heads oriented to the west.

All of the adult skulls were artificially flattened at the forehead and back of the head. Grave goods found with adult remains include columella shell beads, shell ear pins, shell bowls, turtle-shell rattles, and perforated animal bones. Infant remains have with them shell gorgets, columella shell beads, and perforated Marginella shells. In further evidence of social ranking, grave goods at the Warren Wilson site were found only in burials in certain houses.[13] The only surviving artifacts were made from stone, clay, bone, shell, and wood. Chipped-stone implements consist of small triangular projectile points and hand-held flaking tools of the type employed to manufacture the points. There are smoothly ground stone celts, small disks, small elbow pipes, and pottery-burnishing stones. Pecked-stone tools include anvil stones, hammer stones, mortars, and manos. Cut-stone objects consist of mica and various pigment stones such as hematite, limonite, graphite, and ocher. Clay objects include small elbow pipes, beads, animal figurines, disks made from potsherds, and tiny pottery vessels. Awls and other pointed implements were fashioned from the long bones and small bone splinters of deer and turkey. Also found are ornamental bone pins, beads, and turtle-shell rattles. Marine mollusks provided the working material from which various artifacts were shaped. Large round beads were made from the conch columellas, and small tubular and disk beads were fashioned from the outer wall of conch shells. The large beads were used for necklaces or bracelets, and the small beads for necklaces only. Ear pins were made from the conch columellas, and conch shells were used as ritual containers. Circular shell gorgets of the type worn on bead strings for chest decoration were engraved and excised with imaginative representations of a coiled rattlesnake with a forked eye, of

stylized dancers, or in a cross or square form. Perforated Marginella shells were sometimes sewn to the garments in which infants were buried.[14]

The ceramics of the A.D. 1000-1500 Pisgah Phase are of four main types: rectilinear complicated stamped, curvilinear complicated stamped, check stamped, and plain. In addition, pots were sometimes finished on the outside with woven-reed, corncob, cord, or net impressions. The basic vessel form was a globular jar with a decorated, turned-out rim and a collar, but thickened rims, straight rims, and slanted rims were also produced. Rim appendages added for carrying and hanging purposes included loop handles, nodes, vertical lugs, and appliquéd strips. Most shallow bowls were decorated with a thin, pinched, or notched strip around the rim. Pottery clay was often tempered with fine to coarse sand, sometimes with crushed quartz, and rarely with shell or steatite. There was usually a large amount of mica in the clay. Vessel exterior colors were light gray to buff, and interiors ranged from dark gray to black. It is probable that the collared vessel form was introduced to the earliest Pisgah Phase residents from the northwest, along a frontier of expanding Mississippian culture, and perhaps as early as A.D. 1000.[15] About A.D.1450, a merger of Lamar and Pisgah styles resulted in the Qualla-series pottery that is identified with historically documented Cherokee towns.

Pisgah subsistence was equally based on hunting, gathering, and agriculture. Corn was of major importance to the diet and the economy, and other cultivated plants were squash, pumpkins, beans, and sump weed. Wild plant foods such as nuts, fruits, and small seeds were nearly as important as cultivated plant foods. White-tailed deer, wood bison, and wild turkeys were the most valued meat animals, but birds, amphibians, and fish were also hunted.

The Pisgah Phase is thought to represent in the Appalachian summit area the development period of a primarily Mississippian cultural pattern, although some Mississippian traits, such as shell-tempered pottery and extended-body burials that were common to the Tennessee Valley and the Southern

Piedmont, are missing. When we seek an establishment date for the Cherokees, it is interesting that while Pisgah sites discovered thus far contain permanent houses, palisades, and platform mounds, they are not identical to the later Cherokee towns and villages to the south and west. In other words, for some portion of the Pisgah Phase we are not yet dealing with actual Cherokees, but with a pre-Cherokee culture or cultures. The Garden Creek site was an important center in its day, but it does not compare in size and complexity with the great Cherokee centers in the Tennessee Valley, such as Hiwassee Island, or in the Southern Piedmont, such as Etowah. Some scholars have proposed that the town of Etowah was the administrative and redistributional center for a powerful chiefdom, and that the Etowah and other similar southeastern sites were the seats for priest-states having an upper class or caste as rulers of a state cult. But anthropologist Roy S. Dickens of Georgia State University believes that although the Garden Creek site and possibly other mound sites of the Pisgah Phase were the forerunners of the town centers of the historic Cherokees, they were not yet the focal points of fully developed chiefdoms or states. He thinks the Pisgah Phase simply included facets that were significant, and melded finally to become the major Cherokee culture that Europeans came upon in the eighteenth century.[16]

Life in the Qualla Phase

Extensive research has been going on in the southern part of the Appalachian summit area. In testimony to a burgeoning Cherokee culture, by the end of 1972, survey teams had located an amazing sum of more than 1,400 archaeological sites along the broad floodplains of the rivers, along the intermountain lands between the mountain slopes and the floodplain, on the floors of the coves, along the smaller creeks and branches in the mountains proper, on the ridges, and even on the mountain summits. Every part of the region was occupied for at least a short period of time during each of the culture phases. Historic, Mississippian, Woodland, and Archaic artifact types were found in all parts of

the mountains, along with remains of cultivated corn, beans, and squash.[17] Anthropologist Bennie C. Keel of Wright State University in Dayton, Ohio, believes that the Qualla Phase of A.D. 1500 to historic times represents the spiritual and material culture of the Cherokees as it was until it was replaced by the Euro-American material and economic culture in the nineteenth century. Nevertheless, he does not believe that sufficient data will ever be found to determine the exact ethnic or tribal affiliation of the prehistoric peoples of the area.[18]

Ceramics of the Qualla Phase have complicated stamping and bold incising on their exterior surface. Stone arrow tips are small, thin, and well made. Other stone finds are flake scrapers, side scrapers, and small chipped drills. Some gunflints of native manufacture have been found. There are stone pipes, but celt ax heads are the most commonly located ground-stone items that were fashioned during the period. Also found are discoidals, such as the round, thick, and large *chungke* game stones, and small counters that have ceramic additions usually made from potsherds. Stone pins that were worn in the hair or ears have been discovered, and they too have ceramic and shell decorations. Both native and imported shells were used to make beads, gorgets, hair or ear pins, ritual and hunting masks, ceremonial dippers, and pottery scrapers.[19]

The earliest architecture of the Qualla Phase included fairly large circular and rectangular structures that were placed on high, man-made dirt mounds and were employed as combination religious and political buildings. Personal habitations were smaller, rectangular, and set at grade level. In Chapter Two, construction techniques for all of these structures are described. By the end of the eighteenth century, the original habitations were being replaced by the typical frontier-type log cabins made of horizontal logs which were heavily chinked with clay.[20]

Burials were most often made in a simple pit, but a shaft-and-chamber type of grave was sometimes used. The bodies were flexed. Grave goods are rarely found and until the early historic period, ca. 1725, consisted exclusively of aboriginal items. It is evident from findings that trade relationships with Europeans were fairly well established by the beginning of the eighteenth century and that the Cherokees were exchanging furs and hides for French and English guns, blankets, knives, axes, hoes, tomahawks, beads, paint, hardware, and unfortunately, liquid spirits.[21] During the Qualla phase, natives made the most of the natural resources that were available. Hunting and gathering camps were located in mountain gaps and along stream heads. Scattered farmsteads were found in the intermountain zones, and villages were grouped around the central town council-house mounds. It appears that dispersed farmsteads or hamlets were linked to small ceremonial centers – a pattern that researchers believe made rapid growth possible, but also made it difficult to produce the strong, centralized political organization needed to efficiently combat the encroaching Euro-Americans.[22]

Nacoochee and Peachtree Mounds

Other sites important to note in regard to Cherokee history are the Nacoochee and Peachtree mounds. Nacoochee was a Cherokee village that was inhabited from A.D. 1540 to 1819. It included a town council house that was situated on top of a high mound and surrounded by individual dwellings. But little more is known about the history of the site.[23] In the Peachtree site, Woodland and Mississippian traits are blended and fused to make a culturally homogeneous site. Its time range is from before A.D. 1500 to 1830, and Cherokees may have occupied it during that entire period. But the absolute identification of the builders of the site remains questionable, and archaeologists hesitate to label it as pure Cherokee or to assign it unequivocably to any linguistic or ethnic group.[24]

Summary: Settlement and Formative Years

At this point we can say that the veils enshrouding the date of settlement and the formative years are substantially dissolved. It appears that the Cherokees settled in the Southeast about A.D. 1300, and their development took place in two periods, or stages. The first was a formative and more primitive one that extended from A.D. 1300 to 1540, and the second extended from 1540 to perhaps 1750, during which time they flowered into a major nation with a vibrant material and spiritual life. It was not practiced on so grand a scale as that of the middle-American Mayans and Aztecs, yet it was on a scale grand enough to impress anyone.

The only remaining matter is to construct a composite picture of the flourishing period, and considerable help for this is available from the first white traders as they report what they found among the Cherokees of the eighteenth century, and what, it is fair to assume, had been in place and functioning for a considerable period of time. When French and English traders made their first contacts with the Cherokees, the native town sites and population were still grouped in four main divisions. There were the Lower Settlements on the upper tributaries of the Savannah River in what is now South Carolina, the Middle Settlements on the easternmost reaches of the Little Tennessee and Tuckaseegee rivers in North Carolina between the Cowee and Balsam mountains, the Valley Settlements in western North Carolina along the Nantahala, Valley, and Hiwassee rivers, and the Overhill Settlements that were north of the Unakas range and south of the Cumberland range along the Upper and Lower Little Tennessee rivers. All of these places were forested and fertile land that teemed with wildlife and natural foods, springs and streams. The domain was so rich a place that nearby nations had been and were contesting for it against the Cherokees in such fierce and enduring encounters that the region was known as "the Dark and Bloody Ground." To the south and foremost among these nearby nations was the large, jealous, and aggressive Creek tribe, which never ceased to claim land as far north as the Tennessee River. To the west, in what is now lower Mississippi and Alabama, was the large and strong Choctaw tribe. And in northern Mississippi were the Chickasaws, a small tribe whose warriors were so fierce they would do battle at the slightest provocation. The Muscogees were also a thorn in the Cherokee side. Nevertheless, there were moments of peace, and at times one tribe might unite with another against a common enemy.

Intriguing peace belts, called "wampum belts," and spectacular medicine pipes were carried in backpacks by Cherokee leaders and brought as proofs of peaceful intent to councils of peace. Wampum belts used in peace conferences with the Iroquois were preserved by the Cherokees for nearly a century and were carried with them to Indian Territory when the majority of the tribe was finally driven from its southeastern home in 1838. The belts were then in the keeping of John Ross, principal chief at the time of the removal, and were solemnly produced at a great intertribal peace council held near Tahlequah, in the Indian Territory, in June 1843, where they were interpreted by a Cherokee speaker who had seen them delivered to the chiefs of his tribe at the old town of Itsati seventy years before.[25]

Even though there were four main divisions of their population, the Cherokees recognized only two geographic divisions of their country, which they termed *Ayrate,* or "low," and *Ottare,* or "mountainous." The low division included those who were settled along the head branches of the beautiful Savannah River, and the mountainous division those who were settled along the easternmost branch of the great Mississippi. Although the towns and villages were widely scattered, every one was located close to a river or creek where the land was level and fertile — for crop-cultivation purposes, as sources of fish and shellfish, and as places that attracted deer, elk, bear, bison, and fowl. The Cherokees also ate the saltish moss and grass that grew on the rocks and under the surface of the water. Most importantly, running water was needed for the numerous purification rituals that attended every ceremony.[26]

When the year 1735 dawned, the Cherokee nation was large and powerful. There were numerous towns and villages, and white traders claimed there were more than 6,000 Cherokee warriors of fighting age — a dangerous number, the traders feared, to have so close to the small settlements of the intruding whites. Moreover, many of the Cherokee sites were in many places surrounded by nearly inaccessible mountains capped by blue-topped ridges, where only a handful of skilled Cherokee warriors could dig in and hold off for a surprisingly long time even a

force of Indian enemies.[27] The western towns of this period were always engaged in what one trader described as "hot war" with the more northern Indians, while the middle towns were constantly fighting the Muscogees. Losses were inevitable, and before long, several of the finest Cherokee towns along the southern branch of the Savannah River were destroyed and forsaken, and the borders of habitable Cherokee country were steadily shrinking. By the conclusion of the most recent battle, a trader claimed in 1740, the Cherokee fighting force had been reduced to 2,300 men. This was a foreboding portent, and it caused considerable introspection among the Cherokee people. Most traders began to wonder whether any Cherokee town or citizen would long survive. But survive they did, and life continued.

The ability to survive has been, in fact, a remarkable characteristic of the Cherokees, and in the pages ahead we will see that it can be attributed to their religious beliefs and the inner peace those beliefs brought to them. Although some activities were preferred and others were put off as long as possible, as a whole the Cherokee lifeway was an active one. Religious thought and performance dominated other pursuits, and I deal extensively with this aspect of life in the chapters ahead. But the activity that took the Cherokees farthest afield and demanded special attention was warfare of the revenge kind. It was highly organized and undertaken on a massive scale, often requiring travel as far north as the Ohio River, as far west as the lower Tennessee and Mississippi rivers, and as far east as the Atlantic coast. Some current researchers believe it is entirely possible that the broad land claims of the Cherokees were to great extent based on the exploits of war parties that had traveled great distances.

Slightly less in scope was hunting for deer, elk, bison, bear, and beaver, all of whose meat, hides, teeth, and bones were essential to life. As men searched for game, they were often required to travel great distances along rivers, valleys, or mountain ridges. Hunting was the practice of specialists who had been trained to carefully observe the physical and spiritual habits of animals and birds, and who because of this knew the best ways to capture and kill them. As time passed, the Cherokee priests developed intriguing prayer formulas for luring and controlling game that were memorized and employed by the hunting specialists. Some of these formulas are described in Chapter Two. Land cultivation and utilization were not so extensive a pursuit as warfare and hunting, since they were carried out close to home on the river bottoms and nearby slopes. Archaeologists have discovered that the Cherokees wisely developed both primary and secondary living habitats. Examples of this are the Blue Ridge primary habitat and the Valley Provinces secondary habitat. It is entirely possible that the secondary habitats were developed as places to fall back on in times of emergency, such as during natural calamities and warfare. An activity of unknown scope was trade with other tribes, although it assuredly did go on. For example, it is known that Eastern Siouans, Choctaws, and Chitimachas acted as trading intermediaries for the exchange of goods between otherwise warring southeastern tribes, and that the development of trade accounted in large measure for the building up of the entire material culture of the southeast region.[28]

The Cherokees: An Adaptable, Dynamic People

Taken as a whole, the foregoing information about ancient Cherokee life makes it clear that the people had an especially dynamic culture whose composition was the result of adventuring, diverse contacts, mergers, and frequent changes of old lamps for new. This truth gives us our first hint about a Cherokee trait of some consequence in their national evolution, which was an adaptability that welcomed and made use of the new things and ways they encountered. As their story develops and we consider what happens to them, we will see that adaptability was, depending on the circumstance and how one looks at it, sometimes a blessing, often a culprit, and now and then an overwhelming curse. We are,

however, only on the edge of this enthralling story. The veils are only beginning to lift. Dealing with archaeological finds is one thing, dealing with people is another. We must move closer to the Cherokees as human beings who have had the same talents, hopes, dreams, needs, emotions, conflicts, and accomplishments that are common to all of humankind.

NOTES

1. Haywood, *The Natural and Aboriginal History of Tennessee*, pp. 231 ff.
2. Gilbert, "The Eastern Cherokees," pp. 182-184.
3. Adair, *History of the American Indians,* pp. 240-241.
4. Gilbert, pp. 182-183.
5. Adair, p. 241.
6. Gilbert, p. 184.
7. Ibid., pp. 185-186, and Mooney, *Myths of the Cherokee,* pp. 286-287.
8. Gilbert, p. 184.
9. Smith, W. R. L., *The Story of the Cherokees,* pp. 16-17.
10. Swanton, "Indians of Southeastern United States," pp. 114-115.
11. Keel, *Cherokee Archaeology,* p. 233.
12. Dickens, *Cherokee Prehistory,* p. 206.
13. Ibid., pp. 206-207.
14. Ibid., pp. 207-208.
15. Ibid.
16. Ibid., pp. 208-209.
17. Ibid., pp. 211-214.
18. Keel, p. 233.
19. Ibid.
20. Ibid., p. 215.
21. Ibid.
22. Ibid., p. 216.
23. Mooney, pp. 526-527, and Heye, Hodge, and Pepper, "The Nacoochee Mound in Georgia," pp. 4-99.
24. Setzler and Jennings, "Peachtree Mound and Village Site, Cherokee County, North Carolina," pp. 4-57.
25. Mooney, p. 355.
26. Adair, pp. 239-240.
27. Ibid., p. 238.
28. Gilbert, pp. 187-188.

CHAPTER TWO

Physical Appearance, Material Culture, Games

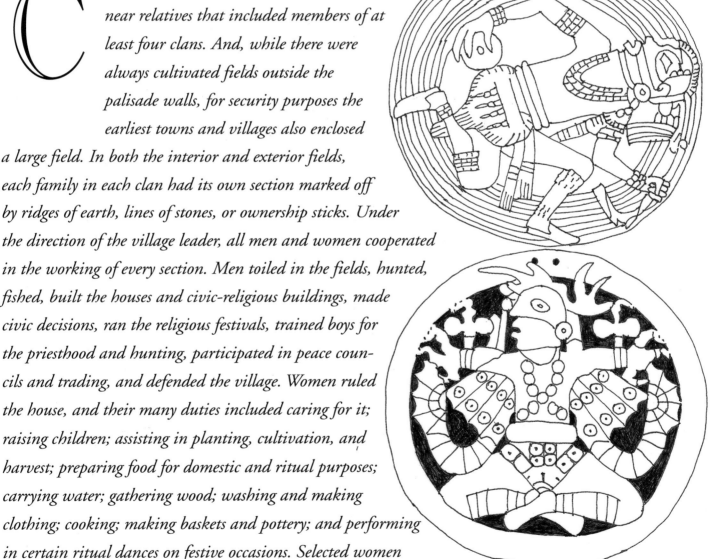

Cherokee settlements were made up of groups of near relatives that included members of at least four clans. And, while there were always cultivated fields outside the palisade walls, for security purposes the earliest towns and villages also enclosed a large field. In both the interior and exterior fields, each family in each clan had its own section marked off by ridges of earth, lines of stones, or ownership sticks. Under the direction of the village leader, all men and women cooperated in the working of every section. Men toiled in the fields, hunted, fished, built the houses and civic-religious buildings, made civic decisions, ran the religious festivals, trained boys for the priesthood and hunting, participated in peace councils and trading, and defended the village. Women ruled the house, and their many duties included caring for it; raising children; assisting in planting, cultivation, and harvest; preparing food for domestic and ritual purposes; carrying water; gathering wood; washing and making clothing; cooking; making baskets and pottery; and performing in certain ritual dances on festive occasions. Selected women shared in council decisions, and Beloved Women determined what would happen to Indian captives.

Inscribed shell gorgets.

Launching log canoes.

Typical male and female attire for inclement months.

White traders described the adult male Cherokee as frank and honest, and in warfare, fierce,
cunning, and unforgiving. He was a lover of freedom
and jealous of his rights. He loved his wife and
children, and in his home, harsh behavior was rare.
The Cherokee woman was mild mannered, amiable,
modest, and industrious. Physically and tempera-
mentally, the mature Cherokees made a favorable
impression. They delighted in athletics and excelled
in endurance. Well featured and of erect carriage,
they were of moderately robust build, and had a
superior and independent bearing. Although grave in
manner and slow and reserved in speech while
participating in public affairs, in private life they
were frank, cheerful, humane, and liberal.

Mature men of the seventeenth and eighteenth
centuries were tall and lank, athletic and sinewy.
Their lips were thin, cheekbones were high, forehead
was narrow, and nose was fat and round. The

Western Cherokees were once called flatheads, and
reference to head flattening during the Pisgah Phase
has been made. But the custom was apparently a
briefly practiced one during the period of early
contact with the Eastern Siouans.[1] The adult hair of
both sexes was coarse, straight, and black, sometimes
appearing brownish red. Children's hair was the same
color, but by comparison, quite soft. Several of
Payne's informants claimed that in more ancient
times, Cherokee men wore beards that seldom
exceeded six inches in length. Some men let their
beards fall loose, but others plaited them, with one
braid hanging from each side of the mouth and one
from the chin. The mustache was either pulled out,
or trimmed to where it did not hang over the mouth.
By historic times the whiskers were being pulled out,
so that the entire face was bare.[2] Cherokee pupils
were jet black, and vision was as keen as that of the
eagle. Complexions were variously described as

Typical male attire in clement months.

Man wearing a typical otter skin for winter.

bear, deer, otter, beaver, and mountain lion, and winter moccasins made of beaver skins. Other male garments consisted of long-sleeved, hip-length hide shirts; tubular-style, fringed hide leggings that had no seat to connect them and were secured to the belt by means of straps; and breeches-like hide breechclouts. The breechclout consisted of two formfitted aprons, one in front and one behind, that were tied above the hips to the same narrow buck-skin belt that held up the leggings, and which extended halfway down to the knees. The aprons were tied together at the man's sides, and the middle of each apron was drawn up between the legs until the two ends could be tied together with thongs. When necessary, the thongs were untied for hygienic purposes. The breechclouts were often dyed, and in the case of the war leaders, were a vivid red.[3] A colorful, broad-woven belt with tasseled yarn ties, made by female finger weavers, was worn over the breechclout, and from this belt at the right side was hung the knife and sheath and at the front by means of thongs a midsized, painted buckskin pouch that was used to carry miscellaneous items such as smoking tobacco, pipes, flint, bullets, patches, mending supplies, and glue sticks.

Men wore hide arm and wristbands, to which dew horn and shell were attached as pendent rattles. In historic times, silver bells were obtained from traders and replaced the horn and shell.

Except for priests, some of whom left their hair long and loose, Cherokee warriors distinguished themselves from their enemies — who shaved, except for a roachlike section, their entire heads — by leaving on the crowns of their heads a long tuft of hair that was as broad as a man's palm, then shaving or plucking around it only a two-inch-wide ring.[4] The rest of the hair at the sides and back was cut short and neatly trimmed. The finished product was something like the tonsure of a Roman Catholic monk. The Natchez men wore, except for a smaller tuft, a similar style, as did the Timucas depicted by Jacques Le Moyne in 1564.[5]

A two- or three-inch-long piece of hollow deer antler was fastened to the tuft by pulling the tuft through it. The way in which the long, thick tuft

cinnamon brown, light yellow-brown, dark as burned coffee, copper colored, deep chestnut, and obscured by red paint or other colored pigments.

Exceptional beauty was common among young women, and women in general had extremities that were small, delicate, and slender.

Daily Attire of Men, Women, and Children

Ordinary Cherokee men — those who did not hold special rank or position — wore belted skin robes that were fashioned from the tanned hides of

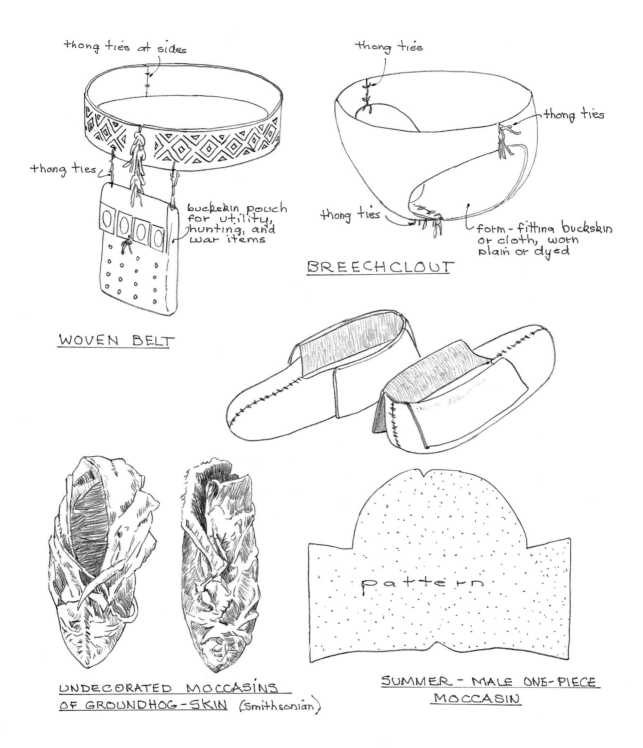

thong ties at sides

thong ties

thong ties

thong ties

thong ties

buckskin pouch for utility, hunting, and war items

form-fitting buckskin or cloth, worn plain or dyed

BREECHCLOUT

WOVEN BELT

pattern

UNDECORATED MOCCASINS OF GROUNDHOG-SKIN (Smithsonian)

SUMMER - MALE ONE-PIECE MOCCASIN

arched gracefully up and fell back made it unnecessary for the Cherokee warrior to have a scalplock. An enemy would have been perfectly happy to cut the tuft itself off where it joined the scalp. The top of the horn tube was ornamented with various items that probably identified the town or larger area each man came from — colored or quill-wrapped thongs with tassels on their ends, beads, feathers, shells, stained deer's hair, and more.[6] The exposed part of the tuft of hair was painted with a thick paste made with red or yellow earth.

In historic times, white traders supplied hollow silver horns to replace the sections of deer antler and also supplied round or quarter-moon-shaped silver

Two views of a massive stone pipe depicting man preparing to throw a chungke game stone, from City Art Museum of St. Louis. This suggests an ancient source for a type of Cherokee hairstyle adopted by the maturing tribe and reported by Payne's informants.

breastplates to be worn on the chest. In winter, it was common for men to wear either an otter-skin headband or an otter-skin cap that was slightly conical in shape and had a front appendage of white opossum hair dyed red. The brim was cut almost round and was decorated with loops or disks made of lead. Male moccasins were of the one-piece style with soft soles. Everyday moccasins were not decorated, but dress moccasins were adorned with quills, cloth, and beads, and in the case of men of status, were painted or dyed. Various kinds of animal skins were used to make moccasins, and winter moccasins other than the beaver type were like boots with the animal hair left on and turned inside to hold the heat. It can be assumed that like the Plains Indians, the Cherokees smoked their winter moccasins over a fire to waterproof them.

Nose rings with attached pieces of perforated shell were worn, sometimes in the pierced middle piece of cartilage, and sometimes at the side of the right or left nostril. Some renowned men were entitled to wear necklaces of mountain-lion skin with the hair left on and with small horn bells attached. Other men wore thong necklaces, to which were appended various ornaments such as gorgets made of stone, horn, metal, and shell.[7] My opinion is that the style of gorget varied according to the community as a means of town or area identification. Great attention was paid to body decoration, and the skin was either painted or tattooed with gunpowder pricked on in various and fanciful patterns. Men's ears were split with knives and stretched to enormous size by the insertion of stone or bone earplugs, after which they were hung with earrings made of stone, shell, lead, and later on, silver pendants and rings.[8] The operation for this is described as one of incredible pain, with the patient thereafter being unable to lie on either side for nearly forty days. To avoid this, some people had only one ear slit at a time. As soon as the patient could bear it, the outer edge of the ear was wound round with wire and the expansion plugs were inserted.[9]

Women wore short, sleeveless, close-fitting deerskin dresses and used fishbone needles to sew them together with deer sinew. The dresses were belted at the waist with broad, woven belts and fastened at the bosom with hasps or broaches made of bone. There was also a hide handkerchief that was worn around the neck and tucked down into the bosom. A bell was attached to the handkerchief. Under the dress was a petticoat that was woven or knitted from wild hemp. This extended down to the knees and had a long fringe that reached the ankles. Women of status were permitted to weave colorful beads and feathers into the fringe and into the body of the dress itself. Women wore no leggings but had deerskin moccasins that were made like half boots, came up to the knee, and had small bells attached at the ankles. These bells worn by the women tinkled as they walked and filled the air with soft music. When the word pictures of both male and female costume are translated into drawings, it is seen that an atmosphere of general beauty prevailed in the towns and villages.

Women worked bear grease into their hair to make it glossy, then sprinkled it with red and yellow earth. Some women let their hair hang straight and loose, while others tied it in classic Greek fashion in a knot on top of the crown. It is said that women plucked out all other hair on their bodies. Like the men, women usually had the rims of their ears pierced and strung with metal ornaments. They also wore multiple strings of beads made of seashells, horn, or turkey bones and overlapped each string in such a way as to nearly cover the chest. Both sexes wore metal finger rings.[10]

Daily attire was fashioned from deer and other skins, but for festive occasions there was cloth made of turkey feathers, mulberry-root bark, and other items. Ornamental articles were made with white opossum hair that was dyed red, yellow, black, and other colors. This hair was spun into threads and dyed yellow, black, or a florid red. The threads were interwoven to make belts and garters for the men, and with the red threads alone, women wove or knit the cap of the Chief War Priest. Sometimes, bear's hair was spun to obtain a black thread that was used to make black cloth. White hair threads were dyed yellow with a certain root called *Ta lo ny* and with black oak bark. Bloodroot was used to make the hair red. Black was obtained from black walnut, butternut, and sourwood.[11]

Young children wore nothing during the clement months and only skin robes and fur-lined moccasins in the winter. Older children, since the Cherokees were very concerned about moral conduct, wore cloth or animal-skin skirts. As puberty approached, the mature costumes of men and women were adopted.

The fabulous costumes of the town priests, the Great High Priest, and the Great War Chief are treated in detail in Chapter Three, where the roles of those men in government and warfare are considered. But in the discussion of clothing, it should be mentioned at this point that the Great War Chief wore as his regular, everyday badge of distinction — on his head, on both arms above the elbows, and on both legs just below the knees where other men wore garters — bands of otter skin with the hair left on. He also had a weasel skin, dressed whole, in which his *U lv sa ta*, or divining crystal, was kept. The crystal was put in the middle of the piece of skin, and the skin was folded around it to make a packet the size of the palm of his hand. The packet was hung round his neck by means of a thong and rested on his chest. All others who used divining crystals carried them in some secret place on their persons, but the Great War Chief carried his openly. Should he be killed in battle, it was imperative that his warriors rescue this stone and preserve it, for the first objective of the enemy was to destroy its power by seizing it and smashing it between two stones.

Headdress for Battle or Ball Game

All warriors and ball players, before engaging in battle or in a game, tied or had tied a feather to their tufts of hair, and attached to the end of this feather another that was three or four inches long and dyed scarlet. The red feathers were considered very sacred. Only those who were pledged to the task as infants, or who were committed to sacred offices by age nine, could dye them. Shortly before a large battle, at the request of the seven principal counselors of the Great High Priest or the Great War Chief, the small feathers were gathered up and sent to a sacred painter or painters to be dyed. But for a small war expedition or for ball play, they could be painted whenever the leader of the event requested it.

The feathers tied directly to the tuft of hair on a man's crown were not painted, and had to be those taken from the right wing of an eagle, raven, mountain hawk, sparrow hawk, long-tailed hawk, or large chicken hawk. Those of the eagle and the large mountain hawk were the most highly esteemed.

The feathers dyed red were those which grew directly under the large tail feathers of the eagle and hawk. They were withheld from public view until dyed and used. When the sacred painter received them, he immediately took them to a remote thicket where he tied them up on bunches and hung them on boughs. The next morning he searched for the materials needed for the dying. If the trees were in leaf, he used leaves, but if not, he used the bark of the root of a low shrub called *Ta lo ny*. This was not the common *Ta lo ny* used for smoking, but another species that was more rare and grew on high mountains. Next, he obtained some of the inside bark of a kind of black oak. He took his materials to the place where he had left the feathers and spread them out to dry in the sun or by a fire. Only then was the painter permitted to eat and drink.

Before breakfast the next morning, he washed his mortar and used it to pound the leaves and bark to a powder, adding a little strong lye that turned the material a beautiful green. This done, he filled his pot with pure water, made a fire with coals that he had taken from the sacred fire kept burning in the town council house, and put the green powder into a water-filled pot. While he prayed for a divine infusion of power into the feathers, he took in succession the bunches of feathers and dyed them by holding each one between the thumb and forefinger of his right hand while he dipped it into the water five times. On the fifth time he let go of it and permitted it to sink to the bottom of the pot. When all of the bunches were in the pot, he placed the pot on the fire and kept it simmering until sunset, when he took the feathers out of the pot, untied the bunches, and spread them out to dry. They were then a most brilliant yellow.

The following morning, the sacred painter, having selected several boys of unquestioned purity to assist him, commenced his search for a root called "the blood." This root was scarce and difficult to obtain. The part that was needed consisted of hundreds of fine hair threads that connected the principal part of the root to the stem. Neither the painter nor the boys was permitted to eat a meal until a sufficient quantity of the root was found and put in a secret place to dry. That night, the painter expected to have dreams that would give him omens concerning the success of the war party. The dreams usually made him sad, and slowed the completion of his work. So once the bloodroots were drying, he went to a place where he could fast and be alone. Not long before sunset, he returned to pound the bloodroot to a powder. He then put a cane sieve into the pot containing the yellow dye and, taking the bloodroot powder in his hands, divided it into equal portions, one of which was put in the pot and the other put aside. Next, he took the feathers, tied them in bunches as before, and again dipped them five times into the pot, praying as he did so that when the enemy saw the Cherokee warriors wearing the red feathers their strength would be taken away, and they would be rendered unable to fight. Finally, he set the pot on the fire, and when it began to boil, put into it the rest of the bloodroot powder. In a short while, just as the sun was going down, he removed the pot, extracted the feathers, and put them away where no one — especially a woman — could see them. Then he ate and slept.

The next morning the painter wrapped the

dyed scarlet feathers in a deer hide so no one else could see them, and delivered them to a messenger. If the feathers were to be used for a large-scale war, the messenger took them to the priest who would carry them while the war party advanced toward the enemy. On or about the seventh night of the march, after observing a vigil, the priest took the unpainted feathers, attached the red feathers to the ends of each with a daub of red clay, and secured the finished items to the warrior's hair tufts. It was the act that served as the final preparation for the battle — and we can see in it and in the involved preparation of the red feathers something of the lengths to which the Cherokees went to obtain divine power and blessings, and thus enhance success.

The feathers of those who survived a battle could be kept for future use, but no effort was made to preserve the feathers of those who fell. For ball-play purposes, the prayers of the sacred painter were different, and the feathers were fastened to the hair just as the game was to begin.[12]

Building Houses

The natives of the Qualla and early historic periods lived in one-, two-, or three-room, one- or two-story, gable-roofed, square or rectangular dwellings. Men did the home construction work and turned out early in the spring to strip from trees the boards and cypress bark needed to cover their buildings. But the work stopped there. As the days grew warmer, able-bodied men turned to planting and to warfare. House building could always be put off, and everyone knew that in the hot summer it was a needless and foolish affair that occasioned much sweating.[13]

When fall arrived and warfare waned, the men of the entire town, frequently with the help of men from neighboring towns, gathered to build houses, and in a single day would erect and finish a good-sized dwelling.

The work was done in an efficient and professional manner. The dimensions of the house were established by drawing lines on the ground, and every man had an assigned task. The timbers were cut and marked, and within a few hours the men were ready to put up the building. Plummet stones suspended on thongs were used to align the walls, much as modern carpenters use them. At regular intervals along the exterior wall lines, strong posts were set deep in the ground and extended above grade for six or seven feet. The posts were usually sassafras and dried locust, which were durable and would last for years. The posts were notched on top. Wall plates were laid on top of the notches. Then a large post, also notched to receive both wall plates and a ridgepole, was set up in the center of each gable end along with a similar post in the middle of the house wherever a partition or partitions would go. On top of the ridgepole, which ran the length of the house, were set and tied at regular intervals — using as ties bark strips or splinters of white oak or hickory — saplings of sufficient length to reach from one side of the house to the other. These passed over the ridgepole. At the place where they touched it, they were notched to make a good joint and at the joint were bound to the ridgepole with bark strips. Sometimes pole rafters were used instead of the saplings. Above the rafters or saplings, running the length of the house, was either a solid, matlike layer of split saplings or bundles consisting of three large winter canes that were tied together. These formed the finished ceiling. To hold up eave boards, strong tree crooks were lashed to the wall plates on both sides of the house and were also fastened to the rafters with the kinds of ties already described.

Since the poplar tree was very soft, the workers used small hatchets to make eave boards of it. An eave board was placed on top of the crooks on each side of the house, and it jutted a foot or so beyond the end of the wall. These were covered with easily split pine or cypress clapboards, and the roof itself was shingled with the bark of the same trees, all of a proper length and breadth. As mentioned earlier, they had been collected in the spring.

To secure the shingles against high winds, a number of long, split saplings reaching from end to end of the house were tied on top of the shingles. Above and at right angles to these, heavy logs were placed on each side of the roof, one end of which rested on the eave boards while the other ends

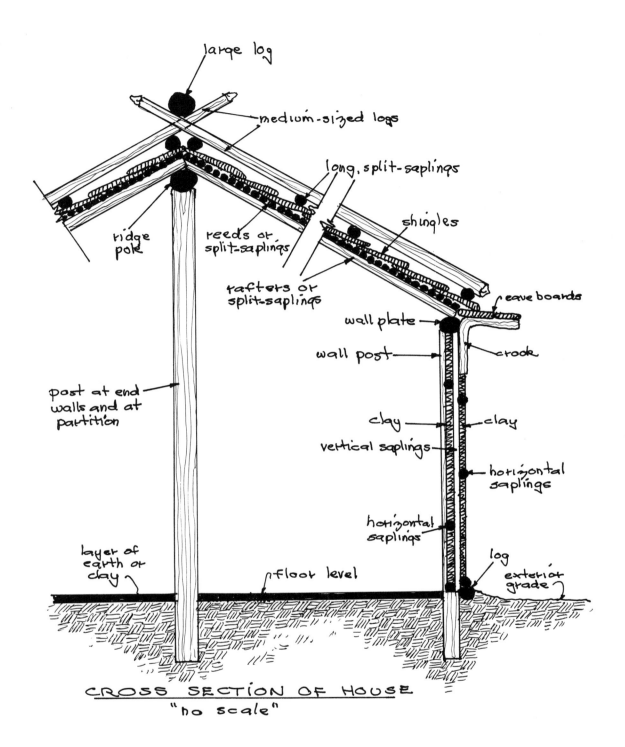

large log

medium-sized logs

long, split-saplings

ridge pole

reeds or split-saplings

shingles

rafters or split-saplings

eave boards

wall plate

wall post

crook

post at end walls and at partition

clay

clay

vertical saplings

horizontal saplings

horizontal saplings

layer of earth or clay

floor level

log

exterior grade

CROSS SECTION OF HOUSE
"no scale"

overlapped each other at the ridgepole for a distance of about two feet. Into the V thus formed, the builders dropped a heavy log and tied the whole securely together.

Exterior wall spaces were filled in with vertically placed split sticks and poles that were tied together and then strengthened by horizontally placed saplings. The sticks, saplings, and poles were then plastered over inside and out with clay tempered with grass. One-foot-square window holes were cut in the walls for ventilation. House doors were made of poplar planks, with two or three crossbars affixed to the inner side, tied on with straps of shaved and wet buffalo hide, which tightened as it dried and made the doors exceedingly strong.[14]

The barrier towns — those most exposed to

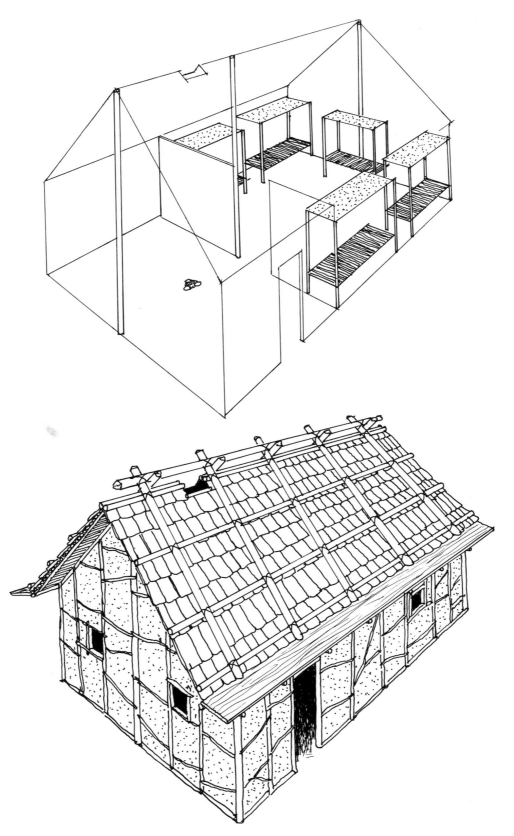

Typical house of late prehistoric period. *Top,* interior view showing hearth in living room and beds in bedroom. *Bottom,* exterior view.

enemy war parties — used very few regular windows and had small windows that were daubed over with clay on the exterior so the enemy could not locate them easily. When an attack took place, these hidden windows could be quickly knocked open and used as firing ports.

House Furniture

House furniture consisted of little more than stools, storage chests, and three-foot-high broad beds that were located at the back and sides of the house, were made of boards, and had white-oak foundations and cane-splinter mattresses covered with bear, buffalo, mountain-lion, elk, and deerskins, dressed with the hair on. It can be assumed that the beds had canopy tops and curtains to keep out the cold and provide privacy.

The beds were raised up on four forks of timber of a proper height to make it difficult for swarming fleas to attack. The blankets of male children were mountain-lion skins, which transmitted to the children the powers of acute smell, strength, cunning, and a prodigious spring, and which gave them the first rudiments of war. Female children were given the skins of fawns or buffalo calves, since these were "shy and timorous" animals.[15]

Stools were made from poplar wood, and wood storage chests were fashioned of clapboards sewn to crossbars with wet strips of buffalo rawhide. Domestic utensils included earthen pots, pans, jugs, mugs, jars, wooden dishes and spoons, and buffalo-horn spoons.[16] Women crafted handsome carpets of hemp that were painted with colored figures as numerous as their imaginations could devise.[17]

Opposite the front door of each dwelling was a small sweat house. Inside this structure a fire was kept burning, and residents sweated there to purify themselves for religious purposes and to cure diseases. There were separate social houses in each village for the women, and wives always retired there when male visitors arrived to see their husbands.[18]

Winter Hothouses

In the colder areas, the people of each town or village provided themselves with large winter hot-houses, whose walls and roof were designed to retain and reflect heat. To build these, they fixed deep in the ground the ends of a number of strong, forked posts that were set up at proportional distances and formed the basis of a circular wall. The posts were of an equal length and reached five or six feet above grade level. To these posts they tied horizontal pieces of the heart of a tough white oak that was flexible in nature. Interwoven vertically in basketry fashion among the oak pieces and from top to bottom of the wall were slimmer pieces of white oak. In the middle of the hothouse and in a quadrangular form, the builders set up four large and very tall pine posts that were notched on top to receive wall plates. On top of the plates were laid in crib fashion a number of heavy logs that were let into each other as cabin logs are, and whose layers narrowed gradually as they approached the roof peak. Above this cribbed structure the builders put down a solid layer of long, dried poles that were notched where they passed over the cribbed logs and were secured with bark ties. A similar layer of poles bridged the gap from the cribbed section to the outer walls, so that overall the finished roof structure was cone shaped.

The hothouse wall was daubed six or seven inches thick with clay tempered with withered grass. As soon as the plaster was half dried, the builders thatched the roof with the longest sort of dry grass that grew in Cherokee country. To do this, they first laid one round tier, placed a row of split saplings on top of it, and tied these to the roof poles and rafters. They proceeded with successive round tiers until the peak of the roof was reached, where an upright pole was fixed that displayed on its top the carved figure of a large eagle. On the rooftop directly below the pole, four heavy logs were tied together in a square form to secure the roof and the pole against high winds. The door of the hothouse was four feet high and so narrow it would admit only one person at a time. It was set up in a vestibule that jutted from the side of the building and led to a short ramp with a winding passageway that secured the interior from strong winds and made a surprise attack by enemies more difficult. Since the hothouses were usually built on high ground, the floor was three or so feet lower than grade. This provided a dirt bench and exterior wall that could serve as a defensive breastwork. Small windows were inserted in the upper wall to enable residents to peek out and see whether enemies were lurking outside.[19]

At the end of the fall season, women built a large fire of dry wood in the center of the hothouse. When the wood was a little more than half consumed, they covered it with ashes and, as the heat declined, struck off some of the top embers with long pieces of hollow cane, one of which was provided as a heater for each broad seat or bed in the hothouse. This ritual was repeated from time to time until daylight. So long as the heaters were used, the hothouse, lacking sufficient windows and air, was hot, smoky, and dark, and during this time most people lay on their beds with their heads wrapped up in loosely woven cloths.[20]

Town Council House

Every town had in its center a circular, fifty-or-so-foot diameter, town council house that sat on top of a man-made earth mound. Adair claims that the only difference between it and the hothouse was in its dimensions and application. Here the old beloved men and head warriors met to discuss and plan civic and religious matters, gathered for social purposes and diversion, and feasted and danced with the entire community. This house was the hub of the settlement, and was furnished on the inside with soft couches to either sit or lie on. Each couch was about seven feet wide and eight feet long, with the seat sloping toward the back or the wall to keep people from falling off when they dozed. Seats were assigned according to rank, and clans sat together.[21] Much more is said about the town council house in Chapter Four.

Food and Drink

Women cooked their food by frying, roasting, or boiling, and the finished products were so delicious that the eastern branch of the Cherokee Nation — those who live in North Carolina where the heart of the ancient domain once was — still prepare many of the dishes in the old way.

There were various ways to make bread. Sometimes the cooks formed it in thin cakes, put it on a heated clay or stone hearth, and covered it with hot coals and ashes. Other times they put a loaf on the hot hearth, covered it with a shallow earthen pan, and put coals on top of the pan. A third method was to set a shallow pan on coals and to bake thin cakes in the pan. They also mixed bread in a shallow basket two feet in diameter. The dough was spread over the bottom of the basket as thick as the desired loaf. The top was smoothed, and the dough was covered with the large leaves of the cucumber tree. The basket was then flipped bottom up onto the hot hearth and removed, leaving only the loaf lying on the leaves. The dough was then covered with the same kind of leaves, and finally with a layer of hot ashes and coals.[22]

Considerable use was made of parched cornmeal. The parching was done by placing the corn in a pot that held sifted ashes, mixing them together, then stirring them constantly as they cooked. The finished product kept well, and was carried on long trips and hunting and war expeditions.[23]

One kind of soup was made of parched cornmeal and grapes. The cooks first boiled the grapes, then mixed in meal until the soup was the consistency of honey. When it was cool, they ate it with wooden or buffalo-horn spoons. As was indicated earlier, they had but few eating and cooking utensils, and vessel bottoms were rounded so they would sit level in a bed of sand or on top of a fire. Earthen oven ware accommodated all of the baking and frying and held various liquids. Gourds were used for carrying water. Deerskin bottles held bear oil, honey, and other thick substances. Sieves, leaching baskets, and mats were made of split cane.

Wars and crop failures often caused the Cherokees to fall back on wild foods. Cane wheat was a species of low cane that grew on the banks of rivers. Its leaves were dried, pounded, and used as meal. *Tse wi na* was a small root resembling a turnip. It was washed, boiled for twenty-four hours, then dried, pounded, and used as meal. If boiled for fewer hours, it would make those who ate it ill. *U la tli ya* was a root that grew in clusters and had vertical extensions like beets. It was washed, cut into small pieces, dried, and pounded into meal. The dough made of it was baked, fried, or boiled. *Kv ni ku tsa ta* was similar in appearance to *U la tli ya*, except that it did not grow in clusters. It was prepared and used in the same matter as the latter.

Kv lo hi was a root that grew in water where the mud was very deep. It was about a foot long and similar in shape to a beet root. Its strong and unpleasant taste was leached out by two methods: it was either washed, placed in a pot of water, and boiled until two fillings of water were used up, or hot water was poured on it until the strong taste was gone. The leached root was then cut into small pieces that were dried and pounded into meal. The bread or fritters made of the meal tasted like flour. *Tu yv sti* was a small root that resembled a turnip, and was probably what was called "Indian turnip." It too was boiled to remove its strong, acrid taste, and mixed or kneaded like dough before it was baked or fried. *U kv na sta* was a sweet root that was white and from six inches to a foot in length. It grew horizontally, just below the earth's surface. The bottom portion was boiled and while wet was pounded in a mortar until it

could be kneaded like dough and made into cakes or loaves. The top of the root was boiled and eaten for greens after being dipped in bear oil. The largest of these roots were found on mountain sides.

Shv ne si grew in pods in spring beds and resembled beans. It must be boiled for twenty-four hours to remove its deadly poison. But after sufficient boiling, drying, and pounding, it formed a meal or flour whose taste resembled that of wheat, and it could be used for all of the purposes of flour. The pods were also made into mush, but after eating the mush, the people must eat no fruit for twenty-four hours, else the combination of foods might kill them. *Shu le* was a small yellow acorn that grew on a species of red oak. While all varieties of acorns would make bread, *Shu le* was preferred. The acorns were dried, hulled, sifted, and pounded. The meats were then put into a leaching basket, and a cloth was tied over the top. Water was dripped on the cloth throughout the night, soaked into the meal, and then ran out through the bottom of the basket. The strong, bitter taste of the original acorn was removed, and the final product could be rendered into bread.

The seeds of ripe persimmons were removed,

Woman working at finger-weaving loom. Typical female attire for clement months.

pounded in a mortar, kneaded like dough, made into cakes, and put on a scaffold to dry in the sun. They could be stored for future use. Bread was made from ripe peaches after removing both the seeds and the skin. Breads of all kinds were dipped in bear oil or oil of some other kind. Dried venison was also dipped in oil. To make bread even more delicious, the dough was mixed with boiled beans, the meat of black walnuts, chestnuts, whortleberries, or some other kind of fruit.

A highly esteemed food grew in the southern swamps. The Cherokees called it *Ta la*. It abounded in Florida and formed the principal food of the Seminoles. It was a species of cane, but had no joints. Growing four or five feet high, it had on its tip a ball that contained the food. The shells of the balls themselves were hard and, like gourds, were used for rattles.

There were several kinds of nutritious drinks. Honey-locust pods were gathered when ripe and put away to dry. To prepare the drink, women put some of the pods into a pot, poured water over them, broke or mashed the pods, then placed the pot in the sun or by a fire where the water would become lukewarm. It was soon sufficiently sweet to drink. Later, hotter water was poured onto the pods to extract the remaining sweetness. Hickory nuts were gathered, pounded, and sifted, and the nut meats were placed in cold water. This resulted in a delicious and nourishing drink. Large quantities of ripe grapes were gathered, tied in large bunches, and hung under the eaves to dry. To make a soup of them, they were boiled and strained through a cane sieve to remove the seeds. The liquid was boiled again and then thickened with a meal such as that of parched corn until it was the consistency of honey.

By 1835, Cherokees had learned to make beer out of persimmons, but no fermented drink was made by the ancient people.[24]

The Manufacture of Goods

The women are described as the chief manufacturers of goods. Buffalo-hair cloaks were made. The hairs were spun as finely as possible, then doubled, and had small beads of different colors worked into

them in figures. Turkey-feather blankets were made by interweaving the long feathers of the neck and breast with hemp or mulberry bark. Since the turkey feathers were long and glittering, this kind of blanket was both warm and pleasing to the eye. Handsome clothes-storage baskets were made of cane. Glazed black earthen pots were made in different sizes, and specially shaped pots were made for weddings and religious uses.[25]

Cherokee men fashioned the most beautiful ceremonial stone pipes of any of the southeastern Indians. The bowls were made of different sorts of stone and were huge. Most stems were made of soft woods and were about two feet long and an inch in diameter. The wood for these was cut into four squares, each of which was scooped out to make a hollow tube where they joined in the center. To the stems were glued or tied buttons, feathers, copper pieces, deerskin thongs, and even enemy scalps. The forepart of the pipe bowl usually came to a sharp peak that was two or three fingers broad and a quarter of an inch thick. On both sides and the top of the bowl were carved reliefs or sculptured images of various animals and men and women.

Men made excellent saddles of wood and hide and used a trimmed bearskin for a pad to sit on. The bridle was simply a rope tied around the horse's neck that was pulled to one side or the other to guide the animal. Cherokee bows and arrows were finely made. Arrow points were shaped for hunting or for warfare, with the latter being barbed so that it could not be pulled out. Points consisted of scooped buck horn, turkey-cock spur, pieces of brass, or flint stone. In historic times, Cherokees became as expert in the use of Euro-American firearms as they were with the bow and arrow. They learned to make new stocks for their guns with only a small hatchet and a knife, could straighten bent barrels, and alter and fix the springs of the lock — although such jobs often took two months of hard work.[26]

Hunting

When young men wished to dedicate themselves to a life of hunting, they made known their wishes to a priest whose business it was to train them. On the appearance of the first new moon in March, the priest gave his pupils a certain purifying drink and had them wash their bodies with it. This was an emetic, and after they were purged they were sent to a river where they immersed seven times, then put on clean clothing. They were ordered to hunt, and when they killed the first buck, they took the tip off the tongue to the priest to offer as a sacrifice.

The same ritual was repeated at the appearance of the first new moon in September. For four years thereafter the candidates were consigned to the care of the hunting priest, and during this extended period they were not allowed to have sexual relations with women. The priest taught them the sacred prayer formulas for hunting and about bird and animal natures and habits. He also taught them how to make the special calls that imitated nature and lured the birds and animals closer. He helped them make the power-infused luring masks for hunting that never failed to bewitch the game and which allowed the hunters to easily get within killing distance. The hunters were told how to give proper thanks for success and how to conserve enough game to assure a supply for future years.

At the end of the four years, the priest prepared for his pupils on the bank of a river a "tent for sweating." He formed a small circle of saplings that were set upright in the ground, then bent the top ends over, lashed them together, and covered them with skins and blankets, making a tent whose shape resembled the top of an umbrella. This tent was called *osi*, the same name as that of the winter hothouse, and it seems to have been identical to the sweat lodges of the Plains Indians. Heated stones were heaped in a pit in the middle of the sweat house, and water was poured on the stones to make steam. As soon as the pupils were in a profuse sweat, the priest ordered them to plunge immediately into the river and to immerse themselves seven times. After this purification ritual they were free to have sexual relations with women.[27]

The rites concerning hunting seem involved and time-consuming, but the dependency of the ancient peoples on game made them understandable.

Hunting specialists were called on to supply the deer meat and skins needed for the rituals that accompanied the great festivals, and as such held a holy office that demanded a close association with the "above powers." Only those who were fully cleansed and properly fit and prepared could carry out the divine will. The meat foods were as much a gift from the above powers as the cultivated and wild plant foods, and to forget this was to ensure failure. Thus, for example, a large company of even those men who

Deer hunter wearing wooden mask and using bow and arrows.

were not specialists but who wished to hunt success-fully usually asked a priest to prepare them. In these instances, he set up for them a tent, called "the tent of sweating," that was large enough to hold the group. Each man had for a seat a deerskin with the hair on. They did not sleep the first night, and at intervals the priest sang the hunter's song. A short while before daybreak, the men got up and, leaving behind all clothing except their breechclouts, went to another tent for sweating, where they crowded in. A helper heated the stones in an outside fire and passed them in to the priest on a pronged fork. The priest put them in the central fire pit and poured water on them. When the men were in a profuse sweat the priest ordered them to bathe, and accordingly all went immediately to the river and immersed them-selves seven times. They then returned to the tent and dressed, after which they drank the medicine for purification. This was a tea made of cedar boughs, horsemint, cane, and old tobacco. It caused them to

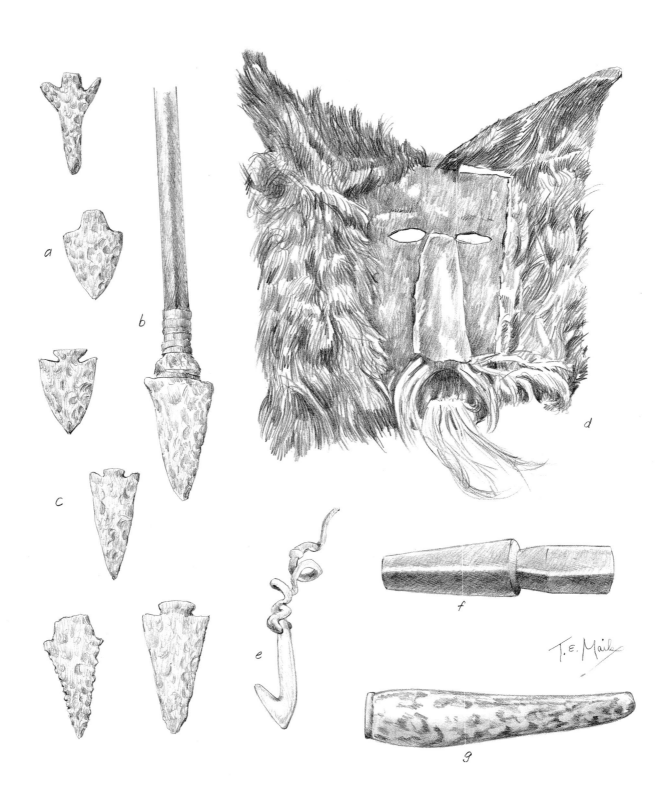

a. bird-hunting arrow points, Museum of the Cherokee Indian. b. lance point, Georgia State Museum. c. war-arrow points, Emory University Museum. d. wildcat mask used for stalking wild turkeys, Museum of the American Indian, Heye Foundation. e. bone fishhook, Smithsonian Institution. f. deer call, Smithsonian Institution. g. wild-turkey call, Museum of the Cherokee Indian.

throw up and thus cleanse the interiors of their bodies. They also washed themselves all over with this same medicine, and cleansed the outside. On that day they fasted until afternoon.

On the next day they again drank the drink and washed with it, but the fasting period was shorter. The ritual was repeated each day until the seventh day, when their first meal was eaten early in the morning. On the night of the seventh day, everyone stayed awake while at intervals the priest sang the hunter's song. Just before daybreak they sweated in the tent of sweating, and at daybreak immersed again. Then, carrying a new fire in a ceramic vessel the priest had supplied, the men went on a hunt. On killing the first deer, they took the meat and offered it to the fire for sacrifice. If a puff of wind came out of the meat while it burned, or if the meat popped throwing pieces toward the east, the sign was good, and the hunt would be successful.[28]

The hunting priest sometimes accompanied his hunting specialists on expeditions. In those instances, he would order them to immerse on seven successive nights and mornings in the manner previously described. The first buck that was killed belonged to the priest, and he offered the tip of the tongue in the usual manner for sacrifice, burning it in a new fire that he had kindled before the hunt began and had brought along. If the meat popped toward the west and indicated poor success, the sacrifice was offered again in a few days, when it was hoped it would pop toward the east and foretell good things.[29]

Only a small number of men became hunting specialists, although all men hunted for game to supply family larders, and performed purification rituals such as immersion.

During a prolonged series of winter hunting expeditions, which — when the need for food was especially severe — might continue for an extended period, the hunters were not permitted to have intercourse with their wives. It was the ultimate form of self-denial, and one that the above powers could not fail to respond to favorably. Some years, this rule would remain in force from the time of the Hunter's

Feast in September to the last hunt of the series during the first spring new moon — a span of six months.

In those instances when the hunting priest did not accompany the hunters, he authorized the leading, or chief, hunter to offer sacrifices in his stead.[30]

A special Hunter's Feast took place each September, when the buck flies first made their appearance. As many hunters as were eligible to do so applied to the hunting priest for cleansing. The customary drink, immersion, and fasting were performed for three days. On the fourth day they sweated and immersed, this time facing alternately east and west until the seven immersions were completed. When they came out of the water, the priest consulted his divining crystal. If they were to be successful in the next hunt, he would see in it deer or other game animals lying down. If not, he would see nothing. That night the hunters were the honored guests for a huge banquet that was prepared by the villagers to express their gratitude for the hunters' efforts throughout the year.[31]

Even when game was plentiful, hunting was a laborious exercise. The men often walked twenty-five or thirty miles over rough ground, high mountains, and deep valleys, fasting regularly as they did so and purifying themselves often. Many prayers were said, and all of the skills taught by the hunting priests were employed.

A typical hunter's formula was as follows: Give me the wind. Give me the breeze. Yo! O great Terrestrial Hunter, I come to the edge of your spittle where you repose. Let your stomach cover itself; let it be covered with leaves. Let it cover itself at a single bend, and may you never be satisfied. And you, O Ancient Red, may you hover above my breast while I sleep. Now let good dreams develop; let my experience be propitious. Ha! Now let my little trails be directed, as they lie down in various directions. Let the leaves be covered with the clotted blood, and may it never cease to be so. You two, the Water and the Fire, shall bury it in your stomachs. Yo![32]

The chief animals and birds shot with the bow and arrow were buffalo, deer, oppossum, squirrel, turkey, partridge, and pheasant, and all such hunting

Men with blowguns. The guns were made of hollow cane and ranged in length from three to twelve feet. Holes were bored with an iron rod, then smoothed with a stick having a stone or metal tip. Small splints of yellow locust were popular for darts. These were smoothed, and thistles were tied with sinew or thread to one end of the splint. Birds, squirrels, and rabbits could be killed with them to a distance of 100 feet. Small rush quivers carried the arrows, and thistledown was transported in a hollowed-out gourd.

was done on foot. To kill small game such as rabbits and small birds, the blowgun was used, and Cherokee men and boys were expert with it. The blowgun was a seven- or eight-foot-long hollow piece of cane through which, by means of blowing, a six- to eight-inch dart was projected. The darts were carried in quivers made of a section of large cane, and a hollow gourd was used to store the cottonlike thistledown plant fibers that the darts were stuck through to seal them in the blowgun and give them greater velocity.[33] The illustrations show how the blowgun was made and used.

Fishing

Fish were caught with bow and arrow, cleverly devised water traps, spearing, bait and hook, and dipping out with baskets.[34] Some fishing was done from canoes fashioned from large pine or poplar logs as much as forty feet long and two or more feet wide. The bottoms, sides, and ends of the canoes were flat, although the ends were slanted to give less resistance to currents. To make a log canoe, the log was hollowed out by fire and adzes. Some of the canoes could carry fifteen to twenty men, yet were so light and maneuverable that the Cherokees could force them upstream against a strong current.[35]

The fishhook might be anointed with spittle

after certain leaves that possessed an attraction power had been chewed. The prayer formula for catching a large fish was designed to lure the fish toward the fishhook or into the trap:

> Listen! Now you settlements have drawn near to hearken. Where you have gathered in the foam you are moving about as one. You Blue Cat and the others, I have come to offer you freely the white food. Let the paths from every direction recognize each other. Our spittle shall be in agreement. Let them be together as we go about. The fish have become a prey, and there shall be no loneliness. Your spittle has become agreeable. Yo![36]

Killing Eagles

Mention has been made of how eagle feathers, especially those of the golden eagle, were prized. It was the great sacred bird of the Cherokees, called "the pretty-feathered eagle," and it figured prominently in their rituals, especially in those things relating to war. In ancient days the killing of an eagle was an event that concerned a whole settlement, and it could be undertaken only by a professional eagle killer who had been carefully chosen and trained for the purpose. Only he knew the prescribed forms of action and the prayers that must be said after the killing to obtain pardon from the "above eagles" for the unavoidable sacrilege, and thus to keep vengeance from being heaped on the tribe.

When the people of a town wanted to have an Eagle Dance to gain war blessings and power, an eagle killer was called on to procure the feathers needed for the occasion. He was paid for his services by offerings taken at the dance, and since the few professionals guarded their secrets carefully, their business was a profitable one.

After certain preliminary preparations, the eagle killer set out alone for the mountains, taking with him his gun or bow and arrows. Having reached his destination, he undertook a vigil of prayer and fasting that lasted four days, after which he hunted until he succeeded in killing a deer. He placed the carcass in an exposed place on top of a high cliff, then concealed himself nearby and began to sing in a low undertone the songs that called down the eagles from the sky. As soon as one

alighted on the carcass, which would be almost immediately if the specialist knew his business, he shot it. Then standing over the dead bird, he addressed to it a prayer in which he begged it not to seek vengeance on his tribe, because it was a Spaniard and not a Cherokee who had done the deed. The selection of a Spaniard in this instance is at once evidence of the antiquity of the prayer, of the early Cherokee presence in the Southeast, and of the enduring impression the cruelties of the early Spanish explorers made on the natives.

When the prayer ended, the dead eagle was left where it fell and the hunter hurried back to the settlement where the people were anxiously awaiting his return. On meeting the first men he said simply, "A snowbird has died," and passed on at once to his own quarters, his work being finished. The announcement was made in this form to further ensure that any eagles who might overhear it would not seek vengeance, for the little snowbird was considered too insignificant to matter.

After waiting four days for the parasites to leave the eagle's body, warriors went to get the feathers. On arriving at the place, they stripped the body of the large tail and wing feathers, and wrapped them in a fresh deerskin. They then returned to the settlement, leaving the body of the eagle where it lay and also that of the slain deer as a sacrifice to the eagle spirits. Back at the settlement, the feathers, still wrapped in the deerskin, were hung in a small, round hut built for that purpose at the edge of the dance ground.

The Eagle Dance was held that night, for the necessary arrangements had already been made. In the meantime, since the feathers were believed to be hungry after their long journey, a dish of venison and corn was set below them on the ground, and they were invited to eat. The body of a flax bird or a scarlet tanager was hung with the eagle feathers for the same purpose. The literal food thus given to the feathers was disposed of after the dance, for the spirit of the food was what was actually eaten. The final act of preparation was to make Eagle Dance wands with the feathers.

Since the eagle was regarded as a great spirit

power, only the greatest warriors and those versed in the sacred ordinances dared to wear its feathers or carry them in the dance. Should any person in the settlement dream of eagles or eagle feathers, he must at the first opportunity arrange for an Eagle Dance and perform the required vigil and fasting. Otherwise, someone in his family would soon die. Should the insect parasites which infested the eagle's feathers while it was alive get into a person, they would, even if they lay dormant for years, eventually breed a terrible skin disease. For this reason the body of the eagle was allowed to remain four days on the ground before being brought into the settlement.[37]

The Ball-play Game

Because of its intensely competitive nature, the ball-play game was related to warfare and was called "the friend or companion of battle." But it was not a religious event. Except for the employment of priests to do conjuring, priests had no other connection with the games.

In each town of significance, a respectable headman superintended ball play. When a young man wanted to play a game, he consulted the headman of his town, and the two of them selected one or two messengers to carry a challenge to another town. The messengers went directly to the designated place and spent some time with the headman of that town before offering the challenge. Once it was offered, the challenged headman asked how large an area he might range over to find players, since in ancient times the players must be famous men of good character who would play honorably and without fraud and deception.

When the challenge was accepted, the headmen of the two towns got together and established a time and place for the game to be held. Each headman then selected an elderly and experienced man to lead his team's seven-day preparatory ritual, "the Ball-game Dance," another man to sing for the players, another to whoop, seven women and a musician to sing and play for the women when they danced on the seventh night, and a priest for conjuring. Seven men were appointed to wait on the priest, and seven more women were chosen to provide the food for a

feast that would be held on the seventh night of preparation.

While witnesses differ in reporting the number of players for each side, with the numbers ranging from nine to as high as fifty, it appears that the usual number was ten to fourteen, plus alternates.[38]

To prepare each team for the game, a fire was lighted in a secluded open place in the woods near that team's town, and about dusk the participants assembled there and seated themselves some distance from the fire. After awhile, the headman called for the players to come forward, and they came with a ball stick in each hand. The whooper then raised something akin to a war whoop, and the players answered, "Wah!" The singer, or musician, then shook his rattle and sang, "Ha hi u, Ha hi u," and the players began to dance, responding, "Hah, hah, hah," to every repetition of the word "Ha hi u." As they circled around the fire, they also made motions with their ball sticks similar to those they made while engaged in play.

After the players had danced four times around the fire, the whooper whooped and ran a few steps away, at which time the players responded "Wah" and walked east to a preselected place, where they locked their ball sticks together in pairs, hung them on a rack, and sat down and rested for about thirty minutes before they danced again. To make this rack, a pole was laid horizontally on two crotched and upright sticks. It was set up on the side of the fire that was nearest the town of the opposing team. When the dance had been done four times, everyone went to a nearby stream and immersed seven times, after which they retired for the night.[39]

Sometimes, a revered former player was chosen to collect the playing sticks from the dancers. He was called "the Driver," and he carried the sticks hooked in pairs over each arm, with the handle of one stick run through the loop of the other to form the inverted V used to hang them on the rack. The playing sticks were two to three feet in length, made of hickory, and bent at one end to form a loop that, with the addition of a netting of cords made of twisted deerskin, squirrel skin, or Indian hemp, made a small racket that allowed the players to catch

Ball players.

and throw the ball. Stick handles were often painted with symbolic designs to give them special power.

At daybreak the next morning, the priest followed the players to the stream, using his deerskin and beads to conjure for them while they walked and while they immersed seven times. There was a lengthy and complicated prayer formula for taking ball players to the water. The ceremony that went with it required a red and a black bead. The priest began by declaring that it was his purpose to inquire into the fate of the ball players and their opponents, and in praying he alternately gave his attention to the two beads. He fixed his eyes on the red bead while praying for his own men and on the black bead while referring to the rivals. He elevated his own men gradually to the seventh and highest heaven, which was the abode of the gods who created and ruled the earth. The opponents he put slowly down under the earth and pictured them as animals that were slow and clumsy of movement.

On behalf of his fellow townsmen, the priest invoked the aid of swift-flying birds that never failed to capture their prey. Birds called on were the wood pewee, the hawk, the great-crested flycatcher, the martin, and the chimney swift. A species of small dragonfly was also invoked, together with a mythical bat who once took sides with the birds in a great ball-game contest with the four-footed animals and who won the victory through his superior skill in dodging.[40]

During the day, the players loitered as a group near the town council house, watching one another to make certain no one violated the seven strict rules of preparation and thus jeopardized their chances of winning the contest.

These rules were as follows:

1. A player could not go near his wife or any other woman during the seven days of the preparatory dances, nor could he associate with women for twenty-four days after he had been scratched — a procedure described later.[41]

2. Ball players were not allowed to eat meat or anything salty or hot. They were restricted to corn bread and to parched corn broth. Even that food had to be received from the hands of boys who took it from women who had placed it on the ground some distance away.

3. The seven men who had been appointed to wait on and watch the conjuring priest could eat only food prepared by the seven women chosen for the purpose.

4. None of the seven female cooks could be pregnant, or afflicted with uncleanness of any kind.

5. The seven men who waited on the priest were usually married, but their wives could not be pregnant or unclean.

6. If the wife of any player was pregnant, that player must follow behind the others when they danced and marched.

7. With the exception of the seventh night of preparation, no woman other than those chosen for specific purposes could come to the place where the Ball-player Dance was held, nor could they walk on the pathways that the players had to use during the seven days of preparation.[42]

To obtain the ball skin, on the second day of preparation the players ordered a number of boys to capture and kill a squirrel with hands or club alone. It must not be shot with a weapon. A Bird Clan man then dressed the skin and stuffed it with deer hair. On the night before play was to begin, he wrapped the ball in a deerskin provided by the priest and then fasted until the game ended.

The dances for the next five nights of preparations were identical to those performed on the first night.

On the seventh night, the seven men who assisted the priest went to a stream bank where he had concealed himself and attended him while he asked in prayer that his players be strengthened and the opponents weakened. The players danced seven times on that night and moved with shuffling steps in a counterclockwise circle around the fire. Their whoops were those of insolence against the rivals, and in his shouts the Driver defied the rival players and their priest to weaken them. Several players at a time charged in the direction of the opponents' town, brandishing their ball sticks like weapons and whooping defiance. Mock attacks on the enemy's town were made seven times during each dance. The closeness of the dancers to the smoke was a form of purification — especially during the last dance before morning, when heavy smoke resulted from a quantity of pinewood that was thrown on the fire.

When the men left to go to the river and immerse, the seven women, who it is believed represented the seven clans, did their dance. Other women could join in if they wished. The women faced the opponents' town and in their dance action stepped on the opposing players. The musician might sing as many as ten songs while the women danced. They stood abreast in a line a short distance from the fire, on the side nearest to the rival town, and just behind the rack on which the sticks were hung. They circled the fire in a counterclockwise direction, the opposite of the Plains Indian dance-circle movement. When the players returned from the stream, the women ceased dancing and were taken by their priest to water, where they washed their faces and hands. They imitated ball playing as they walked, and their singer sang the least-flycatcher song.

Scratchers were used to scarify the arms, backs, and chests of the ball players, and the procedure was considered important to the success of the game. The manufacture and use of scratchers were restricted to priests, and their primary use in this instance was to purify and strengthen the players, although one informant said it was done to make the players harder to catch during a game. Several kinds of instruments were used to scarify players and also warriors in time of war. One was the single fang of a banded rattlesnake attached to the quill of a white duck feather by splitting the quill and binding the fang into it with white thread. The feather symbolized the speed of flight, and a piece of red thread tied to the middle of the quill symbolized the power of lightning. Another kind of scratcher was a bent turkey quill that formed a frame to receive seven sharpened slivers of turkey wing bone that were lashed on with Indian hemp. A turkey-bone scratcher similar to the one just mentioned had no quill base, and it was tied together with white thread and Indian hemp. The usual number of teeth in scratchers was five or seven, and the quills used could be taken from a large hawk or falcon, or a wild turkey.

The scratching was done on the last night before the game. It involved three longitudinal parallel scratches on the players' upper arms, lower arms, upper legs, and lower legs. A half circle, open on the lower side, was made on the chest and back. The total amount of blood let was almost half a pint, and if the blood ran dark, the conjurer drew more until it ran light red.[43]

Before dawn on the eighth day, which was the day of the game, the anxious and excited players were awake and ready to go. Slippery elm was chewed, and the saliva was rubbed on their bodies to make them more slippery when they sweated. A good-luck symbol, made with charcoal taken from the dance fire and consisting either of a cross or a semicircle enclosing a dot, was drawn on the players' cheeks and foreheads.[44] The bodies of one team were painted red, and the other team white.

A pendent extension, sometimes fashioned from a deer's tail but usually made of hawk, falcon, white goose, or eagle feathers, was attached to a player's broad waist belt at the back. The deer tail represented swiftness; the white goose feathers, sometimes worn also in the hair, identified the swiftest players; and the eagle, hawk, or falcon feathers identified the strongest players. Each player chose the kind of tail he would wear, but a false claim would bring ridicule and disgrace. Ball players sometimes wore headbands of groundhog skin, with the aforementioned feathers attached as pendants.[45]

At sunrise the whooper whooped, to which the players, standing in a cluster and facing the ball ground, responded, *"Wah"* four times, then proceeded single file toward the ball ground. The leaders went about a half mile, then paused and waited for the others to catch up. As soon as they did, the entire group went on for the same distance and halted again. The priest took them to a stream where they immersed seven times, then returned to the place of halting to eat a breakfast consisting of corn bread and parched cornmeal.

The meal finished, they stood up, and as a group faced the ball ground. The whoop and the response were repeated, and they again proceeded in single file for another half mile. There were another halt, whoop, and response, and in this manner everyone continued until the ball-ground goal poles were reached. Here the priest laid on the ground his deerskin containing the red feathers and his conjuring apparatus, and the players placed beside it the articles they wished to wager on the outcome. The players again partook of bread and cornmeal and removed all clothing except their breechclouts. They chewed another root given them by the priest and rubbed it on their bodies. The priest's assistant took the sacred red feathers from the conjurer's deerskin and tied them to the hair of the players.

The leading player of the team that had issued the challenge obtained the ball from the priest and held it while an influential speaker came forward to address the players, exhorting them to exert themselves to the utmost and telling them that if they fell they should get up. Even if the opponents' guns were pointed at them and they were about to fall in death, they must go forward.[46] When he was done, the whoop and the response were given, the players girded themselves, thrust their chins out defiantly, and in a slow walk moved in single file to the middle of the ball ground, where they were met by their similarly prepared and countenanced opponents.

Four men, probably two from each town, were selected to keep order and to see that play was conducted fairly, and two tallymen were chosen. Each of these tallymen had twelve small pointed sticks, one of which was stuck upright in the ground whenever the ball was carried through the goal poles. The first team to score twelve goals won the game.

A line had been drawn to establish the perimeter of the ball ground, around which the spectators from both towns, dressed in their finest apparel, were gathered. Goals were made in different ways in

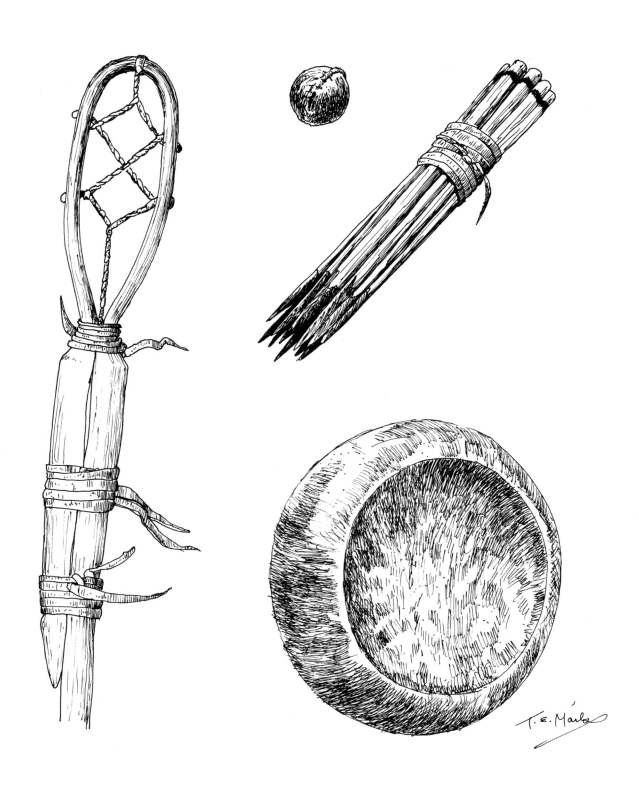

Game items: *Top,* net end of ball-play stick, ball, and markers for keeping score. *Bottom,* chungke stone.

Chungke players.

spectators of both towns applauded and cheered. At game's end, the winners appropriated the wagers of the losers. On their return home, the players observed virtually the same procedure of march they had followed when they came to the ball ground.[48]

Other Diversions

The Cherokees had other games, although surprisingly little has been learned about them.

A favorite played by men was called *Chungke*, and it was both an athletic and a gambling game. Near every town council house was a large square of cleared ground over which fine sand was strewed to make a slick playing surface. Only one or two to a side played at any one time. The game items used were a discoidal stone that had scooped-out sides and resembled a large, thick discus, and eight-foot-long smooth throwing poles that tapered at each end and were daubed with bear oil. The stones were rubbed smooth on abrasive rocks and were religiously maintained and preserved from one generation to another until entirely worn out. They were the property of the town, not the players.

Chungke players stood side by side about six yards from the end of the playing field, and one of them hurled the stone on its edge in as direct a line as he could toward the middle of the other end of the field. The players then ran forward a few yards and threw their poles at the stone in javelin fashion. The pole that lay closest to the stone when the stone came to rest counted the score. Players kept running and throwing at half speed all day long in all manner of weather, wagering as prizes their ornaments and wearing apparel, except their breechclouts.[49]

Other recorded games include a dice game, a hoop-and-pole game played by boys, and an arrow-flipping game played by boys. The numerous known games played by other tribes would indicate that the Cherokees also had many more, especially to while away the long winter hours when not much else could be done. Cherokee children imitated in play and on a miniature scale the occupations of their elders. Social dancing was very popular, and national festivals consumed much of the people's time.

different regions. Some were formed by driving a pair of sticks into the ground. Others consisted of 100-yard-long lines of poles that paralleled each other and were separated by a distance of 100 yards. The playing field that Butrick saw in 1835 was a level plain in a hollow, so that the ground around it rose gradually and afforded the spectators a good view. All stones, sticks, bushes, and logs were removed, and a stake was driven in the center of the field. About 100 yards from the stake on each side, so as to form a playing field 200 yards long, two stakes were driven two or three feet apart to form the goals. A perimeter line was drawn around the field. He does not say how wide the playing area was.[47]

When all was ready, an overseer tossed the ball into the air, and the exceedingly rough-and-tumble game commenced. No quarter was given, and when goals were scored and a victory was achieved, the

Summary

The picture grows clearer as answers to more questions emerge from behind the veils. The large and adaptable Cherokee tribe that was established in a naturally rich and temperate area of southeastern North America in about A. D. 1300 had, by 1650, established impressive towns and villages in four regional centers, two of which were in the middle region and spread over a vast domain. Tasks performed by men and women were evenly balanced. The tribe had functioning cooperatives to carry out the work of planting, harvesting, and building construction. Cherokee appearance and costume were unique and sophisticated, and the most wondrous aspect of this is yet to be described. Warfare was an ever present fact of life and occupied much of the people's time. Houses were well planned and substantial. Foods were varied and delicious. In foodstuffs and in dealing with the elements, nearly every emergency was anticipated and provided for. Even hunting was a province for specialists who functioned in a close relationship with the pantheon of divine beings. All life, in fact, was immersed in religion.

But what of the aspects of life not yet considered? What of government, warfare methods, social units and the life cycle, the always intriguing mythology and healing practices, the divining crystals so often mentioned, and those great annual festivals already alluded to? Are they as fascinating as the aspects of life we have covered?

Indeed they are.

NOTES

1. Gilbert, "The Eastern Cherokees," p. 193.
2. Payne Papers, interview with T. Smith and Zacheriah, Vol. 3, p. 57.
3. Smith, *The Story of the Cherokees,* p. 16, and Gilbert, p. 193.
4. Timberlake, *Memoirs, 1756-1765,* p. 75.
5. Maxwell, *America's Fascinating Indian Heritage,* pp. 84-87.
6. Timberlake, p. 193.
7. Payne Papers, interview with Nettle, Vol. 4, p. 27.
8. Bartram, *Travels through North and South Carolina, Georgia, East and West Florida, the Cherokee Country, etc.,* p. 296, and Timberlake, pp. 57-75.
9. Timberlake, pp. 75-76.
10. Payne Papers, interview with Nettle, Vol. 4, p. 23.
11. Payne Papers, D. S. Butrick, Vol. 4, pp. 275-276.
12. Ibid., pp. 276-280.
13. Adair, *History of the American Indians,* p. 448.
14. Ibid., p. 450.
15. Ibid., p. 452.
16. Ibid.
17. Ibid., pp. 453-454.
18. Gilbert, pp. 316-341.
19. Adair, pp. 451-452.
20. Ibid., p. 452.
21. Ibid., p. 453.
22. Payne Papers, interview with S. A. Nettle, Vol. 4, p. 7.
23. Ibid.
24. Payne Papers, Vol. 4, pp. 266-276.
25. Adair, pp. 454-456.
26. Ibid., pp. 456-457.
27. Payne Papers, interview with Terrapin Head and Nutsawi, Vol. 3, p. 44.
28. Ibid., pp. 43-44.
29. Ibid.
30. Ibid., p. 44.
31. Ibid.
32. Mooney, *Sacred Formulas of the Cherokees,* p. 369-370.
33. Adair, p. 432.
34. Ibid., pp. 432-434.
35. Timberlake, p. 85.
36. Mooney, p. 374.
37. Ibid., pp. 281-283.
38. Ibid., p. 396.
39. Payne Papers, Vol. 4.
40. Speck and Broom, *Cherokee Dance and Drama,* p. 58.
41. Payne Papers, Vol. 4.
42. Ibid.
43. Speck and Broom, pp. 59-62; see also Bartram, pp. 298-299.
44. Ibid.
45. Ibid., pp. 55-57.
46. Payne Papers, Vol. 4
47. Ibid., pp. 112-113.
48. Ibid.
49. Adair, pp. 430-431.

CHAPTER THREE

Life Cycle

T hanks largely to a healthy climate and life-style, Cherokee women seldom had difficulty in bearing children. Although as many as four women might be present to help with a birth, in the usual instance a mother or a grand-mother provided all of the needed assistance. Sometimes a priest was in-vited to pray for a speedy and safe delivery, but men were not otherwise allowed to be present.

As soon as a woman learned she was pregnant, she informed her husband. He spread the news to the entire community, and then built for her an isolated dwelling place where she would confine herself during the final three months she carried the child. Pregnant women were subjected to numerous regula-tions that will seem strange to modern women, some of which are given in Chapter Five under the heading of "uncleanness." But the most important rule was for her to be taken to water at the appearance of each new moon, where she was to pray and be puri-fied. A priest, her husband, and her mother or some other near relative accompanied her. Once there, the priest applied water to the crown of her head, her chest, and sometimes to her face. He also conjured with white and red beads to learn what the child's future would be.[1]

Baptism. Priest purifying infant in the smoke of the fire.

The Cherokee mother, as did Plains and Apache mothers, knelt on a robe with her legs spread wide apart to deliver the child. It was a bad omen if, during delivery, it happened to land on its chest. Should this occur, it was immediately wrapped in a cloth and taken to a creek, where it was immersed in the cold water. As soon as the action of the water disengaged the cloth and caused it to float away, the infant was rescued, dried off, and taken home. It was supposed that any possibility of ill fortune had been carried away with the cloth. If the child fell on its back, the omen was good, and it was spared the water ordeal.[2]

Some, but not all, ancient Cherokees believed that infants were born without souls and that only when the first air they breathed had entered them did they become living souls.[3] Once the birth had taken place, the father or nearest relative buried the placenta on the farther side of two mountain ridges that lay between the places of birth and burial. The Cherokees did not use cradleboards. From the time the child was three or four weeks old, it was carried about in a blanket sling astride the mother's back.

The Naming Ceremony

A day or two after the birth, a priest waved the infant four times over a fire while he addressed on its behalf a prayer to the fire for special blessings. On either the fourth or seventh day after birth, the same priest took the child to a creek or river and commended it to its Creator, praying that it might enjoy a long and happy life. After this, while holding his hand over the infant's mouth and nostrils, he quickly immersed it seven times, then returned it to its parents.

Then the naming ceremony was held, and the name was bestowed by a prominent elderly woman of the community, such as one of the Beloved Women. In most instances, the name was based on the infant's fancied resemblance to some object, on something said or done at the moment of birth, or on an unusual character trait in the infant. Later in life and depending on a person's character changes or achievements, a new name might be earned or given. For example, a Cherokee warrior who killed a

distinguished enemy might, in a public ceremony, be given the name Buffalo Killer. Whatever the name, every Cherokee regarded it as a distinct part of his or her personality and believed that injury would result from any misuse of it. If, for instance, a priest's prayers had no effect while he was treating a patient for a serious illness, he often concluded that misuse of the patient's name was the cause and accordingly went to water where, with appropriate ceremonies, he christened the patient with a new name. The priest then began his healing ritual anew, repeating the prayer formulas with the new name inserted, confident that his efforts would be crowned with success.[4]

Cherokee parents were excessively fond of their children, but in early historic times were criticized by white settlers for indulging even the older ones to a degree that led to their ruin. Most children and young people showed great respect for their parents and for the aged generally.[5]

Daily immersion of the child continued for two years. At the age of four or five, boys came under the supervision of their fathers or elder brothers and were taught how to handle blowguns and bows and arrows. Girls helped their mothers and older sisters and learned by doing. Both sexes learned rapidly and played games in which the activities of their elders were imitated. A child born in the midst of unusual circumstances, such as when strange things were happening on earth or in the heavens, might be raised to become a visionary or prophet, and such a career was particularly marked out for twins. Selected children such as these were kept secluded during the first twenty-four days of their lives. They were not allowed to taste their mother's milk, but instead were given the liquid portion of corn hominy. While such children were growing up, they were encouraged to go out alone and talk with the Little People, a race of dwarfs or fairies believed in by nearly all southern Indians.[6]

Some sons were promised to the priesthood, and on acceptance by the priests were called "devoted sons." As previously stated, the training of boys for hunting was extensive and thorough, and training for the priesthood was even more demanding. It is described in Chapter Six, where religion is considered more closely. The priesthood was to some extent hereditary, but there was also a selective process in which the less likely candidates were weeded out. The priests were advised in advance when a new candidate was to be presented to them. Before the presentation, the parents fasted and for seven days tasted only of a certain root to vicariously bestow special powers on the child. To preserve the purity of children devoted to the priesthood, mothers always delivered them into the care of the grand-mother or some other aged matron during the mother's periods of menstruation.[7]

Marriage

Members of the same clan were considered to be near relatives who were not allowed to intermarry. In ancient times, Cherokees seldom married a second time, since the only second marriages considered honorable were those involving a brother's widow who needed a man to provide for her. The latter custom may account for white claims of polygamy being practiced, for many men were killed in war, and the women greatly outnumbered the men.[8]

There were several ways of making proposals and consummating marriages. Informants do not say which of these applied in given regions, nor do they associate the different approaches with different time phases in Cherokee development. It is entirely possible that customs changed and were unique to different regions.

In one way of proposing and marrying, when a young man wanted to marry a certain young woman, he spoke with his parents and her parents, and sometimes with a brother from each of the partici-pating clans, whose consent was essential. When all parties agreed, a time was set for the marriage, and the priest who would officiate was notified of their wishes. Early in the morning on the marriage day, the priest obtained two roots of a certain kind and laid them a small distance apart on the palm of his hand. Then, with his face turned toward the east, he prayed, asking whether the bride and groom were intended for one another and whether they would live long and happily together. If the answer was that

the couple should not marry, the roots would not move. If the couple would only live well together for a short time before one of them would die, the roots would move together and one root would quickly wilt. In either instance, the priest forbade their marriage, and nothing more was said about it. But if the roots came together and did not wilt before the priest put them down, the omen was good, and the marriage should be consummated. The couple, their families, and friends then assembled in the town council house, and in a brief ceremony the priest commended the couple to God, praying that they might be empowered to live long and happily to-gether. He concluded by telling them that if either should prove unfaithful to the other, the unfaithful one would go after death to the "bad place." As part of this ceremony, it was customary for the bride's brother to exchange personal clothing and ornaments with the bridegroom, and in this symbolic act the two men played out the joining together of the two families, who were becoming one. It was taken for granted that nothing other than adultery could end a marriage established in this manner.[9]

A pubescent young woman about to go through her first menstrual period was immediately separated from the rest of her family and retired to a distant camp where she remained for seven days. During this time no person might touch her, and she was careful not to handle even her own food. Another woman fed her. At the end of seven days she washed herself, her clothing, and whatever else she had touched during her uncleanness, then returned to her family. She was now eligible to be married.

In a second manner of courting and consum-mating, if a young man fell in love with a certain girl before her change, he spoke to her parents about her, and if they were willing to give her to him, he kept the girl supplied with venison, and she was not allowed to marry another person. Once she had undergone her first menstruation, the marriage ceremony took place. It was accepted as a contract for life, and if either person forsook the other, the one who did so was usually publicly whipped by a town official, and the wife had her hair cropped by the women of the town.[10]

Father and son on fishing excursion. Fish were often killed with bows and arrows.

In a third manner of proposal and marriage, when a young man wished to marry a certain woman, he relayed his desire through a female relative who conferred with the mother of the woman. If the mother disapproved, she asked her brother or her oldest son to tell the female relative this. If the mother consented, the young man was permitted to share the desired woman's bed.[11]

In a fourth manner, a purchase contract was entered into. The suitor either devoted his services for a specified time to the parents of the maiden he was courting, hunting for them or assisting in the making of their canoes, or he offered them presents he already had, which usually consisted of clothing for the bride. The maiden could not refuse if the parents approved the match. Then, at the marriage ceremony, she was stripped of any gift clothing by her relatives, who claimed it for themselves, and in that state she was presented to him as his wife.[12]

In another style of marriage ceremony, on the eve of the wedding the groom feasted with male companions in a dwelling on one side of the town council house, and the bride and her companions feasted in a dwelling on its opposite side. The entire town convened in the town council house for the ceremony, where the oldest married men took the highest seats on one side of the council house, and the oldest married women took the highest seats on the other. The next older married men sat directly below the oldest men, and the next older married women sat below the oldest women, and so on.

At a signal, a priest escorted the groom to one end of the open space in the center of the council house, and another priest escorted the bride to the opposite end. The groom received from his mother a leg of venison and a blanket, and the bride received from her mother an ear of corn and a blanket. Then the couple met near the sacred fire in the center of the council house, exchanged the venison and corn, and joined together their blankets to symbolize the mutually supportive functions of the man and the woman in the Cherokee household. After that, the couple walked silently and alone to their dwelling place, which was either in the girl's mother's house, or within the mother's clan's area of the town.[13]

Although divorces were infrequent, they did happen, and all that was required to formalize the parting was a dividing of the blankets, which reversed the act performed at the wedding.[14]

Scholars concur in describing the law against marriage within the clan as the most stringent of all Cherokee laws. Anciently, the death penalty applied to the breaking of this law, and the penalty was inflicted by the members of the offended clan themselves. Whipping was substituted for the death penalty in the early nineteenth century, and later on formal penalties for marriage within the clan were entirely abolished. Adultery brought disgrace to the offenders, and if adultery was proven against a wife, all of her possessions were taken away and she was turned out of the house. When separations were mutually agreed upon and the blanket was divided, the couple's possessions were equally parceled out, and the children went with and were provided for by the mother.[15]

A priest could not marry a widow, a woman who had been divorced by her husband, or a woman of bad character.[16] The marriage of a priest was attended by special ceremonies, and his wife must be approved by his seven counselors. She must be a virgin and of unblemished character. Great honor was attached to her person, and when her husband died, she in some respects filled his place until his successor was consecrated. Most of the deceased priest's official duties were, however, performed by his right-hand man, called "the priest's principal assistant." More is said about that in the next chapter.[17]

Death, Mourning, and Purification

When a father, especially an aged one, was convinced that he was about to die, he called for his children to gather about him. He told them about his situation, gave them advice and instruction concerning their future life, repeated the ancient traditions, and reminded them of Cherokee customs they should never forget.

When death was at hand, all of the children were sent away, and only the priest and the adult relatives spent time with the dying person. Females wept exceedingly, commencing at the moment of death a most doleful lamentation in which they sang over and over, with only brief pauses, the name of the deceased for as long as they could hold their breath. Male relatives seldom wept, but put ashes on their heads and wrapped themselves in worn clothing.[18] During the seven days of mourning no one was to be angry, speak in a light or trifling manner, or eat or drink anything but the lightest kind of food and liquid. Circumstances surrounding the death determined whether the expressions of grief were greater or lesser. Sometimes mourners seemed entirely inconsolable and gave the impression they would weep all the way to their own graves.

A near relative closed the deceased's eyelids and washed the entire body with water or with a purifying wash made by boiling willow root. In each town there was a priest whose task it was to bury the dead. He came soon after death to the house where the corpse was and usually buried it either in the floor directly under the place where the person had died, under the hearth, outside near the house, or in the case of a distinguished chief, under the seat he had occupied in the town council house. In instances when burial was outside, the priest, followed by an adult relative of the deceased, carried the body to its place of interment. Sometimes the corpse was laid alongside a large rock, and a wall about eighteen inches high was built on the other side of the corpse to enclose it. Then, a covering of wood or an arch of stone was laid over it as a roof and stones were heaped over the whole to create what was in essence a small tomb. Other times a corpse was covered by two overlapping wooden boxes, then piled over with stones. Some people were buried in graves that were dug in the earth, and rocks were laid over the graves to keep animals from getting into them.[19]

When death occurred, everything in the house, including the surviving family, became unclean. The personal belongings of the deceased were either buried with him or burned at the grave site. Food and furniture were smashed and thrown away. As soon as the corpse was buried, a priest was sent for to ritually cleanse the house. He entered the house alone to destroy everything that had been contaminated, and to thoroughly clean the hearth. He then kindled a new fire and put on it his water-filled medicine pot that he used for purifications. He put in the pot a certain weed and later gave the tea he brewed to the family members, who drank it and washed themselves all over with it. He also sprinkled the inside of the house with the tea. Then he smoked and further purified the house interior by building a fire with cedar boughs and a certain weed. When this was done, the priest took what remained of his purifying items away and hid them in a hollow tree or rock cleft where they would not be found.[20]

Finally, the priest took the defiled family members to a river or creek, where on the bank he prayed for them and then ordered them to immerse. They did this by entering the water and alternately facing east and west as they immersed seven times. They either put away their polluted garments before going into the water, or while in the water let them loose to drift away and take their uncleanness with them. When the people left the water, new clothing was put on, so that when they returned to their house the mourners were entirely clean. Shortly thereafter, the priest's principal assistant sent a messenger to them, bearing two gifts — a piece of tobacco that would "enlighten their eyes" so they could bravely face the future, and a strand of sanctified beads that would comfort their hearts. He also asked them to take their seats in the town council house that night. The bereaved always accepted this kind invitation, and when they went to the council house they were met by all of the townspeople, who in turn took them gently and understandingly by the hand. Once everyone had done this, the mourners either returned home or stayed to watch while the other people danced a solemn dance.[21]

On the morning of the fifth day after death, while family members gathered around him, the priest took a bird that had been killed with an arrow, plucked off some of its feathers, and cut from the right side of the breast a small piece of meat. After praying, he put the meat on the fire. If it popped one or more times, throwing small pieces toward the family, sons in the family would soon die. If it did not pop at all, the sons were considered safe.

Mourning continued for another two days. On those two mornings, the entire company of mourners arose at daybreak and after going to water to immerse, went to the grave site. There the local women set up a most bitter wailing of the kind already described, and neighboring women often joined in. During this time the Chief Priest of the town sent out hunters to bring in meat for the mourning family. With this assistance, the family, with the help of relatives, prepared food and on the seventh night took it to the council house, where a community feast of consolation was held.[22] Priests were usually paid for their services in clothing.[23]

When the deceased was a husband, the widow was expected to remain single for a long time, and for as much as ten months to let her hair hang loose and uncared for. She neither washed her body nor paid any attention to herself, and her clothes were thrown carelessly on.[24] When her friends believed she had mourned enough, they went to her, combed and dressed her hair, and changed her garments.

Views regarding the future state differed according to what individual Cherokees believed about the powers who created and ruled the earth and its inhabitants.

Those who worshiped the sun believed that at death the soul assumed different appearances and at first lingered about the place where the person had died for as long a time as the person had lived there. The soul then went to its prior place of residence and remained there for a similar time. This retreat of time continued until the deceased had moved backward to its birthplace when, after remaining for as long a time as it had lived there, it took its final leave — either into nonexistence or to a place far away in the west where the deceased was always miserable because it was away from its natural home.

Others believed that at death the soul entered a mystical but living body that was larger or smaller than its own. Whatever the case, the body the soul entered grew smaller each year, until at last it vanished and ceased to be. This group also believed that adulterers and women who destroyed their infants would in some way after death be punished more than other persons.[25]

Those Cherokees who prayed only to the three Divine Beings above believed that all who were free from certain sins and vices would at death go to be with those beings and would dwell with them forever in a place that would always be pleasant and light. But women who had aborted or otherwise killed their children, together with other murderers, witches, adulterers, fornicators, and thieves would go to the Place of Bad Spirits, where they would always scream in torment. When they asked for food, they would be fed with coals of fire. When they asked for a drink, a flaming liquid would be poured down their throats. Any one of sinners such as these who had been killed in war would always whoop and yell in another place, flying around in the air with head down, always wanting to light and rest, but never being permitted to do so.[26]

Social Units

The existing literature does not tell us what exactly the ancient social structure was like — what its foundation was and what aspects of life were built on this foundation to make a strong and cohesive society. To discover what we can of these things, we must turn to the Cherokees who live on the Eastern Cherokee Reservation in North Carolina. Although they have changed in many and significant ways, of all Cherokees, they have in social structure preserved the most and changed the least. Of this much we can be certain — the social structure investigated by ethnologists between the years 1880 and 1940, when the most intensive investigations went on, was not a recent invention. Even though Euro-American influences were everywhere present among the Cherokees, what was discovered had to represent in some important measure the form of social organization that had been practiced in ancient times.

The Towns

The Eastern Cherokees of today are organized politically into five towns that lie within the Qualla Boundary, plus a sixth town that is comprised of the Graham County settlements. The towns are Wolftown, Painttown, Birdtown, Yellow Hill, and Big Cove. They have locally elected officials and are united in a republican form of government known as the Eastern Band of Cherokees. Members of the band council are elected annually by the six towns, along with a chief and a vice-chief. These officials, together with officers of the state of North Carolina and the United States superintendent of the district, govern the band and determine policies to be followed. The band is incorporated under the laws of North Carolina, and the state regulates taxation and administers common law. The federal government regulates education and local welfare work, and the band determines its own land-use policies. More details regarding present government are given in Chapter Ten.

Each of the six Eastern Cherokee towns is made up of one or more local neighborhoods or communities, and each has local organizations that consist of cooperative bodies such as the *gadugi*, or work cooperative, and the funeral and poor-aid societies. The unity of each town and its surrounding communities is most clearly seen in its ritualistic and kinship expressions, its political organization with councilmen, its town ball team, and in some instances a town dance team. One important difference between the present and ancient times is that while once the national capital was the primary social unit, today the town has become this. There is no longer a national capital. Except for the town of Cherokee, North Carolina, serving as the location for band, state, and federal government offices, each town is in effect its own capital.[27]

The Household

The next social unit of importance is the household. Householders are given individual land-tenure grants that remain in force for as long as they occupy and cultivate the granted property. The tenures can be bought, sold, traded, or inherited — just as if they were private property. Land reverts to the band only when the holder of the tenure no longer is considered a bona fide member of the band, which means the person does not possess the required one-sixteenth Cherokee blood.

In the ancient Cherokee household, the husband came to live in the house of the woman he married and, in regard to family affairs, was restricted in his activities and his authority over the children. The mother's line was the primary means of tracing descent, and the mother's eldest brother was the family authority whose commands must be obeyed on all occasions.[28] Much of this has changed.

The usual Cherokee household of today is made up of the domestic family with occasionally a few relatives. Sometimes there are extended domestic families that consist of father, mother, children, mother's kin by blood or marriage, and occasionally a daughter's kin. Households have retained many matrilocal features, although by the 1840s the prevailing trend was already toward the patrilocal type. In a few instances, two or more families who are unrelated live together in a single dwelling in perfect harmony.

The undisputed head of the household is the father, and family names are in English and can be traced back for three or four generations in a patrilineal line. Given names for children are chosen by the father or his kin. Children are expected to obey their father and must defend and uphold him at all times. The father is the economic head of the family and usually is the main wage earner.[29]

The Seven Clans

The next social unit of importance on the Eastern Cherokee Reservation is the clan, of which there are seven. These are known by bird, animal, and descriptive names that find their origin, along with their personal songs, dances, and magical formulas, in the great mythological giant, Old Stonecoat, who was slain many centuries ago. This giant was burned at the stake, and as his spirit ascended on high it sang songs that set forth the rules and regulations the clans were to follow.[30] Going to the water in clan groups for purificatory ceremonies is a custom only recently abandoned, and whenever a priest prays for a family he still mentions its clan name and predicts the future fortunes of the clan's individual members. In all of his conjuring practices, irrespective of the omens derived, the priest of old was extremely careful to get the correct name and clan of the person involved, since other-

wise the power of both the priest and his ministering rituals would be nullified.[31] A council of seven members representing the seven clans was responsible for calling on a priest to pray for favorable changes in the weather.[32] On the Eastern Cherokee Reservation, a council of seven members that represents the seven clans still carries out this function. There is some evidence that originally there were fourteen clans, which by extinction or absorption have been reduced to seven; thus, the ancient Turtledove and Raven clans now constitute a single Bird Clan.[33]

The *Anidzogohi*, or Wolf Clan, in ancient days hunted like wolves, running after game and attacking in packs. They were fond of wolves and raised them in captivity, training wolf pups just as dogs were trained. It was considered bad luck to kill a wolf, although there is mention of a professional wolf killer who used magic to avoid the bad-luck consequences.[34] Wolftown is named after the Wolf Clan.

The *Anikawi*, or Deer Clan, members were once like the deer in swiftness. They kept deer in captivity and through special training became skilled in hunting and killing deer. They used prayer formulas and ritual to ward off divine retribution for any mistakes made in following their profession. A portion of Painttown was once called Deer Place.

The *Anidjiskwa*, or Bird Clan, was fond of birds, and often had captive crows and chicken hawks. Members of the Bird Clan were renowned for their use of snares and blowguns in hunting. Birdtown is named after this clan.

The *Aniwodi*, or Red Paint Clan, members were noted for their skill in ritually employing red iron-oxide paint to attract lovers and gain protection from witches and other harm. They were known as great conjurers in those matters.

The *Anisahoni*, or Blue Clan, was named after a bluish plant that was gathered from swamps and used for food and medicine. The plant was called *sakoni* or *sahoni* and was a kind of narrow-leafed grass that produced berries that looked like young cucumbers. The roots of the plant were used to protect children from diseases, and it was customary to bathe the children at the appearance of each new

Women in typical daily attire preparing food.

moon in a liquid made from the plant's boiled roots.

The *Anigotigewi*, or Wild Potato Clan, were gatherers of wild potatoes. These grew in swampy places along the rivers and were like sweet potatoes, except that they were round.

The *Anigilohi*, or Twisters Clan, obtained its name in one of two ways. One version has it that the name evolved through the word *gagiloha*, "one who twists," later changed to *ugilaha*, "one born twisted" — referring to the fact that they once were a proud people who strutted when they walked and twisted their shoulders in a haughty manner. A second version maintains that the name was derived from *ugilohi*, or "long hair," referring to the clan's love of personal adornment and elaborate hairstyles.[35]

At present, the greatest numbers of clan affiliations of family heads are found in the Wolf Clan, who together with the Bird Clan account for 50 percent of all individuals listed as having clan affiliations. Next in order are the Twister, Deer, Red Paint, Wild Potato, and Blue clans. Most of the citizens of Wolftown, of the Wright's Creek area of Painttown, of Yellow Hill, and of Birdtown are Wolf Clan members. The Deer Clan shares this position with the Wolf Clan in Big Cove.

The clan and the mother's blood were considered as one in essence and in this regard were both subject to a number of mystic ideas and practices. One was that the mother's blood somehow entered the food a woman prepared during her menstrual period, and if a man ate this tainted food it made him ill. Only a Cherokee woman with clan affiliation could cause this sickness. A white woman could not. There was a medicine to counteract the sickness, but giving it to a man caused the woman's menstruation to intensify in its action, and her discomfort to increase.[36]

The idea of blood connection within the clan itself was allied with the blood-revenge principle in which the older brother of a person who had been injured by another was expected to take revenge either on the offender or a member of the offender's clan.[37]

Clan structure was involved and complex, and it served more purposes than that of preventing marriage within the clan and blood line. The clan was inherited through the mother, and the mother's clan was by birth her child's clan. All members of the child's clan except mother and sisters, brothers, and grandparents were known to the child as "brothers" and "sisters." When the child grew up, he was forbidden to marry anyone of this group.[38]

The next most important clan to the child was his father's clan. Everyone in it was known to the child as a "father," a "father's sister," or a "grandmother." Men who married "father's sisters" were known to their children as "grandfathers." Women who married "fathers" were called "stepparents" if they were of a different clan than the child's, and "mothers" if they were of the child's clan. All children of "fathers" were known as "brothers and sisters."

The mother's father's clan and the father's father's clan determined in considerable measure how the individual was considered when marriage was concerned. Everyone in these clans was a "grandmother" or "grandfather," and it was among those clans that one must find a person to marry. Also, toward all of those clans, familiar behavior was permitted.

A person's grandfather on the maternal side was usually of a different clan from a person's grandfather on the paternal side. This was because marriage with a "sister," or woman whose father was from the same clan as one's own, was forbidden.[39]

Wherever one happens to be in any town of the Eastern Cherokee Reservation, he observes a regular form of rights and duties toward clans. A traveling man who needs shelter for the night in a town distant from his own seeks one of his "brothers" of his own clan. When two people meet for the first time, the ordinary form of greeting is designed to ascertain mutual clan affiliations. There are several ways to learn what a person's clan is without being so rude as to simply ask for it. People associate most closely with their own clanspeople, and the membership of one of those individuals may be known to the visitor. Or, it is only necessary to observe one's behavior toward those persons whose clan affiliations are already known to determine a person's clan.

Those who are indoctrinated in the cultural ways know how people should behave and how to behave themselves.[40]

In sum then, the order of importance in ancient Cherokee social structure was the national capital, the town, the household, and the clan. Today it is the town, the household, and the clan.

The Animal and Plant Worlds

As we consider the mother's place in the family and clan, we should remember that both the animal and plant worlds were thought to duplicate within their own existence the Cherokee lifeway. Plants were dominated by a mother figure. Among all vegetables, corn held the first and highest place in the household economy and ceremonial observance. *Selu*, corn, was invoked in the sacred formulas under the name of *Agawèla*, "the Old Woman," alluding to its mythic origin from the blood of an old woman who was killed by her disobedient sons. Since this is an origin myth, it is told in Chapter Five, where other origin material is treated.

In ancient times, days were reckoned from one sunset until the next, months by moons, and the year was divided into winter and summer. Winter began when the leaves fell in September and the Great New Moon Feast was celebrated. Spring started in March, with the first new moon of that month, and it was the beginning of the Cherokee year. Foremost on everyone's mind was the new birth that demonstrated the spring god's victory over the winter god who lived in the north. Because birth and nourishment were involved, earth had to be a female.

Ceremonies of Corn and the Seasons

The first and foremost events of spring were the preparation of the fields and the planting of the crops. The Great High Priest who lived in the national capital and his seven counselors determined the beginning time for this activity so that the fruits of every field would ripen at the same time. To obtain good crops, seven ears from the last year's crop were put carefully aside by the Great High Priest. These were believed to draw the new corn closer and closer until it had ripened and it was time

for the ceremony, when the old ears were mixed with and eaten with the new ears. To assure favorable weather for growth, rites designed to obtain it were performed by priests.

The annual thanksgiving ceremony of the Green Corn Dance, celebrated before the eating of the first new corn, was the most solemn tribal function, for it included propitiation and expiation for the sins of the past year, amnesty for criminals, and prayers for happiness and prosperity for the year to come. Only those who had properly prepared themselves by prayer, fasting, and purification were allowed to take part in the ceremony, and no one dared to eat the cooked new corn until the ceremony was performed. In eating the corn after the ceremony was ended, care was taken to not blow on it to cool it, for if someone did this it would cause a windstorm to beat down on the corn that was still standing in the fields.[41]

Considerable ceremony accompanied the planting and tending of the corn crop. Seven grains, the sacred number, were placed in each dirt hill, and these were not afterward thinned out. After the last tending of the crop, the owner of each field built a small enclosure in the center of his field, then he and the Chief Priest of his town sat on the ground within it with their heads bent. While the owner kept perfect silence, the priest smoked his sacred tobacco, shook his rattle, scattered grains of corn, and sang songs of invocation to the mother of the corn. Soon thereafter a loud rustling sound would be heard from outside, which they knew was caused by the Old Woman as she brought the true corn with its spiritual power into the field. Neither man, however, was allowed to raise his head and look for her until the priest's songs were finished, and by that time she had always done her work and disappeared.

This ceremony was repeated on four successive nights, after which no one entered the field for seven more nights. Then the priest went in, and if all of the sacred regulations had been observed, he would find young stalks. If the owner of a field was willing to pay a sufficient fee to the priest in return for being taught the proper songs and rituals, he could perform the corn-prayer ceremonies himself.[42]

Another custom was keeping a clean trail from the cornfield to the house, since it was believed this would let the corn know that the owner would make regular trips to see to the well-being of the corn and thus encourage it to not wander off as neglected corn would surely do.[43]

In ancient times, one more ceremony was enacted after the first working of the corn, when the owner or the priest went to each of the four corners of the field and wept and wailed loudly. Some authorities have speculated that this act may have been a lament for the bloody death of the Old Woman. As late as 1900, some elderly people on the Eastern Cherokee Reservation were still religiously observing these customs.[44]

Beans were the next most important food plant after corn, but there does not appear to have been much ceremony or folklore in connection with their cultivation. To make their children smile and be good-natured, mothers sometimes rubbed on the lips of their offspring beans that had cracked open in cooking. It was believed that melons and squashes must not be counted or examined too closely while they were still growing, else they would cease to grow. Neither should one step over a vine, or it would wither before the fruit ripened. A person who had eaten a mayapple was never to come near the melon vines, for the mayapple plant withered and dried up very quickly, and its proximity to the melons would cause them to do the same thing.[45]

Tobacco Ceremonies

The tobacco referred to above was used as a sacred incense, an ingredient in purification rites, a conveyer of prayers to the powers above, a love potion, and as a guarantee of a solemn oath in nearly every important function. It bound a warrior to go to war against the enemy, it ratified a treaty of peace, it confirmed sales or other agreements, it sought omens for the hunter, it drove away witches and evil spirits, and it was used in healing. Tobacco was either smoked in a pipe or sprinkled on a ceremonial fire. It was never rolled into cigarettes as among the tribes of the Southwest; neither was it smoked for pleasure. It was the *Nicotiana rustica*, or wild tobacco, and was

called "old tobacco," by the Cherokees. The Iroquois called the same plant "real tobacco."[46]

Tobacco had no power of its own until it was "remade" through ritual that began with its planting. In the spring, in a secret place where no one would see the growing tobacco and thus damage its power, lightning-struck wood was placed by a priest on a small patch of ground and was burned. Then the tobacco seeds were planted, and if it thundered while this was being done, it was a good omen. The crop would be an excellent one. The tobacco was harvested at sunrise one day in the fall and was taken to the bank of a stream, where a sacred prayer formula was said over it four or seven times. By this act, power was infused into the tobacco, and it was "remade."

For additional power, the tobacco was held up to absorb the rays of the rising sun, and since one's saliva and breath were believed to contain the essence of a person's life-force and personality, chewing the tobacco and blowing on it invested the tobacco with even more strength.

When ritually used and prior to being smoked, the tobacco was sometimes spat into the left hand and kneaded in a counterclockwise motion with the four fingers of the right hand. Other ingredients might also be mixed with it. Shredded grapevine helped when one wished to attract a mate. Cedar leaves and certain seeds helped it repel witches.

There were four main ways to use remade tobacco when healing and witches were concerned. It was smoked close to patients so that the smoke touched them; the fumes could be blown around to pervade a general area; the smoke could be blown toward where an individual was likely to be; or the tobacco could be placed where the desired individual would come into contact with it.[47]

1. Mooney and Olbrechts, *The Swimmer Manuscript,* pp. 116-130.
2. Payne Papers, Vol. 4, p. 121.
3. Ibid., p. 235.
4. Gilbert, "The Eastern Cherokees," p. 254.
5. Payne Papers, Vol. 4, p. 121.
6. Timberlake, *Memoirs, 1756-1765,* p. 90, and Mooney and Olbrechts, *The Swimmer Manuscript,* pp. 116-130.
7. Gilbert, p. 341.
8. Payne Papers, Vol. 4, p. 120.
9. Ibid.
10. Ibid., pp. 20-21.
11. Nuttal, in Thwaites, 1904-07, Vol. 13, pp. 188-189.
12. Haywood, *Natural and Aboriginal History of Tennessee,* pp. 280 ff.
13. Gilbert, p. 339.
14. Ibid.
15. Ibid., pp. 339-340.
16. Payne Papers, Vol. 4, p. 120.
17. Ibid., p. 18.
18. Ibid., p. 97.
19. Ibid., pp. 98-99.
20. Payne Papers, interview with G. Hicks, Vol. 3, pp. 38-39.
21. Ibid., Vol. 4, pp. 98-99.
22. Ibid., interview with Nutsawi, Vol. 3, p. 36.
23. Ibid., interview with Chism, Vol. 3, pp. 36-38.
24. Ibid., Vol. 4, pp. 98-99.
25. Ibid., p. 235.
26. Ibid.
27. Gilbert, pp. 201-202.
28. Ibid., p. 203.
29. Ibid., pp. 202-203.
30. Ibid., pp. 207-208; see also Mooney, *Myths of the Cherokee,* pp. 319-320.
31. Ibid.
32. Payne Papers, Vol. 1, pp. 164-176.
33. Mooney, pp. 212-213.
34. Ibid., p. 203.
35. Gilbert, p. 204.
36. Ibid., pp. 206-207.
37. Ibid., p. 207.
38. Ibid., p. 208.
39. Ibid., pp. 208-209.
40. Ibid.
41. Mooney, p. 423.
42. Ibid., p. 423.
43. Ibid., p. 423.
44. Ibid., pp. 131-137; see also Adair, pp. 186-197.
45. Ibid., p. 424.
46. Ibid., p. 424.
47. Kilpatrick and Kilpatrick, *Run toward the Nightland,* pp. 9-12.

CHAPTER FOUR

Government and Warfare

I t is apparent that the female did not play a subordinate role in Cherokee society. Unlike Pueblo, Apache, and Plains women, the Cherokee wife was not even required to build the house. Cultivation work in the fields was shared, with the man bearing the greater burdens. Overall, there was a balance of labor and responsibility, with the woman's prominent place in the home and with the family being offset by the man's prominent place in government and warfare. Therefore, Cherokee women had a sense of self-worth and dignity that undoubtedly showed in their character and appearance, and proved so attractive to European and American traders that in early historic times they coveted Cherokee women as wives. Intermarriages led to such a rapid intermixture of blood that by the turn of the nineteenth century, mixed bloods were common in the Cherokee Nation and becoming an influence to be reckoned with. Nowhere do we find this influence more apparent than in Cherokee government during the nineteenth century, but to see how this could happen at all we must first examine the ruling form of government in prehistoric times.

The wife of the *Uku*.

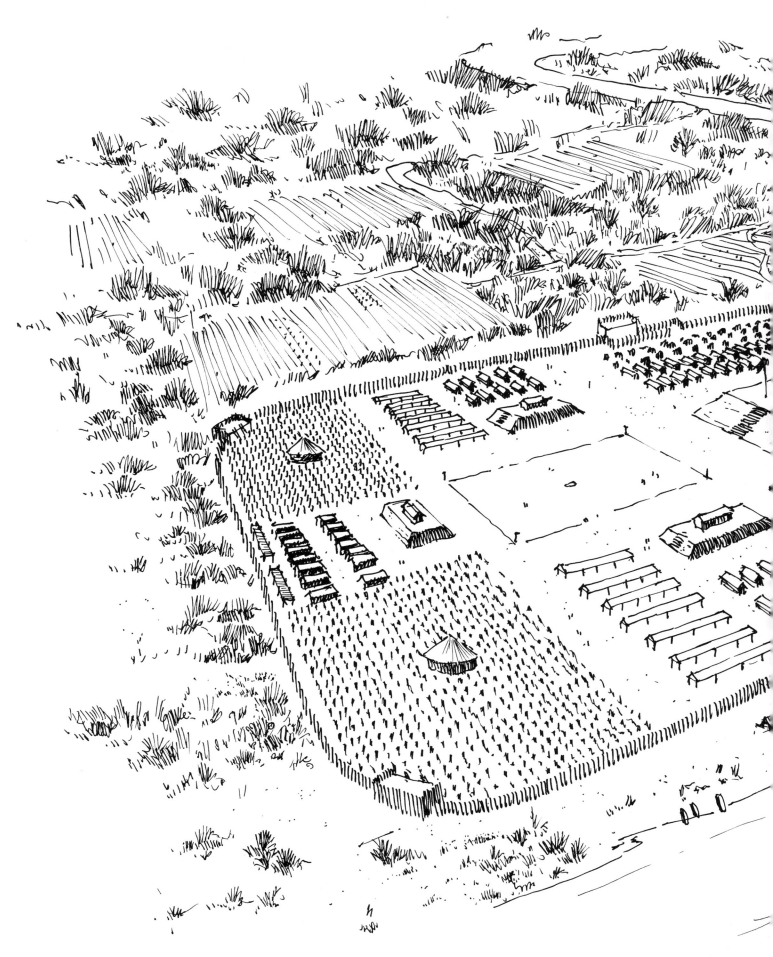

The Cherokee national capital.

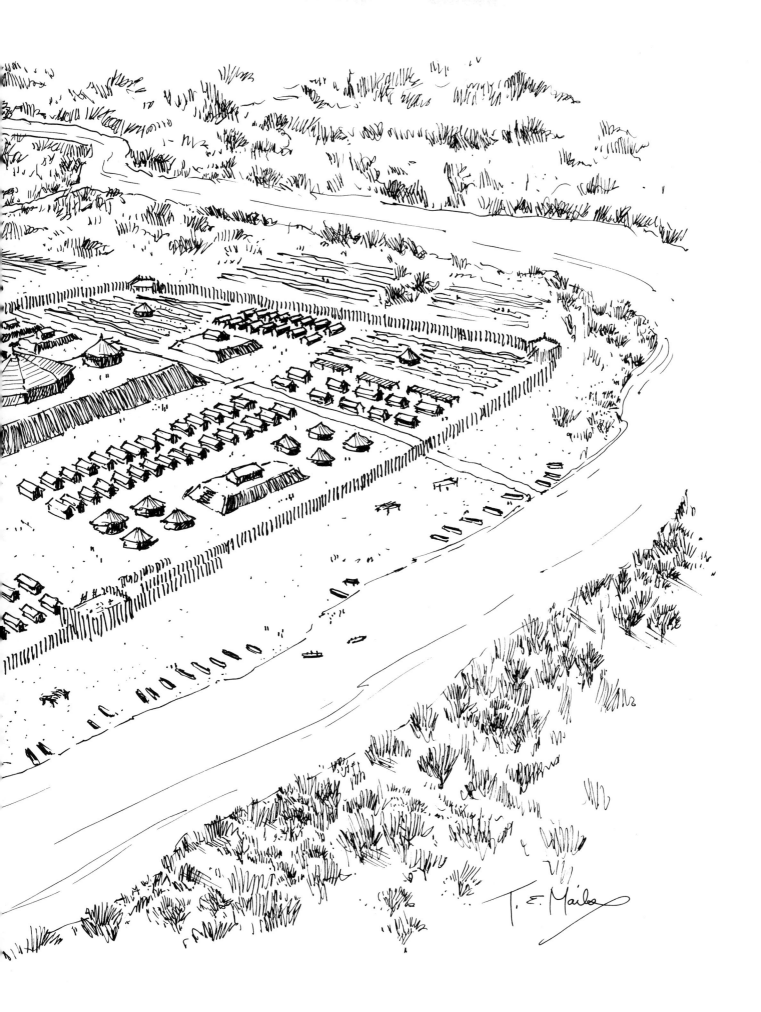

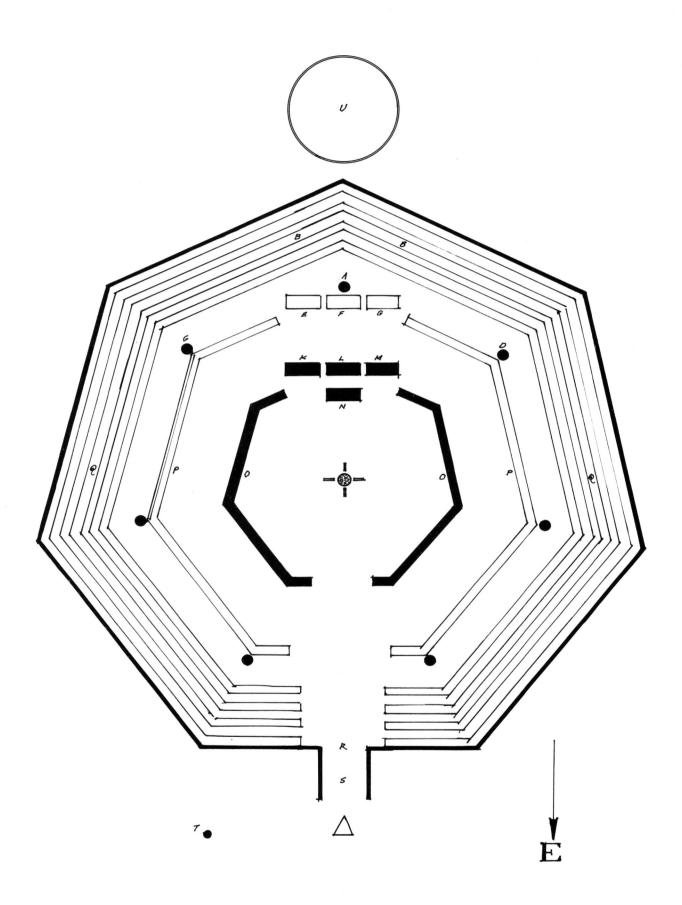

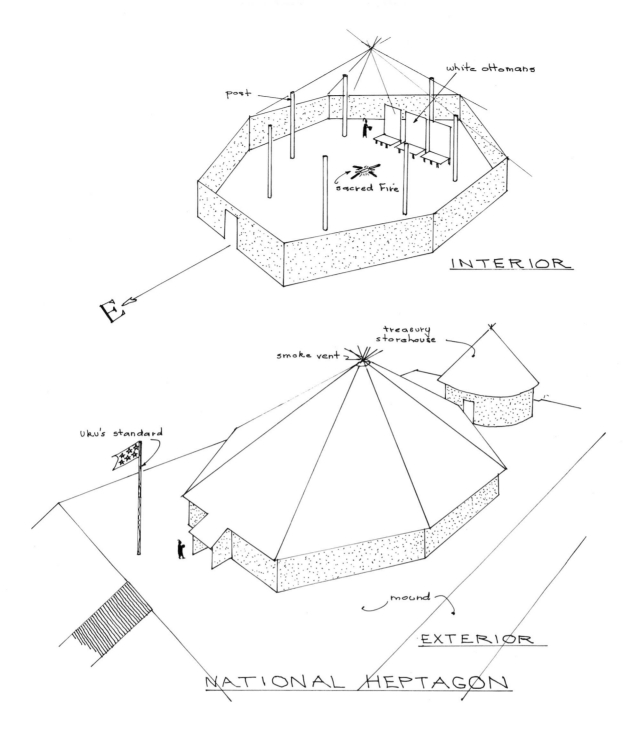

Labels in illustration:

post

white ottomans

sacred Fire

INTERIOR

E

treasury storehouse

smoke vent

Uku's standard

mound

EXTERIOR

NATIONAL HEPTAGON

Illustration on facing page: Floor plan of the heptagon based on information in Payne Manuscript, Vol. 4. **a.** holy post considered the seventh post, and about which the holy things were stored. **b.** holy place, including all that part of the interior west of the two posts. **c., d.** points beyond which no common person could go. **e., f., g.** The three white-painted ottomans for the Chief Priest, or *Uku,* the principal assistant, and the chief speaker. The backs of the seats were as wide as the seats were long and extended up to the joists above. See post detail on page 90. Several pieces of carved wood were put on the seat backs and ornamented with figures such as new moons and oval boards. The seven joists were also ornamented as shown. Except for the ornamentation, everything was painted white. **k., l., m.** middle seat for the Great War Chief, right seat for his right-hand man, left seat for war chief's speaker. **n.** seat used when a new Great War Chief was installed. The war seats were painted red and had backs, but Payne did not learn how high the backs were or how the seats were ornamented. **o.** red seats for the War Chief's counselors and the war leaders of the nation's towns. **p.** white seats for the civil and religious counselors of the nation. On common occasions, others could occupy these seats as far back as posts. **p., q., r.,** seats for national leaders on festival occasions, and for the ordinary citizens of the capital at other times of the year. **s.** entrance portico. **t.** *Uku*'s standard, replaced by Great War Chief's standard in war times. **u.** national storage house or treasury house.

Early Cherokee Government

By A. D. 1600, Cherokee government was already highly developed for an Indian tribe, although some other southeastern tribes, such as the Natchez and the Creeks, had similar approaches in their manner of rule. It is here that we begin to see the true greatness of the Cherokee Nation and experience the heights it had attained. It is here that the Cherokees stand out from the rest, and where we see another facet of their personality that made rapid change possible for them. In their enlightened system of government we find a concern for individual freedom and human rights, a sense of shared responsibility, and an awareness of consequences for acts that mark the best of both democratic and republican control. It was these qualities that opened them up to the adoption of the like principles they encountered in the fledgling federal government of the Americans.

The National Heptagon

In the national capital and situated on a high mound was a huge heptagon, or seven-sided building, at which all national festivals were celebrated, where major war parties assembled before going off to war, and from which a measure of control was dispensed to the entire nation. Contrasted with this were the smaller individual town council houses, which served an average town population of 350 people. As mentioned earlier, the town council house was a circular building, although the members of each of the seven clans sat in it in individual places, so that the interior arrangement was, in a sense, seven sided.[1] Directly behind both the heptagon and the town council house was a round storage building with a cone-shaped roof, sometimes called the treasure house, where some of the important tribal items were kept, and where foodstuffs for the festivals were temporarily stored. I have not found in the literature a diagram of a seven-sided, or heptagonal structure, although there is a recreated small version of one at the Oconoluftee Village in Cherokee, North Carolina. One author states that in ancient days the town council house had seven sides, one for each of the seven clans, and by the

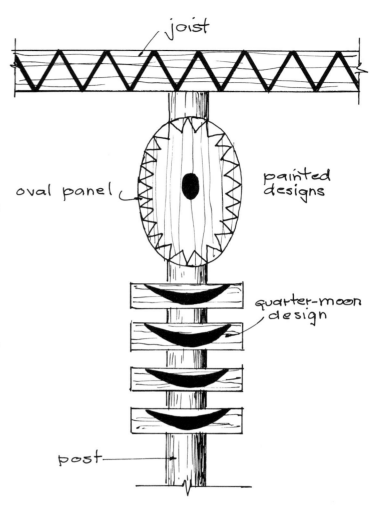

HEPTAGON or COUNCIL HOUSE INTERIOR POST DETAIL

.... redrawn from Payne Papers

eighteenth century the town house had become rounded, although the symbolism of seven remained. But while the idea is reasonable, no source is cited for it.[2]

It is just as probable that the national heptagon was the only seven-sided building in the nation, and that all town council houses were from the beginning circular in shape. I can think of no reason why they should be changed from seven-sided to circular.

It is regrettable that early traders paid little attention to Cherokee arts and gave few descriptions of them. Yet what can justifiably be called fine arts were broadly and competently practiced by all Indian tribes, and the nature of the Cherokee people was surely such that similar fine arts were practiced among them. We find some hints of these in the descriptions of the clothing and a few other things they manufactured, and we find more hints in their civic-religious architecture. By this latter term I mean the principal building in each town that served both civic and religious purposes.

Town Council Houses

The average town council house was fifty feet in diameter, sat on a mound, and except for its circular shape was constructed in the same manner as the national heptagon. The central portion of the room was held up by seven large posts set in a circle half as broad as the building's diameter and connected by wall plates. One end of each of seven slanting beams was laid on top of the wall plates where they joined the posts, and the other ends met and crossed over one another, tipi style, at the roof peak. Log beams connected the wall plates and the outside wall, and the finished roof was cone shaped. The side walls were covered with grass thatching, and the grass was covered with clay, then more thatch, and with this durable plating was rainproof. The roof logs were covered with a layer of saplings and then successive tiers of bark shingles, and a smoke vent was left in its center where the logs crossed. On the east side was an entrance door with a portico to shield it in bad weather. On the interior was the centrally placed sacred fire that always burned. A storage place for the sacred ark was on the west side, along with storage shelves for sacred items. Several concentric rows of seats along the wall provided places for the lesser officers and the clans to sit. Closer to the sacred fire were the seats and bedlike ottomans for the chief officers. The high backs of the latter shielded the storage area from public view, and at the front corners of the seats were five- or six-foot-high upright boards that had carved into them the representation of a full moon and four quarter moons. These carvings were painted with chalky white clay, and on certain occasions black paintings were intermixed with them.[3]

James Adair saw a number of what he calls "the Indian synhedria," but as usual he does not distinguish one from the other. All of them are described as having esoteric features that lent a lavish tone to their interiors, yet he sets forth conflicting details regarding what he refers to as "the imperial seats." Consequently, I take the liberty of attaching the more opulent items he mentions to the national heptagon, and the less opulent to the town council houses. If this is not correct, how, apart from size, would the capitol building be distinguished from the rest?

At the front corners of the three white imperial seats in the national heptagon — each of which was seven feet broad and nine feet long — were white-painted eagles carved of poplar wood, with their wings stretched out, and raised five or so feet off the ground on top of deep-notched boards. On the faces of each of these boards were painted with a chalky white clay the figures of a mountain lion and a man wearing buffalo horns. The latter emblem was a reminder of the fact that every war leader must make three successful war campaigns with the holy ark before he was permitted to wear a pair of a young buffalo bull's horns on the front of his headband, before he could sing the triumphal war song, and before he could dance and sing with a buffalo's tail attached to his belt and sticking up behind him. The eagle was to remind people of the divine attributes the Great High Priest inherited at the time of his installation, and which were retained by his constant prayers and sacrifices. Each of these sacred emblems was painted anew at the annual fruit offering for the expiation of sins.[4]

A Dual Form of Government

As previously mentioned, the ancient Cherokees lived in an alternating state of war and peace which called for a dual organization of tribal government: a white, or peace, organization, and a red, or war, organization.

The white organization consisted of a set of officials aged fifty or more, a large portion of whom were priests, and who performed both secular and religious functions. They ranged in authority from the Great High Priest, whose Cherokee name was "*Uku*," down to lesser officials needed to carry on the minor functions of state. The Great High Priest

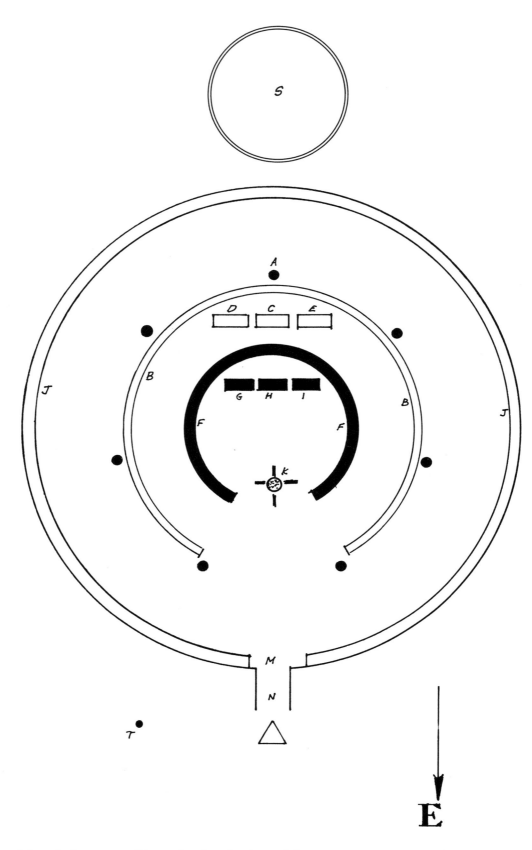

Floor plan of the typical town council house, based on drawing and data in Payne Manuscript, Vol. 4. **a.** the seven posts. **b.** white seats for the civil and religious counselors. **c.** seat for the town white chief and his principal assistant. **d.**, **e.** white seats for the speaker and seven counselors. **f.** red seats for the common war counselors. **g.** red seat for the town war chief. **h.**, **i.** red seats for the right-hand man and speaker. **j.** seats for the common people. **k.** the sacred fire. **m.** entrance door. **n.** entrance portico. **s.** storage or treasury house. **t.** town white chief's standard, replaced by war chief's standard in war times.

had a principal assistant, a great speaker, and seven counselors representing the seven clans, whom he consulted on all matters of importance. The rules that governed the induction of these men into office, their dress, and marriage were similar to those governing his own. It was this group of officials that helped him determine the times of the national feasts and made arrangements for them. In every town of considerable size, there was a court consisting of a priest, his principal assistant, his speaker, and seven counselors. They decided all matters of lesser importance and attended to such religious ceremonies as were proper for individual towns to observe. In smaller villages or hamlets where no such court existed, the people called upon neighboring priests to assist them as circumstances required.

In addition to administering civil law, white officials alone owned the prayers for invoking blessings from sun, moon, and other protective spirits who, assuming it was the will of the powers who dwelt above, could prevent or take away illness, wounds, and even death. White officials could remove the uncleanness from polluted persons and restore them to normal life. White officials and their belongings were sacred and not like ordinary citizens. We are told that in some instances they were not subject to ordinary laws and usages, but not what those instances were.[5]

The red organization consisted of a set of officials who corresponded in rank and duties to the white officials, except that their function was exclusively military. If either of the two organizations was in any way subordinate to the other, it was the red group, since the Great High Priest could make or unmake the war chiefs. In addition, the red officials were at frequent intervals elected by popular vote, while the white officials were either to some extent hereditary or subject to appointment by the Great High Priest. White chieftainships could be transmitted, like clan membership, only in the female line. The son of a chief could never inherit his position and power and was not regarded as of royal blood or even next of kin to his father. Instead, the chief's position went to the son of the chief's oldest sister.[6]

In most instances, red officials acquired their rank as the result of bravery in battle and were surnamed either Raven, Wolf, Fox, or Owl, since those were the foremost symbols of cleverness and bravery. Red officials were honored with victory and scalp dances and sat in places of honor in the town council houses. Since war was an act of killing and involved blood as a polluting agent, many of the ritual acts associated with war were designed to deal with and to remove the effects of uncleanness. Purification was always required after a battle, and divination with crystals and sacrifice to the fire were a standard part of every war expedition.[7]

Like the national capital, each town was governed by its two head chiefs — the white chief in peacetime and the red chief in war. The one exception had to do with those occasions when the nation was being attacked and the white chief took control, which will be explained shortly. The interior seating arrangements of the town council house differed according to who was in control, and Payne's diagrams for them have been redrawn here. Whichever of the head chiefs was in power occupied the central ottoman in the west half of the town council house, and when the red chief ruled he sat closer even than the white chief to the sacred fire.

An assemblage of Beloved Women, also called "Pretty Women" or "War Women," was present at every war council. These served as counselors to the male leaders, and also regulated the treatment dealt to prisoners of war. One of the Beloved Women in historical times was Nancy Ward, and the inspiring story of her life is recounted in Chapter Ten.

The White Organization

The principal officers in the white, or peace, organization were as follows, with categories one through five and ten being members of the priestly caste:

1. The chief of the tribe, or Great High Priest, who is variously called *Uku, Ookah,* and other ceremonial titles.

2. *U lo tv,* the chief's principal assistant, also called "right-hand man" or "the one who fanned him."

3. *Ti nv li no he ski,* the seven counselors who represented the seven clans.

4. *A tsi nv sti,* the chief's messenger.

5. *Ti kv no tsi li ski,* the chief speaker.

6. The council of elder, or beloved, men.

7. The Beloved, or Pretty, or War, Women.

8. *A ke yv gv sta,* the women who warmed water to wash the chief.

9. Lesser officers required for specific ceremonies included: seven hunters, seven cooks, seven overseers, seven fire makers, seven cleansers, musicians, attendants at the *Ookah* dance, and the *Yo wah* hymn singer.

10. *Nv no hi ta hi,* the priest who superintended the building of the hothouse.[8]

The above officials served in the national capital and as officials for the entire tribe. But with the exception of those listed in category nine, since most of the ceremonies requiring these were held at the national heptagon, in each of the larger towns of the tribe the same series of officials was repeated.

Also, while the officials in all of the towns outside the capital were subject to the will of the Great High Chief and his seven counselors, they were often incorporated with them in a governing group when grave decisions confronted the tribe.[9]

On festival occasions, the *Uku* was clothed in a sleeveless white waistcoat and wore a broad woven belt. As soon as he entered the heptagon to begin his duties, a beloved attendant spread out on the *Uku's* white seat a white dressed buckskin and a soft buffalo or bear robe, and placed on top of them beautiful white beads that were a gift from the people. Then the *Uku* wrapped around his shoulders in shawl fashion a consecrated deerskin that was also whitened. This he tied on by knotting together the legs of the skin, tying them in such a way that the legs formed an X on his chest. He also wore a new pair of whitened buckskin moccasins he had made and stitched together with deer sinew. The top portion above the toes he painted, for the space of three inches, with a few streaks of red — not

Left to right, the principal assistant, the *Uku* or Great High Priest, and the chief speaker seated on their ottomans in the national heptagon.

vermillion, for this was a war color — but with a certain red root whose leaves and stalk resembled the ipecacuanha, which was one of the principal symbols for holy things. To the upper part of the moccasins were fastened tufts of blunted wild turkey-cock spurs. Between festivals, the moccasins were stored on the shelves with other consecrated things.

The festival costume of the *Uku* included a magnificent cape made of white feathers and a breastplate made of a white conch shell with two holes bored in the middle of it, through which were passed the ends of an otter-skin neck strap that had a single white buck-horn button fastened to it on each side. His headband was either a wreath of swan feathers or a long piece of swan skin, doubled so that only the fine snowy feathers appeared on each side. Topping this was a cap covered with upright white feathers whose ends curved over and hung down.[10]

Other priests also had white festival costumes, but these are only alluded to by informants and are not sufficiently described to reconstruct them other than by conjecture.

For regular year-round duties, the Great High Priest and the town priests wore chalked, perfectly white deerskin shirts that reached halfway down the thighs, and also breeches made from two aprons, one before and one behind, that were fastened above the hips with a belt, and extended down about halfway to the knees. The aprons were tied at the sides with thongs and then drawn together and tied to form a crotch. Worn over the shirt and breeches was a sleeved coat whose hem came nearly to their feet. It had woven, epaulet-type pieces on both shoulders of the *Uku* garment and on one shoulder of the coats worn by other priests. Bells were attached to the coat cuffs. The trim rolls of the coats were of the same white deerskin, having fringes and tassels that hung down to the knees. White leggings were worn in the winter, and the garters and moccasins that were always worn were also white. Bells were attached to the garters. The cap of the Great High Priest was conical and made from the skins of the underside of deer tails that were dressed with the hair on. Enough of these skins was sewn together to make the cap. This hair was perfectly white and lay close to the skin so that it pointed upward on the cap. Bells were fastened to the back of the cap, and long, upright white feathers were attached to the top of the cap in such a way as to curve gracefully over and hang down on all sides.[11]

Although we have no specific information about them, we can assume that the principal assistant and the chief speaker had differently adorned but similarly shaped hats that were covered with swansdown feathers and topped with feathers that were a little shorter than those worn by the Great High Priest.

All priests had spectacular ritual pipes, which were about three feet long and had whitened wooden stems and stone bowls carved with symbolic figures appropriate to their offices.[12]

The wives of the priests also had a distinguishing dress. This consisted of a short gown and petticoat fashioned from clay-whitened deerskin. The petticoat came nearly to the ankles, and at knee level had a row of bells that encircled it. Their moccasins were white and made like Indian boots whose tops came halfway to the knee. They also wore hide headbands to which were fastened, as badges of honor, animal horns that were about three inches long. Their jewelry was the same as that worn by other women of distinction.[13]

The *Uku* Consecration Ceremony

The consecration ceremony for a new *Uku* gives us good insights into the nature of the office and the extravagance that surrounded it. On the death of the presiding *Uku*, his principal assistant set a date for the consecration of his successor, who would already have been chosen and trained. A messenger was dispatched to notify the chief priests throughout the nation. He was given a special string of braided wild hemp with as many knots tied in it as there were nights prior to the appointed date. Each day the messenger traveled, he was to cut one knot from his string and thus would keep a precise account of the time. He followed a direct course that took him to the central towns of each region, and once the news had been passed to the priests of those towns, they had the responsibility of notifying others

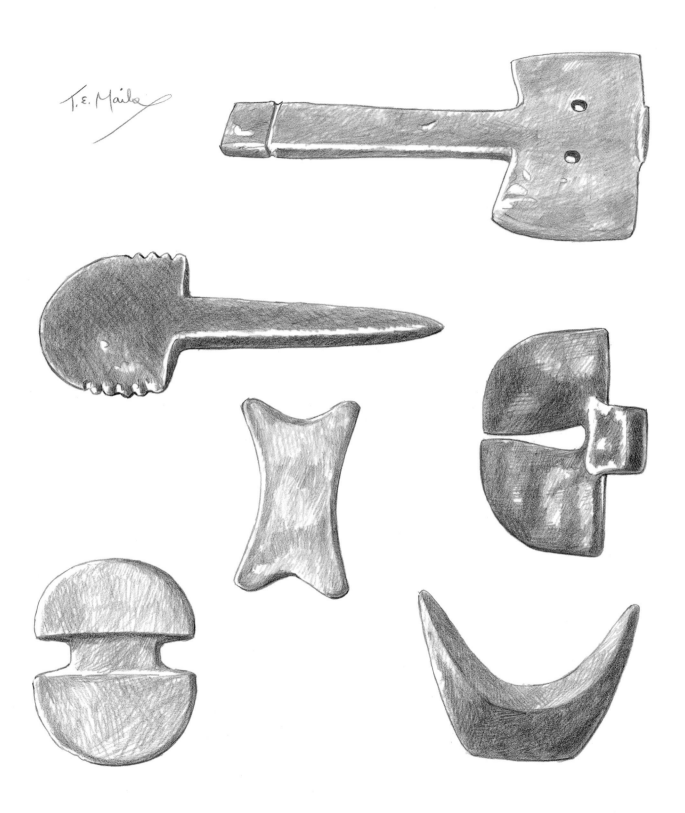

Typical ceremonial objects used by national leaders as symbols of office, Museum of the Cherokee Indian. Those in the middle and at the bottom were mounted on decorated wooden rods.

until the entire nation was informed.

At the appointed time, the nation's priests assembled with their messengers at the national heptagon and sent these messengers en masse to the candidate to request that he accept the office of *Uku*. For decorum's sake, the messengers were to pretend that the new leader, when actually faced with the decision, would be modest and need encouragement and persuasion. The fact was that he was more than ready to undertake the responsibility, and everyone knew it. When the messengers returned and the priests were assured that the candidate would comply with the request and had begun a six-day fast, the priests used those six days to make a special platform of tall and strong reeds, an official *Uku* investiture costume, and a yellow painted scepter. Then, on the seventh day, the priests, along with a vast multitude, went to the candidate's house.

Previously selected persons undressed and carefully bathed the candidate, for he must be absolutely clean when his official clothing was put on him. Then he was dressed in the installation garments of the *Uku*, and his face was anointed with sacred white paint. The installation garments were exactly like the *Uku*'s white festival dress, except they were of deerskin painted yellow, as were even the feathers of the cap.

The platform was brought to the candidate's house, and to affirm his enthusiasm for the job, he leaped onto it and stood upright, taking the yellow scepter in his right hand. Four chosen men then lifted the platform on their shoulders and carried the candidate to the national heptagon, with half of the assembled priests walking in front and the other half behind, all singing. The procession halted three times on the way. When they arrived at the heptagon everyone drew silent, and the people filed in and sat down. The procession of priests bearing the candidate walked silently around the heptagon four times and then lowered the platform to within three feet of the ground, whereupon the candidate climbed onto the back of an appointed person and in this ungainly manner was carried into the heptagon, where he was placed on the previously prepared and centrally located white seat, or ottoman. The seat had already

been covered with a white dressed deerskin, and for the candidate's feet there was a footrest of cane covered with a large buckskin that was dressed white. The other priests seated themselves in prescribed order on white seats that were arranged in a semi-circle, with the most distinguished sitting nearest to the candidate.

The candidate stood up, and except for his breechclout, his clothes were removed by another priest. The principal assistant dipped the forefinger of his right hand into a thick ointment made of white clay and deer tallow. He approached the candidate and, placing his finger on the candidate's head, drew a white line that passed down over his forehead, nose, and chin, and ended on the center of his chest. The assistant then took more ointment and made a line from the top of the candidate's head to the middle of his back. A third line began on the candidate's right thumbnail and ran up the arm to the shoulder and then to the chest. From there, another line was drawn down the abdomen and right leg to the big toenail on the right foot. Finally, the painting was completed by drawing similar lines on the left arm, chest, abdomen, and leg.

Next, the principal assistant presented the candidate with an eagle-tail fan, old sacred tobacco, and a sacred pipe, which was the signal for the candidate to commence smoking with the other priests as a token of friendship and loyalty. But this was not done in the usual manner of handing the pipe from one man to the other. Each priest smoked his own pipe, for the candidate's pipe, since he was being transformed into the *Uku,* was peculiarly sacred, as were his attire, seat, and other paraphernalia. Once this rite ended, his pipe and his bag for keeping his tobacco were hung on pegs on the left side of the upright white planks that formed the back of his seat.

At this point the chief speaker came forward and made a lengthy address in which he directed everyone to pay homage to the new *Uku*, and the people arose and in single file came to do this, bowing before the *Uku* and saying, *"Tsa gv wi tso la,"* to which he replied, *"Ho!"* When everyone had returned to their seats, they sat in silence for the rest of the night and contemplated the significance of the event, the people no doubt praying for divine blessings upon the new ruler and at the same time assuring themselves they would have good success and happiness during his reign. Just before daybreak, the new *Uku* broke the silence with an address to the people in which he promised to exercise his authority in all respects according to the commands of God. When he finished, the people answered in unison as they promised to obey him. Then the candidate was dressed again in his official garments.

About noon, the young people withdrew from the assembly, and the *Uku* stood up and placed his scepter over his right shoulder. With two men putting, in a symbolic gesture of loyalty, their hands under his arms to support him, he walked to the door of the heptagon and from there to his house, where his yellow installation garments were removed and stored away. His common dress was put on, and the ointment was washed from his face. The installation ritual was completed.[14]

In addition to his special costume, the *Uku* had a standard, or flag, which consisted of a long white pole with a carved eagle on top and bearing a pennant made of white cloth or deerskin, four or five yards long, painted with red spots like stars. In instances of great emergency, such as a sudden attack from without, the standard was raised in front of the national heptagon, and the national council would, after assembling for divination with tobacco smoke to learn the nature and extent of the emergency, select those individuals from the overall domain that would be needed to play the key roles in assisting the Great War Chief in defense.[15]

Crime and Punishment

No one says how rampant crime was among the Cherokees, but based on studies of other Indian tribes it was probably not widespread or even a problem of great consequence. But it assuredly did happen amongst the Cherokees, else their laws to deal with it would not have been so stringent as they were. In the punishment of criminals, the eldest brother or the nearest male relative was expected to be the avenger of spilled blood. To handle this justly,

the ancient Cherokees set apart four towns of refuge, one of which was Echota, or Chota, to temporarily protect anyone who intentionally or unintentionally slew a fellow Cherokee. Moreover, every priest's door and yard were places of refuge, and if the slayer even came in sight of the *Uku* while fleeing, the avenger of blood could not touch him.

When a slayer reached a place of sanctuary, the priest of that place either blew his shell trumpet or directed his messenger to call together the people of the town. The person was declared innocent until a court could be convened and examination could be made of the circumstances surrounding the slaying.

Beyond listening to the details of the incident, the Cherokees had their own method of testing a witness. In inconsequential affairs, the elderly priest who served as judge asked each witness whether he had lied when he gave his testimony, then observed the witness very carefully when he replied. The witness usually answered, "I do not lie." In affairs of greater consequence, the judge said to the witness, "What you have now said, is it true in the beloved name of the great and self-existent God?" And the witness replied, "It is true in the beloved name of *Yo He wah*." In a matter of great importance, the judge said the same thing, but put it more powerfully: "Have you now told me the real truth by the great and powerful name of the living God, which proclaims his existence without beginning or end, and by his self-existent and literal name in which I adjure you?" And the witness, assuming that he was properly fearful of God's chastisement of liars, would answer as strongly as possible, "I have told you the naked truth, which I most solemnly swear by this adorable, great, divine, self-existent name, which we are not to profane, and I likewise attest to it, by his other beloved, unspeakable, sacred, essential name."[16]

If the court decided that the accused was guilty of an unforgivable breach of law, he was not publicly condemned, but rather placed in the forefront of a battle line or in some other circumstance that would bring him a noble, or contributory, death. This kind of decision did not, however, apply in all instances besides those wherein sanctuary was sought. Other times, justice might be summary and swift.

The entire clan, not only the older brother, was responsible for the crime of one of its members, and there were no exceptions. It was a system that, while unacceptable by present standards, worked well for the Cherokees, because relatives themselves would usually bring the fugitive to justice to avoid like punishment.[17] For example, the brothers of a murderer would often dispose of him to save one of themselves from becoming the victim of blood vengeance, although accidental deaths could be recompensed by the gift of a scalp taken from a prisoner or an enemy in battle.[18]

The fulfillment of the law in ancient times could be brutal, although we must understand that it was practiced as a deterrent. Criminals who seriously harmed the public by their actions were sometimes stoned to death or killed with a weapon. A favored treatment was to take the individual to the top of a high cliff, where his elbows were tied behind him and his feet were drawn up and tied. Then he was cast headlong over the side and died on the sharp rocks below.[19]

The law of retaliation even applied in trifling offenses. An eye for an eye was the only kind of act that seemed to achieve satisfaction.

The father of a family could not punish his own children, since they were of a different clan from his. If he should kill one, he would be subject to clan revenge on the part of his wife's clan. The mother of the children could kill them, although whether a woman ever did this is not known. Accidental killings might be punished in any one of several ways, depending on the circumstances of the event. The punishment might be one of those bestowed on individuals who sought refuge, it might be by clan revenge, or the incident might be settled with a gift.[20]

After a thorough investigation of Cherokee law, John Phillip Reid states that the Cherokees were a law-abiding people whose ancient customs served them well, allowing them to maintain social harmony in their towns and a sense of common ethnic identity. He is not certain that they understood the importance of law and assumes they just took it for granted. Yet later on, when the ancient customs had become obsolete and their survival depended on the adoption of a new system of jurisprudence, the Cherokees demonstrated a remarkable national trait. They reached back into the very past they were discarding, into their strength as a people, and developed a law consciousness surely rare in history, not merely because they were giving their allegiance to a foreign law, but because of the degree to which they pledged their commitment — trusting their rights, their fortunes, and their future to the rule of the law.[21]

Cherokee Towns

In the Oklahoma Historical Society archives, there is a list of Cherokee towns that existed in 1755 and another list of the names of the chiefs who ruled in early times prior to removal. I suspect that the towns mentioned are only the large ones, and it might be that not all of the chiefs should be called *Uku*. But the lists are useful, and it is worth noting that most of the chiefs had long reigns, indicating either successful administrations or that once in office, chiefs were not easily deposed.

The districts are (1) *Over Hill Towns:* Great Tellico, Chatugee, Tennessee, Chote (or Chota or Echota), Talassee, and Sittiquo; (2) *Valley Towns:* Euforsee, Conestee, Little Telliquo, Cotocanahut, Nayowee, Tomatly, and Chewotie; (3) *Middle Towns:* Jaree, Watoge, and Nuckasee; (4) *Keowee Towns:* Keowee, Tricentee, Echoee, Torsee, Cowee, Torsalla, Caweeshee, and Elejay; (5) *Out Towns:* Tucharechee, Kittowa, Conontoroy, Steecoy, Oustanale, and Tuckasegee; (6) *Lower Towns*: Tomassee, Oustestee, Cheowie, Estatoie, Tosawa, Keowee, and Oustanalle.

The chiefs are Moytoy, 1730-1760; Attacullaculla, 1760-1775; Oconastota, 1775-1780; Hanging Maw, 1780-1792; Little Turkey, 1792-1801; Black Fox, 1801-1811; Pathkiller, 1811-1827; Charles Renatus Hicks, 1827; William Hicks, 1827-1828; and John Ross, 1828-1866.

The Red Organization and War

The principal officers of the red, or war, organization were as follows:
1. *Ska ya gu stu eg wo*, the Great Red War Chief, or

High Priest of War, was called "the Raven" when he scouted or "spied" while the army was on the march.

2. The chief's second, or right-hand, man.

3. Seven war counselors to order acts of war.

4. Pretty, or Beloved, or War Women to judge the fate of captives.

5. *Ska li lo ski*, the chief war speaker.

6. *Ka ta ta ka ne hi*, the warrior who carried the Great War Chief's battle standard, or flag.

7. *Ku ni ko ti*, the Chief War Priest for healing and treating wounds, who had three or more assistants.

8. Messengers.

9. *A tsi lv ti ye gi*, the priest who carried to war the ark containing the holy fire. It was said that he could follow the enemy at night as well as anyone else could in the day. His right-hand man was called *Ko lv nv*. Only the priest and this man were allowed to touch the ark.

10. Three war scouts: the Wolf, the Owl, and the Fox.

11. A special war priest, who did the divination and carried out other religious functions for the Great War Chief.

12. Lesser officers included drummers, cooks, fire tenders, and wood gatherers. A priest who had killed an enemy during a battle was named *Nv no hi ta hi*, and he superintended the building of sweat houses for purification rites.[22]

D. S. Butrick believed that from the manner of his induction into office, the Great War Chief was himself both a priestly and a warlike character.[23]

In cases when any one of the town chiefs was forewarned of approaching enemies who were yet some distance away, he immediately dispatched a messenger bearing this news to the *Uku*, along with a twist of sacred tobacco that was painted red. On receiving the tobacco and message, the *Uku* immediately called for the Great War Chief and his officers. If, after consulting together, this group felt there was no great worry, they did not smoke the tobacco but sent it back by the same messenger who had brought it. If on the other hand they concluded that danger

was imminent and considerable, the tobacco was smoked, messengers spread the news throughout the nation, and the *Uku* had his standard hoisted to notify the citizens of the national capital. At the same time, the *Uku's* personal messenger was dispatched to tell the seven counselors to convene at the national heptagon. As soon as this meeting was held, and always in conjunction with the Great War Chief and his advisers, war plans were made. The red war standard was also hoisted in front of the heptagon, and the red officers painted themselves and their weapons with fresh red paint.

Since the body of soldiers who would gather to defend the nation would be divided into either four or seven companies, the council selected a healer for each company. If only four companies were desired, some companies would be combined. The number needed was determined by the plan of defense. Then seven counselors, one from each clan, were selected to direct each company. Presumably, all of these were members of the red organization. Either a priest of great power was chosen to officiate in divining and offering sacrifices for the entire army, or the counselors for each company selected their own priest.

Each group of seven counselors had its own speaker, called *Ko wo ni gv lv*, who during such emergencies exhorted the warriors to boldness and action by describing the legendary feats of distinguished leaders who had fallen in past battles. He urged the warriors to imitate that bravery and sacrifice, adding that such a death in defense of their beloved land and people was far preferable to life spent in the pursuit of pleasure and trivial things. To soften the thoughts of death, the speaker told them that those who died in battle had only gone to sleep with their beloved forefathers, then he concluded by pointing out that there was a certain fixed time and place for everyone to die, without any possibility of averting it.[24]

One of the sacred prayer formulas used by war priests went as follows:

> Hayl! Yo! Listen! How instantly we have lifted up the red war club. Quickly his soul shall be without motion. There under the earth, where the black war clubs shall be moving about like ball sticks in the game, there his soul shall be, never to reappear. He

causes it to be so. He shall never go and lift up the war club. He causes it to be so. There under the earth the black war club and the black fog shall never be lifted from them. He causes it to be so. Instantly shall their souls be moving about there in the seventh heaven. Their souls shall never break in two. So shall it be. Quickly we have moved them on high for them, where they shall be going about in peace. You have shielded yourselves with the red war club. Their souls shall never be knocked about. Cause it to be so. There on high their souls shall be going about. Let them shield themselves with the white war whoop. Instantly grant that they shall never become blue. Yu![25]

Color Symbolism

The mythological significance of the different colors in Cherokee lore is important here. Red was symbolic of success, the color of the war club with which the warrior was to strike the enemy, and also the other club with which he was to shield himself. The war whoop was likewise represented as red. In conjuring with the beads for long life, for recovery from sickness, or for success in love, the ball play, or any other undertaking, the red beads represented the party for whose benefit the magic spell was wrought, and he was figuratively clothed in red and made to stand on a red cloth or placed on a red seat. The red spirits invoked always lived in the east, and everything pertaining to them was of the same color.

Black was always typical of death, and in the formula just given, the soul of the enemy is continually beaten about by black war clubs and enveloped in a black fog. In conjuring to destroy an enemy, the priest used black beads and invoked the black spirits — which always lived in the west — bidding them to tear out the man's soul, carry it to the west, and put it into the black coffin deep in the black mud, with a black serpent coiled above it.

Blue was emblematic of failure, disappointment, or unsatisfied desire. To say "They shall never become blue" expressed the belief that they would never fail in anything they undertook. In love charms, the lover figuratively covered himself with red and prayed that his rival would become entirely blue and walk in a blue path. The formulistic expression, "He is entirely blue," approximates the

meaning of the common English phrase, "He feels blue." The blue spirits lived in the north.

White denoted peace and happiness. In ceremonial addresses, as at the Green Corn Dance and ball play, the people symbolically partook of white food and, after the dance or the game, returned along the white trail to their white houses. In love charms, the man, to induce the woman to cast her lot with his, boasted, "I am a white man," implying that all was happiness where he was. White beads had the same meaning in bead conjuring, and white was the color of the stone pipe anciently used in ratifying peace treaties. The white spirits lived in the south.[26]

So then, in setting forth the colors of the cardinal directions, red was east, black was west, blue was north, and white was south.

Two other colors are mentioned in the prayer formulas collected by Mooney — brown and yellow. Brown was associated with animals, and yellow was linked to trouble and vexation. The yellow spirits were invoked when priests or medicine men wished to bring down calamities on the head of a victim without destroying the person. Neither color was associated with a particular point on the compass.[27]

War Practices

War prayer formulas were recited by the priests of the different companies for four consecutive nights before setting out to meet the approaching enemy. No taboos were enjoined at such times, and no beads were used for divining. But the warriors went to water in the regular way and stood at the edge of the stream looking down while the priests repeated the formula. If there was enough time, on the fourth night, the priests gave each man a small root that through ritual had been given the power to confer invulnerability. On the eve of the battle, the warriors, after immersing in a running stream, chewed some of the root and spat the juice on their bodies to make enemy arrows or bullets slide off like drops of water.[28]

It is said that almost every man of the 400 Eastern Cherokees who served in the Civil War had this or a similar ceremony performed before setting out and also consulted a medicine man who had a divining stone. Interestingly enough, only two or three of the entire number were wounded in actual battle, and none was killed.[29]

Whenever enemies killed or wounded Cherokees in a surprise raid, word of this spread quickly to the Great War Chief who called for a retaliatory strike, which was a massive and highly organized undertaking.

In declaring a war of revenge, the Great War Chief took control. He and his principal assistant consulted together, and whatever they decided, the entire nation agreed to. Actually, it appears that the consultation was little more than a formality, for the assistant always went along with the War Chief's decision. The two men would sit together, and after stating the circumstances of the situation, the chief would say something like, "It is my wish to engage in war; what is your opinion?" "I also wish for war," the assistant would reply.

The chief then stood up and said, "We will give ourselves up," meaning not that they would surrender, but that by putting their own lives on the line they would comfort the relatives of those who mourned Cherokees whom the enemy had killed. He then took his gourd rattle and went into the yard that surrounded his house, where he walked back and forth, shook the rattle, shouted the war whoop again and again, and sang four times the word *"U gi wa ne e."* After this he returned to his house, sat down, and handed the gourd to his assistant, who went outside and repeated the ritual.

People living nearby heard this performance and relayed the word until it had spread throughout the town. Within minutes, large numbers of warriors gathered at the Great War Chief's house, and he emerged to tell them it had been determined that they should comfort those who were mourning for their relatives who had been killed. The Cherokees would return the blows that had been struck.

Messengers were dispatched to every town and village war chief in the Cherokee Nation, and on receiving the news, these chiefs met with their principal assistants to repeat the war ritual that alerted warriors and summoned them to the town

war chief's house. The counselors of each town appointed women to prepare food for the men in their war party. In the main, this consisted of parched cornmeal and corn bread that was formed in long, six-inch-wide cakes baked on a hot hearth while covered with leaves and hot ashes. Each warrior carried his own provisions and was heavily loaded with them when he started out. He also furnished his own weapons and armor. The armor consisted of a shield and a club used only for defense, and the weapons consisted of war clubs, axes, knives, lances, and bows and arrows. The Cherokee men made perhaps the finest war bows and the smoothest barbed arrows of all Indians. Oak, ash, and hickory wood were used for the bows. For greater flexibility, the bows were coated with bear oil, then warmed by a fire to cause the oil to sink in. War bows averaged five feet in length and had a flat, rectangular cross section. The handle section was one-and-three-quarters inches wide, and the limb width tapered to three-quarters of an inch at the necks. The draw was more than fifty pounds. Strings were fashioned from twisted bear gut and were very strong. Stone-headed arrows averaged thirty inches in length, were made of cane, and were fletched with two split turkey feathers. Designed for forest use, the arrows were excellent for close fighting but tended to plane on longer flights. The release was a secondary, or pinch, grip. Quivers were either made in basketry fashion or of rushes laid side by side. Color was added with dyes and feathers, and they were slung over the shoulder on a buckskin loop. The quiver proper was for arrows only, and the bow was either carried in the hand or slipped through buckskin bands on the side of the quiver.[30]

Once the warriors of each town and village were assembled, armed, and ready, their war chief and their war officers led them in rapid procession for the sometimes long march to the place of rendezvous at the national capital, which was the house of the Great War Chief.

The seven counselors of the Great War Chief met in the national heptagon to decide which of the nation's war priests would serve on the present occasion. Customarily, a considerable number of them were chosen, and once the decision was made, messengers were sent to give notice to those priests. During the war expedition that followed, the messengers served as the priest's assistants.

Notice given, the messengers went to the national heptagon and obtained seven dressed deerskins that were kept for that purpose in the treasure house. The skins were taken to the Chief War Priest, who wrapped his divining crystal in them and gave the bundle to his assistant. The priest then took up his ark, which is described as a lidded earthen pot that contained live coals taken from the sacred fire, and with his assistant trailing behind him, marched through the town to bestow his blessing upon the planned war expedition.

Once the entire army was assembled in the capital, a fast day was celebrated. This consisted of a day and a night that were given over to prayer and fasting. The taboos included a provision that no warrior or priest should eat or sleep, and no one should take anything directly from the hand of another person. Objects to be passed must be dropped on the ground by the passer and picked up by the receiver. On this first and fasting day, the counselors appointed officers for their warrior groups, also doctors, musicians, and cooks, and the towns joined in pairs to form companies.

The three principal leaders of a revenge army were the Great War Chief, now called the Raven because he wore around his neck a raven skin; the flag carrier, who in most respects was considered equal in authority with the Raven, and who carried the Great War Chief's standard that consisted of a four- or five-yard-long, red-painted deerskin flag that was attached to a tall, red pole; and *Ska ti lo ski*, the chief speaker.

When the time came to move out toward the enemy, the three leaders followed the carrier of the ark and marched at the head of the war party. It was said they could track the enemy in the black of night as well as an ordinary tracker could in the daytime, that they could fly, could handle red-hot coals, could not be shot by an enemy arrow, and if the enemy approached could throw themselves down and disappear.

Next in line after the three leaders were the seven counselors of the chief warrior. Then came one after the other the individual companies, each led by its town war chief, who was called *A ska ye gv sta*, and who was followed by his principal assistant, by his own seven counselors and speaker, and by his priests, doctors, and cooks. Town drummers and other musicians marched in the center of each company.

On the morning of the second day, bathing was optional, and that evening, the war standard was set up in the middle of the town sacred square. That night, by the light of huge bonfires, the war party did a dance called *A te yo hi*, which means "going around in a circle." Each warrior moved counter-clockwise around the war standard with his left hand extended toward the standard. Each company followed its own leader, who led the singing, the step, and the various movements.

Just before daylight, the Great War Chief halted the dance and ordered the entire war party to the river, where the men immersed themselves seven times. At sunrise, everyone gathered around the Great War Priest, who swept and made bare a place on the ground, then kindled a fire on it with some of the coals of the ark, whose fuel on this occasion was seven special kinds of wood. Into this fire he first sacrificed rats and worms. Standing on the west side of the fire and facing the east, with his principal assistant at his right and his seven counselors behind him, he held a piece of deer tongue in his hand and prayed to learn what the fate of the war party would be. Then he threw the piece onto the fire. If the fire burned bright and clear and quickly consumed the meat, it indicated that the Cherokees would win the battle, but if the fire did not consume it, it meant just the opposite.

If the latter happened, other rituals were done, and further predictions were solicited to see if the prediction could be changed. A little after sunrise, the priest set up a small table, folded and put seven deerskins on it, and placed his divining crystal on top of the skins. He then moved back a few steps and prayed to each of the seven heavens. While he did this, he first touched the ground with his hands and then slowly raised them, stopping a moment at each heaven until he reached the seventh one. Between each thumb and forefinger the priest held a bead, and if the Cherokees were to conquer the enemy the bead in his right hand would seem to move and, be alive. But if they were to lose the battle, the movement and life would be in the bead in his left hand. Also, if they were to win, blood would flow down the right side of his crystal, and if they were to lose, down the left side.

Whatever the Cherokees learned from the rituals, and despite the gloom that accompanied persistent signs of a loss, there was no giving up. Having come this far, the war party would always go the rest of the way. The Chief Priest wrapped his crystal in the seven deerskins and gave it to his principal assistant to carry, for it was believed that it would strike the priest dead if he carried it in that manner. Also, the priest must wash his hands after he touched the crystal, else wherever he touched his skin, sores would appear.

The priest then put the hot ashes of the fire back in the earthen pot and picked it up. This was the signal for the Great War Chief to call the men to order, and to do this he waved his red war club in the air, then made a speech in which he told the warriors they must not be afraid, for God would help them if they trusted in him. This speech done, the priest made a prayer to the Three Beings above, and the command to march was given. The war party moved off, and before long the Great War Chief and his principal assistant shouted the war whoop and broke into a rousing war song. The warriors joined in, and in high and bolstered spirits the party continued toward the enemy.

The chief speaker chose the path the marchers would follow, selected campsites, and sounded the daily call to awaken and get moving. Certain rules were to be obeyed by the marching warriors; no one was to speak about vain or trifling subjects or about women.[31] While crossing a creek, no one should stop until everyone had passed over, then if necessary the chief speaker would order a halt, and putting off their loads, the cooks would offer the men water.[32]

If while marching a warrior accidentally broke a stick or twig, he had to pick it up and hold it in his hand until the party camped for the night. When, as they came to the top of the mountain or hill, the war party encountered a pile of sacred stones left by earlier war parties, each man would throw another stone on the pile as a prayer that God would spare his life. At encampments by a river or stream, the warriors bathed before bedding down, and at daybreak completely immersed themselves seven times.

It was said that the Great War Chief, in his guise as the Raven, watched the enemy and kept the chief speaker perfectly informed. He directed the necessary preparations, and each night magically went forward two days' march yet was back in camp the next morning. On at least one night, the Great War Chief sent his crystal by mystical means in the enemies' direction, and if it returned covered with blood, it was a good omen and a sure sign to proceed with the battle.

Although acts such as these are put in the category of superstition today, they were firmly believed in then, and among other things kept men's minds focused on the matter at hand and inspired continued confidence. Although it is easy to play out heroics in an imaginary war, facing a real one in which people will be killed or terribly maimed is a different matter. Having been there, I can attest to the fact that those who boast the most about what they will do become quite sober and reflective when the enemy is close at hand. The practices of the Cherokees, however foolish or superstitious they may seem, are simply another testimony to their acknowledgment of their own frailties.

If in marching the war party unexpectedly encountered enemies, the chief speaker told the warriors what to do, and everyone waited for his directions. When the war party reached enemy country, everyone halted while the chief speaker gave a speech of encouragement. This ended, the Great War Chief blew on his battle trumpet, and in return the men shouted war whoops. Then heedless of danger, the Great War Chief, flag carrier, and great speaker led the war party directly into the nearest enemy town, where the Great War Chief went boldly to the closest house, momentarily put his hands on its wall and turned to begin the battle. The speaker and the flag carrier also touched the house, and the latter set the war standard in the ground alongside it and remained there to guard it.

On their return home from a battle, the warriors stayed at their own town council houses for twenty-four days, where before returning to their wives and families, they underwent extensive purification rituals to rid themselves of uncleanness that was contacted during the fighting. It was taboo for them to touch women during this time, and the purification included seven immersions in water each evening and morning. At night there were Scalp, Smoke, and other dances that the townspeople could watch. During those dances the four men who had served as spies wore the bird and animal skins they had used while on the march: that of the raven, the owl, the wolf, and the fox. Each night, when the Great War Chief put on his raven skin and went forward as a spy, three renowned warriors put on their skins and went off in other directions. The owl man went as a spy to the right, the wolf man to the left, and the fox man went back the way they had come. The raven and owl skins were worn around the bearers' necks. A slit was made near the head of the wolf and the fox skin for the warrior to put his head through, and the skin was arranged so that the head hung down on the man's chest and the tail hung down his back.[33]

The twenty-fourth day after returning from a great battle was devoted to fasting, during which time the war priests offered meat sacrifices to the sacred fire and consulted their crystals to determine whether the Cherokees would now enjoy peace and quiet or their enemies would soon retaliate for what the Cherokees had just done. Peace was heralded when the fire burned briskly and consumed the meat offering, and trouble when the fire died down or failed to consume it. A divining crystal was also set up on a stack of seven deerskins, and prayers were offered. If nothing was seen in the stone, the Cherokees could expect an attack at any time. If no war was to come for a month, a new moon would appear briefly in the stone and then repeated moons for every additional month they were to enjoy peace.[34]

Here again, the purpose of seeking omens was preparatory, and kept the Cherokees in a state of readiness for what was to happen. If for some reason the signs were misread and the preparations proved unnecessary, little was lost, for it was better to be prepared and not need it than not to be prepared and get caught flat-footed.

Warriors who distinguished themselves in battle were on their return honored by the gift of a new name that was publicly bestowed by a general council of town leaders. Killer was the highest name, then Raven, Owl, Wolf, and Fox. Such men achieved higher status and with it certain war offices and increased responsibilities.

It was a fixed rule of war that those who kept the camps, such as assistants, counselors, cooks, and musicians, shared the spoils equally with the warriors who fought. Another rule was that in battle, the Great War Chief never retreated, although when other warriors saw that the tide was turning against them, they could take him by force and make him retreat. To honor the Great War Chief's bravery, when he retired he was given an eagle feather with a red strip painted across it for each war party he had led and each enemy he had killed.[35]

Warriors

The prime age for a warrior was twenty-five to fifty years, and all men under the age of twenty-five were called "boys." When war officers reached fifty years of age they retired, and other men were appointed to fill their places. When the Great War Chief retired or was killed, the nation's warriors nominated his successor. This nomination was presented to the *Uku* and to the war chiefs, and if they and their counselors approved, the candidate underwent a momentous and regal consecration ceremony.

As a rule, the consecration took place at the first feast of green fruits to be held following his nomination, but if the feast was some time away, or if there was a national emergency, the consecration could be held twenty days after the nomination was made. In either instance the ceremony was directed by the retiring Great War Chief or, if this chief had

The installation of the new Great War Chief. See color plate No. 3.

been killed, by a past Great War Chief.

Individuals were appointed to prepare the candidate's seat, which was something like a stool with a four-foot-high back and painted red, and when the stool was ready, they were to place it just to the west of the sacred fire in the national heptagon. Other men were appointed to wash the candidate and to dress him in his official robes, which were entirely red.

Four retired war officers of high rank were chosen to spend with the candidate the day and night prior to the day of the consecration ceremony. During this time the retired war officers neither ate nor slept, and they also fasted on the day of the ceremony. At sunrise, wearing red costumes, they conducted the candidate to his heptagon seat. One

of them carried a ceremonial war club made entirely of red stone and walked in front of him, one bearing a red-painted eagle feather walked on his left, one carrying a bag of red paint and a bag of black paint walked on his right, and one behind him carried a magnificent red cape made of eagle feathers. The candidate himself had been washed and was dressed in his clean but common everyday clothes.

On arriving at the heptagon, which was already filled with the leaders of the Cherokee Nation, the group circled it once and then entered to lead the candidate to his seat, which faced east and was situated directly in front of the seats of the *Uku* and the retiring Great War Chief. The new chief's seat was also flanked by four other red seats, two on each side, for his four escorts. The regular seats of the heptagon were arranged as usual around the outside wall, and in front of them was a circular row of red seats for the nation's war chiefs.

While the candidate stood in front of his seat and faced the sacred fire, the four escorts performed a slow dance around him, singing one verse of a certain song with each circle, until they had passed around him four times and four verses had been sung. The men who had walked behind the candidate undressed him, stripping off all of his common clothing save his red-dyed breechclout. After this the man with the war club put it in the candidate's right hand, and the man with the eagle feather put it on the candidate's head. The quill of this feather was inserted into a small, two-inch long, red-painted cane tube that was tied to the larger deer-antler tube holding the tuft of the candidate's hair, so that the feather stood upright.

Then the man with the paint moved to the candidate and with the forefinger of his right hand made seven stripes, alternately red and black, across his face, and one red stripe running from his forehead down across his nose to his chest. Then a red stripe was drawn from the candidate's right and left thumbnails along the arms and across the chest until they connected with the vertical stripe previously drawn. The man with the paint then drew similar stripes from the candidate's big toenails up the legs and across the abdomen until they too connected with the vertical stripe. Finally, he drew red stripes from the forehead to the back of the head that passed along each side of the crown. Now the man who carried the red cape put it on the candidate's shoulders, and the man who had undressed the candidate put on him red garters and moccasins. The candidate was seated, and the four escorts sat down on their red seats.

At this point, the retiring Great War Chief stood up and addressed the audience, charging them to obey without question the new chief and never to go to war without his knowledge and direction. In concluding, he resigned his position and authority and turned them over to the new chief. The new chief stood up then and addressed the audience, saying, "You have now put me in blood from my head to my feet, but in war I shall not bloody my hands by destroying the infants and aged who cannot defend themselves. Yet, if in my path any tribe or individual shall raise the war whoop, and if I see weapons in their hands, I will fight and conquer or die. You have made me your Great War Chief, and I will strive to take care of my young warriors, never exposing them unnecessarily in war."[36]

The new chief sat down, and all who had gathered in the heptagon shouted, "*Hawh!*" Then the civil and war chiefs and the warriors went individually to take the new chief by the hand, calling him their uncle, and acknowledging his superior position while at the same time intimating it was his bound duty to guard and defend them and to lead them well.

It was noon by then, but the ceremony continued through the rest of the day, the night, and until noon the next day, at which time food was brought to the heptagon and served to the new chief and the other chiefs and priests. The rest of the audience retired to seven houses in the town, where food was provided for them. Strangers who happened to be in town, including those from other tribes, were invited to eat in the heptagon after the officers had finished.

On the morning following his consecration, the new Great War Chief arose from his seat, walked to the door of the heptagon, turned, and said, "Now I am going home."

The others, in order of rank, responded, "*Hawh.*"

When all had emerged from the building save one, this last man went to the door and said, "Now I am going home," but received no response. That ended the ceremony, and several of the war chiefs accompanied the new war chief to his home.[37]

The Great War Chief had his own speaker, messenger, and seven counselors. The dress of his counselors was red, but not as vivid a hue as that of the chief. The red eagle feather, along with the bands of otter skin he wore on his arms, legs, and head, was the chief's identifying badge of rank. To the tufts of their hair the seven counselors attached as their identifying symbol a round and symbolically inscribed shell disk to which two small, red-painted

The Great War Chief in full war regalia . . . he contemplates the hair lock of a fallen Cherokee left by the enemy as a warning. See color plate No. 4.

eagle feathers were appended. The chief messenger was distinguished by his special staff, and when the messenger retired or died, the Great War Chief nominated a successor. If the man accepted, the nation's leaders assembled on an appointed day at the national heptagon, where an officer under the direction of the Great War Chief took a staff that was three feet long and wound from end to end with a red strand of beads into the heptagon yard and cried aloud several times, "*A tsi nv sti!*" The messenger candidate then went to the officer, took the staff from him, put it over his own shoulder, and began a slow trot around the council house, singing, "*Hi ta ka ni ha,*" then, "*Qu ha ya wi ha,*" then exclaiming, "*Naskigo,*" to which those inside the heptagon replied loudly, "*Hawh!*" Thereafter, the beaded staff became the new messenger's property and symbol of office.

As soon as the first emergency arose that required the services of the new Great War Chief, he called for a joint meeting of the civil and military councils. When these men had taken their seats, the retired Great War Chief went to the west side of the heptagon where he kept his red-painted bows, arrows, quiver, helmet, shield, and bracelet, and when he returned with them delivered them into the hands of the new chief, at the same time charging him to take care of the warriors that had been entrusted to him.

The bracelet was worn on the left wrist, was made of buffalo hide, and was designed to protect the arm against the released bowstring. The "helmet" consisted of a three-inch-wide thick, buffalo-hide headband whose upper edge held a tightly packed circle of upright feathers painted red.

The shield was twenty-four inches in diameter and made from the thick forehead skin of the wood buffalo. It was boiled and then dried in the sun until hard. Two holes were made near its middle, and the ends of a buckskin band were attached there to make a shoulder loop. Informants don't tell us so, but there was probably a small hand loop as well. The final task was to paint the shield red and to put powerful black designs on it. Then white fur trim was appended to the top edge, and feathers were hung from the bottom edge. Many warriors made and carried such shields, except that theirs were not painted red. It was said that in instances of starvation, some warriors would roast and eat their shields, afterwards being referred to as "shield eaters." As part of their war costume, warriors also wore animal skins in a hooded-cape fashion on their heads and backs, and bird-of-prey feathers were tied to their hair tufts.

The final act of preparation for the new chief was when the retired Great War Chief brought forth his revered stuffed raven skin and put it on the neck of his successor, with the shiny blue-black head and neck of the skin resting on the new chief's chest, and the wings and tail on the back of the neck with long red thongs attached to the tips of the tail feathers.[38] It can easily be imagined that this was a touching moment for all who were involved in the ritual, for the raven skin carried with it not only great power, but many memories of mysterious messages, triumphs, celebrations, and painful losses. I should not be surprised if tears were shed by men who otherwise felt it was incumbent upon them to remain stoic in all but moments of great rejoicing.

When enemies appeared unannounced near an outlying Cherokee town, the town war chief would call out the news in a loud voice for his warriors to assemble. If they failed to hear him, he would begin shouting his war whoop and would continue until the cry spread and brought the warriors in. Once they arrived, he blew on his war trumpet, and they immediately went to engage the enemy.[39]

In instances when the war leaders of another nation made a declaration of war and sent a challenge to the Great War Chief of the Cherokees, the chief consulted with his principal assistant and seven counselors. When everyone agreed, as they always did, that the challenge must be met, the Great War Chief sent a message to the enemy saying that the Cherokees would meet them at the time and place stated in the challenge.

Meanwhile, the Great War Chief sent messengers to the war chiefs in all parts of the nation, and being thus advised, each of these chiefs assembled fifty to one hundred of his men and brought them to the national capital.

Middle Cherokee warrior in battle gear. See color plate
No. 5.

Once everyone was present, the Great War
Chief, wearing his raven skin, addressed them in
words something like, "I see you all here. You have
turned your feet to the darkness. But it is not
because I wished it. If we conquer our enemies, it
will be because God fights for us, and if we return in
safety, it will be God who will preserve us. Therefore,
put your trust in God. The light is his, and he can
make it light where you stand."[40]

Now a huge fire was lighted, the red battle
standard was hoisted, and a ritual of acceptance was
performed. Seven counselors from one company
stepped forward toward the fire, and the Raven
placed his war club on the ground in front of them.
The counselors of each company then sang a war
song that consisted of six verses, each verse of which
was "*Yo wi hi, hi yo wi ye*" repeated four times.
Between the first and second verses, the speaker of
the company came forward to pick up the club and
march around with it, at which time the counselors
would issue their war whoop.

When the ritual had been performed by the
counselors and speakers of all of the companies

present, a war dance, called *ti ge yo hi*, commenced.
It was led by the principal assistant of the Great War
Chief, and the warriors formed a huge circle around
the fire and war standard, with each of them carrying
his weapon in his right hand. Music was provided by
drummers who used a drum fashioned from fired
earth. It was shaped like a widemouthed stone water
jar, and had a raccoon skin drawn tightly over its top.
Small bells were fastened to a thong around the rim,
and rattled as the drum was beaten. The dancers did
not sing but frequently raised the war whoop and
moved their feet in cadence with the sound of the
drum.

The dance ended at nightfall, and the men
walked to the river, where they immersed themselves
seven times, then went to their beds and slept. At
daybreak the next morning, the men bathed again,
and the Chief War Priest offered sacrifices and
consulted his crystal.

The night previous to marching was spent in
entire wakefulness while the Chief War Priest sang
war songs and prayed. Just before sunrise, the priest
ordered everyone to the river, where they immersed
seven times with their faces turned alternately toward
the east and west. They then returned to the sacred
square, where the priest offered sacrifice with a new
fire made specially for this battle and kindled with
the seven kinds of wood used for sacrifices. While
the warriors formed a huge semicircle around him
that left an opening toward the east, the Chief War
Priest himself faced east and put a piece of deer
tongue and old tobacco on the fire, praying for
predictions regarding the battle's outcome. If the
Cherokees were to be defeated or to suffer considerable losses, the meat would pop and throw little
pieces westward toward the semicircle of warriors,
with as many pieces flying off as there were men to
be killed. Families knew then that they should be
prepared to mourn.

This sacrifice offered, the Chief War Priest,
together with his seven counselors, ascended a ladder
to a scaffold, where he spread out a deerskin, placed
his crystal on it, and prayed for further information
regarding the outcome of the battle. If when he
examined the stone there was blood on its right side,

some of the Cherokees were to be killed, but blood on the left side told of enemy dead. If nothing appeared, the battle would be inconclusive, with neither nation victorious.

The order to march was now issued, and the men formed ranks, moving out in the marching order previously given. Soon after starting they sang another war song, the first verse of which was "*Ugi wha v ne*," repeated four times. There were seven verses in all, and between verses the war whoop was sounded four times.

Each day they marched, the warriors followed a course of broken bushes that had been marked out the previous night by the Great War Chief in his role as the Raven. When the war party stopped for the night, the Great War Chief, his speaker, flag bearer, and counselors occupied a place in the center of the camp. The next officers in rank formed a circle around them, and the common warriors formed an outside ring of defense. No one knew how honorable the enemies would be or when they might set an ambush. When night fell, the four men who bore the raven, owl, wolf, and fox skins held them over a smoking fire and prayed with them before putting them on. Then they went out in their respective directions as spies, and if any of them on his return to camp "smoked" his skin again, it was a sign of alarm that told the war party there were enemies nearby. Small contingents of Cherokees were then sent out to look for them and to fight them if necessary, although the enemies spotted were probably spies who were scouting the Cherokees.

When an open-challenge battle with the enemy was planned, the place of halting on the night before the engagement, and not the national capital, was considered the true starting point. At sunrise, the great speaker delivered a message of encouragement to the warriors, and then the Great War Chief blew his war trumpet, which was made of the thighbone of the large white crane and made a noise so shrill it could be heard for miles. Instantly, the warriors raised their war whoop and ran toward the enemy. The Great War Chief went straight forward to meet the enemy leader, and the Cherokee warriors formed wings at his right and left in an attempt to enclose

Lower Cherokee warrior in battle gear.

the enemy. The Great War Chief, unless he was forced to retreat by his men, must either conquer his rival or die in the attempt.[41]

On their return home from that kind of battle, the warriors performed a Scalp Dance in their own towns. The women danced first, standing behind the drummer until he sounded a certain note, and then indulging in what was called "a Snake Dance around the fire." They assumed a stooping posture and stepped slowly in accordance with the beat of the drum. Their song was "*Hu ya nv ni yo*" repeated four times. At times they raised their hands and made motions as if striking an enemy. When the men joined in, those who had taken scalps had mounted them on sticks. They held the sticks by their handles, and with a woman at each man's side they danced as couples, stooped over and moving their feet to the beat of the drum. The war song now, "*Hi no nu*," was repeated four times, and then the words "*Ya a ho yi ne*" added. The head war chief and his wife danced first, then danced up to other couples who arose and joined in, until at length all of the warriors and their wives or girl friends were engaged in the dance.[42]

Fighting Techniques

A general fighting technique of the Cherokees was to set a trap for their enemies in which they formed a V-shaped wedge that caused the foes to at first think they had only a few Cherokee warriors to contend with, when in fact they would soon find themselves completely surrounded.

Whenever a Cherokee warrior had killed a person, touched a dead baby, a human bone, or a grave, he was considered unclean for four days and was required to take an emetic that made him throw up. Then he must bathe in the usual ritual fashion and afterward put on entirely clean apparel. Beyond this, he was not permitted to sleep with his wife for seven nights.[43]

Very little is recorded about the travel details of Cherokee war parties, but a common way to cross broad and deep rivers was for each man to wrap his clothing and weapons in a skin float. He would then jump into the river with the float and push it ahead of him as he swam across to the opposite shore. To make the floats, men carried deerskins and bearskins in their packs. These were spread out on the ground with the hair side turned up. The gear was placed on top of the skins, with the heaviest objects, such as guns, on the bottom of the pile. The skins were wrapped around the gear, and knots were tied in the shanks of the skins to secure the bundle. The floats took only a few minutes to fashion, and little travel time was lost when the war party paused to do this.

To move very large loads across a river, a crude framework raft was fashioned with dry pine branches that were lashed together with strong vines. The completed raft was placed at the river's edge, loaded, pushed into the water, and paddled or poled across by warriors.[44]

The only other battle techniques mentioned by early white observers were that the Cherokees mimicked the voices of birds to communicate with one another, that a favorite method of waylaying an enemy was ambushing, and that whenever an encounter was imminent, the quiver was shifted from the shoulder to the left side, where the arrows could, by the warrior's reaching across the abdomen with the right hand, be more quickly and easily

drawn.[45] This manner of rearranging the quiver for battle use is identical to that of the Plains Indian warriors and suggests that it was a common practice.

The Sacred Ark, Prisoners, and Peace

Although most of what has been stated about warfare comes from the Payne Papers, Adair describes some details that should be included.

As has been seen, the ark held a prominent place in Cherokee life, and it is important to know all we can about it. Adair points out that several of the southeastern tribes used the sacred ark, but unfortunately, as he describes it and the rituals related to it he again does not distinguish the customs of one tribe from those of another. While Payne's informants describe the Cherokee ark as an earthenware vessel, the ark Adair portrays is a square basket. Three of the basket's sides are bowed out in the middle, but the fourth side that rests against the carrier's back is flat. The ark has a cover that is tightly woven in basketry style with hickory splints. The ark is quite small — perhaps twenty inches in length, fifteen inches broad, and fifteen inches high. The designated priest and a "beloved waiter" carried the ark by turns. It contained several consecrated vessels of antiquated forms made by Beloved Women. The priest and waiter were purified more thoroughly than the rest of the company so that the first might be fit to act in the religious office of a priest of war and the other to carry the awesome and sacred ark.[46]

This description of the ark as a basket is most intriguing and suggests that, since it contained consecrated vessels, one of those would have been the earthenware pot that contained the live coals taken from the sacred fire in the national heptagon. Cherokee earthenware vessels did have loops and lugs to which straps could be attached, but such vessels were either hung on pegs or carried by means of a tumpline. It is doubtful that the sacred ark would be transported in the latter manner. A carrying basket of the type Adair describes would seem more secure and less likely to spill while crossing creeks and rough terrain. Most probably, the person who carried the basket would put a long pole on his shoulder and

The bearer of the sacred ark.

then suspend the basket from one end of it by four straps and in such a way that the flat side rested against his back.

The war leader required fledgling warriors, during the first campaign they made with the ark, to remain standing from sunrise to sunset each day the party stopped to rest. They also had to purify themselves by drinking warm water that had been made bitter with rattlesnake root. The ark was deemed so sacred and dangerous that even the ritually purified warriors and the most inveterate enemies dared not touch it for any reason.[47]

Regarding retaliation and the treatment of prisoners, after spending some time on war parties with the Cherokees, Adair believed there never was a people who pursued the Mosaic law of retaliation with such fixed eagerness as they did. He knew them to go a thousand miles for the purpose of revenge — through pathless woods, over hills and mountains, through cane swamps full of grapevines and brier; over broad lakes, rapid rivers, and deep creeks; all the way endangered by poisonous snakes, if not by the lurking enemy, while at the same time exposed to the extremities of heat and cold, the changes of the seasons, and hunger and thirst. Yet such was their overboiling, revengeful temper that they disdained all those things as trifles — so long as they managed to get the scalp of an enemy and by this satisfy their deceased relations.

If equal blood had not been shed in battle, then while the warriors were sanctifying themselves for war they always asked the Beloved Women to delegate captives either to be killed outright or put to torture. No fixed method was used for torturing captives, but burning was one, and in most instances they were dealt with before the Cherokee warriors set off with their ark and other holy things. Sometimes the traveling Cherokees were so embittered they killed every non-Cherokee they met along the way.[48]

If a warrior died a natural death, which was seldom, the war drums, musical instruments, and all other kinds of diversion were put aside for three days and nights.

When the Cherokee Nation made peace or renewed an old friendship with another nation that requested it, the ceremonies and solemnities they used were of ancient vintage and very striking. As soon as representatives of the other nation approached the national capital or the regional town they wanted to arrange friendship with, they sent a messenger ahead to inform the Cherokee people of their amicable intentions. The messenger carried a swan's wing in his right hand that was painted all over with streaks of white clay. The next day the visitors entered the town without weapons and in a friendly parade, and advanced to the sacred square, where their leader was met by the chief priest of the white organization. The two men approached one another in a bowing posture and vowed that both acted in the name of God. Then the priest grasped the wrist of the visiting leader with both of his own hands, and moved them in steps up the man's arm. Finally, he waved an eagle-tail fan over the visitor's head as a pledge of good faith.[49]

The two leaders and their officers entered the heptagon or the town council house, where they took seats — with the two leaders sharing the priest's ottoman — smoked the pipe and ate together. They then drank a bitter liquid called *"Cusseena"* and used ancient invocations for peace. The ritual concluded with a dance. For this dance, the chief priest called on a half-dozen of his most active and expert young warriors, who painted their bodies with white clay and covered their heads with swansdown. The dancers approached the visiting leader and waved their eagle-tail fans backward and forward over his head.

Immediately, the dancers began to sing a solemn song and dance in a bowing posture. Then they stood erect and looked upward while with their right hands they waved the fans toward heaven — sometimes with a slow and other times with a quick motion — at the same time touching their chests with their small gourd rattles held in their left hands. Time was kept with the motion of the fans, and during the dance the divine note, "*Yo*," was repeated. They continued to wave their fans over the visiting leader's head and did not move more than two yards backward or forward as they did so. They were so expert at this and observed the timing so exactly with their gestures and notes that there was not the least discord in their performance.[50]

Summary: Government and Warfare

In summing up the information on warfare, we see that as a whole it consumed considerable amounts of the people's time and energy and it was constantly engaged in during the clement months. Never in all of my studies of other tribes, save a few of those in the southeastern part of North America and those in Middle America, have I encountered a nation whose approach to war was so sophisticated that it varied with the type of engagement. This leads me to wonder whether the ties of the Cherokees were not stronger to their Middle American neighbors than most people suspect. The Cherokees had one approach to being attacked, another to a revenge war, a third approach to a challenge war, and a fourth approach to simply receiving the news that enemies were in the area and needed to be sought out and engaged. How intriguing it is that even the rituals associated with each of those approaches varied! One can only conclude that over the years the Cherokees had, through experience and testing, arrived at ritual patterns that offered in each instance the best chances of success.

While reading the available accounts of Cherokee warfare, one suddenly realizes that even after they acquired horses, there is no mention of their being used in battle. The assumptions must be that in the rough and mountainous southeastern terrain, horses would have been more of a hindrance than a help, and the time-tested Cherokee battle techniques did not lend themselves to using horses.

We see that the Cherokees fought hard and neither asked for nor gave quarter. Yet in Chapter One it was noted that wampum belts were used when the Cherokees wished to make peace with another tribe, and in this chapter we find that the nation had a gracious way to receive those who wanted to make peace with them. Surprising and stimulating people, the Cherokees!

The veils concerning government and warfare being pierced somewhat, we can now move on to the enthralling matters of superstitious belief, mythology, and healing.

1. Payne, Papers, Vol. 4, pp. 106-107.
2. Woodward, *The Cherokees,* p. 44.
3. Bartram, *Travels through North and South Carolina, Georgia, East and West Florida, the Cherokee Country, etc.,* pp. 232 ff.
4. Adair, *History of the American Indians,* pp. 32-34.
5. Reid, *The Law of Blood.*
6. Gilbert, "The Eastern Cherokees," p. 340.
7. Payne Papers, Vol. 4.
8. Ibid., p. 321.
9. Gilbert, p. 321.
10. Adair, pp. 87-89.
11. Payne Papers, interviews with T. Smith and Arrow, Vol. 4, p. 22.
12. Ibid., p. 22.
13. Ibid., interview with Ana (very aged).
14. Ibid., pp. 18-21.
15. Ibid., D. S. Butrick, Vol. 4, pp. 62-68.
16. Adair, pp. 51-52.
17. Gregg, 1904-1907, as cited by Gilbert, p. 324.
18. Nuttal, 1819, p. 189, as cited by Gilbert, p. 324.
19. Adair, pp. 165-167.
20. Haywood, 1823, as cited by Gilbert, p. 324.
21. Reid, pp. 275-276.
22. Payne Papers, Vol. 1, p. 63, and Vol. 4, p. 463; see also Gilbert, pp. 348-349.
23. Payne Papers, D. S. Butrick, Vol. 1, p. 71.
24. Adair, p. 25.
25. Mooney, *Sacred Formulas of the Cherokees,* pp. 388-389.
26. Ibid., p. 390.
27. Ibid.
28. Ibid.
29. Ibid.
30. Adair, p. 28.
31. Payne Papers, Vol. 3, p. 63.
32. Ibid., interview with T. Smith, Vol. 3, p. 63.
33. Ibid., interview with Nutsawi, Vol. 3, pp. 70-71.
34. Ibid., interview with Johnson Pridget and Nutsawi, Vol. 3, p. 64.
35. Ibid., interview with T. Smith, Vol. 3, pp. 70-71.
36. Ibid., pp. 65-66.
37. Ibid., pp. 67-68.
38. Ibid.
39. Ibid., p. 71.
40. Ibid., p. 74.
41. Ibid., pp. 79-80.
42. Ibid., pp. 71-80.
43. Ibid., pp. 79-80.
44. Adair, pp. 290-292.
45. Ibid., pp. 291-295.
46. Ibid., pp. 168-169.
47. Ibid., p. 170.
48. Ibid., pp. 153-165.
49. Ibid., p. 63.
50. Ibid., pp. 176-177.

Healing and the Causes of Disease

In 1738, smallpox brought by white traders reduced the Cherokee population by half, leaving thousands dead and the confidence of the people shattered and in disarray. At first, the deadly virus made slow advances, as though feeling its way along, and since the priests did not know how to treat this strange malady, they pondered for awhile before cautiously applying to the afflicted, as they did for many other illnesses, a regimen of hot and then cold things. When this failed to help, the priests sought through their beads, divining crystals, and sacrificial rituals to determine the source or cause of the disease. Finally, they decided that the spiritual powers who lived in the heavens had sent the sickness as a curse, because the young unmarried people had, during the past year, notoriously violated "in every thicket" the ancient laws regarding sexual intercourse outside of marriage. Proof for this conclusion was found in the fact that the perpetrators had, in performing these shameful crimes, managed to break down and pollute many of the people's bean plots — which to purify again would cause the priests no small amount of work and trouble. Worst of all, the small bean plots of the religious men themselves, which were located next to the town council house used for sacred purposes, suffered in each instance the most damage.

On an occasion witnessed by Adair, the priest of a certain town at last realized that every effort must be made to halt the progress of the disease, and since he was certain it was brought on by "unlawful copulation in the night dews," he decided it would be practical to effect the cure in the same location and at the same time. Therefore, he immediately ordered the afflicted to lie day and night on their backs in the bean plots, and at regular intervals to uncover and expose their chests to the night dews. A further justification for this requirement was that of getting the patients out of their houses so the disease would not spread to others. When the exposure approach failed, the desperate priest repeatedly poured cold water on the naked chests of the victims, and as he did this he dolefully sang his mystical religious song, "*Yo Yo*," and frantically shook a gourd rattle.

Nothing worked, and when the entire body of Cherokee priests had similar failures, they consulted together and decided that the best treatment would be to sweat their patients and then to immediately plunge them into the cold rivers. This was done, and the patients expired instantly. In consequence, the frustrated and embarrassed priests smashed their consecrated pots that for decades had been used for cleansing and sacrifice rituals, and threw away all of their other holy things, imagining they were polluted and had lost their divinely infused power. Soon, even the priests shared in the common fate of their countrymen. Smallpox claimed them, and being naturally proud, when they looked into the mirrors they always carried with them and saw themselves disfigured with no hope of a cure, some shot themselves, others cut their throats, some stabbed themselves with knives or with sharp-pointed canes. Many threw themselves "with sullen madness" into roaring fires and stoically expired there.

Emphasizing further the horror of smallpox and its effect upon the Cherokee people, Adair remembered a great head warrior who had killed a white man who had stolen some of his deerskins. When he saw himself disfigured by the smallpox, he believed it resulted from the offense. Appalled, he chose to put an end to his shame by killing himself.

When the warrior's relatives discovered his intent, they watched him carefully, and took every sharp instrument away from him. The warrior began to fret and then said the worst things about them that the Cherokee language could express. In desperation, he finally threw himself savagely against a wall, but to no avail. Dejected and resenting the opposition shown by his relations, he fell sullenly onto his bed and remained there, refusing to eat. As soon as they left him alone, he arose and, finding nothing but a thick hoe handle, drove one end of it into the ground and threw himself repeatedly on the other end until finally he forced it down his throat. That accomplished what he wanted, and he was laid to rest in silence and without the least mourning.[1]

These stories raise inevitable questions about the competence of Indian healers, although some sympathy becomes due them when we learn how poorly white doctors dealt with smallpox even in the 1800s. As one studies Indian healing practices, it becomes clear that over the centuries they became competent at treating familiar afflictions, but developed no means of dealing with the unfamiliar — those alien diseases brought in by the Europeans. They could not respond quickly, for formulas took time to develop, and the right herbs, plants, roots, and attitudes were found only through intent observation and prolonged prayer and ritual. This is not to suggest they could have cured the epidemics that struck them down in such great numbers, but only to say that they were not even able to try. We cannot judge their competence on the basis of how they dealt with these things. When it came to the application of heat, herbs, plants, and roots, they often effected remarkable and swift cures for common afflictions and for bullet and arrow wounds. An important part of the healer's success was due to the practice of bringing the patient's body into balance by combining natural medicines and an abstemious life. For example, a man undergoing treatment might be forbidden to have sexual relations with a woman, forbidden to eat salt and every kind of animal meat, and required to use a cleansing astringent whose chief ingredient was mountain alum.[2]

Cherokee healers did not employ surgery as we

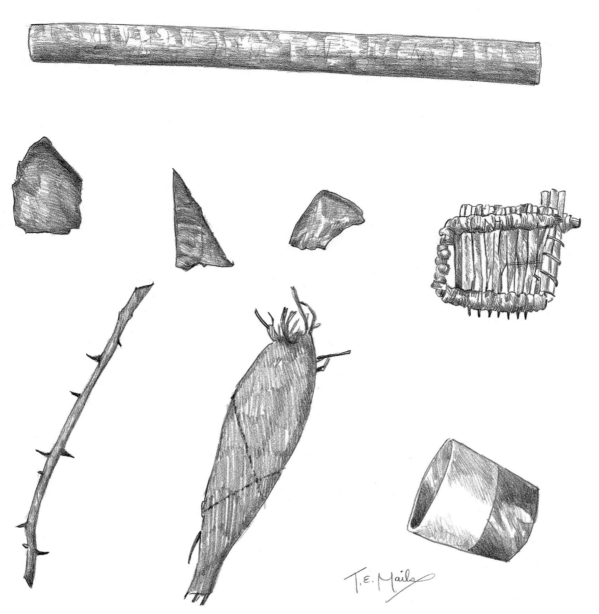

Surgical instruments used by healers — stones, brambles, herb bundle, cup, medicine blowing tube. Redrawn from *The Swimmer Manuscript*, page 54.

know it today. What they called surgery was nothing more than the use of scratching and bleeding with the type of instruments described in the ball-play and warfare material. Their justification for this is found in an incisive commentary Adair makes as he compares the Indian and white surgeons of his time, vowing that he would prefer the former if he had a serious wound. He supports his choice by describing an event that took place in 1749, when he, with friendly Chickasaw Indians, arrived in Charlestown, South Carolina, on the very day that an English surgeon had cut off the wounded arm of an Indian.

When Adair told the Chickasaws what had been done, they were shocked, and stated that the doctor should have exerted the common skills of manhood in so trifling a hurt, especially since the butchery would both disfigure and disable the poor man for the rest of his life. It would have been more humane, they said, to cut off the man's head, for it was better for a man to die once than to always be dying. When the arm was lost, how could the man feed himself by his daily labor? Following the same rule of thumb, if the man had been wounded in his head, the doctor would have cut that off.

Adair explained to the Chickasaws that the wisdom of English laws had exempted the head from such treatment by offering no reward by the severing of it, whereas rewards were received for each joint of the limbs that could be severed without the loss of life, and in addition, the patient who lost a limb would be cared for in a government hospital or home for the rest of his days. But the Indians declared that such brave and hardy men as fathers and warriors would rather be deemed men and work for their bread than be laid aside as useless animals and as burdens to the rest of society.[3]

Healing

In writing about Cherokee healing practices, I am forced in various parts of the book to use the titles "priest," "conjurer," and "medicine man," and I must explain how they came into being and the difference among them.

"Priest" was the original and ancient title given to religious leaders, just as it is today in some churches. But Cherokee priests were both leaders of religious services and healers. The ancient priests served as doctors for warriors who were on war parties, and at home some practiced healing for every kind of ailment, while others specialized in treating certain things. Because of this dual and essential role, priests ranked among the nation's leaders and were greatly respected. Virtually all of them were, either in infancy or childhood, devoted or promised to the task by their parents. All were specially trained by selected priests who knew how to conduct the great festivals and rites. All were authorized to use the sacrifices, the beads, and the precious divining crystals to obtain answers to questions about life, death, healing, victory, defeat, family affairs, and lost objects.

Since all priests conjured — that is, sought out answers and worked up solutions — it was natural for the Euro-American traders to call them "conjurers." During the early historic period this title was appended, not always to the leading priests, but always to those priests of lesser rank who were well known for their healing practices.

Later still, what was in truth a more scornful term, "medicine man," was applied by the whites, and in time it entirely replaced the title "conjurer." As a rule, white settlers thought of medicine men as charlatans who practiced magic and deception and who really couldn't heal anything of significance. The same settlers appended this derogatory title to white men with traveling medicine shows.

My use of the titles will be applied according to the time scale, although I do not care for "medicine man" because of its bad connotations. Nor do I like the title "shaman" any better. "Holy man" or "healer" is more proper and apt. I will use these as the occasion calls for it.

The ancient Cherokees had a descriptive title for healers. They were called *Kv ni a ka ti*, which is a combination derived from *Shv ni*, an arrow, and *A ka ti*, which meant going along or following a course. The title was chosen because the healers followed the course of the arrow in healing the wound made by it. In other words, the treatment was applied directly to the wound or precisely above the spot where the pain was most intense. *Kv ni* was a kind of slim cane that grew on the mountainsides, and it was heavy and had a hard texture. And, since arrows were usually made of it, they were called by this name. When the Cherokees became acquainted with lead rifle balls, they gave them the same name, for they were heavy and used in shooting.[4]

The Cherokee healers believed there were both natural and supernatural causes for disease and death. Some things they knew were the result of common accidents — a man cut himself, a child fell and broke a leg. But the vast majority of problems came from supernatural causes. If anything at all strange attended the onset of a problem, it was thought that someone or something with special powers was angry with the individual and had taken vengeance.

A mythological explanation might be advanced to account for any mysterious, unexplainable, insidious diseases.

Human or animal spirits could be the cause. Usually these did not act on their own. They might be prevailed upon by a witch or some other human agency. Rarely, the sun might send disease, but more often she was called upon to cure disease. The fire might become angry and retaliate if someone threw waste into it, but like the sun, fire was more often invoked against the causes of disease. The moon might be responsible for blindness. He never dispelled disease. A polluted river might strike back at those who insulted it. Thunder was the parent of lightning and in this wise might hurt or kill someone, but thunder was another being who was more likely to help. Animal spirits were invisible, but their presence could be sensed. Their motive for sending disease was mainly self-defense against wrongs done to them. Human ghosts felt lonesome and wanted human companionship. They caused sickness so that people might die and come to be with them. Animal ghosts caused most diseases. These were the reincarnations of animals that had been killed by hunters, and the same animal might have as many as seven reincarnations before going finally to "the night land."

Fellow human beings who could cause diseases included witches and "man killers." Witches were human beings who could steal the life, or vital principle and power of the individual, and add what they stole to their own power. They preferred to attack the weak, and that is why they hovered around the sick and feeble. Witches were indoctrinated into the profession by fasting and at the same time drinking over a prescribed period of days a certain brew made from a beetle-shaped plant. Those who drank it for four days could change themselves into any person or animal living on the surface of the ground. If they drank it for seven days, they could take on the shapes and powers of birds or animals who lived under the ground or flew above it. Witches loved to work at night, and that is when people most often guarded against them with remade tobacco.

Man killers had occult power to change food in a victim's stomach, to change or twist people's minds, and to change a minor ailment to a serious one. Above all, they might shoot an invisible arrow into a person's body and kill him.

There were a number of dreaded diseases thought to be caused by the trickery of a human agent who deluded the patient and the healer by

Priest with a patient being purified by immersion in running water.

sending a disease that looked like one which it was not. Thus the healer made a wrong diagnosis and might not realize his mistake until it was too late. Menstruating women could spread disease to those who touched what they had touched. Even their presence could cause problems. Pregnant women were only slightly less dangerous.

Dreams were causes of diseases, as were signs, or omens.

Neglected taboos and disregarded injunctions worked in insidious ways to cause physical defects such as toothaches and abdominal pains.

Last of all, yet the most dreaded, were the causes of the contagious diseases and epidemics, which were immorality and the evil influences or activities of white people. The latter were thought to let loose epidemics to ravage the Cherokee towns so that the whites could possess the land.[5]

When, in the ordinary instance, a person was taken sick, a piece of good cloth and a few beads were sent to the priest who was known for being able to deal with that particular illness, along with a request that he attend the sick person. The priest's first step was to use the beads to discover whether he would be able to accomplish the healing. If the answer was unfavorable, he simply returned the cloth and beads to the person who had sent them. If, on the other hand, the answer was favorable, the conjurer went immediately to work.

The way in which priests administered their medicines differed according to what they had been taught and come to believe. With the exception of the use of prayer formulas, any two of them treating different patients who had like ailments made their individual decisions about how they would proceed and who they would pray to for assistance.

The first thing the healer endeavored to learn was the location of the patient's pain, for the healer did not so much aim at curing the disease as he did at removing the cause of it. He proceeded by intently questioning the patient as to whether he had infringed upon a taboo, and about his dreams and omens. Investigation might take the patient back months or years before the healer would feel the proper cause had been learned. Even then, if the healer made a mistake, it was not really a mistake, but a wrong diagnosis based on erroneous or insufficient information. Only when the real cause was hit upon could the culprit be forced to leave the patient. Once the cause was found, the proper roots or herbs could be obtained. In doubtful cases, beads could be used to determine whether the healer's guesses were correct. If, in seven days after treatment, the patient was not showing improvement, it was believed that he was afflicted by more than one cause, so either further treatment was undertaken, or a change of healer might be in order.[6]

It is essential to remember that healing consisted of a combination of action and prayer on the part of the healer. The two were inseparable, and one would not avail without the other. Faith was vital on the part of both healer and patient. They must believe absolutely that the illness would be cured, or that there was some good and spiritual reason why it would not be. Present-day doctors are acknowledging how important this is and have determined that the mind can trigger chemical mechanisms in the body that are both detrimental and beneficial. Remarkable cures have been effected by positiveness and optimism alone. Practitioners call it holistic healing that gives patients hope and a sense of control, and they stress that the healer-patient relationship of trust is all important. Thus we must credit the Cherokee healers and their patients for recognizing this important truth hundreds of years ago.[7]

As for curing methods used by the healers, both the intrinsic properties of the remedies used and the careful observing of rules and regulations for the rites and prayers were of equal importance in achieving a cure. Methods of application included administering the medicine in chewed or liquid form, blowing the medicine by spraying it over the patient with a blowing tube, blowing the healer's breath on the patient, sprinkling the medicine on the patient with a small pine branch, exposing the patient to the vapors of the medicine, using a sweat bath and followed by a plunge into a cold stream, massage with warmed hands that had been empowered by the fire, vomiting into the river to get rid of the disease, scratching and sucking on the patient and then burying the extracted cause of the disease, and walking around the patient in a prescribed manner.[8]

Paraphernalia used by the healers was not extensive. It included objects used for divining, scratching instruments, a blowing tube made of trumpetweed, gourd dippers, a gourd rattle (but never a tortoiseshell rattle), and a persimmon-wood stamper used for massaging.[9]

Mention has been made of the healthy region the Cherokees lived in and of their general good health. But as the following list of prayer requests by just one healer shows, ailments we are familiar with were numerous and common. Each of these prayers was directed to some "above being" who was thought to help and who was asked to come and either treat the illness or carry or send it away.

In cases of fever, the healer prayed to the coldest waters to come and cool the fever and ease the discomfort. For a common headache, he prayed to white beings who resided in the north — an old

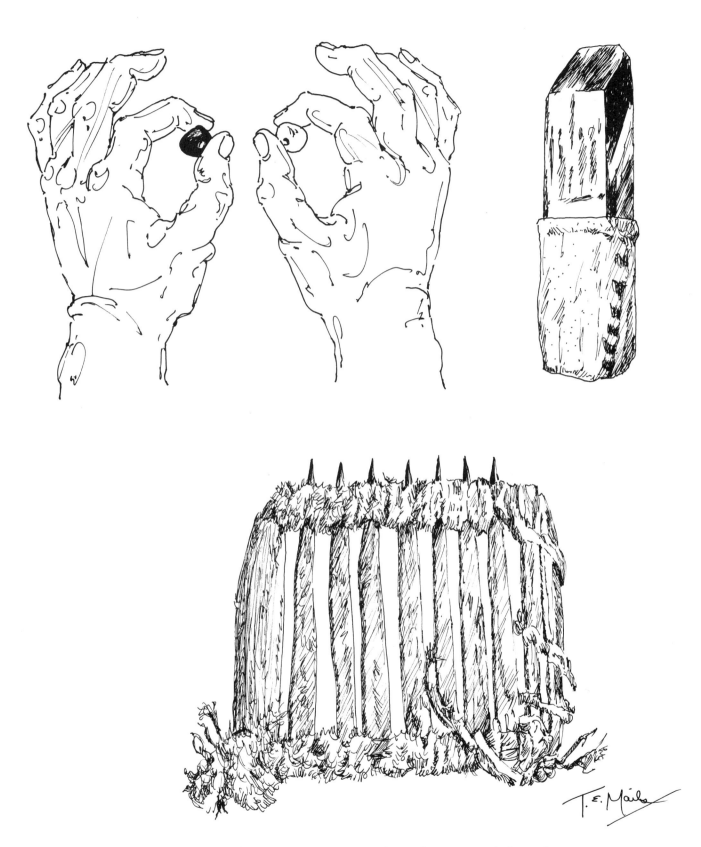

Divining items. Top left, method of holding beads. Top right, typical crystal. Bottom, typical scratcher.

white person and his son. For sore eyes, the prayer was to a great red spider above, asking it to come and take away the redness, inflammation, and pain. For a certain kind of sore eyes, the healer sang, "The wolf is coming" four times. Then he mocked the wood-cock, and blew derisively at it.

For those with a toothache, the prayer was to a red woodcock who was asked to take away the pain — if, as was suspected, the woodcock caused it. Earaches were caused by an evil black bug. So the prayer was to a certain bird above to come down and take the bug away. The prayer was repeated four times, then the healer blew on the patient to transfer the answer he had received. For heartburn, the healer prayed first to the edge of the water, then to a pond of water, then to a mouse above, and finally to a bird called *Tso sta wu.* To stop a cough, the prayer was directed to a great blue being above, and to the red flute above. To treat constipation, the healer prayed to the red man (the sun), to a blue being in the north, to a black man in the west, and a white man in the south.

For colic, the healer prayed to a great star. Measles required a prayer to a great being above called *Ni ta we he u.* The first prayer for rheumatism that was accompanied by swelling went to a great butterfly in the north, asking it to come and fan the joint and take away the pain. The healer then prayed to a little butterfly to do the same. For pains in the bones and lameness without swelling, the prayer was sent off to a great being in the east who had a sharp head, asking him to come quickly and remove the acute pain, since this being was able to do whatever he pleased. The prayer for a broken bone was to a yellow person who lived in the midst of the upper regions, asking him to bring down a red thread and to use this to bind up the broken bone and make it well. For a flesh cut, a song was sung to the earth, the water, the stones, and the wood. Then a prayer was said to certain above creatures — the yellow wolf, the yellow buzzard, and the yellow otter — to come down and heal the wound. The prayer for an arrow or bullet wound was to a kind of being called *Ta ka tsi,* the English equivalent of which is not known.

To heal bruised flesh, the prayer was offered to a great mulberry in the east. For a common sore or sore place, the prayer was to the mother of the water and to a little whirlwind that lived at the edge of the water. For a sore becoming gangrenous, the prayer was to a mulberry in the east and to a blue goose above to come and feast on the worms supposed to occasion the sore. For a thorn or sliver embedded in the flesh, the prayer was made to the wolf and the red dog above to come and heal the wound. Then a kind of song was sung or chanted.

For snakebite, some healers prayed to the raven, supposedly a great being, asking it to go to God and to get him to send down his seven messen-gers to heal the wound. Informants say that the god mentioned here was probably the sun.[10] In all his years with the Cherokees, Adair did not remember having seen or heard of one of them dying from snakebite, although when hunting or on a war party they were often bitten by the most dangerous kinds. Everyone carried in his quiver or belt pouch a piece of the best snakeroots, such as the *Seneeka,* or fern snakeroot; the wild horehound; plantain; St. Andrew's Cross; or one of a variety of other herbs and roots that were well known to those who ranged the woods. Any one of those would effect a thorough and speedy cure if applied soon enough. The mo-ment a person was struck by a snake, he chewed and swallowed some of the root, then applied the same root to the wound. For a brief time after this, the victim experienced a terrible conflict throughout his body caused by both the poison and the antidote. But, Adair claims, the poison was soon expelled through the same channels it had entered, and the patient recovered.[11] Also for snakebite, a certain healer seated his patient on a log in the woods and put a certain root in his mouth. While the patient chewed it, the healer prepared his other medicine — possibly an emetic — and then walked around and around the patient as he sang, "Let this poison go away to the rabbit." He then administered the other medicine, and as he did so he prayed, "Those white men above, past promised to hear. Those past made this snake's teeth white which bit this person. Let them be in vain in this case, and let him get well. Let what those have done and the remedy which I have administered agree. Therefore let the man speedily recover." This same prayer was then addressed to the white man in the north, the west, the south, and the east. Thus, the prayer was repeated five times.[12]

For kidney stones or gallstones, prayers went to the mother of the earth, the mother of the water, the mother of the stones, and the mother of the mulberry. If no relief was obtained from those, the healer often ascribed his failure to witchcraft, to mismanagement on the part of the patient or his attendants, or to some other cause beyond the healer's control. He conjured again to learn whether the person was to live or to die. To do this, he took two beads, one between each thumb and forefinger, a white one for life and a black one for death. He then prayed to the sun for a sign. Shortly thereafter, the beads moved. If the person was to recover, the bead representing life would move with the greater force. If the person would not recover, the other bead did so. If the latter happened, there was nothing more to be done except to smooth the way to the grave by kind ministering to the family by relatives.

Cherokees believed in witchcraft and in what were called "familiar spirits." It was commonly accepted that witches, both male and female, were able to do considerable harm to both persons and property. They received their power from the familiar spirits, who were emissaries of the Evil One. To more easily work out their malicious plans, witches were thought to sometimes assume the form of birds or animals. Priests alone had the power to counteract the evildoing of witches, and even the power to destroy witches without ever going near or seeing them.[13]

A prayer formula used to destroy life goes as follows:

> Listen! Now I have come to step over your soul. You are of the (wolf) clan. Your name is (*A yu ini*). Your spittle I have put at rest under the earth. Your soul I have put at rest under the earth. I have come to cover you over with the black rock. I have come to cover you over with the black cloth. I have come to cover you with the black slabs, never to reappear. Toward the black coffin of the upland in the Darkening Land your paths shall stretch out. So

shall it be for you. The clay of the upland has come to cover you. Instantly the black clay has lodged there where it is at rest at the black houses in the Darkening Land. With the black coffin and with the black slabs I have come to cover you. Now your soul has faded away. It has become blue. When darkness comes your spirit shall grow less and dwindle away, never to reappear. Listen![14]

The formula was accompanied by a fascinating ritual performed by the priest to effect the death of the witch in question. There was also a formula for driving away a witch, and the ritual for that was equally spellbinding.[15]

If a person was suddenly taken with an uncommon disease, a priest was immediately summoned. He first examined the patient, looking intently at him and asking questions about him. He then made tea of some kind of roots and had the patient drink some of it. He also bathed the patient's face and limbs with it. The priest then turned to incantations, to blowing his breath on the patient, and to making manipulations over his body — all the while muttering or speaking in a low tone as he conversed with his secret helpers. In cases of severe pain, the priest gathered bark from a particular kind of tree and burned it to coals. Then after warming his hands by rubbing them briskly over the fire, he pressed them tightly to the location of the pain. He repeated the treatment several times, and quite often the patient recovered. Should, however, the treatment prove unsuccessful, a witch was suspected of being the cause of the trouble. Various methods were employed to determine who the offender was and to punish him. One way was to make a picture representing the accused and to shoot it with an arrow. If that person died soon after, it was conclusive proof of his guilt. A buzzard feather placed over the doorway prevented witches from entering people's dwellings and served as a watcher of the house. There was a spoken charm that accompanied the placement of the feather: "I am going to leave you on watch here. Now you will also be the finder for me of all valuable things."[16]

Warriors who were wounded in battle were carried away by their comrades as soon as possible. When it was safe to do so, the priest took a certain preparation in his mouth, then put his mouth to the

Priest healing patient by applying warmed hands and suction.

wounds and sucked out all of the bad blood. He chewed hickory bark and spurted the juice on the wound. He also chewed a certain root called *Ta ye wo* and spurted it in the wound. As soon as the battle ended and the priest could move his patients to a quiet resting place, he chewed a root called *A ta nu kv le ske*, or "cleansing tongue," and using a cane tube twelve inches long, spurted the juice on the bottom of each wound. After this, the patients were required to fast for four days. This was to show their appreciation to the divine beings for the preservation of their lives and the healing of their wounds. The priests also fasted. As each patient recovered fully, the priest offered a thanksgiving sacrifice for him and prayed as he did on those instances when a man wished for long life and asked the priest to assist him in obtaining it. A person who was wounded by accident was directed to fast for twenty-four hours.[17]

If, while practicing at home, a healer lost a patient, he threw away all of the medicine similar to that he had used and did not employ the same medicine again until a new year had arrived. He in fact ceased to practice at all until the next new moon, at which time he purified himself by drinking a purge tea made of *Kv ne si* and *Ha lo ha ne ka* roots, which caused him to vomit. Then he poured some of the same tea on a hot stone and steamed his hands with it. His excuse for purifying himself so soon as on the first appearance of the next new moon was that he loved his wife, children, and other friends and wished to be ready to attend to them in case they became ill.

Many medicinal plants and roots were known and used by the people themselves in the treatment of common diseases. The caustic and detergent properties of the root of the white nettle served well in the cleansing of ulcers and deteriorating flesh. The bark of the birch tree was considered a specific cure for ulcers. For rheumatism, they used a lead-colored, oval-shaped stone that was thought to be solidified lightning, since it was found near the roots of a lightning-struck tree. A few birds and some wild animals served as messengers of evil tidings, and there was a legend of a large serpent called the ground snake, which was the color of the ground and

was said to foretell death to the one who saw it. If the snake appeared to a group, a national calamity was foretold.[18]

The ancient Cherokees believed that the universe was created for more than man, and that while man had unique qualities and opportunities, he was no more important in the eternal scheme than other created things. Moreover, each created thing — including even the rock that appeared to be inanimate — was actually alive. And, like each cog in a wheel, it could do something no other created thing could do, so that it made an essential contribution to the whole and played a necessary role in the continued existence of all things.

Creation included both visible and invisible entities, the tangible and the intangible. On the one side were the earth and its creatures, and on the other side the celestial objects and the mediating spirits. These were the halves that together made the whole. Beyond them were the heavens where the Above Beings dwelt, and from which, in the beginning, the powers needed for life were dispensed to the whole of what they had created.

Sometimes the Cherokees did not understand why the Above Beings had created some things, since their precise roles in life were not understood. But they knew the things did exist, and that they should not be scorned or abused, else they might retaliate. Also, there were purposes to be served other than those of man. The Above Beings had their reasons for creating them. Knowing what these reasons were and why things were so really did not matter. What did matter was that if each created thing sought to do the will of the Above Beings, then the beings, as they had promised in the beginning of time, would watch over the whole of creation and see to it that what was needed would be done.

Regarding causes, early in their history, the Cherokees acknowledged the existence of the mysterious things they encountered but did not understand by creating a complex realm of beliefs. Scholars sum these up under the headings: spirit people, superstitious practices, signs and portents, dreams, uncleanness, prayer formulas, and myths.

Spirit People

There was a race of spirit people named the *Nunne hi*, or immortals, whose home in the old Cherokee country was in the highlands. They had many town houses, or communal-type dwellings, especially in the bald mountains, the highest peaks of which no timber ever grew on. There were large town houses in Pilot Knob and under the old *Nilwasi* mound in North Carolina, and there was another one under Blood Mountain, at the head of the Nottely River in Georgia.

The immortals were invisible except when they wanted to be seen, and then they looked and spoke just like the Cherokees. They were very fond of music and dancing, and hunters in the mountains would often hear their dance songs and drums beating in some distant town house. But when the hunters searched for the source, the sound would shift and they would hear it behind them or away in some other direction, so that they could never find the place where the dance was. The immortals were a friendly people too, and often brought lost Cherokees to their hidden town houses, where they cared for them until they were rested, and then guided them back to their homes. More than once, when the Cherokees were hard-pressed by the enemy, the *Nunne hi* warriors came to save them from defeat. They were invisible, naturally, but from the miraculous things that happened on the battlefield, the Cherokee warriors knew that the immortals were with them.[19]

The preferred home of the *Yunwi Tsunsdi*, also given as *Nuh na yie*, *Nemehi*, and *Gemehi*, or "Little People," was a rock cave on the mountainside. They were little fellows, hardly reaching up to a man's knee, but they were well shaped and handsome, with long hair falling almost to the ground. They were great wonder workers and were very fond of music, spending half of their time drumming and dancing. They were helpful and kindhearted, and often when people had been lost in the mountains, especially children who had strayed away from their parents, the Little People found them, took care of them, and brought them back to their homes. Sometimes the Little People's drum was heard in lonely places in the mountains, but it was not safe or wise to search for it, because the Little People did not like to be disturbed at home, and they would cast a spell over the stranger who did this, so that he was bewildered and lost his way. Even if he did at last get back to his home, he was ever after like a person dazed.

Sometimes the Little People came near a house at night, and the people inside heard them talking. But the human beings were not to go out and look for them, else they would die. In the morning they would find the corn gathered or the field cleared as if a whole force of men had been at work. When a hunter found a useful object in the woods, such as a knife or a grinding stone, he was to say, "Little People, I want to take this," because it might belong to them, and if he did not ask their permission, they would throw stones at him as he went home.[20]

Once a hunter found tracks in the snow like those of little children. He wondered how they could have come there and followed them until they led him to a cave, which was full of Little People, young and old, men, women, and children. They assumed he was lost and brought him in and were kind to him. He was with them for some time, but when he left, they warned him that he must not tell others about them or he would die. He went back to the settlement, and his friends were all anxious to know where he had been. For a long time he refused to say, but finally he gave in to their pleadings and told the story, and in a few days he died.

Belief in the immortals and the Little People did not end with the Cherokees' conversion to white ways. Two stories from the Eastern Cherokee Reservation show how those beliefs continued in the nineteenth century, and they continue today among the Eastern Cherokees and the traditional Cherokees of Oklahoma.

During the smallpox outbreak among the Eastern Cherokees just after the Civil War, a sick man wandered off into the woods. His friends searched for him but could not find him. After several weeks he returned on his own and said that the Little People had found him and taken him to one of their caves, where they tended him until he was cured.[21] In about 1895, two hunters from

Raventown went behind the high falls near the head of Oconaluftee River on the Eastern Cherokee reservation, and they found a cave with fresh footprints of the Little People all over the floor.[22]

Cherokee lore included other fairies. The *Yunwi Amaiyine hi*, or water dwellers, were prayed to by fishermen who needed help.

Some friendly spirits lived in people's houses, although no one could see them, and so long as they were there to protect the house, no witch dared come near to do mischief.[23]

Tsawa si and *Tsaga si* were the names of two small fairies who, although they were mischievous, often helped hunters. *Tsawa si* was a tiny fellow who

The Little People

was very handsome and had hair falling down to his feet. He lived in grassy patches on the hillsides and had great power over wild game. Deer hunters who prayed to him were able to slip up on deer without being seen. *Tsaga si* was helpful in other ways to hunters who prayed to him, but when someone tripped or fell it was known that *Tsawa si* caused it.

There were several other fairies, all of whom were good-natured and tricky.[24] Among these was *De tsata*, a boy who once ran away to the woods to avoid the punishment of being scratched. He tried after that to make himself invisible. He was a handsome little fellow and spent most of his time hunting birds with blowgun and bow and arrow. He had a great

many children who were just like him in appearance and actions and had the same name. When a flock of birds flew up suddenly as if frightened, it was because *De tsata* was chasing them. He was also mischievous, and sometimes hid the arrow of a bird hunter who shot it off into a perfectly clear space but looked and looked without finding it. Then the hunter realized what was happening and said, "De tsata, you have my arrow, and if you don't give it up I'll scratch you," and when he looked again he always found the lost arrow.[25]

There was one spirit who was not so friendly, and who prowled around at night with either an inner light or a lighted torch. The Cherokees called it *Atsil dihye gi*, "the Fire Carrier," and they were afraid of it, because they knew little about it and thought it dangerous. They didn't know what it looked like, because they were afraid to stop when they heard it moving and saw the light. It might have been a witch instead of a spirit.[26]

Superstitious Practices

Different superstitious practices are mentioned in other places in this book, but what follows here are a few of the best known ones. By reading them carefully, we move behind their charm and learn a considerable amount about Cherokee life and nature — what thoughts occupied their minds, what they feared, how they came to terms with the mysterious unknown, and how they solved problems they could not have solved in any other way than by means of superstition.

Superstitions did not, of course, explain or take care of every problem, but together with the solutions offered by other aspects of life, they did much to achieve the inner peace the Cherokees needed to cope with the unfriendly supernatural powers and adversity that might otherwise have destroyed them.

Moccasins were sewn together with deer sinew, for it was stronger and more lasting than hemp. But it was believed that to eat sinew would breed worms and other ailments in proportion to the number of sinew threads one ate.

A piece was cut from the thigh of every deer the Cherokees killed and then thrown away, for it

was dangerous to do otherwise and would bring sickness and other misfortunes such as spoiling their aim with weapons.

When it thundered, the great chief of the thunder was very cross or angry. When it rained, thundered, and blew hard for a considerable time, the Above Beings were at war above the clouds.

Smallpox was a foreign disease that came from whites or from the invisible darts of angry fate that were pointed against the Cherokee nation because of the young people's immoral conduct.

Words that were repeated in divine hymns while dancing around the holy fire were deemed so sacred that they were not mentioned at any other time.

Women always threw a small piece of the fattest part of the meat into the fire while they were eating, and frequently before they began to eat. This act assured that good things would happen and turned away those things that were evil.

Newly killed venison was waved several times through the smoke and flame of the fire as a sacrifice that consumed the creature's spirit, which was never to be eaten.

Hunters sacrificed the melt, or large fat portions, of the first buck they killed during hunts. Sometimes they sacrificed the entire carcass. This was an offering of thanks for a recovery from illness, and a prayer for success in hunting.

Frequent washing of the body in a river or creek was practiced as a religious duty rather than for sanitary reasons. If the water was frozen over, the ice was broken and the immersing was done anyway. The neglect of this was considered so heinous a crime that delinquent persons had their arms and legs raked with snake-teeth scratchers.

It was supposed and feared that certain kinds of uncleanness might be contracted during the night while asleep, either from witches or some other unknown cause. Therefore, the most religious persons observed the following ceremonies every morning for their purification: On awakening sometime before daylight, they turned onto their faces and sang the following verse four times: *"Hi na tu hu yi, Kv lv la ti, Ha tlo sv gu ti."* They then devoted some time to meditation, sang the same verse again, and continued the ritual until sunrise. Then they arose, went to a nearby river or creek, and while standing on the bank sang the same verse again. They plunged into the stream, and continued to remain under water for as long as they could hold their breath. They then stood up and again plunged in as before, and did this seven times, after which they considered themselves to be cleansed from the impurities of the night and ready for the day.

In one method of gaining the serenity needed to drop off to sleep quickly, on lying down at night the Cherokees sang, or repeated, a prayer that in English says, "Let my soul be in the first heaven, let my soul be in the second heaven," and so on to the seventh heaven. The first heaven was supposed to be as high as the tops of the trees, the second as high as the clouds, the third the moon, the fourth the sun, the fifth more distant planets, the sixth the constellations, and the seventh the place where the Creator resided. In each of these heavens, angels were supposed to dwell, attending to the various duties assigned them in the vast government of the Creator and especially to the needs and well-being of all created things.

To protect them against inward uncleanness in the body, in the beginning the Creator told the Cherokees what they should eat and what they should not eat. They were not to eat foxes, dogs, wolves, snakes, moles, polecats, rabbits, opossums, buzzards, crows, ravens, cranes, fish hawks, eagles, owls, hoot owls, bats, and woodcocks. They were not to eat eels or any kind of water snakes, catfish, gar, or *Tsv wi*, a fish with a flat head and body that resembled a snake. Things that could be eaten were chickens, turkeys, some other birds, deer, elk, buffalo, antelope, and cattle. They were allowed to eat bear meat and to use of bear oil for food and ointment.

After a person had died and was buried, a kind of spirit called *u tse lv nv hi* would often come to the deceased's house and make various kinds of strange noises. These were the souls of persons who had died recently. To combat this, the family would prepare food and carry it to the graves where their relatives were buried. They would leave it on top of a rock or in some other conspicuous place where the spirits could find it. After that, the spirits would trouble them no more.

Witches were living persons assisted by some evil spirit. They were very dangerous and were often encountered outdoors after dark. Witches would frequently sneak into houses and make knocking sounds in various rooms. The father then filled his pipe with old or remade tobacco and smoked it in the rooms and outside the house, blowing smoke in every direction. At length some of the smoke would get into the witches' throats and make them cough. Then the family was secure. The witches would immediately depart and, in seven days or less after inhaling the tobacco smoke, would be dead. When a person was sick in a house, witches would constantly be flocking about as they sought to take advantage of the situation. Therefore, old tobacco was smoked continually. Witches would sometimes get in some corner of the house and sing like an owl or some kinds of birds. The smoke rooted them out too.[27]

Purification

Purification by diets, emetics, prayers, and immersing in water has been mentioned several times and will come up again in the chapters ahead. This is a good place to analyze how the Cherokees understood the act or ritual of purification in which the entire person was cleansed. The Pueblo and Sioux holy men and women thought and still think of the purification ritual as that which, by the rote performance of divinely given commands, turns them into fit tubes or channels through which God is willing to enlighten people and perform his miracles. Purification rids them of any sinfulness or uncleanness that would hinder his use of them. Thus all credit for what is accomplished belongs to God. The ancient Cherokees gave credit to God, yet for the rest believed something quite different — that cleansing by water and emetic rid them of any uncleanness that would make God unwilling to touch them, bless them, and work with them. In uncleanness, there was no hope or optimism. In cleanness it was just the opposite. In the case of the priest, ritual cleansing enabled him to perform successfully and to see, as in the use of divining crystals and meat and tobacco sacrifices, what he could not otherwise see. For were he unclean, the truth might be plainly before him, but his eyes and mind would be blinded to it.

Signs and Portents

The ancient Cherokee signs, portents, and dreams have a fixation with death, illness, and misfortune. Not many of them have pleasant associations. The natural conclusion might be that the people were morbid and unhappy — an idea strongly contradicted by what we already know about them. Furthermore, by carefully studying the following signs and dreams, we discover four important things about them.

First, some of the signs and dreams are about things that seldom, if ever, happened. Thus they would cause little concern among their observers.

Second, because unexplained deaths were unacceptable, people had to have ways of coming to terms with and accepting them and of not accusing the Above Beings of unfairly taking away loved ones. Signs and dreams did both.

Third, signs and dreams prepared people to accept death when it came as a natural consequence of living. They were able to accommodate the fact that all who live must die sometime, and they thought it was better to be ready than to be unprepared. In this regard, Cherokees were fatalists as individuals, and yet optimistic when the nation was concerned. It never occurred to them that the number of deaths would be such that the nation would not survive — another view of life that prepared them for national disasters to come.

Fourth, a positive aspect of the signs and dreams was that they sent the recipient of foreboding news scurrying to a priest for cleansing and restoration. Thus the bad omens had the beneficial effect of keeping people aware of their dependence on the Above Beings and keeping them close to the powers who cared for them. This is how the Above Beings wanted it, so they were pleased, and it kept the people from foolishly attempting to solve all their problems on their own.

There were numerous signs that indicated death. If, on starting a journey, one should frighten a fox and the fox, after running a few steps, looked back and barked, that would mean one of the person's family members or a neighbor would die before his return or soon thereafter. Frightening a wolf, or seeing a snake called *U ka te ni*, large immortals, or Little People meant the same thing. If, while absent from home, a person should see something larger than was common for its kind, it was a sign that some of the person's family was to die soon. If a person saw two squirrels fighting in a tree and they fell off and were killed by the fall, some relatives would die soon. Should someone hear a wailing sound like that of mourning for the dead, some of his friends would die soon. Should one see the apparition or appearance of a friend that soon vanished, that friend would soon die. Should a hen crow, someone in the family would soon die. If, miraculously, a dog talked like a person, it signified there would soon be a catastrophe. If a hominy pestle should move about a house unassisted, it was a sign that all in the house would soon die. A scratching sound or some uncommon noise was a sign of death. Should a tree fall without being blown down and the top point towards the house, someone in the house would soon die. When the Cherokees heard a whippoorwill in the daytime, they supposed it was a witch who had assumed the appearance of the bird. If a whippoorwill came near a house and sang repeatedly, it was a sign that one of the family would die.

Other signs had to do with enemies and warfare. If one heard a *Tsa wi skv* bird singing its name very fast and loud, enemies were near the town. Should an owl light on a peach or other kind of tree in the town and sing, it foretold the approach of the enemy in a few days. When warriors were out on a war expedition, if the people at home heard the Little People sounding the war whoop and the sound was protracted, then Cherokee warriors were killing their enemies. But if the sound was short, Cherokee warriors were getting killed.

Some signs had to do with strangers and visitors. If, while a person was traveling, a little bird called *Tsi ki lili* flew over in the same direction singing, the person would soon meet a stranger. If one of those birds should light near a house or sing in the vicinity, a visitor would come soon. And, should a bird fly into a house, some visitor was coming. When a certain blue bird sang, there would soon be a storm.

If a person who had been trained for holy office desired to know whether he had long to live, he would sometimes determine this by means of a rattlesnake. On seeing one crawling along, he approached it, and stretched out his right hand toward it. If the snake acted angry and began to coil, the person knew he would die soon. But if the snake seemed pleasant, the person put his hand on it and, clasping the body about where the heart lay, he slowly lifted it up, and then put it gently down. If the snake moved off toward the west, it meant the man would not live long. But if it went east, long life was assured.[28]

Dreams

In essence, Cherokee dreams were like our own. They were about strange and unusual happenings of the kind that for the most part transcend life as it really is. Since the sampling of dreams cited here suggests that the dreams could be recalled after awakening, we must ask how the dreamers managed this. Most of our dreams are gone by the time we awaken, and defy recall. Yet the Cherokees put considerable stock in dreams, and even had a ritual way of using seven memory stones that Archie Sam told me about to help recall them. Dreams and signs, or omens, were even thought to be among the causes of things happening. Thus, to see in a dream one of the signs of death, whether or not the dream was remembered in part or whole, was to cause the death, and the same was true of illness and other matters. It is apparent that Cherokees dreamed often, and that most dreams were negative in nature. But as in the case of signs, they also had their positive aspects in keeping one centered in religion and the Above Beings. Unfortunately, while we are told about the dreams, we are not told what dreamers thought when dreams failed to come true.

The following dreams foretold death:

Seeing any person going towards the west was a sign that that person would soon die.

Seeing anyone with an eagle feather in his hand, or to dream of possessing such feathers, was a sign of death.

Seeing a house burning was a sign that one or more persons would soon die in that house.

Seeing anyone floating down a stream of high water foretold the death of that person.

Hearing and seeing any family member or any number of individuals singing and dancing was a sure sign they would all die soon.

Seeing a person with very clean clothes signified that the person would not live long.

Seeing an eagle or crane on the ground or flying low was a sign that someone would soon die.

Other dreams had to do with illness. If someone in a family was ill and another member of that family dreamed of a stream of low, clear water, the ill person was sure to recover. But if the stream was rising and full, either the sick person would get worse, or someone else in the family would get very sick. Dreaming of a living person or animal that in the dream was seen dead was a certain sign of sickness to come. Those who dreamed of seeing a woman would soon have the ague and fever. To dream of seeing water rising around a house was a portent of sickness. If some of the water ran into the house, one or more of the inhabitants would soon die. But if the water fell away without flooding the house, none would die. Seeing clothing on fire was a sign of impending sickness. To dream of eating meat was a sign of sickness. If a sick person saw in his dreams any kind of snake, it was a sign that the snake, through witchcraft, had caused the illness. Dreaming of lice meant the person infested with them would soon be sick.

Other dreams had to do with hunters. Hunters who dreamed of having bread, peaches, or any kind of fruit were being told they would kill a deer. Therefore, hunters prayed for such dreams. If a hunter dreamed of having broken his gunlock, he would kill nothing during the next winter.

Some dreams signified greatness. To dream of flying was a sign that the person who dreamed it would live to a great age. A woman who dreamed of her son becoming an eagle was being told that he would become one of the great warriors.[29]

Uncleanness

After childbirth, a woman was considered unclean for seven days. All of her clothing became unclean, as did her bed, chair, and footstool, and all the vessels she touched. The furnishings had to be purified by smoke and sprinkling and, as was mentioned earlier, she went at delivery time to a tent that was some distance from the house. No one should touch her or anything she touched. If her condition was such that she required a priest's assistance, he took a bird, plucked off its feathers, removed the innards, and offered it as a sacrifice for her. Two or three days after the birth and again on the seventh day, she washed herself and put on clean clothing. On the morning of the thirteenth day she went at daybreak to the river, immersed seven times, put her defiled clothing and blankets under water and washed them, and on coming out put on clean clothes.

In ancient times a woman with child ate little if any meat, and some authorities think this was why she experienced few of the complaints attending present-day deliveries. If a woman wished, she could be out in the field and hoeing the next day.

All females, during their menstrual periods, went to tents and followed generally the same procedure as that just described for childbirth. Females in their menstrual uncleanness could eat only hominy and drink certain liquids.

If, during the woman's period, a man should lie with her, he too became unclean, and must immerse seven times and put on clean clothes. Until he did this he dared not engage in any business whatsoever or mingle with other people. Prior to bathing, he drank an emetic tea for inward purification.

After a man and his wife had sexual intercourse, they were both unclean, and had to immerse in the river seven times. Every garment and place on the skin that had been touched by his sperm had to be washed with water, and both the man and his garments were unclean until evening.[30]

Regarding the uncleanness associated with death, I add these specifics to what was said in Chapter Three about purification: The priest obtained the root of a weed called *Rv na so la*, soaked it in water, and with this water sprinkled the inside of the house. Then he smoked the house with burning cedar boughs. When this was done, he boiled a mixture of crab apples, plums, locust, and thorns, washed the mourners with the liquid, and gave them some of it to drink — which caused them to throw up and cleansed their insides. When a priest was cleansing a family, he was said to be purifying them.

All who touched a dead body, a bone, or a grave contracted uncleanness, and had to remain alone until the uncleanness was removed by purification. I said earlier that this included warriors who returned from battle and who continued in uncleanness and separation for twenty-four days. If they had been wounded, the separation might be for as much as seven years.[31]

Prayer Formulas

The ancient Cherokees had various charms, incantations, sacrifices, and prayers that were used to deal with life's problems and sickness, and over the years these were formalized into statements to be repeated by rote. The main types of prayer formulas were those for love and disease.

Love formulas were employed for attracting and retaining a wife, winning a woman away from a rival, achieving popularity with someone, and working revenge when betrayed.[32] Disease formulas were recited for the removal of the causes of disease, as protective prayers, and as prayers for long life.[33]

Other formulas included those employed by hunters when they went after bear, deer, or fowl. They were designed to lure the game closer so that it would be more easily killed and to make the traps more effective. The gathering of medicinal herbs also called for attraction formulas, and there were ritual prayers for the finding of lost people, animals, and

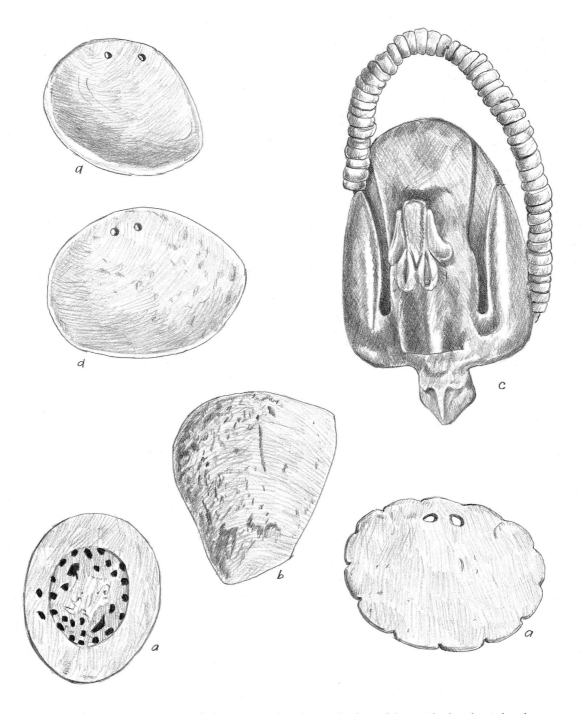

a. shell gorgets of type worn by healers. **b.** shell death mask placed over the face of deceased when buried. **c.** huge chest hanging worn by priest. All items from Museum of the Cherokee Indian.

objects. In conjunction with these, the conjurer might suspend on a string a pebble, straw, bread ball, or brown stone, and the direction of its swing indicated the position of the lost object.[34]

Weather-control formulas were applied to bad storms, to induce rain during a drought, and to stop rain when there was too much of it. Formulas for war and ball play were discussed in prior chapters.

Myths

As a whole, the mythical lore of the Cherokees had to do with the explaining of the origins of things and meanings of the present world in terms of what had happened in the past. Mooney classifies these Cherokee tales in seven groups: cosmogonic, quadruped, bird, snake-fish-insect, wonder stories, historical traditions, and miscellaneous. The collection is massive and detailed, and is necessary reading for those who wish a good understanding of the Cherokees. Most of the events recounted in the myths are explained by relating the adventures of various animal deities as they are organized into a society resembling that of the Cherokees themselves, possessing town houses, towns, trails, and the like, having the same emotional involvements, the same desires, and living in clans. Since, from the animals' point of view, man often mistreated them and sometimes failed to pay them the proper respect, some of the animals' spiritual selves used their special powers to cause diseases in man. To fight this, the Cherokees called in prayers upon the pantheon of animals whose feelings toward man were good and who would aid them, for like was able to cure like, which was a rule that applied in all manner of healing.

Here is a sample of the myths collected by Mooney, the second of two versions of "How They Brought Back the Tobacco:"

> The people had tobacco in the beginning, but they had used it all, and there was great suffering for want of it. There was one old man so old that he had to be kept alive by smoking, and as his son did not want to see him die he decided to go himself to try to get some more. The tobacco country was far in the south, with high mountains all around it, and the passes were guarded, so that it was very hard to get into it, but the young man was a conjurer and was not afraid.
> He traveled southward until he came to the mountains on the border of the tobacco country. Then he opened his medicine bag and took out a hummingbird skin and put it over himself like a dress. Now he was a hummingbird and flew over the mountains to the tobacco field and pulled some of the leaves and seed and put them into his medicine bag. He was so small and swift that the guards, whoever they were, did not see him, and when he had taken as much as he could carry he flew back over the mountains in the same way. Then he took off the hummingbird skin and put it into his medicine bag, and was a man again.
> He started home, and on his way came to a tree that had a hole in the trunk, like a door, near the first branches, and a very pretty woman was looking

out from it. He stopped and tried to climb the tree, but although he was a good climber he found that he always slipped back. He put on a pair of medicine moccasins from his pouch, and then he could climb the tree, but when he reached the first branches he looked up and the hole was still as far away as before. He climbed higher and higher, but every time he looked up, the hole seemed to be farther than before, until at last he was tired and came down again. When he reached home he found his father very weak, but still alive, and one draw at the pipe made him strong again. The people planted the seed and have had tobacco ever since.[35]

In this myth we see that the sacred tobacco is looked upon as essential to mental and physical well-being. When the son goes to get more, he has a hummingbird helper and the guards are lax. Yet even the ease with which the tobacco is obtained does not eliminate the young man's human side. He can be distracted from even this holy quest by a pretty young woman. That's the way life is. But nothing comes of this, and he redeems himself by righting his priorities and returning home in time to save his father and people.

Summary

What does the foregoing information regarding healing and the causes of afflictions tell us about the culture and nature of the Cherokee people of A.D. 1500-1750?

We know that priests, hence religion as a whole, played the dominant role in life, and that religion was inseparable from any part of life. When calamities of any sort befell the people, the priests, as intermediaries, were turned to for solutions. Thus, as stated earlier, the Cherokees were willingly a dependent people. Rather than shame, they found wisdom in this view, and personal satisfaction was subordinated in matters when credit for achievement was concerned. They believed that their own best good was served when the Above Beings, who were not limited as humans were, had control. Priests were turned to, but only because the priest himself turned to the higher powers. The respect of the people for their priests came from the priests' knowing how, in accordance with the ancient teachings, to fulfill their intermediary role.

Even during tribulations such as smallpox, the priests were depended upon. While there was a natural disappointment in failure, any consequence was attributed either to the divine will, to a lack of knowledge as to how to prepare, to a miscalculation in determining the cause or the manner of treatment, or to the abuse or misuse of persons or holy property, so that impending death or other loss did not cause panic and was in fact accepted with stoicism. In this regard we see that the nature of their religion was preparatory. They wanted to know what was ahead so they would be ready for it and not be irretrievably broken when it came. The one thing they could not prepare for was the unknown epidemics brought in by outsiders. But preparation for what they did know was the reason behind the constant divining with the beads and crystals. It gave the priests and the people a way to combat disease, other adversities, and death before they reached out to claim their victims. It is stimulating to note the inner peace such an attitude brought.

While the traditional beliefs and national practices are broadly considered in the chapters immediately ahead, we can see even at this point that the people believed in a vast pantheon of higher and mostly beneficial possessions of power that could be called upon as needed. A combination of act and faith was essential in obtaining assistance, and prayer was an inseparable part of faith. It was to be practiced constantly, and prayer formulas were evolved for special needs and the obtaining of spiritual direction. We notice that both priest and patient expected that prayers would be answered. They began the prayer with a positive attitude. As in the cited prayer formula for destroying life and in the snakebite prayer, there was no expression of doubt. I am reminded of the Hopi Indians who begin each of their annual nine-day rituals by preparing the host of gifts that will be given to the people when, as is certain, God and his helpers bless them by answering their prayers and performances.

As is shown in their seeking of inner balance in healing, good sense was also employed. People were given minds, and the Cherokees knew that the Above Beings intended those minds to be used. They also knew that a moral life was pleasing to the Above Beings and important to personal and national survival, and they did not consider abstinence to be a heinous thing. Fasting and other acts of denial were regularly practiced.

Personal dignity, honor, and shared responsibility were looked upon as valuable assets — as is illustrated in the instance when the man's arm was amputated. People cared about those things and enough about one another to wish not to become someone else's burden.

In the manner of all ancient peoples, there was considerable superstition, for there was no other means of finding answers to certain mysterious happenings and to counteracting those events and portents that were detrimental to and fearful to man.

The Cherokees were practical. They made practical approaches to religion and to ordinary life. Their villages were practical, their civic-religious buildings were practical, and their economic choices were practical. They carefully observed and imitated nature and her creatures to find the proper medicines and effective ways to apply them.

The ancient Cherokees were as human, as culpable, and as fallible as the rest of mankind. They had the same shortcomings and sometimes performed badly — and those instances are noted in the proper places in the book. But for the moment, we can say that had we met a Cherokee in some ancient place, she or he would exhibit dignity, serenity, competence, a sense of place and destiny, and a firm grip on life. Bearing and costume would testify to this. The attitude would be open, and the dark eyes would be sharp and observant as they looked constantly for opportunities that might help the Cherokees shape a better world.

1. Adair, *History of the American Indians,* pp. 245-246.
2. Ibid., pp. 246-247.
3. Ibid., pp. 245-248.
4. Payne Papers, interviews with Nutsawi and Candy, Vol. 4, pp. 584-593.
5. Adair, p. 121.
6. Mooney, *Sacred Formulas of the Cherokees,* pp. 319-340.
7. Mooney, *Myths of the Cherokee,* p. 49; see also Mooney, *Sacred Formulas of the Cherokees.*
8. Ibid., pp. 48-49.
9. Ibid., p. 48.
10. Payne Papers, interviews with Nutwasi and Candy, Vol. 4, pp. 584-583.
11. Adair, pp. 246-247.
12. Payne Papers, pp. 584-593.
13. Wahnenauhi, *Historical Sketches of the Cherokee,* pp. 185-186.
14. Mooney, p.391.
15. Ibid., pp. 384-395.
16. Wahnenauhi, p. 187.
17. Payne Papers, interview with Nutsawi, Vol. 4, p. 593.
18. Wahnenauhi, pp. 185-187.
19. Mooney, pp. 330-331.
20. Ibid., p. 333.
21. Ibid., pp. 333-334. See also Kilpatrick and Kilpatrick, *Eastern Cherokee Folktales,* for delightful stories of Little People, the origin of fire, death, etc.
22. Mooney, p. 333.
23. Ibid., p. 334.
24. Ibid., p. 335.
25. Ibid., pp. 384-385.
26. Ibid., p. 385; see also Kilpatrick, *The Wahnenauhi Manuscript: Historical Sketches of the Cherokees,* pp. 189-190.
27. Payne Papers, interview with Nutsawi, Vol. 3, p. 54.
28. Ibid., p. 54.
29. Ibid., pp. 54-55.
30. Payne Papers, interview with Nutsawi and T. Candy, Vol. 3, pp. 51-53.
31. Ibid., interview with Mrs. Chism, Vol. 3, pp. 85-86.
32. Ibid., interview with Yv wi yo ka, Vol. 3, pp. 86-88.
33. Mooney, *Sacred Formulas of the Cherokees.*
34. Ibid., and Mooney and Olbrechts, *The Swimmer Manuscript.*
35. Mooney, *Sacred Formulas of the Cherokees.*

CHAPTER SIX

Ancient Religious Beliefs

Writing in 1701, William Bartram said the Cherokees were by no means idolaters, unless their puffing tobacco smoke toward the sun and rejoicing at the appearance of each new moon might be so interpreted. So far from idolatry were they that they had no religious images among them, or any idolatrous religious rite or ceremony that he could observe. Instead, they adored the Great Spirit, whom they described as the giver and taker away of the breath of life, with the most profound and respectful homage.[1]

In 1736, James Adair confirmed Bartram's view, saying that although it was well known that the ancient heathens worshiped a plurality of gods which they created to satisfy their own beliefs, the Cherokees did none of this and were devoted to the great, beneficent, supreme, holy spirit of fire, who resided above the clouds and on the earth with purified people. He was, with them, the sole author of warmth, light, and all animal and vegetable life. They did not pay the least perceivable adoration to any images, dead persons, celestial luminaries, evil spirits, or any created being whatsoever. They practiced none of the gestures employed by the pagans in their religious rites, and kissed no idols. Their form of religious worship was more like the Mosaic institution than it was like that of the pagans, which

The principal assistant to the *Uku* prays to the Above Beings through the smoke of the sacred fire.

Adair felt would not be so if the majority of the old natives was of heathenish descent, since all pagans would fight to the death to retain their superstitious worship — even when it had lost all its substance. But the Cherokees did not believe the sun was any bigger than it appeared to the naked eye, and they never prostrated themselves or bowed their bodies to each other in salute or homage, except when they were making or renewing peace with strangers who came in the name of *Yah* — but they always bowed in their religious dances.[2]

In 1760, Timberlake and other early authorities supported Adair's claims regarding the worship of one supreme God and the absence of idolatry among the Cherokees. In 1835, the aged Cherokees whose primary sources took them well back into the 1600s said that as far back as their history could be traced, the nation had been divided into at least two sects regarding their beliefs about divine beings.[3] The first sect was made up of the majority of the people. Its adherents said that more than two beings came down from above and formed the world. They then created the sun and moon and appointed them lords of all of lower creation. After this, the beings returned to their own place above, known only to themselves, where they remained in entire rest, paying no attention to this world. The sun then completed the work of creation, formed the first man and woman, caused the trees, plants, fruits, and vegetables to grow, and continued to order, watch over, and preserve everything on earth. This first sect worshiped the sun and moon and many of the stars. Its adherents also paid divine homage to many birds, beasts, and creeping things, and they worshiped the fire. The other sect embraced the minority, and said there existed above three beings who were always together and of the same mind. The names of these beings were: first, *U ha lo te qa*, "Head of all power," or literally "Great beyond expression"; second, *A ta nv ti*, "United," or rather "The place of uniting" where persons agreed to meet and form a perpetual friendship; third, *U sqa hu la*, the meaning of which could not, in 1835, any longer be learned, but it had something to do with "mind" or "affection." These three, it was said, were always one in sentiment and action and would always continue to be the same. They created all things, were acquainted with all, were present everywhere, and governed all things. When these called any person to come to them, that person must die in the way the beings thought best. These three sat on three white seats above, and all prayers were directed to them. They had messengers, or angels, who came to this world and attended to the affairs of men. The difference between this sect and the former consisted only in the objects of worship and not in outward form or ceremonies. The latter were the same and employed no images. Both agreed that in the beginning all creatures and objects were innocent and harmless, that even snakes had no poison, and that such weeds as became harmful to health were at first created harmless.[4]

Writing in 1890, Mooney adamantly declared that the religion of the Cherokees, like that of most North American tribes, was zootheism or animal worship. Their pantheon included gods in the heaven above, on the earth beneath, and in the water under the earth, but of these, the animal gods constituted by far the most numerous class, although the elemental gods (fire, water, and sun) were more important. Missionaries, he said, "have naturally, but incorrectly, assumed this apportioner (sun) of all things to be the suppositional 'Great Spirit' of the Cherokees, and hence the word is used in the Bible translation as synonymous with God."[5]

Just as adamantly, Wahnenauhi stated, "The Cherokees believed in one God whom they called *Oo n hlah nau hi*, meaning 'Maker of all things,' and *Cah luh luh ti a hi*, 'The One who lives above.' They acknowledged him as their friend and believed that he made everything and possessed unlimited power." In commenting on this statement, Kilpatrick said, "Mooney and Olbrechts (1932, pp. 20-21) theorize that this term for the Supreme Being is a synonym for the sun . . . I discover in Cherokee theology little to support this concept."[6]

Wahnenauhi also said the Cherokees "believed in an Evil Spirit, called in their language, *Skee nah*, and to his malicious influence they attributed all trouble, calamity, and sickness." Kilpatrick responded to this: "There is no universal evil spirit,

Stone bowls for ceremonial pipes: *top and middle,* Emory University Museum; *bottom,* Georgia State Museum.

corresponding to Satan, in Cherokee theology. Properly *Skee nah* is any sort of spirit, but it is usually considered to be a malevolent one. Wahnenauhi derived her connotation from the Cherokee New Testament, in which the term is employed for a devil, or the Devil."[7]

No veil hangs heavier over the ancient Cherokees than that clouding their earliest beliefs regarding the Creator and the origins of their religious customs. In Chapter One, I explained that although the creation and origin material collected by Payne was the most complete available and made very interesting reading, it also included such extensive near duplications of the first five books of the Bible as to cause readers to conclude that early in the historic period the Cherokees began to weave the newly learned biblical material into their origin legends. Thus, what Payne collected in 1835 appears, despite his claims regarding the isolation of his sources from one another, to be a composite, neatly woven and chronological story, that includes both biblical and uniquely Cherokee material.

Nevertheless, of particular value in the study of the ancient culture are those portions of the stories that bear only slight, or in some instances no, resemblance whatsoever to the biblical account, and which set forth the foundations upon which the pillars of Cherokee religion were constructed. These are fundamental to our proper understanding of the culture and to our recognition that what was found by white traders in the early historic period represented beliefs and practices that had been in place for some time.

What follows is an extraction from Payne's creation and origin summary of those things that marked the Cherokee culture at its apex, so that when customs such as the office of the *Uku*, the tending of the sacred fire, and the use of the national heptagon are encountered in the book, it will be remembered that their foundations, or roots, lie in the distant past, and that accordingly the Cherokees attributed their existence to the Creator, or creators, themselves. In the Cherokee mind, these foundations and the pillars built upon them were the express creations of God and not of men, and they were reserved as such. I record them here in essentially my own words, but in the order in which they were set forth in Payne's full creation and origin account.[8]

How dependable is the information gathered by Payne? In recording the historical and moral traditions he received from "professors of the early and orthodox Cherokee religion," he felt he should emphatically declare that the dozen or more highly respected ancients of the Cherokees from whom the fragments were obtained gave them at different times and at different places. No one of the informants knew what had been told by another or had even the same source. And not one of the informants had the slightest notion of his information ever having been extracted from a connected series of records, either oral or written.[9]

According to Payne's informants, the Chief Supreme Being believed in by the Cherokees of the eighteenth century was the same "Mysterious Being" whom the more ancient Cherokees had said was both God and king, appearing sometimes on earth as a man. Except for someone specially consecrated for the purpose, this being's name was to be spoken only on an appointed holy day. It was *Ye ho waah*, and he gave a certain hymn to the Cherokees that could only be sung by selected persons on "occasions of the greatest solemnty." The hymn played a special role in the exciting Cementation Festival, which is described in the next chapter.

The great *Ye ho waah* himself taught the hymn to the first Cherokee priests. The words he used were still being repeated in 1835, but they were no longer understood. They were described as being part of "the old language." Many of the Cherokees living in 1835 remembered the last of the white organization speakers who spoke that revered language and described these speakers as being "most devoutly wedded to the ancient usages." The few old-language words that were still employed in the nineteenth century were unintelligible, and most of them were included in what was called the *Yo wa* hymn. Its chanter and his attendants had to be expressly chosen by the *Uku*, and all of them, before performing for the first time, had to undergo a rigorous testing that included prolonged abstinence from food and sex and the fulfilling of special observances of prayer, purification, and vigils.

Man, Mortality, and Mounds for Civic-religious Buildings

In the beginning, the Three Beings Above employed seven days in the work of creation. The world was created at the first appearance of the autumnal new moon, when the fruits were ripe. Hence, that moon began the lunar year and was called the Great Moon. From this new moon, time was reckoned for all of the feasts of new moons. Man was made of red earth. The first man was red. The Creator, having made man of red earth, blew into his mouth, and that breath became a soul. Some of the ancients used to say that infants were born without

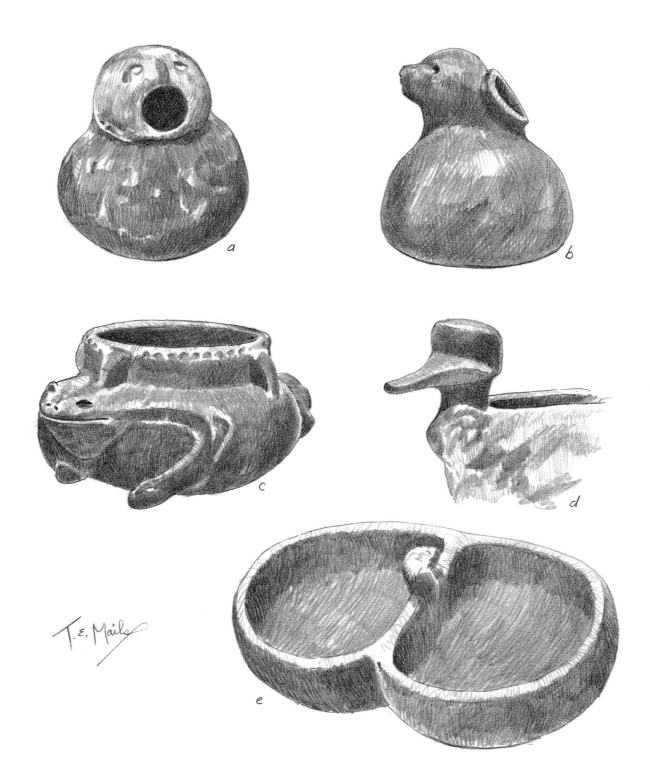

Top and middle, effigy pots: **a.** Museum of the Cherokee Indian. **b.** Georgia State Museum. **c.** Georgia State Museum. **d.** duck effigy bowl, Museum of the Cherokee Indian. **e.** double wedding bowl, Museum of the Cherokee Indian.

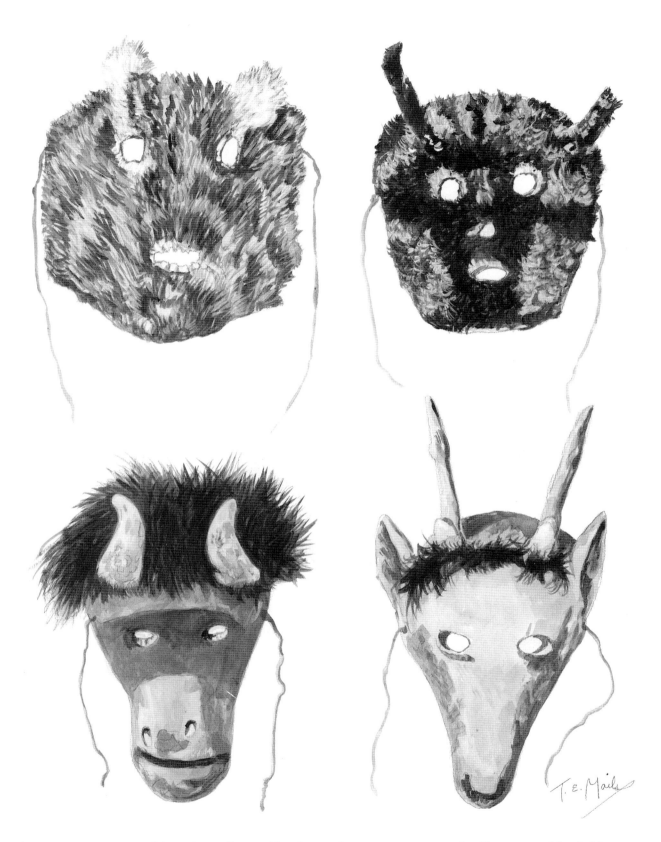

Masks for decoying: *Top left,* used in stalking wild turkeys and in Booger Dance, made of brown woodchuck skin, Denver Art Museum. *Top right,* wildcat, University Museum, University of Pennsylvania. *Lower left,* black buffalo-hunting mask, Museum of the American Indian, Heye Foundation. Lower right, wooden deer-hunting mask decorated with brown animal hair, Denver Art Museum.

Ancient Religious Beliefs   147

souls and that the first air which entered their beings became living souls. The Creator perceived man to be lonesome. Therefore, he took one of the man's ribs and made a woman. The first woman, like the first man, was red. Therefore, the red people were the real people, as their name *Yv wi ya* indicated.

At first, serpents were not poisonous, and no roots were poisonous. Man would have lived forever, but the sun, passing over, saw that the earth was not large enough to support forever all who would be born. So poison was inserted in the tooth of the snake, in the root of the wild parsnip, and elsewhere, and one of the first family was soon bitten by a snake and died. All possible efforts were made to restore him to life, but in vain. Being overcome in this first instance, the whole race was doomed, not only to the death of the body, but to eternal misery.

Not long after the creation, *Ya ho waah* ordered men to build high mounds on which to erect structures for worship, where they might offer sacrifices, assemble for religious instruction, and perform their dances. He commanded them not to despise the lame, the blind, and the deformed or to laugh at them, but to be kind to them and especially to strangers. If they owned any kind of creatures, they must be kind to them and treat them well.

The *Uku* and Eternal Punishment

In obedience to *Ye ho waah*, on certain days the Cherokees assembled for worship at the structures they erected. They met early in the morning. When the people were all seated and silent, the priest commenced his talk. He was called *U ku wi u hi*. No one dared make the least noise while he was talking. By noon he was very tired, yet he continued until near sunset. In his talk, he commanded that *Ye ho waah* must be obeyed in every respect, telling the people they must do all that *Ye ho waah* had directed and never disobey in any secret place, thinking themselves alone, for *Ye ho waah* always saw them and was with them. The people were never to indulge in idle or vain conversation, or call anyone wicked names. They were urged to abstain from all lewdness and from polygamy. Children were ex-horted to be industrious and to mind their parents.

The priest supported his exhortations by holding up to the people prospects of eternal life, assuring them that if they were obedient, they would, when they died, go to *Ye ho waah* and dwell forever with him, where it would be always light — like a pleasant, exhilarating day. But should they be disobedient, they would be miserable eternally in a lake of fire. Just as they got to that place, a terrifying gulch would appear before them, across which they would see a small pole, with a black dog at each end. Being pulled forward by some unseen power, they would proceed to the middle of the pole, and then the dogs would turn it and plunge them into the gulch, at whose bottom was the lake of fire. Some few, however, might be permitted to cross the gulch on the pole, but on arriving at the other side, they would be put into a house of fire, transfixed with large iron spikes, and thus tortured forever. At death, the righteous and the wicked would be immediately separated and the wicked driven forward to the gulch in a different path from the righteous.

Just before sunset, the priest offered sacrifice. The altar he used for this was made of flat stones and was about two-and-a-half feet high. The sacrifice was a piece of meat with a powder of old tobacco sprinkled over it. The sacred fire built on the altar was not an ordinary one but was made as follows: The priest put a hearth stick on top of the altar with a round shallow hole in its upper side. Into this hole he put some of the weed called goldenrod. He then took a slender stick that was two or three feet long, the rounded lower end of which exactly filled the hole in the hearth. Holding this stick upright between the palms of his hands, he twirled it swiftly around in the hearth until the goldenrod caught fire. The woods kindled with the burning goldenrod and used for sacrifice were blackjack and sycamore, and they had to be free from worms and rot.

Besides preaching and offering sacrifice, the ancient Cherokee priests also foretold future events.

The Priestly Office and Devoted Sons

The greatest priest the Cherokees ever had was named *Hasi*, which Payne believed was another name for Moses. He told the people what had gone on from the beginning of the world and what the future would be. He gave them an account of the creation, events before the flood, the flood, the building like a tower, Abraham, the wandering in the wilderness, and so forth. He also gave the people directions as to what to do in all circumstances. He appointed their feasts and all of their ceremonies. He told them how to consecrate their priests, make their Great High Priest, and so on, and ordered them to obey his instructions from generation to generation. He commanded perfect obedience to their Father above and warned them of the misery that would follow disobedience. He said that when he died, another priest would take his place and this would continue down through time so there would always be priests. He said that these priests would give the people of their generation the same kind of instructions and direction he had given. Out of this, the Cherokees evolved their system of consigning "devoted sons" to the priestly office.

There was a special manner in which boys were selected and educated for the priesthood among the Cherokees, and part of this required the use of the divining crystal.

In instances when a birth was expected in a family in which the priesthood was hereditary and it had been predetermined by parents that their expected child, if male, would be devoted to some sacred office, a priest was forewarned and was on hand to receive the infant when it arrived. If indeed the child was a son, the priest administered to him a consecrating drink. Since the child was unable to fast, the parents were required to fast in his place. For seven days they were required to chew nothing but a certain root, only once each day a little after sunset.

Devoted sons were raised with particular caution and care. During the mother's menstrual periods, when she was considered unclean and especially was not permitted to come into contact with holy things, she protected her infant son's purity by delivering him either to his grandmother or some aged matron. Boys promised to the priesthood were not permitted to wander about like other children. They could not sit or eat at a neighbor's house lest

they touch anything that an unclean female had touched.

Even though a devoted son was vigilantly supervised by his parents and relatives, the priest who was present at his birth always watched over him, and monitored him carefully as he grew older. Countless days of fasting and nights of watchfulness impressed upon the young pupil the solemn responsibilities of the career to which he was promised, and numerous lessons were taught about the various kinds of food that certain orders of the sacred brotherhood must abstain from. For example, a boy being prepared to become the chief speaker for war must never taste frogs or the tongue or breast of any animal.

But the formal training of a devoted son really did not begin until he had reached the age of nine or ten. At this point the priest to whom he was entrusted would at daybreak lead him up to a mountaintop, give him a purifying drink, and instruct him to "Plant his eyes upon the spot whence the sun was to rise, so as to catch the first beams of that luminary, from which he was not to withdraw his gaze until the light died away in the west." If during this period he did not once avert his eyes from the sun, he would be forever qualified to fulfill his duties both day and night, but if even once he looked away, everything he had worked toward would be lost. Payne does not explain how damage to the boy's eyes was averted.

During this first day's probationary period and throughout the following night, the priest remained with his pupil, and both of them fasted, with the night being spent in walking back and forth and the imparting of knowledge about high and holy themes.

At the time of the following moon, the priest took the boy to an even more secret part of the mountain where no female eye could penetrate and there taught him the mysteries of the divining crystal — how and where it was to be used and what must be said and done during those ceremonies in which it was consulted. This session lasted for six days, together with the first day making a total of seven days. Fasting was continued. Nothing was eaten for the first two days and first night. A little after sunset

"Devoted son" being trained for the priesthood in mountain retreat.

on the evening of the second day, the priest and the boy chewed on a certain kind of root. Then they fasted until after sunset the next day, when they again chewed the root, and they continued this procedure until the seventh day and night, when both the fast and the watchfulness were ended.

On the morning of the eighth day, the priest took out his divining crystal and used it to see how long the boy would serve in the capacity for which he was destined. Setting the crystal where it would catch the first rays of sunlight, the priest inquired of it whether the boy was to live to an old age. If so, an aged man with gray hair and a white beard would appear in the crystal. If not, the man seen would have black hair and a black beard. Once this message was received, the priest took the boy to a nearby creek and directed him to stand in the water with his face turned toward the east. While the boy did this, the priest took a similar position on the bank and prayed. He then ordered the boy to entirely immerse himself seven times in the water, with his face turned alternately to the east and to the west. When the boy finished, the priest led him to a ritual house and offered sacrifice for him. To do this, the priest cleared a space on the ground and lighted a holy fire. He tossed into the fire the tip of a deer's tongue and a little mush. If the boy wished to be a war priest and a piece or two of the meat popped toward the boy, it indicated that he would be slain by enemies. But if the pieces flew away from the boy, he would have a long and successful career. If the boy wished to be a White priest, to fill the office of a boiler of the sacred herbs, or to serve in any of the other of the sacred orders, the appearances of the sacrifice and the inferences from them would differ accordingly.

The greatest number of youths a priest might have in his charge was seven. They would on occasion visit their holy guide, and he would pass a day and night with them in watching, fasting, and teaching. When at last the priest knew he was near death, he would gather his pupils around him and repeat his instructions, selecting one of them to be his successor, and as his final act he passed on to this youth his divining crystal. The pupil thus honored sometimes took the crystal immediately, but more often waited until his mentor had passed on and been buried.

It was only to such persons as those just described that the secret mysteries were disclosed by the ancient Cherokee priests. To make them known to the uninstructed would assure death either suddenly or not long to be avoided, both to the betrayer and the listener. Hence it was with extreme difficulty that any information upon the subject could be lured from the old priests, even in 1835, and especially if the information was being sought for any Caucasian person, all of whom were believed to feel a contempt for the ancient faith — which the Cherokees could not abide. This is why Payne and Butrick found it impossible to gather more nearly complete details and to give an account of the deeper mysteries and forms of prayer and incantation taught by the priests to their pupils.[10]

The Sacred Ark

While the Cherokees were migrating in earliest times, *Hasi* told them to make an ark of the covenant in which to carry the sacred fire and other holy things. This ark would represent the everlasting bond between the Creator and the Cherokees, and the army that carried the ark before it when it went to war would be invincible.

The Divining Crystals

Even Cherokees who knew nothing about *Hasi* called the divining crystal often referred to in these pages *U li sa tu*, or "light." Others called it *Hasi catouvhi*, "the word of *Hasi*," or *Hasi uti sw ta*, "Hasi directed them," indicating that the crystal was introduced and used by the direction of *Hasi*. In ancient times too, when any Cherokee was particularly distinguished for his singing ability, the old men would say, "He is *Hasi's* singer," or, "He sings like *Hasi*," or, "He sings the song of *Hasi*."

Throughout the years that followed, the divining crystal formed an essential part of the paraphernalia of the ancient Cherokee priest. Though it was not always part of his dress, it was essential to his vocation.

The Cherokee name used for the divining

crystal in 1835 was *Ooh lung sah tah*, with the first syllable pronounced like *ho* in the word "who," and meaning "Light that pierces through," as through a glass. Light, stated simply, was *I ka ka ti*, but *Ooh lung sah tah* was more significant, implying both a light piercing through what it fell upon and a light conveying, through the substance of which the object was composed, instruction to the observer.

So sacred was the divining crystal that it was certain death for anyone to touch one who had not been sanctified and initiated for the purpose. The regular priest would sometimes wear his crystal suspended on his breast by a neck thong, but always hidden from public view by his clothing. Exceptions were the *Uku* at the Propitiation festival and the Great War Chief. Everyone else who carried divining crystals kept to themselves even the knowledge of the places where they were worn or carried, and those crystals that were not being carried about were either kept as treasures in a holy box called an ark, or carefully wrapped in seven deerskins.

There were five sizes of divining crystals, each hexagonal and composed of crystalline quartz. Some informants said that in the earlier times the stones were diamonds. Payne did not learn how the crystals received their power. His informants only knew that each priest possessed one and that all of the sizes were consulted with equal confidence and held in equal honor.

The largest of the crystals was used for divining, or seeking to learn, the outcome of war, and the method of employing it was described in Chapter Four. The crystals used by the White priests were smaller than the war crystals, and there were four of those that varied in size according to their use. The largest was employed to ascertain whether sickness would come to an individual, a family, or a town. A sacrifice was offered by the priest, and in one of three manners the crystal was set to catch the first rays of the morning sun — either on top of seven folded deerskins, on top of a post covered with fawn skin, or in a crevice of a house. If the omen was favorable, a bright and unclouded blaze of light would appear in the stone. But if the omen was unfavorable, the crystal would look blue and smoky, and as many

persons would die as appeared lying down on its right side.

This same size crystal was, on certain occasions, consulted for the same purpose by large bodies of people. One of these instances was the great, or first autumnal, moon, when the Cherokees began their lunar year. Before sunrise on the appointed day, the priests of each town would gather all of the men, women, and children into the town council house and seat them in rows with their faces turned toward the east. Then he would open a crack in the east wall and set his divining crystal there to catch the first rays of the rising sun. He backed up until he was four feet from the crystal, and with his eyes riveted upon it and his face toward the sun, he offered a prayer. As he prayed, the crystal shone brighter and brighter, until a brightness as dazzling as that from a mirror with the glare of midday full upon it reflected from it to the ceiling, where the light moved back and forth. The light descended lower and lower until at last it would glance toward the seated people. Over those who were to die before the return of another new moon, the light would pass without the least illumination of their persons. Credible witnesses of this ritual declared positively that they had known instances in which those Cherokees the light failed to rest on as it passed among them all died within three months. During this ceremony, the priest never touched the crystal. He simply stood where he was and repeated his prayers.

The next smaller crystal was used for recovering lost or stolen objects. The priest set the crystal in the sun and prayed for information. Where a theft had occurred, he would see the thief and the stolen object in the crystal.

The hunting crystal was smaller still. After an appropriate prayer and adjusting the crystal to catch the morning sunlight, if a buck deer was going to be killed, it would be seen in the stone; if a doe, a tinge of blood would appear; but if nothing would be killed, nothing would be seen. A crystal used during the chase would be set on a wooden stool placed at a riverbank and covered with seven folded deerskins. Success was indicated when the cover was raised and a multitude of deer horns could be seen in the crystal, and failure was indicated when there appeared no more than a few or none.

The smallest divining crystal was used to discern how long a person would live. If the inquirer was to attain old age, a figure with gray hair and a long white beard would appear in the crystal.

A way of interpreting a crystal that differed from all of the others was used by men who were jealous of their wives and suspected an affair was in progress. But a priest who had this kind of crystal was seldom consulted until the men had tried for themselves a different mode of conjuring for information, for they were reluctant to disclose jealousy, even to a priest. The different, or private, means consisted of the following: The man took two white beads and blackened one of them, making the white bead a symbol of innocence and the black bead, guilt. He placed the white bead between the thumb and forefinger of his right hand and the black bead between the thumb and forefinger of his left hand. Both hands were then placed on the ground, and as he lifted his hands until they were raised as high as possible above his head, he asked, using actual names, "Has (such a man) of (such) a clan dishonored me?" So long as both beads did not move, he continued the questioning from man to man and clan to clan, until all of the suspects in the seven clans were exhausted. But if the black bead moved when he mentioned any man's name and clan, the husband took it as an indication that his wife was guilty, and thus watched her until he found proof.

Sometimes though, it was necessary for the jealous husband to go directly to a priest. In such instances, the priest would set out his crystal and pray for information. If the wife and another man were innocent, the appearance of the crystal did not change. But if there was guilt, those having the affair appeared in the crystal. The priest would then pick up a handful of flies he had killed for the purpose, and solemnly pronounce the evil that would descend upon the wife. He declared that if when he opened his hand one of the flies came to life again, it would instantly fly to her, settle on her body, and burrow its way into her; with bitter tortures she would in seven days feel it gnawing its way into her heart and she

would die. Such women invariably died on the seventh day. Whether or not the fly received any assistance from the husband or the priest was not reported.

So dearly did each priest prize his crystal that when he knew he was going to die, if he had no favorite disciple to whom he wished to bequeath it, he would go alone to the woods. As soon as he discovered a tree in which a woodpecker had picked an opening, he would bury the crystal there and stop up the hole with clay and bark in such a way as to render its discovery impossible. He did this because if the stone was found lying about after his death with no properly authorized person commissioned to take charge of it, it would, without exception, mean the death of every person in the priest's family.[11]

Conduct and Morals

Long ago the Cherokees had a white post set up with a white skin, or cloth, fastened to the top. This post was to remind them to keep their hearts as white as the white skin and to lead their thoughts back to the commandments given to their fathers, which were written on something white. Those laws forbade all acts of sin. Before the post was lost, the people behaved better than they did afterward. They did not lie or talk foolishly. The old people used to tell the boys it would be bad to grow up in sin, for they would go to a place of misery and punishment. But if they did right, they would go to a good place.

The National Heptagon and the Town Council House

While *Hasi* was with *Ye ho waah* on the mountaintop, he was commanded to instruct the people to build a certain building and to carry it with them on all of their journeys. This building had either four or seven posts. In bad weather it was covered with a kind of cloth made of deer hair and turkey feathers. It was taken down when they traveled and was set up when they encamped. Four white seats for the priests were connected with this building. On the upright boards forming the back of the seats were four pieces of carved wood with a half-moon and other designs on each.

Uncleanness

Long ago, the Cherokees were afflicted with some terrible diseases. One of them differed from smallpox, yet like it, occasioned dreadful sores in the flesh. When anyone in a family was taken with this disorder, the diseased person was made to live alone, being removed to a hut or tent that was set up some distance from any other habitation. The priest was sent to cleanse the family dwelling vacated by the diseased, as if some person had died in it. After this, should anyone touch the diseased, he would be as unclean as if he had touched a dead body.

Clan Distinctions

When the Cherokees traveled to a new country, each clan kept distinct, not intermingling with the other clans. The clans were distinguished by having feathers of different colors fastened to the rims of their ears. Each clan was composed of the descendants of one family and, being of the same blood, its members were forbidden to intermarry. Each clan encamped by itself. This rule of keeping distinct was continued in later times. The Cherokees had seven-sided council houses, with each clan occupying seats in its own side. The men sat on one end of the seats, and the women on the other. Each clan was in all respects considered to be one family.

The Standards of the *Uku* and War Chief

There was one standard under the special direction of the priests. This was a long pole with the bark taken off and the wood painted white. An eagle tail was tied to the top. The standard was raised by the direction of the *Uku*, and when they marched it was carried by two men. The priests called it *U ni ky wi u hi*. There was another standard under the direction of the Great War Chief, *A ska yv gv stu eqa*. This standard was painted red and had a red cloth fastened to its top. It was raised only to call the people to war. When a warrior saw it, he uttered the war whoop and ran to it. The war dance took place around this standard.

Healing and the Causes of Disease

Of two great kings, or high priests, the greatest

of whom lived before the flood, the second great king lived after his red people made their journey through the wilderness. He taught them many things about the virtues of all kinds of roots and herbs, trees, shrubs, and so forth, and how to administer these as medicines. He also taught them all of the charms and verses which they sang when administering the medicines. In the second king's day, the Indians generally were wise. He also formed the two kinds of little spirits called *A hi ta we hi*. One kind was evil and used witchcraft to make people crazy and to kill them. The other kind was good. They would cure victims who had been poisoned, and they taught priests how to obtain their assistance when someone was bewitched. They also used the ends of their forefingers to rub people who had muscle pains, and they had a root called "black" with which they could massage away cramps. For dizziness, the little spirits soaked a root called *ti li wo tv he ski* in water, then blew the liquid on the human patient's head. In later times, the good little spirits taught those techniques to the priests and, when called upon, would lend assistance.

Migration Myths

At first there were twelve tribes of Indians. But after awhile one of the tribes violated the law of *Ye ho waah* by intermarrying. Therefore, he reduced the number of tribes to seven and caused them to scatter. All of them traveled a great distance and came to a great water. After building rafts and crossing it, the different tribes went north, west, and south. Those who went to the north settled in two towns, one called *Ka no wo gi* and the other called *Nv ta gi*. Together, they were accepted as the grandfathers of all of the Indians, and their tribal name was *A quv ni kv*.

The Loss and Regaining of the Sacred Fire

The sacred fire the Cherokees received from *Ye ho waah* was not brought with them when they came to this country, but priests were sent back to retrieve it. It was kept burning until about 1735, a hundred years before Payne gathered his information. It was then in the council house at *Tu gu la*. In a battle with whites, the council house was destroyed. Some people think the fire was extinguished — others believe it is still burning deep in the ground.

The End Time

The Raven, an old Cherokee known to be more than 100 years old in Payne's time, said that when he was a small boy, he used to hear the old men predict the destruction of the world after four generations. The Supreme Being would cause a storm to arise out of the east which would rain pitch until everything was covered with it. Showers of fire would follow, everything would be set ablaze, and the whole world would be consumed.

Revisions and Additions

Payne's informants carefully distinguished between the most ancient religious beliefs of their people and the additions to, or revisions of, them over the passing years, stressing at the same time that the revisions and additions were quite ancient and thus carried as much weight as the original pillars. None of these newer things included slippages into idolatry, and in no instance were the ancient precepts abandoned in favor of the newer revelations.[12]

Revision of the Mortality Legend

A number of beings were engaged in creating all things. The sun was made first. The intention of the Creator was to have people live always, but the sun, after he had passed over the earth, told the Creator there was not land enough, and that rather than living forever, the people had better die. But the Creator was not convinced. At length, the daughter of the sun, being with the people, was bitten by a snake and died. The sun on his next return to earth asked where she was and was told that she was dead. He was willing at that point that people might live on earth forever, but told them to take a box containing her spirit to where her dead body was and not to open the box until they arrived there. But temptation overcame them and, just before they reached the body, they opened the box and peeked in to see the spirit. When they did this the spirit escaped, and the fate of the daughter became the fate

of mankind — they would not live on earth forever and must die.

Second Revision of the Mortality Story

A number of beings, more than two and probably three, came down and made the world. They then attempted to make a man and woman of two rocks. They fashioned them, but while attempting to make them come alive, another being came and spoiled their work, so that they could not succeed. The three beings then made man and woman of red clay, and because they were made of clay, they were mortal as clay is. Had they been made of rock they would have lived forever.

Other Cherokees ascribed their mortality to another cause. Soon after the creation, one of the family was bitten by a serpent and died. All possible means were used to bring him back to life, but in vain. Being overcome in this first instance, the entire race was doomed to follow, not only to death, but to eternal misery. These beings, having created earth, man, and woman, then made the sun and the moon and constituted them gods with entire control and management of everything made up to that time. It was their responsibility to proceed in this work until creation was complete. At this point the beings, having employed seven days in their work, returned to their places in the heavens and paid no further attention to the earth they had created. Of their exact place above, no one had any knowledge but themselves.

Origin of the Sun and the Moon

The Supreme Creators, having in seven days created the sun and moon and given form to the earth, returned to their own abode on high, leaving the sun and moon to finish and to rule the world, about which the beings gave themselves no further concern. Hence, whenever the believers offered a prayer to their Creator, they meant by the word, "Creator" either the sun or moon. As to which of these two was supreme, there appeared to be a wide difference of opinion. In some of their ancient prayers, the Cherokees spoke of the sun as a male and the moon as female. In other prayers they

a. effigy figure used in rituals, original located at the Etowah mounds near Cartersville, Georgia. Reproduction in Georgia State Museum. b. effigy bottle, Museum of the Cherokee Indian. c. bird stones said to be worn by healers as a badge of office, made by Woodland Indians who were ancient ancestors of the Algonquian tribes, Museum of the Cherokee Indian. d. hematite plummets with bas-relief designs, either used as weights or worn as chest ornaments, Spiro Mound, Oklahoma, but similar to Cherokee items. e. stone ear spools with carved designs, Spiro Mound, Oklahoma, but similar to Cherokee items.

invoked the sun as the female and the moon as male, because the moon was vigilant like a hunter and traveled at night.

A prayer to the moon as Creator was used in conjuring against drought, wherein the moon was asked to throw certain beads around the face and neck of his wife, the sun, and thus to darken her face so that clouds might form and come to the towns from the mountains.

In one of the most ancient prayers, to be repeated early in the morning when going to the water, the sun as Creator was implored to grant the petitioner a long and blissful life here in his only place of happiness. In many instances, a second request was for the sun to take the petitioner's spirit, bear it with him until he had ascended to the meridian at noon, and then restore it to him. The same prayer, with the exception of the last clause, was repeated at night.

The expression, *"A ke yv ku gv, Squa ne lv nv hi,"* "Sun my Creator," was a common one in the ancient prayers, and men used it to gain assistance in obtaining the love of a desired female. The sun became in time the superior being in Cherokee devotions. It was to him, or her, they first appealed to give efficacy to the roots and herbs they sought for medicine to use in healing. If, however, these plants failed to effect the cure, the moon and not the sun was believed to have caused the illness, and so they turned for help and comfort to the moon. At the appearance of each new moon, the Cherokees paid special homage to him, entreating him to take good care of them during his term of rule.

There were many inferior deities besides the sun and moon, but the sun and moon were considered as supreme over the lower creation. All that was made by them was subject to their direction and employed in their service, wherein each created thing was assigned special duties.

Origin of Fire as Intercessor

Fire was the most active and efficient agent appointed by the sun and moon for the benefit of mankind. When any special favor was needed, it was made known to the fire, and accompanied by an offering of deer meat and tobacco. The fire was considered the intermediary being nearest to the sun and received the same sort of homage from the Cherokees. This homage was extended to smoke, which was named "fire's messenger," and believed to be always ready to convey petitions to the Above Beings. A child was waved over the sacred fire and smoke shortly after birth. Children would be brought before fire, and its guardian powers were entreated for them. Hunters waved their moccasins and leggings over fire to secure protection from snakes. For the same protective reason, it was a custom in very remote times to put newly hatched chickens into a kind of open basket and wave them over fire.

Some old Cherokees believed that fire descended directly from above. Others spoke of it as an active, intelligent being in the form of a man who dwelt in distant regions beyond wide waters, whence their ancestors came. Some Cherokees came to believe that a portion of fire was brought to North America by their ancestors and thereafter was sacredly guarded. Others believed that, after crossing the wide waters while they migrated, the Cherokees sent back for it to the man of fire, from whom a little was carried back by a spider, wrapped in her web. After this, the fire was kept in their original national heptagon, or rather, in a hole or cave dug under it. But this building was captured by enemies and destroyed, after which some Cherokees thought the fire was lost, and others thought it only sank deeper in the ground to avoid unhallowed eyes and still exists there. After fire's disappearance, new fire was always made at particular times of the year and with various ceremonies associated with the national festivals.

Origin of the Four Cardinal Directions

Older Cherokees said the Creator — supposed in this case to mean a *Ye ho waah* who supervised the affairs of the universe and whose abode was the center of the sky immediately overhead — in the beginning directed certain lines from a center place to points upon the earth that white men called "north, south, east, and west." To each of these

points the Creator sent newly created beings of
different colors: in the north was placed the blue
man; in the west, the area called, "the region of the
setting sun," the black man was placed and named
Ewe kah waisk hee, "the fearless"; to the south was
sent the white man, the man of purity and peace; but
the first and most important of all was the red man,
and he was placed in the east and signified the sun.

These four lines, or directions, were in their
spirit form existing on high as the vice-regents, or
agents, of the Supreme Beings and the mediators
between them and creation, of which the sun, or "red
man," was the first created. To these four beings
power was given over the world. To each of them,
Cherokee supplications were to be addressed in a
regular succession. Whatever was addressed to the
black man would forthwith be attended to, and for
all that related to goodness, the white man was to be
invoked. But over the four directions the Creator
reigned supreme, enthroned above in the center of
the place where those four lines met. His eye at once
beheld them and mankind. He knew everything that
anyone in this world could do or think, and he knew
what was best for each created thing. To him, after
first invoking in order the men of the east, the north,
the west, and the south, must be offered the final
and most fervent of mankind's prayers.

What follows is a typical prayer, drawn forth
with utmost difficulty from one of the most aged
and intelligent of the Cherokees living in 1835. The
man was in the habit of using it himself and regarded
it with special veneration. Brief as it is, it contains in
the Cherokee original some words of the "old
language" that by 1835 had become obsolete.
Among them is *Ho yannah,* with which it com-
mences. At sunrise, the supplicant ascended by
himself to the top of a high mountain, and there
gave this petition:

"*Ho yannah* to thee, oh Almighty One! Hear
my prayer; the prayer of him who is of the acorn
clan! I have purified my feet from the dust of the
earth on which I am a dweller, until they are white
enough to bear me to the high places, even above the
tree tops, where I may commune with thee undis-
turbed by anyone who can interrupt my attention;

for there, minds encounter no obstruction from the
things of the world, but can look straight at Thee
and see Thee clearly. Shake not from Thee our
minds, oh Almighty One! Ours of Seven Clans of
the Red Clay. Thou hast already driven off from him
who now supplicates before Thy throne the power of
the evil bewilderer of slumbering hearts, and in so
doing for mine Thou hast shown love. Continue that
guardian love, oh Almighty One, and suffer not my
heart to fall away from its devotedness to thee!"

Priest and owner of cornfield calling for Corn Woman to come and bring life to the just-planted corn.

Thunder

Thunders — for there were supposed to be many stationed and dwelling in different places — were each charged by *Ye ho waah* with special duties. They were revered and worshiped. A legend said that a certain exemplary Cherokee man, after having fasted for seven days, went to the top of a stupendously high mountain during a thunderstorm and there saw with his own eyes the thunder beings and the place where they came from.

The Morning Star

The morning star was an object to be feared. Long ago, a wicked priest used witchcraft to commit murders. The Cherokees joined forces and planned to slay him. Hearing about this, the priest gathered up his "shining instruments of mischief and flew upward to a certain height, where when he paused his instruments made him look like a star. He then became fixed in this position in the sky and was prayed to as the motivating, empowering, and acting spirit for all who desired to use witchcraft to kill others; that is, he bewitched the proposed victim and did the actual killing."

The Old Corn Woman and the Woman of the East

From earliest times in this country, a female being was held in special honor and was identified with the life principle of Indian corn, or maize. Most of the "all-night" dances paid homage to her in some way, and she held a special place in planting rites and the Green Corn festivals. There was a legend that told how she was the one who brought corn into being and imparted life to it. There was also a legend about a greatly revered woman called "the woman of the east."

The Seven Stars

The celestial cluster that the Cherokees called the Seven Stars was regarded with particular reverence. Payne was not given any of the prayers that were addressed to it, but he did receive a legend about its having sprung from a family of eight brothers who once sneaked into the town council house and beat the sacred drum kept there for ceremonial purposes. Some of the elders of the town caught and reproved the brothers, who became angry, seized the drum, and flew upwards into the sky with it, defiantly beating upon it as they went. Finally, seven of the brothers became seven stars. The other brother, however, fell back to the ground so hard that his head stuck deep into it, and he became a cedar tree. This tree would stand forever, and it had the peculiar ability to bleed like a human being whenever it was bruised or cut.

Payne's informants told him there were many other celestial objects that were considered to be "ancients" and these varied in "figure, color, and office." Each was stationed in a different part of the sky, and prayers were often directed to them. A few of the Cherokee informants who mentioned the Seven Stars thought they might once have been distinguished persons who, after their deaths, had been deified by the Cherokee people.

NOTES

1. Bartram, *Travels through North and South Carolina, Georgia, East and West Florida, the Cherokee Country, etc.,* p. 495, and Timberlake, *Memoirs, 1756-1765,* as cited in Adair, *History of the American Indians,* p. 20.
2. Adair, pp. 20, 21 and 51.
3. Payne Papers, Vol. 4.
4. Ibid., pp. 209-210.
5. Mooney, *Sacred Formulas of the Cherokees,* p. 340.
6. Kilpatrick, *The Wahnenauhi Manuscript: Historical Sketches of the Cherokees,* p. 185.
7. Ibid.
8. Payne Papers, Vol. 1.
9. Ibid., pp. 3-5.
10. Ibid., pp. 53-63.
11. Ibid., 53-62.
12. Ibid., pp. 5-29.

CHAPTER SEVEN

The Religious Festivals

Eagle Dance wands.

I t is commonly thought that we know more about the Indian tribes of the Great Plains than we do about most other tribes. This may be true where the overall culture is concerned, yet even the aged Plains holy men I have been with lament that because of white pressures, vital parts of their national ritual life were put aside in early historical times, are now irretrievably lost, and the people have suffered greatly because of it.

Bearing this in mind, it is my opinion that John Howard Payne's greatest contribution to our knowledge of the Cherokees lies in his detailed accounts of the annual cycle of splendid national and local festivals, for without his information, there would be only the scantiest references to turn to, and this part of Cherokee lore would also be lost.

Payne takes us into a wondrous world of incense, pomp, and circumstance as he describes the most primitive rites that included both the greater, or major, festivals, then those that were minor and occasional, and finally the changes that preceded their utter confusion and demise, which are described in Chapter Eight.

Most of these religious festivals were also called dances, since they always featured dancing. As was noted earlier, the Cherokee dance was always done in a counterclockwise direction, since it was believed that movement in this direction brought more success in what one hoped to achieve and greater blessings from the Divine Beings. So the dancers moved counterclockwise in a circle around the sacred fire, always having the fire, and thus the center of the circle, at their left hand.[1]

When we consider the festivals, it helps to know how the Cherokees measured and counted time.

Days were counted by sleeps. Quantity was counted by tens, using their fingers. Numbers were marked on the ground by units, using X for ten. Twenty was *Tahre Skoeh*, or "two tens"; 100 was *Skoeh Chooke*; and 1,000 was *Chooke Kaiere*, or "the old one's hundred." By swiftly adding together their tens they found their totals and called this "scoring on the ground." They had no proper name for a pound weight.

Records of passing days were kept by knotted strings of various colors and makes or by notched sticks. These were used by the head warriors and leaders of the different towns to number the winters, moons, sleeps, and the days when they traveled, especially to plan secret acts of war. As each day elapsed, a knot was loosened, or a notch was cut off or made according to previous agreement, calling those days that were used up "broken days." Thus

they proceeded day by day until the whole time had expired, and they knew with certainty the exact time of the planned periods.

The Cherokees thought of their year in terms of seasons: spring, summer, autumn, or the fall of the leaf, and winter. Years were remembered by what had happened in any of these four periods, somewhat after the manner of the winter-count robes of the Plains Indians. There was no name for a year, and its length was measured by its twelve lunar months, or moons. The Cherokees also had no proper names for the sun and moon and used one word, with a note of distinction, to express both. For example, the Cherokees called the sun *Eus se A nan to ge*, "the day-moon, or sun," and the moon *Neus se A nan to ge*, or "the night-sun, or moon." They counted the weeks by sevens, and the parts of the day by three sensible differences of the sun's position. Sunrise they termed "the sun's coming out." Noon or midday was "sun in the heavens." Sunset was "the sun is dead," or, "the sun is fallen into the water."

Their lunar year began with the appearance of the first new moon of the vernal equinox, and each month thereafter consisted of twenty-nine days. When each new moon appeared, "the people made joyful sounds and stretched out their hands towards her — but offered no public sacrifice to the moons themselves." The various seasons of the year were named according to the planting, ripening, and harvesting of the corn and fruit. The green-eared moon was the most beloved and sacred moon, for the first fruits appeared then, and in thanksgiving seven of each of these were ritually offered to the Above Beings to sanctify the rest.[2]

Confusing as it may be, we should note that the Cherokees actually had two points of beginning during their annual ceremonial cycle. The first beginning was associated with nature's cycle — with the renewal time for the whole of creation — and opened with the First New Moon of Spring Festival. The second beginning was linked with the lunar year and opened with the Great New Moon Festival of autumn. Their reasons for this make more sense as we examine the festivals in detail in the pages ahead.

Musical instruments used for ceremonial dancing: *Top*, gourd and turtle-shell rattles. *Bottom left*, turtle-shell leg rattles. *Bottom right*, water drum.

The Ancient Major Festivals

In ancient times, the Cherokees held an annual series of six major festivals, and each festival had its own rituals and manner of proceeding. All were celebrated at the magnificent national capital, where virtually the entire population of the nation would assemble in response to a summons sent out by the *Uku*. On such occasions, generosity and good will was the rule — every home in the capital was open to visitors, and hospitality was freely and abundantly provided.

The First New Moon of Spring Festival was celebrated about the time the new grass began to show itself.

Second came the *Sah looh stwknce keeh stoh steeh*, which was a preliminary event known as the New Green Corn Feast. It was held when the young corn first became fit to taste.

Third was the *Tung nah kaw hoongh ni*, which was the Mature, or Ripe, Green Corn Feast. It followed the New Green Corn Feast by forty or fifty days, the time being determined by the corn's having become hard and perfect.

Fourth was *Hung tah tay quah*, the Great New Moon Feast that took place on the appearance of the first new moon of autumn, and it was the actual beginning of the festival cycle. At the conclusion of this chapter I explain why.

Fifth came *Ah tawh hung nah*, the Propitiation and Cementation Festival. It occurred ten days after the New Moon Feast.

Sixth was *Eelah uahtah lay kee*, the festival of the Exalting, or Bounding, Bush.

Attending a Great National Festival

To feel what it was like to attend one of the great national festivals, let's pretend it is early spring and we are invisible visitors to the national capital at the time of the Festival of the First New Moon of Spring. Along with thousands of Cherokees from all parts of the nation, we arrive there on the day before the festival is to begin. As we approach the main entrance gate that will allow us to pass through the tall, palisaded walls, we see other people arriving on foot and in square-sided log boats that are thick on the river. The boats are rapidly beached and appear like giant clothespins laid neatly out side by side along the sloping beach that fronts the town's wall.

No sooner are the boats secured than the passengers pick up their baggage and head for the entrance. Everyone is dressed in his or her finest clothing, and we see that the ornamentation varies according to the region people come from. The soft sounds of tiny bells fill the air, and the younger women laugh gaily and chatter like magpies as they look around to see who else is there. Their dark eyes flash, and framing bronzed and temptingly beautiful faces is their coal-black hair, either piled in a bun on their crowns and stuck through with carved bone or shell pins, or hanging free over shoulders and backs to flow like swaying palms. All of the women are slim and energetic, and as they move about, the shining beads and glistening feathers woven into their dresses are like dancing pinpoints of light. The older women, who have come here many times over the years, wear even more sumptuous dresses than the younger ones, and they are more sedate and officious in their actions. The wives of the priests and chief warriors are arrayed in chalk-white buckskin dresses and have decorated capes thrown over their shoulders. Their hair is piled higher than that of other women, and some is etched with traces of grey. Their bearing is regal, as befits their positions. Wives of leading warriors can be told from the rest by the touches of war red on their otherwise white costumes.

Even the little children who are urging their parents to hurry are dressed in finely made cloth and buckskin. Well trained, they are anxious to get inside, but they know the rules and stay close at hand while the necessary things are attended to.

The men move about more slowly than the women. They smile at the sight of special friends, but their manner is that of the proud warrior. They wear the costumes that reveal their achievements in battle, and those sons who are not yet old enough to join their fathers in combat proudly carry their fathers' shields and weapons. Most men wear no war shirts, so that their scars can be seen as marks of special distinction.

The women and girls have unloaded from the boats baskets filled with foodstuffs carefully preserved over the winter months. The men shoulder containers of deer meat and the meat of other animals and birds. All of this will be taken to the large storehouse that sits behind the Heptagon and kept there until needed for the festival feast.

The sound level rises as we pass through the open gate and enter the capital, merging now with a boisterous throng of happy people who, in the spirit of the spring that marks Earth Mother's triumph over Cold Maker and celebrates new birth, greet one another with particular fondness after the long separation of the winter months. Warm expressions of joy come from fellow clan members who are seeking one another out. Large as the capital is, it is jammed with people, for 10,000 or more are crammed into an enclosed space about a half-mile square — more than enough to house its 1,200 or so regular residents, but barely enough for this huge and active multitude.

In all parts of the town we see pale gray columns of smoke rising up from hundreds of cooking fires. Preparations are under way for the feast of celebration to be held this night, and the rich smell of roasting meat and corn saturates the air. The people nearest us part to make a path for a large hunting party led by seven hunters with colorful feathers attached to their hair tufts. The men carry on long poles several dozen newly killed deer. One of the men has on his shoulder three hides whitened with clay. Another man holds out in front of him with both hands a small deer-hide packet. People look at him with awe. They know the packet contains the tip of the tongue of the first deer killed, and that it will be used for ritual sacrifice during the ceremonies.

The hunters head straight for a twenty-foot-high, huge and rectangular mound of earth that sits in the center of the town. New green grass covers the mound's sloping sides and flat top. Sitting pretentiously on the mound is the giant national heptagon that seats more than a thousand people. Its roof is like a grey, cone-shaped and multifaceted hat that is topped by a fierce-visaged, carved wooden eagle

whose details are smoothed over by decades of wind and rain. The heptagon's seven sides are clearly marked by the light and shadows on each of them. In front of the heptagon is a tall white pole that holds the Great High Priest's flag which, as a gust of wind strikes it and causes it to stream out, displays a field of red stars on a white background.

For the moment, the sacred square fronting the heptagon can hardly be seen, since it is covered by people of all ages who are engaged in animated conversation. But off to the sides of the heptagon mound and at each cardinal direction we can see smaller mounds that bear the houses of the Great High Priest, his principal assistant, his chief speaker, and the Great War Chief. Even smaller mounds hold the houses of other men of rank who play essential roles in government and warfare. Taken as a whole, the town's appearance is like that of a clean and

Turkey-tail fan.

simplified Mayan city, and it has a distinctly religious feel. As we move around we discover that it is laid out on a modular gridiron pattern, with broad streets bisecting it on east-west and north-south axes. Each of the smaller mounds has grouped behind it rows of neat, gable-roofed houses where clan members live as a unit. In the rear of these are the circular-walled winter hothouses, and in each of the four corners of the town is a large field whose corn and beans will be safe from marauding enemies in case of a siege. In the middle of each field is a large, round, two-story-high storehouse with a cone-shaped bark roof. Spaced out at regular intervals along the palisaded wall enclosing the town are high log bastions where even now lookouts stand watch, and on which warriors can take defensive positions in time of war. Outside the wall are dozens of fields for corn, other vegetables, and fruit trees.

Of particular interest are the rows of long, gable-roofed shade arbors that shelter the festival visitors and people who must visit the capital on business during the regular course of the year. Some visitors stay in the homes of fellow clanspeople, but the homes won't hold everyone now, and others will use the shelters for the duration of the festival. Just in front of each family, or group of families where clanspeople prefer to be together, is a fire on which one or more clay pots sits heavily in the midst of one of those rising columns of smoke we saw earlier.

We stop to watch excited children at play, but our attention is diverted by four aged Beloved Women who walk by in their sumptuous white dresses and broad headbands. Just behind them come two stern-visaged priests with their white knee-length skirts, and their tall basketry hats festooned with white down and wing feathers. Hanging on their chests are large carved-stone fetishes that denote the creatures they pray to for help in healing. A war leader walks by in his long and splendid cape of turkey feathers, his face etched with striking designs and his paint-impregnated hair tuft arching up from his head like water from a fountain. Our delight mounts as we slip back into a time hundreds of years before our own, and we want to go on looking forever, but a drum booms out from the top of the

Heptagon mound, and instantly the people grow quiet. For the first time we notice that the light is waning. Sun is dropping down into the great water far to the west, and in the east Moon is edging above the horizon. Inside the Heptagon the *Uku* and his assistants are making their final preparations for the great festival. Women hurry back to their living places to ready the last things needed for the feast soon to be held . . . and tomorrow morning the festival will begin . . . .

The First New Moon of Spring

Sometime prior to the first new moon of spring, the *Uku*'s seven prime counselors met at the national heptagon and appointed certain honorable women to perform the Friendship Dance. When this dance ended, the counselors counted the nights from the last new moon and consulted a divining crystal to determine when exactly the first new moon of spring would appear. These things done, the counselors sent messages to all of the towns of the nation to announce the day the forthcoming festival would begin. The counselors also ordered the hunters who resided in the capital to provide meat for the occasion. They were to kill deer, turkeys, and any other wildlife permitted for festival food, and were to preserve those provisions and bring them forward on the appointed day. One buck deer they were to dress whole, which meant that the skin, entrails, and feet were to be removed from the body, but the liver, lungs, and heart had to remain. This skin, together with those of a similarly prepared doe and a fawn, must be whitened with clay. Finally, the counselors appointed seven men to oversee the feast and seven women to oversee and do the cooking.

On the day before the new moon was to appear, most of the citizens of the Cherokee nation assembled at the national capital, and the hunters brought in their meat and placed it in the storehouse located on the west side of the heptagon. Notice was given to the *Uku* that the dressed whole deerskins and the other dressed white deerskins had been deposited, and the principal assistant was sent to move them into the heptagon. At this time, other Cherokees who had been out on hunting excursions

The First New Moon of Spring Festival: the principal assistant sprinkles flower buds from old wild tobacco on the three deerskins. See color plate No. 7.

during the winter came alone or with their families to add to the storehouse supplies the meat and skins they had collected. These, together with the contributions of other kinds of foodstuffs from other people, assured that abundant supplies would be on hand for the festival celebration. Scarcely anyone arrived at the national capital empty-handed.

While the people were arriving, the altar that stood in the center of the heptagon was refurbished by the principal assistant. It consisted of a conical mound of fresh earth, on the flattened top of which a circle was drawn to receive the sacred fire. Inner bark was laid on the circle, ready for use. This bark was to be freshly taken from the east sides of the seven kinds of trees whose wood was employed on this festival occasion — white oak, black oak, water oak, blackjack, basswood, chestnut, and white pine — all of which had to be free from blemishes and worms.

On the evening of this first night of assembling, bonfires were lighted, and everyone feasted and visited, after which a Friendship Dance was performed by the women. During it and afterwards people were permitted to sleep, for on the following morning the festival would begin, and the people would need their strength.

Sometime before dawn, the leaders of the Cherokee Nation filed into the heptagon and took their seats in the appropriate clan areas. The rest of the population crowded around the heptagon exterior on the mound top and in the sacred square and streets down below. The principal assistant took the three white-dressed deerskins and spread them out next to the altar fire, with the heads pointed toward it. Then he took a vessel filled with the fresh blood of a fowl or some other creature and, using a little weed as a brush, sprinkled the blood on the skins, then drew a long, straight line from the nose to the end of the tail. He laid a divining crystal on the blood line on the buckskin and dropped on all three skins flower buds from old wild tobacco that had been gathered the previous year.

Soon after sunrise, the *Uku* ordered the entire population to the river, on the banks of which seven large tables had been set up, and where bench seats parallel to the water were arranged for the leaders. On the way to the river everyone was to look straight ahead, neither back nor to the right or left. This was to prove that their minds were fixed on the ceremony and not on other things. In this procession, the seven counselors carried seven containers filled with medicine roots, the chief speaker carried a large container filled with small flags, the principal assistant came next to last and carried seven deerskins that were folded one inside the other and contained the divining crystals. The *Uku* came last of all.

Once they arrived at the river, the people were allowed to look wherever they pleased, and the assistant placed the seven skins on the centers of the tables. The people sat down and maintained silence while the assistant took from the large container a great number of sticks, each about six inches long, with skin flags mounted on them. He carried these to the river and, with the help of assistants, at the distance of a stick's length from the water's edge first touched the water with the end of each stick, then one by one stuck the flags in the sand, leaving short intervals between them. When they were finished, the sticks formed a long line parallel to the water's edge. This done, the assistant urged everyone to pay strict attention to the flags directly in front of them and to notice whether anything came out of the water there, for if bugs, worms, or something else crawled out and fought near a flag, the person closest to that flag either would soon die or be grievously distressed. But if nothing appeared, all would go well for them.

After a respectable period of watching, the assistant directed everyone to plunge into the river with their clothing on and, facing east, to immerse entirely seven times. This order included infants, who were to be immersed by their mothers.

While the immersing was going on, the *Uku* unfolded the seven deerskins and exposed the seven divining crystals they contained. Then he covered the tabletops with medicine roots. When the people emerged from the river, beginning with the oldest men and proceeding according to age, they approached a table one by one, walked four times around it, then stopped while they wet the tips of their right forefingers with their tongues and drew them down the length of a divining crystal. They next put the wet fingers to the tops of their foreheads and drew them down over the nose, lips, chin, and on to the pit of the stomach. Finally, each person took a piece of medicine root from the table and, looking straight ahead, walked away from the river and back to the town. Here, they changed into clean and dry garments. The common people performed this wet-finger ritual first, and the priests and the people of rank last.

The balance of the day was devoted to fasting, with infants being denied nourishment until the afternoon and the rest of the people until after sunset.

As sun was setting, the people assembled in and around the heptagon, where near its altar, whose fire had been kept burning all day long, the white-dressed deerskins still remained. When everyone was ready, the *Uku* and his principal assistant took positions on the west side of the fire, facing east, and the *Uku*'s seven counselors formed a semicircle behind and around them. The *Uku* picked up from the deerskins the flowers of old tobacco that had earlier been placed there and flung them onto the fire, where as they burned they emitted an incense-like odor. After this he took the tip of the tongue of the buck deer that had been dressed whole, and threw it into the fire. While it burned, everyone watched it intently, for if bits of it popped to the east that was an omen of life, and if west, that was an omen of death for someone in the nation.

Once this sacrifice had been offered, the dressed-whole buck was cooked, and small pieces of it were distributed to the people. A prodigious amount of thick mush made with newly pounded meal was dispensed with the deer. Tradition required that each person was to receive a taste of both meat and mush. Distribution took a long time, but part of the ancient rule was that the food must be consumed before dawn. Then the rite of scratching was freely administered with snake fangs, flints, or fishbones used to cut long gashes on the limbs of participants. The medicine roots distributed at the riverbank were also chewed, and the people rubbed the juice of them on themselves and on their children. However, some of the root was kept for similar use at the appearance of each new moon until autumn. During this night, only infants were allowed to sleep. The women spent most of their time doing the Friendship Dance, and at sunrise on the following morning the First New Moon of Spring Festival ended, with everyone free to return to their homes.

The white-dressed deerskins and the skins of all of the animals killed for the festival became the property of the *Uku*, who also received a share of the other provisions contributed. Anything left over was equally shared by the town residents.

The day after the festival ended, the *Uku*, acting through his seven counselors, set the date for a Sacred Night Dance and announced that on the seventh day after that dance, new fire would be made by seven chosen men.

Messengers were dispatched to give notice of this, and on the evening of the seventh day the people of the national capital and representatives from all of the other towns and villages gathered again at the national heptagon, where the entire night was passed in the performance of a Sacred Night Dance.

Early the next morning, the seven chosen men began to make the new fire. One man was delegated as the official fire maker and the other six as his assistants. According to the ancient way, a round indentation was made in a block of wood, and a small quantity of dried goldenrod was dropped into it. Then a stick, the end of which just fitted the indentation, was twirled rapidly between the hands of the official fire maker and the assistants who "spelled" him until the weed caught fire. This fire was now transferred to the hearth, and from it hot coals were taken to designated homes near and far by women who had been assigned to do this.

The old fires in the homes of the capital having been everywhere extinguished and the hearths having been scrupulously cleansed of their old ashes, new fires were built as replacements. As soon as those who lived elsewhere returned to their own homes, they used coals they had obtained from the heptagon's sacred fire to duplicate this procedure of cleansing, rebuilding, and lighting. Then, as an offering of thanks to the Above Beings, the tongue of the next deer killed by the husband of each house was sacrificed to the new fire in his own home.[3]

The New Green Corn Feast

To assure that the rate of corn growth would be simultaneous throughout Cherokee country, instructions were given by the *Uku* through his seven counselors as to how the planting should be regulated, and reminders were issued at regular intervals that proper watches must be kept over the growing fields. As soon as the corn had reached the stage when it was ready for the New Green Corn Feast, messengers were sent out to advise and convene the entire nation. The chief messenger had a special assignment: he was to gather as he traveled seven perfect ears of corn, one ear from a field of each of the seven clans. On his return, he was to deliver the seven ears to the seven counselors, who would receive them and then make the necessary arrangements for the New Green Corn Feast.

The first step was to order all of the capital's hunters into the wilderness for a six-day hunt. Then the *Uku*, his principal assistant and the counselors entered the heptagon and began a six-day fast. When the chief hunter of the hunting party downed his first buck deer, he cut a small piece from the right side of the tip of its tongue. He wrapped this in old leaves that had fallen from trees the previous year and put it in a pouch to bring back to the *Uku* for sacrificial purposes.

The Ripe Green Corn Festival: *Top,* bird's-eye view. *Bottom:* Great War Chief being carried on sedan-chair platform.

On the evening of the sixth day, the hunters returned, the people gathered at the capital, and each family brought with it an offering of every kind of fruit available in their part of the land — either already cooked or edible in its natural state. The deer meat brought in by the hunters and the food offerings were placed in the heptagon's storehouse. The leaf-wrapped tip of the tongue and all of the deerskins were delivered to the *Uku*, who was not permitted to eat deer meat until after the tip of the tongue had been sacrificed to the fire.

The sixth night was observed as a night of watching. No one, save infants, was allowed to close his eyes, and part of the night was spent doing, both inside and outside the heptagon, a traditional religious dance, the movements of which were done silently and solemnly. Thoughts were concentrated upon God's faithfulness in the past and present, and because of this the assurance that it could be depended upon in the future.

At sunrise on the morning of the seventh day the festival proper began when the seven counselors delivered to the *Uku* the seven ears of corn brought by the chief messenger. Upon receiving them, the *Uku* commanded the people to abstain that day from all labor and levity. Meanwhile, the altar in the heptagon was refurbished as it was in the First New Moon of Spring Festival, and when the same types of tree bark had been placed upon it, seven fire makers lit a new fire for the forthcoming sacrifice. Then the people assembled in and around the Heptagon.

Just before nightfall, the *Uku* took between his right thumb and forefinger the tip of the buck's tongue, and in his left hand seven kernels of corn, one from each of the seven ears. He gazed upward as he slowly raised both hands high above his head, and then he uttered in a reverent voice a thanksgiving prayer using words that had been handed down from time immemorial, which were never to be altered or abused. The prayer expressed heartfelt gratitude to the All Beneficent Beings for having permitted the fruits to show themselves and for allowing the people to behold and enjoy them. It also implored the beings to unite the corn and the meat in such a way as to guarantee good health to the nation throughout the coming year and make such bounty available until life's end.

This prayer having been offered, the *Uku* tossed the meat and corn into the sacred fire and over these sprinkled old tobacco leaves ground into powder. Then, as the people in the heptagon leaned forward in anticipation, the principal assistant and the seven counselors intently watched the fire and the burning sacrifices. If the fire burned quietly and the popped-off pieces of meat went in directions other than westward, all would go well with the Cherokees, but if smoke settled over the altar in a bluish cloud and meat fragments popped westward, sickness would attend the forthcoming year.

Once the portent was known, the principal assistant ordered that the food for the feast should be arranged in and around the sacred square in front of the heptagon in such a way that everyone could sit down and begin to eat at the same time. The exceptions were the *Uku*, his principal assistant, and his seven counselors, who by tradition had to abstain from eating until after sunset, and even then were only allowed to eat provisions that had been kept from the preceding year. The feast ended the first part of the festival, and many of the people returned to their homes.

At the end of seven days, those who stayed or lived close enough to the capital to return once again assembled in and around the heptagon, this time for a banquet of new fruits in which the *Uku* and his assistant and counselors shared. This ended the second and final part of the New Green Corn Feast.[4]

The Ripe Green Corn Feast

Forty or fifty days after the New Green Corn Feast ended, the Ripe Green Corn Feast was held. The cornstalks would have grown tall by then, and the ears of corn would be hard and perfect, delightful to smell and behold.

At the *Uku*'s order, his seven counselors went to the fields to ascertain the state of the corn, and if it had developed as they expected, they called for the performance of a certain kind of religious dance that everyone knew heralded the time fixed for the feast, which would follow the dance by about twenty days.

The capital hunters were sent out as usual, and ranking officers were notified to be ready to carry out their respective tasks at the appointed times. Among the special requirements for this occasion was that an arbor made with green boughs must be constructed in the sacred square. Also, a beautiful shade tree was to be set up there and a large booth that contained several rows of seats.

On the day after the religious dance, messengers went to all parts of the country to announce the time fixed for the festival, a time that had with marked emphasis been set in the beginning of time by the Creator for the entire nation to convene.

On the day prior to the first day of the festival, the hunters and people arrived with their food offerings and stored them in the heptagon storehouse. The arbor and the booth had been made ready, and a beautiful shade tree that had been cut down at the base of its trunk — a bushy-topped tree whose branches stretched out wide — was hoisted into place with its trunk set in a deep hole that was dug in the center of the sacred square. Every man provided himself with a green bough and, when all of these preparations were finished, the people were ready to begin the festival with a victory dance on the following day.

This was a time of unmeasured exultation, and the people burst into an enthusiasm of joy. While the women and children watched, men took turns performing the festal dance peculiar to this commemoration, and when in the morning the men met in the sacred square, each one held above his head in his right hand his green bough. As the leader struck up the music with his rattle and started the movement, the other men fell in behind him with rapturous expressions on their faces as they imitated the green corn that filled the fields of those who were virtuous. They ran, leaped, sang, and exulted. Even though they appeared to be in wild disorder, they followed ancient rules and were guided by their leader, who during each of seven dances led them seven times around the tree trunk and under the shade of the branches that represented the sheltering arms of the Creator.

To enhance the victory aspect of the dance, the Great War Chief joined in it, wearing a red cap, a white robe, leggings and moccasins, with his arms covered with otter skins, seated on a sedan-chair type of platform that was carried around the tree by six men. The seats in the booth were occupied by the *Uku* and the other men of rank from all parts of the nation.

The Ripe Green Corn Feast continued in this manner for four days. Each evening at sunset, the men ceased dancing, deposited their green boughs in a safe place, and then retrieved them the next morning. Although women were not permitted to enter the sacred square while the men danced during the day, after sunset, social dances were held that included both men and women. In these dances, wives followed behind their husbands, and single women and girls followed their brothers or young men of their own clans. On the last night, a great feast was held, and then the people returned home.

The Ripe Green Corn Feast was so important that it outlived all the rest and was known, in an altered shape in 1835, as the Green Corn Dance. The oldest informants did not believe that even the form just described was the most ancient of all, even though they were not able to discover what that earliest form was. Still, it seemed to be well understood that there was once a Festival of Green Shades that was more distinct and exclusive in its characteristics than even the Ripe Green Corn Feast.[5]

The Great New Moon Festival

The fourth of the great festivals was held when the first new moon of autumn appeared. The *Uku*'s first act was to send his seven counselors out to determine when the new moon would appear, which was when the leaves began to turn yellow and to fall, sometime in the early part of our October.

The Cherokees believed that the world was created during this moon, and therefore, this was the first of all moons and began the lunar year. Accordingly, they named it "the Great Moon" and arranged their series of New Moon feasts by it.

The seven counselors carefully counted the nights from the preceding moon, the waning of which they solemnly observed. But if clouds hid the moon, a divining crystal was employed to learn what they needed to know. Once they could say for certain when the great new moon would appear, seven nights before its arrival the capital hunters were sent out and, as before, hunted for six days and returned on the seventh. Seven other men were appointed to prepare seats and tables and to make certain that the traditional rules for feasting were followed. Seven honorable women were selected to oversee the preparation and cooking of the food.

On the very day when the great moon rose in the sky, the hunters gave the old-leaf-wrapped tip of the tongue of the first-killed buck deer to the *Uku*, along with seven deerskins, and deposited the rest of the deer meat in the national heptagon's storehouse. That same day, the entire nation gathered at the capital, with each family contributing to the *Uku* for his own purposes seven or more ears of hard corn, beans, dried pumpkins, and a sample of every sort of produce they had raised. Beyond this, in preparation for the feast, each family deposited in the storehouse something of the same foodstuffs.

That night, only infants were permitted to sleep, and the women performed a religious dance.

In the morning, the festival got under way. Before sunrise, the *Uku* ordered everyone to the river and, as in the spring new moon ritual, the people were arranged in lines, flag sticks were placed by the water's edge, and the people watched for what might come out of the water near them. Everyone immersed the usual seven times and, upon emerging from the water, came one by one to tables where divining crystals were set up on end and medicine roots were deposited. In praying on this occasion, however, as the bathers left the water they held the palms of their hands out toward a crystal. Those who saw themselves standing erect in the crystal would live until the next first spring new moon appeared. But those who saw themselves lying down would die before that moon arrived. The latter went aside to pray and to be alone for awhile. Then as they went to the town to change to dry garments everyone picked up a piece of the medicine root. The people of higher rank performed the same acts as the common people, but only after the common people were finished.

The foodstuffs were prepared and set out, and with exceptions about to be mentioned, about nine o'clock that night, everyone feasted. The exceptions were the *Uku*, who had to sacrifice the tip of the deer's tongue before he ate, and the counselors and certain other leaders, who ate when the multitude had finished. Also, those whose earlier omen had been that they were to die before the first spring new moon were required to fast until midnight. In the evening, each one of them gave the *Uku* either a deerskin or a piece of new cloth, after which he took them again to the river, where he spread out on the table the deerskin or cloth, set his divining crystal on top of it, and sought in the crystal further information regarding the life of the giver. Once again, the owner of the cloth held out toward the crystal the palm of his hand. When he looked into the stone, if the omen had changed and he was to live, he saw himself standing erect and his skin color unchanged. If the omen was still that he was to die, he either appeared for an instant and then promptly vanished or saw himself with a blue complexion and reclining. In the latter instance, the matter was put aside for four weeks until the next new moon appeared, when the crystal and his palm were again employed. If the same dire portent appeared, his death would surely occur before long. If on the contrary the vision of himself finally stood erect, he had gained a reprieve, and to express his gratitude he was directed to face east and immerse seven times in the river.

Only infants might sleep on the night after the entire multitude had bathed, and the women, as was usual to end feasts, devoted most of the night to a solemn religious dance. The next morning, the people returned to their homes, and the Great New Moon Feast was over.[6]

The Propitiation and Cementation Festival

A day or two after the Great New Moon Festival ended, the seven counselors gathered at the national heptagon to set the date for the beginning of the significant and solemn Propitiation Festival, whose beginning was always to be seven nights later. This would not seem much time for people to return home from the prior event, but for those in and near

The Cementation Festival: two men exchange garments to "cement" their everlasting relationship in symbolism of the renewed relationship between the Above Beings and the people. See color plate No. 9.

the capital it posed no problem, and we must remember that others were accustomed to the annual schedule, so they were always in a state of readiness. Then too, we can assume that those who lived farthest away simply remained at the capital until the Propitiation Festival was held.

The Cherokees expressed at this festival their most intense devotional feelings, especially to the beings whom they believed were the source of all of their blessings. It was at this festival that the ancient and mystical *Yowah* hymn was specially chanted. The origin of this hymn was described in Chapter Six.

The dual Cherokee title for this festival was derived from a peculiar bond between two Cherokee men. It could best be described as a vow of eternal brotherhood that sprang from such a deep friendship between the young men that it prompted them to a solemn act of lifelong devotedness to each other. This cementation, or joining together, was publicly plighted on the first night in the sacred square, with the two men silently exchanging garment after garment until each was clad in the other's clothing. When this was done, each man accepted that he had given himself to the other and that from that moment forward they were one and indivisible. It was an alliance that embraced all that is implied in perfect unity — reconciliation, friendship, brotherly affection, and much more.

While the two men were in the process of uniting, they were said to be *ah nah tawh hanoh kah,* "about to make friendship," and the union itself was called *ah tah hoongh nah,* "friends made," giving the Cementation Festival its name.

The uniting of the two men had an even higher purpose, for it symbolized the state that united each Cherokee on earth with the Creator Who Dwelt Above. Moreover, the nature and dignity of this festival were emphasized by the title that was given for this occasion only to the *Uku: Oonah wheeh sayh nunghee,* "One Who Renews Heart and Body, the purifier from all defilements, spiritual and corporeal." During the time he directed the ceremonies of this festival he was also called *Oole stool eeh,* "One who has his head covered," because he officiated with his cone-shaped cap on. While other priests concealed their crystals, on this occasion his was worn openly on his chest, wrapped in a skin and suspended by a string around his neck. This was to emphasize his eminence as an instructor in moral and religious duty, to which end he had seasons set apart for visiting the different towns throughout the nation.

A second name by which this festival had become known in 1835 was Physic Dance. The use of this title, along with others that were over the years given to the festival, provided added evidence of the festival's special character, since the Cherokee

Headdress worn by the seven men appointed to cleanse and exorcise the national heptagon and capital.

word for "physic," or "emetic," applied equally to that which healed both soul and body and distinctly signified that the festival occasion was one of conciliation, purifying, healing, and renewal.

The Cherokee word for "physic" was *Nungh wah tee.* When a house was to be purified, the cedar boughs and whatever else was employed was called *Nungh wah tee.* This title was also applied to the purifying water used by someone after he had touched a dead body. Furthermore, the combining of the words "physic" and "conciliation" was related to the fact that the Cherokees regarded those diseases which required a physic as having been sent down from above to punish some offense among the people, and the physic was part of the restoration of good relationships between the Above Beings and

Headdress of the men who cleansed and exorcised the heptagon and capital.

man. To such divine curses Payne traced the almost exclusive employment in his own time of what were then called conjurers, or medicine men, who treated diseases. The Indian doctors in that day were universally admitting that they accomplished their objectives by the assistance of incantations. Those who had lost all other traces of the ancient ceremonies and had no idea of their original significance — no knowledge of the early priesthood or of the dignity of the primeval *Ah tawh hungh nah* — nevertheless adhered to the peculiarly mystical part emetics played in the rites relating to the expiation of sins.

After the head counselor had given a special and solemn address about the importance of this festival to the other six counselors, the seven of them dispatched messengers to the towns of the nation to direct the people to meet at the national capital on the evening of the sixth day. Seven women were summoned to lead the women's dances, and musicians were appointed to aid them. Seven wives of seven counselors, one from each of the clans, were appointed to assist and to fast. Seven men were called upon to clean the national heptagon and to use sycamore rods to exorcise all of the buildings in the capital. Seven more men were sent to seek certain woods needed for the purification rites. To all of the above people, attendants were assigned.

The maker of the sacred fire and his six assistants were commanded to have a new fire ready on the morning of the seventh day. A special attendant was assigned to the *Yo wah tee kah naw ghistee* — the priest who would chant the *Yo wah* hymn — and whose job it was to dress and undress the chanter for his water purifications and for his official duties. For both the chanter and his attendant, subordinates were appointed. If the priest who had been designated to chant the *Yo wah* hymn had died during the preceding year, the seven counselors appointed at this time a substitute, who then retained the office for the duration of his life.

Once all of these appointments had been made, on the following morning the *Uku*, his principal assistant, the seven counselors, the seven women from the seven clans, and the chanter and his assistants began to fast. Only after darkness fell and only once in each twenty-four-hour period for the next six days were they allowed to taste food, and even then very little of it.

The rest of the preparations for this festival were the same as those for the New Green Corn Feast, except that simultaneously with the hunt, seven kinds of wood for purification were sought. In earliest times these consisted of evergreens: cedar, white pine, hemlock, mistletoe, evergreen brier, heartleaf, and ginseng root. Although the top of the ginseng died in winter, the root did not, and for this reason it was included among the evergreens. By 1835, it was not always possible to obtain all of the ancient woods, and substitutes were made. These included bark from mountain birch, which grew only in shrubs; willow roots that grew on the banks of streams and for a long time had been washed by the streams; swamp dogwood roots that had had the same washing as the willow roots; mistletoe; spruce pine; and the bark of the *a ta sv ki*, or perfume wood.

The seven woods were placed in a cane basket expressly made for the occasion and on the evening of the sixth day were stored in the treasure house. The kills from the hunt and the other foodstuffs were stored at the same time, and while this was going on, the nation's citizens gathered in and around the sacred square. During the first part of the night, the women danced while individual musicians took turns singing and drumming for them. When the dancing ceased, everyone but a select few slept, for at sunrise on the seventh day, the propitiation part of the festival would begin.

As for the select few, long before daylight and before the new fire makers could build their fire, the seven men who had been appointed to cleanse the national heptagon and to exorcise the buildings of the capital were awake and busy. For this task they wore on their heads broad cloth bands. The front was decorated with a plume that consisted of a round stick covered with the skin of the underside of a deer's tail with the white hair left on. They swept every inch of the heptagon's interior, removed the old ashes from the cone-shaped altar, and repaired the altar by renewing the earth upon its flat top and bringing it up to its proper height, which was about a foot above ground level.

The Cementation Festival: the exorcisers at work with their sycamore rods. See color plate No. 9.

Then the seven fire makers started the new fire in the stick-and-hearth manner already described. They kept it burning with seven kinds of wood: blackjack, locust, post oak, sycamore, redbud, plum, and red oak. This wood had to be broken from the lower dry limbs of the trees and only from the east side of limbs. None of it could be taken from fallen branches already on the ground.

The main furnishings and interior posts of the heptagon were given a new coat of whitewash. These included the three ottomans provided for the *Uku*, principal assistant, and chief speaker, and the upright planks that backed them. Also whitewashed were the bench by the altar that held the fourteen dipping gourds, the sacred purifying cauldron, and the seven central posts and their connecting plates. The seats of the three central ottomans were also covered with whitened buckskin. Spread on the earth floor in front of the ottomans were whitened buckskins, and untanned deerskins were hung on a framework above each of the ottomans to form a canopy. All of this work had to be completed before sunrise.

At sunrise, the seven men who had done the cleaning, or exorcising, placed the sacred cauldron near the new fire. Then they walked around the fire and the cauldron four times, exclaiming at intervals, *"You, You,"* and raising a whoop. This done, they took the seven white dipping gourds from the bench, went to a stream of running water — the only kind considered to be alive — filled their gourds, returned, walked once around the fire and cauldron, poured the water into the cauldron, placed the gourds back on the bench, and went to tell the *Uku* that the cauldron was ready.

The *Uku* and his principal assistant proceeded to the treasure house, where the assistant picked up the basket containing the seven woods. With the *Uku* following him, the assistant left the treasure house and walked toward the entrance of the heptagon. When they were close to the entrance, the assistant paused while the *Uku* offered a prayer. This done, they continued. Upon entering the heptagon there was another stop while the priest offered in a low voice a second prayer, whose purpose, like that of all other prayers for this festival, was to ask that

the people might be cleansed from all the pollutions and impurities of the preceding year.

The two men then circled the altar once and stopped while the *Uku* sprinkled the powder of old wild tobacco on the fire. He then took the wing fan of a perfectly white heron, and while he prayed, waved it four times over the hot cauldron in such a way as to waft the steam in every direction. Three more times the two men circled the altar, and each time they did this the *Uku* sprinkled the tobacco on the fire and prayed while he waved his fan over the cauldron. Now the *Uku* ordered his assistant to place the sacred basket in the cauldron and, after holding the basket in both hands while he moved it in a circle above the cauldron, the assistant slowly immersed it. The two men circled the altar once more, the *Uku* waved the steam away again, and they retired to their seats. From that moment on, the cauldron and the fire were watched day and night by the seven counselors.

The select few and the *Uku* were not the only ones awake and up by now. Before dawn, women had extinguished every fire in every home in the national capital, every hearth was carefully cleansed, and all ashes and firebrands were thrown away. The women then went to the heptagon and took from it coals to light new fires in their homes. A piece of the first meat cooked on this new fire was always sacrificed, and no food whatsoever could be tasted on this day until after the new fire had been made. Those families who had come from other towns carried with them on their return home special receptacles holding coals for their own new fires. Upon arriving, they removed all traces of their old fires and then built new ones, observing the same rules as those mentioned above.

Soon after the *Uku* and his principal assistant were seated, the people assembled in and around the heptagon. When all were present, the seven attendants of the seven cleansers, each carrying a white rod of sycamore, went to the altar and called upon the cleansers to come forward. When they did this, each attendant gave the one he served his sycamore rod. The leader of the seven then sang the note *"Ayh,"* to which the other six responded *"Wah."* The leader sang *"Eh ah"* seven times, then resumed his former note, *"Ayh,"* to which the others again responded with *"Wah!"* pronounced quickly. The leader then left the heptagon and was followed by the rest of the cleansers. It was now only a little after sunrise.

When the cleansers were gone, the attendant who had been appointed to wait on the chanter went to the middle of the heptagon and by name loudly called for him to come forth from his seat. When the chanter had done this and had taken a position facing east, the attendant went to the storage place where the white robes were kept and returned to dress the chanter in them. He also placed in the chanter's hand either a white painted gourd filled with pebbles, called "a rattling gourd," or a perfectly white shell rattle fastened on a stick. The attendant returned to his seat and, after a moment had passed, the chanter shook the gourd and sang the note, *"You."* Then he walked solemnly around the altar and to the door of the heptagon where, after changing his note to *"Eeh,"* he left the building.

The seven cleansers were outside the heptagon and ready to begin their cleansing of the town when the chanter emerged. At this point, the leader of the cleansers, followed by the other six, walked around the heptagon until they came to the treasury storehouse, whose roof eaves they repeatedly struck with their sycamore rods. After this, the leader laid his rod on his shoulder and, followed by the other cleansers, descended from the mound top and went in single file from house to house, with the leader singing a short chant between houses that always ended before the next house was reached, with the other cleansers responding, *"Hah."* They continued in this wise until they had struck the eaves of every house and other type of building in the town, after which they returned to the heptagon, circled it, again struck the eaves of the treasury house, still singing and responding as at first, and finally reentered the heptagon, where their rods were stored in the storage place and were not touched again until the next day. It was then a little before noon.

As for the chanter, he continued to sing the note *"Eeh"* that he had been singing when he left the

heptagon. He did this while he climbed a ladder onto the heptagon roof and ascended to its peak, never drawing his breath until he reached the top where, as the people crowded around down below and gazed up at him, he now sang the grand and mystical *Yo wah* hymn. This hymn had seven verses, and each verse had only one line that was chanted four times in a distinct tune. Thus, the seven verses were chanted in seven different tunes and were as follows:

VERSE 1. *Hi yo wa ya ka ni*

VERSE 2. *Hi te hu yu ya ka ni*

VERSE 3. *Hi wa ta ki ya ka ni*

VERSE 4. *Hi hi wa sa si ya ka ni*

VERSE 5. *Hi a ni tsu si ya ka ni*

VERSE 6. *Hi yo wa hi ye yo ya ka ni*

VERSE 7. *Hi a ni he ho ya ka ni*

After chanting each verse, he shook his rattle and struck the note, *"I."* When the hymn was finished, he began to descend. As he did so he struck the note *"I"* as before, only this time holding it until he had come down, reentered the heptagon, and walked around the fire until he came to the spot where he had been robed. Standing as erectly as possible, he then cried loudly, "I am heard!" whereupon the entire assembly cried out an exalting, *"Hawh!"* His attendant then came to him, removed his white robe and put it back in the storage place, whereupon both men went to their seats and sat down.

The seven cleansers arose then and took from the bench seven whitened gourds — not the same gourds used earlier that morning to fill the cauldron with water. Each cleanser dipped his gourd in the cauldron and handed it to the headman of his own clan, who drank from it, rubbed some of the liquid on his chest, then passed it on to the members of his clan, who in turn performed the same ritual. The ritual was completed by midafternoon, and when it was done, the *Yo wah* hymn was sung a second time. Children participated in this rite, and the tasting and rubbing were repeated from time to time throughout the balance of the day. After first partaking of this purifying drink, infants, but not grown persons, were given a little nourishment.

Two hours before sunset, the *Uku's* principal assistant ordered everyone to go to the water. While they stood on the bank, the *Uku* prayed for them and then ordered them to bathe. As they waded in, the men went upstream and the women and children went downstream. Everyone quickly faced east and plunged entirely under water. Then they quickly faced west and did the same, alternating between these directions thereafter until they had immersed seven times. The Supreme Beings who dwelt above had ordered them to do this, and not to wipe the water from their faces until they had plunged seven times. Some people followed the custom of wearing old clothing, and while in the water, they disrobed and let the old clothing float away. This carried all

Child applying medicine to abdomen.

their impurities away with it, and upon emerging they put on new clothing they had brought with them. Those who did not remove their clothing nevertheless changed to clean dry garments, so that, on returning to the national heptagon, all were newly clad.

The *Uku* and his principal assistant walked at the rear of the procession as everyone returned to the Heptagon, where those with assigned places within it entered, and the rest stood silently outside. The *Uku* prepared now to offer the sacrifice. He went to the west side of the fire and faced east. His principal assistant stood by his side, and the seven counselors stood behind them and formed a semicircle around them. The *Uku* placed the piece of deer's tongue between his right thumb and forefinger, held the hand containing it high above his head, and prayed. Then he dropped the tongue on the hot coals and sprinkled it with old wild tobacco. Together with his assistant and the counselors, he intently watched to see what would happen. The number of deaths that would occur during the year would be determined by the number of times the meat popped. As regards sickness, if the smoke rose instantly toward the heavens, all would be well, but if the smoke formed a bluish cloud and did not rise directly, there would be much sickness among the people. Next, the *Uku* took seven deerskins, folded them, and placed them on a bench. He set his divining crystal on top of the skins and prayed. If the people were to be healthy, the crystal would flash a clear, unclouded blaze. If not, it would look smoky, and those who would soon get sick and die would be seen in the crystal.

As sunset approached, the *Yo wah* hymn was again chanted, and just before sunset the great speaker ordered that the meat and other food already cooked by new fires should be distributed to the people for the feast. The fleshy pieces of meat had been pounded, boiled, and cooked separately from the bones. Bread had been made from dried, new corn; pounded mush was prepared for the elderly people. These, hominy, potatoes, beans, and all other kinds of vegetables were brought forward, arranged for eating, and the people ate. But the seven counselors and the seven women who had fasted with the counselors during the previous six days were not allowed to eat until after dark, and the *Uku* and his assistant could not touch food until late at night. As for the chanter of the *Yo wah* hymn, he could only eat once each twenty-four hours during the four days of the festival, and even then it had to be after dark. He was also required to immerse just before eating and at daybreak each morning.

On the first night of the festival, the people danced a religious dance until midnight, at which time those who desired could rest. But a vigil must be kept for the entire night, and some of the women performed a religious dance whose nature stimulated and energized them. The Zuñi Indians of New Mexico keep such a nightlong vigil today during their famed Shalako dance and have told me that one must be awake if he hopes to see the gods when they come, else he will only know about them and never truly see them. Further, the gods appreciate this special effort on the part of the human beings and accordingly bestow their blessings upon their nation.

On the second day, the houses of the capital were again exorcised, and meat was again distributed to the homes to be cooked on the new fires for that evening's feasting. The above-mentioned ritual leaders continued to observe their rules for fasting, but the *Yo wah* hymn was not sung, and when the food was called for a little before sunset, the eating was not organized. The people were allowed to eat where and as they pleased.

The third day of the festival was a duplicate of the second day, and the fourth day's rituals resembled in every particular those of the first day. The *Yo wah* hymn was sung twice on the fourth day, once at noon and once about sunset. The houses were cleansed again, food was disbursed to be cooked, the people immersed, the sacrifice was performed, the divining crystal was consulted, and the leaders of the ceremony continued to observe their fasting rules.

Thus, the *Oole stool eeh*, his principal assistant, the seven counselors, and the seven women fasted ten days successively, eating only once in twenty-four hours; and the chanter of the *Yo wah* hymn fasted in the same manner four days. All of the people — men, women, and children — fasted two days, on which days even infants fasted until noon. Also, everyone except infants spent two whole nights, the first and fourth, in entire wakefulness. Soiled garments were put off at immersion time, either in the water, before entering, or immediately on coming out, and then the people clothed themselves in clean apparel. Besides this, everyone immersed on two occasions for a total of fourteen times. All in all, the amount of purification was extraordinary!

Except for a light supper no one was allowed to eat on the fourth night, and all were required to remain awake. The women passed the night in a religious dance. On the morning of the fifth day, sacrifices were again offered. The *Oole stool eeh* took the purified pieces of wood from the cauldron, held them in his hand until they had ceased to drip, wrapped them in a piece of buckskin, and exclaimed, "Now I return home." After the people responded, *"Hawh!"* he walked with his principal assistant and chief speaker toward the east side of the heptagon and put the articles in a place where they would never get wet. Then the three men left the heptagon so quickly that people thought they had disappeared by magic. Now the chanter rose to his feet, said, "Now I depart" and, when the people responded, *"Hawh!"* left the heptagon. In the same way, the seven counselors rose and departed. Then, after waiting a few minutes, the people stood up and went silently to their homes and resting places. Throughout this departure the most perfect order and dignity prevailed, and the people retired free from all pollution. The Cherokees were considered purer immediately after this festival than at any other time of the year.[7]

The Exalting, or Bounding Bush, Festival

The date of this final annual festival was set during the Festival of the First Moon of Autumn. Once the people had assembled in the national capital, a man previously chosen for the purpose appeared suddenly in their midst with an open-topped box in his hands. He danced slowly around, singing as he went, and each person he passed threw a piece of old wild tobacco into the box. When the box was filled, he departed.

The Bounding Bush Festival: man with the tobacco box. See color plate No. 11.

On both the first day and the first three evenings of this festival, spectators sat around the perimeter of the sacred square, while the *Uku* and other dignitaries sat high above them on benches placed at the front edge of the heptagon mound. Pairs of costumed men who stood side by side and who were separated from one another by pairs of side-by-side costumed women, danced around a huge fire in the sacred square. Six men – consisting of the lead pair, two men who were in the middle of the dance line, and two men at the rear of the line – bore in their right hands eighteen-inch-diameter wooden hoops with two straight sticks attached to them in such a way as to meet in the center and form a cross. White feathers were fastened to the ends of the sticks. The rest of the dancers held in their right hands green boughs of white pine.

The dances ended at midnight, at which time the hoops and green boughs were carefully deposited in the Heptagon with the other consecrated religious articles used in the ceremony, and they remained there until the participants were ready to begin the next night's dance.

After dark on the fourth night, fires were built, prepared food was brought out, and everyone joined in a joyful feast. At midnight, the man with the box returned, and as he walked among the people, he sang:

> *"U hu ni tu tu*
> *A ni hu le ya."*

He made four circuits to reach them all and gave each person an opportunity to take from the box a piece of tobacco. The people then plucked off pieces of pine leaves from the boughs of all but four

The Bounding Bush Festival: dancers with hoops and white pine boughs.

of the dance-team couples, crushed the leaves in their hands, and mixed the leaves with their tobacco. This done, the people formed huge concentric circles around the sacred square fire. At a signal from the *Uku* they closed slowly in upon it, holding out their hands as if they were about to throw the crushed leaves and tobacco, and singing, *"You you."* But at intervals they would suddenly pull their hands back, as if reluctant to sacrifice the offerings. When at last they did reach the fire, they as one person threw their offerings into the fire, and with this gesture the final great festival of the year ended. The annual cycle, however, was only at midstage.[8]

Ancient Minor Festivals

Minor festivals were celebrated at the capital and in the individual towns at the appearance of every new moon, at the beginning of each quarter of the year, and sacrifices were performed on each seventh day. The most ancient of the new moon festivals resembled the Great New Moon of Autumn Festival, although in a condensed form. They were led by local priests.

The quarterly New Moon Festival bore the same general characteristics as the monthly festivals, but was somewhat more involved. Along with the other parts of the ceremony that were performed, when people came to it, they always brought some of the medicinal roots they had taken from the tables at the Great New Moon of Autumn Festival. These roots were placed in a consecrated cauldron that sat near the town council house altar. While the cauldron was being heated, the officiating priest chanted a long hymn. When the brew was ready, a small, consecrated gourd was used to give a taste of it to each person present, who immediately thereafter drank water. When all had tasted the brew and water, the priest chanted again, and the people were ordered to the river to immerse seven times, dipping in the same rapid manner as they had at the Great New Moon of Autumn Feast. Once this purification act was carried out, the people were dismissed and returned to their homes.

By 1835, the traditions associated with the seventh day's sacrifice were sinking slowly into the lost category. Some informants said that in ancient times adults fasted throughout every seventh day while little children fasted until noon. Then everyone went to a river or stream and immersed. Other informants said that *Ye ho waah* had commanded the people to, on every seventh day, rest from all work and show their adoration for him by holding their hands entirely still while they rested their palms open and upward on their knees. If any parents labored on that day, they, or some of their children, would die. Also, ordinary things were not to be discussed. The people must confine themselves to talk about the Supreme Being that dwells on high.[9]

Festival Modifications and the *Ookah* Dance

As in remotest times, religious assemblies were convened in individual towns in every instance of public apprehension or calamity, for as has already been mentioned, the Cherokees ascribed all suffering — mortal diseases especially — to the displeasure of the beings who dwelt above. The beings themselves had told them nothing could prevail against their wrath except the propitiation rites. Therefore, in all such instances, these were resorted to.

The *Ookah* Dance

There was an occasional festival held in the national capital every seven years, and it bore no resemblance to the rest. It was entitled The *Ookah* Dance, because its purpose was to allow the *Uku* to offer his personal thanksgivings and adoration to the Creator, and on this occasion he was called *Ookan,* or "Thanks Giver." It was a feast of extreme rejoicing, not of sacrifice, and was required of the nation and its leader by the Creator himself. Every seventh year, at the end of summer and the beginning of · autumn, the people of all ranks and ages were to appear at the national heptagon for the purpose of giving thanks and rejoicing together with the *Ookah*.

The precise time for this wonderful festival was set by the *Uku* and his seven counselors, who then dispatched messengers throughout the nation to notify the people. Seven hunters from the capital were sent out to hunt during the seven days prior to the festival. Their kill was brought in on the seventh afternoon and distributed to the town women, who

The Ookah Dance was held every seventh year, with the *Ookah,* or *Uku,* being carried to his throne in the sacred square.

then cooked it for public use. By early evening of that same day, the entire nation had assembled at the heptagon, where the *Ookah*'s seven counselors appointed men to direct and order the banquets, women to superintend the cooking, an aged and honorable woman called *A ke yv gu stu,* or "honored matron," to warm the water that would be used to bathe the *Ookah,* two priests to bathe him and one to undress and dress him, a priest to carry him, a priest called *U lo tee* to fan him, a man called *Kv nv wi sti ski* to sing for him and lead the music, and a man to prepare his thrones. Under the supervision of

the latter, a tall throne with a canopy and footstool, carefully whitened, was erected at a midway point between the *Ookah*'s home and the sacred square fronting the national heptagon. A similar throne was also set up in the center of the sacred square, around which a broad circle was drawn, swept clean, and carefully guarded by priests to make certain that no unconsecrated person stepped on or entered it.

Seven days were required to do the preparatory work, and on the morning of the eighth day, the festival proper began. All of the priests, preceded by the *Ookah*'s seven counselors, went in procession to

The Religious Festivals   185

the home of the *Ookah*. They sang ancient chants as they walked, and when they arrived they found the honored matron waiting there with the warm water. The priest appointed for the purpose approached the *Ookah* and undressed him. Then the two appointed priests bathed him carefully, as one would wash a little child. This done, the man who had undressed him came forward again and dressed him in the yellow garments he had worn on his installation day. The priest appointed to be the bearer approached the *Ookah,* turned his back, and the *Ookah* climbed on, putting his arms around the bearer's neck and his legs around the bearer's body like a little boy would do when his father carried him.

Then, with the singer and the man bearing an eagle-tail fan by his side, the *Ookah,* preceded by half of the nation's priests and followed by the other half, was carried to his canopied white throne, with all but the bearer singing as they marched and the happy people crowding around and joining in. When they reached the first throne, the *Ookah* was allowed to sit on it for a moment while he and his bearer rested. Then the march and the music continued until they reached the sacred square, where he was again enthroned. Here he remained for the entire night, attended by his principal assistant, his seven counselors, his speaker, and his bearer, all of whom maintained a silent vigil while the rest of the people danced in the streets and in the national heptagon.

On the morning of the second day, the *Ookah* was lifted up from his throne and carried into the broad circle, where he was set down on his feet. He then began to dance a slow step, keeping always within the circle and constantly looking both right and left. As he passed each spectator, he bowed and received a bow in return. Just in front of him was the man with the fan, ready to fan him whenever he required it, and at his left side was his musician. Following him in single file and imitating his dance step was his principal assistant, his seven counselors, his speaker, and the other priests. After they had danced once around the circle, the *Ookah* was taken back to his seat, where, while his eleven immediate attendants kept watch over him, the other priests stood some distance away and watched. At this time

no woman was allowed to enter the sacred square and especially could not approach the circle where the *Ookah* danced.

Sometime after noon the men who ordered the banquets had the food spread out on the tables and called for the people to be seated, whereupon the *Ookah*, acting through his speaker, directed that everyone should eat. But the *Ookah* and his assistants and attendants fasted until sunset, when the speaker brought them food. After eating, the *Ookah* was carried back to his home in the same way as he had been carried away from it in the morning. Arriving there, his official yellow clothing was removed, and he was dressed in his ordinary dress.

With the exception of the bathing, the first day's ritual was repeated each day of the festival. On the fourth and last day, after the *Ookah* had danced, he was placed upon his throne, consecrated anew by his principal assistant, and by this act was reinvested with sacred and regal power. The yellow dress was worn only on this occasion and at his original installation. Any other time he sat on the white ottoman in the national heptagon and attended to his regular duties, while he, his principal assistant, and his chief speaker wore white clothing.[10]

Common to All Festivals

When he had completed his review of the entire round of festivals, Payne felt he should mention four things not yet covered that were applicable to all of the festivals alike. One was that the national heptagon, the sacred square, and wherever any part of the religious ceremonies took place could only be entered by Indians, and even then only by those who had qualified themselves by the fulfilment of certain requirements. An exception was that if a person charged with a crime could make his way unobserved into the heptagon or sacred square during a fasting time, or could get within the *Ookah*'s view, that person was absolved of his crime and could not be punished.

A second was that during a religious festival, no one was to touch an unclean person or thing, and no drunkenness was allowed.

Third, among the customs observed at some

festivals, if not all, was the gashing of limbs of young men and boys who requested it. Aged priests did this with sharp flints, carefully watching the faces of their subjects as they cut the long lines, filled bowls with blood, and then dashed the blood against the wall of the sacred place outside of which the ceremony was performed. At the least flinching, the priests cut still deeper. The intent of the gashing was to show the Above Beings how fully the subjects were willing to undergo whatever was necessary to secure divine blessings.

Finally, nothing could be more urbane than the bearing of the Cherokees at these festivals. There was no expression of superiority, no sourness, no affectation; they were considerate of one another. If by chance a conversation took a direction someone thought objectionable, even the highest among the priests simply and mildly remarked, *"Yay lee quawh,"* "That will do," or, "That is enough," which was always sufficient to put an end to the matter.

The Essence of the Festivals

It remains now to express some thoughts regarding the annual cycle of festivals and to consider what exactly they accomplished for the Cherokees. When we do this, momentous things become apparent, and our esteem for the Cherokees rises. For what we experience is vastly more than the thought patterns of a primitive people, and all of us can profit by applying their religious principles to our lives.

Earlier, I explained that the annual cycle of Hopi Indian ceremonies was preparatory in its nature, and that the Cherokee orientation was a similar one. This fact, among others, becomes undeniably clear as we examine the essence of the festival cycle. As we do so, please recall that in the Cherokee mind the cyclical idea found its origin in the annual cycles of nature.

In the Great New Moon Feast of Autumn, called "the Commencement" by the Cherokees, we find a ceremony that is held toward the end of nature's year and yet is actually a beginning. The Cherokees commence their annual cycle by — as the fruits of all of their crops are harvested and shared — *acknowledging* that the Above Beings are blessing

them and expressing in ritual their awareness that they are being watched over. Thus, the cycle begins on a strong and *positive* note. All is well between man and God, and it will continue to be so.

The Cementation and Propitiation Festival follows immediately, in which the union of the Above Beings and mankind is symbolized by the two men who perform the cementation rite. The fact that the Above Beings have blessed them so abundantly in itself proves to one and all that *nothing stands between the beings and them.* By the intense *purification* of man and his possessions, any barrier or hindrance man might have willfully or unknowingly placed between the beings and himself has been put aside and done away with. The gates to and from heaven are thrown wide open! Confidence abounds!

The Bounding Bush Festival is the natural climax to the assurance just celebrated. *Unrestrained joy* is expressed as the Cherokees acknowledge the source of their blessings, and thanksgiving is offered as the sacred tobacco is given to the fire by one and all. However, overconfidence can become a problem for man. He might begin to think he has accomplished his blessings on his own, or that he has received them because he deserves them.

So *winter* follows, and in its frigid atmosphere and bleakness the Cherokees are reminded over a prolonged period of time that without the beings, they are close to helpless where survival is concerned. As the fields become barren, the game retreats, the snow piles up, the sleet cuts at flesh and bones, even the bravest begin to wonder, and the tribal elders sit by fires and tell children and adults reassuring stories about how for countless centuries winters have come and gone. The beings do not forget those who love them.

Then, sure enough, the snow melts, the winds subside, the rains turn warmer, chunks of ice float down the rivers, and the first blades of green grass poke their friendly heads through the surface of the soil and look up at the sun. Mother Nature is renewing creation! Life is coming back. She has triumphed again over Cold Maker, and in concert with all creation the Cherokees are called to renewed celebration. The Above Beings have not forgotten them. It is time to plant again, to call upon Old Woman Corn Mother and to rejoice. The First New Moon Feast is celebrated, in which the old fruits provided as testimonies in past years are now consumed, and the new fires that symbolize fresh beginnings are kindled.

Can all of this really be true? Is it not, considering the nature of man, too much to hope that the beings have so much love for the Cherokees? But look! Out there in the fields the fruits are showing themselves. Old Woman Corn Mother did come when she was called. She did implant true life in the corn. There too are the beans and the other vegetables. Fruit is appearing on the trees. The streams run full. Out in the hills fawns are prancing around. The beings are coming down and revealing themselves in what they create anew. Now there must be total purification of the people so they will be fit for the union that is taking place. The New Green Corn Feast is called for, and the people will taste the corn as a tangible proof of hope and assurance fulfilled.

Finally, the ultimate victory is proclaimed with the harvest of the mature and ripe fruit. In the midst of its pungent aromas, *exultation and rapture* are expressed with abandonment in the Mature Green Corn Feast, and with this pageant of joy the annual cycle of major festivals comes to an end. But the next year lies ahead, and to assure that the blessings will continue, the annual cycle of festivals must go on and on.

"Must?" we say. But will the events of history immediately ahead permit this to happen?

Summary

Some final notes . . . It is obvious that as warlike as the Cherokees were, they were also deeply involved in religious practice and by no means gave over the majority of their time to battle during the clement months. Also obvious is that as many people as possible were given responsibilities in the annual rites, making everyone feel important and needed.

And one thing more. We can see that on a national scale the Cherokees wisely played out in ritual form a series of six steps that could and can still be applied in individual lives. For the overall

needs of the individual are the same of those of the multitude that makes up the nation, and they can be fulfilled by taking the same steps: beginning with *firm confidence* that God will answer the petitions we are about to offer up; acknowledging that one is forgiven and there are *no barriers that prevent the union with God*; unrestrained *joy and thanksgiving* for what one has received — then there is winter; then comes the celebration, together with the whole of creation, of *renewal and new birth*, and the assurance of the continuation of life; next comes *the tangible proof* in the tasting of the new fruits; and lastly *a dance of rapture* to mark the ingathering of the harvest that one knew from the cycle's beginning would certainly come!

Notice the extreme emphasis upon purification during the rituals and upon the color white that symbolizes it. Notice also that in the Cherokee cycle, although each festival includes rites that are duplications of those in other festivals, it also has rituals that are unique unto itself. Although we can assume that those were handed down from ancient times and that the Cherokees were certain they came directly from the Above Beings, we can also deduce that in the individual festivals, or meetings with the Above beings, one was expected to develop approaches that were unique and appropriate and which would in each instance produce the desired result. Thus, no two festivals in the annual cycle could ever be alike. Repetition was to be avoided, for one was never to be careless where the Beings were concerned, or to take for granted the divine and human relationship.

NOTES

1. Payne Papers, Vol. 3, p. 26.
2. Adair, *History of the American Indians,* pp. 77-83.
3. Payne Papers, Vol. 1, pp. 72-79.
4. Ibid., pp. 79-84.
5. Ibid., pp. 84-88.
6. Ibid., pp. 88-92.
7. Ibid., pp. 151-152.
8. Ibid., pp. 152-162.
9. Ibid., pp. 115-116.
10. Ibid., pp. 116-117.

CHAPTER EIGHT

Transformation of a Culture

We leave Chapter Seven on a reasonably high note. Our picture is that of a vibrant and fascinating culture with much to offer and whose citizens are pleased, fulfilled, and optimistic. No one will ever know what exactly the common people thought of their life, leaders, and form of rule. But the nature of the great festivals themselves indicates warm and free acceptance. There was no conscription, no force, no shaming of people into conformation. Still, the Cherokees were about to, in a relatively short time, give much of it up and exchange it for something new.

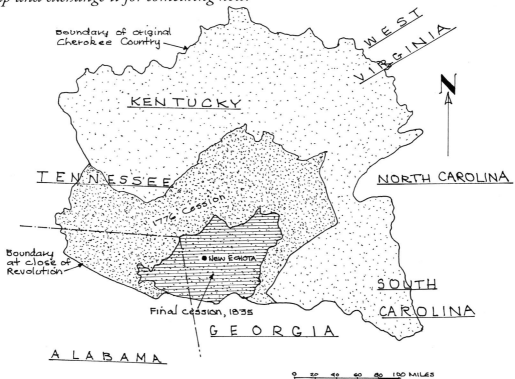

CHEROKEE LAND CESSIONS

Does this prove that Cherokee beliefs were tenuous and shallow, or that they were a fickle people deserving little compassion? I think not. There is far more to the surrender than at first meets the eye, and we must withhold judgment for a time. As the gripping story unfolds in the pages ahead, it will be seen that where Indians are concerned, what seems on the surface to be dead may underneath be very much alive. They show outsiders their faces but keep their hearts and souls to themselves. History has taught them it is best to do this, and in this chapter we encounter the history that taught the Cherokees this important lesson. In future chapters we will see how they have dealt with it. For now though, we should empathize with them and try to understand what must have been going on in their hearts and minds as the transformation got under way. It is so easy to assume that what was inculcated and forced upon them was for their own good, far better than what they had, and that they must have known it. Some thought so, but they were not full bloods. After we know the entire story we will need to ask ourselves some serious questions as to who exactly was converted and to what extent. For the transformation picture shows us what happened to, and the responses of, two distinct sides of a coin: the full blood and the mixed blood.

We will see that whites, and particularly the politicians and the missionaries, had a disconcerting tendency to lump the two sides together, and to describe their conversion and progress as if what was happening to one were happening to both. In a sense it was, but the rate of attrition was significantly different, and time will prove that long after the whites thought the old culture was given up, some of it still existed among the full bloods and is present today.

Early Expeditions to the Cherokees

The A. D. 1540 meeting between the Cherokee tribe and the de Soto expedition was a quickly passing event, and nothing of significance came of it for either party. Life for the Cherokees proceeded much as it has been described in the previous chapters, until in 1667 a British trading and explor-

atory expedition led by Henry Blatt came to visit the tribe. That year is probably the most significant and pivotal year in Cherokee history, for although no one recognized it at the time, it marked a turning point of greatest magnitude. Why? Because other traders from Virginia and South Carolina followed Blatt, and by 1690 a trader named Daugherty was residing with the Cherokees and had established a pattern of close fraternization that was to have a profound effect upon Cherokee development. At this point in time the proud Cherokees felt they had nothing to fear from a few traders who they thought were more dependent on them than they were on the traders. After all, it was Cherokee country they were in, and the Cherokee culture was powerful and highly developed. They were a grand and glorious people who were riding the rolling crest of a wave of influence and prosperity.

Unfortunately in this instance, the Cherokees were true to their adaptable nature. They were most curious about these newcomers and about their views, habits, and skills. There just might be something here the Cherokees could make use of. Nothing untoward was suspected. They knew nothing about the outside world or what was going on in it, and it appears they decided that the wisest course would be to keep the whites around and learn what they could from them.

Thus, and quite innocently on the Cherokees' part, began their conversion from a profoundly spiritual, warring, hunting, and semiagricultural nation to a wholly sedentary group of agriculturalists who would follow to a considerable extent the white manner of life. Difficult as it may be to comprehend how the Cherokees could give up under any circumstances such a rich and satisfying culture as we have witnessed, the answers become plain as the next 125 years speed rapidly by. In retrospect, we can see that the Cherokees and the intruding whites were on an ill-fated collision course, and that eventually the outnumbered and outgunned Cherokees would have no choice but to accept what came. Yet it is hard to believe that such graphic change as did take place could come about so quickly.

By the year 1700, imported metal weapons and

cutting tools were replacing the old stone and bone implements. Not long after that, the use of shell, stone, and feathers for arts and crafts vanished like a mirage. A steady stream of opportunistic white traders continued to infiltrate the country, bringing with them new agricultural methods, and for use in trade, guns, metal ornaments, trinkets, and whiskey. Many of the traders took unto themselves Cherokee wives and settled down in Cherokee towns. Before long their mixed-blood descendants were engaging in stock raising and the typical pioneer industries of the white colonial settlers. Within only a few decades mixed-blood descendants would also become the ruling class in Cherokee society, replacing the old form of white and red government, and they would exert enormous influence in the transformation of the native culture.

While no one tells us this in so many words, it is certain that early in Cherokee-white relationships the full-blooded Cherokees were straining mightily to hold onto traditional life while they at the same time moved into an eighteenth century that included whites who strongly opposed that tradition's continuance. We can substantiate the idea of straining by observing that sometime in the early 1700s, the resistance of even the most fervent Cherokees began to buckle, and as inevitably happened in instances of white intrusion into Indian lands, the unsure people let themselves be talked, by both whites and fellow mixed bloods, into altering their festival procedures. For awhile after that, national events continued to be celebrated in the capital, with the only exceptions being those instances of domestic or sectional sickness when families, and occasionally groups of families, were permitted to perform the rites in their own homes or towns. But as white power and the number of mixed bloods continued to increase, the power and appeal of the capital declined.

I do not mean to suggest that mixed bloods were insensitive to what was happening, or that they didn't care, but the mixed-blood youths had white or partially white parents to convince them that the old ways were heathen and counterproductive. Early in the historic period these children were persuaded and began to pull away from the ritual life. The full

bloods held on, but even among them, at first individuals and then towns as a whole began to act on their own and according to their personal convictions. Ultimately, most everything the Cherokees did became so modified and mixed up that the old ways came close to losing their effectiveness entirely.

Causes of Change

Where causes of change are concerned, historians tend to deal primarily with political events — but not in the case of the Cherokees, for religion and not politics was the core of ancient Cherokee life. The whites recognized this and planned accordingly. Punch a hole in Cherokee religion, they reasoned, erosion would set in, and in time the dam would give way. When it went, everything else of consequence in traditional life would go with it. With some exceptions, that is close to what happened. Payne collected excellent accounts of what exactly occurred in the demise of the spiritual world of the Cherokee nation, and for those who find merit in the ancient ways, it is not a pretty picture. I touch upon it in several places in the material ahead, but for now I will consider the political changes.

Opportunities to Capitalize

Whites who were careful observers of the Cherokee collapse saw numerous opportunities to capitalize upon what was happening to them. In 1735, Attakullakulla, who was the civil, or white chief of the nation and who resided at Chota, was taken, along with a small group of other Cherokees, to visit London. The Indians delighted the English residents and had their own eyes broadly opened to the attributes and strengths of white civilization. When they returned home, the English traders and officials made the most of this, and over the next twenty years carefully cultivated the Cherokees by offering to help whenever the Cherokees needed it. Attakullakulla was especially responsive, and in 1757 he would be instrumental in persuading the governor of South Carolina to construct Fort Loudoun to strengthen England's control over the area and to encourage more trade between the Cherokees and the eastern coastal towns. In addition, the chief invited at this time several more traders to set up headquarters in Chota and to take Cherokee wives.

In 1736, a Jesuit named Christian Priber, whose mission was both religious and political, came to the Cherokees and spent nine years with them. He gained considerable influence with tribal leaders, becoming a kind of unofficial secretary to the principal headman. But he served both the church and the French government, and his primary goal was to disrupt tribal relations with the English colonists. He did pursue some religious and educational ends, and in time compiled and had ready for publication a dictionary of the Cherokee language. But the manuscript was lost when he was captured and imprisoned by the English. Later, the Roman Catholic Church made sporadic attempts to further missionary work among the Cherokees, including token efforts in the educational field, but had limited success.

In 1738-1739, the smallpox epidemic previously referred to raged until half of the population had died — from 9,000 to 10,000 men, women, and children.

About 1740, the Cherokees obtained their first horses, and a horse trail was opened up between what later became Augusta, Georgia, and Cherokee country. By 1760, the tribe possessed large horse herds, and by 1775, each man owned from two to twelve mounts. Cattle were introduced by a renowned and farsighted Cherokee woman named Nancy Ward, and hogs and domesticated bees were probably introduced at the same time. The cultivation of European fruits had begun as early as 1670, and domesticated potatoes and coffee were among the many items brought in during the eighteenth century. In 1770, an Englishman arrived with spinning wheels and looms and by 1791, ordinary English farming tools would be in general use.[1]

Gradually and steadily the Cherokees were surrounded by and becoming part of a white man's world upon which they were increasingly dependent for food, shelter, and clothing. To the east were the English and what were becoming Americans, to the west were the French, and in the south were the Spanish, with all three of these contesting for trade advantages and for every bit of land. The old cooperative efforts of the Cherokees became more and more obsolete, and by the end of the nineteenth century the neighborhood cooperatives were nearly gone. Skins and textiles as mediums of exchange were replaced by white currency. Most produce was handled through white markets, and Cherokee young people began to learn the white man's trades. As white exploitation and control of the natural resources of the southern Appalachians continued, the old Cherokee system of economy collapsed. Except for deer, rodents, and birds, the wild game was disappearing. Fishing was subjected to severe restrictions, and even the Cherokees' efforts to raise livestock were limited by hampering regulations. Forest areas were denuded of trees as lumbering interests bought up and then exploited timber rights. Mining and chemical interests moved in to excavate the ground and to pollute and poison the plants and streams. Finally, waterpower interests came to build dams across the beautiful valleys, and numerous lakes appeared where formerly Cherokee homesteads had stood.[2]

Government too was changing; the old system of clan-tribal loyalty was giving way to demands for a republican form of government, and the people were emerging from the matriarchal system that had been the basis of their society for centuries. Into this flawed political scene stepped the rival and waiting forces of the English and French, whose divergent interests acted to pull the Cherokees even farther apart. The French had the superior diplomatic machine, but the English were better able to supply the guns, ammunition, and other resources the militant Cherokees desired, and an uneasy alliance was formed with the latter nation. In the last half of the eighteenth century, a rivalry for tribal control that whites had secretly encouraged developed between the leaders of the towns of Great Tellico and Chota and kept the tribe in a constant state of turmoil. Factions from both places began to bargain on their own with the whites, promising loyalty or military aid in return for more favorable trading privileges. Some Cherokee leaders figured out what was going on and sought to turn the tables on the foreigners. Before 1763, the French were being played off against the British, and after that date the Cherokee leaders shrewdly pitted against one another the colonies of Virginia, North Carolina, and Georgia. Throughout this period the crafty tribal leader Attakullakulla dominated tribal policy by grasping the import of white colonization and steering tribal policy away from the old ways of life and into closer cooperation with the settlers. It was during his reign that the sedentary life of farming actually replaced hunting as the dominant economic factor, and warring ways against neighboring tribes gradually diminished. Also, it was he who bargained for colonial forts and military garrisons to protect the Cherokees from their warlike neighbors.

Unfortunately for the Cherokees, these cooperative efforts alleviated but did not solve their problems, for tribal settlements remained squarely in the way of the relentless tide of white settlers, and the inevitable result was a series of wars with the whites that would last from 1756 to 1794 and result in the virtual annihilation of the Cherokee settlements.

Nancy Ward holds a position of great significance in Cherokee history, and must be mentioned here. In 1738, Tame Doe, the sister of Attakullakulla, gave birth to a daughter named Nancy, who in time became the last true Beloved Woman of the Cherokees, and who in her views regarding Cherokee and white relationships was an ally of Little Carpenter. In the early 1750s, she married the noted war leader, Kingfisher of the Deer Clan, and was at his side when in 1755 he was killed by Creek warriors at the battle of Taliwa. She immediately picked up his weapons and rallied the Cherokee warriors to overwhelming victory. Her first tangible reward was a black slave who had been left behind by the retreating Creeks, and legend has it that this was the beginning of black slavery among the Cherokees. Back at Chota, she was chosen to fill the vacant position of a Beloved Woman. It was believed that the Supreme Beings often spoke to the people through the beloved women, and they were given absolute power in the question of what to do with prisoners taken in war. Nancy did not hesitate to use

the power. She was also head of the influential woman's council that consisted of a representative from each clan, and she sat as a voting member of the council of chiefs. In the late 1750s, she married an already wed white trader named Bryant Ward, who before 1760 left her and returned to his white wife and children in South Carolina. In 1772, an English diplomat named Robertson visited Nancy's home at Chota, which he described as being furnished in a barbaric splendor that befitted her high rank. She was then thirty-five years old, and he pictured her as "queenly and commanding."[3]

Numerous settlements had been made on Cherokee land in direct violation of royal decree from England, and when the Revolutionary War broke out, the Cherokees once again sided with the English. In 1776, the Cherokees prepared to attack simultaneously the frontier settlements of Virginia, the Carolinas, and Georgia. The responsibility assigned to 700 warriors from Chota was to strike the settlers who lived in the Watuga area. As much for the Cherokees' sake as for that of the settlers, Nancy Ward helped Isaac Thomas and two other white men to escape from Chota in order to warn the Wataugans. This act established Nancy's reputation as a friend of the settlers. When in October 1776 Colonel William Christian led nearly 2,000 troops in a devastating retaliatory raid, out of respect for Nancy Ward he spared Chota, while most of the other Cherokee towns were ravaged.

In 1780, at a time when most of the Watauga men were away from home and engaged in the King's Mountain campaign, the Cherokees again prepared to attack the settlements in the Watauga area. Nancy Ward warned the whites a second time, but when the soldiers returned from King's Mountain and learned of the threat, they were enraged and set out to teach the Cherokees a lesson they would never forget. Despite Nancy Ward's pleas for mercy and friendship, Chota was destroyed along with other towns, and for a short time she and her family were placed in protective custody. When they were released, they returned to help rebuild the town, and on July 20, 1781, she was the featured speaker for the Cherokees when the reeling people reluctantly accepted a peace treaty with the Wataugans. When the Treaty of Hopewell was made in South Carolina in 1785, she offered another dramatic plea for continued peace between the Indians and whites. Once the unhappy war years were ended she lived in Chota, where although it was no longer the capital of the nation, it was still a city of refuge, and from all over the nation she took into her home orphaned and homeless waifs, including mixed breeds. Nancy Ward died in 1822, a truly remarkable woman who earned a permanent place of honor in Cherokee and white history.

Another Cherokee leader who must be mentioned is Tsunu-lahun-ski, whom whites called Junaluska. After a stunning massacre at Fort Mims by the Creeks, General Andrew Jackson went after the perpetrators, and in accordance with the terms of a previously made treaty, Chief Junaluska went with 500 Cherokee warriors to assist the general. While on a scouting mission, Junaluska overheard Creek warriors plotting to surprise and kill Jackson, and he risked death by swimming across an ice-chunk-filled river to warn the general. On March 27, 1814, after Jackson and his troops had been routed by the Creeks, Junaluska and his warriors joined him at Horse Shoe Bend in Alabama to fight and to play what became the crucial role in winning perhaps the greatest battle in Indian history.

The Cherokees relate that, during hand-to-hand fighting, Junaluska struck down a Creek warrior who was about to run a bayonet through Jackson, and that after the battle ended, Jackson swore an everlasting friendship with the chief. Unfortunately, the chief believed him, and in the years ahead had good reason to regret his trust.

The First Protestant Missionaries

During the last half of the eighteenth century, the first Protestant missionary efforts of significance were made among the Cherokees. But the goals of the natives and the whites differed considerably, and none of these early attempts was successful. The missionaries wanted to convert the "heathens" and save their souls, but the Cherokees wanted to read and write, so as to better compete in the white man's

world. In 1757, a protestant clergyman named John Martin came to the Overhill settlements on the Little Tennessee River, but he concluded that while the Cherokees wanted instruction in white ways they were not ready to be converted. His replacement in 1758 agreed. In 1763, Little Carpenter asked the colonial authorities to send a minister to instruct his people, and the group of Cherokees who visited England in 1765 repeated this request. But a succession of Protestant clergymen who came between 1783 and 1799 had little success in accomplishing what either party hoped they would.

The outbreak of the American Revolution had already embroiled the Cherokees in a storm of opposing forces. Because of their existing blood feud with the Americans and their long relationship with the British, the Cherokees joined the latter in what proved to be a fatal war against the revolutionists. Since the Cherokee hunting grounds had greatly contracted, the Americans were able to simultaneously attack them from all sides, allowing Tennesseans to wipe out the Overhill towns, and Carolinans and Georgians to ravage the Middle and Valley settlements.

Some Cherokees fled to the hill country of northern Georgia, where during a period of comparative peace and respite from 1794 to 1836 they managed to build up a thriving community governed by mixed bloods as a dependency of the United States. Further changes came now in the disposition of the tribe as a whole. The traditional faith of the people had been thoroughly shaken, first by the fact that their priests were not able to deal with the smallpox epidemics that had repeatedly swept through the tribe, and further by the fact that their supposedly invincible towns had been several times devastated by the whites. Thus confused and doubting, most Cherokee people became willingly responsive to the persistent efforts of Moravian, Presbyterian, Baptist, Methodist, and Quaker missionaries who began their work about 1801.

Over the next thirty years, the Cherokee nation would undergo changes that, because they moved the tribe closer to what whites considered to be civilization, were for mixed bloods welcome and good. On the other hand, because they moved the nation away from traditional life, the full bloods considered the changes to be unwelcome and bad.

The first actual school was established by the Ross family at Kingston, Tennessee, in 1799, when J. B. Davis was hired to teach the Ross children. But he also accepted children from the neighborhood and had perhaps twelve students. In 1799 the Moravians asked permission of the Cherokee council to establish a mission school. Some full bloods objected, and the school, located in Spring Place in northwest Georgia, did not open until 1801. By 1802, the tribal council was already unhappy with the nature of the mission and threatened to expel the Moravians unless they placed greater emphasis upon teaching, spent less time preaching, and agreed to clothe and board up to thirty students. The mission did improve in those areas and over the next two decades did some successful teaching.

In 1803, the Presbyterian Church established a mission at Hiwassee, Tennessee, and their poorly endowed school opened in 1804 with twenty to thirty Cherokee students in attendance. A typical day began with prayer and washing. Then there were "scriptures and praise," followed by public prayer and lessons until breakfast. After an hour of recreation, there were additional lessons until lunch. After lunch, there were more lessons and work, ending in a spelling session just before supper. After supper came hymn singing, prayer, and bed.

Despite the emphasis upon religion, the first conversion of a Cherokee student did not take place until 1810. Cultural differences and the fact that the students could neither speak English nor had a written language of their own are cited as reasons for this. In order to surmount the impasse, the missionaries forced the children to accept the clothing, food, and manners of the whites. They were instructed in table manners and opened and closed each meal with a prayer, and they were dressed in homespun cottons that were either donated by Presbyterian congregations or made by the wives of the male schoolteachers. But the students could not accustom themselves to sleeping in beds, so they slept on the floor.

Outside Cherokee country, whites as a whole

remained skeptical about the ability of the "savage" Indians to learn. To counter this, in 1805 the Reverend Gideon Blackburn took his pupils to a treaty meeting between representatives of the Cherokees and the United States, where before a large audience of Indians and whites they were publicly examined. "Each scholar read such a portion as was requested. The different classes then spelled a number of words without the book. Specimens of their writing and ciphering were shown, and the exhibition closed by the children singing, with a clear and distinct voice, a hymn or two committed to memory."[3] In conclusion, the American commissioners expressed great joy over the progress of the students and wished Blackburn everlasting success in his missionary pursuits. But financial difficulties and mission-board doubts continued to plague the mission schools, and church boards regularly questioned whether the missions should be continued. In the late fall of 1807, a Presbyterian committee visited both the Hiwassee and Sale Creek schools and examined eighteen students. Of these, they found that "twelve could spell well off the book, ten read the Bible and other books pretty well . . . ten could repeat the Shorter Catechism in part, one only the whole, five write a tolerably good hand, one had studied arithmetic as far as through compound interest. The remaining six had made some progress in spelling and reading. The most of them for their age and time in school had made good proficiency."[4]

Skelton states, "It is well to remember that these schools were being started at a time when many still regarded the Indian as an inferior race, and some of the very motivation of the missionaries seemed to reflect what became known at the close of the century as the 'white man's burden.'" In this regard he notes the remarks of agent Meigs, who upon witnessing one of the public examinations of the students, said, "It is impossible, at least for me, after reflecting on what I have seen of these children, at this and sundry other exhibitions, not to be convinced that the minds of these people are capable of the highest improvement."[5]

Religious and domestic changes, intermarriage, loss of confidence, whiskey, the contributions of mixed bloods, and the mission schools all were having their inexorable effect on the Cherokees. By 1810, the old system of blood revenge for private wrongs had been superseded by a system of regular civil courts. In 1817, what would become the famous Brainerd Mission School was established, and soon after that mission schools spread across much of the Cherokee Nation. Before 1820 the death penalty for marrying within the clan was abolished in favor of whipping. These changes more than anything else interfered with the system of clan rule, and clan dominance in political integration and political functions came to an end. Only its ceremonial status was retained. Organized legal sanctions replaced the older rules for individual behavior. The death penalty for practicing witchcraft was abolished, and somewhat later it was declared wrong to even recognize the crime itself. This attempt to do away with belief in witchcraft fractured the old system of ritual laws and allowed it to be replaced with specific penal sanctions, such as laws against theft and murder.

The Reverend Cephas Washburn wrote at this time — although in truth it appears to be in reference to only that part of the nation's citizens he was acquainted with — that with such influences silently at work on the very foundations of Cherokee society, it was not to be wondered that astonishing changes would take place in the entire nation. And indeed there had been great change since he and his fellow workers first came among them. At that time there were not twenty men in the nation who wore hats and pantaloons. Now there were not more than twenty who did *not* wear pantaloons, and the great majority wore white-style hats. The majority of the females now wore bonnets, many of them of the leghorn type. There was among both sexes, but especially among the females, an extravagant fondness for white-style dress. The Cherokees nearly all lived in comfortable cabins, many of which had plank floors. They had tables, knives and forks, plates, cups, saucers, chairs, and other amenities. Their houses were generally as well furnished and their food was generally as abundant and as well prepared as was common in the white settlement. The people used coffee and sugar daily. All had more

or less land under cultivation where they raised corn, both Irish and sweet potatoes, and most kinds of garden vegetables. Little serious regard was, Washburn claims, paid to their heathen rites. The Green Corn Dance was now observed by a very few, and not as a religious ceremony but as a scene of amusement and revelry. When a war party returned from a successful expedition, some would attend a scalp dance, but it was only a scene of boisterous joy and drunkenness. Considerable superstition still remained. The more ignorant among them believed in witchcraft and conjuring. To the former they ascribed many of the evils which they endured, especially when affected with unusual diseases, and they applied to the latter to relieve them from their evils. They were improving in the points previously referred to. As far as the whites and most mixed-blood Cherokees were concerned, worthwhile progress was being made. Ancient superstitions were yielding to the influence of religious instruction. The Cherokees had, it was thought, many fine attributes such as patience, fortitude, courage, and hospitality. The affections among parent and children, brothers and sisters, and all the other relations were very strong. Respect for the aged, Washburn states, was manifested by everyone.[6]

The Festivals

Contrary to what Washburn claims about Green Corn ceremonies being observed by a very few, Payne, whose informants were members of the full-blooded communities, reports that in the 1820s the Green Corn Festival was still well attended and held annually. It commenced after the corn had ripened and continued in different towns throughout the main part of the autumn months, but admittedly in an altered and suspect form. Priests were now "conjurers," and unexplainable modifications were made that caused the once great religion to flounder badly.

Hundreds of full bloods gathered at each town, but thanks to the inroads made by the missionaries, mixed bloods, settlers, and state and federal governments, their enthusiasm was waning. Compare what we are about to consider to what we found just a few decades ago. There is performance now, but no longer the passion of old; petition, but wavering faith; the thrust of the ancient way is present, but its application is such that it hangs on by a thread. In disapproval, the Above Beings seem to be distancing themselves from the Cherokee people.

No rule was enforced regarding the number of days to be devoted to the Green Corn observance. A dance might continue for anywhere from three to seven days. People usually spent the first day visiting in and about the town council house and danced a little at night. On the second or third day, the principal exercises commenced. The chief conjurer of the town in which the festival was held led the dance. He advanced, singing, into the square, level yard in front of the town council house, and for accompaniment shook a small gourd with gravel enclosed in it — the sound of which was believed to resemble the rattles in the throat of the dying. Presently he was joined by a considerable number of men — women did not participate in this dance. Some brought rifles and pistols charged with powder and wadding and others had clubs, poles, and branches of trees. They formed a single-file column behind him.

The leader led them several times around the yard, then in zigzag fashion repeatedly crossed the yard backwards and forwards until the dance line had traversed it from one end to the other. The line of dancers now exhibited a serpentine appearance, and because their movements were perfectly regular and simultaneous, frequently presented the picture of a huge water snake undulating on the smooth surface of a lake. Meanwhile, an irregular firing of guns was kept up, and when the firing tapered off there was considerable hallooing and shouting. This dance continued for the greater part of the day, with rest intervals for refreshments that consisted mainly of bread dough made by folding together Indian corn, beans from the new crop, and long green blades of corn, and then boiling it. At night the common dance was performed. Excessive drunkenness and its consequences generally prevailed, especially toward the close of the dance. On these and similar occasions the old men seemed as if they were seriously

absorbed in the fulfillment of a solemn duty, but the greater part of the more youthful Cherokees only assembled as a lark and for something less than the purest reasons.

It appears that both of the Green Corn festivals were being blended together, and that from the outset of their acquaintance with firearms, the Cherokees made use of them in their celebrations, firing away in such festive joy that the women and children would stop up their ears and run for their lives.

As for the Great New Moon Feast that once began the revered annual cycle, on the first appearance of the new moon of autumn, the people of each town assembled at the dwelling of the conjurer, who on this occasion had two assistants who were subject to his orders. Seven days prior to the festival, these two appointed seven men to hunt and seven men and seven women to fast. One of the assistants chose seven men to sing for the women dancers. The first of these took his place, began his chant, and the women started to dance. The leader of the women — who had strapped around her calves terrapin shells that were partly filled with pebbles that gave a measured tinkle as she moved — was followed in single file around the fire by the other women. The first singer performed for about forty-five minutes, then withdrew and rested while another singer took his place. This method was followed until all seven singers had performed, at which time the dancing ceased.

Before sunrise the next morning the conjurer gathered all of the men, women, and children into a convocation house that had been expressly prepared for the occasion. The people were seated in rows, with their faces turned toward the east. Opening a crack about a foot long in the east wall, the conjurer set his divining crystal in it and prayed as he consulted it regarding its omens about the life or death of everyone present. This done, he put the crystal away, and the people went outside. The women busied themselves with cooking, and the men gathered wood, gauging their time so as to have everything in readiness by noon. One assistant was assigned to the task of obtaining the proper kinds of bark needed to make the fire on the altar of a smaller structure called the "house of sacrifice," and the other assistant watched the seven men and seven women to make certain they did not break their fast before the proper time.

Meanwhile, the conjurer chose several men to clear a path to a neighboring stream, to prepare seats for the people, and to erect two tables for him to spread his deerskins on — one at the riverbank and one at the convocation house. While they did his bidding, he went alone up on a mountain to sing and pray. He came down in time to meet the people at noon, the precise moment of which both he and they ascertained by fixing in sundial fashion a stake perpendicularly in the ground and watching it while the sunlight struck it.

He immediately ordered the people to follow him to the convocation house where, as soon as they were arranged in rows and stood with their faces to the east, he prayed with them, but as was proper for the most sacred prayers, in a tone too low to be audible. He then spread on the table, with the flesh side up, the skins of a buck deer and a doe. On top of the skins he placed folded pieces of colorful new cloth that had been given as offerings for the ritual. On top of these he laid seven six-inch-long strands of beads, one for each clan. Each woman had with her a six-inch-long string that had three beads on it — one red, one white, and one black. She wet her beads with spittle, and the mothers did this for their infants, then beginning with the oldest woman, they walked up in single file to place them on the doe-skin. The men had similar strands of beads and put theirs on the buckskin. When everyone had done this, the cloths and skins were folded up in such a way as to leave only the hair side of the skins visible, and the two assistants picked them up.

The people were told to go to the bank of the stream, looking straight ahead as they walked. When they arrived they were to fix their gaze on the water. Once everyone was out of the convocation house, the assistants followed with the folded packets, and the conjurer brought up the rear of the procession.

At the riverbank, the packets were placed on the previously prepared table, then unfolded and arranged as they had been in the house of convocation. The bead strings were now in full view and laid out according to the age of the owners, with the beads of the oldest coming first.

The assistants set up in the sand a line of tiny flag sticks, and the people watched them for omens. When the conjurer felt enough time had been spent in watching, he began to consult the bead strings. Beginning with the string of the oldest man, he took from it two of the beads — a white one to symbolize life and a black one to symbolize death — and placing one of these between the thumb and forefinger of each hand, he held them up as high as he could, then slowly lowered his hands, praying all the while. If the white bead seemed to move the more actively of the two and as if seeking to escape, all would be well with the owner. If the black one was more active, the reverse was true. When every string had been used in this wise, the conjurer cast the entire lot into the stream and urged the people to quickly follow them in. The women entered it with their clothes on, and they and the children went a short distance downstream from where they had been seated. The men stripped and then went in the opposite direction, a little upstream from their seats. Everyone immersed four times while they faced east, always so swiftly that the beads of water remained on their heads as they straightened up, then they quickly turned about and immersed three times while they faced west, making a total of seven times. The two assistants immersed also, and no child was excepted. Everyone was required to plunge entirely under the surface of the water and on coming out to put on clean, dry clothing.

While this purification ritual was being performed, the conjurer set a medicine root on the table for each person, and also placed his divining crystal there. Then he went through the types of conjurations previously described. When the people emerged from the water, they received their pieces of medicine root and returned to the village. The conjurer's assistants brought back the folded but empty deerskins and cloths, and followed by the conjurer, they entered the house of sacrifice, while the people went to the convocation house.

The assistants had prepared the altar and fire with the seven kinds of bark, and now the conjurer made his offering. It consisted in this instance of the piece of deer's tongue mixed with as much mush as would fit on the blade of a knife, and over this a sprinkling of old tobacco. The conjurer revealed to his assistants the omens he deduced from the offering, and one of the assistants went to the convocation house and made them known to the people. If any were going to die, the total number was proclaimed, but no names were mentioned. If none was to die, the people were simply told that all of them would be present at the next meeting.

At this point, women brought the cooked food into the convocation house and set it on benches. Just before sunset, everyone ate together, including the two assistants. But the priest remained in the "house of sacrifice." After a time, he put away the skins and cloths, and when the others had finished their meal he went to the convocation house and ate.

When it was dark, the seven singers sang once more while the women repeated the dance they had done on the preceding night. Only infants were allowed to sleep on this night. In the morning, the people returned to their homes, taking with them the roots they had been given at the water. From time to time they chewed these and rubbed their bodies and arms with the juice. Most people tried to make the root last until the first new moon of spring.[7]

Variations were also employed when the Cementation and Propitiation Feast was celebrated.

A circle was formed on top of the altar with seven different kinds of wood, and radiating out from the circle like the spokes of a wheel from its hub were seven strings of white beads that represented the seven clans. The strings were placed on the altar by one member from each clan and were said to be pointed towards the wood. Two fire makers put dry goldenrod on a basswood hearth board, and pairs of fire makers twirled a basswood stick on this until the goldenrod ignited and could be used to start the fire on the altar.

For divination, the returning hunters gave the conjurer the skins of a buck deer, a doe, and a fawn. He spread these out on the west side of the fire, with the heads turned towards the fire and the east. The hair sides of the hides were down. He then took a small bunch of weeds or grass and dipped it in fresh blood, either that of deer or fowl, and drew with it on each skin a line of blood that extended from the head to the tail. After this he set his divining crystal and seven strands of beads on the middle of the blood line on the buckskin. He looked carefully at the crystal, for if the people were to be sickly, the crystal would be smoky and blue, and if they were to be healthy, it would shine brilliantly. Next, the beads were consulted. One after the other he picked up each string of beads and examined it, determining what they portended concerning health by the kinds of movements the beads made.[8]

As for the Bounding Bush Festival, the man with the open-topped box no longer appeared, but the other aspects were retained. It too was performed at those seasons when it best suited the people's convenience and inclination, although people knew that in earlier times it was always observed annually on the latter part of the first autumnal new moon.[9]

The Cementation Festival was resorted to for relief in every case of public distress, but in so modified a form that it no longer accomplished its purposes.

Payne believed these changes were introduced by the worshipers of the sun and moon, and by the men now called conjurers, who were commonly allied with the sects just mentioned, although many of them worshiped nothing except themselves — a far cry from the priesthood of old. Surprisingly, the people were settling for this.[10]

In the first of two recorded variations of the Cementation and Propitiation Festival, when pestilence or "fever" was feared or prevailed, the people of the town assembled and asked the seven counselors of the town conjurer to make arrangements with him to prevent or stop it. One of the counselors passed this request on to the conjurer, while the other counselors chose a *Yo wah* chanter, a person to dress and undress him, seven men to hunt, seven women to lead the sacred dance, and one or two musicians. The festival was to commence on the evening of the seventh day following.

The conjurer went immediately to find the herbs and roots needed for the occasion. There were seven of these, and they were the same medicines as those used in the old national Cementation Festival. As each plant was gathered, the conjurer uttered over it a special prayer that named the purpose for which it was destined and asked that it would receive the power to accomplish that purpose.

Seven kinds of wood were brought in and arranged in a circle for the fire, and seven strands of beads were added that pointed toward the circle. The wood, although sometimes kindled by a twirled stick, might also be lighted with a flint stone. Before the altar fire was lit, some of the wood was set to one side to make the fire needed to boil the herbs.

The people began a fast at sunrise on the seventh day, and a little before sunset they assembled in the town council house, with each clan sitting silently and as a group. The festival got under way with the center white ottoman being occupied by the conjurer and his principal assistant, and their feet resting on especially prepared cane matting. The seven counselors and the speaker occupied the other two ottomans to the right and left of the center seat. Since these seats were always on the west side of the house, the door being on the east side, these officials always sat with their faces toward the east.

The old fire had been cleared from the altar, and the new fire built in its place. The hunters had brought in the skins of a buck, a doe, and a fawn, and the conjurer folded them and laid them down by the fire. A whitened cauldron was filled with spring water and set on the separate fire provided for it. The herbs were dropped into the cauldron, and a buzzard's wing was laid across the cauldron's top. With his face turned toward the west, the conjurer prayed to the setting sun, and while he did this the seven counselors began to watch the cauldron, continuing thereafter to watch it day and night for the duration of the festival.

The musician now took his place and raised his voice as he struck his drum. The seven women who were appointed to lead the dance came forward and in single file moved with a slow step around the fire and the cauldron. Behind them, forming circles

within circles, came the other women, and last of all the younger girls. When this dance ended, the *Yo wah* chanter and the seven cleansers, or exorcisers, proceeded in every respect as they once did at the parent festival. And when the chanter and cleansers had cleansed the town and returned to the town council house, the women resumed their dance and continued it throughout the night.

At sunrise on the following day, the conjurer faced east and prayed. The herbs having been thoroughly boiled in the cauldron, he dipped seven gourds into it and gave one to each of the seven counselors. They tasted the liquid, and then each handed his gourd to the members of his own clan, who passed it among themselves until everyone had shared it. The *Yo wah* hymn and the exorcisms by the seven cleansers duplicated what was done on the previous day. All of the people fasted until sunset, and at its approach, divination ceremonies were carried out, again using the three deerskins, with the addition that one by one each person went to the conjurer with a marked white bead and wetted it with spittle. The bead was placed on a skin — the men's beads on the skin of the buck, the women's on the doeskin, and the children's on the skin of the fawn. The conjurer kept these beads so that he might, in case any of the people became ill later on, determine by consulting their beads what would happen to them.

At this point, the people were told to make ready the dining areas in the sacred square and to put the prepared food there. But they were not to begin eating until they were notified that the evening sacrifice was finished and had been told what things were learned from it.

The conjurer, his assistant, the seven counselors, and the speaker remained in the town council house to watch for the omens of the sacrifice. With his face turned toward the setting sun, the conjurer put the tip of the deer's tongue on the fire. He sprinkled over it powdered old tobacco, and he prayed that he would learn whether the dreaded pestilence might be driven away. This prayer and sacrifice had to be witnessed by the departing sun. If sickness were to prevail, smoke would gather in a blue cloud and hover over the flames. If sickness were not to prevail, the smoke would rise straight up toward the sky. Also, if the sickness could not be prevented, the divining crystal would take on a blue tint and the entire town would appear in it. Those who were to die would be a peculiarly dark blue, and the others would by comparison look bright. If good health was forthcoming for everyone, the crystal would grow more and more brilliant. Whatever the omens, they were made known to the people, who by this time were already seated at the dining places. At the conclusion of the report, the people were directed to eat, and everyone commenced at the same moment.

The second through the sixth days were repetitions of the first day, except that the fasting lasted only until noon, and the second through the sixth nights duplicated the first, except that the dancing ceased at midnight. On the seventh day, everyone fasted until sunset. The prayer and sacrifice rituals of the first day were repeated, after which everyone ate, and that night was a duplicate of the first night.

On the morning of the eighth day, the conjurer took herbs from the cauldron, held them up until they ceased to drip, placed them on a buckskin, folded it, then together with everyone else departed in the same manner as at the close of the ancient Cementation Festival.

The second modification of the Cementation Festival was employed when smallpox was present or a threat, and it was not introduced until the original Cementation Festival had become thoroughly corrupted by those who worshiped only the sun or moon. Rife among these people were surprising new ideas regarding the source of this terrible disease.

One source was an invisible spirit or, as some said, a "kind of devil" called *Ko sv kv u ski ni*. He was always inclined toward evil, was the bestower of the sickness, and was only restrained by the Above Beings until they set him loose to destroy. Another was that of two tormentors, spoken of as two devils, who were spirits of a quiet disposition who usually let people alone. The female of these was the color of a ripe chestnut burr. She was entirely covered with fine prickles that let loose whenever she touched anyone, and they raised the fine red pimples characteristic of smallpox. The male was the color of the ripe pokeberry hue, and whoever he touched exhibited the blackness that the smallpox pustules afterwards assumed. It was believed that these spirits did not sleep, except for a short time about midnight. Accordingly, anyone who wished to escape them must do so at that time, and if someone wished to return safely home from a place he was visiting, that hour should be made the most of while dead silence was maintained. Also, the two spirits always prowled in wide-open places, so those who wanted to avoid them used bypaths in the woods. Moreover, despite the threat posed by the spirits, no one was to speak a word against them or let other Cherokees know that the spirits were regarded with dismay.

Whenever it was suspected that these evil spirits were haunting a neighborhood, the people assembled and chose seven men, one from each clan, to take the necessary precautions needed to ward them off. These seven elected a conjurer to officiate and sent one of their number to give him notice. The conjurer began immediately to gather the seven kinds of herbs that were needed. On the fourth day following, and at a little before sunset, he brought the herbs to the town council house. At sunset, the ceremony began with the people silently assembling in the house. The new fire was already lighted, using the same materials and forms employed at the fast for fevers, and there with it was the filled cauldron, the herbs, and the watchers of the cauldron. Those who presided occupied the same seats and maintained the same silence as the conjurer and his assistants did at the fever feast. All was as still and as solemn as at a house of mourning, and no one slept that night.

When the sun rose the next morning, the conjurer faced it and prayed to it. He then distributed the liquid from the cauldron. The people did not eat until noon, and the conjuror and his counselors did not eat until sunset. Only those who had to gather food left the town council house, and even then only at the midnight hour when the evil spirits would be sleeping. Then they hastily returned.

People were allowed to sleep, and the only drink permitted was spring water.

Dead silence was maintained at the town council house during the second through the fifth days, with nearly the same rites as those of the first day being performed. Exceptions were that on the second, third, and fifth days, an herb drink could be tasted whenever anyone desired, and on the fourth day the consecrated drink from the cauldron was distributed as it was on the first day.

The sixth day followed the same routine as that observed on the second and third days, but the seven counselors sent out early in the day all of the hunters who had guns. Their kill was brought in that same night and, along with the tip of the tongue for the sacrifice, was deposited in the storehouse.

On the morning of the seventh day, the conjurer prayed to the rising sun, the consecrated drink was distributed as on the first day, and everyone fasted until sunset when, the meat having been cooked by the women and long dining tables prepared, the food was set out and the people sat down at the tables. The conjurer, counselors, and speaker remained in the town council house to perform the sacrifice and to determine its omens. Once the portents were proclaimed, the order was given to eat. It was considered vital that the closing prayer and sacrifice on this occasion should be witnessed by the setting sun, and the evening rites were the same as those enacted on the first evening of the fast for fevers.

The seven counselors having previously selected a man to preserve a portion of the sacred fire, that portion was from that moment kept in a secret place and carefully guarded. It could never be employed in cooking, no torch could be lighted by it, no coal from it could be thrown where it might be extinguished, and it must be kept burning for the duration of the keeper's life.[11] We are not told what happened to it after he died, but it may have been that another keeper was appointed to take his place.

The conjurers of this period had rites they employed in times of drought, when a change of temperature was needed, or when devastations from storms either were feared or had already occurred.

Although these rites were obviously based on the ancient festivals, they too were tainted with new customs.

When the soil in a given area became so dry and parched that townspeople were desperate for rain, they would assemble at the town council house, where they would ask the town conjurer's right-hand man to take charge of the arrangements. The preliminaries included the sending out of seven hunters to hunt for seven days, and the appointment of seven men and seven women, one from each clan, to fast for the seven days immediately prior to the ceremony. On the evening of the seventh day the hunters returned and the fast ended. The people assembled at the town council house, and the rite began. A male courier was selected to carry to the conjurer the hunter's deerskins and a piece of deer's tongue, along with a request that the conjurer perform the appropriate ceremony for the emergency. Also, the courier was to remain with and assist the conjurer until the ceremony was completed.

If the request of the people was for him to "bring down rain," the conjurer's first act was to spread out on the ground and next to the fire a deerskin whose flesh side was turned up. He prayed while he sprinkled old tobacco dust on the fire and then sacrificed the deer tongue. After this he carried to a nearby creek a string of beads that was long enough to reach around a person's neck and had seven swan feathers attached to it. He placed at the water's edge a flat stone whose upper side was smooth, doing this in such a manner that the smooth portion was even with the surface of the water, and laid on top of the stone the string of beads and feathers.

This done, the conjurer prayed to the moon, calling him, "husband of the sun," and then prayed to the sun. Once more he prayed to the moon, imploring this being to take the necklace and put it around the face and neck of the sun, so as to darken her face and make it possible for clouds to come from the mountains. This prayer finished, he shook a terrapin-shell rattle and afterwards prayed to the little men at the north, who were "the little thunders," entreating them to send clouds and rain to the very spot where his deerskin was spread on the ground. Finally, the conjurer begged the greater man in the west, who was "the great thunder," to come in all of his strength and majesty and to bring with him the clouds needed for abundant showers.

If the foregoing appeals were ineffective, the conjurer called upon the Woman of the East. This being had long ago promised that whenever the other powers failed the Cherokees, she would if sought provide plenty of rain, always without thunder. It was said that no appeal for rain made to the Woman in the East was ever known to fail, which, if it weren't for knowing that ritual must follow its prescribed course, would cause one to wonder why the Cherokees didn't just skip the others and pray to the Woman of the East in the first place .

When the conjurer finished his prayers he withdrew from the creek for a time, then returned to invariably find that the stream had risen sufficiently to indicate that rain was falling in the higher elevations, and that the beads and the feathers had floated off the stone. Then when the rain did reach the town, if it came down more heavily than was desired, the conjurer offered a sacrifice of old tobacco to the Woman in the East, imploring her to hold back the torrent.

The moment the first drops hit the ground the citizens of the entire town assembled at the town council house to honor the being or beings who were believed to have sent the blessing, and they performed there in their name or names a nightlong solemn dance of thanksgiving. The persons who were appointed to fast remained inside the town council house until their seven-day fast ended, and food was brought to them there.

Although it was difficult in 1835 to determine the exact significance of the Woman of the East, she was often directly or indirectly alluded to in Cherokee traditions, and with great deference. Payne speculated that she might be the first woman created — the one who by legend was said to have been destroyed by her sons — and thought the following story and the forms of ritual connected with it had her in mind.

Certain Cherokee conjurers believed in an ancient tale that related how the corn once died, leaving upon earth a seed, and that the spirit of the corn instructed the spirit of the seed to use conjurers to look up to its Mother Corn Above whenever it was in trouble. When the people wanted rain, the conjurers prayed for clouds to be sent, first to the great mountains, second to the plains, third to the otter, and last to Mother Corn Above, who was responsible for the white seats, or snow, that capped the mountaintops. They prayed that she would ask the moon to send clouds from the mountains that would bring rain to the corn in the fields below. When the prayer was done, the conjurers waded into a stream until they were waist deep, then sang to the four beings just named. As they sang they threw water into the air with both hands and watched it fall like rain back to earth. If rain was to come soon, a snake would soon swim towards them.

If the weather was too cold and the people wanted it changed, they assembled at the town council house, where seven men were selected to gather seven large bundles of sticks. There had to be one bundle each of peach, plum, mulberry, locust, blackjack, or "a low kind of red oak," grapevine, and one of a large kind of whortleberry that grew in the old Cherokee country east of the Mississippi, on or near brooks, and some eight or ten feet high. When these bundles were brought to the town council house, the conjurer made a fire of them, and threw its coals into a terrapin shell full of old tobacco. This was a sacrifice to the Woman of the East and a prayer to her for warm weather. As soon as she complied with the request, she was honored with an all-night thanksgiving dance.

When the weather was too warm, the conjurer prayed to a great red man in the north to send cool air, and while he prayed he sacrificed to the red man the leaves of Spanish oak and ivy.

If the conjurer wished to learn whether high winds were coming and what their nature would be, he would build a sacrifice fire and sprinkle old tobacco on it. If the winds were to be a destructive kind, the smoke would fly in every direction, but if not, the smoke would rise straight up. If a gathering storm threatened to blown down trees and cornstalks, the conjurer would do battle with it by lighting his pipe and going outside where, with eyes blazing and hair flying and a string of old tobacco leaves in his hand, he would blow tobacco smoke toward the clouds, since it was believed that the Thunder Beings were waging a fierce war and by their clashes producing the storm. Then he prayed that the fire and the smoke would turn away the storm. [See color plate No. 2.]

The *Ookah* Dance was never modified. At whatever point in time the last *Uku* surrendered his position, it simply ceased to exist.[12]

At this point we can answer one of the questions we began with. If the old religion was slipping away, in what sense was it going? The answer is in modifications that led to confusion and doubt. The Cherokees should have known better, for the Above Beings had made it clear that changes or modifications of the ancient precepts were beneficial only if they were a matter of advancing and keeping up with progress. But if the modifications were simply attempts to conform in order to be accepted or popular, they risked a disastrous result and religion was not the only thing being modified; so was government. We are about to witness the shattering climax of that questionable move.

The Republican Government

Copying in its main features the characteristics of the United States government, a republican government was set up in 1827 at a convention in New Echota, and John Ross was elected principal chief, thus beginning a long and remarkable career as a Cherokee leader. There were also democratically elected representatives, and legislative, judicial, and executive arms. Cherokee country had previously been divided by law into eight districts, and four representatives were elected for each of these districts. The tribal legislature consisted of two houses, a national committee, and a national council. Four circuit judges were provided for, and courts were held in each district on an annual basis. A ranger was provided in each district to care for stray property. Taxes were assessed to pay for tribal debts, road repairs, schoolhouses, and the like. Penalties were

enacted for horse theft, and liquor traffic and slavery were regulated and restricted. Polygamy was at first discouraged, then finally done away with.[13] There were also appropriations voted for the establishment of a national press and the printing of a national newspaper.

Although a recalcitrant group of North Carolina full-blooded Cherokees, who are described shortly, steadfastly refused to cooperate with white ways and authority, the other and mostly mixed-blood part of the tribe was rapidly becoming anglicized. By 1830, the transformation of these Cherokees was nearing completion. Mixed-blood offspring had grown up to be prosperous merchants, traders, planters, slave owners, writers, tribal statesmen, and teachers who lived in impressive Euro-American-style homes and embraced the social mores of the whites. Included among these were names now famous, like Ross, Vann, Ward, Adair, Lowry, and Rogers. Whereas the North Carolina Cherokees owned only thirty-seven slaves, the more affluent Georgia Cherokees owned 1,223.

Referring to these Georgia Cherokees and seconding what Washburn had written earlier, the Reverend Samuel Worcester said in 1827 there were indeed a depth and earnestness about the Cherokees at this time such as was seldom found in any people. Two years of residence at New Echota had convinced him that the outlook for the Cherokees was indeed hopeful, that the civilization of the whole people, as well as their evangelization, was not an impossible dream.

Following the last session of the Cherokee general council, he scarcely recollected having seen any members who were not clothed in the same manner as the white inhabitants of the neighboring states; those very few who were partially clothed in Indian style were, nevertheless, very decently attired. He had seen there only one Cherokee woman, and she an aged one, who was not clothed in a decent long gown. In New Echota only one woman, and another aged one at that, was willing to be seen on the streets in her original native dress. Three or four who in their own houses still dressed in Indian style hid themselves with shame at the approach of a

Top, the Reverend Samuel A. Worcester, missionary, translator and publisher in Georgia and Tennessee from 1825 to 1835 and in Indian Territory, at Park Hill, from 1835 to his death in 1859. *Bottom,* the brick residence of Chief Joseph Vann, at Springplace, Georgia, built about 1800. John Howard Payne and Chief John Ross were once imprisoned there.

stranger. Among the elderly men there was yet a considerable number who dared to retain part of their Indian dress. The younger men almost all dressed like the whites around them, except that the greater number wore turbans instead of hats, and in cold weather blankets frequently served for cloaks. Regular cloaks, however, were becoming common. There yet remained room for improvement in dress, but that improvement was coming with surprising rapidity.

Cherokee women were spinning and weaving cloth. Most of their garments were made from cotton they produced in their own fields, though some came from northern states. Calico was worn, and silk was common. Numbers of the men wore imported cloths, broadcloths, cottons, and wools that were made into clothing by their wives, although the greater number of people were clothed in cotton.

Except for the arts of spinning and weaving, little progress was being made in manufacturing. A few Cherokees had become mechanics. Agriculture was the principal employment and support of the people. It was the mainstay of nearly every family. As for the people who still hunted for game, if any of these were to be found in the nation — for Worcester certainly had not found them or even heard of them except from the floor of Congress and other distant sources of information — he did not know of a single family who depended in any degree of consequence on game for support. It was true that deer and turkeys were frequently killed but not in sufficient numbers to be depended on as the prime means of subsistence. The land was cultivated with very different degrees of industry, but Worcester believed that few Cherokees lacked an adequate supply of food. The ground was uniformly cultivated by means of the plough and not, as formerly, by the hoe only.

The houses of the Cherokees were of all sorts, ranging from elegant painted or brick mansions down to very mean cabins. The mass of the people, however, lived in comfortable log houses, generally one story high but frequently two, sometimes of hewn logs and sometimes unhewn, commonly with a wooden chimney and a floor of the puncheons that

New England men called "slabs." Their log houses were poorly furnished. Most had scarcely any furniture, although a few were furnished elegantly, and some decently. Improvement in the furniture of their houses appeared to follow improvement in dress, and at that time the progress was rapid.

Regarding education, Worcester said the number of Cherokees who could read and write English was considerable, although it was only a fraction of the whole population. Among such, the degree of improvement and intelligence varied. The Cherokee language, as far as he could judge, was read and written by a large majority of those between childhood and middle age. Only a few who were beyond middle age had learned to do this.

As for the progress of religion, he cites the number of members in the churches of the several denominations who were then among the Cherokees. The whole number of native members of the Presbyterian churches was about 180. In the churches of the United Brethren there were about fifty. In the Baptist churches he guessed there were probably as many as fifty. The Methodists, he believed, counted more than 800, of whom he supposed the greater part were natives. Many of the "heathenish customs" of the people had fallen entirely, or almost entirely, into disuse, and others were fast following in their steps. The total number of members was 1,080, yet he went on to assert that he believed that the greater part of the people acknowledged the Christian religion to be the true religion, although many who made this acknowledgment knew very little of that religion, and many others did not feel its power. Through the blessing of God, however, religion was steadily gaining ground.

"But," Worcester concluded, "it will be asked, is the improvement which has been described, general among the people, and are the full-blooded Indians civilized, or only the half-breeds? I answer that, in the description which I have given, I have spoken of the mass of the people, without distinction. If it be asked, however, what class are most advanced, I answer, as a general thing — those of mixed blood. They have taken the lead, although some of full-blood are as refined as any, but, though those of mixed blood are generally in the van, as might naturally be expected, yet the whole mass of the people is on the march."[14]

On the march indeed! If so, it was still a meandering and a stumbling one for more than a few Cherokees, and we must consider these to possess a well-founded picture.

There is a strong and unmistakable note of confidence and triumph in the Reverend Worcester's comments. And in this he echoes what other whites of the time chose to believe, that the Cherokees and their southeastern neighbors — for what was happening to the Cherokees was happening to them also — were becoming civilized, that is, becoming what in the white mind represented acceptable civilization. Thus, the eradication of the old Cherokee culture was assured, and the rapid conversion of those people whom whites thought represented all Cherokees proved this. Yet, as in the case of Washburn, what Worcester describes in truth represented only the mixed-blood part of the Cherokee nation, and a fractional part at that, albeit a substantial one. His broader application was wishful thinking on his part. The rest of the nation *was* changing, but neither so rapidly nor so willingly or completely as he stated. There was still ample evidence that the ancient beliefs were deep-seated, and that while some customs were being put aside, others were going underground to surface another day.

In 1835, a man known as J. P. Evans communicated to Payne some vivid sketches of Cherokee character, customs, and manners that were derived from personal observations made during a residence of more than two years with "the full-blood recalcitrants in the old nation east of the Mississippi." His time period is established by his reference to Sequoyah's having invented his syllabary "a few years ago," which would place it around 1825. The "old nation" he referred to was that part least influenced by whites.

Evans began by admitting there were at that point in time few individuals among the Cherokees who had not conformed in some degree to the customs and manners of the whites. But there were also communities that clung tenaciously to the old

customs and that on many occasions exhibited the original character of the tribe.

Within the chartered limits of North Carolina, Georgia, and Tennessee, the Cherokees were still divided into towns and clans. Although each town had its own headman, the town was not a close cluster of dwellings contained within a small space as among the white settlers. It was a small colony spread over some miles. The town was not composed of a single clan, for clans did not have any relationship to the size of a town or the number of its inhabitants. There were no natural boundaries to the Cherokee clans, and the members of different clans were intermingled. A Cherokee could as yet tell what degree of relationship existed between himself and any other individual of the same clan. A man and woman of the same clan were not allowed to become husband and wife, but this custom was beginning to crumble, and the disregard of it was disgusting and portentous in the eyes of the tribal elders.

Even though new laws based upon Euro-American laws were being put into practice by the council of the Cherokee Nation, the influence of the headmen of the old towns remained considerable in those matters of minor importance they presided over and about which they made binding decisions. In all criminal and important cases, however, the written laws had supplanted the ancient customs. Murderers were no longer subject to the revenge law, and in the courts that had been instituted by the written laws, trained judges presided and trial by jury was guaranteed.

Hospitality remained a prominent feature in Cherokee culture, and the idea of eating whenever one was hungry was scrupulously complied with. To such lengths was this custom carried out that in many towns an invitation was not a prerequisite to eating. It made no difference whether the visitor was a stranger or a relative, and no compensation was expected for food, lodging, or supplies for one's horse.

The taciturn temperament of the people still prevailed, and visitors frequently entered a house in silence and shook every member of the family by hand without uttering a word or moving a muscle of the face. But this was not always the case. Morning and evening greetings were common, but the custom was observed more frequently on meeting a white person than it was among the Cherokee themselves. Old men, on meeting, were seen to grasp each other's arms between the elbow and shoulder, which was a mark of particular friendship. When approaching a dwelling, it was customary to give as a warning two or three sharp yells while yet some distance off.

Cherokees who were not influenced by the manners of the whites never bent their necks or bodies when saluting a person, but there was something in their manner that more than compensated for this. They remained in an upright position and shook one so cordially by the hand that the one they were greeting was always impressed with a feeling of deep sincerity. A prominent trait in Cherokee manners was that of speaking one at a time. Evans found it remarkable that while speaking in public the Cherokees did not make use of gestures or motions of the limbs. Lengthy harangues from town heads did not include a single gesture. The speaker stood with his fingers interlocked throughout the entire oration. Even at sermons fervently preached by white missionaries, the Cherokee interpreter relayed the sermon to the flock without gesture or motion of any kind. Yet in private conversation Cherokees did just the opposite, using motions that were illustrations and accompaniments of words resulting from developed habits.

Whether on horseback or foot, when a man and woman traveled together the man went in front and the woman followed. This was partly a social custom, but it was also a defensive one in early times, for the man was best prepared to meet the enemy. No matter how many Cherokees might be traveling together, they all proceeded in single file, and women and children always occupied a position at the rear of the line. Cherokees who were going from one place to another did not consider themselves at leisure, but trod away with might and main without entering into any conversation of consequence. They frequently carried large burdens, and at the same time the women bore their infant offspring in blanket slings on their backs.

The dress of the females was now copied from the whites. The dress of the men consisted of a short, buckskin hunting shirt, in the construction of which considerable taste was displayed. In winter a beaded belt was worn around the waist. Coarse, homespun pantaloons were the most common, but some older men disdained their use and wore deerskin leggings. Moccasins were extensively used by both sexes, but shoes were coming into vogue. A blanket served as a cloak by day and a bed by night.

Dwellings in general consisted of insignificant log huts. Hothouses were still being made but now were simply small, low-roofed huts constructed of small logs, mud, and clapboards. To make the roof, a layer of thick planks was first laid on and then a thick coat of mud covered with bark shingles. A small entrance door was placed in the wall. All visible avenues through which air could find admittance were carefully sealed off with mud. Burning coals were confined in a central hearth, and fuel that produced little or no smoke was used. Evans said that a white man could scarcely exist in such a habitation, yet during the winter months many of the old Cherokee men spent most of their time in the hothouses roasting potatoes and parching corn. Young people who lacked adequate bed coverings also spent their nights in these houses.

Every town had either its town house or a particular spot of ground appropriate for dancing and for holding council meetings and courts. The town house was still built in a circular form and had perpendicular walls six or eight feet high. But it was not placed on a mound. The rafters ended at a point, giving the finished roof a conical form, and they were supported by seven interior posts. The distance from the floor to the highest point of the roof was fifteen to twenty feet. Inside, planks were laid horizontally along the walls to serve as seats. The roof exterior was covered with tree bark held on with hickory shrub or white-oak strips. A doorway was provided, and opposite this on the interior was an angular wall that deflected wind. Outside the door was a small portico providing additional protection. In front of the town house on the east side was a square and level yard made smooth for dancing.

Evans said that the old Cherokees remained extremely superstitous, believing in the power of numerous charms, incantations, spells, and enchantments. They seldom trusted in medicine alone for the cure of disease but also resorted to conjurers — and with perfect confidence in their skills. The conjurers on their part claimed to be able to ascertain whether a sick person would live or die. After invoking a spiritual being, they usually cast beads belonging to the sick person into a stream of water. If the beads floated, it was considered a good sign. If they immediately sank, the patient was considered lost. Along with a favorable reply came the necessary revelation that revealed the proper remedy for the illness.

The Cherokees least influenced by the whites were of a copper color. Their features were regular, and their form on the average was better than that of the whites. Cases of deformity or defects in muscular or bony conformation were seldom experienced. Evans claimed that the crookback or spindle shank could hardly be found in the old nation.

The Cherokees delighted in acts that added to their strength and health. Their diet in the summer months, and of many Cherokees for the entire year, consisted principally of hominy, potatoes, and bread made of cornmeal and beans. Those who ate considerable meat possessed more muscular strength than those who subsisted mostly on vegetables. Yet the latter could better endure hardships and bore up better in exhausting tasks than the former. So well assured were the people of this fact that consumers of meat were excluded from the lists of ball players.

In his view, many of the subjects Evans observed had sunk into the lowest depths of ignorance, superstition, and vice. He could hardly conceive that human beings could be brought lower. Yet there were many who, though they were ignorant of "the arts of civilization," exhibited considerable native dignity. They were high-minded, honorable, candid, sincere, and hospitable. And to the honor of the nation, the majority was peaceable, industrious, and as well versed in farming and the arts as a majority of the whites by whom they were surrounded. There were also many individuals who would grace the most

refined society. The clouds of heathenish darkness and low superstition, Evans said, which overshadowed many other tribes, were rapidly dispersing for the Cherokees, and considerable numbers were living under "the benign influence of Christianity."

Ball play was yet a favorite sport with the full-blooded Cherokees, and to excel in it was considered a proof of manhood and added greatly to a man's respectability and standing in his community. Men entered the lists of players with as much enthusiasm as if they expected their performance would gain them unbounded fame and renown. The game was as violent as ever, and a new dimension was rearing its head — after the games there was often drinking and quarreling among both players and spectators.[15]

When in Chapters Nine and Ten the Eastern and Western Cherokees are treated, there are references to a number of dances that would seem to have no precedent in Cherokee culture and appear to have sprung out of nowhere. But Evans laid the groundwork for these when he described a few dances he observed in the 1820s that apparently had ancient roots and were a regular part of Cherokee life. Those dances he does not mention were surely done also, but he, like so many other whites, either paid no attention to them or was simply not permitted to see them.

One dance was more frequently performed than any other, and therefore Evans calls it "the common dance." To hold one of these, the only thing needed was a proclamation by the civil head of the town stating that a dance would take place in a certain number of nights at the town council house or dance ground. It seldom happened that such a dance was not held for want of participants, but if there was a shortage of whiskey, the dance was certain to end at an early hour. And, even while it did last, it lacked the usual animation and energy.

At sundown, a keen, shrill yelling and whooping were heard in all directions near the place of dancing, which indicated that the people were gathering, for as already mentioned, it was customary for the Cherokees to scream or whoop on approaching a house, and they frequently did this when they left a place. Depending upon the number of people involved, the dance was either held indoors or in the yard in front of a dwelling. An hour or two after nightfall, the people were all present and ready and silently awaited the signal to begin. Presently, a male dance leader stepped forward — either voluntarily or by solicitation. He walked once or twice around the fire that had been built in the center of the dancing place, then invited others to join him. Sometimes a drum consisting of a keg with a skin stretched over its open end was struck a few times as a signal. The leader started to sing and stamp his feet in quick time and in this manner moved counterclockwise around the fire, immediately followed by other men who imitated his movements and who answered his shouts in a brief chorus that resembled a boat song. In a short time the men were joined by one or two women who had fastened to the calves of their legs rattles consisting of the shells of terrapins with small pebbles in them. Any other person who wished to dance could now participate. Generally, an equal number of males and females were engaged at the same time, but this was not a rule that had to be complied with.

Stamping in quick succession with one or both feet at a time, Evans said, usually constituted the Cherokee manner of dancing. The leader generally sang extemporaneously, and the air was filled with a combination of high and low sounds issued in rapid succession, with but few variations. Evans felt it was disagreeable and monotonous, and not being able to speak or understand much of the Cherokee language, he speculated incorrectly that the leader was relating his love adventures, misfortunes, and triumphs, or boasting of his manhood, his influence with the fair sex, and his dexterity in various performances.

The men and women did not dance alongside or fronting one another, but proceeded in "Indian file" with the men in front and the women next. Boys and girls who were being initiated into the dancing art at an early stage brought up the rear. The leader made a great many "grotesque" motions and contortions, slapping his hands together and raising them alternately one above the other, all the while turning and twisting and bowing "ludicrously." (What mistakes people make about Indians when

they don't first seek understanding!) The motions and gestures of the leader were repeated by his followers or sometimes done simultaneously with his, for through constant practice the performers were able to anticipate him.

Any person could commence or leave off dancing when he wished. Frequently, a large number of people were engaged at the same time. Towards the close of the dance they interlocked hands and formed the figure of a coiled serpent with the leader leading them in as many turnings, windings, and eccentric evolutions as was possible in the space available. Since the line of dancers was a long one, its sudden turns never failed to produce confusion, and the dance ended precipitately with bursts of laughter, hallooing, and yelling. Repetitions of this dance, conducted by different leaders, the drinking of whiskey, and quarreling and fighting often consumed an entire night.

A woman's dance was a more rare occurrence than the common dance, but it was inaugurated in the same manner by the town head. When the hour of dancing arrived, an old man, usually the oldest in the dominant clan of the town, commenced singing a dirgelike air while he beat time on a keg drum. Like all Cherokee beats, this one did not possess much variety. However, Evens found that some parts were "a little touching" and, in the mind of one accustomed to civilized society, added somewhat to the gloomy feelings produced. Before the old man had spent much time in singing, two or three women came forward with their terrapin rattles on and kept time by stomping as they skillfully moved around the fire. In a short time, most of the women present joined in the dance, and the performance was continued for as long as the whim of the old man prompted him to sing. After resting for a half-hour to an hour, the singing was resumed by the same man or by another, and the dancers again danced. The night of the woman's dance usually ended with a common dance and finally with the same kind of drinking as previously described.

Evans felt that if all other Indian tribes danced like the Cherokees, some writers had greatly misrepresented them, for there was no variety in the movement of their feet. They stamped in rapid succession with one or both feet at a time and when stationary simply jumped up and down on both feet. This constituted their only steps in dancing. Today, we know that what he was describing in this instance was the common stomp dance that is currently performed in Oklahoma.

The Beaver Dance originated as a celebration of a successful beaver hunt, and it was said by informants that in former times the skin of that animal was exclusively used in the dance. But in the 1820s beavers were scarce, and the Cherokees substituted the skins of other small animals. Every person who intended to join in this dance brought a short stick or a club, and thus prepared, both men and women began a common dance, or something very much resembling one. Previous to the beginning of the dance or immediately thereafter, an old man took a rope twelve to fifteen feet in length and tied the skin to the middle of it. Taking an end in each hand and throwing the center of the rope over a peg driven into the ground, he stood prepared to move the skin by alternately pulling on the ends of the rope. After dancing for a half-hour or more, a man and a woman broke ranks and approached the skin in the manner of hunters with brandished clubs — the man in front and readying himself to strike the skin a blow while the old man whipped the skin back and forth by pulling on the rope. When the hunter had made his attempt he threw down his stick and retired. Then the woman tried and, after her, all of the other dancers. The amusement provided by the dance resulted from the awkward and usually unsuccessful attempts to hit the skin, for the old man was an experienced manipulator. Whenever a person missed, there were hooting and derisive laughter from other dancers. When everyone had had a turn, the remainder of the night was spent in common dances.

The Eagle Dance was seldom done in the 1820s, but people remembered that the capture of the eagle had given rise to the dance and that the ritual was supposed to be continued. When it was performed, it was without having captured an eagle, for the eagles had retreated from intruding civiliza-tion and sought safer places in the deep recesses of the forest. But some eagle feathers had been pre-served to be used at the ceremony.

Owing to its rare occurrence, the Eagle Dance never failed to draw a large crowd to the town council house or dance yard. The performers were chosen from among the most athletic and active young men, and these convened a short time after nightfall in a private place where they painted themselves in a manner similar to ball players and decorated their heads with feathers. They then arranged themselves in lines four to six deep, so that the arrangement was something like that of a platoon of soldiers. This was the only time in Evans' experi-ence that he saw a dance line of this kind.

The long, shrill war whoop was sounded by the dancers, immediately after which they moved forward in quick time, dancing and answering in a short chorus to the singing of a person appointed for that purpose. Although the motions of their feet were quick, they proceeded at a slow rate by mincing their steps. They halted frequently and, before setting off again, issued a war whoop that was so deafeningly shrill it stunned the ears of those specta-tors who were unaccustomed to it. Thus the dancers proceeded until they reached the yard or the interior of the house. They then seated themselves and joined in a song that was part of the dance. Shortly after this was finished, an old man bounced to his feet with a war hatchet or club in his hand and related the adventures of his youth with as much warmth of feeling as he could muster. Since there were few surviving warriors left in the nation, the elders were forced to resort to different memories and related a number of fabulous anecdotes, some of which were pure fiction. These tales were sometimes repeated three or four times, and both men and women joined in.

When the others had made their contributions, the old man commenced singing and dancing, at the close of which he flourished his weapon over the heads of the dancers.

Evans described another dance, which present day ethnologists entitle the Booger Dance. It con-sisted of three or four men who were disguised by masks that were made of large gourds which had openings for the eyes, nose, and mouth and were garishly painted. The performers represented beggars who were on a long journey, and their disorderly clothing reminded Evans of the crafty Gibeonites who appeared before Joshua as ambassadors from a distant land. Evans doubted whether Garrick ever acted a part on the English stage that conformed better with nature or reality. Never had he seen low life and old age acted so well as by these Cherokees who were so disguised.

A man went to the seated performers and asked them various questions: Where were they from? Where were they going? The first of them usually answered that they had come from a far distant land whose name they made up. Other questions were asked of them, and the answers given never failed to produce great laughter among the audience. When the questions ended, the performers were invited to dance, and they performed after the manner of the eagle dancers, except that their dancing and accompanying gestures were so ludicrous and such exact imitations of the characters they represented that the giddy onlookers were convulsed with laughter.

Immediately after this display, the principal performance commenced. The masked characters advanced into an open space in the center of the house or yard, and while the old man sang for them, they danced in a stooped-over position and glided around the fire with a movement of the feet so rapid as to resemble the twirling of a top. It consisted of a trembling or rapid vibration of the muscles and, at the same time, a regular and brisk movement forward, requiring the utmost exertion of muscular power. But the effect of the dance appeared to depend mostly upon a variety of obscene gestures and movements that Evans was not willing to describe. The remainder of the night was spent doing common dances.

Among those Cherokees observed by Evans, the Green Corn Dances were still taking place annually, commencing after the corn had opened and continuing at different towns throughout the greater part of the autumal months. Each place appointed for holding a dance was attended by a multitude of people. There appeared to be no standing rule in regard to the number of days to be devoted to the observance of this festival. It sometimes continued for three days and other times from four to seven. The first day was ordinarily spent in lounging and conversing around the town council house and in the immediate vicinity, and in a little dancing at night. On the second or third day the main portion commenced.

The head of the town in which the festival was held led the dance. He advanced singing into the square level yard in front of the town council house and shook a small gourd rattle. After a few moments, the leader was joined by a considerable number of men, some with guns and pistols charged with powder and wadding and others with clubs, poles, and branches of trees. With the leader at the head, the column of dancers proceeded several times around the yard, and then crossed it repeatedly, going backwards and forwards until they had traversed the yard from one end to the other. During this maneuver, the line of dancers, now numerous and in single file, exhibited a serpentine appearance, and since their movements were perfectly regular and simultaneous, the spectators got the impression of a large serpent swimming on the smooth surface of a lake. All this time, an irregular firing of guns and pistols was kept up, along with hallooing and shouting. The dance continued for the greater part of the day, with rest periods for refreshments that consisted principally of bread made from the new crop of Indian corn and beans. This bread was made by enfolding green blades of corn in dough, and boiling it. The cakes made in this manner were facetiously termed "broadswords" by the whites, and interestingly enough I found they are made today on the Eastern Cherokee Reservation.

The remainder of the time was spent in similar performances and at night in performing the common dance. Excessive drunkenness and its accompaniments generally prevailed — especially towards the close of the dance. The old men, Evans concluded, seemed to be seriously engaged in the performance of a solemn duty, but the greater part of the young people treated it like play.[16]

We can return now to what was going on politically among the people of the Cherokee nation in the 1820s.

Encroachment by White Settlers

The encroaching white settlers progressively reduced the area of Cherokee tribal lands to northwestern Georgia, western North Carolina, and eastern Tennessee, but the reduction at the same time permitted a consolidation and unification of the Cherokee Nation. New Echota became the new national capital, the Cherokees undertook new enterprises, and once again the nation flourished. The Presbyterians and Congregationalists united in their missionary efforts, and the missionaries, principally the Congregationalist, Samuel A. Worcester, built schools and churches throughout the nation and encouraged the Cherokees to persevere and achieve in their new life. Through Worcester's influence, mission-school graduates were sent on to academies and colleges in New England, and the result was well-informed and dedicated tribal leaders such as John Ross, Elias Boudinot, Boudinot's brother, Stand Watie, John Ridge, and Charles Hicks. It was a most rewarding time, and the mixed bloods were convinced they had at last achieved acceptance, that they at last had equality, and that they had finally become what the whites wanted them to be. Perhaps they even thought of themselves as white — after all, a goodly number did have more white than Cherokee blood in them.

In 1809, a brilliant yet unschooled and illiterate Cherokee mixed blood named Sequoyah, whose German father's name was George Gist, began to invent symbols to represent words. Over a period of several years he astonished Indians and whites alike by developing a Cherokee syllabary, an eighty-five-character system that reduced the tribe's language to written form. Dr. Worcester saw what Sequoyah's invention offered the people and arranged for movable type to be cast of the alphabet. A press was installed in New Echota, and in the spring of 1828, the first Cherokee newspaper, The *Cherokee Phoenix*, whose manager was Elias Boudinot, was published. Its name was carefully chosen, for it would remind people of the legendary bird of Egyptian mythology that rose from the ashes to live again, and it became the symbol of Cherokee resistance.

The newspaper's columns were printed in both English and Cherokee, using the Sequoyan syllabary. The laws and constitution of the Cherokee Nation were also printed. While many of the mixed bloods were literate in English, the full bloods were not. The new alphabet in a matter of months enabled most of the tribe to read and write in their native language, and the Cherokees became the first Indian tribe in the United States to have a written language and a newspaper in its own syllabary. In honor of this, the great trees bordering California's Yosemite Valley were later named the "sequoyia giants."

Things seemed to be going extremely well for the tribe, but under the surface the Cherokee situation was a perilous one. Georgia was protesting about the idea of having a tribal government within her borders and claiming the right to use force if necessary to rid the state of Indians. The Cherokees were seen as a handicap that prevented Georgia from progressing at the rapid rate other states were. And the number of white settlers coming into Georgia had become so great they joined in the clamor for the total abolition of the native Indian government

Cherokee transformation costumes.

ᎦᎵᏉᎩ ᏚᎴᏏᎯ (Sacred Seven)

ᎠᏂ ᎦᏙᎨᏫ   A NI GA TO GE WI   (Wild Potato)

ᎠᏂ ᎩᏆᎯ   A NI GI LO HI   (Long Hair)

ᎠᏂ ᏬᏗ   A NI WO DI   (Paint)

ᎠᏂ ᏩᏯ   A NI WA YAH   (Wolf)

ᎠᏂ ᎧᏫ   A NI KA WI   (Deer)

ᎠᏂ ᏥᏍᏆ   A NI TSI S KWA (Bird)

ᎠᏂ ᏌᎰᏂ   A NI SA HO NI   (Blue)

ᎠᏂ ᏴᏫᏯ   A NI YUN WI YA   (Principal People)

Cherokee characters from Sequoyah's syllabary.

and the substitution of rule by the state of Georgia.

It was now that the mixed bloods learned a bitter lesson, and one they would never forget. They had made a fatal miscalculation. Not in their wildest imaginings had they considered that the whites would treat them the same as they would the Cherokee full bloods. To whites though, an Indian was an Indian, and any fraction, however small, of Indian blood was sufficient to make that determination. Ignoring the tremendous advances and concessions both the mixed-blood and the full-blooded Cherokees had made, the responsive and powerful machinery of the federal government began to turn. In 1838, in one of the best known and most tragic events in American Indian history, the "Trail of Tears" took place, when all but an approximate 1,000 escaped refugees were brutally rounded up and forced to move to Indian Territory, in what is now Oklahoma.

Actually, small bands of Cherokees had succumbed to white pressures and moved west as early as 1795. By 1817, a community of several thousand of them had settled between the White and Arkansas rivers in northwestern Arkansas. That same year the United States government signed a treaty allowing the Cherokees their new domain, and all of the Eastern Cherokees were invited to join them. The invitation was declined, however, and in 1828 the Arkansas Cherokees were persuaded to sign yet another treaty — this time exchanging their Arkansas territory for a seven-million-acre tract in Indian Territory.

Three-fourths of the nation still remained in the east until, that is, continued harassment began to convince some of them that removal was inevitable. The leaders of this group, who came to be known as "the Treaty Party" and who believed that the tribe should sign an agreement accepting removal to Indian Territory, included Major Ridge, John Ridge, Elias Boudinot, and Stand Watie. Aligned against them were Chief John Ross and most of the full bloods, who stubbornly refused the entreaties of the Treaty Party and the repeated attempts of the United States commissioners to obtain a cession treaty.

Also remaining firm was Junaluska, who steadfastly believed that the man whose battle and life he had saved at Horse Shoe Bend, and who in 1828 had become president of the United States would never betray the Cherokees. But when to his horror the chief learned Jackson advocated removal, he pleaded with the president to honor his oath and to remember that his war successes at and after Horse Shoe Bend had played a significant role in his election. But the president refused to listen, and the disillusioned Junaluska cursed the day he had saved Jackson's life and reputation. "If," the chief said, "I had known he would break his oath, I would have killed him that day at the Horse Shoe."[17]

The state of Georgia shortened its leash and continued to claim that the separate government of the Cherokees violated states' rights. Its legislature enacted a law annexing the Cherokee country within her borders and placing it under the jurisdiction of state laws. In 1830, the act took effect, causing John Ross to bring a suit against the state in the United States Supreme Court in 1831. The case was dismissed on the grounds that the Cherokees were a "domestic dependent nation" with the United States as guardian, and therefore could not bring actions before the state courts.

Jackson was also disturbed. "It is absurd," he said, "to think that an independent nation with power of making its own laws and of making treaties with other nations could exist within the limits of a sovereign state," and from this time forward a relentless campaign was waged to complete the removal. Persuasion was tried, and when it was rejected, Ross and his followers were forbidden to hold council meetings. Their lawmaking power was taken from them, and they were given no protection by the state. No Cherokee was permitted to be a witness in a lawsuit in which a white person was the defendant. The moment gold was discovered near Dahlonega, Georgia, the state promptly seized the area and applied to it the state's own laws. All customs and laws of the Cherokees were declared null and void, and the mining area was divided into lots and at a lottery sold to whites only. Federal troops guarded even the mines of the Indians, and kept them from digging there. When the Georgia

Chief John Ross

courts ruled against this, the governor ignored the ruling, for there were also lead, iron, and silver to be mined along with limestone and marble.

Both the mixed-blood Cherokees and the white missionaries had naively assumed that state and federal governments heartily approved of the missions' efforts to enlighten and civilize the Cherokee nation. But they were wrong. Civilized Indians, however nice that sounded when compared to "uncivilized savages," became competitive Indians who could articulate their positions and rights and thus became a greater threat than ever to white plans for Indian removal. The Cherokees were not only doing well, they were doing too well, so next, the missions were attacked in a subtle but effective way. Every white man in Georgia was required to take an oath of allegiance to the state. Since missionaries, teachers, and others friendly to the Indians were loath to do this, they refused and were quickly arrested. Among them was the Reverend Worcester, who, though his presence had been approved by the president, the Indian agent, and the Cherokee Nation itself, was arrested, sentenced to four years of labor, and put in prison. The others recoiled at that, took the oath, and remained free. Worcester's case and that of the Cherokees were favorably appealed to the U. S. Supreme Court, and his release was ordered at the same time as the rights of the Cherokees to government protection was proclaimed. But two years passed before Worcester was allowed to leave the prison.

In the meantime, President Jackson was caught in the midst of a dilemma. On the one hand, Georgians expected him to rid them of the Indians and threatened a rebellion if he refused. On the other hand, the Cherokees asserted their land rights and reminded him of his prior promises to protect them. He vacillated, but not for long. Knowing where the real power was, he defied the Supreme Court, saying, "John Marshall has rendered his decision; now let him enforce it!"

The Cherokees claimed they were the original owners of the land and remained an independent nation with whom treaties could be and had been made. Jackson replied that they were merely occu-pants and neither owners of the land nor an independent nation. They had been allies, he said, of Great Britain, whose power by virtue of the Declaration of Independence and the Treaty of 1783 became that of the thirteen colonies, including North Carolina and Georgia.

The Cherokee missions having been closed, the *Cherokee Phoenix* was now seized by the state, assuring that in the Cherokees' time of greatest need they would be deprived of the only vehicle they had to spread the news of what was going on. Protest after protest was sent to Washington, while with deliberation, candor, and for a time at least goodwill, the Cherokees rejected the order to move west. Congress got into the act, and the discussions regarding removal were heated and prolonged, with the Whigs favoring Indian rights and the Democrats siding with Jackson. Daniel Webster, Henry Clay, Davy Crockett and others made passionate speeches in which they criticized the administration for its unjust, dishonest, cruel, and shortsighted treatment of the Indians.

It was inevitable that a full-blown split would develop among the Cherokees themselves, and finally it did — with the minority party under the leadership of the well-educated and naturally affable John Ridge, who regarded further resistance to removal as useless and believed removal to be the only way out of a desperate situation, vying openly now against the majority party led by Ross.

Rival delegations went repeatedly to Washington, D. C., and bitterly contested council meetings were held in the Cherokee Nation. Finally, in February 1835, the rival Cherokee factions met again in Washington, and in March the Ridge party signed a treaty ceding all Cherokee lands in the East to the United States in return for a promised $4,500,000.

In October, the Cherokee people in full council rejected that preliminary treaty. The Reverend J. F. Schermerhorn, who had been appointed by the United States government to negotiate a treaty with the Cherokees, met with them at New Echota, Georgia, in December. On December 29, 1835, members of the Ridge faction signed a treaty to relinquish Cherokee lands in the East in return for

The removal and the Trail of Tears begin.

T. E. Mails

payment and the right to occupy the same land in Indian Territory already settled by the Western, or Arkansas Band of Cherokees, plus an additional smaller tract in what is now southeastern Kansas. Payment was allowed to individual Cherokee emigrants who left improved property in the East, and every Cherokee was to remove west within two years after the verification of the treaty by the United States Congress and a vote of the Cherokee Nation. The Senate ratified it on May 23, 1836, by a majority of one vote. Yet there were 17,000 Cherokees affected, and at a council meeting at the treaty was declared null and void, and John Ross immediately sent off a thunderous protest signed by thousands of Cherokees.

Ridge and his followers packed up their belongings and left for Indian Territory. The final appeal by John Ross was sent off in February 1838:

> "For adhering to principles on which your great empire is founded, are we to be despoiled of all we hold dear on earth? Are we to be hunted like wild beasts, our women and children, our aged and sick, to be dragged from their homes, packed in loathsome boats and transported to a sickly clime? Already we are thronged with armed men; forts, camps, military posts occupy our whole country. We acknowledge that power of the United States; we acknowledge our own weakness. Our only fortress is in the justice of our cause. Our only appeal on earth is to your tribunal. To you then, we look. We have not forfeited our rights. If we fail to transmit to our sons the freedom we have derived from our fathers — it must be — not by an act of suicide; it must be not with our own accord. Will you shield us from the horrors of the threatened storm?"

President Martin Van Buren, Jackson's successor, was immovable. General John Elias Wood and 3,000 regulars were sent to disarm the Cherokees and begin the removal process. In one of his letters Wood admits, "the whole scene is a heart-breaking one. I would that I might remove every Indian tomorrow beyond the reach of white men who, like vultures, are watching ready to pounce upon their prey, and to strip them of everything they have." When General Dunlap of Tennessee was called out to prevent an uprising, he told his soldiers that he "would not dishonor the Tennessee arms by execut-

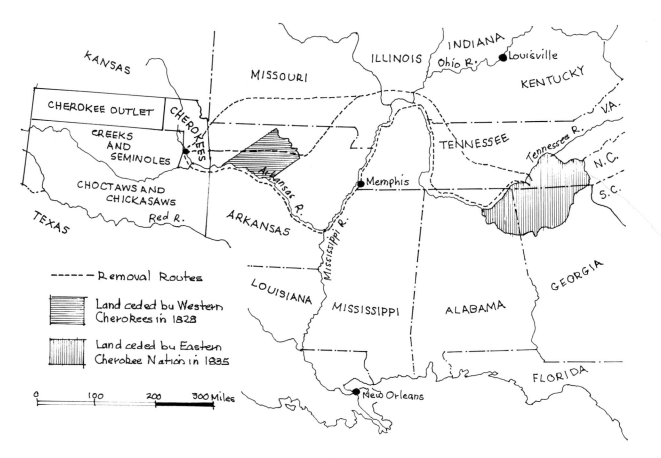

CHEROKE LAND CESSIONS & REMOVAL ROUTES, 1828 - 1838

ing at the point of a bayonet, such a treaty."[18]

When General Wood gently suggested to the Ross Party that a decision to stay might bring death, they responded, "It will be death if we go. Why not stay here and die among our mountains?"

In May 1838 General Winfield Scott came with 7,000 heavily armed soldiers, consisting of regulars, militia, and volunteers, and the cruel roundup intensified. Even refined and cultured families were dragged from their homes while in the midst of meals or sleep and placed under arrest. Sometimes, as they were herded away, they looked back to see their homes being taken over by whites, and other times they looked back to see their homes in flames. In August 1838, one group met for the last time in the chapel of an abandoned school and celebrated Holy Communion, after which they visited the cemetery to tell their loved ones good-bye, and handed themselves over to a General Scott, who claimed to be Christian.

On June 9, 1838, Captain L. B. Webster wrote

to his wife:

We arrived at Ft. Butler on the 7th but did not establish this camp till today, which is on the north side of Valley River, just about its entrance into the Hiwassee, and about one mile from the Fort. We are said to be in the thickest settled portion of the Cherokee country, and the least civilized. There are about six thousand in our neighborhood — their houses are quite thick about us, and they all remain quietly at home at work on their little farms, as though no evil was intended them. They sell us very cheap anything they have to spare, and look upon the regular troops as their friends — My man just returned with four fine chickings for which he only paid fifty cents. Eggs are but a shilling a dozen and butter the same per pound. These are the innocent and simple people, into whose houses we are to obtrude ourselves, and take off by force. They have no idea of fighting, but submit quietly to be tied and lead away. If there is anything that goes against my conscience it is this work, and I would not do it, whatever might be the consequences, did I not know that there are thousands that would, and probably with much less feeling towards the poor creatures . . . Orders are out to begin operations on the 12th. Inst. and I expect to see many affecting scenes before the business is over. Those that were in Georgia have already been collected, and sent to the principal depots, from whence they are sending to the West as fast as possible.[19]

Although those Cherokees who hid in the mountains were never found, soldiers herded the rest of the tribe into hot and miserable, essentially roofless stockades, where more than a few became sick and died. Initially the Cherokees were to all move at once, but it became obvious this would be impossible. So the people were organized into detachments of approximately 1,000 persons, each of which was supervised by its own officers. In June, the first detachment went by boat up the Tennessee and Ohio rivers and across the Mississippi River. Many died of heat and other privations, and the remaining Cherokees successfully begged to put off further departures until cooler weather arrived. Finally, on October 1, 1838, they one by one started out on the 800-mile journey to Fort Gibson, Indian Territory. All of them endured indescribable suffering, ranging from inadequate transportation and food, storms, blizzards, bad roads and sickness to broken hearts. The last contingent began its journey overland on December 4, 1838, having horses and wagons enough to carry only the provisions and some of the sick and aged. With them they carried the sacred fire and never allowed it to go out. It was midwinter and bitterly cold when they reached the Mississippi in southern Illinois. The river was full of floating ice, and a thousand poorly clad Cherokees, many of them sick and dying, some with only a single blanket, lying on frozen ground alongside friends already dead, waited until the ice was cleared so the crossing could be made. So they might find enough game for food, the contingent divided, with one portion taking the northern trail that passed by Springfield, Missouri, while the other portion went through the more southern part of the same state. It took the thirteen contingents from three to five painful months to make the journey, and it is estimated that one-quarter of the travelers, 4,000 Cherokees, died either in the roundup or along the

way. In addition, more died of exhaustion after they arrived at their final destination, Fort Gibson, the eastern gateway to Indian Territory.

Indian Territory was itself a phenomenon in the lives of the Indian tribes of North America. Before 1825, it had been chosen to become the detention camp for displaced Indians, and by 1850, approximately one-third of all Indians would reside within its boundaries — sixty-seven tribes of them, as widely divergent as some of the Plains tribes from mid-America and the West, the Senecas from Ohio, the indigenous Osage, the Kiowa, the Comanche, and the Five Civilized Tribes. Of the latter, the Choctaws were the first to be removed, beginning in 1834 with most arriving by 1835 and some straggling in as late as 1848. Next came the Creeks, whose first emigration was in 1835, after a token move in 1828, and the last in 1837. The Chickasaws followed from 1837 to 1840. The Cherokees were next, beginning with the first early emigrants and finishing with the larger and complete removal in 1838-1839. Last of the five to relocate were the Seminoles of Florida. They fought a bitter war with the United States that lasted almost seven years and cost the government nearly fifteen hundred soldiers, many civilians, and twenty million dollars in expenses — along with the utter destruction of Seminole property. The Seminoles began to move in 1836, with some arriving in the 1840s and 1850s, and others remaining in Florida.

When finally they were all settled in Indian Territory, the Cherokees were in the northeast corner and bordering them on the south were the Choctaws and on the southwest the Creeks. The Chickasaws were immediately west of the Choctaws, and Seminole country was a narrow band that lay between the Creeks on the north and the Chickasaws on the south.

Summary

From this point on, the story of the Cherokee tribe must be told in terms of a geographically divided people: the smaller group of Eastern Cherokees living in North Carolina and the larger group of Western Cherokees living in what, in 1907, would become the state of Oklahoma.

Considering what we know at this crushing moment in their history, it is not too difficult to imagine what conditions were like for these wretched people as they attempted to pick up the pieces, of which there were pitifully few, and go on with their lives. As I ponder this, I am forced to wonder whether they thought back to the great days that once were, when the magnificent festivals were celebrated and the name of the proud Cherokees rang loud in the land . . . did they wish they had done some things differently in their relationships with whites . . . and did they remember another time and the Phoenix bird? We will see.

NOTES

1. Gilbert, "The Eastern Cherokees," pp. 360-361.
2. McClary, "Nancy Ward: The Last Beloved Woman of the Cherokees," pp. 352-364.
3. Skelton, "A History of the Educational System of the Cherokee Nation, 1801-1910," a letter dated December 14, 1807, from Gideon Blackburn, Maryville, Tennessee, p. 37.
4. Ibid., p. 40.
5. Ibid., p. 41.
6. Washburn, *Reminiscences of the Indians,* pp. 16-17.
7. Payne Papers, Vol. 1, pp. 136-147.
8. Ibid., pp. 147-149.
9. Ibid., pp. 150-151.
10. Ibid., pp. 151-152.
11. Ibid., pp. 152-162.
12. Ibid., pp. 163-170.
13. Gilbert, pp. 365-366.
14. The Reverend Samuel Worcester, as cited in Bass, Cherokee Messenger, pp. 95-102.
15. Evans, "Sketches of Cherokee Character, Customs and Manners," Payne Papers, Vol. 4, pp. 1-39.
16. Ibid.
17. Freel, "Our Heritage: The People of Cherokee County, North Carolina, 1540-1955," pp. 26-27.
18. Ibid.
19. Ibid.

CHAPTER NINE

The Eastern Cherokees

Several references have been made to the divisions between the full bloods and mixed bloods that developed in the Cherokee nation from 1667 to the time of removal in 1838. Beginning as a hairline fissure, it widened continually until it became a canyon, thanks mainly to white intrusion into Cherokee political life and intermarriage. At first, the mixed-blood children hewed fully to Cherokee culture and values, and their thought and behavior patterns were Cherokee. But unrelenting persuasion by white fathers drew the mixed-blood children and most Cherokee wives steadily away from Cherokee traditional life and into the white culture.

THE EASTERN CHEROKEE RESERVATION

Decline of Cohesion

To summarize what has already been said about this, sometime during the first half of the eighteenth century, the ancient culture's cohesiveness began to give way. The national capital and the priestly caste progressively lost their force, and somewhere along the line the office of the *Uku* and all that related to it terminated. With it went the rich and vital cycle of national festivals, and the ritual focus shifted to the individual towns and the individuals themselves, so that long before the removal and its consequences the central aspects of the ancient culture were gone. Removal — and this term can be applied to both the Eastern and the Western Cherokees, for the former were equally dislocated insofar as their lives were concerned — was only the swift clean blow that at last jarred the full-blooded Cherokees loose from their dreams and from what they had once been. After 1838, there were no illusions, either for the dazed Eastern Cherokees, or for the mixed bloods and the full bloods who sat forlornly in the north-eastern corner of Indian Territory. So as we begin to consider the Eastern Cherokees, the question is not that of observing a continuation of the ancient life. It is a question of observing how they survived, which is a miracle in itself, and what, if anything, of the old ways were retained.

Losses in warfare to both white and Indian enemies during the last half of the eighteenth century shattered Cherokee optimism and upset the tribe's economic base. The people were forced to question both their own competence and their relationship with the Above Beings they had depended upon for so long a time. They were a weakened and demoralized nation that was ripe for total conversion.

Mission schools that moved in at the turn of the nineteenth century seized upon this and furthered the process of tribal deculturalization. Once the minds of Cherokee students had been sufficiently exposed to white ways and Christianity, the break between the old and the new, the mixed bloods and the full bloods was, whether or not anyone recognized it at the time, complete. The fissure had become a canyon that could no longer be bridged.

By 1815, or by 1820 at the latest, all of the mixed bloods were either shying away from or avoiding entirely traditional life and its supposed stigma, and whenever ongoing traditional life is described from this point on it may be safely assumed that virtually all of the participants are full bloods. (Let me insert here that in the last decade, mixed bloods have exhibited a strong desire to learn more about their ancient heritage, and to be openly proud of their Cherokee blood.)

Also, while the initial division of the Cherokee tribe was a cultural one, the tension it produced led inevitably to a political and geographical spilt. At the same time the mixed bloods found their center in New Echota and Georgia, not all, yet a substantial number, of full bloods withdrew to the remoter parts of North Carolina. By this geographical division, the nation already altered by adulterated blood was weakened further. Full-blooded leaders still participated in national politics, for as a nation all Cherokees continued to share common problems. But the participation of the full bloods was a peripheral one, and political control remained in New Echota and in mixed-blood hands. This is not to say that all mixed bloods cared nothing about traditional life or were insensitive to the needs and views of full bloods. John Ross is a prime example of mixed-blood concern, for as we know it was he who led the fight to remain in ancestral land and for more than economic reasons. Did he suspect, or have some vision about, what was going to happen to the Cherokees? We do know that he did everything he could to assist John Howard Payne when he came to collect data about the ancient life. And it is doubtful Ross would have done this had he not known it was an important thing to do.

Accordingly, John Ross remains in full bloods' eyes a hero of considerable proportions in the Cherokee cause, and he is fondly remembered by the Eastern Cherokees. But the tribal division was present, and it was to play an unanticipated role at the time of removal. For while an approximate 1,000 of the most remote North Carolina Cherokees had time to learn what was going on and to lose themselves in the caves of the high mountains, the other full bloods and the more affluent and accessible mixed bloods of Georgia, North Carolina, and Tennessee were caught flat-footed, and were the first to be seized and herded into holding pens. Later on, a few dozen captives escaped from the pens and joined the refugees, where together they fearfully waited and wondered whether General Scott would send troops to search for and root them out. As we learn in a moment, Scott did know they were there, but for some reason or another chose to leave them alone. Perhaps he planned to return from Indian Territory and capture the fugitives. I'd like to think that his conscience was troubling him, and that in spite of government orders he had decided to let them go. It might be that he knew 400 of the refugees had already become citizens of the state of North Carolina and had the legal right to remain there. In any event, the situation was solved for everyone by an unexpected incident involving a man named Tsali.

The Sacrifice of Tsali

It is said that, while on his way to Indian Territory, Tsali killed a soldier and with his terrified family escaped from the line of march and fled to North Carolina, where he joined the people in hiding. When word of this reached General Scott, he vowed that he would return and capture all of the refugees — unless Tsali, his two sons, and a brother would give themselves up. The fact that the slain soldier had prodded Tsali's ailing wife with an unsheathed bayonet and caused the struggle made little difference.

William Thomas, a white man who had years before as an orphan been adopted by Yonaguska, chief of the Middle Towns along the Little Tennessee and Ocanaluftee rivers, and who was now a successful Indian trader, was conscripted to carry the following message to Tsali, who was known to be hiding in a cave in the rugged Nantahala Mountains. If Tsali, his sons, and his brother would surrender, General Scott would allow the other Cherokees who were in hiding to remain in their land and to return to their abandoned homes or to build homes for themselves. If, on the other hand, the wanted

persons refused to surrender, the general pledged to turn his army lose in the mountains to hunt down "like wild dogs" every Cherokee man, woman, and child and to send them off to Indian Territory.

Tsali thought about the choices for awhile and then answered, "We will come down. No band of soldiers could ever take me alive, but if my people can stay, we will come."[1]

Tsali, one son, and his brother were executed by a firing squad of four Cherokees — who some say were compelled to do the execution, and others say were chosen by Tsali, who wanted his own people to do the shameful job.

According to most accounts, including those in Eastern Cherokee literature and that set forth in the dramatization of the event in their annual pageant, it was this gallant self-sacrifice that led to freedom for the rest of the Cherokee refugees, although their economic condition was pitiful, and for years after that, the United States government simply ignored them and left them to go their own way. Those who had lived in the area returned cautiously to their homes, doing what they could for those who had no homes to go to. One way or another they got along and survived, but surely the shocking news came to them about the tragic toll of deaths along the trail, and they must have wondered what was happening to the Cherokees who did make it to Indian Territory. So in most respects they drifted about like an anchorless boat in a strong current while they tried vainly to assess their present and future, which at the time seemed bleak at best. Moreover, they knew all too well that what the state and federal governments had done to the rest of the Cherokees might at any moment be done to them — for who could ever again trust the white man's motives or promises?

Early Years: Settlement Along the Tuckaseegee

Finally, William Thomas, described at this point in his career as "champion of Eastern Cherokee rights," was made their agent. Already, upon Yonaguska's death in 1839, he had been elected principal chief of the Eastern Cherokees, and he would be the only white man ever to be so honored. He was an articulate man and repeatedly pleaded the

Eastern Cherokee case in Washington. At last, some money, a tiny fraction of the five million dollars promised at New Echota in 1835, plus a small amount for confiscated possessions, was paid to the Eastern Cherokees. Adding to this what little they could scrape up on their own, they purchased from whites some of the Qualla Boundary land along the Tuckaseegee, and at last they began to settle down. After considerable effort, Thomas got the leaders in Washington to agree that the Treaty of New Echota did not legally apply to the Cherokees residing in North Carolina, and in 1846, a treaty was signed in Washington that allowed the Cherokees to stay. However, the state did not recognize them as legal land owners until after the Civil War ended in 1865, and in the interim Thomas held the deeds in his own name.

Several towns, or more accurately, communities, were laid out, and the individual headmen occupied these with their small groups of followers. The towns are the same as those that make up the Eastern Cherokee Reservation today.

Only the scantiest reports exist of these tenuous years of reestablishment, but we do know that the Eastern Cherokees were strongly influenced in their life-style by the white neighbors that surrounded them, and we learn what Cherokee subsistence was like by looking at what we know about the settlers. About 1830, the Scotch, Irish, English, and Dutch who had left their homelands in search of freedom began to settle in the mountain regions of North Carolina. They brought with them what they wore, a few bedclothes, seeds for planting, cooking utensils, a few pewter plates, and some spoons. The father had his rifle, a saw, hoe, ax, adz, auger, and a steel plow point. There was also a banjo or a fiddle, and since these were a God-fearing people, a Bible. They were known for their honesty, self-respect, pride, and old-fashioned speech. Their medicines were home remedies involving herbs, roots, and barks similar to those employed by the Cherokees, and their superstitions were so rife they even added to their own some of those observed by the Indians. Corn, wheat, oats, and rye were the chief crops, and cultivation methods were crude. There were enormous vegetable gardens, Irish potatoes, sweet potatoes, and beans. Drinks consisted of milk and teas. Practically all meat was wild game, for that had not been eliminated in this backcountry as it had in other areas of the Cherokee domain. It still included deer, buffalo, elk, bear, raccoon, hare, turkey, and pheasant. Cattle types included Durham and Ayrshire. Sheep were raised more for their wool than for the mutton, and the wool was used for clothing and blankets. Chickens were raised for food, and professionally arranged chicken fights were one of the great sporting events of the times. There were a few horses, but most work was done with oxen. Hound dogs were used to hunt and provide protection from wild animals. The women used roots and barks to make dyes and raised silkworms to make thread. Flax was popular, and even linen tablecloths were produced. The men built forges, and blacksmiths established their trade. In time, gristmills were built to relieve the slow and tedious task of making bread.

Although little of the above was completely new to the Cherokees, they had never before had such a steady and encompassing exposure to it as they had now, nor had they been so called upon to readjust their lives in order to survive. Their decision was to adapt again and in general to copy the whites, however repugnant an idea that might once have been to them. In 1848, the Cherokees were manufacturing their own clothing, plows, other farming utensils, axes, and even their own guns. They had the same domestic animals and did the same cultivation as their white neighbors. Most were Methodists and Baptists. They had their own courts, except on festive days dressed like whites, and they lived in small log houses. While no first-person information is available concerning religious practices, we know from what was learned later in their history that some were continuing, so that those who were members of Protestant churches were also keeping one foot in the traditional world. But this foot was not enough to keep what had happened to the mixed-blood children from happening to the full-blooded children, for formal education began to work among them a serious disruption in cultural views.

Of special interest is the fact that some white settlers of that time owned black slaves and that wealthy families had as many as six. Some Cherokees obtained slaves too, with prices ranging from $60 for a girl to $250 for a boy, and $100 for an old man. The whites had no regular courts, and lashing was the usual punishment for crimes, sometimes followed by jail. Many a Cherokee must have watched with utter fascination as an offender's feet and hands were placed in stocks, he was stripped to the waist, and the sheriff administered the sentence with a long horsewhip. There were also government stills to provide liquor and brandy — to the settlers first and then covertly to the Indians.

Cherokee recreation shifted now to quilting bees, cornhuskings, logrollings, house-raisings, horse races, and various games. They continued their social dances, whose roots were in the ancient lifeway. Their Christian religious assemblies were held in the schoolhouses until churches were built, and worship services continued for hours on end, with social hours before, after, and sometimes during worship.[2]

1860-1910

Thomas served as a Confederate colonel in the Civil War, and 400 Cherokees enlisted in his company, called "the Thomas Legion," along with fourteen companies of white infantry, four companies of cavalry, and engineers and artillerymen. As mentioned earlier, virtually the entire Cherokee unit returned unharmed from the battlefields. About 1870, the Eastern Cherokees were finally united in a second federated government that was incorporated under the laws of the state of North Carolina. In its composition, this government remains virtually the same today as it was then. In 1874, a congressional commission was appointed to study the Cherokee situation. In 1875, the government made the Cherokees wards of the United States. And in 1876, Congress passed an act confirming an award of roughly 50,000 acres of Qualla Boundary land to the Eastern Band. Thomas died on May 10, 1893, and is remembered by the Eastern Cherokees as the best white friend they had ever had.

It should be emphasized that throughout these early years, and for this time period at least, the Eastern Cherokees clung to at least a semblance of their traditional religion and native form of leadership. When word of this reached the anthropologists and ethnologists who retained a consuming interest in what ancient Cherokee life had been like, Bureau of American Ethnology anthropologist James Mooney hurried to the reservation, where he worked on and off in Big Cove from 1887 to 1890. He collected sacred myths, animal stories, local legends, historical traditions, and the intriguing sacred formulas that had been recorded by a principal medicine man named Swimmer. It was then and in the years following that a few new discoveries were made about the ancient lifeway, and in particular about the nonfestival dances that ethnologists only suspected had existed, for outside Evans' report to Payne, which most researchers had never read, there were no records of these. Further on, these dances are described, but first we should record that in the late 1880s, Mooney was shaken to learn that with nearly everything either having been taken from the Cherokees or undermined, they remained what the outside world would have to classify as "poor and miserable." He would write, "In the old days when the Cherokee was the lord of the whole country from the Savannah to the Ohio, well fed and warmly clad and leading an active life in the open air, he was able to maintain a condition of robust health notwithstanding the incorrectness of his medical ideas and his general disregard of sanitary regulations. But with the advent of the white man and the destruction of the game all this was changed. The Eastern Cherokee of today is a dejected being; poorly fed, and worse clothed, rarely tasting meat, cut off from the old free life, and with no incentive to a better, and constantly bowed down by a sense of helpless degradation in the presence of his conqueror. Considering all the circumstances, it may seem a matter of surprise that any of them are still in existence. As a matter of fact, the best information that could be obtained in the absence of any official statistics indicated a slow but steady decrease during the last five years. Only the constitutional vigor, inherited from their warrior ancestors, has enabled them to sustain the shock of the changed conditions of the last half century. The uniform good health of the children in the training school shows that the case is not hopeless, however, and that under favorable conditions, with a proper food supply and a regular mode of living, the Cherokee can hold his own with the white man."[3]

Despite his fascination with Cherokee myths and formulas, Mooney reflected upon the matter of conjurers and wrote in the 1890 *Journal of American Folk-Lore* a surprisingly negative article on the "Cherokee theory and Practice of Medicine," based upon what he had learned and witnessed among the full bloods in Big Cove. In this article he began by stating that, "One of the most prevalent errors in regard to the Indian is that he knows every plant of the field and forest, and that the medicine man outranks the white physician in his knowledge of the healing art."[4] He then argued that the Indian doctor is not to be compared with the educated physician who has devoted years to study under trained specialists. The medicine man's knowledge of herbal remedies, Mooney asserted, is about on a level with that of the ordinary farmer's wife, while the best of them are far inferior to her in regard to nursing and the commonsense care of the sick. Although the white doctor works upon a disordered organism, the Cherokee doctor works to drive out a ghost or a devil. Treatment is generally in the form of taboos that must be observed for four days. The ordinary treatment at Big Cove was rubbing, or the simple laying on of hands previously warmed over the fire. This fire was not the hearth fire, but one specially kindled for the purpose. Sometimes the medicine was blown from the mouth of the doctor onto the body of the patient, according to certain rules. In one case, for instance, the doctor blew first upon the right hand, then upon the left foot, then upon the right foot, and finally upon the left hand, thus describing the figure of a cross. In every instance a prayer or sacred song accompanied the application.[5]

There were also a number of precautionary health-preserving ceremonies that were commonly observed, but Mooney was careful to point out that these were religious rather than sanitary. Chief among them was "going to water" with the conjurer.

He concluded his article with what I think is an exceedingly important admission as he admitted that as he studied Cherokee medicine practice, his disappointment over the misconceived ideas of disease and the lack of practical therapeutic results soon gave way to admiration of the systematic consistency of theory and practice, and ultimately was replaced by respect for the deep religious spirit which animated it all. Every doctor was a priest, and every application was a religious act accompanied by prayer. In these prayers the doctor first endeavored to show his contempt for the diseased spirit by belittling it as much as possible, so as to convey the impression that he was not afraid of it.[6]

Thus, Mooney reinforces what I said earlier about the positive aspects of ancient methods of healing, and he might well have added that the Cherokee doctor's attitude was conveyed to the patient, who himself grew less fearful and more willing to fight back. Admittedly, a patient's optimism and faith do not solve all medical problems — and they are not intended to — but the recognition of them at least removes the ancient practice from the stigma of pure primitivism and superstition and may account for the Cherokee full bloods' continued unwillingness to turn their backs on their healers, however archaic their approach.

Actually, Mooney hadn't seen the worst of the Cherokee conditions, for things had begun to change for the better about 1880, when the Quakers established the school on Cherokee land he referred to and sought to give the Cherokees moral and religious training. From the beginning, the government cooperated with the Quakers, and after twelve years, took over control of the school. White teachers were made the "ideal" for Cherokee youths to emulate, and attendance at the schools was compulsory. Discipline was harsh, and students dared not speak a word of Cherokee in the presence of the teachers. More and more Cherokees joined the churches as Baptist and Methodist missionaries worked among them, yet most of the full bloods still clung to what remained of the old religion. But living conditions were better than they had been, and encouraged Cherokee men began to improve their small homes and to pay more attention to the cultivation of their small tracts, while Cherokee women started to weave and to sew with more enthusiasm.

1910-1929

Information about this period is also scarce, but fortunately the archives of the Museum of the Cherokee Indian at Cherokee, North Carolina, include a most helpful copy of the handwritten minutes of the 1913 to 1915 meetings of the people of the Big Cove District as they met to create and implement an organization whose purpose was to "promote agriculture, stock raising, fruit growing, home building, habits of industry and the general welfare and prosperity of our people." I could easily have summarized the minutes in a few paragraphs, and I do include only a portion of the material available. But summarizing would take away the flavor of the time and remove us from the voices and personalities of the men who were involved. Note that I say "men," for women were not included in this decision making, although a female treasurer appears in the minutes of January 24, 1914. On the surface, the minutes appear quite ordinary, but on reading between the lines one can build an impressive picture of the Eastern Cherokees' progress, their economic situation, and their manner, mind, and pace of life during this little-known period of their development. Notice particularly how formal the Cherokees were and how well acquainted they were with rules of order. Yet they kept the meetings personal. An individual could speak his piece, and the human dimension of Cherokee life was evident at each meeting. Here we find simple but fascinating answers to what items cost then; how aware Cherokees were of the world around them; how forthright they were in their views, confessions, and appraisals; how ready they were to meet the present and future; and how ready the state and federal governments were to help them do this.

Twenty-six names are listed as organizing members of the Big Cove Farmers Organization, and I repeat them here, since everyone will want to know what kinds of names the Cherokees were using in 1913. It makes our union with them more personal,

and the history less remote. They are John Wolfe, Charles Lambert, York Cornsilk, William Driver, Tom Swimmer, Johnson Thompson, Going Bird, Wesley Driver, Johnson Wolfe, Johney Swayney, Tarquet Wolfe, Owen Wolfe, William Long, Elijah Welch, Runaway Swimmer, Soggy Hill, Mose Powel, Arsene Thompson, Ward Wolfe, Eli Bird, Adam Welch, Josiah Blackfox, Justus Toorli, Corneeta Welch, D. Climbingbear, and John Davis. Still other names appear in the minutes, and we can assume they represent members who joined the organization after it began.

The first meeting was held on December 13, 1913. Observe that an interpreter was still required to translate Cherokee into English and vice versa. Notice also that the pace was unhurried, as if the men were not too sure at this point that the proposed organization would benefit them. And picture the scene in your mind as the men gather in a small, nondescript hewn-log or plank building, with windows that are only holes cut in the walls, a potbellied iron stove for heat, unpainted walls, bare puncheon floors, benches to sit on, and perhaps one small table for the officers about to be elected. Light is furnished by lanterns or candles. The men's hair is shorter than it used to be, and it is parted on one side. But the cinnamon-brown skin tone, the broad nose, the thin lips, and the wary brown or black eyes are still there. So is the broad frame. Around their necks are tied soiled polka-dot bandannas. It is winter, so they wear narrow-brimmed felt hats; woolen coats or jackets; long-sleeved cotton or wool shirts; denim overalls; and dust or mud-covered heavy, high-topped work shoes or boots. They are quiet and pleasant. A few shake hands when they meet, but most say nothing. They just find places to sit, and then wait for the meeting to begin.

The minutes of this historic first meeting follow, and as will be seen, it was a brief and non-committal one. It was historic only in that it constituted a beginning. What needed to be done was done, and that was all.

> The first gathering of the farmers meeting was held. At this meeting the work that was being carried out by the Superintendent James Henderson was

interpreted by Mr. James Blythe, both of the Eastern Cherokee Training School.

The meeting was especially for the benefit of getting acquainted with our new Superintendent who at this time spoke of organizing a society called the Big Cove Farmers Organization.

Temporary officers were appointed. Pres. John Wolfe. Sec. Johnson Owl. Tran. Sec. Daliskie C. Calahoun.

A committee of two was appointed to meet the founder of this organization at Cherokee in order to set the time these meetings will be held.

The days being set every two weeks on Saturday.

The committeeman are William Long, York Cornsilk.

After appointment the meeting was opened for questions. Very few questions asked.

The meeting adjourned.

Temporary Sec. Johnson. Owl

Dec. 27, 1913

At 1: p.m. the meeting called to order by the temporary Chairman John Wolfe.

On account of Mr. James Henderson the Superintendent of the Eastern Cherokee Training School being absent, Mr. James Blythe acted as our instructor.

The meeting was opened for questions. Not any. Any new business was called for. There was none.

On account of the religious meeting to be held on our next meeting day, Mr. William Long motioned for the meeting to be held next Friday week but not carried on account of school in session.

The second time Mr. William Long motioned that we meet here next Saturday week at 9:00 a.m.

Mr. John David seconded the motion and carried.

A motion to adjourn was made and carried.

The meeting adjourned.

Temporary Sec. Johnson Owl

Jan. 10, 1914:

At our regular meeting day being set to meet at 9:00 a.m. on account of our lack of promptness caused a delay of two hours and at 11:00 a.m. the Superintendent spent three quarters of an hour in issuing checks to the needy people of our race in our Township also to the members of the Council.

At 11:45 the Temporary Chairman called the meeting to order.

And without any program the Superintendent was given the first chance to deliver what he had to say being interpreted by James Blythe.

James Blythe gave us a talk on the ways we ought to use the money that is appropriated to us by the

Commissioner of Indian Affairs.

William Long gave his experience in preparing for his life's work and the mistake he has made. [Ethnologists would love to know the content of this talk, since Long became a principal informant regarding Cherokee lore.]

The Secretary was called on to read the minutes of the last meeting.

The minutes being interpreted by Mr. James Blythe.

Johnson Thompson made a motion that we meet here on the last Saturday of each month seconded by Tom Swimmer and carried.

The meeting was then opened for questions.

There being no questions the Chairman gave us a talk on changing our 1913 ways to 1914 which was for the benefit of our welfare.

Mr. William Long motioned for adjournment and seconded by Johnson Thompson and carried.

The meeting adjourned.

Temporary Sec. Johnson Owl

Jan. 24, 1914:

At our usual place of gathering the President of our society called the meeting to order at 12 o'clock.

The Secretary was called upon to call the roll.

Next came the reading of the minutes of the last meeting, being interpreted by Mr. James Blythe.

Mr. James Henderson the Superintendent of the Eastern Cherokee Training School was given a chance to explain the Constitution and the By Laws of this organization being interpreted by Mr. James Blythe. A misunderstanding was made between the president of our society and the chief of the band of Indians this being made in the way it was interpreted. [This was an unfortunate but frequent occurrence that led to constant problems between Indians and whites. The pity is that white officials often dispensed information and never bothered to ask whether or not the Indians truly understood it.]

Also the meeting day was argued on, but the By Laws settled that argument.

Next came the votes for permanent officers, and the following were elected: Pres. John Wolfe. Vice Pres. Johnson Thompson. Sec. Johnson Owl. Tran. Sec. Dalisk C. Calahoun. Treas. Miss Lizzie Wolfe.

Next came the program committee of three were elected: William Long, Arseen Thompson, Eli Bird.

After election came the instruction speeches from the following: James Blythe, James Henderson, Johnson Owl, Arseen Thompson, Johnson Thompson.

Then Johnson Thompson made a motion that we meet here on Feb. 28, 1914 at 10 o'clock a.m.

Seconded by Tom Swimmer and carried.
Motion to adjourn made by Johnson Thompson
seconded by Tom Swimmer and carried.
The meeting adjourned.

Johnson Owl

Feb. 28, 1914:
The meeting called to order at 12 o'clock.
The secretary was called upon to call the roll, 10 of
the members being absent.
The programs for the two meetings were asked to
be read for Feb. 28 and March 28, 1914. This being
interpreted by the translating secretary, Caliskie C.
Calahoun.
The program was carried out very good especially
Soggy Hill brought out the most instructive talk on
farming which we all know was of great benefit to
our organization and other farmers of today.
 At 2:30 p.m. 20 minutes recess was given for
lunch.
At 3 p.m. the meeting was called to order by the
chairman.
Roll call by the secretary, 8 being absent this time.
Next came the organization funds, the standing
committee announced that every individual as a
member of this organization pay down 5 cts. as a
beginning tuition of our organization. And 25 cts.
every two months. Seventy cents were collected
from the organization, sixty cents to be placed in
the hands of the treasurer and ten cents in the
hands of the chairman to buy writing paper with.
Johnson Thompson made a motion that the
meeting adjourn seconded by Elie Bird and carried.
The meeting adjourned.

Johnson Owl

March 28, 1914:
Time being set to meet here at 9 a.m.
But on account of our lack of promptness caused a
delay of one and three quarters of an hour.
At 10:45 a.m. the meeting was called to order by
the chairman.
Roll call by the secretary, not enough members to
open our meeting.
At 11:10 Roll call again the second time. The same
as the first.
At 11:50 Roll call the third time.
Reading of the minutes of the last meeting by the
secretary translated by the translating secretary.
Reading of the program for March 28 and April 25,
1914.
Address by the Chairman, and recitation by
Josephen Colonahaski. Speech topic organization

by Arseen Thompson.
Next came a debate. Resolved that the horse is more
important to the farmer than an ox.
Affirmative speakers: York Cornsilk, Tom Swimmer.
Negative speakers: Johnson Wolfe, Soggy Hill,
Arseen Thompson.
Judges: John Wolfe, Daliskie C. Calhoun —
decided in favor of Johnson Wolfe and negative
speakers.
Twenty five cents tuition collected from organiza-
tion. Twelve cents taken out by buy:

1 memo	10 cts
1 postage	02 cts
into the treasurer's hands	13 cts
total	25 cts

A letter of thanks to be wrote to the Commissioner
by the secretary in reply to a typewriter circular sent
to us by the Supt. of the Eastern Cherokee Training
School. The Circular was to encourage the Indian
farmers, especially to our organization.
Tom Swimmer was behind with his tuition 5 cts
and was ordered to sweep the floor after adjournment.
Soggy Hill is informed to hustle up the tuition that
is not paid from the members.
Four new laws passed. 1st. that all of our meetings
open at 9 a.m. and close at 4 p.m. 2nd. that when a
member is to leave the room while the meeting is in
session he is to get permission from the Chairman.
3rd. that when a member wishes to be discharged
or expelled from this organization he should leave
all of the tuition which he has paid. 4th. every
member should bring dinners to every meeting day.
Motion to adjourn by William Long. Seconded by
Soggy Hill.

Adjourned."

April 24, 1914: [Spring]
"At 10 a.m. the meeting called to order by the
Chairman.
Roll call not enough members to open the meeting.
At 10:20 a.m. Roll call again.
Reading of the minutes of the last meeting.
Reading of the program for April 25 and May 23,
1914.
Program for May adopted.
Program was carried out excellent.
Mr. _____ from Washington spoke very highly
of our program, so let us keep it up.
12:30 dismiss for dinner.
1:00 p.m. the Chairman called the meeting to
order.
Roll call.

Soggy Hill gave us his report [regarding the collection of past-due tuition] but a failure. He acted as a marshal.

Mr. James Henderson the Supt. also praised our program.

Tuition collection $2.80.

Soggy Hill made a motion that we accept an offer by the Supt. and seconded by York Cornsilk and accepted to furnish us windows and desks.

Corneeta Welch, Soggy Hill and Tom Swimmer were chosen to fix up the new organization room.

William Long made a motion that every new member who wishes to join this organization shall pay the full tuition as other members have. Seconded by Elie Bird. and carried.

William Long made a motion that every member shall make a full payment in June 1914 in dues. Seconded by Elie Bird and carried.

Johnson Thompson made a motion that Tarquet Wolfe and Jonney Swayney be put off the roll in June if they did not pay their tuition by then. Seconded by York Cornsilk and carried.

William Driver made a motion that we have an officer to see about our dues or other necessities. He shall be elected for a term of 12 months, and he shall go by the title of a Marshal. Seconded by York Cornsilk.

Chas. Lambert and Arseen Thompson were nominated for this office. Arseen Thompson got the majority of votes.

Johnson Thompson made a motion that we adjourn. Seconded by Tom Swimmer and carried.
    Adjourned."

May 23, 1914:
"At 10 a.m. the Chairman called the meeting to order.

Roll call 14 members absent.

Reading of the minutes of last meeting interpreted by the translating secretary.

No program for May 23, 1914.

Reading the program for June 27, 1914 and translated by the translating secretary. Approved by the organization that three committees be appointed by the Chairman to make a program for May 23, 1914.

James Blythe chosen to speak on the subject Indian. It was very interesting.

James Henderson spoke an instructive talk but very short.

At 11:45 a.m. Dinner.

At 1 p.m. the Chairman opened the meeting.

Roll call took place.

New business. William Driver made a motion that the Chairman choose a committee of three to borrow money for the benefit of this organization, seconded by Runaway Swimmer the committee chosen are as follows: William Long, Arseen Thompson, Johnson Owl.

Fair 1914

Sept. 29th. and Oct. 1, 1914. And this fair will be known as the Cherokee Indian Fair. The admission fees will be 25 cts.

Elie Bird as a program committee drops his office. Two candidates nominated: Johnson Owl, Chas Lambert. Chas Lambert has the majority of votes.

Johnson Owl made a motion seconded by Johnson Thompson that we adjourn. Carried.

The meeting adjourned. Total collection .75 cts."

June 27, 1914:
"At 11 a.m. the Chairman of the Farmers Union of the Big Cove opened the meeting.

Minutes of the last meeting were read for May 23, 1914 and translated into Cherokee by our translating secretary Daliskie C. Calahoun.

The program for May 23, 1914, which was postponed, was lost by the committee and abolished.

Programs for June 27, 1914 and July 25, 1914 were read and approved by the organization.

At 12 o'clock dinner.

At 1:00 p.m. the Chairman called the meeting to order.

Roll call by the secretary.

The program was well rendered.

Marshal's report was a failure.

Tarquet Wolfe and Johnney were put off the roll on account of not attending the meetings and paying their fees.

At 4:30 p.m. the meeting adjourned. Amount collected $2.50."

The collection of minutes for the monthly meetings continue in this wise from then through July 24, 1915. Highlights of the August 15, 1914, meeting were the selection of a committee of five to complete the work of arranging for the Indian Fair and the forming of a committee of three to choose a building for the fair exhibits to be set up at the Cherokee school. A motion was made that the meeting-room desk and floor be scrubbed with a broom (costing 30 cents), and a motion was made to purchase a lock for the door. At the September meeting, Johnson Owl made a motion that all of the money in the treasurer's hands be drawn out to pay for the printing of tickets and posters to "help along our Cherokee Indian Fair at Cherokee." The secretary wrote a check for this. William Long made a motion that a breastwork be built on the bank of the river just above the society building to insure that the riverbank would not be washed away. In October, Tom Swimmer spoke about cattle raising. In December, Dawson Gorge of Wolfe Town and Ben Bushyhead of Bird Town were added to the rolls. At the March 27, 1915, meeting, Going Bird spoke on corn raising, Johnson Wolfe spoke on gristmilling, Word Wolfe spoke on plowing, and Tom Swimmer spoke on raising and fattening hogs. The influence of the federal and state governments, the schools, and the white settlers can be clearly seen in the Big Cove Farmers Organization, and the implementation of the annual fair will prove to be a significant step for the Cherokees as a whole, for the annual fair continues to be held and has become one of the tribe's economic staples.

1929-1945

In 1929, there was still no real town on the Eastern Cherokee Reservation, and except for the government school and the agency buildings, there was no electricity. Cherokee Station itself consisted of three large stores, one small store, a warehouse, two dwellings, and some small outbuildings. Taking these statistics at face value, it would appear that little was going on among the people, but the truth is that the Eastern Cherokees were, after nearly a century of wondering and despair, coming back to life. Nothing supports this better than a document found in the archives of the Cherokee Museum, at Cherokee, North Carolina. Like the minutes of the Big Cove Farmers Organization, it contains little more than simple facts, but once the facts are put together, they tell a thorough and informative story. It is introduced as "The Census of the Eastern Cherokee Tribe of the Eastern Cherokee Reservation of the Cherokee, North Carolina jurisdiction, as of April 1, 1931, taken by L. W. Page, Superintendent." He begins by giving the total population as 3,199 — so in the ninety-three years since the removal, the population has tripled, and we will see that two-thirds of them are mixed bloods.[7]

Other details are as follows:

"Number entirely self-supporting from their own industry and thrift 3192.

Number who make no effort at self-support: none.

Number of able-bodied Indians to whom rations were issued: none.

Number of Indians who wear modern attire: all.

Number of Indians eligible to vote. Right of franchise questioned.

Last election approximately 100 voted under protest by judges of election.

Number of Indians able to speak English: unknown.

Number of Indians who read and write the English language: unknown.

Number of adult Indians who won county or State prizes on agricultural products exhibited at Cherokee Indian Fair: 500.

No crimes committed. Manufacture and possession of liquor 3, Indians 3.

Two Indians arrested for drunkenness, in State court. $30.00 fines.

Type of Work	No. engaged	Production	Value
Total	475		$42250.00
Basket making	25	3500	5000.00
Beadwork	30	1500	3000.00
Blanket weaving	none		
Lace making	none		
Pottery	20	700	700.00
Farming	400		33550.00

Indians engaged in trades, professions, and industries, hired by others:
    Total 36 yearly earnings 42000.00
    Skilled 4
    32 others in Indian Service.
Total value of tribal property $880,220.00
"   "   " Indian homes, barns, corrals   20,500.00
"   "   " furniture in Indian homes   5,000.00
"   "   " livestock, poultry, etc.   32,784.00
"   "   " all individual Indian property   64,784.95
"   "   " all types of land, 63260 acres   76,200.00
Raise wheat, corn, hay, and rye.
Have 100 horses, 100 mules, cattle — beef 271,

cattle — dairy 126, sheep 110, hogs 321, turkeys 75, chickens 6557, other fowls 120, bees, hives 250.

Eastern Band of Cherokees total 3199: Male 1711; Female 1488; Full-blood 842; Mixed blood 2357. Forty-two births during year. All other additions 39. Deaths during year 10. Eight marriages, legal procedure. Between Indians seven. Between Indians and whites one. One Divorce between Indians. Marriages existing June 30, 1930, 563. No. churches eight. No. who attend church 3199. Protestants, no Catholics. Three Missionaries. No Y.M.C. members. No Y.W.C.A. members. Twenty-two Boy Scouts, no Girl Scouts. No other societies. One Government mill on reservation. This is a saw mill.

Agency employees consist of a farmer, a forester, a field nurse, two police privates, two clerks, and a weaver. The services of the last named employee are divided half and half between boarding school and reservation Indians. No Indian courts exist. They are amenable to the laws of the state the same as white citizens . . . our Indians receive every consideration in the courts.

The old-time Indian dances on this reservation have passed out of existence. The only survival of this old-time custom is a ceremonial known as the 'Ball Dance.' This dance is held the night before a game known as 'Cherokee Ball.'

The Baptists support a full time missionary; 75% are Baptists. M.E. Church North has a missionary. M.E. Church South has assigned Rev. William Hornbuckle, a seventh-eights Cherokee, 45 years of age, to spread the Gospel among the people. He was raised on the reservation and educated at the boarding school here. He has built a church. There is a half-score or more of old-time fire and brimstone preachers, who preach and work with the missionaries. They are lacking in education and training. Preach in sing-song style. Their influence is good. The liquor traffic is well in hand. Relentless warfare against illicit liquor business on the reservation. They do not use peyote or mescal and there are no drug addicts among them. These Indians are not given to gambling.

Last year the Tribal Council passed a resolution appropriating $5,000.00 each year for a period of five years for the purpose of buying seeds, equipment, and live-stock, et cetera, for selling to the Indians under the reimbursable plan. With this appropriation, one hundred and thirty-five Indians were aided in their farming operations last year. For the most part this aid consisted in the purchase of seeds but included in this number there were six key men set up in the sheep business. Each man was furnished with ten sheep as a start. This venture seems to have borne much good fruit. We are setting up a dozen or more this season and have purchased more than a hundred head of sheep for that purpose. The country is well adapted to sheep raising, and has wonderful industrial possibilities for the people of this reservation.

The Council appropriated $1,500.00 last November for the construction and operation of a reservation cannery. There were formerly two large lumber operations on the reservation but they were discontinued because of the establishment of the Great Smoky Mountain National Park. This leaves many Indians without work. Very few of them are willing to leave home to look for work, in fact few are in a position to leave and few do.

Some of the homes are modern and up-to-date as farm houses go. Some have been painted and the premises are well kept, but as a rule they are generally built of logs, and sealed on the inside and outside with clapboards. The less progressive have one room, most of them have two or more rooms with a lean-to for a kitchen-dining room. In some of the houses kept by returned students, the floors are kept scrupulously clean, the walls are plastered with newspapers and pictures cut from magazines. On the outside is usually found a neatly kept garden. The fence is usually of pickets sharpened at the top, and it is the exception when one does not find shubbery and flowers . . .and in some instances various varieties of fruit trees.

The Cherokee Indian Fair which was started here in 1914 is the one great event in the community life of these Indians. They look forward to it from one year to the next. Last year they reaped a harvest of something like $6,000.00 paid to them in premiums on exhibits, sale of baskets, and other native products, as well as services for putting on free acts furnished for the entertainment of fair visitors. L. W. Page, Supt.

The reservation lies in the extreme southwestern portion of North Carolina, in the counties of Swain, Jackson, Graham and Cherokee. The reservation proper, often referred to as the Qualla Boundary, lies in Swain and Jackson Counties and consists of 50,000 acres or less. In the counties of Graham and Cherokee, there are something like fifty-three scattered tracts aggregating 13,000 acres. This 63,000 acres form only a small part of that vast region comprising western North Carolina, northern Georgia and eastern Tennessee which was at one time the original home of the great and powerful Cherokee Nation. It became easier for them to hide in the mountains fastness and elude their captors. Thus they did with varying success until the treaty of 1846, which provided that all Indians not removed to the west would be allowed to remain in their native homes.

Their agent in the person of W. H. Thomas, who had been raised among the Indians and was their friend, began the purchase of the lands which constitute the present reservation of these people. Titles to all lands purchased by Thomas were taken in his own name. He became involved in debt and to secure the debts owed by him, he gave deeds of trust on a great deal of the lands purchased by him for the Indians, and to further complicate matters, the State of Carolina made grants to white settlers which were in conflict with the lands purchased by Thomas.

In order to protect the interest of the Indians, an Act was passed by Congress in 1870 appropriating the funds and providing means looking toward the adjustment of the tangled state in to which these lands had fallen. Thomas had been sued by his creditors and foreclosure proceedings instituted.

In 1874, a commission was appointed consisting of three members. A degree of award was made, and in 1876, Congress passed an Act confirming this award. Thus, the Qualla Boundary stated as 50,000 acres, was on October 9, 1876, conveyed to the Eastern Band of Cherokee Indians. The Qualla Boundary and other lands thus acquired and occupied is a rough, rugged, mountain section. It forms a part of the Blue Ridge Mountain chain and lies at the foot of the Great Smoky Mountains. Some of the peaks attain an altitude of 6,000 feet.

There is one boarding school . . an average attendance in excess of 375, and two day schools have more than fifty pupils in attendance. A twenty-two bed hospital is maintained at the boarding school but agency patients may be admitted and treated there. A physician is also employed and his services are free to both students of the school and agency patients.

This reservation is healthy. The climate is equable, the average temperature is not more than 72 degrees. There are no mosquitoes.

The boarding school takes the student through the primary and intermediate grades, and two years of high school work. There are no mission schools, and with the exception of a small one-teacher school in Graham County, seventy miles distant, there are no contract schools.

There was also an increase in the per capita cost allowance in the govt. boarding school. This permitted the full ration of milk, eggs, fresh fruit and vegetables for the students' table. Heretofore, practically all of these items used on the students' tables were produced on the school farm, which were good as far as they went but not sufficient to furnish the full ration allowance.

At the Birdtown day school, a new two-room school building was completed . . .ready next school term . . . no material improvements at Big Cove day school during the past year . . . new kitchen-dining room . . . and the noonday lunch was established at both schools.

The lands of the Eastern Band are held by them in common. They have never been allotted in severalty — act passed but not allotted. Timber on the reservation is taken out and sold under the permit system. On the first Wednesday in each month, the Chief, Assistant Chief, and the Supt. who compose the business committee of the Council, meet to receive applications for permits and to attend to other tribal business. Last committee day fifty timber permits were issued ranging in amounts from two cords to ten, mostly of pine or poplar for sale to pulp mills. The position of forester was created during the last fiscal year.

Judge maintains that since these lands were never a part of the public domain, they could not be considered exempt from taxation by the state. An appeal has been taken from this decision and it is understood that the case will ultimately come before the United States Supreme Court for decision.

For several years past, the right of these Indians to vote in the State and National elections has been denied by the state election officials. Last year they were allowed to register and vote in Swain County, but in Jackson County they were denied that privilege, even those possessing education and intelligence were turned down. The Indians feel, and rightly so, that they are being grossly discriminated against, and so far, only partial success has resulted in the efforts to give them full and complete citizenship which they deserve and should have. A. E. Clancy, Supt.

The Agency has a very efficient and industrious field nurse in the person of Mrs. Lula Gloyne. It is planned to organize Mothers' Clubs. A forester, Mr. Clarence Balizat, has recently been appointed.

A plan to encourage better living conditions among the people is being initiated. Visits by teachers to the homes will be encouraged.

It is planned to give special attention to the care of the old, infirm, and needy and each case will be carefully investigated by the field nurse to determine whether the case is a worthy one or not. Report 1931

By the mid-1930s, the fear of removal had eased, and conditions were rapidly improving. Cherokee had a modernized school with twelve grades that emphasized academic, industrial, and vocational achievements. A teacher had even been employed to teach the mixed bloods the native language that had fallen into disuse. Many graduates were going on for further study. New civic buildings had been erected, and old buildings had been improved. A new government hospital had been completed, and the people were receiving free medical and dental treatment. Homes were being built, and considerable intermarriage with whites was taking place. Photographs from the time show that the more progressive women were wearing short-sleeved and belted cotton or calico dresses, white ankle socks, and slip-on shoes. Their hair was cut fairly short and worn straight or in natural waves. Aprons were a standard part of the costume. For daily wear, men wore cotton shirts with the sleeves rolled up, denim overalls or belted trousers, and work shoes. Girls wore knee-length dresses, wool jackets, and their hair was straight or in wrapped braids. Boys had short hair, and wore cotton shirts and denim overalls. It appears that all children aged ten or under went about barefooted. For dress occasions, men had vested black or brown suits that

were worn without ties. Their felt hats were creased down the center and were narrow brimmed. Radios were in existence, along with pianos and organs.

But the majority of the full bloods remained in the outlying districts, where they lived secluded lives and clung to some of the ancient ways. They could be seen coming and going along the narrow mountain trails and crossing rivers on quaint wooden hanging bridges. Often a woman would carry a child in a blanket sling on her back and at the same time a bushel of cornmeal in a basket. They sang the old hymns in their native language. The older women wore long, full dresses and tied kerchiefs over their hair. They remained reticent, stoical, and seemingly indifferent to strangers, yet proved to be friendly to all whites who made a sincere attempt to know them. Conjurers, or medicine men, were still preferred over the white doctors in the government hospital, and the old superstitions were maintained. Only on Saturdays or on council and association meeting days did these folks come into the town centers.

Some forms of the old manner of government were still being maintained in the 1930s, but the Bureau of Indian Affairs was the ultimate authority. The Cherokees had a chief, vice-chief, and twelve councilmen who represented the six townships. Except for the educational and medical facilities, the people were self-supporting. A tribal fund assisted the aged, sick, and needy, and provided the final rites, caskets, and graves for the dead. A cook and food were sent to the home of the deceased. The old custom of placing grave goods with the deceased was abandoned, and the burial services were Christian.

When in the 1930s serious sickness came to a family, the local cooperative poor-aid society stepped in and took over the farming and housework until the family was back on its feet again. When death did occur, the cooperative became an undertaking establishment. Other than performing a few miscellaneous tasks of little consequence, relatives or immediate kin were not asked to carry out the funeral arrangements or burial. The corpse was washed, dressed, and then lay in state for a day or so on a slightly tilted viewing board while relatives and friends came for a last look. The friends of the family watched the corpse day and night. When everyone was ready, the funeral society brought the coffin, placed the corpse in it, then an ordinary Christian funeral service was held, and the coffin was taken to the cemetery.[8]

Near the town council house in what had now become the main reservation town of Cherokee was a mission house provided by the Southern Baptist Convention, whose chief resident supervised the numerous Baptist churches on the reservation — many of whom now had mixed-blood pastors who were exceedingly passionate about their work. There was also a single Methodist mission.

The main industry was agriculture, but except for a few progressive farmers and one small farm that was cultivated under school management, the Cherokees used a steer, hand plow, and hoe, and they tilled the hillsides, where the ground was more fertile and easier to work. To supplement their farming, they made extra money by craft work. During the inclement months of winter the men fashioned bows, arrows, blowguns, and carved items, while the women produced pottery, baskets, and beadwork. These products were sold during the summers to the thousands of non-Indian visitors who swarmed to an ever expanding number of tourist shops in Cherokee. Modern cabins, cafés, and inns were being built where excellent lodging and meals could be had. In 1937, a natural amphitheater was developed, and a colorful historical pageant was presented in it. The production was so well received and successful that it became an annual event and a mainstay of Cherokee life. The tourist season climaxed with an annual fair in October, whose quiet beginning we saw in the 1914 minutes of the Big Cove Farmers Association meetings. Here visitors could see some of the old life recreated — fragments of old dances like the Eagle, Beaver, Butterfly, War, and Green Corn; blowgun contests, bow-and-arrow contests, and ball play. There were also farm and garden exhibits, and special Cherokee foods were available.

Ethnologists who came to the reservation during the 1930s and early 1940s found there had been a leveling of social classes in Cherokee society.

A complete secularization had taken place. The power of religious officials and Beloved Women had been done away with. There was now democratic equality, modified only slightly by the presence of a privileged caste of whites who were married to Cherokees and considered themselves "white Indians," and by mixed bloods who possessed a greater amount of land or other wealth than their purer-blood Indian neighbors.[9]

Government schools had set into motion a decline in the old manner of family control. Parents no longer advised their children in regard to a marriage partner. Clan affiliations continued to control mate choices, but to less and less a degree. The mother's brother was no longer a power in the family, and the transmission of family names had shifted from the mother to the father. The age of consent in marriage was now fifteen for girls and seventeen for boys. But earlier marriages than at these ages often occurred. Late marriages were also common, and the persons involved in these frequently used love charms and rituals provided by medicine men or women to gain the affection of the ones they desired. After marriage, the husband farmed, looked after the stock, cut wood, hunted game, fished, or visited other villages. The wife did the household chores, looked after the children, cooked, sewed, washed the clothes, and sometimes followed her husband around in his visits. In all public meetings, such as the ball game, dances, church services, and the like, the women always congregated by themselves and apart from the men. Each party regarded the spouse's parents with great respect.[10]

Some elements of ancient Cherokee life were entirely gone. There was no retaliatory warfare, no blood revenge, no ritual performance to deal with taboos. Replacing these were white culture traits — just as cattle, turkeys, chickens, and hogs had replaced deer, buffalo, and bear in the diet.

Everything else that was left of the ancient culture had suffered alteration and abbreviation and was removed from its original context. Artifacts that were once in common use, such as the flute, trumpet, blowgun, and bow, were now made only for tourists, or in small-sized toys for children to play with. Instead of singing all of the verses of songs used for dances, only the first and last and perhaps one or two of the other were sung. Some of the great dances that were once given on only the most special occasions and in prescribed seasons were now indifferently performed in public for tourists, without censure and for monetary gain. The Above Beings were no longer consulted in these matters. These ceremonial changes paralleled the decline and disappearance of aboriginal traits noted in other fields. In the 1930s, while there were still many types of social dances being held, only scant traces of the ancient ceremonial cycle could be found, and those in the form of a dozen pitiful dances given at odd times in one or two of the villages or in competition for cash prizes at the annual fair.

The trend was away from independence, whether political, economic, or cultural, and toward a complete dependence upon tourists and the federal government for all of the means of existence and education. So thorough and profound was the sequence of changes leading from the past to the present that visiting ethnologists, Gilbert in particular, thought it probable that if present tendencies continued the tribe would be completely deculturalized, so far as aboriginal elements went, within another generation — by 1975 or 1980.[11]

Gilbert's aged informants named for him eight dances that had disappeared within the last fifty or sixty years: the Pheasant, Raccoon, Round, Snake, Buffalo, Pigeon, War, and Women Gathering Wood. The Eagle Dance, they said, would have suffered a like fate were it not for white ethnologists who supplied the natives of Big Cove with imported feathers. Certain of these dances were reduced to sheer entertainment and obscenity before they disappeared. The Medicine Dances were among these. In the early nineteenth century they were serious affairs, but at the time of their disappearance had become mere burlesques. Only the Green Corn Dance retained any measure of its original ceremonial position and significance, and the Ball Dances that accompanied the ball games still had some substance. The dance, then, no longer played the role

it once did. The modes of ritual cleansing by water and emetic having all but lapsed and the use of native medicine and conjuring having fallen into evil days, there was not as much use for the dances. As mentioned above, this is not to say that dances were entirely eliminated, and reference will be made to a number of social dances that were being performed in the 1930s and 1940s. Also, spontaneous revivals of dances had occurred from time to time in several of the villages, but the kind of enthusiasm and reverence we once saw for the old festivals did not accompany them.[12]

Other things were disappearing also. When Gilbert compared the meanings of forty signs given in the Payne manuscripts to what existed in his time, he discovered that twenty of the signs had lost all meaning. Changes in interpretation from death to mere sickness had occurred in eight of the signs. Some sign meanings were lost when cultural habits, such as war and hunting, no longer existed. Only twenty of the signs still held their original interpretations.[13]

As for new fire rites, Gilbert did find traces of them in Big Cove, where several of the medicine men employed new fire in their work. In fact, he says, its use as a magical force was probably known all over the reservation. But he experienced great difficulty when he attempted to gather worthwhile information on this topic, for it had become an esoteric matter of the greatest importance, being used in their rites for sending witchcraft power against an enemy, and its effects were thought to be fatal if not counteracted in time.[14] New fire, then, had changed from a public rite of meaning understood and shared by all of the people to a secret rite performed by the medicine men and women for their own purposes. Its public function had become a private one, and Gilbert felt this paralleled the case of witchcraft as it had shifted from being a public act punishable by death to that of a merely private act of no public significance. In his opinion, ancient public ritual, that fortress of the full bloods who once clung so tightly to it, had degenerated into nothing more than black magic.[15]

Dances in the 1930s and 1940s

Superintendent L. W. Page claims in his census statistics that the old-time Indian dances on the Eastern Cherokee Reservation had passed out of existence by 1931. This was not true, and either he was not a careful observer, or he believed that the dances being done in no way represented the ancient ones. Several ethnologists who were visiting the Eastern Cherokees at that very time saw many dances whose roots extended back to ancient times, and while these lost much of their luster because they were done in ordinary clothing and no longer served the original religious purpose, the Big Cove band was boasting of never having ceased its native dancing. In other words, while their meaning for the people during the transition period and in 1931 was different, the dances continued to serve a worthwhile purpose.[16]

According to Gilbert, there were, in fact, sixteen dances that were current among the Big Cove residents. Frank Gouldsmith Speck and L. Broom, with the assistance and guidance of Will West Long, whom they portray as a most authoritative Cherokee, name twenty-nine dances they either saw personally or learned of at Big Cove during their series of investigations that ranged from 1928 to 1944. Winter Dances included the Booger or Mask Dance, Eagle Dance, and Bear Dance. Summer Dances included the Green Corn Ceremony and Dance, and the Ball-players' Dance. War rites consisted of War or Snake-mask Dance, Warrior or Brave Dance, Victory or Scalp Dance. Formal rites included the Beginning Dance, Friendship Dance, and Round or Funning Dance. Animal and other rites were numerous, and consisted of the Beaver Dance, Buffalo Dance, Pigeon Dance, Partridge Dance, Groundhog Dance, Horse Dance, Chicken Dance, Knee-deep (Spring Frog) Dance, Pissant Dance, Corn Dance, Raccoon Dance, Gizzard Dance, Bar-the-Way Dance, and Women-Gathering-Wood Dance. Besides these, there were intermission pastimes, contests at the conclusion of dance night, and animal-hunting formulas and rites consisting of large animal-hunting masks, bear-hunting formulas, deer-hunting formulas, turkey-hunting formulas, eagle-hunting formulas, and the hunting-song formula for general use.[17]

In most of these dances, both men and women participated, but men led and did the singing. A few dances were done only by males and a few only by females. Most dances were led by a singer who carried either a drum or a gourd rattle, who might or might not participate in the motions of the dance. The rank and file of the dancers followed the leader in single file and might accompany the leader's singing, might finish out his initial phrases, or might reply in antiphony. A woman with tortoiseshell rattles fastened to her calves usually followed immediately behind the leader and kept time for his singing by stomping to shake her rattles in rhythmic sequence.[18]

The drum was made of a small section of hollowed buckeye trunk whose open end, or "head," was covered with woodchuck skin held down by a hickory hoop. The outside was carved or painted. For use, the drumhead was soaked in water, and the hoop was pounded down over the skin until the skin rang when struck lightly. Enough water was poured into the drum to allow the singer to remoisten the head either by shaking the drum or turning it upside down. The drumstick was made from a piece of hickory or black walnut, was slightly less than a foot long, and had a small knob on one end. Gourd rattles were made of hollow, dried gourds with either the neck or a hickory stick serving as the handle. Most rattles were left unpainted, but a few were painted with red or black designs. Some Birdtown rattles had rattlesnake-rattle or hawk-feather pendants attached to the top of the gourd. Turtle-shell leg rattles consisted of cloth or hide pads that had attached to them clusters of four or five whole shells with pebbles inserted. The more ancient form had four deer hooves dangling from the uppermost shell.[19]

Other items used in the dances were pine boughs, sticks, eagle-feather wands, pipes, masks, and robes or blankets of various kinds. Although body paint and costumes of skins and feathers were used in ancient times, in the 1930s and 1940s, other than for the masked Booger Dance and the dances performed at the annual fair, only the plain overalls or shirt and trousers of everyday male life were worn, and the dances had little visual effect.

Most dances were done at night, with certain of them performed in the early part of the evening and others given in the hours after midnight. If we include for the moment the dances that had recently lapsed, the evening dances were the Eagle, Booger, Beaver, Women Gathering Wood, and Pigeon. Friendship and Ball dances might continue all night. Booger dances usually preceded an Eagle Dance, after which a Friendship Dance was held. Other times there was a Pigeon Dance, followed by a Beaver Dance and a Booger Dance. If an Eagle Dance was given, the Pigeon Dance was omitted, or vice versa. Booger Dances almost always included a Bear Dance given by masked performers. About 2:00 a.m., the different dances might be held in the following order: Coat, Groundhog, Corn, Knee-Deep, Buffalo, Ant, Quail, Chicken, Snake, Raccoon, Bear, Horse, and finally, when full daylight had arrived, the Round Dance, followed with another Eagle Dance or by a game of women's football. The Green Corn Dance was performed at any time during the day, but once begun never ended until after dark. Until the mid-1920s, the people at Big Cove believed that certain dances, such as the Eagle, Booger, and Snake, were to be given only at certain seasons, for if these were done in the summer, bitterly cold weather or a rash of snakebites would inevitably follow. So the proper time to hold these dances was the frosty season that extended from November to March. But by 1930, the disappearance of the old-time conjurers and the curses they could impose for breaches of rules eased people's fears, and they were holding these dances in the summer months.[20]

Dances could be held either indoors or outdoors, but the majority was held indoors. Sometimes a regular and periodic round was made of all the houses in a given community, with each weekly or biweekly dance being held at a different house. At Big Cove, all of the dances were held at houses located in the valley flats, which were more accessible, and which had level sites for dancing.

The number of song accompaniments for a given dance could range from one to fourteen, but the average number employed was four. A song consisted of an individual melody sung with a series of meaningless words or syllables that represented or symbolized ancient towns and places, and of poetic phrases that represented the sounds of nature. In the Friendship Dances, syllables and melodies were improvised, and in the course of several hours as many as forty or fifty songs might be sung. Most of the syllables and the accompanying melodies were repeated without variation, except that vowel tones of some of the syllables might vary in the numerous repetitions. The average duration of a single dance with its four songs and their repetitions was from a quarter-hour to a half-hour.

An alternate order of slow and fast melodies was maintained, with the faster tempos predominating toward the end of the dance. The steps used in dancing varied only slightly from dance to dance and consisted of simple rhythmic walking steps in time with the drum or rattle. In fast time, a quick hopping motion was employed. In the Booger Dance, the performers used any kind of step they wanted to. Much of the dancing was done with the upper parts of the body — especially the arms, shoulders, and head.

All kinds of conventionalized and naturalistic motions accompanied the dances. But except for the Green Corn Dance and the Ball Dance, the dances of the 1930s had no connection with agricultural, hunting, warring, healing, or national preservation pursuits. Hunting methods and the habits of various animals were still imitated, as were the movements of sowing seeds and the tilling of the soil, but these were incidental motions that were lost in a maze of meaningless movements. The basic purpose was now a social one, intended for having a good time and for the making and renewing of acquaintances.

The clapping of hands was a common feature of the Friendship Dances, which were symbolically related to the bear and expressed the joy and happiness being experienced by the participants. Bears were thought to clap their hands when pleased, so much clapping was indulged in. In the ancient past, whenever a family had lost a member by death, their neighbors would give a Friendship Dance to help the family forget its sorrow.

In the 1930s, the *gotogwaski*, or "caller," was the organizer of the night's dancing, and it was he who called off the names of those who were to lead the individual dances. At the end of a song, he would shout out words of encouragement and applause. Note the difference between what he actually said and what Evans thought he was saying back in 1835. The caller always selected the best and strongest singers as leaders. The leader started to walk around in a circle singing his song and at first was followed by only one or two old men. Next, other men joined the circle, then the woman with rattles on her legs, and finally came a vast number of girls, boys, men, and women who were circling around the room at a faster and faster rate. After the song ended, the entire group made a wild dash for the door and fresh air.[21]

The two dances of special importance were the Friendship Dance and the Booger Dance.

Aside from the pungent smell of old tobacco permeating the air and the constant spitting, the Friendship Dance was one of the most fascinating aspects of life at Big Cove. Gilbert felt the dance held a gripping power as great as any opera in white society, for its drama and music were the prime expression of the socially significant facts of Cherokee existence. In the renewal of their old-time mating memories, the older people found their chief consolation as age advanced. In the sexual glamour of the occasion, the young people found their chief recreation. In the general cheerfulness the atmosphere generated, those who mourned for deceased relatives were comforted.[22]

The Friendship Dances Gilbert witnessed were a mix of a large number of dances whose common purpose was to provide the social atmosphere young people needed to find a spouse among potential relatives. In this dance young people got acquainted. There was a great amount of teasing and joking between relatives. Young men would scratch the young girls' hands with their fingernails, slap them lightly, or feint blows at them, poke at them, or otherwise tease them.

Other familiarities indulged in during the Friendship Dances consisted of men placing their hats on the heads of their female partners, putting their coats around them, putting their arms around their shoulders and necks, and performing various overhand movements with them. The dance motions were designed to overcome shyness and reserve on the part of the young people — strictly along the permitted line of the familiarity relationship with specific relatives. "At the dance a man must find a wife, and there is only one way to find a wife and that is to select her out of the group of women with whom he can carry on relations of familiarity."[23]

The typical Friendship Dance began with a few of the older men circling around the room. The woman with the rattles then joined in the circle and after her came the older women followed by the younger men and women. Round and round the circle went, gradually picking up speed and volume as more people joined in the "magic ring." Finally, when the crowd had become too great for the size of the room, and the heat, sweat, and dust were oppressive, everyone would give a final whoop and rush forth into the open air.[24]

The Booger Dance retained particular social importance. Its performers were called Boogers, Bogeys, or Buggers. Considerable paraphernalia and preparation were needed for the dance. Primary were from six to twelve masks made of gourds, wood, or pasteboard, and from six to ten gourd rattles and a drum with a groundhog-skin head. The male organizer of the dance collected from all of the women present shawls, blankets, or sweaters to clothe the Boogers.

Six men sat down on chairs or benches on one side of the room. These included a drummer, or leader, and five assistant music makers who held gourd rattles. The six were known as "callers," whose function it was to sing and call the Boogers. When the callers had completed their sixth song, the Boogers entered one by one, their faces concealed by masks and their bodies by various wraparound materials, and hobbling in various comical positions and with odd motions. They endeavored to do everything in a topsy-turvy, or backwards, manner.

There were usually seven Boogers, and as the

Carved Booger Dance masks from Museum of the American Indian, Heye Foundation. Top left, warrior. Top middle, black man. Top right, Indian. Bottom, Cherokee log cabin redrawn from photograph by James Mooney around 1888-93, Negative no. 1000-A, Smithsonian Institution, National Anthropological Archives.

seventh song was played they danced in a circle about the room and attempted to frighten those children who were clan relatives to them. They also teased the grown-ups who were their familiar relatives. All of the spectators did their utmost to guess which of the performers was their familiar relative.

At the end of the seventh song, the Boogers seated themselves in a comical fashion and with clumsy gestures on a log at one side of the room. While they did this, the organizer was asked by the head caller to put some questions to the Boogers. The first question was generally, "What is your name?" or "Where do you come from?" The organizer then went to the first Booger and repeated the question. To this the Booger gave a whispered reply, and the name he chose for himself was always either obscene or ludicrous. He gave as his place of origin some remote or fanciful location. He might "joke" a familiar relative in a neighboring town by using his name. After the initial questions, the first Booger got to his feet in some ridiculous manner and clowned around in a solo dance. During the dance the music maker or chief caller repeatedly called out the name of the Booger, and as he did this the Booger went through motions and gestures that fitted the name. The steps of this solo dance were utterly unlike those of any other Cherokee dance and consisted of a series of heavy hops done in rhythmic time. When the first Booger finished, the other dancers took their turns.

Following this, the organizer asked the Boogers to do a Bear Dance together. When this dance was finished, the audience joined in and danced with the Boogers. As the dance proceeded the Boogers teased their familiar relatives, especially the women, in obscene and ridiculous ways. When the dance ended, the Boogers left the room and went away to some remote area where they removed their costumes, then slipped away to their homes so they could not be recognized. Once the Boogers were gone, the rest of the people held a Friendship Dance.[25]

After studying the Booger Dance, Speck and Broom decided that as it was done at Big Cove it was more than a continuing and simple cultural form being held in an isolated geographical pocket. They

saw in the dance a record of the anxieties of a people — their reactions against the symbol of the invader and their insecurity in their dealings with the white man. In this dance, the Big Cove full bloods were relating their reactions to the invasion of the white man, as most clearly expressed in the cultural changes and the 1838 removal, to the spiritual forces of nature with which the Cherokee had once successfully coped through their rituals. By performing the Booger Dance now — the Booger being the white man — the power of the white threat was somehow lessened. To put this another way, the Cherokees were better able to deal with the reality of whites when they were able to place the problem in a familiar ritual context. Once the white invaders had been disguised as boogers, or mythical animals and frivolous demons, they were reduced to something the Cherokee could deal with.[26]

After completing his research, Gilbert concluded that the Eagle Dance was, even in 1940, probably the most important and most revered of the Cherokee dances. He recalls that the eagles were said to have gathered together and teased each other just as men did in the Eagle Dance[27] and that the dance was once held in the fall or winter when eagles were killed. But in the 1930s and 1940s it was being held whenever anyone wanted to hold it. He also points out that in addition to its function as a celebration of the killing of an eagle, the ancient dance had several subordinate elements, such as the Scalp Dance that celebrated victory in war and the Peace Pipe Dance that celebrated the conclusion of peace.[28] In contrast, the chief function of the 1930s Eagle Dance was celebrating victory in the ball game. In this performance, all of the elements of the ancient Eagle Dance were mixed together, and the Scalp Dance portion was a solo dance in which the male performer could dance out his story and boast of his bravery.[29]

True to their boast, in the Big Cove community more than in any other on the reservation the old-time methods of dancing were being remembered and carried on the longest, although a considerable interest in dancing and periodic indulgence in dances was found at Birdtown, and some of their dances were not being done in Big Cove. They included the Witch Dance, in which the performers imitated eye goggles with the use of their fingers; the Gagoyi Dance, whose curled-up or twisted evolutions resembled those of the Ant Dance; and the Parched Corn Dance, which was an addition to the Green Corn Dance.[30]

In 1946, John Witthoft reported on "The Cherokee Green Corn Medicine and the Green Corn Festival." In this report he stated that the Green Corn Festival seemed to have been the last important major ceremony to survive among the Eastern Cherokees, mentioning that Mooney, in 1914, claimed that he saw the last Green Corn Dance performed there in 1887 and a related festival in 1914. However, Speck observed and described a Green Corn Ceremony that still existed at Big Cove, although it was not held at any fixed time, and seemed to have lost all connection with the yearly agricultural cycle. It was performed for curative purposes for persons suffering from specified ailments and was accompanied by a feast provided by the patients and their families. Will West Long functioned as a leader of that Green Corn Feast whenever its performance was required.

We recall that in the ancient festival, the priest consulted his beads or crystal to determine which individuals would survive the year. Where the indication was negative, a ritual associated with the Green Corn Feast was held at night that included dances and nightlong vigils. The proper formulas were recited by the priest, and divination was continued until some assurance was received that the person's life would by some means be perpetuated until the next green Corn Festival was held. Witthoft believes it was probably this secondary phase of the ceremony that had survived and was being performed in the 1930s and 1940s. It was a curative rite done in association with the medicine man's forms of diagnoses and therapy. The Cherokee had also preserved a green corn medicine, that, while it was no longer preceded by a cleansing emetic, was made and administered by the head of each household to his family. This was an individual and not a community function and was performed wherever the

family's green corn was ready to eat. Its purpose was to prevent the colic that resulted from eating the green corn, especially in the case of children. The emetic served also as a medicine to prevent the increase of stomach and intestinal worms that flourished in green corn, which could do great damage to a person. None of the really conservative Cherokees of the Big Cove settlement would even taste green corn if they had not taken the medicine, which consisted of the leaves of four or more weeds or plants that were crushed in the hands and pounded together in a mortar, then steeped in warm water until the solution was ready to be drunk.

Beyond this, two rules, whose basis was found in the green corn myth of the Corn Mother, were still followed in the eating of the green corn. One must not blow on a roasted ear of green corn to cool it, else a violent thunderstorm would erupt, for the Thunders were the sons and husband of the Corn Mother and would resent such disrespectful treatment of her. And since the Corn Mother's body had lain outdoors on the ground for four days after she had been killed by her sons, the cob remnants had to be kept in the house for four days after the feast.

Witthoft concluded his article with two enlightening accounts of the origin of corn, one given by Mollie Sequoyah and the other by Moses Owl. Both of them differed in important features from earlier accounts given by other informants, but indicated to him the continued strong conservatism of a certain minority of full-blooded Cherokee households on the Eastern Cherokee Reservation, particularly in the Big Cove and Birdtown communities.[31]

Dance Masks

Dance masks played an important role in ancient Cherokee ritual, and many kinds were made. But by 1940, the only masks being used for dances were the Booger masks. The rest were being fashioned for museums and tourists, although they were carved in the old manner as replicas of former types.

To outsiders, Indian masks are always fascinating and add to the mysterious aspects of performances. Yet they mean far more than this to Indians.

Will West Long and son Allen carving masks with mallet, wedge, and carving tool. Redrawn from photographs in the Museum of the Cherokee Indian.

In Hopi belief, when a performer dons his Katcina mask, he becomes the Katcina he represents. Thus a transformation occurs, and the man is now as much or more spirit than he is man. Among the Iroquois, false-face masks were carved into the trunks of living trees, then were cut out, retaining by this process the "life" of the tree within the mask. Cherokee masks do not seem to have served the same purposes, for each mask was infused with its own power, and it did not transmit that power to the man who wore it. Therefore, a performer's dance was designed to help the spectator understand what the mask's power was and how it dispensed its power. When a hunter wore his mask, it was the mask and not the hunter who became one with the game being pursued and either drew it closer to the hunter or enabled the hunter to find it. Also, photographs taken in 1932 of Will West Long and his son, Allen, as they carved masks, show them first cutting a five-foot-or-so-long log and then dividing this log into sections, each of which was large enough to make a mask. They used an ax and a knife to carve each section into a finished product. My drawings show the process. As previously stated, masks were also made of gourds and animal hide, and these were painted with strong colors and had chunks of fur and hair added to make them more powerful and frightening.

In December 1940 W. N. Fenton and Lester Hargett interrogated Will West Long, Speck and Broom's informant, probably the same "William Long" mentioned in the 1913-1915 minutes of the Big Cove Farmers Organization, about dance masks and the Eagle Dance. Long, who died in 1946 at the age of seventy-seven, was accepted by ethnologists in general as a leader, an authority as a priest would be in a rite — a mentor and leader in the performances.[32]

A number of the various types of masks were on exhibit in the Cherokee Chieftain Craft Shop, operated by Louise and Ross Caldwell. Will made them on regular order, and they sold for five dollars to seven-and-a-half dollars. When he made them on consignment he was paid three dollars for plain wooden masks and five dollars for dyed ones. He created about twelve types. Of these, Fenton and Hargett saw a warrior mask with a feather on its forehead, a medicine mask with horns, a bear hunter's mask, and several Booger Dance masks.

Will reported that he had made sets of masks for Mooney, as had the Owl family; one or two sets for M. R. Harrington; as many as sixteen complete sets for Olbrechts; and sets for Speck, Burnett S. Mason of Cincinnati, and many others, including L. Broom of Duke University.

Included in these sets were dance masks of all kinds that were of a generalized type: a warrior mask, with one or two feathers in front after the custom of the ancient Cherokee warrior. The ordinary warrior wore one feather, and two feathers signified a war leader, who might also have another feather that slanted back at the rear of the head. A medicine mask was always ugly and had horns and ears. A conjurer, or curing, mask was discussed by Will: "This is more powerful than the Warrior, it is always ugly, and has horns and ears. The Medicine man prays for a cure, asks God in Heaven for aid, and then frightens the sick person who gets well. The prayer is whispered." If the person were very sick, the conjurer went to water, where he used beads to divine night and morning at the edge of the water. He slept only in the daytime. If the beads gave hope after four nights of vigil, a member of the sick person's household fetched the doctor, who prepared everything. He put on the mask and prayed, using a doctor mask like the one just described, and scared the sick person. This reference on Will's part was to a time before he was born in 1840, and he added that a sick person who got well would kill a wild fowl, a duck, or a white chicken, then cook and eat it. The meat must be fowl and preferably white. There was a deer hunter's mask that had antlers of wood and was difficult to make, sometimes being covered with rabbit skin that was the color of a deer; a magical mask that had rattlesnake rattles carved on its forehead and was regarded as a powerful mask that could kill or cure, although it was not regularly used for medicine; and a hunter's wild-turkey mask, in which groundhog skin was used for the face, and the ears were those of a wildcat — the groundhog skin was now scarce, groundhogs having retreated into

Great Smoky Mountain National Park. Hunters wore this kind of mask to stalk wild turkeys. The hunters would sneak up behind a log near several turkeys, put the mask on, and stand up. The mask knew that wild turkeys were curious and would come close, wondering whether the mask was a true wildcat that preyed on wild turkeys. In an emergency, a mask could be improvised. Once Will and his brother went hunting. They came upon wild turkeys and lacked masks. His brother took the leaves of a nearby tree and used these to improvise ears. He blackened his face with charcoal and called the turkeys close. The two men then shot them, getting one apiece.

The ancient Cherokee priests used rabbit, young woodchuck, deer, bear, and wildcat skins to decorate and add power to the masks they fashioned for themselves and others. But the white traders in Cherokee who marketed the masks for Will and his son had objected to the use of fur to decorate masks, because they believed it was an addition to please the white tourists. However, Fenton and Hargett say the traders were wrong, that the ancient people used fur for eyebrows and in historic times added long whiskers and other embellishments to satirize white men, blacks, and members of other races with whom the Cherokees came into contact. The two ethnologists also say that since the traders had created a market for masks, it had become impossible to hold a masked dance. The traders bought up the masks so fast that the mask makers couldn't keep a set on hand.

The set included a bear hunter's mask that was a replica of a bear's face, dyed black. In connection with this, Will described an incident that happened at a certain Booger Dance where a performer wore a black overcoat and a black bear mask. Another masked man led him around by a string while the performer danced like a trained circus bear. Will thought this was a fine stunt.

There was a buffalo hunter's mask that had horns, gourd masks of the type used in Booger Dances, a black-painted black mask, and finally a Chinese mask. Will claimed that the old Cherokee people had foretold the coming of whites, blacks,

and Chinese, and that the appearance of these characters in Booger Dances satirized the various cultures.

When Fenton described to Will the Iroquois false-face ceremony, it caused Will to remember a time when M. R. Harrington brought to the Cherokees an Iroquois mask with long hair and tin eye sconces and then demonstrated its use to the people. Will had never seen anything like it and supposed it was a medicine-man mask. But the mask behaved strangely, and Will was quite frightened. "It came in whining and crawling around the fire and picked up hot ashes and scattered them and blew on someone. The Cherokees don't go to the fire and scatter ashes, and they don't blow ashes on patients," Will said, although fear was a commonly used element in healing. The Cherokee healer would occasionally act as if he were going to throw a knife at the patient. Will recalled seeing this done to a boy with a backache, who was frightened by the knife and got better. Toothaches were similarly treated with fright. Instead of blowing hot ashes on a patient, Cherokee medicine men used their warmed hands to transfer heat from hot coals to a child's stomach. This treatment was often applied to a child who had overeaten. Sometime parents took the white ashes from a hot fire log and rubbed them on their stomachs so they wouldn't get sick.

The Booger Dance, Will said, was formerly a ceremony, but it was only held for fun now. It was usually done in conjunction with an Eagle Dance. He explained that the Booger dancer carried no rattle, but the singers used a water drum and rattles. The Boogers said funny things. Of ten or twelve performers, one might carry an old rifle, another a horse skull hung on the front of his garb, another a dead rooster on a string while he whispered in confidence to the interpreter that it was a wild turkey. Boogers always whispered and never spoke out. When the interpreter asked them who they were, they gave funny names like "Cow's tail." If the question was, "What do you come here for?" they answered something like, "We come hunting grease, we are looking for meat and lard." Some Booger performers dressed like women, putting handker-

Eagle dancers of the 1930s.

chiefs over their heads and carrying babies in shawls. Those who wore cornhusk masks often carried babies.

Will said that the Cherokee Eagle Dance was originally associated with warfare and the celebration of a victory. Warriors would return with scalps, and one night would be appointed to hold a Victory Dance and the Booger Dance at the same time. In this ceremony, a line of dancing men carried eagle wands. One warrior would leap out in front to dance for several seconds and would cry *"Hi!"* while raising his hand with the arm bent at the elbow. "Now I am going to tell you what I have done!" the warrior would shout. "By this scalp you can see what I did!" He would then show the scalp or scalps he had captured to all present and tell his story.

In the Victory Dance the singers had gourd rattles and eagle wands and stood in line and walked slowly. The dancers held only the scalps, and the scalp holders recounted their war records in turn. There were two kinds of Eagle Dances, of which the Victory Dance cited above was the least ancient type. In the later type, two dancers carried feather fans and rattles as they hopped about, and the dancers wanted a present from the spectators before they performed. Sometimes there were two, six, or eight pairs of dancers in a dance. Fenton thought the Eagle Dance which Will demonstrated was very reminiscent of the Iroquois Eagle Dance.

Will insisted that the Cherokee dance fan had only five feathers, and that five were sufficient if the feathers were broad, otherwise it might take six or seven. He also insisted that the twelve feather fans that John Ax made for James Mooney, which are now in the collection at the Smithsonian's National Museum of Natural History, were not Cherokee. Both Will's and Ax's fan specimens were decorated at the ends of the sticks to which the feathers were tied. At one time, Will tied onto his fans with red thread a wild-turkey feather. But now he used only a piece of red cloth and attributed the change to another demand made by the white traders. The five feathers were spaced out by the use of a radial spreader thong. The illustrations show the fans, or wands, more clearly than they can be described in words.[33]

Sports

In the 1940s, sports were social events. Chief among these were ball play, the women's football game, basket game, match hunts, various children's sports, and various kinds of matches such as archery, rock casting, pitching stones.[34]

The Eastern Cherokees Today

Joyce Johnson, a Cherokee from Tulsa, Oklahoma, and I compiled a list of thirty-four present-day communities on the Eastern Cherokee Reservation. Of these, Cherokee is the largest and most prominent, since it serves as the administrative headquarters and is a year-round tourist center. It is located on U.S. Highways 441 and 19 near the entrance to the Great Smoky Mountains National Park and the southern terminus of the Blue Ridge Parkway. The other communities are: Whittier, Soco, Birdtown, Piney Grove, Jericho, Old Mission Road, Rock Springs, Old No. 4 Road, School House Hill, Smoky Mountain Trail Camp, Shoal Creek, Camp Creek, Long Bird Road, Old River Road, Cold Springs, Yellowhill, Goose Creek, Paint Town, Shoal Creek, Big Cove, Toe String, Big Witch, Washington Creek, Blue Wing, Hoot Owl Cove, Grassy Creek, Union Hill, Wright's Creek, Wolfe Town, Adams Creek, Nation's Creek, and Soggy Creek.

A visitor whose knowledge of the people is superficial and based on erroneous data finds disparate elements that must lead to confusion, for there are numerous faces presented.

The first face is that of commercially oriented Cherokee, North Carolina, where there are glaring billboards, modern motels, and overstocked gift shops whose curios are mostly imports from Latin America and the Far East.

A second face is that of the tribal government functioning in the Tribal Civic Center as a fully modern body in the modern age — overseeing the outdoor pageant, *Unto These Hills,* the Oconaluftee Indian Village, the Museum and Cultural Center, and the Qualla Arts and Crafts Mutual, Inc.; appropriating tribal funds; passing bills and resolutions concerning the tribe; overseeing public services such as fire and police protection, garbage disposal, street safety and improvement, health services, emergency relief, and assistance to the needy. The tribal government also works with and supervises to some extent the non-Indians who operate most of the motels, campgrounds, restaurants, gasoline stations, stores, and souvenir and specialty shops. Since the 1960s, the tribal government, working through the Qualla Housing Authority, has worked with the Bureau of Indian Affairs to acquire hundreds of new and improved homes. A principal chief and vice-chief are elected from the reservation at large and serve four-year terms. The chief during the time we visited in 1983 was John A. Crow, and the vice-chief was Leroy Wahnetah. Council members represent the six townships of the reservation, and are elected for two-year terms. The tribal government cooperates with the federal government in the operation of schools and a hospital, maintaining the roads on the reservation with the exception of U.S. highways. The federal government provides a forester, soil conservationist and, through contract with the state, a farm and home demonstration agent. The Cherokees also receive services given by various state and federal agencies, such as the Veterans Administration, TVA, state experiment stations, and others. Reservation lands continue to be held in trust by the government. Individual Cherokees hold possessory rights to certain tracts, and such holding can be bought, sold, willed, or inherited among the people themselves. However, such holdings cannot be sold or willed to non-members of the band, and cannot be leased to non-members without consent of the tribal council and the BIA, a provision established to keep the Cherokees from becoming landless. Law enforcement is under state law and the sheriffs of the individual counties included in the reservation. Trials are held in State courts. All Cherokees are U. S. citizens, and are entitled to full voting rights. Among the thirty or so churches on the reservation are fourteen Missionary Baptist, three Methodist, one Episcopal, one Pentecostal Holiness, one Roman Catholic, and one Mormon. In some of the churches, the sermons and hymns are conducted in the Cherokee language.

A third face is presented by variations in characteristics and life-styles. Tribal enrollment is something over 10,000 persons, of which 5,000 reside on tribally owned lands. Like outsiders, they have different physical characteristics, thoughts, and life-styles. Around 7 percent are full bloods, and twenty percent are a quarter Cherokee or less. Dwellings of various makeup are scattered throughout the valleys, coves, mountainsides, and ridges of the 56,000 acres comprising the reservation. Some are very new, some are very old. Owners with different professions, degrees of education, and occupations live side by side. Most still speak the Cherokee language, but also speak English. Some have attended college, and some have no public schooling at all. An ultramodern high school building provides educational facilities for 600 students in grades seven through twelve, and serves as a community learning center. The Bureau of Indian Affairs operates the school, but there is also a Cherokee advisory school board. Besides these things there are a Rescue Squad, a Lions Club, a chamber of commerce, a foster parents' organization, labor groups, homemaker and 4-H clubs, Scout troops, and a credit union.

A fourth face is presented by the historical association and museums, the village, the pageant, and Qualla Arts and Crafts. These are where one facet of the lifeway and remembrances of the people is preserved.

The splendid and modern museum that was completed in 1976 features exhibits treating all phases of Cherokee life, including minitheater exhibits related to the Trail of Tears removal, Sequoyah, John Ross, and William Thomas. There are displays of artifacts and crafts, both ancient and contemporary. The archives of the historical center contain an impressive selection of materials relating to the Cherokee Nation's history. A reference library is available to research students, and to all visitors.

Oconaluftee Indian Village and the Botanical Garden and Nature Trail perpetuate in living form the history and heritage of the Cherokees. The village is a full-size replica of an early eighteenth-century Cherokee community, and during its open season from mid-May through Labor Day, locals don somewhat authentic costumes and recreate some of the ancient activities. Guides conduct tours of primitive log cabins, a seven-sided council house, and give lectures in a sacred square. People demonstrate basketry, pottery, finger weaving, beadwork, flint chipping, corn pounding and food preparation, canoe making, weapon making and woodcarving, blowgun demonstrations, and the preparations of materials. Next to the village is the Botanical Garden and Nature Trail. Here are more than 150 species of native plants with their common botanical names, a stream and bridges, a Cherokee vegetable garden, and a notched, hewn log house that was moved from its original location on the reservation and restored.

The pageant, *Unto These Hills,* is performed in a magnificently situated outdoor amphitheater, and most effectively tells again the story of Tsali and the other early chapters in the struggle for survival of the Eastern Cherokees. Some have acclaimed it as "the greatest outdoor Indian attraction in America." By its twenty-sixth year, more than three million persons had witnessed the play.

The Qualla Arts and Crafts Mutual was first organized as a craftsmen's cooperative in 1946, and then incorporated in 1955. Its purpose was to secure for its members better pay and a continuous market for their handicrafts. Also, because the craft tradition was dying out, a major effort was to be made to improve the standard and accuracy of workmanship. This led to a resurgence of interest and industry by both adults and children. A series of facilities was rented as the cooperative grew, until in 1960 a building program was undertaken that has subsequently been enlarged to where it includes working space plus areas for sales, storage, and exhibitions. Today the cooperative has more than 300 members and is a financial success, and contributes substantially to its members' livelihood. By 1981, reported sales were $440,598, with a net profit of $143,086. The quality of the work is extremely good. Prominent among the crafts workers have been Eva Wolfe, Helen Smith, Carol Welch, and Allen Long of Big Cove, and Amanda Crowe and Virgil Ledford. Eva specializes in double-weave river-cane baskets, and in 1977 was awarded by the National Endowment for

the Arts a craftsman's fellowship grant to create an exhibition that was shown in the Renwick Gallery of the Smithsonian Institute. Helen weaves white-oak baskets, and also uses river cane and honeysuckle in her baskets. Carol makes white-oak baskets so well that she provides most of the income for her family. Amanda is recognized as one of the most prominent, creative, contemporary American Indian sculptors in the United States, is a noted teacher, and was awarded an honorary doctor of fine arts degree by the University of North Carolina at Greensboro. Virgil is an outstanding sculptor and carver, both of Cherokee and non-Cherokee items. Allen is the last surviving maker of traditional Cherokee masks for sale to the public.

The fifth face of the Eastern Cherokees is seen in the more remote communities, such as Big Cove, where a semblance of the old life that existed in Mooney, Speck, and Gilbert's time can still be found. Among her many talents, Joyce Johnson is an excellent cook, and uses a number of Cherokee recipes. Thus she was anxious to discover what the Big Cove residents were eating in 1978, and how they prepared it. Being a Cherokee who came with letters of introduction, she was well and openly received, and learned a great deal.

One of the prehistoric dishes was bean bread, made with flour corn. The Eastern Cherokee women still prepare it, and call it "flour corn." Dried pinto beans are boiled in water until they are tender. The corn is skinned with wood ashes, and the ashes are sifted and placed in an iron or pottery pot. To make it in the old way, when the water in the pot begins to boil the corn is placed in it and stirred at intervals to keep it from sticking. Then when the corn is thick enough to bubble, the pot is removed from the fire. The corn is placed in baskets and taken to a stream where it is sifted and washed. When the corn is clean, it is allowed to drip until it is dry. Then it is pounded with a corn pounder, consisting of a log and a piece of tree, and mixed with the beans. Balls are formed, and these are cooked in a pot of plain water, with no salt or other seasoning, since seasoning causes the bread to crumble. When it is done, the bread balls are eaten. The Eastern Cherokees still coat their bread balls with rendered back fat or hog fry.

Another dish is called "broadswords." Corn balls are flattened out in the palms of the hands. Then corn blades gathered when they were green are tied together by the ends and hung in the shade to dry. When the women want to make broadswords, they make the blades limber by dipping them in hot water. The balls are wrapped in the blades (hickory, oak, or cucumber leaves are acceptable substitutes for the corn blades), tied with thread, and dropped into boiling water.

Joyce has eaten the bean bread made in the old way in both Oklahoma and North Carolina, and cites a modern way of preparing it. Beans are added to cornmeal, baking soda, and salt. The mixture is placed in a cornbread pan and cooked.

She tasted chestnut bread for the first time in North Carolina, "Possibly because we don't have chestnut trees around here (Oklahoma)." It is made in the same way as the bean bread, but fine-chopped chestnuts replace the beans. Where the bean bread is red because of the pinto beans, the chestnut bread is gray in color. Carrot or sweet-potato breads are also made.

Joyce was told that some of the Big Cove women still fixed fish soup the old way. The fish is gutted, strung on a stick, and hung over either an inside or an outside fire, being turned now and then until it doesn't drip anymore. It is then placed in a dry paper sack and tossed on a shelf until needed.

The Eastern Cherokees have a sweet grass they pick for greens, and they have sochan, "which is very strong," Joyce said, "and I don't like it." They have cresus, and they have ramps, which are like the wild onions used in Oklahoma. The ramps look like lily of the valley, and have a broad leaf. Since they are so strong, they are picked while they are young. "The smell just nearly knocks you down," Joyce said. Ramps are in the garlic family but are similar to a green onion, and have a root the size of a walnut. The women dig down and cut the plant off just above the root. "They say that if you have eaten ramps you can smell it for three days, and I believe it."

The Cherokees cut the greens and leave them about an inch long. They fry meat in a cast-iron pot, then take the meat out and fry the onions in the grease until brown. Then they beat up chicken eggs — "in the old days they would use either bird or chicken" — and stir them in with the onions. "And that's the way they fix the ramps. It's also the way we fix wild onions here in Oklahoma."

They eat a lot of wild mushrooms, and use a lot of sassafras and spicewood for tea.

There's an abundance of wild apricots, which the women call "old field apricots." These are dried and used to make drinks. Apples are also dried.

Considerable cabbage is cooked and dried.

It seems they dry a lot of their food. They have "leather britches," which are green beans. These are broken off in inch-and-one-half-long lengths and strung on a string, then hung or laid out in the sun to dry. The beans are brought in at night, and during rainy weather. To prepare the beans for cooking, they are soaked in water overnight, then cooked like green beans usually are.

There are at least three different kinds of wild grapes, and many other kinds of fruit.

Joyce learned that the people eat frogs, and it seems they just skin and parboil the entire creature.

Fish are plentiful, and eaten often. The Cherokees boil the fish in water, then drop in a little cornmeal and some lye or soda. This is their fish and mush which "they feed to people who are sick."

They have a wild potato that they use to make potato soup. But what they like best is a hominy drink. To prepare this they shell corn and soak it in lye until the skin can be removed. Then they beat the corn in a corn beater until it is small, after which they sift the powder from the remaining kernel. This is cooked until done, and thickened a little with cornmeal. It is called "crack corn," and is drunk hot or cold. It is often kept until it sours, and can be kept for four days unless the weather is extremely hot. "This is the customary drink if friends come to visit, or if you have been working in the fields." The Cherokees eat a lot of soured food and drinks.

There is a succotash that is very good. It is made of brown beans, cooked until tender, and mixed with hominy. Large pieces of black walnut are put in it, and the whole is thickened with pumpkin.

When animals are butchered, a blood pudding is made from the blood. Joyce ate a piece of groundhog, but found it had a very gamy taste. Groundhogs and raccoons are parboiled until tender, and then baked. Bear meat is also baked. Sometimes bear meat is ground up like patties and then fried. There is also bear sausage used for breakfast. Joyce was told that in the old days, when the Cherokees were having trouble raising the corn, they used instead swamp potatoes, cooking them and then beating them to make a meal that could be used in cooking.

They make a cornmeal gravy, adding only water, salt, and pepper. If they have milk, they use milk in the skillet in which the meat has been cooked. Otherwise, they use a clean skillet. They add cornmeal and cook it until it is like a gruel, then eat it with bread for breakfast.

There are blackberries, huckleberries, strawberries, dewberries, and gooseberries. The strawberries grow wild, and the ground is covered with them. Joyce said, "They are like our dandelions in Oklahoma." There are also raspberries and elderberries. Elderberry wine is made, and also strawberry cobbler and blackberry cobbler. There are wild plums, wild cherries, and crabapples. There are homemade jellies for breakfast. Ground cherries, persimmons, field apricots, fall grapes, fox grapes, possum grapes, hickory nuts, walnuts, hazlenuts, and butternuts add to the larder.

Besides the sassafras and spicewood teas, they also make a sweet drink out of sumac, and it is called "shoo-ma-kid."

There are chestnut bread, bean bread, wild-potato bread, hominy bread, flour-corn bread, sweet-potato bread, and molasses bread.

"The flour corn is evidently a different kind of corn than we grow in Oklahoma . . . It seems to be fuller," Joyce said. The corn is not harvested when it is ripe. At every house a cornfield with dry stalks and the ears of corn still on them can be seen. The Cherokees only pick the corn when they need it. They just leave it to dry on the stalk, and use it all winter that way.

Every house has a good-sized and spread-out garden, and a large cornfield. The gardens consist in the main of corn, beans, cabbage, and potatoes. Corn is planted in the flattest areas, and potatoes are planted on the hillside slopes. Each bed is separate from the others.

We wanted, more than anything else, to research in the Big Cove area, where it is known that people still believe in imitative magic, signs, omens, portents, and witches. By good fortune Joyce met at a symposium in Cherokee a couple who not only live in Big Cove, but were more than willing to help. They began by inviting Joyce, Ray, and Victor Gatlin, Joyce's brother, to visit them, and even to stay with them. They would tell what they could, would provide introductions to family and friends, would show them the area, and would take them to other communities of interest.

The first visit to the home included an experience that Joyce, Ray, and Victor will never forget, and one that gives us a special sense of the haunting flavor of the area. Big Cove is a remote community, and not a town, that is about fifteen miles from Cherokee, and has, aside from its blacktopped main road that bisects it, dirt side roads so rough they put the worst of Oklahoma's to shame.

As they visited, Joyce learned that a man named Wilson, who was an herb gatherer for medicine men and women in the Big Cove, Soco, and other areas, had been paid about $300, and had mysteriously disappeared.

The next day was spent in Cherokee, and was a busy one, and the trio returned to Big Cove about dusk. Just beyond the Baptist church building that was near the West home, they came upon a man who was standing stock-still and unblinking in the middle of the road. Victor had to swerve the automobile around him to miss him, and after going no more than a half-block farther, stopped and backed up, because all three of them thought the man might need help. But the man was gone, despite the fact that a high bank ran down to the creek on one side, and there was a sheer mountain on the other. So they went on, agreeing to say nothing to their hosts, who might well think them "crazy."

Eastern Cherokees redrawn from photographs in Bureau of American Ethnology, Bulletin 99, plates 5, 8, and 12: Top left, the oldest of the medicine men. Top right, Will West Long. Bottom left, a prominent midwife. Bottom right, a medicine woman.

But no sooner had they arrived when the wife said, "Let me tell you the strangest thing about Wilson. People have been seeing him in different places. My sister-in-law, who lives nearby, got in her car and started it. Then she saw Wilson in her rear-view mirror. She jumped out to talk to him, but he wasn't there! Then about dusk another couple saw him standing on the road with an ax sunk in his back! There are others who say they saw him, and this afternoon his jacket and some blood were found near a rock down on the road. We know what it is. He's trying to lead people to where his body is so they can bury him."

The next morning, while the wife was showing them around, they drove by the place where Joyce, Ray, and Victor had seen the man standing on the road. They stopped at the spot, and directly across from them was the rock near where the jacket and blood had been found. When Joyce described to her what the man had been wearing — an army cap and a white T-shirt under a khaki shirt — it was precisely what Wilson had been wearing when people last saw him alive.

Later on, Joyce met a Big Cove girl who worked at the museum, and the girl told her that something strange had happened to her on the morning after Wilson disappeared. She was driving on the road near the Baptist church and saw him standing there. She slammed on her brakes and called out, "Wilson, where have you been? Everyone's looking all over for you." Then all at once, Wilson wasn't there. She got out and looked around, but couldn't find him. That evening when she arrived home she learned that his jacket and the blood had been located right where she had seen him.

This account, unfortunately, has no fitting climax. When Joyce, Ray, and Victor returned to Oklahoma, Wilson had still not been found. But Big Cove is there . . . a strange and wondrous place where the essence of the ancient world still pervades the lives of the inhabitants. Even in Cherokee the mention of Big Cove causes brows to raise, and when a visitor wishes to go to Big Cove, there will be frowns. "Big Cove people are the mean ones . . . . There's a lot of drinking and fighting out there . . . .

Some will even shoot at you if you go near their houses."

Joyce learned there was some truth in this. Men were often beaten up and cut up. Young people were finding ways to get drugs. A resident named Don West was head of a boys' club whose aim it was to get boys away from the bad environment, and in general to do something about the unfortunate situation.

One instance given was of a certain man's son-in-law, who came drunk one night to the door, and no sooner had the man opened the door to talk to him than the son-in-law, without a word, slit him from chin to navel, and laid him wide open. The man was taken by ambulance to the hospital and lived, and Joyce met him.

At the same time, Joyce found that Big Cove people were the friendliest, nicest, and most hospitable people she had ever met. The talking and visiting were wonderful, and the house would fill with visitors. The homemade food was superb, the best she'd ever eaten.

Very few Cherokees live in the town of Cherokee, their homes being in the communities already listed that are spread out over a large area. Snowbird, for example, is about eighty miles from Cherokee. A community consists of a church and a few houses. Big Cove children ride a bus to school in Cherokee. The majority of the community churches are Baptist. Preaching is of the "hell-fire and brimstone" variety, and is very popular with the people. Nearly every family is represented at every service, even though an unrepentant drinker might be called up in front and made an example of. Preaching is still done in the Cherokee language, and the Eastern Cherokee dialect is slightly different from that used in Oklahoma. Bu, Joyce says one can still communicate without difficulty. She thinks that the Eastern Cherokees have more "traditionals" who speak both the English and Cherokee languages than is the case in Oklahoma, and says that as the Big Cove people talk they switch regularly back and forth from English to Cherokee. She and I agree that Cherokees look about the same in both places.

Outside of Big Cove, intermarriage with non-

Indians is common, and yet the Eastern Cherokees are more "clannish" than the Cherokees in Oklahoma. In Big Cove, for example, an extended family owns an entire hillside, and couples who marry are given their own land within this area. There are family dinners and get-togethers, and they help one another whenever help is needed. They even have, in continuation of the old ways, a "Freelabor Community" organization. All men sign up for this, and each year cut wood and do other tasks such as winterizing houses for the elderly single women, the older couples, and widows. The special task for able women is to care for the sick and disabled. There is no charge for this. "We just see that people are taken care of."

Some people in Big Cove have television, but only for one or two hours a day, and the reception is poor. Lots of men work in the forestry department, while others work for the tribe. Some men are supported by working wives. Those who work year-round have comfortable homes, but the majority work only during the summer tourist season. In the winter, some produce crafts that will be sold during the summer. When it is asked, "What is traditional about the residents of Big Cove today, since they don't even have stomp dances?" the answer is given that Big Cove is where the full bloods still live, and is the home of the least acculturated Cherokees.

But Big Cove has its own souvenir factory now, where junk Indian items are made, and there is a quilting cooperative. Do the people feel bad about the Cherokees who dress up in Plains Indian costumes to be photographed by gullible tourists? By no means. "Those people make from $300 to $500 a day! In just four months they make enough to live on for the rest of the year!"

Hearing this, I was reminded again that as you enter Cherokee you see for two-and-one-half miles nothing but row after row of motels, shooting galleries, carnival attractions, ice-cream and cotton-candy vendors, and five of every six buildings is a gift shop. Prices are so high the Cherokees can't even afford to purchase groceries there. They shop in their home communities. Most of the businesses are owned by whites who live out of state. The tribe is

supposed to get 10 percent of the profits, and may, but people say that they seldom or never look at the books for fear of offending the owners.

Joyce feels there is by far more traditional life in Oklahoma, for it is practised there with hog fries, ceremonial dances at grounds, and all-night sings at churches such as the Old Green Corn Church, yet she relates many more things regarding the Big Cove people that are of considerable interest.

There is a creek in front of Karen and Don West's house where a multitude of frog eggs can be found. The frogs are called "turkey frogs," because their croaking sounds like turkeys gobbling. In a bedroom was a plastic bowl filled with tadpoles that were being kept as pets. Each day, dirt was put in the bowl to feed them, and the family went often to observe their "pets."

Many of the dogs of Big Cove are called "bear dogs," and they are trained to hunt bears. All of these are ferocious, and when they are not hunting they are chained up. Although in the back areas of Oklahoma dogs are everywhere in the Cherokee communities and every home boasts from eight to twelve, the typical Big Cove home has only one or two, and some homes have no dogs at all. At one house Karen took Joyce and Ray to visit, there was on the floor a large cast-iron skillet full of corn bread and meat. Karen explained that this was what the owner cooked each day for her two bear dogs. She purchased the canned meat — a kind none of the Cherokees would eat — in town, cut it up, and mixed it with cornbread.

Some men wore overalls, but most wore khaki pants and brown or gray work shirts. Their shoes were a high, brown, lace-up type similar to army issue. The younger men went bareheaded, but the older men wore hats or caps. Older women wore old-style long dresses that reached almost to the ankle. Nearly every woman wore a scarf around her head. Younger Cherokees wore jeans and T-shirts.

Big Cove had a recently opened corn mill where the Cherokees took their corn to have it ground into meal or crack corn.

Since the Cherokees of Oklahoma still have medicine grounds and dances, Joyce was asked by the people of Big Cove to give a talk about this. After the talk, a women asked her to stay the night at her home. Joyce couldn't, but returned the next morning. She said, "People came in and stayed all day and night talking, and they slept on the floor and on the divan and were there for breakfast the next morning. But I got to meet so many people this way, and the conversation went from A to Z and we covered everything."

Karen had told Joyce that there was a family of Little People living behind her house, and pointed out to her the rocky area where they stayed. It was a natural ravine, and ran from the top of the mountain down to the rear of their house. There were no trees or vegetation in the ravine, which itself was cone-shaped, with the larger end near the house. Karen said that her husband's family had had a corn patch up on the mountain and had talked about building their house up there where they would have a better view and breeze, but decided against it. The way she said this made Joyce feel the decision also had something to do with its being the Little People's ground, and emphasizing this probability was Karen's comment that the hillside had been in her husband's family for generations, and while the old people had planted corn there, the rocky ravine had never been disturbed because the Little People lived there. Old family members even told Karen they had seen a Little People wedding, in which the man wore a top hat and the woman wore a long dress. Young children were warned early in life to be careful when they played around the ravine, for Little People were known to carry off young children. (More on this subject is in Chapter Eleven). One night while Joyce and Ray were visiting with Karen and her family, Joyce heard, about 3:00 a.m., the loud voices of several men talking outside and behind the house. She was in the front of the house, and insists that if she had moved to the back the volume would have been so loud she could have taped what was being said. "But the Big Cove people just went on talking, and assured me it was the Little People and not to worry."

Among pictures Joyce wished she had taken was one of an old log house where a woman lived. It had no plumbing, running water, or electricity, and appeared to be a very small one-room cabin. About eight feet from it was a new frame house "with all of the conveniences" that the government had built for the woman, and her son was making payments on it. But the woman preferred her cabin and refused to live in the new house.

Another photograph of an unkept, two-room house was also passed up because her hosts, who are understandably proud of Big Cove, felt it did not represent the best there. But on the porch of this house was a tiny old Cherokee woman wearing a long dress and apron and a scarf, who looked like she must be in her nineties. The house was falling apart, and there were no screens or doors. A youth in his twenties stood in the doorway, but Joyce was told there were twenty people living in the house. The old woman was using a galvanized dishpan to feed a big white hog. There was no fence on the property, and the animal ran wild. Off to one side was a nearly collapsing outhouse.

The people of Big Cove are troubled by wild boars. Residents claimed that some even mated with domestic hogs. Karen asserted that the woods were full of the boars, and that they frequently got into the gardens and tore them up. Garden pests included bugs that ate up tomatoes as fast as the residents could plant and raise them. They couldn't raise lettuce, radishes, or carrots for the same reason. So they picked a wild lettuce that grew there.

Joyce was taken to another house that had been fixed up by the government. A new electric stove sat in the kitchen, but it was piled over with pans, cans, and potted herbs. The woman preferred her ancient wood stove.

Bears, rattlesnakes, and watermoccasins are very bad in Big Cove. Snakebites are an everyday occurrence, but the people "don't think anything about it." The night before Joyce and Ray stayed at a certain house in Big Cove, a large black bear had jumped onto the roof of the house next door.

Since the government is building homes for the Eastern Cherokees, many of the old cabins are being torn down. But the new houses are in many instances not being taken care of. Picture windows have been broken out, and have only sheet- plastic coverings. Yards are often piled with trash. Few of the households have clotheslines. The custom is to string a line across the front porch. It was explained that the women wash by hand, and with the line on the porch they needn't carry the clothes far to hang them up. There were no doors in the interiors of the houses, and quilts were tacked up to close openings. There were no rugs or curtains. Exterior doors were not locked, because there were no locks. On the inside of the front and rear doors was a bar consisting of a piece of wood with a bent nail in its center to keep the doors closed. "But the door wouldn't stop a bear or a snake if it wanted to come in, for though it was made of planks, there were one-and-one-half-inch cracks between the planks," Joyce said.

Joyce was told that the old houses were very cold in the winter, and she could see why. In the corners of some houses the chinking was falling out from between the logs and you could see daylight between them. She worried because she "could just see a rattlesnake coming through the cracks and getting into her bed."

Joyce and Ray and Karen West drove from Big Cove to Snowbird, a distance of about thirty miles, because Joyce had been told by full bloods at a symposium that Snowbird was where the more traditional Cherokees lived. But when they arrived, they didn't see any residents. They hid, as people usually do at Big Cove. What houses the visitors did see were painted white, or were recently built government houses.

Present-day Little People working the cornfields of the Cherokees at night.

Joyce talked with the medicine doctor at Big Cove, Almaneeta Sequoyah, for some time. She suspected that his medicine was not as strong as it once was, and Karen thought that might be due to the fact that more whites than Cherokees used his services. But Karen also told her several stories about surprising cures he had worked in the past year, and Joyce concluded in the end that he must be a "good doctor." It appeared that he had learned a great deal from the white man regarding payment, and knew that white patients could pay more.

They went to see another medicine doctor, but he was away from home, and Karen thought he might, as was usual, be off somewhere socializing with cronies.

There is a medicine woman who in her earlier years had been very good at her work, but was now eighty-five years old, nearly blind, and could not go out and get her own herbs any more. So for awhile she had had this seventy-eight-year-old man who "went out and got the herbs for her doctoring." He also picked herbs for Almaneeta. But this old man was dead now. After looking for him for a long time, they had found his body up in the hills, and it was so decomposed they couldn't tell what had killed him.

Joyce was also told about two men who had frozen to death up in the mountains. The cove people were "constantly" losing people who had been out hunting or walking. "They do a lot of walking, and they walk fast." So they think nothing of going across the mountains to see a friend in a remote cabin. On a visit to one family who had a still, she was told how the Cherokees were always losing people in the mountains, and that signs asking people to help find someone were posted regularly.

There are no longer any dance grounds on the Eastern Cherokee Reservation, and except for social purposes and at the Oconaluftee Village, no dances are done. That aspect of life has ended. We heard there was an old man who still remembered about fifty of the songs, and that the last dances they had held on the reservation were social dances in the yards of people's houses. "There was no fire, finally no one knew or wanted to learn the songs, and it just died out."

Joyce learned there is, besides Allen Long, a Big Cove man who still made masks, but that he hides them under a table whenever anyone comes to visit. There is also a George Littlejohn, who makes bows and arrows that are identical to those described by Adair.

More than a little discouraged by the commercialism of the Cherokee, North Carolina, community, and saddened by the passing of a lifeway that she cherishes, Joyce was delighted to meet a part-Cherokee doctor named Garrett, who has a number of medical degrees, and who worked at the Cherokee hospital — a building in a lush setting with its interior walls hung with Cherokee artifacts and art. Dr. Garrett wore both the Cherokee and the white man's hats, and was an apprentice medicine man to Almaneeta. He was doing what he could to collect the old songs, and encouraged medicine men to come into the hospital to help the staff treat patients. Where at one time the old people considered the hospital to be a place where they came only to die, they now came with revitalized hope, and the senior-citizen survival rate had risen to 70 percent. The old people were so pleased they were even bringing herbs to the doctor. Joyce had been to the reservation three times before she met the doctor, but learned from him now about things she had never seen or never knew existed. He wore a divining crystal and had a small, personal medicine bundle. He told her that to have a proper medicine bundle, you must include in it something that goes back to your beginnings, and sent her to see where he obtained his — the locations of the two nearest ancient townships and grounds. She found there old fishing weights, pottery shards, and arrowheads. One of these was the village of Kituwah. Its site is a cornfield now; the other site is plowed ground. Their whereabouts are not to be revealed.

Joyce was amazed at what Dr. Garrett knew and could predict, especially at what he told her about herself. He had a second crystal that had a small spur on it, and gave it to her saying, "This is you," and that the spur represented the new beginning that was taking place in her life as a rejuvenated Cherokee.

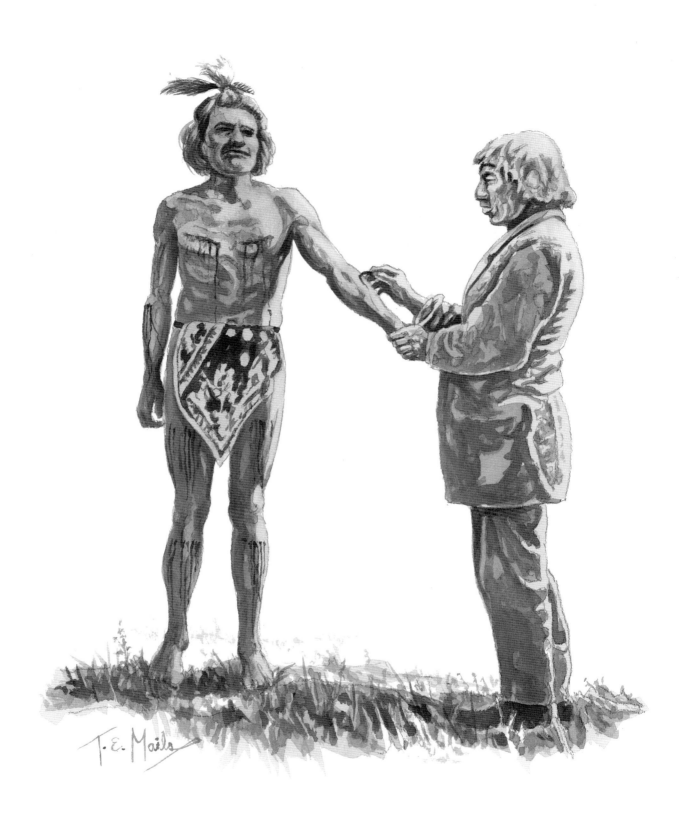

Ritual scratching of ball player. Redrawn from photograph by James Mooney in 1888. Negative no. 1042, Smithsonian Institution, National Anthropological Archives.

Ball players. Redrawn from photograph by James Mooney. Negative no. 477, 748-f., Smithsonian Institution, National Anthropological Archives.

Further encouragement was obtained at a Conference on Cherokee and Iroquois Studies held at Cherokee in April of 1978. Papers presented by several white scholars included "Classifiers and Noun Incorporation, Morphosyntactic Characteristics of Cherokee Classificatory Verbs and Onondaga Noun Incorporation," by Hanni Woodbury of Fordham University, and "The Natural Acquisition of Morphology, the Teaching of Iroquoian Languages," by Marianne Mithun and Mary MacDonald, of the Anthropology Department, State University of New York, Albany and Ahkwesahsne, New York.

Among those Joyce met and visited with at the conference were Floyd Lounsbury, who is recognized as the Mooney of today, and the most knowledgeable authority on Cherokee and Iroquois language and culture; Jack Campisi, the Oneida historian; Pauline Bennett, granddaughter of Chief Sampson Owl, who works in the library of the museum; A.W. Sequoyah, who was in need of certain herbs for medicine purposes; Jacqueline Fiorato, who read a paper and is from the University of Paris, France; Carl Vyspirman of the University of Georgia History Department, who gave an impressive paper on the removal; Robert Toineita, a member of the Eastern Cherokee council, with whom Joyce talked for a long time about their government and problems; James "Bo" Parris, who is the postmaster and a Baptist minister, who knew "where all of the people lived way back in the hills," and volunteered to take her there to find anyone she wanted to see; Dorothy Robbins, who is doing research on Cherokee herbs and legends; Nancy Cohseen, a fascinating full-blooded woman who has lived all her life among the full bloods around Cherokee and knows all of the old beliefs and traditions; William Snell, from Tennessee, who read a paper on Candy's Creek Mission; William C. Sturtevant, from the Smithsonian in Washington, D.C.; and two men who were doing research in the museum archives — Jim Lewis and Bill Anderson of the Department of History of Western Carolina University, North Carolina.

It was also here that she met the Karen and Don West referred to previously.

A Beloved Woman

In addition, Joyce met a most fascinating woman named Maggie Wachacha. Since the duties that accompanied the Beloved Woman, or War Woman, had disappeared with the end of Cherokee-white hostilities, those titles had not been passed on to anyone else until about 1938 when they were officially bestowed upon Maggie. After that time she sat on the council of the Eastern Band, but did not hold an elected office. She seldom spoke at council meetings, but when she did her words were respected and listened to. Her official title in the council was "Indian clerk." She wrote the minutes of each council meeting in the Cherokee syllabary, and Joyce was told that her records were frequently referred to, and were considered by some to be more reliable than the minutes taken in English by other clerks. The high esteem in which she is held by the Eastern Cherokees is evidenced by the fact that she is the only female to have a tribal building named for her. The Maggie Wachacha Building serves as the center for all tribal communications. She was born in 1895 in Little Snowbird Township, to Will and Caroline Cornstalk Axe. Maggie is of the *Ani go ta ga wi* Clan, and passed the clan membership to her only daughter, Winnie. Maggie married Jarrett Wachacha of the Deer Clan, *Ani kawi,* in 1935. She was attending council sessions long before she became tribal clerk because Jarrett was an elected member from Snowbird Township. The "Indian clerk" title passed to her when Will West Long resigned as clerk about fifty years ago. During the early days when the council met, Maggie and Jarrett would walk in two days the sixty miles from their home in the mountains of Santeelah to Cherokee. They would start out at 3:00 a.m. and walk until they reached a friend's home, where they would spend the night. Early the next morning they would walk on to Cherokee, where the council meetings were held. Later on, when they had the money they would catch a train, leaving Andrews, North Carolina, at midnight and arriving in time for the council meeting the next day. After Winnie was born, Maggie made the trip with the child in a blanket sling on her back, either walking or on the train. During the council meet-

Girl and woman with child in carrying blanket. Redrawn from photographs in the Museum of the Cherokee Indian.

ings, Winnie was laid on her back underneath the bench Maggie sat on, and behaved well.

Maggie assumed many roles for the tribe, the community, and her church. She taught the Cherokee Indian class for Zion Hill Baptist Church for many years. She also kept the minutes for the church meetings for many years, and was chosen as the first Cherokee recording secretary for the Little Snowbird community. She had very little formal education, attending school only three months each year for three years, and even then as seasonal work permitted. And yet Maggie Wachacha taught herself to read and write the English language, and carved for herself a remarkable career.

So, although at the Eastern Cherokee Reservation the ancient lifeway is to most intents and purposes gone, it is by no means forgotten by everyone, and still cherished by some. Among white and Indian scholars, and both in the town of Cherokee and back in the coves, there are individuals in whose blood run the fond remembrance and heritage of a noble and resilient people whose ways and talents rank with those of the finest civilizations the world has known. Outsiders who visit Cherokee should be aware of this and seek to learn about and feel it at the coves, the museum, the village and the pageant, not being blinded by the dazzle of the tipi-shaped shops and trading posts with their wooden tomahawks, tin-can drums, and plaster-of-paris plaques, or by the untrammeled commercial development that year by year replaces more and more of the lush ancestral land.

NOTES

1. Fitzgerald, *The Cherokees,* p. 41.
2. Freel, *Our Heritage, The People of Cherokee County, North Carolina, 1540-1955,* pp. 46-53.
3. Mooney, *Myths of the Cherokee,* p. 333.
4. Ibid., p. 44.
5. Ibid., pp. 48-49.
6. Ibid., p. 49.
7. Oklahoma Historical Society.
8. Gilbert, "The Eastern Cherokees," pp. 256-257.
9. Ibid., p. 370.
10. Ibid., p. 256.
11. Ibid., pp. 370-371.
12. Ibid., p. 369.
13. Ibid.
14. Ibid.
15. Ibid., pp. 369-370.
16. Speck and Broom, *Cherokee Dance and Drama,* pp. 21-22.
17. Ibid., p 21.
18. Gilbert, p. 257.
19. Speck and Broom, pp. 21-22.
20. Gilbert, pp. 257-258.
21. Ibid., pp 259-260.
22. Ibid., p. 264.
23. Ibid., pp. 263-264.
24. Ibid., p. 264.
25. Ibid., pp. 261-262.
26. Speck and Broom, p. 3.
27. Mooney, pp. 281-283.
28. Ibid., p. 496.
29. Gilbert, p. 263.
30. Ibid., p. 266.
31. Witthoft, "The Cherokee Green Corn Medicine and the Green Corn Festival," pp. 213-219.
32. Speck and Broom, p. viii.
33. Museum of the Cherokee Indian, Cherokee, North Carolina.
34. Gilbert, p. 268.
35. Ibid.
36. Ibid., pp. 268-269.
37. Ibid., p. 270.

CHAPTER TEN

The Western Cherokees

For weeks after Tsali made his heroic gesture, the 1,000 or so refugee Cherokees in North Carolina cowered in terror in the caves, for considering what had already happened, they could not be certain that General Winfield Scott would keep his word. It was a terrible time for them, yet the conditions for the 16,000 Cherokees who had been rounded up were far worse. Most authorities agree that 2,500 of the captives either died during the roundup, or from malnutrition, exposure, and brutal treatment during their few months of imprisonment. Of the 13,500 who did survive to begin the woeful march to Indian Territory, we learn that 1,500 more, an average of two per mile traveled, died along the way and were hastily buried in lonely and poorly marked graves.

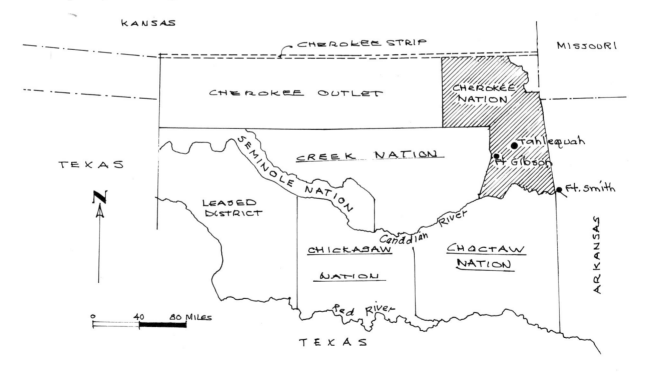

LOCATION OF THE FIVE CIVILIZED TRIBES IN INDIAN TERRITORY IN 1860

Land, homes, and other possessions having been rudely stripped from them, the Cherokees were herded along like cattle, most always in wretched weather, and never with adequate transportation or provisions. What agonizing thoughts must have clouded their minds — the emptiness of possessing nothing and not knowing what lay ahead, the errors they had made over the decades and their complicity in change that had led to this, the fact that the Boudinots and the Ridges had betrayed a sacred trust, the guilt and shame that came from recognizing how little whites must think of them to treat them so meanly, the wondering why the Above Being would abandon them to such a crushing fate. Although treatment by the soldiers was not so inhumane as that received by the American soldiers during the infamous death march at Bataan of World War II, it was inhumane enough to result in a death toll that was comparable in the percentage of lives lost. To cap all of this off, as the survivors straggled into the compound at Fort Gibson, Indian Territory, they were not given promised farm equipment, and the foodstuffs they received were unfit for human consumption. Despite this, the survivors were immediately sent into their new land. Only a few of the resident Cherokees who had arrived in Indian Territory from 1808 to 1828, and no members at all of the Ridge Party, were on hand to meet them or to offer help — a fact that in itself told the new arrivals they were not the only ones who harbored animosities. As an omen, it did not bode well for the future.

These already settled Old Settler and Ridge parties totaled only 6,000, so the newcomers outnumbered them two to one, and in any accommodation would outvote them. It was obvious that future control of the nation would soon become a serious issue. Since these established residents had arrived in Indian Territory in good financial circumstances and with adequate possessions, they had long ago settled into a comfortable lifeway akin to that of the neighboring whites, and they resented the idea of losing control. Moreover, they were established in the choice locations such as the rich Verdigris River valley and were not about to relinquish what they had to the newcomers, although some of the Old

Settlers were cordial enough to tell newly arrived relatives that they were free to go wherever else they wanted and settle down.

It should be mentioned here that while much of Oklahoma's terrain is flat, has little foliage, and is uninspiring, the northeastern portion given to the Cherokees is in most of its parts exceptionally beautiful, with a succession of lovely wooded hills and valleys rich with trees, lakes, rivers, and creeks that in the early days were a haven for deer, coyote, wolves, prairie chickens, quail, and other wildlife. In this wise at least, the exchange of lands was not an unfair one. Mixed bloods who came early to the territory often praise it in their writings. The initial problem for the removed Cherokees was that their eyes were too misted over with sorrow to at first see and appreciate the new land.

From the beginning then, the newcomers had to shift for themselves, with the mixed bloods heading for sites along the Illinois River that offered the best business opportunities and were near the Old Settlers at Park Hill and Takatoka and the full bloods heading for the wooded backcountry where they had always felt the most comfortable and secure. Except for the political arena, two years of mourning and of moping over dislocation would follow, until finally a few individuals, including John Ross, decided it was time to put mourning aside, get on with life, and began to goad the others into action. After that, reestablishment was remarkably swift. More substantial houses were erected, other properties were refurbished, and the newcomer Cherokees went back to work.

In another sidelight worth noting, during the spring of 1840, a Cherokee named Elezier Butler returned to Georgia to recover what he could of his possessions, fully expecting the entire country to be filled with white settlers. To his astonishment he found that the settlers had moved on toward the west, and that most of Cherokee country was empty and as quiet as a tomb. He and the Cherokees he reported this to were greatly perplexed. Why, they wondered, had the whites gone to such lengths to wrest from the Cherokees something so cherished if they didn't want it? No answer was forthcoming.

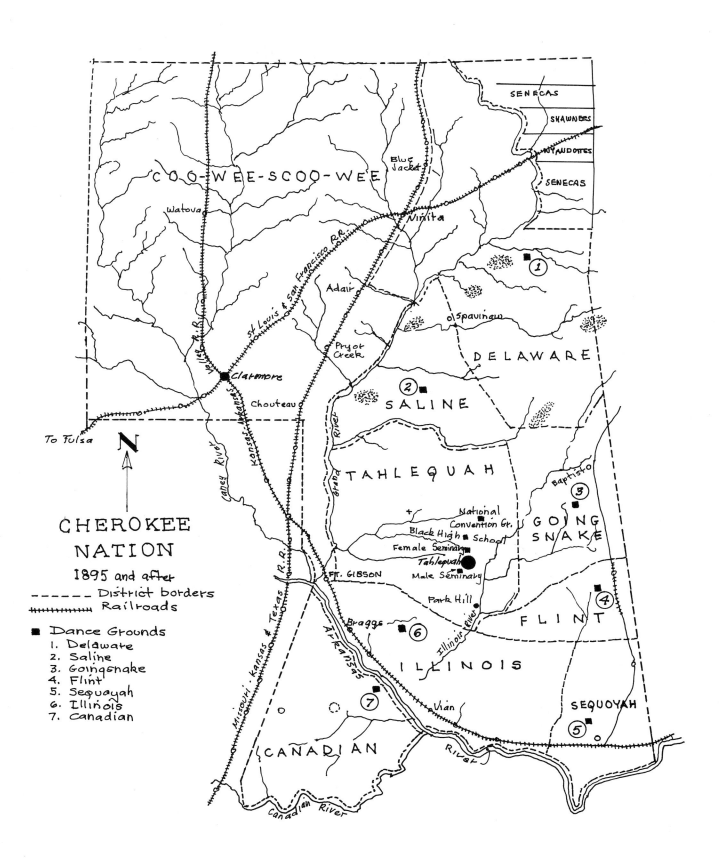

SENECAS

SHAWNEES

WYANDOTTES

SENECAS

COO-WEE-SCOO-WEE

Watova

Blue Jacket?

Ninita

Adair

① Spavinau

DELAWARE

St Louis & San Francisco R.R.

Neosho R.R.

Pryor Creek

Claremore

Chouteau

② SALINE

To Tulsa

N

Caney River

Kansas-Arkansas

Grand River

TAHLEQUAH

Baptisto

③

GOING SNAKE

National Convention Gr.

+

CHEROKEE NATION

1895 and after

------ District borders

+++++ Railroads

■ Dance Grounds
1. Delaware
2. Saline
3. Goingsnake
4. Flint
5. Sequayah
6. Illinois
7. Canadian

Black High School

Female Seminary

Tahlequah

Male Seminary

Park Hill

④

FLINT

Missouri-Kansas & Texas R.R.

FT. GIBSON

Braggs

⑥

Illinois River

ILLINOIS

Arkansas

⑦

Vian

SEQUOYAH

⑤

CANADIAN

River

Canadian River

Getting Established in Indian Territory

Wise statesman that he was, John Ross knew that two interrelated projects were of paramount importance. The first was to give his people something to take their minds off of the Trail of Tears and to redirect them toward the future, and the second was to forge a union of the old and new settlers that would do this. Ross believed he could accomplish the latter by reminding the Cherokees that a lack of unity had cost the nation dearly in 1835 and 1838, and stressing that failure to unite now would unquestionably lead to civil strife — even to internal warfare — and ultimately to an even greater disaster. Stabilization of the nation was an imperative!

Within a month after the last contingent of the removed Cherokees had arrived in Indian Territory, negotiations with the Old Settlers were begun. The initial hope was to find common ground on which the two governments could merge, but the attempt did not go well. The bitterness on both sides was too deep to allow more than a token beginning.[1] On the first Monday in June 1839 at a convention held near Fort Gibson, a union of sorts was effected when the newcomers, who were known as the Ross Party, persuaded some of the Old Settlers to come over to their side. But others did not come, and when the Ross Party proposed that a new constitution should be submitted to the vote of the entire nation, the Old Settler chiefs refused on the ground that their own government was entitled to remain in control until the regular October session of their council, when the Ross Party would be free to vote and any changes in the laws could be legally made. When the members of the Ridge Party sided with the Old Settler chiefs, the Ridges were bitterly denounced for having in the first place signed the treaty of New Echota.

Additional background is needed to understand what happened next. In about 1828, the Cherokee Nation had enacted a law that imposed the death penalty upon any person or persons who signed away or exchanged Cherokee lands without the consent of the national authorities and the people. Major Ridge himself was the principal author of this law, and was among those who had killed Chief Doublehead for

having signed the Treaty of 1805. With this in mind, Ridge, when he himself signed the removal treaty in 1835, had said with a sigh, "I am signing my own death warrant." Motivated by anger and believing themselves to be justified by these facts, unknowns from the Ross Party went secretly on June 22, 1839, to Major Ridge, John Ridge, and Elias Boudinot, and brutally murdered them. Stand Watie was also marked out for death, but he was forewarned and escaped. The killings were acts as devastating as the Trail of Tears itself, for they revealed a house more viciously divided than ever, a nation that, not being able to do anything about the whites who had so grievously cheated them, now turned fully upon itself. The leaders of the Ross Party vigorously denied they had instigated the shameful crimes, but the denials did not convince the Old Settlers and the Ridge followers. A feud began that presaged in its horrors the Civil War that would soon rock the entire American nation. For the next six years small-scale battles raged, with killings and house burnings being common. More than thirty assassinations were recorded.

Nevertheless, in the midst of the beginnings of the violence, on July 12, 1839, the convention did adopt a formal Act of Union, in which the Eastern and the Western Cherokees were declared one body politic under the title of the Cherokee Nation. At Tahlequah in October 1839 a constitution was drafted and adopted. John Ross was elected principal chief, and a convention of Old Settlers meeting at Fort Gibson in 1840 approved the constitution. Joining them in this were two bands of Arkansas Cherokees who had migrated to Texas in 1819 and 1831, then had been driven out of Texas and come to live with the Old Settlers. Therefore, on paper at least, the Cherokees in Indian Territory were a united people living under a constitution and laws of their own making.

Assisting vicariously in what ultimately became a workable settlement was an intertribal council attended by representatives of local nations, eastern nations, and the Plains nations that had been crowded into Indian Territory. This council lasted four weeks, and the Cherokees, with considerable practice at making peace, were able to serve as arbiters for the assembled nations. Recognizing this outstanding contribution, in 1846 the United States negotiated a new treaty with the Cherokee Nation. It provided for a patent to be issued by the United States to secure all lands in the nation for the common use and benefit of all the Cherokees, a general amnesty for all past offenses in the nation, the adjudication of all Cherokee claims, and the adjustment of other matters that had long awaited settlement. This satisfied the concerns of both the Old Settlers and the Ross Party, and at last there was peace.

The Cherokees continued to act as intermediaries between tribes and between the government and tribes, finally becoming known as "the Peacemakers of the Plains." Cherokee guides for white parties passing through hostile Indian regions wore distinctive hunting coats trimmed with red yarn fringes, and their presence was usually a guarantee of safe conduct and whatever assistance might be needed.

The more enterprising mixed bloods of the tribe increased their control over national affairs, although they had to accomplish what they did on their own, for the five million dollars promised in the Treaty of 1835 proved to be worthless. The government simply appropriated it in exchange for relocation costs and the land the nation had received in Indian Territory. During this period, life remained quite different from what it had been before the removal. No town organizations had been set up by the Old Settlers, no town council houses had been built, and no ceremonial dances were being held. Ball play was occasional, and all-night social dances were rare. The Ross Party mixed bloods cared little about these things anyway and soon joined with the more progressive of the Old Settlers who already operated farms, stores, and even small plantations.

The demoralized full bloods looked to John Ross for leadership but otherwise retreated like turtles back into their shells. Most of them were Baptists by now, and Baptist church buildings became the focal point of full-blooded communities. Stomp dances were resumed, and going to church

services was counterbalanced by the continuation of Cherokee medicine practices. The removal had standardized full-blooded culture.[2]

Since there were no town council houses, no ceremonials, and families were scattered throughout the nation, culture and authority took upon itself a revised and uniform characteristic. The kin units were broken up, sounding the near-death knell of the lineage and clan rule (I say "near" because, as we will see, it was not final.) The husband became the family head and economic provider. By 1860, emphasis lay heavily on the paternal side. By 1890, kinship organization had taken on a generational pattern, and English family names had become the rule.

The year 1841 saw the establishment of a public school system with a national superintendent. It was financed by appropriations of the national council from Cherokee educational funds provided for in treaties negotiated with the United States. Dwight Mission had been moved from Arkansas to Indian Territory in 1829, and some other mission schools functioned, but their establishment was now limited by law. By 1843, there were eighteen public schools in operation, and in 1851 two seminaries for higher learning were opened to Cherokee students — a National Female Seminary located three miles southeast of Tahlequah and a National Male Seminary one-and-one-half miles southwest of the town.

The *Cherokee Advocate* newspaper published its first edition in September 1844, and it was the first newspaper in the territory to have its columns printed in English and a native language. The Park Hill Mission Press, located at Park Hill and run by the Reverend Samuel A. Worcester, printed its materials in Cherokee as well as in the languages of many other tribes. The mission press at Baptist Mission published part of *The Cherokee Messenger* in Cherokee and was the first periodical in the territory, its first issue being published in August 1844. In 1857, Ross reported to his council that the evidence of progress by the Cherokee people was of the most cheerful kind and contrasted favorably with their condition of fifty years before. There were well-cultivated farms yielding abundant crops of grain, well-filled public schools, large and orderly assemblies, and quiet neighborhoods, which in all the districts showed marked improvement and furnished a sure indication of the "susceptibility of all classes among the Cherokee people for thorough civilization." Before Worcester's death in 1859, his presses had printed more than thirteen million newspapers, textbooks, almanacs, and tracts from the Bible in the Cherokee, Choctaw, and Creek languages.

As the outbreak of the Civil War drew near, mixed bloods who had either brought black slaves with them or again become slaveholders began to form secessionist organizations, and in 1859 the full bloods in reaction formed the Keetoowah Society. This name was derived from *Kituwha,* the ancient town of the old nation that is said to have consisted of the most conservative element of the tribe. Its purposes included the promotion of Cherokee nationalistic aims and the counteracting of the influence of the Blue Lodge and other secret seces-

sionist organizations among the wealthier slaveholding classes, chiefly made up of mixed bloods and whites. The Keetoowahs claimed loyalty to the Union, favored the abolition of black slavery, and said they had combined in a secret organization for self-protection. They were also known as "Pins," since they wore two crossed straight pins as a means of identifying one another. During the Civil War, the Pins rendered service to the Union in a number of bloody military encounters, while most of the slaveholding Cherokees, who made up the wealthy and better educated class, allied themselves with the Confederacy. Once again, the nation was divided.

A further reason given for the formation of the Keetoowah Society was the revival of the old religion, and while church alliances were continued by its members, greater emphasis was placed upon the establishment and use of dance, or "medicine," grounds.

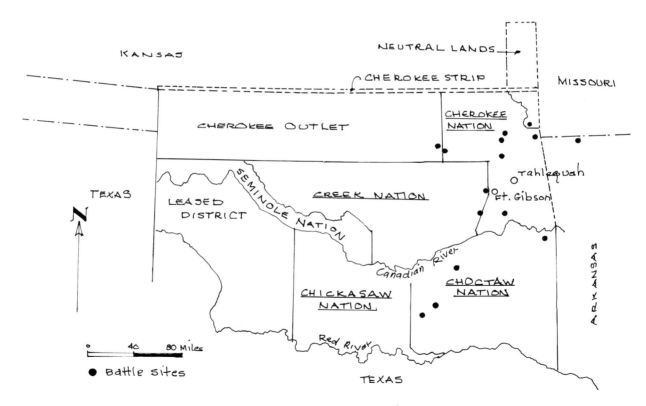

LOCATION OF CIVIL WAR BATTLE SITES IN AND NEAR THE CHEROKEE NATION

Top, the typical graduate of the Cherokee Female Seminary in 1903. *Bottom*, the Cherokee Male Seminary.

When the Civil War erupted in 1861, John Ross, with the backing of the Keetoowahs, declared for strict neutrality. But under constant pressure from the Confederacy, the Cherokee Nation signed an agreement allying itself with the South. It raised two regiments, one under the leadership of Stand Watie that consisted of mixed bloods and another of mostly full bloods under a Colonel John Drew. The full bloods, however, still angry with the southern states which had cooperated in their removal, soon deserted to the Union side and together with loyal full-blooded Creeks fled to Kansas. Stand Watie had little formal military training, yet became the only Indian officer who attained the rank of brigadier general in the Confederate Army and was the last Confederate general to surrender to Union forces.

By war's end, much of the Cherokee Nation's property had been devastated — homes burned, orchards razed, stock stolen, and public buildings knocked down. Some authorities say there was not a house left standing in the Cherokee Nation. But the resilient people built once more, and before long, life had returned to where it had left off in 1861. In 1866, a treaty was signed in Washington, D.C., that provided for the resumption of Cherokee government, and a new era of progress got under way. After more than forty years of devoted and outstanding service as principal chief, John Ross died on August 1, 1866. A realignment of political factions was effected, and the full bloods and other elements were brought together in a new organization known as the Downing Party, while Chief William P. Ross led the National Party. Lewis Downing was chosen principal chief in 1867, and at last the old feuds and factions gave way to common concerns, dominated at this time by relations with the federal government, which was increasing pressure to open Indian Territory to white settlement. In particular, focus was on the rich grassland in the Cherokee Outlet. In response in 1879, the Cherokee national council passed a law providing for the collection from outside cattlemen of fees for grazing privileges in the outlet, an area already abused by thousands of cattle being driven overland from Texas to shipping points in Kansas. When collections proved difficult, the

Cherokees changed their minds, and in 1883 leased all grazing privileges in the outlet for five years at $100,000 a year to the Cherokee Strip Live Stock Association, an organization of cattlemen whose headquarters were in Caldwell, Kansas.

The year 1889 witnessed the first run for white settler homesteads at the opening of "Oklahoma Country" on April 22. Negotiations began for the purchase of the Cherokee Outlet by the United States. An agreement was finally reached, and Congress ratified it on March 3, 1893, paying the sum of $8,595,736.12 for 6,574,487 acres. The outlet was then, on September 16, 1893, opened to white settlement with the most spectacular run for claims in the history of the territory.

The encroachment of white settlers on Indian Territory lands was by no means a new thing. By 1870 the railroads were laying their knifelike tracks through the heart of the Cherokee Nation. The death of John Ross was a particular blow to the full bloods, for without his balancing leadership, they were no match for the entrenched and worldly-wise mixed bloods, who overrode the objections of the full bloods and inaugurated a permit system that allowed white cattlemen and farmers to use Cherokee land by paying a fee or by working as tenants for Cherokee landowners. In the end, the subdued full-blooded Cherokees themselves had adopted so many white cultural traits they could, on the surface at least, hardly be distinguished from frontier whites.

It was during this turbulent period that what are popularly known as "the last two Cherokee warriors" earned their titles, and in so doing excited even the most complacent of the Cherokees. Zeke Proctor, who later became a famous sheriff, accidentally killed Polly Chesterton, the Cherokee wife of a white man who had been adopted by the tribe. The Cherokee courts assumed jurisdiction over the matter, but Chesterton successfully appealed to the federal court at Fort Smith, Arkansas. While Proctor's trial was being held under federal auspices at the Whitmire schoolhouse near the present community of Christie, Oklahoma, a deputy marshal and a posse, along with members of the dead woman's family, arrived outside the schoolhouse to

Redbird Smith.

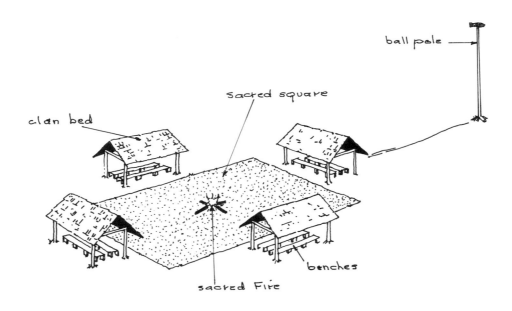

ball pole

sacred square

clan bed

benches

sacred Fire

Top: view of typical stomp ground. *Bottom,* the ground on Greenleaf Mountain, Oklahoma, where Watt Sam officiated as the medicine maker, redrawn from photograph in Bureau of American Ethnology Bulletin No. 98.

await the verdict, and if Proctor was adjudged guilty, to take him into custody. For some unknown reason, a gunfight broke out between this group and the supporters of Proctor, and the posse suffered the greatest damage. In all, nine men were killed outright, and two more were mortally wounded. Later, Proctor was tried again and declared not guilty, and in 1873 an amnesty treaty with the government was worked out.

Christie, a Cherokee who longed passionately for freedom for the Cherokee nation, was falsely accused of the murder of a deputy marshal, and after escaping, he carried on a four-year war with the government authorities, even recruiting a small army from Keetoowah members to help him. Finally, in 1892, a posse with a small cannon surrounded the small fort the Christie group had built, blew the fort apart, and killed Christie. His tombstone in the cemetery at Wauhillau, Oklahoma, reads, "He was at one time a member of the Executive Council of the C.N. He was a blacksmith and was a brave man."[3]

Lewis Downing was chairman of the Keetoowah Society during the Civil War period, and was also assistant principal chief. He handled these responsibilities well, and was elected to the position of principal chief in 1867 and 1871. He died in 1872 while still in office. William P. Ross was selected to fill the unexpired term. At this point, the Keetoowah Society divided into small groups run by local chiefs. In 1874, Budd Gritts reorganized the society, was elected its chairman, and the organization was reunited. A member named Dennis Wolf Bushyhead received Gritts' support and served as principal chief from 1879 to 1887. These were the last times the full bloods had anything resembling control of the nation, for as the Western Cherokees entered the 1890s, the mixed bloods regained their authority and established new national policies. Here we see distinct patterns of full-blood and mixed-blood life developing and encounter the important Redbird Smith movement, which centered itself in the dance aspect of the ancient religion that had for a half century been neglected — for so long a time, in fact, that outsiders believed it was gone forever and forgotten. To me, it is nothing less than astonishing

that while the full-blooded westerners put their ancient forms of religion aside in favor of political developments, the full-blooded easterners carried theirs on, and then as the easterners began to let their old religion drift away, the westerners experienced a rebirth of it! The Above Beings do indeed work in mysterious ways.

1880-1890

To illustrate how far removed the old religious practices were from full-blooded life in 1880, they are said to have believed that the last decade of the 1800s marked the end of true Cherokee culture for the western portion of the nation. As we will see, this forlorn opinion was not entirely true, but the changes that did occur in this brief ten-year period were momentous.

Contributing heavily to the progressive demise of the old culture were the laws being passed by Congress whose aim was to strip the Cherokee Nation of its independence and to provide for the illegal settlement of white migrants on Indian land. By century's end, 25,000 whites had joined the 75,000 Indians in Indian Territory. Intruders in the Cherokee portion were settling down in what became rough frontier towns that fronted the several railroads that ran through the nation. Criminal and property laws were seldom enforced, and in cases where they were observed in Indian vs white issues, the decisions always favored the whites.

The full bloods were more confused and apprehensive about these things than were the acculturated mixed bloods, and as was their tendency, responded by further isolating themselves. When the idea of land allotment was proposed by the federal government, the mixed bloods, many of whom were by now owners of beautiful homes with orchards, gardens, flowers, vines, fruit trees, and large cattle spreads, fought it only until they knew they couldn't win. Then they embraced the concept as if they had thought of it themselves. The full bloods found the idea contrary to the ancient belief in shared and cooperatively tended lands, and ignored it in the hope it would go away on its own.

The typical full-blooded community of the

year 1880 had as its center a log church building and was made up of two or three extended families whose log homes were spread out along a stream course. Most homes were a single room, but some were of the "dogtrot" variety with two rooms that had a roofed but open passageway separating them. There was no outhouse, but there was a separate smokehouse for storing and preparing meat, and later, canned foods in jars. Crops consisted of corn, cotton, and beans, and there were small gardens. The aim was to be self-sustaining. Fish and wild game, principally deer, provided perhaps half of their sustenance. Hunting was done with guns acquired from whites, with bow and arrow and, as in the old days, with blowguns. Food was prepared in the old ways with the log and stump pounders. Hogs and cattle were raised, as were milch cows, but not to such an extent as by the mixed bloods. Peach and apple orchards were cultivated, and the fruit was dried for winter use.

Full-blooded families lived in individual homesteads, but the larger tasks, such as planting, harvesting, plowing, house building, hog slaughtering and rail splitting for fences, were done communally. Leadership was provided by "Little Captains," who were the local officers of the Keetoowah Society.

Flour, sugar, coffee, tobacco, and clothing were purchased at country stores run by mixed bloods or intermarried Cherokees and whites, and at stores in the railroad towns and urban centers. Extended families made on foot or by wagon trips of a day or more to procure these supplies. Men cut their hair shorter and wore typical frontier-type shirts and trousers, along with western hats and brown, knee-high miner's boots fashioned by native cobblers. Older women wore full-length dresses and scarves, while younger women began to adopt the more fashionable white woman's clothing of the time.

After the "run" in the Cherokee Outlet, land payments bolstered the Cherokee economy, and individual improvements of properties took place. Within the family itself, emphasis shifted in mounting degrees to male control, although the mother still oversaw and shepherded the children. Clan relationships were being ignored by many, although not entirely dispensed with. The nation's legal system provided for civil marriages in the courthouses, but the full bloods preferred to have either a service by their local Cherokee preacher or a simple blanket marriage. Divorce was still accomplished by a "dividing of the blanket."

The prevailing religion among the full bloods was Baptist, but each Baptist community church was virtually autonomous. The parishioners built the log church buildings and maintained them, adding brush shade arbors for use in the hot summer months. Communal quilting bees, social dinners, and other activities took place there. Most communities had a native lay preacher who both farmed his own land and ministered to the congregation. Services were conducted in the native language, and there was a Cherokee-language Bible — some of whose passages were shaded to follow the older religious thought patterns that were still acceptable, while other passages were couched in obscure statements to make it easier for the minister to skirt ancient concepts that did not fit in with "proper" Christian thought. Standard Baptist hymns were translated into Cherokee, and the people composed many of their own. The music was altered to fit the native melodic pattern, and the change gave it a medieval European flavor. The hymns were joyful and robust and proved to be a great attraction for the Cherokees.

It is doubtful that the Cherokees understood the doctrinal teachings in the same way as the white Baptists did, or that they embraced the Baptist moral code. But my own research indicates that the conversions were in many instances so thorough that the converted individuals came to have nothing but disdain for the ancient religion.

Political and religious life were intertwined. Meetings and dinners were held on the church grounds during the day, and political meetings were held inside the church building at night. In the fall, about the same time the old Green Corn Ceremony had once been held, there was a four-day church convention with singing, preaching, and friends being reunited. The missionaries were passionately against stomp dancing, even for purely social purposes, and condemned it in their sermons, so as might be expected, the practice underwent a gradual decline. Nevertheless, a small segment of conservatives who did not participate in the Baptist religion rebelled against the idea, and in time became the catalyst for the Redbird Smith movement.

Except for the fact that it was no longer used in annual ceremonies, conjuring for healing and other divining practices did survive the decade and continued to be employed as described both in this chapter and in earlier chapters. Also, many of the religious concepts of the Redbird Smith movement were derived from the formalized religious prayers of medicine men who had been and were then writing them down in books in the Cherokee syllabary. Although the variety of herbs being used was more limited than it was in the old country, there was a sufficient amount. Conservative preachers often became medicine men and medicine men became preachers, with the church members seeing no conflict in the arrangement. The ancient myths were retold, and most full bloods retained their knowledge of these. The belief in Little People continued, and further on more will be said about that. Superstitions also prevailed about a world populated with spirits, witches, and black magic, wherein bad rituals could cause misfortune, sickness, and death.

During this time, there was a short-lived period of cooperation between full bloods and mixed bloods in tribal government. Tahlequah was the capital of the nation, and the capitol building later served as the Cherokee County courthouse. The capital itself became in time the only real urban center in the nation, and it was fully controlled by the now numerically superior and more cosmopolitan mixed bloods. So factions developed again, and eventually the division pervaded every aspect of Cherokee life. The fact that the mixed bloods no longer spoke Cherokee and the full bloods refused to discuss affairs in English made communication difficult. Intermarriages between mixed bloods and whites only served to cause a further dissolution and widened the gap.

Actually, there were few "full bloods" who by then did not have a white ancestor or two, but if a person's parents spoke Cherokee, that person was still looked upon as a full blood. The approximate population in 1885 was about 25,000, made up of 9,000 full bloods, 12,000 mixed bloods, and 4,000 black freedmen. The blacks did not hold the same place in Cherokee society as they did among the other "civilized tribes." Most worked for and never with the mixed bloods and were controlled by them in voting situations.

Cherokee political practices duplicated those of the white frontier politicians of the period. Candidates stumped the countryside for votes and held political rallies. There were violence and whiskey drinking at voting time, and the distances full bloods had to travel to polling places made it difficult for them to muster any strength.

The Cherokees did develop in this decade a court system modeled after that of the federal government, with a supreme court and lesser courts for each district. But here again, while the mixed bloods strove to duplicate exactly the federal government procedures, the full bloods shaped the system to fit their own concepts and their leisurely manner of doing things. Yet it is claimed that once a decision was reached, justice was swift and direct in those courts run by a full-blooded judge. Throughout this period, however, while the Cherokees were going about their business, the federal authorities worked steadily to strip authority from the Cherokee courts and to put it in the hands of federal courts. And slowly but surely, United States marshals replaced in each district the Cherokee sheriffs and deputies; often with men such as the famous white judge, Isaac Parker, of the federal court at Fort Smith, who ordered the hanging of eighty-eight white and Indian "outlaws" and sentenced another eighty-eight to the same fate.

Cherokee Nation bylaws for 1892, Article 8, Section 615, established the following districts as precincts for holding elections, and the delightful names alone are worth noting:

Cooweescoowee District

Vinita, Chelsea, Claremore, Catoosa, Coody's Bluff, Coo-y-yah, Silver Lake, Rogers, Jobe Parker, Goose Neck, Ske-a-Took, Oo-La-Gah, Adair,

Chouteau, Riverside, Lenapah.

Canadian District

Lookout Point, Webbers Falls, Briar Town, Texanna, Brushy Mountain.

Delaware District

Charles Thompson, Court House, Johnson Thompson, Richard Taylor, Timber Hill, Fairland, Ballard, Vinita, Afton, Beck, Cave Springs, New Town.

Goingsnake District

Reese Mitchell Mill, Oak Grove, Court House, Rabbit Trap School House, Baptist (near Long Prairie), Prairie Grove, Pea Vine.

Illinois District

Fort Gibson, Court House, Vian, Tah-Lon-Tes-Ky.

Flint District

Court House, New Hope School House, Broken Canoe, Hungry Mountain.

Saline District

Rogers Salt Works, Stand Rowe, Court House.

Sequoyah District

Muldrow, Sweet Town, Swimmer School House.

Tahlequah District

Tahlequah, Elm Springs, Ketcher Town, Manard, Bug Tucker, Yah-Tun-ner Vann, Hicksville.[4]

An 1898 list of towns and settlements in the Cherokee Nation that were not surveyed includes ninety-eight sites.[5]

Another listing from the year 1900 gives the populations of some of the incorporated towns: Adair, 268; Bartlesville, 698; Catoosa, 241; Claremore, 855; Collinsville, 376; Fort Gibson, 617; Gans, 136; Nowata, 498; Pryor Creek, 495; Tahlequah, 1,482; Vinita, 2,339; Webbers Falls, 211; Afton, 606; Bluejacket, 303; Chelsea, 566; Fairland, 499; Grove, 314; Hanson, 182; Lenapah, 154; Oologah, 308; Sallisaw, 965; Vian, 296; Welch, 334; and Westville, 296.[6]

The principal chiefs who served from 1839 to 1906 were John Ross, 1839 to 1866; Lewis Downing, August to October 1866, and 1867 to 1872; William Potter Ross, 1866 to 1867, and 1872 to 1875; Charles Thompson, 1875 to 1879; Dennis

Wolf Bushyhead, 1879 to 1887; Joel Bryan Mayes, 1887 to 1891; C. Johnson Harris, 1891 to 1895; Samuel Houston Mayes, 1895 to 1899; Thomas Mitchell Buffington, 1899 to 1903; William Charles Rogers, 1903 to 1917. During the Civil War, in 1863, Stand Watie was elected principal chief of the southern Cherokees and was recognized as such by Confederate Cherokees until 1866.[7]

Cherokee Education

The Cherokee educational system was by now as good or better than that of some states. Nancy Hoyt opened a subscription school in Tahlequah in 1845, but this was replaced by a public school in 1846, whose teacher was Caleb Covel. By 1867, thirty-two public schools were in existence, and the education of Cherokee children was heavily stressed. In 1870, there were two high schools and 100 primary schools. Fourteen primary schools and one high school were provided for black citizens. Twelve mission schools still functioned, plus an orphan asylum. Noncitizens had subscription schools for their children. Naturally, the schools were managed in such a way as to benefit the mixed bloods more than they did the full bloods. Schools were provided equally for all districts, but the mixed bloods insisted on an all-English curriculum, and the language barrier made teaching and learning difficult. Because of the anxiety of full bloods to learn, the results were discouraging, and dropouts were common. Language use became a heated issue, and by 1874 the schools in full-blooded settlements were reformed, with the use of Cherokee language and texts permitted. One consequence was that from 1875 until the 1890s, the male and female seminaries were crowded with full-blooded students.

The Keetoowah Society

The interest alone from the sale of the Cherokee land to the United States was sufficient to maintain the Cherokee courts, schools, government, roads, and other necessary services, and financial help for these was not required from the Cherokee citizens.

After years of discussion about the allotment

and dissolution issues, the Keetoowah Society decided to act to retrieve and retain in land and religion what either had been lost or was in danger of being lost. In 1896 they met in special session and appointed Redbird Smith — a charismatic man with a shock of wavy hair, a thick mustache, and piercing eyes — and a committee to accomplish these ends. Since Redbird's messengers would carry their secret messages at night, his followers were called Nighthawk Keetoowahs. Smith was a local Society official, a staunch traditionalist, and an excellent leader. Pig Redbird Smith, Redbird's father, had had a large part in the organization of the Keetoowah Society in 1859 and was president of the Cherokee senate in 1870. Before his death in 1871, he searched for a man to teach his son, Redbird, the ways of the Keetoowahs and to give him spiritual guidance. Creek Sam, a Creek, Cherokee, and Natchez, was chosen, and he was the father of White Tobacco Sam, Archie Sam's father. Creek Sam was told that Redbird would be left in his care for teaching and advice in medicine and ritual, and to this day, as Redbird's birthday is celebrated at his old ground each year, Creek Sam's picture is hung alongside his.

Redbird's first move was to recover the seven sacred Cherokee wampum belts that, it is said, were being kept by an unnamed former chief. Smith believed that a translation of the symbolic writings on the belts would enable the Keetoowahs to reconstruct the ancient Cherokee faith and ritual, and to this end he took the seven belts to the elders of the Cherokee Nation, and even to those of the Creeks and the Shawnees.

We were able to obtain from the descendants of Redbird Smith descriptions of only three of the belts: The smallest one is about three inches wide and about two-and-one-half feet long. It is white, with seven pieces of one-half-inch wide white buckskin worked into it crosswise and spaced at equal distances apart. The pieces represent the seven clans which are sworn to eternal peace. Another belt has a blue background, with a peace pipe and a tomahawk worked into it in white beads or cloth, and its meaning is that the pipe and tomahawk unstained with blood symbolize peace and brotherly love for all

mankind. The largest belt is six inches wide and six feet long. It too has a blue background, and has a one-inch-wide white stripe through its middle and a white square at each end. In one of these squares are the figures of two men with clasped hands, symbolizing sworn allegiance to each other as they travel life's pathway together — and they are a strong reminder of the Cementation Ceremony of old. The other square has characters worked into it that explain the secret rituals of the Keetoowahs. Also shown in old Keetoowah photographs is a sacred pipe whose bowl was made of stone obtained in Tennessee in 1865. It is claimed to be the last peace pipe made by the Cherokees. An inscription of the back of the photograph states that the stem is made of bois d'arc, is about two feet in length, and that the entire pipe weighs about three pounds.

During Redbird's visits to the Creeks, the Four Mothers' Society was formed and became the instrument that united into one resistance organization the majority of the full bloods of four of the Five Civilized Tribes — Cherokees, Choctaws, Chickasaws, Creeks and Seminoles. In makeup, it resembled the old intertribal councils, and it retained lawyers and sent delegates to Washington to argue its cases.

Stimulated by this, the full-blooded Cherokees in many parts of their nation reinstituted the all-night dances that had not been done since 1837. Included in these was a small group of Natchez, who revived an old Natchez-Creek ceremonial ground in the southwestern part of the Cherokee Nation, and Cherokee and Creek full bloods came in droves to the dances held there. It was at this ground that Redbird Smith and his committee met for business sessions. At first, the format was for Baptist services to be held in the daytime and Indian dances at night, but the Baptist services were soon discontinued. And at the meetings of the Keetoowahs, only all-night dances were performed — using burnt offerings of tobacco and of the head, tongue, or heart of a deer, squirrel, or white chicken. There were both stomp dancing and feasting, and extensive reference is made to the modern versions of these dances in the pages ahead.

The Keetoowah council at the Redbird Smith ground in 1916 and the seven wampum belts. Redrawn from photograph in the *History of the Cherokee Indians,* p. 487. On the ground in front of them are ball sticks, scoring markers, and a water drum.

In 1897, the first commercial oil well in Indian Territory was drilled in Bartlesville, and inspired by this, in 1898, Congress passed the Curtis Act that called for the dissolution of tribal governments, the abolishment of tribal law courts, and in particular the forcible allotment of lands belonging to the Five Civilized Tribes. The full bloods, acting through the Four Mothers' Society, refused to accept this, and in 1902 Redbird Smith and several other leaders were arrested and jailed for not enrolling.

Albert Carter, who was a youth at the time, reported in an interview given to me in 1978 that in the early 1900s, angered Keetoowahs were "ready to kill all of the white people in Indian Territory."

Apparently, word of this threat got out and sounded an alarm throughout the territory, for on May 16, 1903, Keetoowah leaders attempted to defuse the situation in what proves to be an informative letter written to Federal Judge Joseph A. Gill, in Muskogee, Indian Territory.[8] The letter tells us a great deal about the nature of the society, and its eloquence has the additional significance of revealing the high educational level of those who wrote it:

Dear Sir:

We have had our attention called to an article in the Muskogee Times, of recent date, purporting to be an interview with you, wherein you are represented as having said that you have instructed a Commissioner of your court to make a tour of the Cherokee Nation, and get after the Keetoowahs, that this Society takes the same attitude in the Cherokee Nation with respect to the policy of the Government, as that taken by the Crazy Snake band in the Creek Nation; that it has opposed the work of the Commissioner to the Five Civilized Tribes, and given much trouble to the Government; that you propose to stop their obstructive methods, and the intimidation of would-be allotters; that a man who was recently murdered by the Keetoowahs because he had selected his allotment; that the Commissioner referred to had been instructed to run down the Keetoowahs who did this; and that the leaders of the Society will all be in jail before long.

Whether the newspaper article referred to correctly represents your views or not, such injustice has been done the leaders of the Keetoowahs, and the whole Society, by this publication, in misrepresenting the purpose and objects of the Society and the attitude of its leaders toward the work of the Commission, that we feel called upon in justice to ourselves and the Society, and in order that you and the general public shall be advised of our position, to take notice of it, and make answer to the statements it contains that could only be justified by ignorance of the objects of the Keetoowahs.

In the first place we wish to emphatically and without qualifications to deny that the purposes of the Keetoowahs are the same in the Cherokee Nation as those of the Crazy Snake band of the Creek Nation, as we understand the purposes of that band, or that the Keetoowahs or their leaders have continuously opposed the work of the Commissioner to the Five Civilized Tribes, or that they have given trouble to the Government. We also deny that the Keetoowahs as an organization have advised, counseled or countenanced the murder of a man, or set of men, or violence of any kind, on account of allotment of land, or on any other account.

If any Keetoowah was connected with the murder of the men referred to in said article, the fact that he or they, if there were more than one, is a member of the Keetoowahs does not signify an organized effort to intimidate allotters, as has been persistently and we believe maliciously reiterated in the press and by the enemies of the Indians, who appear to desire to make money out of their land.

The Keetoowah Society was organized in 1859, and the basic principles of its Constitution are loyalty to the Government of the United States, and the preservation of the property of the Cherokees, for those to whom the treaties intended it should go.

It is composed of Cherokees by blood, who can speak or understand but little, if any, English, and they are, therefore, at a great disadvantage in getting their views on the attitudes toward the important changes in progress, respecting the holding of property by the members of the Cherokee tribe, before the public so that they can be understood.

The fact that the Keetoowahs have always been loyal to the United States can be amply remarked by any stranger who may out of curiosity or for any other purpose visit a convention of the Society. The stranger will observe that nearly all of the older members wear in the lapel of their coat, a button of the Grand Army of the Republic. The Society furnished a great majority of the Cherokees who risked their lives and property by joining the armies of the Government in the Civil War.

The Keetoowahs have had and now have some positive views with regard to the partition of the property of the Cherokee tribe, and they have at times differed with the officers of the Government on the methods and plans adopted for that purpose. But in doing so they have always submitted their views to the proper authorities, in a respectful and orderly manner, as the records and files of the Commissioner and the Interior Dept. will amply prove.

There is another organization, within the Cherokee Nation, which we understand is composed of former members of the Keetoowah Society. This organization is known as the Night Hawks. It is a secret society, and we know no more of its objects and purpose than the general public. We do not intend to speak for them, but as for us, and the Keetoowahs, we would be glad to have any investigation made that may be thought desirable, because we believe that if our real feelings were known and understood, they would be respected, even if just what we think out to be done is impracticable or impossible.

The Keetoowahs have been so vilified, and lied about, that we appreciate how hard it will be to put us right in the minds of the people. We are charged with the responsibility for a failure on the part of the full bloods to enroll, because they do not rush to the land office and take their allotments. The full-blood Indian, as is well known by those familiar with the Indian character, is timid and suspicious, because he is not acquainted with the ways of the whites, who has so often been the victim of cheats and frauds who take advantage of his ignorance. He is deliberate in all of his business dealings, and becomes confused when hurried, yet he is abused because he does not come to the land office and take his allotment in low grade public lands while there are many more intelligent citizens unlawfully in possession of thousands of acres of the best land, to the exclusion of would-be allottees.

Why is the machinery of the court not put in action to compel those people to relinquish their unlawful holdings, either by taking their own allotments, or otherwise, so that others may exercise their right by allotting their excess? Many citizens of the Cherokee Nation would take their allotment at once if they saw any disposition on the part of the officers of the Government to enforce the law against this class of violators, but this is not done, while the poor and ignorant are abused for doing nothing more than exercise their right to allot only such lands as they may desire.

1890 to the Present

The Keetoowahs were by no means alone in their opposition, for the Cherokees as a whole opposed any proposals to organize Indian Territory as a state. But the same congressional act that had ratified the sale of the outlet provided also for the appointment of a commission to the Five Civilized Tribes, whose assignment was to work with each of them to secure agreements for allotments of their lands in severalty and to disband their governments preparatory to making Oklahoma a state. Furthermore, it was a commission that intended to succeed in its task. It was known as the Dawes Commission, and although its attempts to begin negotiations were at first disdained by the Cherokees, a series of three meetings was at last held, and at the end of the third, on August 7, 1902, an agreement was approved by the representatives of the Cherokee people.

Most members of the Cherokee Nation were now enrolled, and every enrolled man, woman, and child selected an allotment of 110 acres of average land from the tribal domain.

Active Cherokee resistance to government pressures crumbled at this point, and again the full bloods did what they always did in stressful situations — they withdrew. The Keetoowahs first pulled out of the Four Mothers' Society and then refused to participate in tribal affairs or in the new agreements between the United States and the Cherokee Nation. Full-blooded Cherokee informants are reported as saying, "We just depended on our religion from then on."[9]

It was actually in 1896 that the true stomp dance was revived, although to avoid publicity it was at first known only as a social affair. Soon after this, George Missingshell, a Creek, started a fire near his home on Blackgum Mountain, about a mile from the Redbird Smith home. There were so few capable dancers at this time that George himself had to wear shakers and show the women how to use them. Next, a fire was lighted on Greenleaf Mountain, and this became the Sulphur Spring Ground, which is today known as Medicine Spring. Released from jail, in 1902, Smith constructed a ceremonial dance ground in his home community on Blackgum Mountain. It was called the Deep Branch Fire and later on, the Illinois District Fire. (In 1985 it was known as Redbird's Ground, although the chief was Charlie Tee Hee.) Within a year after Smith's release, there were twenty-three grounds in the Cherokee Nation. At first, each ground had only a fire keeper and conducted a minimum of ritual along with its all-night dances. Redbird himself pushed his followers to follow the seven-clan rule, which he believed was according to God's law. But by 1916, a generalized Cherokee ceremony was in use, as well as the old White Town form of government organization. The seven-clan law was reinstituted with the aid of the ancient wampum belts. By the time Redbird Smith died in 1918, those belonging to the grounds said that "the old rule was complete again."[10] What happened to the grounds from then until now is told in the interviews with my own informants.

Since the full bloods represent the continuation of at least some portion of the ancient culture, my emphasis has been and will be upon them. But the Western Cherokee mixed bloods developed their own cultural pattern, best seen from the turn of the century forward, and perhaps as best typified in the Indian Women's Pocahontas Club of Claremore, which was organized on June 29, 1899, in Oowala community of Cooweescoowee District of Indian Territory. The Cherokee word *oowala* means "life and light," and in what the club has achieved, it has certainly been that for its members.

From its beginning, Oowala itself was a community that expressed progress. Its first school opened in 1881 in a small log house that had been used as a granary. The teacher was paid by subscription from parents and other patrons. Harvey's readers, the Eclectic geographies, and Ray's arithmetic were used for the basic courses for the ten months of the year that the school was open. Pupils furnished their own books, chairs, and tables. Later

on, a modern school replaced the log building, and the teacher was paid by the Cherokee Nation.

A general mercantile store was opened in 1882, followed by a post office, blacksmith shop, harness shop, and sawmill. In 1885, a Presbyterian Church was established and became a center of community activities. Young women of the time are reported as having versatile skills, being well educated, able to garden, cook for roundup or harvest crews, drive wagons, ride horses, do fine needlework, make their own clothes, play musical instruments, sing, dance all night, and graciously entertain visitors.

Originally organized for purely social purposes, the Pocahontas Club soon accepted male honorary members and took on a literary aspect. Members met in homes where they enjoyed contests, guessing games, music, art, and scholarly papers — many of which reveal a surprising interest in Cherokee prehistory and history — and always ended with elaborate refreshments. There were also picnics, swimming parties, hayrides, jackrabbit hunts, social stomp dances, and hill climbing.

In 1904, the club records reported that young Cherokee mixed-blood men were going with shipments of cattle and horses to booming markets in Kansas City, Saint Louis, and Omaha, arriving at these destinations in the finest tailor-made suits, handmade boots, and big cowboy hats. While in these cities, the men attended such events as the opera. The well-known historian and physician Dr. Emmet Starr of Claremore was elected president of the Pocahontas Club in 1906. The club's most illustrious member was Will Rogers, who in his youth seldom missed a meeting and was always the life of the party. As time permitted, Will returned to meetings throughout his life, the last one shortly before his untimely death with Wiley Post in their airplane crash at Point Barrow, Alaska, on August 15, 1935.

After 1908, so many of the female club members were getting married, establishing homes, and rearing families that regular meetings lapsed, and from 1929 through 1935, no meetings at all were held. In 1937, the club was reorganized, with the principal emphasis upon the literary side and in

Present-day full-booded basket maker at work. At top is drawknife bench operated by foot pedal. Lower left shows the steel last used for forming baskets with rounded bottoms. Right shows the initial weaving pattern on the last top, and the underside of the homemade drawknife.

particular upon Cherokee heritage and culture. Among the dozens of themes covered after that were clan relationships, the matter of being Indian in a white world, Sequoyah, famous Indians, and the early history of the Cherokees. In the 1940s lists were being regularly read of Cherokees and other Indians who had made the supreme sacrifice in World War II.

In May 1947, the Pocahontas Club became a member of the National Congress of American Indians. In 1949, the club's golden anniversary was celebrated, and in that year members began to commit their recollections to writing. The year 1959 saw twenty-nine members traveling by chartered bus back to the old Cherokee Nation, visiting Arkansas, Tennessee, Georgia, and finally North Carolina, where they saw the drama, *Unto These Hills.* Later, they publicly lamented in a letter to Luther H. Hodges, governor of North Carolina, that the Cherokee boys and girls of his state were not allowed to attend public schools. "If," the women said, "after over a hundred years, the Cherokee people are still being suppressed, we should be very glad that our ancestors came to Oklahoma."

In 1976, the club members published *Cherokee Recollections,* a delightful limited-edition book in which the history of the club and many of its members is set forth, and the historical notes just given are gleaned from it. The club continues today with its literary pursuits and historical interests, with special emphasis upon charitable work among needy families, at the Indian hospital at Claremore, and in providing financial assistance to school students.

Although the Cherokee government was to have disbanded in March 1906 in preparation for Oklahoma statehood, the rolls did not close until November 1907, when Oklahoma became the forty-sixth state, and their government continued in modified and restricted form under an act of Congress until June 30, 1914. Principal chief William Charles Rogers, a thirty-second-degree Mason and a Shriner, continued in his office until his death in 1917 to sign the deeds in the transfer of Cherokee lands. The Cherokees were now citizens of the state of Oklahoma — a name derived from two Choctaw

Joel Bryan Mayes, principal chief of the Cherokee Nation.

Present-day full-blooded woman pounding corn in ancient-type pounder.

words: "okla," meaning "people," and "humma," meaning "red," or literally, "red people" — where their expertise in government gave them singular prestige and prominence. Many were delegates to the state constitutional convention. Other Cherokees have served in Congress and in such professions as judges, artists, writers, actors, dancers, teachers, engineers, and architects. Dennis Bushyhead was an outstanding lawyer and judge. Will Rogers has been mentioned. Emmet Starr became a well-known historian of his tribe. N. B. Johnson became chief justice of the Supreme Court of Oklahoma and was one of the founders of the National Congress of American Indians. Ida Collins Goodale was among the women who pioneered the Oklahoma State Federation of Women's Clubs. Cherokees have served with distinction in both world wars, and more than a few are buried in the Argonne Forest in France. Rear Admiral Joseph James Clark, of World War II, is a native Oklahoman of Cherokee descent.

After 1914, the office of the principal chief of the Cherokee Nation became appointive and later was vacant for many years. It was reinstated as a nominal office — until recently without salary or expense allowance of any kind. Its main duties include improving the Cherokee economic situation, promoting the interests of tribal members in the various government welfare programs in the Bureau of Indian Affairs, and acting in an advisory capacity in the tribal lawsuits brought before the Indian Claims Commission. On April 16, 1941, President Franklin D. Roosevelt selected J. Bartley Milam for the job, and in 1947, President Harry S. Truman reappointed him. W. W. Keeler, chief executive officer of Phillips Petroleum Company in Bartlesville, Oklahoma, succeeded Milam as chief, and Keeler was succeeded by Ross Swimmer, who later was assistant secretary of the interior and head of the Bureau of Indian Affairs in Washington, D. C. The present principal chief of the Cherokee Nation is Wilma Mankiller.

Of special interest to me personally was my coming across as I did my research for *The Cherokee People,* relatives by marriage that I had not known I had — in particular Stephen M. Lewis, who traced his descent back to the pioneer families of Jamestown in 1607, and through the Randolphs, Washingtons, Carters, and Lees, and who was, as I am, a direct male relative of the family of the famed explorer, Merriwether Lewis. Stephen died in 1907, at the age of eighty-eight years. His son, Alexander S. Lewis, settled in Dawson, Tulsa County, Oklahoma, where he married Elizabeth P. Dawson, a member of the Cherokee Nation. A son, Stephen Riley Lewis, was born to them in 1873 and was educated in the Dawson community and at Hillside Mission, a Quaker school near Skiatook. In March 1898, Stephen married Minnie Carter of Cooweescoowee District, who was the daughter of David Tecumseh and Emma Carter. She died in December of 1898. In 1907, Stephen married Elizabeth Belle Schrimsher, daughter of John Gunter Schrimsher, who served as a captain in Stand Watie's regiment and later became a judge and a Cherokee senator. Stephen was admitted to the practice of law in 1902, in 1910 to the Supreme Court of Oklahoma, and in 1916 to the United States Supreme Court.

NOTES

1. The principal secondary sources for my information on the Western Cherokees are those listed in footnotes two through nine, plus Skelton, A History of the Educational System of the Cherokee Nation; Tyner, The Keetoowah Society in Cherokee History; Bass, *Cherokee Messenger;* Woodward, *The Cherokees;* and Foreman, *Indian Removal.*
2. Foreman, *The Five Civilized Tribes,* pp. 367-412.
3. Steele, *The Last Cherokee Warriors,* p. 107.
4. Oklahoma Historical Society.
5. Ibid.
6. Ibid.
7. Wright, *A Guide to the Indian Tribes of Oklahoma,* p. 74.
8. Foreman Collection, Oklahoma Historical Society.
9. Thomas, The Origin and Development of the Redbird Smith Movement.
10. Ibid.

CHAPTER ELEVEN

The Final Veil

T he last of the veils I hoped to penetrate was that of discovering what, if anything, remained among the Western Cherokees of ancient thought patterns, secular customs, and religious ways. When, in early 1975, Joyce and Ray Johnson and I first explored the idea of pursuing this, we were, to my great joy, able to compile a remarkable and surprisingly large list of source individuals to contact and interview — surprising because it is commonly accepted that little of consequence remains to be seen and explored. But the list itself proves otherwise. Also, although for a short period of time during the latter half of the nineteenth century the old religious ways were not visible, they were being remembered and missed, and beginning with the turn of the century they surfaced again to be continued thereafter until the present day. Taken together, the interviews we have had account for the material that follows. Some individuals contributed bits of information that are woven together to make tapestry pictures. Other individuals gave interviews so valuable that they are individually cited.

First and foremost would be Archie Sam, youngest son of White Tobacco Sam, who was chief of the Medicine Spring dance ground when we visited there in the 1980s. Little did we realize in first considering him what a dear friend Archie would become and what a fount of knowledge and inspiration he would be.

Netche Gray was in his eighties. He made ball-play sticks and also coconut, gourd, and turtle rattles. We could learn from him how he made these.

Eliza Sumpka, who lived in Muskogee, also made turtle-shell rattles and could give us further details about them.

Sam Blossom lived in Salina and made *Knnuchi* (also spelled *Kenuchi* and *Connuche*) balls, using a rock in the "old way" to pound and break the hickory nuts. He also owned one of the old corn pounders — a chopped-out log and a wooden pole — and used it to pound the corn and nuts.

Ezekiel Vann, also known as "Sig," was from Salina and was a respected medicine man and a Baptist preacher. When later on, Joyce made her first trip to the Eastern Cherokee Reservation, it would be Sig who directed her to come by his house to pick up some medicine which he called "pomigilian" for Almanetta Sequoyah, the medicine man of Big Cove already referred to. Sig's instructions were that Joyce was not to let anyone else touch it and that she was to personally give it to Almanetta, for it was a "very powerful medicine." Sig also told her he was going to insure a safe journey for her, Ray, and her brother, Victor, by treating them with remade tobacco. He went into another room and brought back a medicine bundle of faded, coarse, and dark red material, about five inches square and tied with a string of white cloth. The actual medicine itself was wrapped in the cloth. It was bright red, had been pulverized, and was formed into a lump about the size of a golf ball. He did not completely open the bundle, lifting just the corners of the cloth slightly while holding it in his left hand, using the blade of his pocketknife to scrape out only a tiny portion. He doctored them with it by rubbing it on their foreheads, and then handed Joyce the medicine for Almanetta. At this time, Sig said he had never before given any of the "pomigilian" to anyone, nor had he admitted to anyone that he had any, because it was so powerful it was dangerous. Whether the treatment accounted for it or not, Joyce did complete a successful series of trips to the Eastern Cherokee Reservation.

James Vann was 101 years old, lived at Stilwell, and was a medicine man. But he could only be talked to with the aid of a skilled interpreter.

Nancy Kingfisher lived at Salina, was in her eighties, and could tell us some interesting stories about the old days.

Howard Tyner lived at Vian, and in 1949 had written an excellent thesis on the Keetoowahs, during which time he interviewed the society president, Jim Pickup; Keetoowah Chief Stokes Smith; and also Levi Gritts. When contacted, Howard generously offered us the use of his notes and any of his copies of society minutes and correspondence.

William Glory was the chief of the United Keetoowah Band, and when contacted said he would be happy to have us come and talk with him.

John Hair was the assistant chief and was equally open to an interview.

Jenny Wycliff was a medicine woman who might prove very useful.

Betty Jumper lived just outside Tahlequah. She still had the papers and books that had been used by her father, medicine man Willy Jumper.

William Smith was the head of the Stokes ground, and it was essential that we meet him. His father was Stokes Smith, the son of Redbird Smith. William lived with his children and grandchildren alongside a dirt road about fifteen miles outside Vian and was a medicine man of some renown. He worked for the railroad during the week and was only home on weekends. But on these weekends there were always people coming to him for medicine. When we arrived there one Saturday, there were twenty-five pickup trucks parked nearby whose occupants were waiting to see him. When William was home, he would sit out in front of the house in a chair so people would know he was ready to treat them, or if he was not in the chair, people would know he was inside ministering to someone. Patients respectfully waited their turn.

Jasper Smith was an uncle of William's and one of the seven medicine men who served the Stokes ground. He granted us an interview.

Crosslin Smith of Marble City was a brother of William Smith, was studying to be a medicine man, and promised an interview.

Charlotte Rogers lived at Fort Gibson and knew a great deal about Cherokee history. She is nearly blind. Since the Cherokee way is to sit and

Creek Sam - 1908

Creek Sam, redrawn from Bureau of Ethnology Bulletin 137, plate 74.

listen while someone talks, she would not allow the use of a tape recorder. But she had many interesting things to say about her Uncle Stokes and also photographs that have never been shown or published. One beautiful picture is about fourteen by twenty inches and shows four men holding the seven wampum belts. An eight-by-ten photo shows Stokes in his later life holding one of the belts and standing near the fire as he talks about the belt. In a third picture of the belts, her uncle holds also a huge, red stone-headed peace pipe. Charlotte has also a sheet of paper with the seal of old Keetoowahs printed on it. The actual seal was broken, but Uncle Stokes had held it together to make the print. These items plus others are kept in a secure place in an undisclosed location and are only available to those whom Charlotte trusts.

Albert Carter lived at Gore and remembered many things about the early years. Among the intriguing things we first learned from him was that when he was young, the Cherokees in his area, most of them Nighthawks, decided to move west to a new location. Eventually, thousands of them were gathered in the valley where he lived and they camped there for about a week. Then for some reason unknown to him they changed their minds and returned to their homes.

Charlie Tee Hee lived next to the old Redbird Smith ground and was its chief.

Jim Wolf lived near Stilwell and had the original fire-starting "flint" of the Four Mothers' Society. He invited us to camp, dance, eat, and visit with him at his home and dance ground.

Joyce had already talked with a certain individual whom we will leave unnamed who was studying to be a medicine man, and we hoped we could talk with him again. He had told her that he made the choice to study on his own, and had not been chosen for this by medicine men. In consequence, he was experiencing conflicts that were "killing" him and had decided not to study anymore. Some two years before, he had put his papers in his barn because he believed there was evil connected to the affair. We did not get to see him, for at age forty-two, he had a sudden and fatal heart attack. This same "curse" was said by certain Cherokees to have applied to A. K. and J. K., ethnologists who had collected some papers from the old medicine men, had translated them, and were "using them to make money for themselves." Word had been passed that they would not live to an old age to enjoy their profits, and it was also said that both of them had died early. "They were not capable of handling all the power that goes with such knowledge," our source said.

There was a woman in Tahlequah who made good-luck and love charms for the Cherokees. Customers told her what they needed a charm for, and she made it.

Virginia Catendon could heal burns. This was her speciality.

Tom Bunch was about sixty years old and had in his possession a number of papers written in the Cherokee language that contained interesting things about the early Cherokees.

Living near Stilwell was a sixty-eight-year-old medicine woman whom we would try to see.

Eliza England at Peavine community was an elderly Cherokee, but not a traditionalist. She went to church and had never been to a stomp dance. Yet she had some beautiful stories to tell about the way she was raised.

Joe Duck was a medicine man who did conjuring. His medicine was reputed to be so strong that many Cherokees were afraid to go to him for treatment.

Charlie Watts was another medicine man worth seeing.

Walter Fargo was eighty-four years old, lived near Muldrow, and had a lot of Cherokee stories to tell. Sidney White was eighty-seven years old, was a maker of ball sticks and also had stories to relate.

There were a conjurer who lived near Chently and a medicine woman who lived at Strang, Oklahoma.

Over a period of time, Joyce, Ray, and I went individually or together to see and interview most of the people just listed. Later, other names were added to the list, and in the pages ahead their information is cited along with the rest. In failing to see some of the prospective informants, we discovered that many of the healers had no telephones and were often away doctoring patients. An additional thing we noticed was that all of the medicine people had four or five noisy dogs, but no cats. We thought this odd and wondered whether bad luck might be associated with the latter.

As we talked with individuals and visited the stomp grounds, the number of tape recordings and notes grew to far more than are included in this book. There are in fact enough to make a second volume this size. But even this information will startle those who believe that the old ways and beliefs are gone in the Cherokee Nation of Oklahoma. A day may or may not come when that is true, but for now the lore is still rich and inviting.

Barker Dry

In the 1970s, it was not too late for us to gather some revealing firsthand accounts of life in the Cherokee Nation at the turn of the twentieth century. We went first to see a storytelling ninety-year-old named Barker Dry, who was born in 1889 and whose sparkling eyes and ready smile masked a genuinely crusty disposition. He was a prime example of the converted full-blooded Cherokee who, although he claims he is fully a Christian, at the same time finds his true self in Cherokee culture. When asked what a true Cherokee was and whether he felt he really was one, he answered that he had been God-fearing since he was a child, but he was forty before he realized he needed to be converted. "I used to get roaring drunk," he said, "and I thought it felt good. But it was nothing compared to what I've got now."

"How did he feel about the ancient faith?"

He replied that he had seen different ways of worshiping that he thought were pagan. And he admitted he had gone to stomp dances but only to be sociable. "I couldn't see no sense to it. I never did like to see Indians wearing costumes or feathers on their heads."

Part of his attitude stemmed from the fact that while his father was a full blood, his mother was a white woman who remained afraid of Indians and the old Indian culture. Yet the parents met and were married in Indian Territory.

When we asked Barker where he thought the Indians obtained their admirable ways, Barker's wife answered for him, saying, "In the beginning man was made to worship God. He has to worship something, and the Indian learned this by being in and among nature. Before Jesus came, man lived under the law. After he came man had to be born again and live under the blood. Pentecost is the important thing." Barker nodded his head in agreement.

Prodded into further thought, he puffed out his cheeks, let out a long sigh, and began by telling us that the nature of people was so different it seemed like he had during his lifetime lived in three separate worlds. "The first people," he said slowly, "who came to Indian Territory were hardly more Indian than a hog was. Most of them came out of Arkansas, and had so many bootleggers giving them whiskey you would find bottles lining the roadsides.

"Then back when I was a kid of about twelve we wore knee britches that we kept buttoned. Then styles began to change. The dresses got shorter. Before this, people had good feelings toward one another, more friendship. Now there's modernism, and the blind are leading the blind. You have to lead the life, be born again. It makes you walk right and talk right. Now there are twelve churches around here that are all different kinds. The singing is really shouting, and the people are laying on the floor. It's a wonder they don't get stepped on. Back then in the churches there was no shouting. The Baptist church is on a cold trail today, and people should use the King James Version of the Bible, because that version is the best and plainest.

"But," he went on, "back in the days when I was seventeen or eighteen, the Cherokees had meetings in the church houses every fall, about September. And it seemed like there was lots of love. People would help each other out with work and food. There was hogs, flour, sugar, and there was a green coffee for a dollar a bunch. There was no such thing as the vaccinating of cattle or hogs or humans. Of course, there were different kinds of diseases, but not the millions that are around now. I don't know whether white doctors have done any good or not."

Barker is an authority on the caves in the backcountry, and we spent some time talking about these and about people who once lived in them. That led him to tell us about some of the Cherokee outlaws, such as the Wycliff brothers, who were Nighthawks, and who once saved him from a beating by a bigger man. There were a lot of Nighthawks who lived in his home area, and he attended some of their stomp dances, which were held at special grounds. Two of these places were prominent gathering sites. One was Chewey, and the other was the location of a Baptist church named Elm Prairie. Both places were going at the same time. People would come to there on foot and in wagons and during the day would visit and play ball with sticks. At night, they would dance. He had seen as many as 10,000 people at some of these gatherings that began on Mondays and often lasted as long as a week or ten days. This was when he was about sixteen years old, so it would be around 1904.

At this time the Nighthawks were fighting to keep the white people from coming into Indian Territory. The Cherokees had some land and some freedom again and didn't want to lose it. But even the Keetoowahs were divided over what to do about this, and finally the Nighthawks broke away from Redbird and the rest. Even though Barker's uncle was one of the leaders at the Redbird Smith ground, Barker paints Redbird as a charlatan who duped his followers. "He was a fortune-teller, and even had a gas connection to the fire to fool people. And his leaders were backing him up. He was the preacher and he was doing all the talking about what he was going to do and how he was going to get the land back from the whites. He told people to not do this and to not do that. Then he had them raise several thousand dollars to send him to Washington, but when he got there he didn't even see the president."

Animated by remembrances of the old struggles, Barker was prompted by a visiting Cherokee friend to tell us a couple of stories that included some interesting insights into the early days.

The first one was about a man who lived about a mile and a half from Barker's house and whose name was Hale Beet. He wore his hair down to his shoulders and was a big fellow. One day he got sick and in no time at all died. Barker was not there to see this, but later on all of the old people were talking about what happened next. Hale had been laid out for viewing on what was called a "cooling board," and they planned to bury him on the fourth day after death. Then along about ten or eleven o'clock on the first night they saw the sheet that covered him move, and they discovered that he was still alive!

Barker explained that, as a rule, a deceased person was kept inside the house, where friends would gather and sing. They would bring food and help the family out in other ways. Then on the fourth day the preacher would come to the house and preach a sermon. When he was finished, they put the body on a blanket and hoisted it into a wagon, and the mourners would follow the wagon on foot to the cemetery.

The second story was about Barker's stepdad's brother's boy, John Stover, who was hung for having committed some terrible crime. They had his suit and his coffin all ready to bury him, but the rope didn't kill him. So they turned him loose, and John lived for about fifteen years after that. Once he told Barker, who asked him what had happened, whether he went to sleep when the rope choked him or what. "I went to this place — I never seen nothing like it — where God told me he wasn't ready for me. He said, 'I'm going to send you back. I'll call you when I'm ready, and that's when you will die.'"

Life in the early days, Barker said, was of the rough-and-tumble frontier kind. Men would get drunk and shoot out candles, kill cats, and even one another for no other reason than sport. For whiskey, there was a still near his home to which people would take a bushel of corn to trade. Whiskey was worth about two dollars a gallon then, and the marshals never did a thing about it.

He told us about a certain day when he and his sister were walking along the road and kicking up the dust with their bare feet, and they came upon a giant rattlesnake. He went to find a rock to kill it, but his grandmother, who was working nearby, told him in

Cherokee to leave it alone. When we asked why he thought she had said this, he answered that everyone said she was a bit off and was one of those old-time witches, a conjurer who could perform evil spells and make herself into whatever she wanted to be. That was why people would get into fights. She caused it.

This grandmother had come over the Trail of Tears when she was only two or three years old. She came from Georgia, and told Barker how they marched and about women having babies on the way. The women would have their babies in the wagons and then stay behind for a day or two before they caught up with the rest of the group. The Cherokees would build fires each night as they attempted to stay alive, and she said they were driven like cattle. It was such a terrible experience that she wanted to forget it, but she never could. Even as a child it had been etched in her mind, and it was beyond forgiving. Nothing the whites could do would ever make it right. Perhaps that was why, Barker said, she had become a witch. She wanted to get even the only way a Cherokee ever could.

Continuing with the subject of witches, Barker told another story about something strange that had happened when his stepdad was only a boy. There was an eccentric old man who lived just across the hollow from him. The old man got very sick, so when the boy and his father heard about it they went over there to see what they could do to help, and they found the old man about dead. On the way home they climbed over the top of a rail fence, and as they did so turned to see behind them an old dog that looked real sick. For some reason they suspected it was a witch, so the boy picked up a rock and threw it, striking the dog between the eyes. The dog gave a loud yelp and then turned and went back where he had come from. The next morning they went back to see the old man and found him dead in his house with a deep gash right between his eyes.

A story was related about an elderly neighbor named Aggie Miller, who had never gone to school. But she could predict things, and while he was still a boy she told Barker there was a day coming when people would have to pay taxes on dogs, cats, everything. She also foretold airplanes.

There were a number of herb doctors who lived around Barker's house when he was young. One was "Old Man Fester," and he was Barker's grandmother's "buddy." Sam Lacey was another herb doctor. One time, Barker's father became quite ill, and his grandmother, convinced that someone was causing the sickness, went to see Fester about it. Fester went out into the woods and came back with something to make a tea. He placed this in a dishpan belonging to the grandmother, added water, and made the tea. The grandmother had his father drink it, and Barker watched wide-eyed as his father's stomach swelled up like a balloon. Finally, he vomited into that pan something that looked like frogs' eggs with black spots on them that looked like flies. The grandmother took the pan away and down a trail. Barker does not know what she did with it. But when she returned, she had been "told" who was causing the sickness and said that the person would not live long. And that man got sick in the same way as Barker's father, except that he vomited up real wood chips and blood, and he died. "This is one thing I know is true," Barker said, "I saw it happen, and I know the old man who caused it died."

Barker related how the witches had had a certain kind of power "back there," but added that there weren't many of them left. This was because life-styles have changed so much. Back then they were more dedicated to what they did. Now they weren't and had succumbed to the ways of the white man's world.

We were told about a certain verse in the Bible that Barker's "pappy" had used, concerning how angels had troubled the water. Then he mentioned how just the night before, the preacher was preaching on that subject and saying how it pertained to the waters of the soul. "Now," the preacher went on to the congregation, "you can do this, but you don't want everybody to know it. You want to be by yourself and do it very secretly. And you go where there is running water, fast running water, and it wants to be running south, and you want to be on the west side, and that's where the Little People, the Little Ones, work." Then the preacher pointed out that people just say they aren't going to water because the water is muddy or they don't want to get their clothes soiled. "But the truth is," he concluded, "they just don't want to be bothered."

"But," Barker added, "now I'll tell you, it doesn't have to be a river. It can be a running stream of any kind, and you can have an enemy and go there and find out about him. You can take a certain kind of bag and put water in it, and bring it back and put in a pan. Then you take some little white, black, and red beads and put them in the pan and make them float on the water and you will find out how many friends you have and who they are — whether they are whites or Negroes or Indians — and you put them down and watch them. They are just sitting there at first in groups of seven or eight. Then quickly one from a bunch and one from another bunch will take off and go way over to one side. That's how many friends you have, don't you see?"

It was mentioned at this point that George Wycliff, whose father was a medicine man, had told how young men had often come to his father and complained they were troubled because something had happened between them and their girlfriends to "fuss up" the relationship. Finally the father told them to meet him at 4:00 a.m. down by a certain creek. There was frost on the ground, but he had them strip anyway and immerse seven times. After one exposure to this they felt miraculously cured. But the father said they had to do it for six more mornings. The boys never came back, and never asked for another cure.

Barker had never seen crystals that had been used for divining and believed the medicine men had ceased to use them before his time. He knew also about people changing into animals such as foxes, bears and, of course, the dog he had already mentioned. As for the Little People, he had not seen them personally, but claimed there once was a bluff over by Twin Oaks where the Little People lived. They were said to have looked like children and to have played there. Other Indians he knew said the Little People were full bloods, and they would have nothing to do with that hill. It was red dirt, and to Barker it sure looked like a place where kids had a

playground. "Now," he said, "the hill has been cut down and a highway goes right through the middle of it."

A story was told about people who live today who say they get messages from Little People who are described as being about twenty inches tall and sometimes living in people's houses. One woman went to visit a certain man at his house in the country and knew no one else would be around because he lived alone. But he wasn't there, so she left. Later on she saw him, and he told her he was sorry he had missed her when she came to visit. She was startled, and asked how he knew she had been there. He replied that the Little People take care of his house and watch over it when he is away. They told him she had been there, and even described what she wore and the color of her car.

Our interview with Barker closed with another miracle story, this one about a man who was certain that he had killed an opponent in a fight and hid the body. But the next day the opponent showed up alive, and the man could never figure out how this could be. Then Barker said, "I've just told you a little bit, and I don't know whether you believe it or not." One thing I was certain of, despite his conviction that he was thoroughly converted to Christianity, it was clear that Barker Dry had more than a little of the old Cherokee left in him. We left him in the middle of another lecture on vaccinations . . . . "They're putting stuff in their blood and everything else . . . . they break your blood up. They weaken your blood. They do everything," he declared. As we went out the door, his wife whispered that Barker had just got out of the hospital and hadn't enjoyed being there a bit.

Lydia Sam McLure

Archie Sam's older sister, Lydia Sam McLure, gave us some extremely helpful information about 1920s living conditions; schooling; her father, White Tobacco, and his medicine practice; her brother Archie; and the early dance grounds.

From the fifth grade on at the Cherokee Sequoyah School, she and the other female students studied, among other things, American and Oklahoma history, hygiene, and homemaking. The latter included considerable work experience in the laundry, kitchens, making beds, cleaning rooms, and washing dishes.

Students arose at 7:00 a.m. and ate breakfast. School classes started at 8:30 a.m. and continued until lunchtime. They resumed at 1:00 p.m. and let out at 4:00 p.m. The white culture was stressed, and the Indian cultures were either disparaged or ignored.

The boys wore standardized drab-brown suits, and the girls wore mostly white blouses and black skirts, with bloomers to match the skirts, and high-top button shoes. When dresses were worn for special occasions, the hems reached nearly to the floor, the sleeves were long, and the necks were high. Again, there were bloomers to match. Underneath all this in both winter and summer was "long-handled" underwear, but the summer variety was of a lighter weight. Students raced home during summer vacation to change to simpler and lighter garb and couldn't wait to go barefoot.

The contrast between the disciplines of school and the freedoms of home was a sharp one, but they "had to get used to it." An education was considered essential, and once they were accustomed to school they were glad they were there. "Our classmates became our friends, and our teachers were good to us. Some of the teachers were white, and some were Indian."

The young people had parties on holidays and especially enjoyed Valentine's Day. The girls and boys were allowed to be together then, and by the time Lydia was sixteen, boys and girls were even sharing the classrooms. Male and female students lived in separate dormitories housing thirty to forty students each. In the earlier years placement was determined by age, with a division of the students into little, middle sized, and large. Finally, when more dormitory buildings were added, the oldest students were housed in individual rooms of two or three students each.

Most preachers who led services at the Sequoyah School spoke English, but on occasion an Indian preacher would fill in. School emphasis was on learning to speak English, and students were disciplined if they spoke their native language to one another. But the native language was allowed when family or friends came to visit. Visits could be made at any time and were carried out in dormitories or out on the campus grounds. If visitors wished to remain overnight, all the student need do was inform the office, and beds and meals were provided. Playing "hooky" was frowned on, but if a student was homesick or didn't like school and decided to run away, the administrators just let the student go. Male students tended the gardens and cared for the stock, but the girls did neither of these, nor did they can the vegetables.

Lydia completed her high school years at Haskell Institute in Lawrence, Kansas. Students from most of the Indian tribes came there, and she feels it was a good school. The administration was tolerant to a point. You either had to be in your room when they called the roll or else have a good excuse, because you would be punished by having to do extra work and receiving a loss of privileges. Also, students were expected to keep up with their studies. The competition was keen, and "as it always is when there are a bunch of girls, some were mean and would do anything to get ahead of you." Every Sunday, students went into town for church services that consisted of a Sunday-school class, a morning service, and an evening service. While most of the churches in Oklahoma were Baptist, each Haskell student went to the church of his or her own denomination. Church services were held at Haskell Institute for faculty members, and students were free to attend, but most went into town.

Lydia graduated from Haskell in 1932, but has lost all contact with former school friends and has never been back, not even for a class reunion.

Braggs was one of the towns the Sam children were now and then taken to by their father, White Tobacco Sam. His trips were made at one- or two-week intervals. Sometimes all of the children were taken, sometimes just one. It depended upon how much money the family had to spend. The longer trips to Muskogee included a train ride, and that was a real treat. Moreover, they would stay a night or more in a hotel that had a "real" dining room. "Archie was just a little boy then, and we older children had to drag him around all the time." Picture shows were always included in the itinerary. They were silent films. "By the time you tried to read what it was all about they were showing another picture. But it was fun, and then you could get in for only ten cents. Ice cream was five cents, and fifteen cents would do you all day." Their father would put them in the theater and tell them he would be back when the show was over. She guessed he took care of his farm business affairs while they were doing this, but said he might also have been meeting with other medicine men.

In those early days most of the people walked to the dance grounds, but some came in buggies. Where the Sams lived, the only close neighbor was Uncle Charlie. The other ground members lived two or more miles away. Some came from Gore and other towns, and somehow knew when anything was going to go on at the dance ground — and they just started coming.

Most of the houses of the time were built of logs and were a gable-roofed, shingled, single-story, single unit partitioned into two or three rooms, with the kitchen usually being in the rear room. Others consisted of two units with two or three rooms in each, connected by a wide, roofed-over breezeway called a "dogtrot." In the hot summers, families often slept in the dogtrot and usually ate their meals there. Some families had iron or rock stoves out in back of the houses for summer cooking. Springs were everywhere, and every home had its own well or cistern.

Among Lydia's earliest memories are those of her father talking about Little People who lived near their home. He said they would visit with him and tell him things. But she guessed that the other children and she were "too mean to see or hear anything like that." She thought he probably told them what they said, but it was so long ago that she had forgotten. She did remember that he said the Little People would come to get him and talk to him and show him things. She imagines that the conversations had to do with his medicines. "We called

them dwarfs, but he called them Little People, and said they were real, and smart just like humans."

Lydia guessed that her problem was that she was only seeing things with her "natural eyes," for her father had said she had to see beyond the human in order to see things like Little People. He would always go to their ranch to perform some of his medicine rituals and once said that while he was there and concentrating on what he was supposed to do — someone had asked him to determine whether everything was going to be all right for that person — he looked up and saw feet, then he continued to look up and saw that they belonged to a tall woman wearing a white dress. She looked down at him and touched his thigh. The only thing he could think of was that it was an angel of God telling him that something good was going to happen to the person he was inquiring about.

As to what her father knew about the practices of witchcraft or bad medicine, Lydia was not certain. But she recognized that he knew whenever something was not right. He could sense it. In such instances he would just have to keep doctoring himself for his own protection.

She told us that in his medical practice, White Tobacco Sam helped only those people who requested it. His aim was to make them healthy and was in large part preventive medicine. He also wanted the Cherokees to grow and be strong in the traditional way, so he always urged them to continue in it from year to year. If he knew people were having bad thoughts and wanted to make trouble, he had a medicine for this and would treat them in absentia. They wouldn't know this was being done or by whom, but the treatment would change them. "Got knew my father's spirit and heart," Lydia said with a faraway look in her eyes, "that he was trying to help his people, and in order to do that, increased his knowledge."

Lydia explained that White Tobacco Sam was trained both by his father, Creek Sam, and by other medicine men who knew he would be helpful to his people and would not tell what he had learned from them. She did not know how old White Tobacco was when he started his training but did know that he doctored people for as long as she could remember.

Sometimes White Tobacco would go alone into a room to make his medicine, and sometimes he would prepare it in front of everyone. But the children grew so used to it they seldom paid attention to what he was doing. Among other items employed for healing, he used herbs and roots, and the way he prepared them was determined by the illness he was treating. Sometimes he washed the herbs in water until they were very clean. Other times he wrapped the herb in a cloth and then pulverized it with a hammer or a rock. Then he would put it in a pot of water and make a tea. Other times he would make a poultice or would strain the herb or root and drink the juice of it. He had a small and very old piece of hollow cane that he used to blow his breath into the boiling pot either four or seven times while he prayed. Except for his children, he would be alone while he did the blowing, "because we were so little he didn't pay no mind to us, and he knew we wouldn't run out and tell everyone what he was doing."

A glass or cup was used to serve the medicine to the patients. Ordinarily, they would drink it, but sometimes White Tobacco would bathe parts of their bodies with it. On occasion, he took patients "to the water" for treatment. Lydia doesn't know what he did there, but does know that he used both the water and tobacco for ritual cleansing. He treated various kinds of illnesses and would always know through his medicine power what kind of illness it was. If there was a white doctor at Braggs in those days, she never knew of it, because she never went to a doctor except for her father, who always doctored her.

While she was at Sequoyah, the Cherokee students were never let out of class to attend traditional ceremonies. "They were training us to lose our tradition," she said. "We were being brainwashed, but we didn't know it." Her father knew it, but he was also wise enough to know that the traditional life would one day die out, and he told the children that all along. He said, "You are going to come up where you know nothing about the old ways. You are going to be mixed in with white people and will lose everything you once knew and lived. So you have to get an education for your future. I won't always be with you, and you will have to face it on your own. Go to school and learn everything you can." He also told her and the other children things "they would never have thought of, and everything he said came true." Since White Tobacco felt this way about the future, except when medicine was being taken, his stomp ground was open to everyone, Indians, whites and other races alike.

On the days when he prepared the medicine, he would be alone at the stomp ground while word of his doing this would be spread to the members, who had to be prepared in advance to receive the medicine and were not supposed to eat or drink anything until after the medicine has been taken. Those taking the medicine had to stand within the dance square, sometimes called the "dance circle," in front of their clan beds. The men came first about noon. They would line up and drink from a common dipper — always enough of the medicine to make certain they would throw up — but some would also wash their faces with the medicine. When the families arrived that night and took the medicine, most of them would take only a little and would not throw up. And it was a rule that the medicine was to be entirely used up, and none was to be taken home.

No woman having her menstrual period was allowed on the stomp ground at any time, and Lydia said the leaders were so strict about this that "they almost went around lifting the women's skirts to be sure before they dispensed the medicine." The medicine men even isolated themselves in a building until someone had made certain about the women. "They are supposed to stay away from those things." Even in the people's homes, the women were not supposed to sit with the family at meals during their "times." If a woman was absent, everyone knew why, and White Tobacco Sam never treated a woman "while she was in that condition." None of this was because the menstrual period was thought of as a bad thing. It was just a tradition.

When we mentioned that the last time we had been at the Stokes ground the women were even sitting on the benches in the beds and that the grounds were changing in several ways and not following the traditions, Lydia commented, "Like my daddy said, they are just going to lose out, and there will be a mixture of everything. And what medicine they do use is not going to be any good. If they don't keep up their cleanness it's not going to work. That's what's wrong now."

When it was added that one leader was charging people to enter his stomp ground and that some wondered whether this might keep his medicine from being as effective as it should be since it was not part of the tradition, Lydia said, "That's right. My father told us that when the medicine men were teaching him they said the fire and ground was a free gift from God handed down from generation to generation. White Tobacco was to help his people, and if anyone wanted to give him something of their own free will

that was to be accepted — but it was to be whatever the person wanted."

The conversation changed to the medicine practice of being able to put people to sleep, and Lydia said she had heard a lot of people say they could do this, "put families to sleep, hide them, and different things like that."

On another day, we had asked a certain medicine man whether if someone came to him and asked him to make bad medicine, he would have to do it. He answered that he would, because they were there to serve people. Even if he didn't feel it was right, he had been given the knowledge and would have to go ahead and do it. When we wondered whether or not this might be wrong, he replied, "No, because the ones who do the bad are going to have to account for it. We are not the ones doing it, they are. So I don't

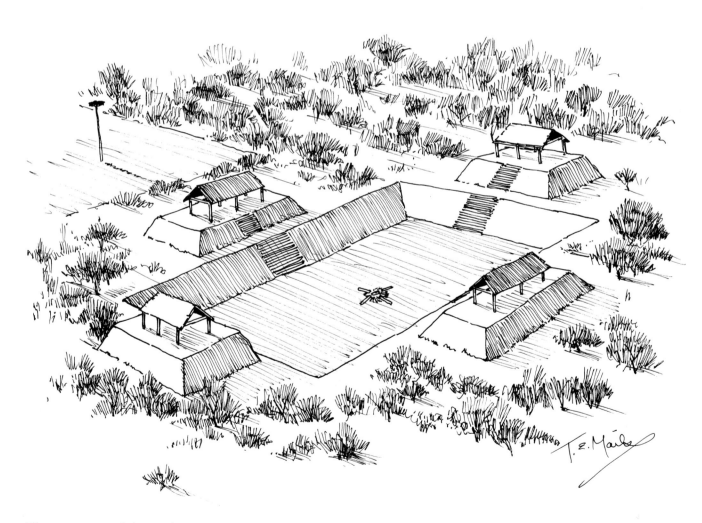

The stomp ground that Archie Sam hoped to build.

feel I am doing bad or should be held responsible. It's the decision of the one to whom the charm or tobacco has been given."

"Did White Tobacco Sam feel like that?" we wanted to know.

"Well," Lydia said after some reflection, "in a way I guess he did. But many times he'd say he had to study about the request and see what he was led to do. Sometimes he didn't feel led and didn't do it. He'd just tell the person he would rather not do things he knew shouldn't be done."

Commenting in general about the changes that are taking place in Cherokee life, such as stealing and other things that go on now, Lydia said she thought it was because "a lot of it is dead. I think that half of the power is gone. There may be some power, but I don't think it's strong enough. There are too many mixtures, and they are not keeping the rules like they should be. And there are so many things that can hinder the effectiveness of the power."

Returning to the matter of White Tobacco and his practice of medicine, Lydia informed us that while he usually stayed at the house to treat a patient, he sometimes went away from the house for awhile to find out what was really wrong with them. "I guess," she said, "he just went out there and studied about it like a doctor does today, and while he did this God would show him what was wrong." Archie had told us that White Tobacco even had a cure for cancer, and Lydia confirmed this. She was never at home when he did his cancer cures, but he told her about one instance, and she knew the man, "and his cancer got healed up." All of this ability had ceased to exist at the death of White Tobacco, because he had not trained anyone to take his place. "Unfortunately," Lydia said, "we were centering our lives in whatever was handy at the time. We didn't really stop and realize what that knowledge would mean to us now."

Archie had already told us the same thing. "We never looked for tomorrow. If we were satisfied with the day it was enough. We never really believed a time would come when we wouldn't have this knowledge."

Lydia did make one vain attempt to preserve the words her father used to doctor himself and to help others. While she was still living at home with him she tried to learn things for her own good. "Of course," she explained, "I couldn't read and write Cherokee. So I tried to write it down in English. But I lost the book, and after I left home I forgot all about it. I didn't keep it up."

All four of the Sam children knew their father had books in which he had written down his medicine secrets, both in Creek and in Cherokee. Lydia was certain he had kept a record of everything he had learned. Watt Sam, White Tobacco's brother, who had also been taught by Creek Sam, was supposed to have written records too, but Lydia knew nothing of where his records might be.

While White Tobacco had traveled a fair distance for some of his herbs, most were available near the house, "And he knew quite a few of them." They were kept in a separate building, where they were hung up in bunches.

White people also came to him to be cured. "A lot of them believed in him," she said. He never charged them a fixed amount. Once they saw that the medicine was working, they were free to pay whatever they liked. Most patients came to him at his house, but if they were too ill to travel, he would go to them.

Lydia was only two or three years of age when her mother died, and Archie was just a baby then. She remembered nothing of her mother, and her father raised and taught the children — mostly by example, for he didn't talk much. They lived next to the dance ground, and she mentions that she often saw the shell rattles hung on the fences to dry. Her aunt, Susy Sam, was a shell maker and also a shell shaker for the dances.

On the subject of shell shakers, Lena Screechowl was mentioned. She was a Creek and was so good with the shakers that everyone praised her for the tone and the way she danced. She could be heard above the others, and Lydia said this is because she kept in step with the leader.

Joyce Johnson told us that she knows of a plant that has a pod on it that contains an oil that is rubbed on the shells to make them sound better.

Archie Sam

This stirred a vague remembrance in Lydia, but she admitted that she hadn't been interested enough to give much thought to such ideas. When she was little, she was told that shell shakers had a method of treating the shells before a dance, but she didn't learn what the treatment was. She did recall that in those early days there were sometimes enough shakers to make an entire circle around the fire. All of the dancers lined up with the elders in the inside line, and others according to age were in the lines outside them. The best shakers always led. Moreover, people came more for the dancing than for the eating and visiting. Lydia told us that she had owned the second pair of Carnation milk-can shakers that were ever used at a dance ground. Tiger Buster had made the first pair for his sister, and the second pair for her. This was "back in '35 or '36." It wasn't long before Lydia had an opportunity to sell them but refused because they had been especially made for her and had sentimental value. As long as she had danced she used those cans. Once other women found it hard to get turtles, they too accepted the cans. Mainly, Lydia wanted hers for practice dancing. Other youngsters joined in, and sometimes they would practice all night. "It was a lot of fun, and we had no other entertainment of consequence. We would build our own fire near someone's house who could teach us how to start exactly with the leader's step and on the right foot."

Joyce asked, concerning when they went around the circle, "Doesn't your leg kind of shuffle twice like this, and then you come down hard on your heel — the first one is on the toe and the second on the heel — isn't that what gets the sound?"

Lydia explained that the important part was where you put the shakers. "You have to put them where your muscles are, right here. When you stomp your feet your muscle automatically shakes the shells according to the movement of the leg. The shells or cans should be just on the side and slightly to the back." She had used a soft pad under the leg rattle that covered both the calf and the ankle. Even then "It would eventually slide down and hurt you." Joyce told her about the half-inch-thick foam-rubber pads

she had seen at one dance and said it did an excellent job of holding up the leg rattle. Lydia liked the idea, "because by the time you've gone two or three times around the circle the thongs loosen and the rattle begins to slide down." Some women tie theirs so tight they cut off circulation, and their legs turn purple.

Asked about cooking at the grounds in the old days, Lydia said two women would be chosen to do it. The members would usually donate money to buy a beef or hog, and once in a while someone would donate an animal. Besides this, they would have beans, other green vegetables, bread, and perhaps coffee. People brought whatever they wanted to bring, "Just something like potluck." Cooking was done in large iron pots. Beef was cut into chunks and boiled or fried in pork fat. Pork was boiled. White Tobacco and other men would help with the frying, but the women did all of the boiling. There was a lot of meat, and cooking was begun in the morning while the meat was fresh. About one or two o'clock the meat would be done, and everyone would eat. What was left over was divided equally among the families and kept for their night snack.

If enough members were there early in the morning, they would play ball and after every seven games would have soup drinking. Two or three of the children of families that would come would play ball every Sunday, usually beginning after the noon meal, but sometimes they would play all day long. Once in a while, these families ate together, but not always. For the most part, the children used only their hands to play ball, because the sticks could badly injure someone. Joyce chuckled and told how at a recent game at the Medicine Spring ground, she had seen a woman player leap on a man's back while he was after the ball. And as he carried her the length of the field she sank slowly from his shoulders to his hips to his legs, yet she wouldn't turn loose. Everyone was laughing wildly by the time the goal was reached.

White Tobacco never doctored at the stomp ground anyone who was injured in a ball game. He also joined enthusiastically in the games and loved to dance. "He was interested in people more than anything," Lydia said, "and would dance all night long. Never slept a bit. The rest of the family did the same, but boy, when we got home we were dead to the world."

There were several men White Tobacco could call upon to lead the stomp dance, although he and Watt were the only ones able to lead the animal dances. Even then, Watt did not know all of these, so White Tobacco led most. Regrettably again, nearly everyone else thought this would go on forever and made no attempt to learn the animal-dance songs. "Eli," Lydia said, "my older brother, knew more than any of us. But at his age he forgets too. Then again, once we started to school, we were only home for three months during the summer, and that was all the dances we participated in and could learn anything about."

We wanted to know whether Watt Sam had any children. "He has three living," Lydia replied. One daughter, Sally, had died. None that Lydia knew of carried on the traditions. His oldest daughter, Katie, lived in Tahlequah, the younger son, George, lived in Tulsa, and the older son, John, lived in McAlester, Oklahoma. Lydia did not see them. "If Katie knows anything about the old ways she doesn't talk about it. But when they were kids they used to go to Redbird's ground and belonged to the Keetoowah Society. Watt's children were also sent away to school . . . George and Sally to Sequoyah, and Katie and John to the Chilocco Indian School, which accepted students from various Indian tribes."

In time, even administrators of the Sequoyah School added Choctaws, Creeks, and Seminoles to the Cherokee students who were already there. And some of the mixed bloods had so little Indian blood in them they couldn't be told from whites. Several of the children, such as the Sams', could speak no English when they first started. There was a girl who was assigned to teach Lydia and others, but most of the English was learned through routine usage. "It was hard for me, because I would go home and speak my Cherokee language, then return to school and try to switch to English. It was real hard. Daddy could speak English, but he would never use it to talk to us. He would correct us if we said an English word wrong, but if someone came to visit who only spoke

English, we would have to interpret for him. He wouldn't budge."

When asked if she regretted the way she had been brought up, Lydia quickly replied that she didn't. More than anything else she missed not having a mother. White Tobacco never remarried and really didn't have time to raise the children himself. He had to work at his medicine practice, and Eli, the older brother, was only home for a short time. "Mostly it was just my older sister, Paula, and me and Archie that grew up together. Then, of course, Paula died."

By the time Lydia was big enough to stand on a chair she had to wash the dishes and learn how to cook. "I remember the first biscuits I ever made. I don't know how they tasted, but Dad just bragged on me. I guess he wanted me to learn. But everything we did he bragged on. And, whether anyone taught me or not, I soon learned. Of course, what they taught us in school really helped. But it was different from home cooking, going by recipes and learning how to measure what was in the food. Besides, I had already learned how to boil beans and to fry potatoes and vegetables. It was nothing new to me."

At home they had milch cows, chickens, hogs, and horses. Planted crops consisted of corn, cotton, and feed for the animals. White Tobacco would never let the girls work in the fields. If necessary, he would hire someone to help him and would say, "Girls work in the home, not in the fields." Lydia grew up knowing little about farm work, then married a man who was raised on a farm and couldn't understand why she didn't know more about farming.

Joyce mentioned that Eli had told her about a certain "spirit" who was down around the Medicine Spring ground and how he thought it was the same animal or something that was supposed to have followed the Cherokees over the Trail of Tears, adding that White Tobacco always told people he had to "feed this thing."

Lydia commented that her father used to say that he had buried — she didn't know what it was — something related to this spirit. And he told her this something was supposed to guard the stomp ground and was more dependable to watch over it than any person would be. If a stranger came around, the thing would follow him and make a strange noise. But the thing didn't hurt anyone. "He just scared the people to death." Word among the Cherokees was that a spirit like that had come with the people all the way from Tennessee and Georgia. They heard it walking in the bushes and breathing deeply. And they knew it was protecting them so that some of them would reach their destination. But they didn't know what it was. This thing White Tobacco buried had to be treated at intervals by saying certain words over it, and as long as this was done, Lydia said, "We were never afraid because we were protected."

Like so many other things we'd like to know about, Lydia, whose grandfather had come over the trail, knew only what she had read in books about the dreadful experience, and could tell us nothing. "So many died and so much was lost that the old people didn't want to talk about it."

William Glory

William Glory, who was head, or chief, of the United Keetoowah Band, told us that to be a leader among the Cherokee people one has to be chosen. Regarding the Keetoowahs, William told us they go back many centuries, and that in his opinion it was only when they left the Iroquois confederation that they called themselves by the name that people later translated into "Cherokee." He also says there were seven mother towns in the old Cherokee country and that there were Keetoowahs in each of these towns.

As for the Keetoowahs at the time we visited with William in the 1980s, the United Band had members in all parts of the United States, with 2,260 on the rolls. William said that as a federal corporation created by an act of Congress, the Keetoowah organization had more authority than the tribe itself, and that it was still the most useful and strongest legal entity the Cherokees had. "Even though we do not meet regularly, we are still here," he said.

The society's membership is open to men and women. Once it was only for full bloods, then it admitted half bloods, and finally quarter bloods. "We would like to have our own hospital but can

only use Indian money for this, else we can't discriminate. We are using politics to accomplish this, and we are attempting to put individuals in positions of power."

Concerning the future of the United Keetoowah Band, William said prophecy was being fulfilled. "Right now the leaders are being pushed aside by the younger generation. There was a period when no one would admit they were Cherokee. Then in the early '60s we won that big lawsuit against the government, and now they are coming out everywhere and saying they are Cherokees. But the Keetoowahs are the only ones who are strong and are keeping the traditions. Nevertheless, if we are going to compete with the white man we must have an education equal to his. We should not ask our youth to live entirely in yesterday's way of life. The leaders and the people must keep pace with the times. But the elders need to be appreciated and honored. One man among us, for example, has given himself unselfishly for our cause and to maintain our traditions for 100 years of his life, yet he is ignored by everyone and given no credit."

William's grandfather was a medicine man, wanted William to help him, and trained him about nature and how to use it. William affirms that faith is the basis for success in healing. "One can read in books about healing but without faith can only go through the motions." The healing must be done through living things. "A lot of power is in that running stream of water out there," he said. "Compared to a pond it is a living thing."

As to what one needs to learn, he stated, "When human life comes into this world it brings all it needs with it. But people must use it, else it will lie dormant. By the same token, nature puts life into the water. The water imparts this to the plants, the plants pass it on to the animals, and so forth. So life is a cycle."

He told us that Cherokee full bloods are attached to nature, and that Little People are an example of the life power that is in nature. "If adults and children have the right qualifications and talents, the Little People can and do steal them away from the world and teach them. The Little People can do anything they want to, but they won't teach a child as much as they will an adult."

His grandfather saw the Little People often — sometimes where they lived, and sometimes they came to his house. He told William they were messengers and intermediaries. Usually there was no conversation between the grandfather and the Little People. Sometimes the Little People would come to visit, sit down, stay for awhile, but say nothing. Other times his grandfather would not see them and would only sense their presence. But just by their being there a message was imparted. Later, understanding of what they had come for would dawn on him, perhaps as a premonition. The grandfather would try not to think about the visit, just continue working, and one day the answer would come. On one occasion he felt compelled to go up on a hill and meditate. After awhile a story about the Keetoowahs came into his mind. Later on, he found a record of this exact story in the files of the Oklahoma Historical Society.

William told us that near Salina there is an area where the Little People live. They like to be in areas that abound with such wildlife as rattlesnakes, raccoons, squirrels, and birds. About any time of the year, those who have the right faith can hear them there. He has seen them with his own eyes. They speak Cherokee, but in a dialect he doesn't understand. They have no distinctive features. Except for their size they look like ordinary human beings. Their skin is brown, and they wear a common type of primitive dress. One Little Person he saw wore a leather breechclout but no other clothing. His long, black hair hung loose, and he was using a coiled rattlesnake for a stool to sit on.

Sig Vann

Sig Vann, in 1978, had been a Baptist preacher for twenty-five years and a Cherokee medicine man for twenty years. His church was located about two miles from his house, and the people who attended it really enjoyed it. His parents were Baptist, and as a child he was baptized by immersion in a creek. "In those days we did this whether the water was hot or cold. Nowadays we do it in a house." His folks were raised in this area, and so was he. "I've been here all of my life," he said.

How did he become a medicine man?

He didn't know it was going to happen. Some old people saw that he could do it and began to teach him. The lessons started when he was about fifty years of age and had some gray hair. The first step for anyone who wants to do this is that you have to believe in the medicine — that it will work. The second step is that you must be the right person for the job and have the right attitude. He told us about a certain medicine man who lived in Stilwell, whose medicine was strong and whose specialty was treating snakebites. This man was old and knew that he should train someone to take his place. He had two sons, and five of his medicine-men friends got together and fasted and had visions about whom should be chosen. They told him they had learned that the oldest son was too smart for the job, and that the other son was too greedy and would use the medicine for evil purposes. So they chose his son-in-law, and he accepted that and began the training. It continued for eight years, and the old man died. Still, the son-in-law wasn't ready, so he continued to train by using the old man's notes. He was still not practicing at the time. Sig also told us this. The medicine men say that a healer or conjurer should not in any event practice until he has gray in his hair and has his own family.

Sig claims he can treat any kind of illness, but doesn't begin to doctor anyone until he knows whether God will permit him to treat that person. He talks to God about it, and God knows what kind of treatment is to be used.

"Does he use formulas?"

"I have it in my mind and don't need to say it out loud," he answered. "God is here, and he knows. I use seven prayers, but let me say again that if I offer a long prayer and don't mean it, it won't accomplish anything."

He uses his hands on his patients and does not blow on them with his mouth or a tube. Each patient is treated differently according to the type of illness. Sometimes patients are treated immediately, sometimes after a period of time has passed, and sometimes herbs are used. He bases his decision on how the patient looks and is feeling. For arthritis, one of his treatments is to use his hands after first warming them at a fire. "If," he said, "more people believed in the medicine I could do more than I do." As an example of this, he cited an instance whose details he did not want disclosed in which he healed within a day a hospital patient whom white doctors had not been able to cure. His payment consists of whatever the patient wishes to give him and is rendered after the healing is accomplished. It might be food or it might be money.

He often takes a patient to water, using a nearby creek. Sometimes they just stand on the bank, and he pours the water on. "I know this sounds silly," he says, "but it sure works! I can tell whether a person believes by the way he looks. And if I see that he doesn't I don't treat him. It won't work any more than if I'd go to a white doctor and didn't believe he could heal me."

Does his entire congregation believe in his kind of healing?

"Some do and some don't. There are no whites in the congregation, but there are members who speak only English. These are the ones who are more likely not to believe."

Can he do things other than curing illnesses?

"A white woman came here from Tulsa about three weeks ago. She had lost her husband and son. They just took off one day without saying where they were going. She was crying, and I told her not to. She said the FBI had already looked, and that she had offered a $2,000 reward. She would settle for just knowing they were alive. I went off by myself to find out what the situation was, and learned they were both doing fine. They were off in a certain direction, and she would see them again. I told her that and she was happy. A week later she returned to tell me that everything I had said was true."

In instances like this, Sig sometimes uses a silver coin to gain information. He explained that he can hold it anyplace or over water while he asks his question just one time, and the coin will move in the direction where the lost or absent person or thing is. He goes off alone when he does this because he doesn't like to have anyone watch him. "No one is supposed to find out what you do." He is not training anyone to do this "because it is hard to find the right people."

Sig knows how to make bad medicine, but doesn't use it. People do come to him to have him counteract evil medicine. When he does this, the evil stops. As for medicine men changing themselves into animals in the way the older medicine men are said to have done, Sig says he knows that it is still being done, but hasn't seen it personally.

Joyce mentioned a medicine man who had lived at Pryor about twenty-five years before whose medicine was known to be strong. Bud Welch had told her how this man had come to his house one bitterly cold winter day and stopped long enough to warm himself by the fire. He had only a shirt on, but when he left he refused the offer of a coat. Worried that the man might freeze, Bud went out on the porch and called out to him. But instead of the man there was a big wolf running up the road. Two days later Bud saw the medicine man, and he was perfectly fine.

Sig stated that the strong medicine men are about gone, and added that he doesn't brag on himself because medicine men are not supposed to do this. He doesn't carry medicine with him when he's away from the house. He has made a written record in Cherokee of his work, but hasn't given it to anyone since it is useless to give this to someone who doesn't believe. He said more than one person trained him and all of these were dead now. They usually only trained one person at a time, and that person must study hard and remember everything. Even the herbs were getting harder to find.

He still made a special medicine for those who wanted something they could use to make a certain person love them more. It consisted of black tobacco and a special chant. "I could spend all day telling you about things like this, and I still wouldn't be through," he said. "Suppose a girl hates you and won't see you and you want her to come back and make love to you. Well, that medicine I make works. That's no joke." He explained that it had to have a little twist and be a very old kind. The best variety had short leaves and was raised on a certain hillside. There was only one sacred spot for this, and it was in North Carolina. He had gone there only two months before we talked to him to get some. "I went and stayed a week. If a person smokes enough of it, the one he wants will even cry because they want so badly to see him."

For some of his divining, Sig uses a piece of special animal hide. "When you want to know anything you have to watch it. It will move and will tell you anything. It will write in Cherokee, or you can place money on top of it. You can also hold a string above it and steady your hand and the string will move itself. It is really God who tells you these things. You can't do it by your own power. Nobody is smart enough to do this. You have to have God first, and let him tell you. There's no mistake to it. All you need to do is read His letter. You can ask God just like we are talking now. But you have to go to Him first and not try to do it on your own power. Let Him tell you. Then you have to know how this hide moves, and if you know that then you know what it is saying."

Sig told us how on one occasion the hide had led him to go to the town of Jay, Oklahoma. An old friend there had been hunting for two or three days for a lost horse. No one he asked had seen the animal. When Sig arrived the man told him how he had looked everywhere for the horse, and then decided it may have been stolen. Sig went off into the barn by himself, consulted the hide, and learned that the horse was some 400 or 500 yards off in a certain direction, and dead. When he told his friend, the man laughed at him. But he went over there and looked and found out it was true. Then the friend offered to give Sig anything he asked to teach him how to do this. But Sig didn't want to sell the way. "I'd rather keep it for myself," he said.

At this point in our conversation, Sig lamented that it was sad that the younger generation didn't believe in these things. A lot of the old ones were passing away, and the opportunity to learn it was going with them. No one was being trained, and the knowledge was being lost.

Jim Wolf

Jim Wolf was a medicine man, the head of the Four Mothers' Society, and had the only Four Mothers' dance ground remaining among the Cherokees. His home was in the Rocky Mountain community near Stilwell. He spoke to us almost entirely in Cherokee, and Joyce and his wife, Maudie, served as translators. A good part of our time together was spent in discussing the matter of lands that Cherokees are losing because of non-payment of taxes, and he emphasized that much of his time was occupied in trying to put an end to this.

His dance ground, known as the Rocky Mountain or Four Mothers' or Flint ground, is about a quarter-mile from his comfortable, modern home. It originated with his father shortly after the time Redbird Smith started his ground in 1902. The original fire had been moved four times since its original location "on the other side of Stilwell," the last move to its present location occurring when the old folks were dying out, and Jim wanted it. He told us that he didn't know the dates of the moves, or the previous locations. Only stomp dances are done at the Flint ground, because no one knows how to do the animal dances.

Jim confirmed that Redbird had started his ground as a Four Mothers' ground, and added that all of the Five Civilized Tribes involved in the Four Mothers' movement began grounds at the same time. In 1987, the Chickasaws still had a Four Mothers' ground, but the Choctaws didn't have a ground at all. Jim mentioned that the Nighthawk Keetoowahs still meet at the ground, and that at these meetings the elders bring out their Nighthawk jackets and talk about the old days.

Jim claimed that Redbird's ground had originally only four beds, and explained that while his ground appears to have seven beds, it really only has four, but within these there are seven places for members of the seven clans to sit. The ball pole at the Four Mothers' ground has a ball on its top rather than a fish. The ball is made from a section of walnut tree, and birds have pecked a large hole in it. We saw a group of young people playing on the ground with pairs of ball sticks and were told that the scoring is one point if the ball hits below the painted black band about three-quarters of the way up the pole, four points if it hits between the band and the wooden ball, and five points if it hits the wooden ball.

The leaders of the Four Mothers' ground no longer, as they once did, sacrifice live chickens to the fire. Jim told how, when he was a little boy, his family went to a Fourth of July ceremonial dance at Sugar Mountain. Jim and his brother arose early one morning and were about to have breakfast when they saw an old man come to the fire with four live chickens. He one by one split the chicken's tongues with a knife, then tucked their heads under their wings and fed them to the fire by placing them in a shallow hole in the fire's bed and raking coals over the top of them. Albert Carter had already told us that he had seen chicken sacrifices offered at other grounds but made no mention of the tongue splitting.

When ceremonial stomp dances are held at the Flint ground, they sometimes, but not always, have dinners. Medicine is seldom used, because it is extremely hard to get the herbs and the seven medicine men that are needed to do it correctly. Besides, there are often not enough people attending to make it worthwhile. In Jim's opinion, the medicine doesn't affect the success of the dance anyway. He believed it is not directly connected with the dance and is instead related to the well-being of the people. "It strengthens them." When they do have the medicine, it is taken at the end of the dance and at sunrise. Then the people who have taken it carry away with them the good effects of the dance, and this lifts them up during the following days and causes them to be good to one another. Jim insisted that at Redbird's ground also the medicine was given after the dance had ended, and just once a month. Maudie inserted here, "If people would come, we would use it more often and we would all be stronger."

The Wolfs were trying their best to keep the ground going and they didn't want to lose it through indifference or unbelief. "But white influence is causing the younger generation to lose faith in it,

although more teenagers are taking part than did a few years ago." One of the Wolfs' sons had vowed he intended to learn how to care for and to continue the ground. There are also twenty-three grandchildren that are being encouraged to take part, and the extended family alone is enough to keep the ground going "if they will only do it." But, there is no one being trained right now. Also, the grandchildren do speak little or no Cherokee, and they are not trying to learn it.

"They are ashamed to speak Cherokee," Jim lamented, "and say it's boring."

Jim was aging and ready to retire, although when someone came to him for treatment he still did it. "But," Maudie said, "when he's gone I don't know what we are going to do."

As for knowing how to move the fire, Jim told us he could do it if he needed to, but that he didn't plan on it. The fire would remain where it was.

When we left, Maudie told us that Jim would be glad to tell us a lot more if we only had someone who could translate it well enough. She explained that her father was a white man, and that it was only after her mother had died that her mother's grandmother had taught her to speak Cherokee. So she wasn't competent to translate all Jim wanted to say. It was an insight that seemed to sum up in a general way the problems facing those Western Cherokees who believe the ground should be continued.

Dance Grounds

Since the ongoing stomp dances and dance grounds represent the clearest continuation of the old Cherokee culture, I was anxious to learn as much as I could about them, and since no one else has done it, to record this for posterity. Fortunately, the Cherokee ground chiefs and the ground members were exceedingly gracious and cooperative in providing this information, and my hopes were more than satisfied.

To begin, let me say that Evans cannot be faulted for having, in 1835, reported that Cherokee dancing was not as exciting to watch as was Plains Indian dancing. This is only true if the viewer fails to find it exciting to see a people of such an exalted history who, as they dance, leave the present and slip slowly back into time . . . to a time when they see again with inner eyes and remember they are a part of a great nation at the time of its glory. In their mind's eye the dancers are immersed in the splendid ancient cycle of annual festivals, and Evans simply missed the point. Those who wish to avoid the same thing happening to them as they watch the Cherokees dance today must know what is happening in the dancing and understand it well.

As of 1978, there were in Oklahoma four Cherokee active ceremonial dance grounds, plus one practice ground. The term for a dance ground is *Gateo Unalas Deske,* which means something like, "stomp and singing ground and ball field." The Stokes ground seemed to be the strongest of the five grounds, because it had enough men to fill the offices, tend the fire, lead the dances, play ball, make the medicine, and in general to carry on the old traditions. Because of this, we gave it our primary attention. The Stokes leader, or chief, was William Smith, a small, serene man with drifting eyes who wore denim jeans, a colorful cowboy shirt, cowboy boots, and chewed tobacco. Its members were the only ones to hold ball games, dances, and feasts during the winter months — although these might last for only a few hours rather than all night. And they were the only ones who met every month.

Stokes included an accumulation of Cherokees who once attended one of the earlier twenty-three grounds whose fires had died out when the memberships were no longer sufficient to support them, and new members at Stokes were being received regularly, the only stipulation being that they must be Indian. Stokes was, at that moment, the newest of the grounds, and it had been formed in the mid-1950s by Stokes Smith. The coals for its fire were taken from the Redbird Smith ground.

The music at Stokes seemed less affected by Creek influences than at the Redbird and Medicine Spring grounds. And the Cherokee language was used more often than it was at the other places.

The Stokes ground functioned as both church and community center for its members, and the reverent way the members felt about the ground was expressed by William Smith at an annual celebration in July of Redbird's birthday:

We first want to welcome you to this annual event in commemoration of the great chief Redbird Smith's birthday. This is an annual event, and it takes a tremendous amount of work to plan, prepare, and notify people. And we are certainly happy to see such a great turnout.

We want to enjoy this celebration. The dance and song are going on throughout the night. We want the children to enjoy everything these people have planned. In doing so we are asking your cooperation in every way possible. In asking for your cooperation we are also including conduct, that it would be in a manner acceptable — as if you might be in a churchyard in whatever denomination you might belong to. This is the kind of cooperation and respect that we would like to have.

So many times in ceremonies of this nature many fun seekers, people who want to go out for a lot of fun, bring with them certain indulgents like alcohol. We want to make this clear — that we do not allow beverages of this nature on the ground. And if it be the case that some individual is on the ground, there have been people who have been designated to watch for this, to look for things like this. And they are instructed, if they find an individual like this who has been indulging, to approach the individual in the most hospitable manner, the kindest and fairest way they know how to communicate with the individual. And the individual is allowed to leave and go to places where they do allow for intoxicants to be taken into the system.

Please remember that the dances and celebration at this ceremonial is an ancient thing. It was true in the East similar celebrations were conducted down through the years. And today we still can come and enjoy an Indian Cherokee Keetoowah Society ceremonial.

And I believe that a fellowship of this nature for all people who would like to go to a place like this have the right to enjoy the fellowship of your kinsman or the fellowship of the strangers you might meet at a place like this. These are the rights that are extended to you, not by this organization only, but it happens to be the civil and basic human rights that everybody has. So please let us have your cooperation and your good conduct. Thank you.

The Stokes Smith ground has been known by two earlier names: the Illinois District Council ground and the Buffalo District Council ground.

The dance ground represents in the Cherokee mind the ancient town sacred square, and the sacred fire serves as the center and focal point for all activities. The sacred fire itself sits on top of what appears to be a mound of compacted ashes about three feet high and ten feet in diameter. An iron rod that stands upright on the east side of the mound is used to tend the fire and serves as a leaning post for those making speeches. As was done in ancient days, four green logs that are never allowed to be consumed during a ceremony are placed around the fire in such a way that one tapered end is on the edge of the fire, and the other ends of the logs radiate out and point toward the four cardinal directions. Around the fire is a broad, smooth, square area that is leveled and used for dancing, speech making, ritual smoking, and other formalities. Around the perimeter of this broad area are placed the clan beds, or houses. There may be seven of these, or four, in which case more than one clan will share a bed. Some Cherokees believe that all of the grounds started with four beds, and that sometime after 1930 the number was increased to seven. Each of the clan beds measures about nine by twelve feet, and has a gabled, shingle roof, no walls, and three or four plank or split-log bench-type seats. Behind three of the beds at Stokes are additional seats, with room between these and the bed seats to build a warming fire in the winter. The origin of the clan bed is uncertain. It appears that it came into existence sometime after the town council house was no longer a focal point for community activities. It could be an adaptation from another of the southeastern tribes. Again, the clan bed may, among the Cherokees, be no more that a way of reinstating the clan concept and after that a means of preserving it.

At Stokes, to the west of the ceremonial area and on a lower elevation is the tall ball pole, looking something like a slender telephone pole that tapers toward the top. On the peak of the pole is a four-foot-long, crudely carved, unpainted wooden buffalo fish, or garfish. To the north of the ceremonial area is a cooking and eating site, and east of this is a storage house, some ten feet square, where the pots for medicine making are kept. Sometimes this storage house serves as a meeting place for the men when they want to have a private talk.

Outhouses are located at the northeast and the northwest of the eating area, and there is a small branch creek about a hundred yards west of the square. Camping and parking areas are on the south side of the ceremonial area.

The Stokes ground has running water and electric lights. There is a long shelter and table for communal eating, and there are huge cast-iron pots for cooking on old wood-burning stoves. The only areas cleared of weeds are the sacred square and the ball field. Most of the original trees remain.

Ball games are played every Sunday, unless the weather is bad or a Saturday meeting is scheduled. On Saturdays, ball play is done in the afternoon. Ball games and medicine taking precede all of the night dances. With one exception, soup drinking, usually *Kanuchi,* is indulged in after every seven ball games. Sometimes ball games are postponed, so the soup drinking is not done every Saturday. In warm weather, additional dances are sometimes done. Those who desire these can ask the ground chief to hold them. Notification as to when dances will be held is by word of mouth only, although in instances of postponement or on those occasions when special dances are to be held, William will send a card to those who live some distance away. It is said that the ground members maintain such close contact with one another that everyone knows when something apart from the usual will be done.

The Stokes organization still attempts to follow the old Nighthawk Keetoowah constitution. It has the required officers, consisting of a chief, an assistant chief, a councilman and a medicine man from each of the seven clans, a treasurer, secretary, interpreter, and a speaker who relates, when it is necessary, the purposes of the society. No person is eligible for office if he does not speak the Cherokee language and is not an Indian. He does not have to be a full blood. A man who is married to a white woman may not hold office. In the past, such a man was not even allowed on the ceremonial ground. But now he can attend and dance. The rule is justified by concern about divided loyalties. "A Cherokee man who marries a white woman might not approve of the Keetoowahs," it is said.

As stated by William Smith, the primary purpose for the present meetings at the ground is to hold the ceremonials, to sing the "Great Spirit songs," and through the fire to call on the Great Spirit in prayer. When the leaders have set the time to meet at the ground, they are required to notify the chief fire keeper to light the fire early on the morning of the day the meeting is to be held. This fire must be started with flint rock and a certain punk. Once the meeting has begun, or as they put it, "worship is being held," fire keepers must keep the fire going. They "feed" it a certain offering and must pray for blessings while they do so. The leaders also pray and ask for blessings, and anyone who wishes to may join them.

Once the ground chief has decided what to use for the offering that is to be fed to the fire, the fire keepers must try to obtain it. According to William Smith, this should be a meat offering, but sometimes tobacco is used instead.

At one of the Stokes dances, the first speaker was Robert Bush from Marble City, who prayed for a long while. Then C. Smith, who lives at Vian, a brother to William, spoke. The fire keeper was a red-haired boy from Marble City. Once the prayers and speeches were finished, offerings were collected, a record of which was kept in a book.

Dance leaders for that night were Bill Fields, Bill Johnson, a Creek Indian, Woody Christy, Frank Tee Hee, and Bill McLemore, who was thirty-five years old and was studying to be a medicine man. Betty Smith, William Smith's wife, was the head shell shaker, and there were another Creek and two aged Seminole leaders who had also come to the Stokes ground to lead in singing.

At this dance, we saw something we had not seen before — ritual smoking. In the wintertime and at monthly meetings, ritual smoking is done during the day, but in the summer it is done in the evening at the monthly meeting and prior to the stomp

dance. The ground chief usually prepares the pipe, but he was absent on this occasion, and Robert Bush did it. The pipe and a bag of tobacco had been placed on the mound near the upright iron rod. As Robert said a reverent prayer, he picked the pipe and bag up, filled the pipe, then lighted it with a coal taken from the fire. While he did this, the members remained seated in their clan beds, but at the conclusion of the prayer they quietly arose and began to form a huge circle in the square. Members of one clan led off, indicating that they are the main clan at the ground, and as they passed the next clan bed its members fell in behind them, and so on until the beds were empty and a single line had formed around the square. Robert stood to the east of the fire, and smoked seven puffs on the pipe while holding the bowl level and pointing east. He then rotated the pipe in a counterclockwise movement and handed it to the person behind him, who moved up to take his place. The pipe itself never moved from its position. Instead, the circle of people moved slowly counterclockwise until everyone who wished to smoke had come to where the pipe was and smoked it, including women and children. When the pipe ran out of tobacco, Robert refilled it and relit it just as he had at the beginning of the ceremony.

Some of the people drew in deep drafts, and you could see the smoke rising very clearly from their mouths. Others, especially children, drew short drafts. After each person had smoked his seven puffs, he turned to his right and resumed his place in the circle. The last man returned the pipe to Robert, and Robert turned to face the fire. He knocked the pipe's remaining ashes onto the fire as a sacrifice, said another prayer, and returned the pipe to its prior position on the ash mound. The line of people walked counterclockwise until the clan members had reached their beds. They stood here until the chief said another prayer, then they sat down, and the ritual smoking was completed.

While it is often noisy at the ground, with everyone visiting, dancing, running, yelling, and talking, it was extremely quiet during the tobacco ritual. Even the children kept silent, and it became a truly beautiful moment. Everyone knew this was

Girl putting on turtle shakers and preparing to dance at the new Tenkiller Lake ground inaugurated on October 21, 1978.

tobacco that had been ritually treated by the medicine men, that it was supposed to cement peace and friendship, and that it would bring good luck to the people who belonged to the ground.

The emetic medicine can be taken shortly after noon or anytime during the afternoon. Members fast before receiving it, and a meal follows its taking. Usually, four lines are formed to the west of the pot — two of men and two of women. The medicine pot itself is positioned just north of the fire and west of the cooking area. A medicine man dips out the liquid with cans. Some members only drink it, while others drink part of it and use the rest to bathe their hands, face, and chests. Some people fill small vials with it and take these home for private use later on. It is a rule that a person always faces east while he drinks the medicine.

Willie Jumper, who formerly was the head medicine man at Sugar Mountain and is now deceased, gave us a list of the ingredients used in the medicine along with some instructions for the proper preparation and use of it.

They use a small, red root of Cherokee huckleberry, which some call snakeroot, which is not the real huckleberry the whites know of, and add flint weed — a wood medicine that is a red willow wood. This red medicine is the basis for many of the medicines that the medicine men use — most will have red root in them. Also used are pine and cedar leaves. The root, weed, and leaves are placed in a pot of water and boiled. Then the brew is set aside to cool, and the medicine men start working on it. They blow on it through a cane tube, then insert the tube into the liquid and make bubbles. When they have done this four times, it is ready to drink — which means it is pure medicine. Only one piece of cane is used. The medicine men share it.

When you drink the medicine, it makes you throw up and cleans out your insides. It purifies you, and a teaspoonful assures good health. You must drink it while it is warm. If you drink more than a teaspoon you will throw up after two or three minutes. If you are not in good health, the medicine will lie on your stomach and bother you. If you are in good health it won't bother you. And if you can

stand a full drink without throwing up you know that your health is very good.

Certain medicine men are "stronger" than others and can make a stronger medicine that works faster. "You are," one informant says, "supposed to throw it up because it is going to clean out your system one way or another. You can tell the ones who have not taken it before, because they don't know how to use it and throw it, and they have to run to the outhouses because it works as a laxative."

At the Stokes ground, the tobacco that is used for protection and good health is prepared for everyone at the same time. A shallow box that sits on the east side of the fire and measures two feet wide by four feet long is lined with deerskin and then filled with a mixture of homegrown and ordinary tobacco. Each family brings a sack and receives a share. Cherokee medicine men commonly recommend the tobacco of the Stokes ground for those who are in need of some.

As previously mentioned, the Stokes ground follows the Keetoowah constitution. It is customary that when a married man becomes a member, his wife and children join also. Regarding initiation, the constitution says the following:

> He shall come to the fire to be initiated and shall stand where there are four corners, all members including women and children. The principal chief shall attend and stand on the east side. Second chiefs shall stand on the west side, and the captains. And he shall enter through the gate, and one captain shall lead him through. And the second chief shall accept him. The chief then shall lead him towards the fire. Then the fire keeper shall accept him. Then the captain shall lead him to the principal chief, bringing him to where he stood, and shall be accepted there and instruct him. He shall prove he has joined of his own accord. And after his acceptance then the captain shall lead him seven times around the fire. And then he shall be shown to his clansman seat. He shall then be placed among all the members standing, and they shall all shake his hands, accepting him as a member.

There are about ten shell shakers at the Stokes ground. They usually take turns, with two or three of them dancing at one time. If, however, the leader wishes, they might all dance at the same time. If an older man who is respected and is a good leader leads a dance, it is the custom for everyone present to join in. In such instances, there may be as many as ten circles formed around the fire, with the inner circle being the smallest and the outer circle the largest. Whether or not a man is a good leader can be told by the number of dancers and shell shakers who follow him. Sometimes a woman stomps so hard she has to leave the dance line to tighten the ties on her shakers. She might return immediately, or another shell shaker might move up to take her place.

William has several pairs of old terrapin-shell leg rattles that he loans to women who have none of their own. Older Cherokees say that in earlier years on a day before a dance, one would drive along a road and see dozens of shell rattles hanging out on the fences. Exposure to the sun helps the tone.

Leg rattles may have anywhere from six to fourteen shells, with the smaller number being worn by little girls, although it is said that more make it easier for a learner, since you don't need to stomp so hard to make the sound. Comments are often made about the capabilities of the shakers. If one is very good, other dancers will say, "You ought to see her shake the shells," or, "She can really shake shells."

To do the job right you must know exactly when to stop and start and when to reverse directions. The steps must be executed in such a way as to sound out loud and clear in close conjunction with the leader's song accents. If even one of the shell shakers misses this, the comment will be heard, "She doesn't know how to shake shells." Also if there are good shakers and a good leader and they are doing a new dance, the spectators will stand up in front of their beds and watch appreciatively.

Technically, the last stomp dance ends the night's activities, although the Old Folks' Dance is yet to come, and some of the traditionalists say that the dancing as a whole is a time to enjoy yourself, for the dance is not part of the ritual. The ritual proper consists of what has taken place beforehand — the ball game, the medicine taking, the smoking of the pipe, and the speeches. "Then you are supposed to have a good time at the dance. This is the time for

having fun," they say. Yet it is obvious that by the nature of the dances, far more than fun is derived from them.

Dances usually begin around 9:00 or 9:30 p.m. and continue throughout the night. The reason for this is that God can see the fire more plainly at night and in seeing it knows that his Cherokee children have not forgotten him and are following him. The caller calls the people together and the speeches and announcements are made. Then the money needed to defray expenses is collected. After this, the caller calls for the leaders, shell shakers, and dancers. The first dance is always the Friendship Dance. Then stomp dances are held until sunrise. As the sun comes up the last dance is held, which is always the Old Folks' Dance. Then there is a prayer, and everyone goes home.

Since most of the ground members live close to the ground, they return home to rest after the ritual is completed. Those who have come from far away go to their tents, vans, or campers, some of which are hooked up to electrical outlets. At dark, which in the summer is around 8:30 p.m., they begin to reassemble near the dance area, although those who are in vehicles might remain there, talking quietly. Some of the men stand in small groups and visit, and the women sit in small circles of chairs and do the same. The fire is already burning, and the pungent smell of the smoke permeates the air. About 9:00 or 9:30 p.m. the caller calls out to the people to assemble, and the fire keeper stokes up the fire. More logs are piled on, and the sparks shower like clouds of fireflies high into the sky. Large logs are used, and they are built up in a cone shape. Before the stoking, "It is a nice fire, not a high fire. Then a high fire is made for dancing." As the call to come and dance rings out, you can hear car doors opening and closing, and the shuffle of feet moving toward the dance square. Visitors set up chairs in front of their vehicles, while members go to their clan beds. A few people may talk softly, but most are silent. Those who do talk follow the custom of speaking in Cherokee.

When everyone is ready, the chief of the ground gives what might be described as a sermon in which he admonishes the people to follow the old Keetoowah ways. He says that to sing and dance all night, raising the song up to heaven with the smoke, is God's way. He tells them he prays to God to teach the adults and the children the ways to sing. He cautions everyone to be good and peaceful, and to cause no trouble at that ground. He asks them to be honest, and to join in the ceremony.

As stated, the money for upkeep and food is then collected. The treasurer counts it carefully and, as all of the officers look on, records it in his book. On those occasions when a member has had a severe illness or some serious misfortune, another offering is taken to help the member out. When the collecting and recording are done, the chief makes a public announcement of the amount collected.

The chief then turns the meeting over to the fire keepers, who call for the dancing and singing to begin. The calls and the speeches used by the chief and the keepers at this time are unusual in that they have a musical tone and do not sound like normal speech. "They are not songs, and they are not magical formulas. They are just kind of a prayer within a speech. They start on a low pitch and then rise and fall and rise and fall. It almost sounds musical."

When they call out in Cherokee for the dance leaders, a rough translation goes like this: "In this place here tonight we are walking. Now sing while we go into the air. Here comes the Number One singer."

When they call in Cherokee for the shakers they say, "Dance, hurry, turtles, turtles, turtles, hurry! Hurry, turtles!"

The caller chooses the leaders by going around and talking to them. He mingles with the crowd and talks to them. He asks a man if he wants to lead, and if he does not wish to, the caller goes on to another man. Usually, as he makes his choices, a *"Yo! Yo!"* is heard from the others, which means, "Good! Good!" or "Yes!"

When the night grows long and the dancers begin to tire, the caller will oftentimes liven things up by selecting a leader who knows how to lead a dance in a special way. Once he has picked this

leader, he moves to the east side of the fire and calls for the first seven men to come forward. Usually, the assistant fire keeper echoes this call. Then one or both of them calls for the shell shakers. If the women are slow to move, the caller will yell, "Turtles, hurry up, hurry turtles!"

The Friendship Dance at Stokes ground was usually led either by Ed Grass or Houston Tee Hee. Whichever one led, the other served as his second. The dance itself had an introduction, then seven songs that are separated with a refrain and a stomp dance. Archie Sam sang as many as fourteen verses for the Friendship Dance, and it is usually a very long song, in fact the longest song they dance to, and some members need to stop now and then "just to survive." At times the friendship song is begun at the ball pole and "brought into the ground." When this is done it means that everyone is welcome to come and dance, including Creeks and Seminoles. The custom may in fact be derived from a Creek form. Also, at some of the present-day Creek grounds, visitors are not allowed to dance until after midnight, and at some of the older grounds visitors must get the chief's permission to dance with the members. "Each ground," they say, "has its own rules, so when you go into a ground and you are not familiar with these it is best to wait until after midnight to dance. Until then, only members are free to participate."

Between the first and the last dances at Stokes the stomp dances are held. On occasion they also do the Horse, the Gar, the Mosquito, or the Double-head dances. It depends on whether or not they have a leader for these. Most of the leaders do not know the songs, for the animal and clan songs have been forgotten by most. It is for this reason they mostly dance the stomp dance, and if the others are done it is after midnight, since they are "variety" dances, and are employed to liven things up when the people get tired.

Once the fire keeper has called for the dance leaders, the men enter from the west side of the square. They advance single file to the east side of the fire, and prepare to dance the Friendship Dance. They line up behind the leader, facing east, with their backs to the fire. The women take positions in another line that is closer to the fire and stand between but slightly behind the men, also facing east.

After the men sing the introductory part of the song, the leader gives a signal with his hand rattle, and the women take positions in line so that they alternate with the men, with the shakers in front, and the other dancers following. While the rest of the first verse is sung, the women and men join hands and walk in a counterclockwise circle around the fire.

The leader's hand rattle is important because he uses it to direct the dance. By making certain sounds with it, he can tell them what the next verse will be and can control the tempo. The dancers always pause between one verse and the next. Verses are introduced by the use of the rattle and certain voice sounds only, and the men echo what he says. During each verse the dancers move in a counterclockwise circle. When all of the verses have been sung, everyone pauses while the leader lays his rattle down by the fire. Then the dancers drop their hands and, walking at a natural pace, circle the fire. At this point the leader introduces a double-time stomp dance, and it completes the Friendship Dance.

Women use only one kind of dance step, while men use three. One of these is a natural walk. Another is a flat-footed stomp. The third is a flat-footed kind of hopping step that is done in place. Each one is a response that shows the men are in tune with the leader and know what he is doing or about to do.

At Stokes, the men use hand movements, but as a rule the employment of hands in conjunction with the rattle sounds depends upon the ground. Some don't use them at all. The Stokes leader uses gestures to signal the changes, stops, and starts in the dances. When he raises his hand above his head with the palm facing forward, it means that the end of the song is drawing near. The shell shakers change their step to a flat-footed sort of jump, and the men also jump flat-footed. This usually happens about ten beats before the end of a song.

Another hand movement by the leader is related to the sacredness of the fire, and the men who

are in the inner dance circle repeat it as they turn to face the fire. Their foot movements are from side to side so that they are circling the fire sideways as they extend their hands toward the fire, raise them to the sky, and then lower them. "They are praising the Lord." Then they turn around and dance counterclockwise for one verse, after which they turn again to the fire and repeat the hand movement. All the while they are doing this the leader is singing part of a song, and the men echo it. At other times during the dance, the dancers will hold hands. At the end of a Stokes stomp dance the leader gives a hand signal, and the shell shakers give a single, sharp shake. Everyone slows down, and another shout, usually from the men, marks the end of the song. A long, high-pitched shout of approval follows, and everyone says, *"Ha do, wa do,"* which means "Thank you." The leader might say this also.

In a few moments the caller calls for the next leader, and the dance cycle is repeated. Each stomp song, depending upon who leads it, can take from three to fifteen minutes.

Another kind of stomp dance is called a Stake Dance by the Creeks but a Friendship Dance by the Cherokees. About halfway through this the leader signals with his hand or rattle and everyone joins hands. Then he walks away to the ball pole with everyone following him in a long line. They form a circle around the pole, facing it, and in unison sing a slow prayer song. When there is no ball pole, they form this circle just outside one corner of the dance square. Either way, after the song and still holding hands, they return to the square, where they perform a fast kind of double stomp. When the line is long, those at its end often have difficulty keeping up, because when the leaders turn the corners they really swing the ones on the end.

In a variation of this Friendship Dance, the leader moves around the dance circle and about every sixth person raises his arms and weaves in and out around the other dancers. Then at a signal they return to their places, and the dance ends.

The Old Folks' Dance is everyone's favorite. To begin this, the dancers line up around the fire in the same way they do for the stomp dance. At Stokes,

William Smith led this dance. At the Medicine Spring ground, Archie Sam always led it. During the first part, as the dancers walk around the fire, the leader sings "Ya Ho" four times. After each phrase, the men whoop. Everyone participates in this final dance. "It is a ritual one always does, because it is supposed to keep you healthy and to bring you back for the next ritual. A dancer never cuts across the square to get to his seat. If he finishes up some distance from his seat, he must continue around the circle until he reaches it. Cherokees believe you are cutting your life short every time you cut across."

In the Old Folks' Dance they sing "Hi Yo Ho" many times. The number varies from twelve to twenty-one. The leader determines the amount. But each time he sings this, the men answer in kind. During this time they are all dancing the stomp dance, and the shell shakers are doing double shakes. During the third part of the song the leader sings, "Yo, Ho," four times, and each time the men answer, "He, He." The dance ends with a shout of approval, and the chief of the ground offers a prayer and a speech. At this point, they all go to their camps or to their homes. "The ceremony has been held, and the Great Spirit songs have been sung. And he has been called upon in prayer through the fire."

Terrapin shells are the preferred and most widely used leg rattles. These are the ancient type, but at some ceremonial grounds the shells have been replaced by five-and-one-third-ounce evaporated-milk cans. The Stokes ground will not allow the use of these. One of the older members said, "God did not give us the cans, so that is our reason for not using them." But those grounds which do not have a sufficient supply of terrapin-shell rattles allow the use of cans. Yet in any dance those women with the shells go first, and those with the cans bring up the rear.

The whole shells of small terrapins are used, and quarter-inch holes are drilled in the backs at one-inch intervals. Flint, river gravel, or even marbles are inserted, but river gravel is considered the best. Sandstone is avoided by knowledgeable shaker makers, since it deteriorates rapidly and has a fuzzy sound. The rectangular backing, or pad, to which the shells are attached can be leather or cloth. Some we have seen are pieces of blanket, others are the tops of old high-button shoes or engineer's boots, and Archie Sam used the tops of worn cowboy boots to make some of his. A standard-sized pad for a woman would be eight-and-one-half by twelve-and-one-half inches. The pad must be a thick and substantial one, and since the shells themselves are quite heavy, it takes a brave woman to use twelve or fourteen. The average number worn at the Stokes ground is eight.

The shells are tied to the pad with leather thongs and are placed side by side and one above the other, so that a shaker having nine shells would have three rows in each direction. The pads are narrower at the bottom than at the top, so as to fit the leg, and the shells have the head end pointed upwards since they are larger at this end than at the tail. Four leather thongs are attached by one end to the corners of the pad and are used to tie the shaker to the leg. Each string wraps twice around before it is tied. Some women use an additional thong that reaches above the knee and keeps the shaker from slipping down. Usually, these are the shakers with the most shells. All women first wrap their calves with something — a piece of blanket, or quilt, or towel — and put the shakers on over this. We have seen younger girls who used foam-rubber padding. Over this the shaker is tied so that the greater number of shells are on the outside of the leg. Since the shakers are continually working loose during a dance, they are tied on very tightly and affect circulation, yet they are worn throughout the night. Some of the older women who have stomp danced all of their lives have permanent marks on their legs to show for it.

There is a medicine that is rubbed on the inside of the pad and sprinkled on the shells "to make them sound louder." A certain kind of berry is used for this, and it is applied one time only on the morning of the dance. Another medicine is made from black seeds that are soaked overnight in water. When this is rubbed on the shells, "It keeps the shells from going dead."

Terrapins that are to be used for dance shells are gathered alive and kept alive until they are needed. The insides are removed by running a knife blade along the inner surface of the shell, cutting as close to it as possible. The shell is not supposed to be scarred, and the meat closest to it is carefully scraped out. Informants told us that only the female turtles are used for the shakers. We wanted to know how one told the difference between a female and a male and learned that when you pick a male up and he pulls back into his shell, the rear parts of the shell will also close tightly together. The female shell does not close tight, leaving a gap between the top and bottom sections of nearly a half-inch. I found myself wanting to see a turtle do this, and if it doesn't, some biologist will surely write and tell me so.

The turtle innards are cut out while the turtle is still alive. Eliza Sumpka told us that the turtles are taken back into the woods where first a ceremony is done, and then the meat is removed. "The hearts are still beating." After the final scraping, the shells are washed, dried, and then soaked in Pine Sol to keep the odor down. People who do not know how to do this correctly invariably have shell-odor problems they cannot get rid of. Also, inexperienced people use both the western and the eastern box turtles, while the older Cherokees who manufacture shakers use only the eastern box turtles that are so plentiful in the Cherokee hills. Of late, a certain kind of spotted turtle from the west has been used by a few people who make their own shakers.

When a shell shaker shakes her rattles correctly, the steps are such as to cause the pebbles to move vertically, giving off a soft sound as they hit the top and a loud sound at they hit the bottom.

Lydia Sam McLure told us about the first set of milk-can rattles ever made, and in 1978, Archie Sam had these in his possession. Around 1928, Archie said, a group of Cherokees from the Notchietown community started a practice stomp ground. Since they were short of terrapin-shell shakers, Tiger Buster made for his sister the first set of milk-can shakers. He told Archie that he had spotted these cans in a trash pile and took them to White Tobacco Sam, who was the chief of the ground. White Tobacco approved of them, and the shakers were made. Later, people from other grounds saw them in use and duplicated them.

Each of the two shakers has twenty of the five-and-one-third-ounce milk cans attached to it — forty for the pair. The cans are tied together with baling wire so that the first row forms a semicircle. There are four rows of five cans each. Each can has forty evenly spaced nail holes in it, with thirty-two knife slits made in vertical lines between the rows. Holes made in the tops and bottoms of the cans were used to empty the cans and to string them together with buckskin thongs. Each can contained enough small stones to cover the bottom of the can, and one informant told us that he uses a snuff can full of pebbles for each milk can.

Those first pairs of shakers weighed about six pounds each, and the women who wear the cans today say they are much easier to use than the shells. They are lighter and do not come undone as easily. They are also easier to tie onto the leg.

The hand rattles used by the dance leaders are made from gourds, turtle shells, or coconut shells. They are not used for every dance — only for certain songs — whereas the shell shakers are always in use.

Eli Sam showed us how he used his coconut-shell rattle. He held it firmly in his right hand and, while he deftly rotated the handle, struck the shell against the palm of his left hand.

Eli's rattle was a very old one, and we were able to examine it carefully. It had on its surface twenty-four quarter-inch round holes spaced two inches apart and arranged in rows. The gravel in it appeared to be river gravel. The original stick handle had broken off, yet what remained was so tightly wedged it couldn't be removed. So Eli drilled other holes in the top and bottom and inserted a drumstick for a new handle. The end of the drumstick that pro-truded through the top was painted red and had black horsehair tied to it with red thread. The handle end had a hole through it to receive a wrist loop that would also be used to hang the rattle up on a wall.

At his Flint ground, Jim Wolf used a gourd rattle fourteen inches long and five inches in diam-eter at the head end. It has no holes in it. The dried seeds served the purpose of the pebbles. Where in one place the gourd was worn through, it was patched with adhesive tape. For storage, it was hung from the ceiling of his house by means of a suction cup taken from a rattlesnake-antidote kit. It is obvious that, unlike the rattles used by some tribes for ceremonial purposes, Cherokee rattles, excepting perhaps those used by healers, are not considered to be sacred objects.

Water drums are not always used for the dances, but one is always present in case the leaders want it. The preferred wood for the drum body is red cedar. Elm is sometimes used, but it splits easily. Crockery vessels used as small butter churns have even been used. groundhog or woodchuck skins are considered best for the drumhead, because they are thin and pliable. Tanned deerskin is a second choice, and even rubber-tire inner tubes might be employed when the skins are not available. For tuning, in the usual instance two inches of water is poured into the bottom of the drum, although one drum maker told us that he fills it to the length of his extended thumb. The top cover is stretched over the opening and most often secured by a hoop made of hickory or metal, although one drum we saw had a thin strip of inner tubing stretched around the head to hold it on.

At the Redbird Smith ground there is a double-headed drum that was crafted by Netche Gray. It has hard rawhide covers that are fastened by nails to a tubular wooden frame that is fifteen inches in diameter. The drumstick is padded. The drummer warms the drum in the sun in the daytime to improve the tone, and at night it is warmed by the fire until the skin stretches tight. When it is beaten, it is held vertically in the drummer's lap.

The drummers at the Four Mothers' Flint ground do not hold their drums in their laps. They stand at the edge of the square and hold the drum waist high by one arm and hand while they use a padded stick in the other hand to beat on it.

Some drumsticks are fashioned from hickory limbs and have knobs at one end. The average diameter of the handle is three-eighths of an inch, and the length is twelve inches. For his drumsticks, Netche Gray used the tip end of a fishing rod, not the old cane, but the modern kind of store-bought rod. He padded these with leather and claimed he could get more action out of them then he could with the stiff sticks.

In the usual dance, the drums are only used a few times. Experienced leaders say there is no reason for not using a drum, and people who would like to can request it. After watching and participating in a number of dances, we concluded that the use of the drum depended to some extent on the shell shakers. If there are a lot of them present, the drum is not needed, for whenever they are short of shell shakers the drum is invariably called upon.

For additional sound, the male dancers on occasion shout and make animal noises to supplement the singing and their repetition of what the leader calls out. Add to this the stomping of the men's feet, the dry-rain sound of the hand, shell, and can shakers, and the hand clapping by men at some points in the songs, and you can imagine what it is like to be at a dance. The women are not allowed to sing, clap, gesture, or play a drum or rattle other than the shell or can shakers, and they always follow the men into the square.

The words sung at the dances are not definable. Some of the words are only phonetic sounds with no meaning. Dance leaders told us that while the words had meaning long ago, they were sung in a language intended only for religious songs so that ordinary people would not know what was being said. No one alive knows the true meanings. "It has been lost for a long time." The leaders do know which sounds are animal, or clan, or gospel. They can tell you which ones belong to a stomp dance, a hymn, a gospel song, a medicine song, or a magic song. But what they are singing are songs that have been passed down for so long a time that the exact meanings are lost.

But guesses are made. One leader we talked to feels that a fair translation of a portion of the sounds of one song is as follows: The leader says, *"He yo who knee he ya,"* meaning, "This is your part," so all of the men answer, *"He o ha, He o ha."* Next the leader says, *"He ya woha le ma,"* which means, "This one you started," and the men say, *"Yo ha, Yo ha, La na, La na."* Then the leader says, *"Ha do ha la na,"* which means, "Start it quickly," and the men answer,

"Yo ha, Yo ha." All of this is repeated either four or seven times. Then the leader says, *"Ya lo sa le hey,"* which means, "God."

In another song the leader says, *"Hey de wa, Yo na,"* which means, "Taught me," and the men answer, *"Yo ha, La na"* and *Day ka, No ho gay do,"* which means, "Song the way it went." And the leader says, "It's beautiful." So what is being said is, "Taught me song is beautiful; song the way it went; God taught me." It is, this individual says, one of the few songs we can actually translate into present-day Cherokee.

One leader may use obscure Cherokee words and another leader only phonetic sounds. Each leader also makes his own choices as to how many times and in what way he sings these.

A man in his eighties told us that when he was little, because of the similarity in sounds, he and other children would be told by their parents that all of the songs really meant was, "Catch a white man and throw him in a fire."

Most of the songs are religious: "You go through a prayer and it is like singing a gospel song."

A younger member at one ceremonial ground said that some songs had translatable words, but only God could understand the others. He believed that some of the old people really knew the meanings of the songs, but did not know the words. He also said that he and some others were trying to find out what these words really meant.

We did discover two explanations for the animal cries. One is that they are done when the dancers are excited, happy, and having a good time. The other is that the men do them according to their clan affiliation.

At all of the grounds, the numbers four and seven are controlling factors. Seven male singers start every dance, and the phrases are repeated four or seven times. Some grounds that once had four clan beds now have seven. Possibly the four beds were used during the period of the deemphasis of the clan, then changed to seven during the Redbird Smith revival of the clan rule. There are the four directional logs at the fire. The members stand in four lines to take the medicine. Seven puffs are smoked on the pipe. During initiation, the fire is circled seven times. At the Stokes ground, seven points are scored when the fish atop the ball pole is hit. A soup feast is held after every seven ball games.

Harmony and peace receive particular emphasis at dances. There is to be no conflict or fighting. If a dance is not going right, if the beat is off, or if the leader or shakers feel something is wrong, the song will be ended early. Sometimes they will stop in the middle of a song and wait. "Everything must fit in harmoniously and everyone must know what to do and do it right." The singing must be done in unison, and one must not come into it late.

"This," Joyce said, "is what Archie is stressing about our ground right now. It is a practice and not a sacred ground because we are not strong enough as a group to be what is required to have a sacred ground. There must be a certain feeling . . . and I admit that it works to have this feeling. There are nights when it seems that everything and everyone is so beautiful. The fire is so bright that you can see the outline of every dancer. This is a good fire, and on the best nights it burns more plainly than on the others. The feeling must be one of friendship. If anyone should cause trouble or if there is friction of any kind the dance might stop and not resume until early morning. If the leaders can discover the problem and get rid of it, the dance will go on. If not, it won't. They only continue in a peaceful and harmonious atmosphere."

For most ground members the stomp dance is a vital part of the true Cherokee religion, for only when they dance around the sacred fire and sing the sacred songs do the traditional Cherokees feel they are properly and adequately worshiping the God who first blessed them in ancient times and has, throughout their history, given them continuing life and hope. "This is what we are going for," the people say, and many ground members no longer attend a church. They do read the Bible and can quote it, yet they say they do this only because they see and accept the similarity between their religion and that set forth in the Bible. "Our fire is a bridge between us and God. Mortal man is not perfect enough to directly present himself to God, but the smoke from the fire — and it does not need to be the sacred fire at the grounds — goes up to Him. This is why we smoke the pipe. Its smoke also goes up to God."

There is a certain way that the fire must be handled, moved, or used to start another fire in another location. If these things are not done correctly, the fire in the new location will have no power.

Joyce tells how one night when she went to her ground she could see that Archie was upset about something. Later that night, he told her that someone had "bothered" their fire, and that during the next week he would bring out a medicine man and some of the other men to fast, take medicine, and to sit up all night in an attempt to learn what had happened. Then, before the dancing started that night, Archie brought out a medicine man to sprinkle medicine all around the fire. This was to assure that the dancers would not be harmed in any way.

At the time we were researching, there was a new ground that was opening up at Warner, Oklahoma. When two of the Warner men came to get some of the Medicine Spring coals to use to start their fire, Archie was concerned that the men did not know how to move it properly. His medicine man told him not to worry, for the men drank and were not pure. They did not know how to handle the fire and would be taken care of. When Archie visited Joyce a short time later, she asked about the two men, and he said he had been told that one of them was already dead.

Archie told us there were prescribed rituals and ways for doing all religious things. He doubted there was any man alive who truly knew how to handle the fire and believed it was sad that this had not been taught to someone before it was lost. "Possibly," he said with resignation, "there will be no more fires, because men do not have the knowledge to rekindle or move them."

Of the fires in the Cherokee Nation, three have seven clan beds. Medicine Springs is the only one with four beds. Also, regarding the seven kinds of woods that are to be used in the fire, it is getting harder and harder to locate them, and some fires must be kindled with substitutes.

Rufus Smith, who was the grandson of Redbird Smith and who lived near Stilwell, told us how he felt about the Cherokee grounds and religion and the use of the wampum belts in connection with these:

The stomp dance and fire is religion for the Cherokees just as the churches are religion for the white man. Many people think of the stomp dance as pagan, but we believe in one God who is a spirit just as church people do. And we have our own oral bible that was handed down to us by our ancestors for hundreds of years before we ever heard of the white man. And surprisingly to whites, many of the stories are the same. I don't know why they should be surprised, because God revealed himself to us just as he did to them. We have our own set of commandments just as the white people do, though we have seven rather than ten. Yet the same subjects are covered, for some of the commandments are combined.

A long time ago, God realized that though his people were getting smarter, they were also getting more forgetful. He knew they had to have something tangible to remind them of the same commandments he had given to Moses. So He gave the seven commandments to the Indians. For the Cherokees, instead of putting them on stone, he told them to do beadwork strips with pearls, and to sew these onto a seaweed base, for it was very durable. And although the wampum belts were once scattered, they have endured through the years.

When the Cherokees were driven out here along the Trail of Tears, my great-great-grandfather didn't know who had the belts, and he became concerned about getting them together. He knew the people would need the wampum belts in the new land. However, he did not live long enough to find the wampums. So before he died, he told his son, Redbird, to continue the search. It took Redbird many years and much hard work to locate them. It is said that during an ancient war the wise men of the tribe selected seven men who were thought to have the best chance of surviving it, and a belt was given to each one of them. After the war, the seven men were scattered, and probably some of them had died. Nobody knew where the sacred commandments were.

My grandfather found one of the belts right here in Adair County. The man who had it originally had grown old and died. To keep the wampum from falling into the wrong hands, the man had buried it. By the time Redbird found out about the belt and came to get it, the man had been dead for seven years. But his granddaughter knew where he had buried it. When they dug the belt up, it was as fresh and new looking as when it was first made. That seaweed had to be strong to survive underground that long.

After many years, when Redbird had at last gathered up all of the belts, it was revealed to him where he should start the stomp ground, and where the sacred fire should be placed. Up to that time he had been participating in the Four Mothers' Society. This included four tribes, but it was revealed to him that there should be a stomp ground for the Cherokees. There should be seven arbors, one for each of the Cherokee clans. He did as he was told and put the seven wampum belts in a safe place where they would be preserved for future generations.

A person who can interpret the wampums can preach indefinitely on them. They contain all of God's will for his people. I have two pictures of the belts. One shows Redbird displaying them and the other shows Nighthawks doing the same. Redbird had to go to Washington, D.C., on behalf of the Nighthawks, and he needed proof that he really represented the Cherokees. These photographs gave him the proof. Every so often the chief will bring out the sacred wampum belts and display them to the people to remind them of God's word to them. The sacred fire is kept burning at the stomp ground. It is a symbol of the spirit, or Creator. Its smoke is a messenger though which our prayers pass up to him. The fire is still made from seven kinds of wood, and there are three men whose job it is to keep the fire burning. There is a pit in the center of the stomp ground, and the fire always burns in it. It is only the top of the fire that has to be cleared away and fresh wood added. The fire has been kept burning for as long as we have any record. It was brought over the Trail of Tears, and we will never let it die.

I should mention that one seldom sees full-blooded Cherokee adults correcting their children in public. Only twice did we see children admonished at dances. Once was when children were playing around some old logs, and one of the leaders told them in a loud voice in Cherokee to watch where they were playing, for there was a nest of rattlesnakes in the logs. But the logs were left there and not moved, even though it was within twenty paces of where the members' cars were parked, and people were milling all around. The other time was during the day when some of the children were playing too close to the kindled fire and trespassing on the dance square. Then adults told them to get out of there. Otherwise, children did what they wanted to. They yelled, talked, and no matter how small they were, if they could walk they joined in the dances. The Cherokee belief is that as children grow older they will have, by watching, listening, and imitating, learned the ways and will know how to think and act.

Our research about the grounds and the fire leaves several questions unanswered, but the most important of these is what happened to the fire between 1838 and 1902. Was there a fire or fires previous to Redbird's that had been started with the coals that were supposed to have come over the trail? If not, where was the fire kept until then, and by whom? Archie Sam believed that the fire was lighted at the site of what later became the Medicine Spring ground, and he might be right. But we have no proof, and are left with the feeling that we should pursue this further around Stilwell, since this is where the first Cherokees came to Indian Territory and are believed to have settled down.

Archie Sam

There was no better student of or fuller participant in Cherokee culture and the dance than Archie Sam, chief of the Medicine Spring ground. During the course of our many visits together, Archie often protested that he did not know as much about medicine practice and the grounds' secrets as did his older brother, Eli. But this was modesty speaking, for as will be seen, Archie was one of those rare individuals who learned to live harmoniously in both the traditional Cherokee and the white worlds. He learned from his father, White Tobacco, the value of an education in white schools, and he came to appreciate this. But he also learned to know and to be what he was: a Natchez-Cherokee first, last, and always. And he came to believe that any Cherokee who did not pursue his roots was destined to feel in some important degree anchorless and that something essential was missing from his life. In truth, he would have no burning and central life-force to give him meaning, impetus, and stability as he faced the high winds of life. So cooperating in this book was a particular joy for Archie, and no one wished more passionately than he to see it finished and published. Unfortunately, that was not the case for Archie. He died suddenly on May 23, 1986. But I take comfort in knowing that some of his life and thoughts will live on here, and may bear fruit that for the moment I can speculate about but am not able to predict.

As a boy, Archie followed his father, White Tobacco, everywhere he went, but since his father was not given to conversation, most of what Archie learned from him was by observation. His father's teaching method was to teach a part of some subject just once and then expect Archie to remember it. Later, White Tobacco would add information about the subject and might at the same time ask Archie what he had retained. Archie said that while his father was a master at remembering oral communication, he was not, so a lot of what his father said "just slipped away." Eli, who was Archie's older brother by ten years, was taught more than Archie and remembered more, but, Archie said, Eli never made any use of what he learned.

Archie remained at home until he was about twelve years of age, when a truant officer came to the house and told his father that Archie had to go to school. After the man left, White Tobacco told Archie that he had to do as the man said, and then, even though his father spoke little English, he immediately began to teach Archie the alphabet and how to write the numbers one to fifty. He also took Archie on a walk to the school so he would know exactly how to get there. Where there was a creek that flooded over at times, White Tobacco felled a tree to make a bridge and said, "You will go over this. There will be no excuses." Archie went to the local school for three or four months, then asked to be

sent to a boarding school. The balance of his educational experience has been given in the preface, along with his occupations until he took over as head, or chief, of the Medicine Spring ground, and some details of the Sams' family life have been given to us by Archie's sister, Lydia Sam McLure.

In the first of our discussions, Archie talked a lot about his grandfather, Creek Sam, of Cherokee and Natchez descent, who, at the request of the Cherokee council, served as teacher and adviser to Redbird Smith. He taught Redbird the old ways, the rites, the ceremonies, the healings, the ball play, and about such things as the *Ga do gi,* or cooperative working group. In Indian Territory it was sometimes called "the Piecemeal Society," and it continued to function until land allotment took place. In 1917 or 1918 a man named Chester Poe Cornelius was hired by Cherokee leaders, including Redbird Smith, to improve the Cherokee fortunes. Cornelius was a full-blooded Oneida Indian, an attorney, and a charismatic individual who mesmerized the Cherokees with a utopian dream of self-reliance, freedom, and prosperity, and promised to lead them to its fulfillment. He became in their eyes almost a god, and they saw him as the fulfillment of an ancient prophecy. By the time they learned differently, he had gotten them to sell or mortgage their land, put the proceeds in his own bank account in Gore, and absconded with the funds. This proved to be, Archie said, one of the worst setbacks the Cherokees have ever experienced.

Regarding the sacred fire, Archie told us he had been taught that in 1729 the last sacred fire had gone out, and this was at Natchez, Mississippi. Then the people went to the use of the sacred ashes that were eventually carried over the Trail of Tears. The fire went out because people were accepting too many white ways and just let it happen. Then they regretted it and went into the mountains to ask God for guidance. It was here that they were taught to use the ashes instead of the live coals, but the ashes had to always be those of the fire that had been kept since the beginning.

"Going to water" was another rite that was close to extinct by now. Some Western Cherokee medicine men still did it, and a few old people followed the custom for personal reasons. But that was all. This was very sad, because "it helped tremendously to live by the water and to use it in ceremonial functions." This was one of the reasons for the revival of the Medicine Spring ground which, when Archie started to use it, had lain dormant for nearly forty years.

The practice of going to get advice about medicine herbs from the dead was also passing away. Archie knew the last man who could do this. He would go out in the woods alone, and the deceased medicine people would come to him, speaking in harsh gasps so that it was hard to understand them. Afterwards, they led him to where the right herbs were.

Crystal use for divining had come to an end too. Archie had known a few men who in the early days in Indian Territory had used crystals. Once, the brother of two sisters who had been raped and killed came to one of these men to find out who the criminals were. The medicine man looked into the crystal and identified them. These men were subsequently found, tried in court, and convicted. Also, many years ago a man who had a crystal and could prophesy with it came to visit White Tobacco, who asked him to look into it and tell him what the future held for the Cherokees. The man put the crystal in water and saw a picture on its surface showing that the traditional life would decline until a day came when the Cherokee youth would raise the Cherokee Nation up again — as Cherokees who were proud of and living the traditional life — but within the structures of a white world.

Gone was the eerie practice of "calling dead people back to talk to you and to give you advice and understandings." They would come into the room "at a different level," that is, floating in the air. White Tobacco told Archie that when he wanted to call someone back he used an old dialect that only trained people would understand. When the dead did return, White Tobacco could see them and hear them talk, but a person who lacked his medicine training could not do this. White Tobacco had also a secret formula he chanted when he wanted to ask the

spirits to take care of his house while he was away. Certain items were required to properly ask for this help. Some medicine, a pipe, and remade tobacco were placed outside on the ground at the same time the call was issued. But if the spirits didn't come right away, the Little People might come along, take the medicine, and give it to the sick. Apparently, this was what had happened when on one occasion the Sams' log home burned to the ground.

Archie didn't think there was any medicine person left in Oklahoma who could change himself into an animal. But he was certain that at one time some could do this. His father knew a man who could change himself into anything he wanted to in order to accomplish whatever he had in mind, and Archie was "willing to bet his life" that his own father was very good at it. "But he never admitted it or let us see him do it, because our lives were going to be so different from his."

Archie said that in the early days in Oklahoma when food supplies were very low and the people were desperate, certain medicine men could do something like Jesus did when he fed the 5,000. Taking a little food, they could cause it to multiply. "But this was only done in times of emergency, and the fact was that you were eating nothing but air, but because of your faith it filled you up." This happened mostly in the 1920s and 1930s.

Where are the Cherokee dead when they are away? They have gone to different planets and are called back from there. There are four levels of planets, and as soon as a person leaves this physical level he goes to the next higher level. Actually, the deceased person is in a state of being in which there is no time. He slowly moves through the levels if he has lived properly in this life. If he has done this, he will ultimately reach the highest level, where God is, and God will want to keep him there.

Another change had to do with the grounds. The ceremonies held at the grounds went well until Cornelius did his "dirty work." After that, attendance at the grounds dropped off, and one by one the grounds closed. Another change was the length of time spent at the grounds. Whereas people used to stay three or four days, they now stayed just a day and a night. "There used to be so many campfires that at night it would look like a city." People came with cook stoves, pets, all they needed, and after the dance remained several days to visit. Then they lost faith in their leadership, in the Nighthawks, and in the religious way of feeding the fire with a chicken. This is when they went from four to seven beds. But "The beds do not necessarily represent clans. They represent the four cardinal directions. The four main clans should be in the beds, with the leading clans determined by who rules the ground. "Why," Archie exclaimed, "they even mixed the sexes in the beds. You can't do that! The woman is too strong for the man. She has the power to nourish and create life, but there are certain things that are connected with this that are very damaging. Menstruating is a very negative power. The proper way is for the men to sit in the beds, and the women around the beds. It's all right if the women pass through the beds to get to the dance square.

"That," he went on, "is one key to a powerful dance. The other thing is that from the start you must have people who are united in body and mind, people who are going through the rituals as one person totally united. If this is so, then the sacred fire picks up and sends out waves like a radio station. If everyone is putting out the same waves, then the outpouring through the fire and smoke is sure to reach God. Unity is a fantastic power. Nothing needs to be spoken when this is so. God feels it and responds. No audible prayer can be as strong."

Archie was instrumental in organizing a group of Cherokees, Cherokee-Natchez, and Creeks or part Creeks to bring back the fire at Medicine Spring. Swanton mentions this ground in 1928 and includes a photograph of it.[1] Archie decided, since so much needed to be relearned, to begin with a practice ground that would be located about a mile southeast of the old ground, which is a few miles north of Gore, Oklahoma. The inaugurating ceremony took place there on September 27, 1969. The ground was, at that time, the only one to have four beds. The basic idea was that once the members were fully trained and ready, operations would be transferred to the original ground, where ashes of the original fire

still were. Archie had great things in mind for the Medicine Spring ground that I mention farther on. But for now the ground is closed. We shared many of his thoughts regarding it, some of which are nicely summed up in a talk he gave on December 12, 1976, at a University of Oklahoma symposium entitled "Public Policy and the Sense of Place in Oklahoma." He gave me a copy of his notes and his permission to use them:

> A long, long time ago a messenger from heaven came to live among the Indians. He was a kind and humble man. We knew he was from heaven and not one of us because he would shine in the dark. He said his message from heaven was that Indians should care for and help one another, that Indians should live by the word of God, and that if they did they would be blessed with a happy life. He told the Indians about man's relation to God, man's relation to man, and man's relation to nature. Earth was God's creation, and man was put here to take care of it. The trees, rivers, mountains, flowers, and animals are part of God's design, and man should preserve it for the coming generations to enjoy. The messenger taught Indians how to get wild foods from the forest, and also how to plant food by the slash and burn method of farming.

> Today, in the hills of Cherokee country, ceremonial tobacco is grown by the slash and burn method. When the Indians followed the messenger's word they were blessed time and time again, and were able to share their blessings with the entire world. Indians have made the greatest contributions anyone has made to the world. They developed and nurtured seventy-five percent of the world's agricultural products. The white men who first came to North America found that the Indians had tremendous wealth in food supplies, and later on the Indian food products were distributed to the entire world.

> But it was prophesied a long time ago that Indians would turn away from their heritage and ceremonies, and would become weak and lost. Still, when the prophets gazed into their crystal stones they saw in the far distant future a young generation rising who would appreciate the values of their heritage and ceremonies and would become a strong race of people. For this reason the traditional Cherokees are desperately trying to preserve their songs and dances.

It was further prophesied that when a non-Indian understands the Indian way of life and its value system and dresses like an Indian, the Indians will have found a true friend. So today, at our ceremonial grounds, we have many non-Indian friends. I personally remember when the non-Indian neighbors would come to the ceremonial grounds to play ball and dance. They were accepted as friends. They were true friends of the Indians.

Historians usually call the Indians who once lived in the southern states "Southern Indians." Cherokee Indians are part of a major cultural group called, "Woodland Indians." They came from southern states to Oklahoma. The dances of the Cherokees are different from the powwows of the Plains Indians. It is very important to the Cherokees that the songs and dances be performed at ceremonial grounds under proper conditions. It is very important that we keep our songs and dances as traditional and pure as possible. And we must hand them down to the next generation just as they were handed down to us. Ceremonies are the very heart of the Indian way of life.

The messenger who came from heaven brought us the Sacred fire. He said it was one-seventh of the Sacred fire that is in heaven. It was to be used as a means of communicating with God. God wanted the Indians to always have the Sacred fire. When the ceremonial rituals are performed in front of the Sacred fire as an act of worship, the smoke of the fire will carry the requests into heaven. The messenger told the Indians that God said to build a big fire out in the open when performing rituals, and to do this at night. Then He would look down and see the Sacred fire burning bright and know that His children had not forsaken His word. He would bless them, and they would have a good life. The Sacred fire is central at the ceremonial ground, and it has been this way since time immemorial. Many years ago the sacred fires were kept burning all the time by men who were assigned to this task. They were kept burning in Holy Temples that were placed on top of high mounds to guard against rain and floods. When the local area of an Indian settlement was no longer able to support life, the Indians moved to another area and took the fire with them. Men of strong faith, dedication, and training were chosen to move the fire, since untrained men would offend it, and this must not happen. A good fire was their means of survival and salvation.

Then, encroachment by white people into the Cherokee domain created havoc in the Cherokee way of life and drastically changed the Cherokee society. As a result, they were not able to keep the eternal flame and embraced the Sacred Ashes concept. The fire was no longer kept burning all of the time, but was relit for ceremonial occasions. So the continuity of the Sacred Ashes has never been broken, and today, the Sacred Ashes are relit as before.

"Tribal Town" is a name we give to our ceremonial grounds because it is a community gathering place where tribal dances are held. The dances begin about two hours before midnight, but each ground has its own customs concerning ceremonial functions.

The "Long Dance" and the "Common Dance" are the first four dances performed by the members. The fifth dance is the "Friendship Dance," which cues the visitors to start dancing. From here on there is common, or stomp, dancing, and various animal dances. These are performed for the rest of the night. The animal dances include the Horse, Duck, Garfish, Beans, Alligator, Fox, Buzzard, and Mosquito.

The ceremonial priest, who is in charge of the dancing, goes around and selects who is to lead each dance. Then he announces and calls for the dance. The leader of the dance will sing about ten songs for each dance. The women will dance with leg rattles, one rattle just above the ankle on each leg, called "shakles." The women dance with shakles to lend color and rhythm to the dance. A wet drum and a hand rattle are also used. For animal dances the leader uses the hand rattle.

The "Buffalo Dance" is a daytime dance. It is performed at dusk and before the sun has gone down. Long ago, the Cherokees before they went on a hunt performed this dance at this time of day. This was when the buffalo were bedding down for the night and was a lullaby song to sing the creatures to sleep. In the song they prayed to the Supreme Deity, giving thanks for the buffalo and also apologized to the animal world, saying they would take only what they needed. The song is so old that we no longer know the words. But we have been told about the Buffalo Dance, and we do it to keep the memory alive.

A dance that is nearly as colorful as the Buffalo

Dance is the "Mosquito Dance." It also survives from antiquity. A long time ago the Cherokees danced for four nights in succession. By the third or fourth night the dancers began to tire, and sat more than they danced. The ceremonial priests then asked the singer to sing the Mosquito Dance. He did this with a drum as his only announcement. The women would get up and start dancing around the fire as they hummed low like a mosquito. Then at a signal from the singer, they would dart into the crowd and begin to jab the laggard dancers with pins, like a mosquito biting. This would wake everyone up and create a lot of laughter. Thus revived, the dancing would go on.

The "Drunk Dance" is also meant for fun and laughter, although no drinking of whiskey or beer is allowed on the grounds. It is performed at day-break, and is the next to last dance. In it, the men and women dance like they are drunk. In this dance only, the women take off their rattles and sing. They are spiritually drunk with joy and gaiety. The dancers have come to dance all night and have done it. They are victorious! In our society, when one finally attains his goal, there is a tendency to relax and celebrate the accomplishment. This is what the Drunk Dance is all about. Indians have a Drunk Dance, and whites have office parties.

When the Drunk Dance is finished, the "Olden Dance" is begun. This completes the dancing. Tribal Town has been part of Cherokee society for a long time. Once, in each Cherokee settlement there were two tribal towns, a main town, and a minor town. They were called the "white town" and the "red town." White town was headed by a hereditary chief. Ceremonies were held in the white town. White town was the place where social, economic, and political causes were heard and acted upon. In early American history, the signing of treaties with the United States government was done at the white towns. The "Red town" was headed by a young man who was capable of leading in war, because it was a war town. The leader of the red town was chosen by the hereditary chief of the white town.

In the year 1838, when the Congress of the United States was forcibly removing the Cherokees from the southern states, the Cherokee state of affairs was miserable. Homes, farms, livestock, and other personal property were destroyed by the Indian haters. All of the well-known tribal towns were destroyed by the white man. Only the unknown

tribal towns, of which one was Gulaniye, survived. It was located at the junction of Brasstown Creek and Hiwasse River, near Murphy, North Carolina. In the wake of the removal to the new homeland, a small band of Natchez and Cherokees prepared to move their ceremonial ashes and fire. Beloved old men of Gulaniye gathered at their ceremonial ground and fasted and kept an all-night vigil in preparation. At dawn, four containers of Sacred Ashes were removed from the heart of the fire, and the ceremonial ground was closed forever. The old men faced east and prayed that the fire would be relighted when their destination was reached and that it would be with the Cherokees forever. The Sacred Ashes were carried to the new home in secrecy, just ahead of the main column of marchers by four of the most trusted, strong, and dedicated men. Each of them had a special container strapped to his body. Chances were that one of the four would reach his destination. Only one fire, that of Gulaniye, was carried over the infamous Trail of Tears. When the destination was reached, the fire was relit at a new ceremonial ground that is now called "Medicine Spring," which was named after a historic sulphureous spring. It is termed in the feminine gender, and called "The Mother fire" of the Cherokee Nation. It is maintained by Chero-kees who are fulfilling the prayers of the beloved old men of Gulaniye, including the keeping of a white and a red town, just as it has been with the Chero-kees from a time unknown to mankind.

Archie will never see his dreams for the Medi-cine Spring ground reach fruition, but in the hope that someone else will pursue them, I include here a diagram of the ceremonial tribal town he planned to build at Medicine Spring in the near future. It included a recessed, rectangular-shaped, Mayan-type dance and ball-play area, that was ten feet below grade and had at each of the four directions a mound that was twenty feet above grade level to hold bed houses, or arbors. It was his belief that such a ground would provide atmosphere and beauty through its architecture and would be conducive to inspired and reverent ceremonials.

Since the fire was so central to Cherokee religion, we wanted to learn everything Archie knew about it, and at every opportunity we pressed the issue.

He said that only a few years ago, the

Keetoowah people were claiming that when his grandfather, Creek Sam, had come over the Trail of Tears he had been the one who brought the fire. But Archie knew that Creek Sam had only been twelve or fourteen years of age at the time and doubted that the *Gulaniye* elders would have put that much trust in such a young person. It was certain that Creek Sam had made the journey, and that he knew what had transpired along the way, "Because this is the knowledge we have today — what he related to us." But the fire carriers would have been the most dedicated and strongest men, those who stood the best chance of being able to complete the trip.

Archie stressed also that the fire led the people on the journey to Indian Territory. Yet is was important to recognize that the fire "is movement," and as such it was not part of the people themselves. It is probable that most of the Cherokees didn't even know that the fire was going ahead of them. Elders told Archie that the ashes were carried in sections of hollow cane that were capped by larger sections. And there were four carriers to make certain that at least one of them would get through.

The fire carriers were anywhere from two hours to a full day ahead of the main body. This group came through the Goingsnake District, stopped at Fort Gibson, and finally settled on top of Braggs Mountain. Later, the fire was moved several times, with the last move being made in 1916 or 1917. . . "to the old place, back of where our practice ground is now. A man named Garrison lives on a corner about a mile from where you turn off 10A to our place. It would be about 200 yards back of his house." This was the area called Sulphur Spring and the ground was first known by that name. Written records were kept of this, and Archie believed his father might have had them but lost them when their home burned to the ground.

Archie told us something of how they moved the fire. First they had to prepare the grounds. "They went down and cleaned up the place. They got it ready. Then, about evening they went down there and kept a vigil all night. The next morning the two men who had been selected and trained for the mission went to the regular ceremonial ground,

picked up the ashes, and brought them back. They put the ashes in the center of the new ground and built a fire on top of these. Then they went through a series of four all-night dances, and when they were finished, the fire had a new home."

He believed there was no one alive who knew precisely how to move the fire. "We don't know all of the secrets," he said. "I know what I just told you, but I don't know all of the secret chants and exactly how the people were doctored with medicine. The men who carried the ashes had to go through certain rituals to assure that they were properly empowered and that the spirit of the fire would accompany them — that is, agree to go with them. I know who went, who brought it back, who built the fire on top. Eli was one, and Ahama Phillips was another. Emma Campbell and Anna Washington were still living and had been a part of it. Three others that played central roles have become Christians and no longer come to the ground."

"What about the fires at the new grounds that were being established, such as at Warner and Nobles? Could they be strong if no one knew the proper method to move the ashes?"

"Probably not," Archie replied, "and it's dangerous. I wouldn't even go up there." In regard to a third and older ground, Archie said he would even be reluctant to smoke their tobacco, because it was being purchased from Arkansas farms where women might have touched it. "Women should never see that tobacco."

Joyce inserted that her father told her that his father had raised the sacred tobacco in Tennessee. He kept the plot separate from his other tobacco and tended it separately. He also had a medicine man come in and specially "fix" the tobacco – it was "treated entirely separately."

She went on to say that when she had gone to the Stokes ground a little over a year earlier, the women brought their own chairs and sat to one side of the beds. But when she had been there the past weekend, perhaps because William Smith was absent, there wasn't one chair, save hers. The rest of the women sat on the beds. Even fourteen- and fifteen-year-old girls "were out there smoking the pipe."

"Seems like something's wrong, doesn't it?" Archie replied with a knowing look in his eyes.

Joyce stated that she had asked Albert Carter whether in the old days everyone had lined up and smoked the pipe. He said, "No," and not at every meeting either. They only smoked the pipe when the medicine man or the chief thought they needed it because there was friction of some kind . . . "maybe two or three times a year."

Archie commented, "According to the old book I have, the pipe ceremony was held just once a year, and about the time the ancient 'Friends Made' ceremony was held." He suggested that we ought to get together with Albert Carter and "pump this information out of him, because Albert isn't given to talking freely about medicine things. Eli is the same way."

Joyce told Archie that once while Ray and she were at Redbird's ground, she had asked Albert about the sacrificing of chickens, and he replied that he didn't want to get into that. But he did admit that the entire bird was tossed into the fire as a sacrifice. Archie explained that when the chicken was taken out to the fire you had to "twist its head and push it in under its wing to make it stay still."

Young as Creek Sam was when he came over the trail to Indian Territory, he was already in training to be a medicine man, and from the time he was a grown man until the day he died he was recognized as the most knowledgeable medicine man among the Western Cherokees. This is why he was chosen to train Redbird Smith, and also trained White Tobacco. This is also how Archie's father came to be chief of the ground. It was passed down to him.

"Who was the first medicine man at Sulphur Springs?"

Archie didn't know, but it might have been his father. "This is the reason I told you to be sure and ask Eli questions. There's a lot of things even I haven't asked him yet. He's much older than I am. Him being the oldest son, he had a lot more influence with my daddy. They could work together just like two friends. I was different. When Eli is around, I have no place." (Eli died without having been

interviewed. And, by the time we could have had a worthwhile talk with him, his mind was wandering badly — one more instance of valuable information forever lost.)

Was the Sulphur Spring ground the only one going at the time of its inception?

"No. The Redbird fire was there, and there was one at Yellow Green Leaves. The place is under water now."

When did the Sulphur Spring ground close?

"Sometime in the early '30s. From 1916 to 1934 or 1935 they danced and had green corn and everything there. Then the government bought up the land and moved the people away. Then the war came along, and we were shipped off and the old people died out. But people still came to White Tobacco for medicine and counseling, and the ashes weren't disturbed. They were still there, waiting to be moved. All I need to do is go up and see a certain man who can locate the exact position of the fire. As soon as I do that and I have enough support we will have to go through certain ceremonial functions. Since the fire is already so close to our ground we will move from the practice ground to where it is. But we have to be able to carry it through. You can't just do it one time and go home and forget it. Besides, I'm not spiritually strong enough to do it now. There are no informed singers, no dance leaders. We're still weak."

"Let me ask you something else," Joyce said. "When you were back in the time of Redbird's, Stokes, and the Medicine Spring grounds, weren't Creeks coming to those dances too?"

Archie answered, "There's always been a mixture. In my estimation there is no such thing as a pure Cherokee ground."

At this point, we asked for directions to get to Jim Wolf's Four Mothers', or Flint ground, and I include Archie's answer to show how complex it is to make any trip into the backcountry of northeastern Oklahoma to find a ground or an individual.

"OK," Archie said. "Start from Tahlequah going toward Stilwell. And maybe four or five miles before you get to Stilwell, you'll see a Stony Point fruit stand, a pretty good-sized one. It's out on the highway on this side. And you go on down that hill to where there's a sharp turn that goes this way. Go back to the right, and you go quite a ways, and you run into a real nice bridge. The road goes on but the bridge crosses that creek, because the road and that creek run parallel all the way down, then it crosses over. Then you go a little ways and you take a left, and you go along there and you come to a church. Now you've gone too far, and you have to backtrack about a quarter-mile and take the road that goes up the hill. Turn left onto what's kind of like a one-track road. You meet a car, you might have to get off. It's one of those kind. It's kind of like a mail-route, though. His house is about a quarter-mile from the dance ground."

"Do you come to the house or the ground first?"

"Well, there used to be several directions they'd come in, but if you come in the way I'm telling you, you'll come to the grounds first. You won't even know there's a grounds there, actually."

Such colloquial pictures were typical for making our trips, and we made many such. Astonishingly enough, with only these directions, Ray Johnson took us unerringly to Jim Wolf's house. He was accustomed to sorting out the backcountry travel problems. On occasion he would stop the car and ponder a bit, but mostly we just bounced straight on in over the kind of ruts and ridges that an auto repairman has blissful dreams of.

On returning to the subject of the grounds and the problem of doing improper things there, Archie stressed that if the members were not doing what "the Man upstairs" told them to, then they were wrong. It was like committing a sin that ultimately would be paid for. Moreover, the members must understand that the primary good served by the ground was that of the people as a whole. Individual good was secondary. Personal benefit and comfort were not the principal aim. Involved too was unity with the Cherokee Nation and Cherokees of the past, and the longevity of the nation. In centuries past, someone had danced for present-day people, and by this guaranteed that they would have the

ceremonies. "So are we going to cut it off now?" Archie asked. "Are we the ones that are going to be guilty of this and who will face that tribunal someday?"

"What did he mean by tribunal?"

"They might ask us what we did with all these things that have been passed on to us . . . What did you do with them?

"Who were 'they?'"

"The next generation. If I fail to pass it on, then I've broken the line that has continued on since the beginning of time."

"All right," Joyce said, "you talk about the way you were told, and about the One above. But you haven't been going to church. Do you, and other Cherokees and Natchez like you, feel there is one Supreme Being who rules all, and to whom you must also account for your actions?"

"Yes."

"Did your father, White Tobacco, feel the same way?"

"Yes. He said our ceremonies came from the Man up there."

"And he used the word 'God?'"

"Yes."

"Did he ever go to church, or know anything about the Bible or the Christian religion?"

"He was around Christian people and exposed to it, but he followed the traditional religion. He believed that all primitive people recognized God up there . . . one Supreme Being. Once there was a Baptist church near Gore that he took us children to. I think it was called Cedar Creek. But he wouldn't go inside with us."

"Did he have a Cherokee or Natchez name for God that he used?"

"He used a Creek word. You have to understand the history of this world. The ceremonies have been going on for a long, long, long time. And 2,000 years ago they created Christianity, and Christianity came over here, and the two ways clashed. The Indians already had a religion that suited them. It was compatible with their way of life and beneficial. It suited their tastes and the way they lived. It served their purposes and they liked it. Then they were told it was wrong and had to ask what was wrong with it. This was what God handed down to us. Why should we give it up? If that's the way he wanted us to live, why not leave it that way?" The Supreme Being said he would bless us if we did what he told us to, and would punish us if we broke his laws."

This strong affirmation took us back to the grounds, and we sought more information regarding them.

"What about the old days when they had the all-night dance? Would people come for the medicine in the afternoon?"

"Yes."

"And were political questions addressed at the grounds?"

"Let me clarify this. There were other dances, other gatherings that were purposely designed for political and secular problems. People would come to these and talk. But there was no medicine. These dances were just plain dances, just pure dancing where they'd get merry and whoop it up all night long. They had deer or some other kind of feast. They might also have 'breakfast with the chief.' It's a Natchez custom."

"Did Choctaws or Seminoles come to the early grounds?"

"The Seminoles came once in a while, and the Quapaws now and then. So did Senecas. That was about it. Some came from quite a distance away. Usually there were about ten Cherokee and Natchez families who were all good singers and dancers and shell shakers. They were the core of the people who did our animal dances."

"Who decided who led the dances?"

"The priest would go around. He knew what singers were present and what they could do. And when the time came he'd say, 'Sing fox, or . . .' The chief is not the priest. The chief has nothing to do with it. At my ceremonial ground if I elect a priest, he will call the shots."

"And the priest is not always the medicine man?"

"No."

"The priest is just a knowledgeable man?"

"Yes. He is out there to do his job, which is to keep the dances going throughout the night."

Joyce said she had noticed that at some grounds the leaders all sat on one bed. Archie replied that at his daddy's ground and at his practice ground the chiefs always sat in the Bear Clan bed, but he didn't know why this was so. His father was of the Bear Clan, but Archie was of the Wind Clan. Archie had tried to find out what clans in ancient times were seated in the different beds, but no one knew the answer. All Archie knew was that it was the south-eastern Indian tradition.

We asked if it was Natchez, and he answered, "No." But he went on to say that the organization of the Natchez was "the most complex, most complicated social system the world has ever known. The head chief would have children, and they would come down link by link until they were on the bottom of the social ladder. I hate to talk about it," he said, "because its so complicated that I catch myself saying contradictory things. But a chief had to marry a commoner. They had four levels of society. And the first girl born to the chief's wife was called 'White Woman.' She had sons, and her oldest son was the next chief in line . . . and they couldn't marry into other royalty. I wish I had asked more questions about this when I was young, when the elders were living and available for questions."

We talked about a certain individual who had been in training to become a medicine man and how his family believed that the studying had literally "bothered him" to death, because he was doing something that was not right for him to do.

"Maybe he didn't live right," Archie said in a sad tone. "Something was wrong somewhere. He was appealing to these spiritual things out there . . ."

What did he mean by "spiritual things"?

"I'm not talking about God. I'm talking about something down here on our level, something that we can appeal to. If you had a bad medicine, you wouldn't appeal to God, you would appeal to those spirits out there. They are here. They have been here all of the time, and they will be here when we are gone. They are immortal things, and they make things happen. There are good ones, and there are bad ones. They even tell a person to do this or that, and he does it. But you need to be careful about getting into this. Things can happen, like they did to that man who got into medicine when he shouldn't, and died. There's a man I know who has some old books in his home, and he can read Cherokee real good. He began to read those books and started to understand them. Then things began to happen at night. Somebody would come into the house and get a drink of water or close a door. Or they would cough outside so loud it would wake him up. He told me he shut those books up and put them away!"

We wanted to know what Archie thought about Little People, and what role they played.

"Well, they're out there . . . but I think more people say they saw them than really did. I've never seen one."

We mentioned that Eli had said there were some Little People at the old ground.

"Well, they are out there, everyplace you go. They were always there."

"How do you know?"

"Well, I don't see any reason why they should move away."

"Has there been any evidence of them lately?"

"No. Because we don't live there anymore."

"But when you lived there, there was evidence?"

"Yes."

"Where they there for protection?"

"No. They were there because it was their home."

"Are they peculiar to the Cherokees?"

"It appears they have their own language and know the languages of the other tribes. The older people said they could understand what the Little People were saying when in the wee hours of the night they would go past the house. They'd be talking. Sometimes you couldn't understand them but knew they were saying something. I never did think they played any particular protective role for any family. They would help you, but you had to ask them like you do anyone else."

"What do they look like?"

"Well, I was told they were just little people, that's all. I never did ask anyone if they looked Indian, white, or Chinese. All I heard is they were just like midgets. They had their own life-style. There were certain things they liked to do. It was said that in their own community they have their own joker, leaders, and serious people. They have followers, and they have thinkers. They have trouble-makers, and they have good people, and they have pranksters."

"How far from the dance ground was the valley where the Little People lived?"

"Well, you can see it down there . . . down past the women's toilet . . . that's where they live."

"Can they make themselves invisible or visible whenever they want to?"

"The truth is, if you are a person whose mental attitude is that of grousing and griping when you take the medicine at the ground, they won't even come close to you, no matter how badly you want them to. And that's why medicine men have to keep themselves pure. Just because you know the chants, you can't go out there and take a book and start reading it, because you don't have the other things it takes for you to qualify to do the things you need to do. I feel sorry for people who just get a book and think they can then do this or that. It's kind of like getting to be a doctor through a correspondence course."

Joyce recalled that she had seen one old man's medicine book and in particular a love formula . . . the kind men used to draw women closer to them or that women used to make themselves more attractive and desirable. This formula called for the white bird to come down and also for the use of tobacco and a chant.

Archie commented that love formulas were a trivial sort of thing. Some were a little stronger than others, and some were just one-time things used by people looking for one-night stands.

Had he heard about prayer formulas for putting people to sleep?

"You can put a whole house to sleep," Archie said. "You can knock on the door and the owner will come to it in a trance. And he will say he has a lot of meat, or tobacco, or groceries, or an ax, or money. And if you ask for it, he will give it to you. But you must give something in exchange for it. The guy will never know what he did. Sometimes if a person has hurt you badly, you will feel justified in doing this. Sometimes you can go to the door and tell him to follow you. And you can take him as far as you want, and leave him there. I don't know whether or not this ability is dying out."

Joyce commented that she couldn't get medicine men to admit whether or not they could do this. Archie answered that even if they told her about the custom, they would never admit they could do it.

In the old days, Archie said, such things were the basis for a lot of fun. Old people would sit around and tell jokes about how girls would become pregnant by one who put them to sleep, and they never knew a thing about it until they discovered their condition. But no one was ever sure whether they had actually been put to sleep, or were pretending. Anyway, the test for such a pregnancy was that children of such unions did not grow into adults, and no one ever saw this happen. Archie often listened in on this kind of joking when he was a child and told us that in so doing he had learned a lot about life. He remarked at this point that he thought each medicine man had back in those days his own special formula, but while he had learned a couple of these, he never tried them out to see whether or not they worked. He was afraid they might backfire on him, for as his father had taught him, there were two sides to everything.

I wondered aloud as to how seriously we should consider present-day medicine men and women, since some we interviewed seemed to have picked up so little knowledge they couldn't possibly do much with it. On the other hand, Lydia claimed that White Tobacco had cures for most everything.

"That's right," Archie said. "And Lydia told me about something that had happened one day while I was away on a trip. A couple brought to Daddy a baby with a harelip. In about two minutes Daddy got everything ready, gave it to the parents, and told them how to use it. And they went home and a year later brought the baby back, and its lip was normal. Isn't that something?"

Did Archie know for a fact that most all of his father's cures had died with him and that he hadn't trained anyone else?

"I don't know for sure. I haven't talked with Joe Duck, who I think has all of the books. At least, he told Maude that he has them."

"You think your father gave them to him?"

"Yes, because he frequently stayed at George Duck's; he was Joe's old man."

"But Joe was already in training then?"

"Yes. He was there, and very possibly about my age at that time. They say he's a good medicine man, and there's always a lot of patients' cars out in the yard. You can't just go up there and chat with him all day long, because he's got different people going in and out from all over the country, different states, whites and Indians."

"He was like your father, then, who would treat both Indians and whites who came?"

"Yes. But he wouldn't talk in English with a white man. That was his way. And even when he was around whites he wouldn't talk it. But he sure corrected me when I made a mistake in English while I was interpreting for him. He had to be pretty smart in it."

"Is that why the ethnologists went to Watt Sam instead of Creek Sam . . . because Watt Sam would talk to anyone? And was Watt Sam truly a medicine man?"

"Watt Sam was a great medicine man, but he was not a ceremonial medicine man. He didn't make any medicine at the ground."

As for the charms currently being made by some medicine people, Archie said there was no way to tell whether they actually worked or not. "How does the person know whether it was the charm or their own ability to make friends that did the trick?"

Archie told us how, in the early days in Indian Territory, one man from the *Ga do gi* group would carry on the old custom of taking his drum to the fields, and while the people worked together he would beat out a rhythm and sing to them to lift their spirits. The songs were planting songs that appealed to the otherworld spirits and to the animals to bring good crops.

When I asked why he thought appeals for help

were made to animals when in the old days animals were thought of as causes of diseases, Archie replied that a person must assume it was his own fault if he caught the disease. Whenever one slighted an animal or treated it badly, and when certain rituals concerning the animal were not done, then whatever bad came of this was the person's own fault. But those things were gone now anyway, and not even human beings were being given respect.

A certain writer had, back in the 1800's, said that he had seen a Bear Dance done in the Cherokee Nation. And I asked Archie about it. He thought they once did it at Redbird's ground, but the singers who could lead it were gone and nothing of it has been preserved. There was a man living at Tahlequah who had the eagle feathers needed for the Eagle Dance, and he had shown Archie how to do some of the steps. Archie had invited him to come to the ground, and the man had said that he would, but he never came.

Regarding summer festivals held in Oklahoma, Archie had heard speakers at certain ceremonial grounds telling their members how the new year began in August or September, and how the Cherokees used to have a seven-day-long dance at that time at Redbird's ground, and a four-day-long dance at other places. The medicine was used also. But these dances were discontinued because, among other reasons, it was so much work preparing for them — going after the necessary herbs, getting the medicine men, and preparing the medicines. People just weren't that interested anymore. They only wanted to do social dances.

"Moreover," Archie said, "the main thing is that we are losing all of our medicine sources. Hardly any of the herbs that we need to use in our ceremonies are being found. These hills used to be full of them, and now they aren't. If you do find a place where there are some, you don't dare tell anyone. If you do, when you go back there won't be any. And even when you do go and get herbs, you have to get them at certain times and in a certain manner. You must also develop a certain attitude about it. You must arise before sunup and go without eating. No food can be eaten until the herbs are collected and

prepared. It's hard, and I don't know how the old medicine men did it."

After conversing one day about healing information that was said to have been written down but no one knew now where it was, Joyce mentioned an October Medicine Dance she had heard of. Archie frowned and said he knew nothing about that, but he did know about and had seen a Gun Dance that was supposed to be like a War Dance. Yet it seemed different than the War Dance he had been told about. They did a Green Corn Dance at Redbird's before Archie's time, and another kind of corn dance at Medicine Spring in the early 1930s. There was once a Friendship Dance that was strictly for women, but the Friendship Dance now being used at Medicine Spring was employed to "start participation in a dance, to get people going." At present, there were daytime dances and nighttime dances, common dances and special dances. Ceremonial dances had to be done on certain months and at certain times of the day. They also lasted for a precise period of time and were accompanied by a feast.

What some Cherokees called the Beginning Dance, Archie called the Round Dance. He said that at one time, each ground had its own manner of starting its dances and different songs for these, but that was another thing that was gone. "We still have our manner of starting at our ground. It's a prayer dance. We ask God's blessing to make certain everyone will have a good time and have the strength and ability to do it, and that everyone will enjoy themselves and friendships will be cemented. The whole thing has to do with asking for salvation for our people, that they will be here for a long time, and they will be blessed. Of course we have to dance all night to have this fulfilled."

Long ago, he said, there was a Clan Dance, but that was another one that was gone now. There was a Bean Dance that everyone still did, and Archie thought it might be one of the oldest dances still in existence. Its performance was like celebrating the receipt of a gift at Christmas.

Ceremonies held at Medicine Spring were begun first thing in the morning with religious services. The attitude of the people was reverent and solemn, and the services were carried on until ten or eleven o'clock. Everyone who wished could share in this. The aim was to heal the body by cleansing oneself mentally, physically, and spiritually. Only then were they ready to speak to God through the fire and in the dances.

Eli was the one who had told Archie that during the October season they used to have what they called a "chief's breakfast." Something of each kind of food that had been prepared the day before was placed on the chief's bed. Then everyone would come and take a bite, and what was left over was offered to the fire by one of the leaders.

Joyce mentioned several dances she had heard of from others that Archie knew nothing of. These included a Feather Dance, a Rhythm Dance, a Masked Dance, and the Big Turtle Dance. He had read about the Booger Dance performed by the Eastern Cherokees, but knew none of its songs. "It never worked down here in Oklahoma," he said.

He did not believe that any of the grounds had ever been used for healing purposes. They were for the benefit of the group and not the individual. All healing was done at private homes. He stressed that, as a rule, medicine men treated only men, and medicine women treated only women, for there were things that happened to each that only a healer of like sex could treat.

"I know," Archie said, "that there was a lot of times women would get sick, and while my daddy treated them he hated to do it, because it was not his proper function."

Archie did not learn any actual medicine procedures from his father and never became a medicine man. He wanted to, and he waited for the right time to do it, but the right time never came. His father had talked to Eli and to him about this, and Archie knew a little about how to treat certain diseases. "But he never taught me to chant, because I wouldn't listen."

"Millions of dollars have been spent trying to find a cure for cancer," Archie said. "When I was growing up I learned English early and could translate it into Cherokee. One day, when a white man with cancer came to my daddy, he had to talk to me. I told my daddy what he said, and after the man left, Daddy went off into the woods and in an hour and a half he was back. I don't know what he got. The white man came back the next day to pick up the medicine, but there were strict rules to go with it. You can't eat and you must follow the rest. I never learned what the medicine was, but the man was cured. As I told you, Daddy said he couldn't teach me a lot — especially about the medicine — because I was going to live a different life in the city, where I couldn't use those things. He probably would have taught me if I hadn't gone to school."

As for the makeup of the Cherokee Nation today, Archie said there are four types of people.

First, there are the old people who live back in the hills. They don't go to the grounds, but use the churches as a substitute. Everything else they do is traditional.

Second are those who work in the towns and cities and try to live in the white man's world but still go to the grounds.

Third is the group which knows nothing about the Indian world but goes to powwows for social dancing.

Fourth is the group which turns its back on everything Cherokee and lives as whites do. These are the end products of the mission schools, and some of them are full bloods.

What did Archie think the future holds for the Cherokees?

Well, we have already talked some about that, and it's plain to see that while signs of hope are there, we don't really know. It depends on so many things. I do think there has to be a plan . . . a way . . . an approach. But it has to be balanced. If someone wants to be a traditionalist, fine. But he must also hang his hat on something else. Preachers who are also medicine men already do this. Traditionalists have something special to build on, but they can benefit from the Bible, although it's a hard book to read and understand. But why can't we couple the two . . . because it all come from the same God. For example, the Bible talks about power coming from the four directions, and so do we. Look at our color symbolism. The Cherokee colors used for ceremonial purposes are red, blue, black, and white. Black is associated with the west, blue with the north, white with the south, and red with the east. Each of these colors teaches us vital things about life, and when prayers go to these directions, the power to deal with and to understand success, death, failure, happiness, and much more comes to us. I'm even more concerned with the significance of the number four than I am with the different colors. The world is put together in four directions: north, south, east, and west. We say we go through four cycles of life, the last one being old age.

Did he know the story of the "black panther" that came over the trail with the Cherokees and what it meant to them?

> I know what the story means to me, but not what it has meant to people at other grounds. Redbird Smith claimed that it was something that had come out of the heavens. It's not really a panther, its more like a dog man that looks like a panther, and each fire has its own. They are out there: apelike, long hair on the face, some say only one leg and one foot. Anyway, when the Cherokees were on the trail they could hear this thing coming with them. My grandfather heard it and told us so. And my daddy told me that when he was a little boy, about eight or nine years old, his mother went out to pick berries and he went along. And he got up close to a tree and saw this thing. It was up on a tree branch and seemed to be asleep. But he had the training and knew what it was; it was the thing that had been involved with the life of the people, and had been living among them for centuries.

Joyce wondered whether Archie could translate for us a Trail of Tears song whose words were written in Cherokee. He couldn't, so she just told the story.

"It starts up slow, when the Cherokees left their homes and started out. They went to the trees and were kissing them and telling them good-bye. The soldiers made fun of this, not knowing the Cherokees were saying farewell to the people they had buried there. So then they started out, and at nighttime when the soldiers wondered how they could keep the young people from running away, the soldiers would march some of the old folks around the fire until they were exhausted and couldn't care for themselves, knowing that the young people would never leave them in that condition. So when you get to the part of the song where it goes fast, that is when the old folks are dancing around the fire."

Archie stirred a bit, grew pensive, and said, "It's prophesied that someday we are all going back en masse, just like we left, not piecemeal, but we're going back."

Well, Archie won't be going back, and except when they visit there or when they dance and slip back in time to the ancient world, I doubt that other Western Cherokees will either. And that is precisely why some will keep dancing and remembering.

The Western Cherokees Today

And what of tomorrow? When I visited the Cherokees in northeastern Oklahoma in the 1980s, primarily in the areas where the full bloods lived, I learned that the full-blooded and nearly full-blooded population was reported to be close to 15,000 and expanding. The number of people who spoke Cherokee, despite what some informants had said to the contrary, was also growing, and it was expected that within a decade there would be significantly more who would speak both English and Cherokee. Part of this was due to the fact that the people who lived in the more remote communities had less schooling than whites and blacks, which left them at home where they were continually exposed to the native language commonly spoken by the older people. It was a situation that had changed little in the past forty years. Many Cherokees in these areas were quitting school at an early age, and only a few of them were graduating from high school. Those who did graduate often moved away to the cities where their only exposure was to the English language.

At least half of the people over thirty-five years of age could read Cherokee, and most learned it after they were thirty years of age. By the same token, no more than half of these could read English well, although the number who could was increasing.

Perhaps half of the back-area Cherokees had steady jobs, and a large percentage could not hold jobs because of old age, disabilities, or other problems. Those who did work held, for the most part, unskilled jobs. As a whole, the people were by national standards poor, although blacks who lived in the back areas were generally poorer.

As in the outlying communities of the Eastern Cherokees, Oklahoma Cherokee families made do by sharing the work and responsibilities, allowing those who could work to do so and those who couldn't to continue on.

Cherokees who live in Tulsa, Oklahoma City, and the other urban areas fare like other Americans, as do most of those Cherokees who live and work in and around the Cherokee capital, Tahlequah, whose population is something over 10,000. The Cherokee Nation tribal complex is a modern and well-equipped headquarters under the able direction of Principal Chief Wilma Mankiller, and includes meeting and working rooms, offices for the Bureau of Indian Affairs, an Arts and Crafts Center, and industrial offices. There is none of the high-pressured commercial atmosphere found in Cherokee, North Carolina.

On June 29, 1969, a splendid outdoor theatre that has artificially cooled air and an outstanding lighting system and acoustics was completed at the Tsa-La-Gi center in Tahlequah, and since then the pageant *Trail of Tears* has been performed there each summer for what, by the mid-1980s, had amounted to more than 500,000 spectators from every state in the union and more than 100 countries. Included in the pageant is the hauntingly beautiful dance of the phoenix that symbolizes the ability of the Cherokees, like the legendary phoenix bird, to rise up and fly after every great tragedy. As we know, there have certainly been many for the Cherokee people.

Within walking distance of the theater is the Cherokee National Museum, a splendid structure built with concrete, steel, and sandstone. Surrounded by a reflecting pool at its entrance are three of the remaining porch columns of the Cherokee Female Seminary that was constructed on this site in 1851, then burned to the ground in 1887. The museum is a 24,000-square-foot building in which there are displays depicting Cherokee history from the earliest known times to the present. They also have a bookstore, research archives, and displays of contemporary Indian arts and crafts that are as well arranged as in any ranking city museum. Next to the museum

is a recreation of an ancient Cherokee village, where during the tourist season costumed people portray, as the Eastern Cherokees do in their village, ancient Cherokee life. In the works when I was last there were a modern Cherokee national museum that would further illustrate Cherokee history with professionally designed and prepared displays; a Cherokee hall of fame that would recognize the contributions of Cherokees who had made significant contributions to the nation; and a Cherokee national archives that would house what was hoped to be the most thorough collection of material written by or about the original Cherokees and their descendants.

In the tribal literature, it is stated that the economic impact of Tsa-La-Gi on northeastern Oklahoma and Oklahoma tourism as a whole is measured in terms of many millions of dollars, providing many jobs for Cherokees and having a great economic impact in the area of tourism.

Ross Swimmer, who preceded the present principal chief, Wilma Mankiller, gives much of the credit for Western Cherokee resurgence to William Wayne Keeler, the chief who preceded him and who put the superlative talents that guided Phillips Petroleum Company to work for and among the Cherokees.

Keeler, with special help from his personal assistant, the well-known writer Joyce Sequichie Hifler, did much to advance the Cherokee people in the way of development, including an industrial tract, housing and land loans, trade and technical schools, self-help home improvement, educational loans, publications, research, the preservation of national history, development in cooperation with the Cherokee National Historical Society, and formation of an arts and crafts center. He also organized the tribal offices and officers for more efficient service. Not the least of his contributions to the tribe was, after many years of effort together with tribal attorney Earl Boyd Pierce and others, the receipt from the United States government of $14,789,000 in additional compensation for the Cherokee Outlet lands. Keeler also succeeded in his goal of having the principal chief elected to office by the Cherokee people, rather than appointed by the president, and the first election since Oklahoma statehood took place on August 14, 1971.

Swimmer did his best to carry on this legacy. Among the accomplishments of his years as principal chief were the purchase of 45,000 acres of once worthless land from the federal government and the transformation of it into tree farms and cattle pastures where young people are learning ranch management and cattle-breeding techniques; the doubling of tribal assets to around $25,000,000 and the highest rate of employment of any American Indian tribe; the construction of more than 2,000 Cherokee-built homes in eastern Oklahoma; and negotiation for industrial parks to house companies that would provide more capital and add to the employment base. His principal aims for Cherokees included a continuation of the traditional life that gave them an identity and a sense of place, and the economic freedom to enjoy these. I think it not surprising that he was chosen assistant secretary of the interior and director of the Bureau of Indian Affairs in Washington, D.C.

As for those traditionalists whom I came to know so well during the years of research, Joyce and Ray Johnson became more involved than ever in the Cherokee culture; both Albert Carter and Barker Dry lived and were active well into their nineties. Sig Vann became ill and was for a time unable to serve his congregation but he went back to preaching and healing before his retirement. Almanetta Sequoyah, the Eastern Cherokee medicine man from Big Cove, is dead. Doctor Garrett left the Cherokee hospital to become deputy director, Office of Program Operations, Indian Health Service. William Smith still presides over the Stokes ground. Charley Tee Hee, Elmer Dennis, and Jim Wolf have died, as have Archie Sam, Lydia Sam McLure, and Eli Sam. It may be that the Medicine Spring ground will be used no more.

The functioning grounds of today are Redbird, Stokes, and Rocky Mountain Four Mothers' Flint. (Creek); and the Blackbird, which is a practice ground. None of these is located where the original twenty-three grounds were. Some Cherokees attend the Seminole grounds, saying the Seminoles still have the traditions that the Cherokees have either lost or are, for any number of reasons, in the process of giving away.

Joyce, Ray, and I attended on the night of October 21, 1978, the "initiation" dance for a new stomp ground on a mountaintop near Tenkiller Lake, and it was exciting to be there when a new ground would be born and look to the future. It was to be a Natchez-Tsalagi-Creek ground. Its grounds chief would be John Mulley, and the assistant chief would be Robert Sumpka. Eliza Sourjohn Sumpka would be the dance leader.

When we arrived at the ground, which was in a pleasant wooded location, a fire was burning and a ball game had been planned. But not enough people were present to play. There were twelve adults and three children. Women were preparing the evening meal, including the frying of bread and hog meat.

We were too hungry to wait and went to a local restaurant to have dinner, and Jim, Celia, and Albert Carter accompanied us. When we returned to the ground at 8:15 p.m. the crowd had swelled to forty-five persons, including twelve children.

A "naming ritual" was held from 8:30 p.m. to 9:15 p.m., in which ten men, mostly young, and six women were named. I was told that this was a rite similar to baptism, so that when these people would come to the ground thereafter they would put everything else aside and not think of it while they danced. It was like the narthex of a church building, where the worldly thoughts are to be put aside before the nave is entered, so that God will have people's full attention.

Some of the names given were old clan names taken from deceased Cherokee and Creek people who had achieved prominence. They were bestowed by those elders who remembered them. Other names were of more recent vintage. All was done by lamplight, and as each person was named he or she was given a quarter. Eliza apologized for this, saying it was an emergency situation. Usually, the naming gifts were more generous. She also reminded the people that deceased relatives lived on at the ground, and were present in spirit to see these things done.

Next, at about 10:30 p.m., the named people assembled within the dance square and, with the women standing on the right, formed a single line facing the lighted fire. When they were ready, the rest of the people came to shake hands with them, called them by their new names, and welcomed them in what was called an honoring ceremony.

Directions for the entire naming ceremony were given by Eliza, and the chiefs did not join until the handshaking was finished.

The dancing proper started at 10:40 p.m., with the leaders circling the fire four times, after which the chief and the assistant chief started to sing. The others then joined in. The usual number of dancers was twenty-five, including two shell shakers and four can shakers.

We learned that a formal ground dedication was set for November 4, and we did not stay very late. My wife, Lisa, was carrying our first child and was alone at the motel, for pregnant women were not allowed at the ground. Most of the people present were relatives of Joyce's, and there was a wonderful openness and friendliness. I found myself wishing them every success, yet wondered where their fire had come from and, depending upon the way it had been moved, whether it would be able to perform its hoped-for task.

I end with the mention of this new ground because at the time of its beginning, we heard from several nonmembers negative comments about the possibilities for its survival. And yet eight years later,

in 1986, the ground was still going . . . and that is a good sign. It may be that all of the existing grounds will lapse someday, but from what I have discovered of Cherokee tenacity I fully believe that others will take up where they leave off, and that with the help of the Above Beings the fires will be successfully moved. Why do I believe this? First, because they should be preserved. Second, because the hopes so often expressed herein ought to be fulfilled. And finally, because portraying a lifeway in pageants and in recreated villages is worthwhile, but not a true substitute for the real thing. Viewing is never the equivalent of participation. Surely that is why the mixed-bloods are turning in ever greater numbers to their Cherokee history for sustenance. They too cannot abandon the common sharing of tragedies, the proud and illustrious heritage of a people who accomplished so much and about whom so many wondrous mysteries have existed.

1992

Six years have elapsed since I concluded the writing of *The Cherokee People*. During this period the Eastern Cherokees have made some economic progress, and the city of Cherokee is growing steadily as new shops are added and a convention center is planned. Tourism increases, and despite our national recession in 1991, attendance at the *Unto These Hills* pageant matched that of 1990. A friend reported to me that the tribe was experiencing some financial difficulty as they try to keep up with government standards and requirements.

I also learned there is a substantial surge in interest in Cherokee heritage. Ceremonial types of dances are being held, and elders who formerly were reluctant to talk are opening up to retell legends and remembered tales.

Under the able direction of Dr. R. Michael Abram, the Cherokee Heritage Museum and Gallery has become a focal point for contemporary Cherokee artists to exhibit their works, most of which are rooted in traditional life. The present chief of the Eastern Band of the Cherokee Indians is Jonathan L. Taylor.

Chief Wilma Mankiller of the Cherokee Nation of Oklahoma has proved herself to be an able and sensitive leader, worthy of national attention. On August 18, 1991, she was featured in *Parade* Magazine as a person "who overcame personal crises and went on to be elected the first woman Chief of the Cherokees: (she) is bringing self-sufficiency to her people." The article points out that her accomplishments in economic development, health care and tribal self-governance already are legendary in the Native American community. While in 1975 nearly all Cherokee income came from the federal government, today more than 50 percent of the tribe's revenues are from its own enterprises. On June 15, 1991, Mankiller was reelected with 83 percent of the vote. "We can look back over the 500 years since Columbus stumbled onto this continent and see utter devastation among our people." she says, "But . . . we are very hopeful. Despite everything, we survive in 1991 as a culturally distinct group." She is confident that this will continue.

In the backwoods, the stomp grounds are still in place and functioning with varying degrees of success. The important Redbud ground lost its chief and suffered a decline in membership until three years ago, when attendance at dances averaged only twenty to thirty members. Then one of the elderly female members had what she describes as "an awesome vision," in which she was told to tell the ground chief that during the dances, prayers must be addressed to both the Cherokee supernaturals and to Jesus. When she told the ground chief about this he responded favorably, and attendance has swelled to several hundred enthusiastic members for every dance. The old and the new are alive, and we can rejoice!

Appendix

CHEROKEE SOUNDS

The following is a simplification of the Cherokee phonetic scheme as given by Speck and Broom, who learned it from Will West Long, whom they call "a Cherokee purist." As stated in the preface, I omit the accent marks. Those who wish these marks and further information are referred to Speck and Broom, *Cherokee Dance and Drama,* pp. XIV and XV; Mooney, *Myths*, pages 188 and 506; and Mooney and Olbrechts, *The Swimmer Manuscript*, pages 11-13.

Vowels

a as in "father"

u as *oo* in "moon"

a as in "sun"

i as in "pin"

e as *aw* in "law"

i as *ea* in "seat"

a as *a* in "take"

e obscure *e* as in "the" when occurring before initial consonant

Semiconsonants

y, w approximately as in English

Consonants

d voice as in "do"

G intermediate between *g* and *k*

D intermediate between *d* and *t* unvoiced, as *T* in "hit"

K unvoiced as in t "king"

g voiced as in "go"

n,m as in English

s,z as in English

l as in English

c equal to *sh* as in "fish"

l unvoiced

dz as in "adze"

dj as in "Jim"

tc unvoiced, as *ch* in "church"

ts unvoiced, as in "ants"

CHEROKEE HISTORICAL SITES

Alabama

The presence of the Cherokees in Alabama is similar to that of Georgia, that is, the Cherokees moved southward from the Great Smokies only in the historic period. Alabama was occupied chiefly by the Creeks as well as the Choctaw, Chickasaw, and Seminole. There was much mound building activity in ancient Alabama (Moundville, Florence, Russell Cave), but these areas are related to tribes other than the Cherokee.

The mountain lake region in northern Alabama is where the Cherokees settled. Manitou Cave near Ft. Payne is a Cherokee word meaning "The Great Spirit." Also, the site of the Cherokee village, Will's Town, is where Sequoyah lived in the early 1800s.

Many museums in Alabama have Indian relics, and although it is not known what tribes are represented, it seems unlikely that many of them could be Cherokee. These museums are the Regar Memorial Museum of Natural History in Anniston and the Alabama State Museum and Huntsville Museum, as mentioned in the letter from the Alabama Department of Archives and History.

Georgia

Most of the historical sites of the Georgia Cherokees exemplify their culture after it had been influenced by the white man. In some instances, the Cherokees drove out other tribes, as the Creeks, for example, or the white man, as in the destruction of Traveler's Rest.

The Vann House: The Vann House was built by James Vann, a Cherokee, in 1804 and is an example of the Cherokee culture at that time. The house has hand carving inside and out; bricks for the house were made on the plantation there, and the hinges were produced in his blacksmith shop. The house is a historical commission site and is located near Chatsworth, three miles west on U.S. 76. Open Monday - Saturday 9 a.m.- 5:30 p.m., Sunday - 1 p.m.- 5:30 p.m.

Traveler's Rest: A pioneer home and early hotel (circa 1835), which was destroyed by the Cherokees. The tribe had a village site nearby, which is referred to as the Turnbull Site on the Tugaloo River; it is thought to be the historical Cherokee town of Tugaloo. (Traveler's Rest is located in Toccoa.)

New Echota: New Echota served as the capital of the Cherokee Nation from 1825 to 1838. The first copy of the *Cherokee Phoenix* was printed here. Exhibits include tools used by the Indians, scenes of farmers and early leaders, a Cherokee Bible dated 1861, an original copy of the *Cherokee Phoenix*, a replica of a tombstone, a copy of the laws of the Cherokee Nation, a scale model of the grounds of New Echota at the time of occupancy, replicas of the Cherokee supreme court building, and the site of the Oothcaloga Mission House. New Echota is located northeast of Calhoun (U.S. 41) on Georgia 225. Open Monday through Saturday 9 a.m.- 5:30 p.m., Sunday 1 p.m.- 5:30 p.m.

Rome: The Martin Archaeological Museum at Shorter College. The only thing relating to Indians was an extremely small collection of pottery shards (Lamar stamped) and game stones from the Coosa County Country Club.

I wanted also to see the Chieftains, but it was closed that particular day. The Chieftains was the home of John Ridge. Ridge was quite wealthy, and this site demonstrates the influence of the whites on the Cherokees. This is also the site of the U. S. Cherokee treaty that removed the Cherokees to Oklahoma. The Chieftains is also the location of an old Indian trading post. Open Wednesday 11 a.m. - 3 p.m. and Sunday 2 - 5 p.m.

Also near Rome is a 16th century Cherokee village known as the King Site, which is being excavated. It is located beside the Coosa River near Foster's Bend in Floyd County.

Eatontom: The Rock Eagle Effigy, a huge rock formation made from milky quartz and measuring 102 feet by 120 feet, was apparently made by some Indian tribe, although it is not known which tribe. The purpose of the structure has not been decided upon. Open year round.

Augusta: The Hollywood Mound, a Cherokee historical site (at least thought to be by some archaeologists), is located here. The Augusta Museum reportedly has archaeological exhibits among its collection, but I do not know whether they are of Cherokee origin.

The Mackay House, also in Augusta, has some Indian artifacts, but of which tribe, I can't say.

Nacooche: Although not a historical site to visit, the Nacoochee Mound is thought to have been inhabited by the Cherokee.

Rossville: The Ross Mansion is a restored home of John Ross, principal chief of the Cherokee Nation from 1828 to 1866. In addition, Ross was a merchant, planter, and statesman as well as leader of the group opposed to the Cherokee removal. Some of the items in the Ross House include a large rare photograph of John Ross in a gold frame, a picture of Daniel Ross, a picture of John Ross after a McKenney and Hall print, a picture of Houston Benge Teehee, a Cherokee Testament, a hand painted picture of the Ross house, an Indian basket, an Indian mat, an Indian doll, a Ross coat of arms, wool hand-loomed Indian rugs, a Cherokee hymnal, the last picture taken of John Ross, a black and white print of the Ross house before restoration, a print of the Ross house from *Scribner's Monthly Magazine*, May 1874, two black and white prints of Indians, a seal of the Cherokee Nation, and a framed picture of John Ross.

North Carolina

North Carolina is, of course, the heart of both the ancient and historical Eastern Cherokees. After they were driven southward from the northern United States by the Delawares, (as one legend has it), they stayed in the Great Smoky region, venturing occasionally into the surrounding states of South Carolina, Georgia, Alabama, and Tennessee.

Besides the Qualla Boundary/Cherokee City, there are numerous other places in North Carolina which have Indian artifacts: Person Hall, University of North Carolina at Chapel Hill, Raleigh State Museum, Art and Science Museum at

Statesville, Park Natural History Museum at Albermarle, Museum of the American Indian at Boone, Schiele Museum at Gastonia, Rowan Museum, Inc. at Salisbury, Greensboro Historical Museum, Indian Museum at St. Andrew's College, Moravian Archives in Winston-Salem, Mint Museum of Art in Charlotte, North Carolina Museum of Life and Science in Durham, Wachovia Museum in Old Salem, and the Charlotte Natural History Museum.

The Cherokee Harvest Fair is held in Cherokee in October. This is the only occasion at which the ancient Cherokee dances are performed.

The various archaeological digs in North Carolina that have been assigned to the Cherokees are the Peachtree Creek site near Murphy, and the sites of Kituhwa, Nununyi and Nequassee of western North Carolina.

The North Carolina Department of Archives and History must have a collection of artifacts, because in *Sun Circles and Human Hands,* there are photographs of a Cherokee cooking pot and a Cherokee wooden dance mask credited to the North Carolina Archives.

Museum of the Cherokee Indian, Cherokee: On view at the museum are the following exhibits:

Stones tools and weapons: Fashioned slowly by hand, these played a major role in the life of the American Indian.

Mineral Display: Typical specimens from the mineral-rich Southern Appalachian Mountains are shown in this revolving display.

Indian Corn: Depicts the evolution of this colorful symbol of Indian culture.

Cherokee Pipes: Unlike the white man, Indians generally smoked pipes only during tribal ceremonies—not for pleasure. The Cherokee believed smoking would frighten away evil spirits.

Bone Ornaments: Deer, bear, turtle, and turkey bones provided the ornaments often worn by the Cherokees.

Seashell Ornaments: Though their homeland was far from the ocean, the Cherokee obtained seashells for ornaments by trading coastal Indian tribes.

Game Stones: Indians played games with stones like these.

Oconaluftee Village Crafts: From the "living village," which represents a Cherokee town of 200 years ago, various aspects of Indian life are shown at fifteen stations. Next to the village is the beautiful Cherokee Nature Trail.

Model of Ancient Burial: Indians often were buried with favorite ornaments worn during life.

Mortar and Pestle: The Cherokee ground up corn into meal with the heavy wooden mortar and pestle. The large end was held uppermost.

Bannerstones, Birdstones, Boatstones: Bannerstones were symbols of tribal authority. Birdstones were worn by medicine men. Boatstones were charms worn by Indians traveling in canoes to ward off disaster.

Origin of the American Indian: It is believed that Indians have been in North and South America for at least 20,000 years—having migrated from Asia over a land bridge or on the ice along the Bering Straits into present Alaska.

Dug-Out Canoe: Hollowed out by controlled burning and the use of stone tools.

Pottery: Exhibit shows both present-day and ancient Cherokee and Creek Indian pieces. Designs in the clay are applied by hand.

Original Cherokee Territory: 1884 map shows original Cherokee land claims in parts of eight Southeastern states and territory ceded by Indian treaties.

Henderson Collection: Crafts from the collection of James Edward Henderson, first superintendent of the Cherokee Indian Agency.

Cherokee Printing: Examples of printing in the Sequoyah syllabary.

Sequoyah: Inventor of the only syllabary in the Indian language.

John Ross: Longtime Cherokee Chief who waged a campaign in Washington, D. C., to prevent the removal of his people to Indian Territory west of the Mississippi.

Early Trade Items: Trading was an important part of the relations between Indian tribes and the white men.

Pistols: The pistol at the top is a military-type flintlock made in 1837 in Massachusetts. The other pistols in the case are replicas.

Will Thomas: White Chief of the Cherokee who was instrumental in the establishment of the Qualla Boundary Reservation.

Medicine Man: Exhibit emphasizes the importance of the medicine man in Cherokee life.

Cherokee Stickball: A favorite Indian game, like field hockey, still played today.

Steps in Basketry: Depicts steps in making baskets from river cane or wooden splints.

Trail of Tears: Traces the 1,200 mile route followed in 1838 by the U. S. Army in removing 17,000 Cherokee from their homes in the Southeast to Indian Territory—later Oklahoma.

Removal Clothing: Two articles of clothing worn on the Trail of Tears are shown at left. At the right is the "surrender document" signed by the Cherokee Council.

Removal List, Lottery Deeds: On the left is a list of the Cherokee removed westward from Ft. Butler, near present Murphy, North Carolina. On the right are lottery deeds issued by the state of Georgia for land seized from the Cherokee Nation.

John Burnett's Story: Contains possessions of John Burnett, a United States Army soldier and friend of the Cherokee, who participated in the removal westward.

Will Rogers: Oklahoman and part Cherokee, probably the greatest and most loved of all American humorists. Visited here periodically.

*Asterisks indicate exhibits interpreted by audiotape programs.

South Carolina

The Cherokee Path was the most famous of the Indian paths which served as early avenues of commerce. Today, highways follow the trail. As mentioned in the brochure describing it, the Cherokee Path Trail ran northwesterly through the state up to the Overhill Settlements in Tennesseee. One town not mentioned in "Cherokee Path Trail" is the town of Tennessee, whose original name of Tamassee meant Sunlight of God. The name is said to derive from the legend of a Cherokee fire prophet, who attributed his power of healing to a large ruby. From far and near Indians came to the village with their ailments and wounds. When the prophet died, the hill where he was buried with the stone was called Tamassee.

Also located in South Carolina is the historical archaeological site of Chauga in Oconee County.

There are many museums in South Carolina which have Indian relics, including the Charleston Natural History Museum, Florence Museum, Andrew Jackson Historical State Park in Lancaster (Indian relics 1750-1850), The Greenwood Museum, and the University of South Carolina Institute of Archaeology and Anthropology. Apparently the Catawaba tribe is empha-sized more than any other tribe as the following excerpt from "News from the South Carolina Museum Commission" states:

"The dynamics of the invasion and settlement of North America by Indians will be displayed in order of their appear-ance and will depict changes as they occurred right up to the present time. While all major native Americans will be represented, the culture of the Catawbas will be singled out for major treatment. The Catawbas will be a continuing concern of the State Museum in its research, reference collections and living history programs as well as in its exhibition galleries."

The above passage regards the forecoming policy of the South Carolina State Museum which is in the planning stages.

Information on archaeological and historic sites is available from the South Carolina Department of Archives and History, the Institute of Archaeology and Anthropology at the University of South Carolina in Columbia, and the South Carolina Museum Commission.

Tennessee

The Cherokees had a strong foothold in Tennessee. Arriving in eastern Tennessee just prior to the white man's arrival, the Cherokee found the Creek tribe and eventually settled in the areas of Tuckuseogee, headwaters of the Little Tennessee and the Tellico River, which is known historically as the "Middle" region of the Cherokees and the "Upper" region which consisted of towns on the Valley, Nottely, and Upper Hiwassee Rivers. The "Valley" settlements refer to the Upper region and the "Overhill" settlements are in the Middle region. Many of the archaeological sites located on the Tennessee River have traditionally been ascribed to the Cherokees.

The historic period brought the white man into the Tennessee and a confrontation with the Cherokee. The Cherokees forced out a garrison at Ft. Loudoun, a British colonial fort and occupied it for more than a year. The excavations there have produced material representing the Cherokee culture of the 18th century. The Ft. Loudoun Association Museum is probably the location of these artifacts.

Other museums in Tennessee that have Cherokee artifacts are the McClung Museum, University of Tennessee in Knoxville, Kirkland Hall (Prehistoric Indian Artifacts) at Vanderbilt University in Nashville. The Tennessee State Museum is also in Nashville.

ETOWAH MOUNDS

The Etowah Mounds and village sites, the largest and most important Indian settlement in the Etowah Valley, were occupied between A.D.1000 and 1500. Etowah, the center of political and religious life in the Valley, was the home of chiefs who directed the growing, storage, and distribution of food. Here the population of the area gathered for great religious festivals.

At its peak there may have been several thousand Indians living in this fortified town, surrounded on all sides except for the river section by a wood post stockade and a deep moat. Within the palisade the people of Etowah built windowless houses, using a post framework, clay-plastered walls, and grass thatch or cane mat roofs. A basin-shaped clay fireplace was built in the center of the earthern floor and smoke escaped through a hole in the roof.

Seven pyramids were grouped around two public squares in the town. Using baskets full of earth from borrow pits near the moats, the Indians constructed these mounds. The largest, called Mounds A, fifty-three feet high and occupying several acres, dominated the scene. A clay ramp stepped with logs led to the tops of the mounds, where temples or residences for chiefs and priests stood. These structures, built like houses, were larger and more elaborately decorated.

Elaborate religious rituals centered on the burial of chiefs. Several hundred burials have been excavated around the base of Mound C and beneath the floors of funeral temples that stood on its summit. The dead were buried in elaborate costumes, accompanied by special paraphernalia.

Etowah Indians were skilled in many crafts and used copper, shell, cane, flint, wood, clay, and bone to make hundreds of different items. Pottery was one of the most important Etowah crafts. Wood was carved into masks, ornaments, and rattles; copper was shaped into decorative ornaments; and shells were made into bead necklaces. Baskets and matting were woven from cane and cloth from plant fiber, hair, and feathers. Sewing implements, weaving tools, hairpins, and fishhooks were cut from bone; and stone was used in the manufacture of axes, arrowpoints, and knives.

Etowah had close contact with other areas in the Southeast. Marine shells from Florida, flint from Tennessee, copper from North Georgia and pottery made in the Mississippi Valley all found their way to Etowah. Decorations found on pottery and religious objects are typical of a wide area of the Southeast.

Cultivation of crops provided the Indians with their most important food resources. Most of the valley was one stretch of corn. Besides a variety of corn types, the Indians grew beans and pumpkins. On wooded hills lining the valley, they gathered wild nuts, fruits, and roots. The Indians did not raise food animals, as hunting and fishing provided their meat. Excavation of refuse areas indicates that deer and turkey were the most important game; mussels and fish were obtained from the river.

In the 1880s the Bureau of American Ethnology of the Smithsonian Institution received many spectacular artifacts from the village and Mound C. During the late 1920s, Phillips Academy of Andover, Massachusetts, undertook three short seasons of excavation, uncovering exotic and interesting specimens; these were distributed to various United States museums. Both institutions felt that Mound C had been completely explored.

In 1953, the Georgia Historical Commission purchased the property. Since then, Commission archaeologists have found more than two hundred ceremonial burials and associated artifacts in Mound C. The latest archaeological techniques have provided new information about mound construction and cultural developments. Archaeological research continues at this exceptionally well preserved site. Results of some of the archaeological excavations that were done in the summers of 1964 and 1965 are exhibited in an in-place burial building constructed over the excavated area.

In addition to the preservation of the remaining mound group, an interpretative museum has been developed. This museum exhibits the many unusual specimens found by archaeologists at this site. One outstanding exhibit is a pair of male and female mortuary figures carved from white marble and having traces of their original paint.

The Etowah Mounds Archaeological Area has been designated a U. S. Department of the Interior National Historic Landmark under the provisions of the Historic Sites Act of August 21, 1935. This award is reserved for sites possessing exceptional value in commemorating and illustrating the history of the United States of America. The Archaeological Area is also on the National Register of Historic Places of the United States Department of the Interior.

CHEROKEE PETROGLYPHS

Georgia

In the *Tenth Annual Report of the Bureau of American Ethnology 1888-89,* Washington, 1893, in "Picture Writing of the American Indians - Georgia," Charles C. Jones, Jr. describes a petroglyph in Georgia as follows: "In Forsyth county, Georgia, is a carved or incised boulder of fine grained granite, about nine feet long, four feet, six inches high, and three feet broad at its widest point. The figures are cut in the boulder from one-half to three-quarters of an inch deep. It is generally believed that they are the work of the Cherokees. . . . It will be noted in it (the boulder) that the characters are chiefly circles, including plain, nucleated, and concentric, sometime two or more being joined by straight lines, forming what is now known as the 'spectacle shaped' figure. (This boulder is currently on display at the University of Georgia, Athens)."

Dr. M. F. Stephenson mentions sculptures of human feet, various animals, bear tracks, etc., in Enchanted Mountain, Union county, Georgia. The whole number of sculptures is reported as 146.

Mr. Jones gives a different resume of the objects depicted, as follows: "Upon the enchanted mountain, in Union county, cut in plutonic rock, are the tracks of men, women, children, deer, bears, bisons, turkeys, and terrapins, and the outlines of a snake, two deer, and of a human hand. These sculptures-so far as they have been ascertained and counted-number 136. The most extravagant among them is that known as the footprint of the Great Warrior. It measures eighteen inches in length and has six toes. The other human tracks and those of the animals are delineated with commendable fidelity."

This particular area is apparently similar to the one James Mooney mentions in his *Myths of the Cherokees:* "Track Rock Gap: A gap about five miles east of Blairsville, in Union county, on the ridge separating Brasstown creek from the waters of Nottely river. The micaceous soapstone rocks on both sides of the trail are covered with petroglyphs, from which the gap takes its name. . . . The carvings are of many and various patterns, some of them resembling human or animal footprints, while others are squares, crosses, circles, 'bird tracks,' etc. disposed without any apparent order."

In *Cry of the Eagle, History and Legends of the Cherokee Indians and their Buried Treasures* (published by the author in Cumming, Georgia in 1969), author Forest C. Wade discusses signs and symbols carved on trees and stones that he claims were made by the Cherokees. These symbols tell of hidden treasure, gold which the Cherokees hid before their removal westward. These markings are found around the area of the author's home, Forsyth County, Georgia. The back of the book contains photographs and drawings of these secret signs and symbols. The location of these markings are Hurricane Creek, Vikery Creek, Etowah River, Bannister Creek, all in Forsyth County; Rising Fawn's (Cherokee chief) homesite on Settendown Creek in Cherokee County; a large stone near the Freeman old millsite on Long Swamp Creek; trail markers knee tree, pull tree, saddle tree, stunted tree, humped tree; the Etowah riverbank in east Cherokee County; and the Hickory Log District in Cherokee County, Georgia.

Tennessee

The following is an account of petroglyphs in Tennessee from "Picture-Writing of the American Indians" in the *10th Annual Report of the American Bureau of Ethnology 1888-1889.*

"He (John Haywood) also gives the following account: On the south bank of the Holston, five miles above the mouth of French Broad, is a bluff of limestone opposite the mounds and a cave in it. The bluff is 100 feet in height. On it are painted in red colors, like those on the Paint rock, the sun and moon, a man, birds, fishes, etc. The paintings have in part faded within a few years. Tradition says these paintings were made by the Cherokees, who were accustomed in their journeys to rest at this place."

CHEROKEE ARTIFACTS IN MUSEUM HOLDINGS

Selected Items from the Emory Museum, Atlanta Georgia

Bannerstones or weights used as throwing sticks from the Archaic Period into the Woodland Period. Banner Stones were made of granite, steatite, rose quartz, diorite, slate, hematite, and porphyry.

Gorgets made of various stones and carrying one or two holes.

Bevelled arrow heads.

Pottery fragments.

Deptford check stamp with incised punctate strap handle, one of the earliest examples of Southeast carved paddle stamp.

Indian drills which were turned by hand or by means of a wooden shaft.

War points with heads not firmly attached to the shaft so that if the shaft were pulled from the wounded enemy, the head would not come out.

Javelin points originally attached to short wooden shafts and thrown by means of atlatls or spear launchers.

Dart points used to kill small game.

Fish net sinkers.

Universal tool found on east side of Kinchafonee Creek, Lee County, Georgia. Used as a scraper knife, saw, skinner, and awl.

Fire-stick holders.

Hide scrapers.

Portable paint pot.

Arrow heads used mostly to tip arrows used in hunting game.

Spear heads and knive blades.

Indian beads.

Indian ceremonial pipe found near Hutchenson's Ferry in Coweta County, Georgia. Loaned by J. W. Wellborn, Newnan, Georgia.

Opal from Indian mound in North Carolina.

Indian paint pot, a naturally occurring concretion often filled with a red or yellow pigment.

Portion of an Indian pipe from Tumlin Village Site in Cartersville, Georgia.

Indian game stones used to play a type of "heads" or "tails" game. The design is on only one side.

Indian calumet pipe, rare because of its fine workmanship. Found on George Graf's farm near Atlanta, Georgia. Loaned by George Graf.

Effigies of soap stone (steatite).

Indian ax heads.

Banner stones.

Grinding ax (Pestle) and mortar fragment.

Large Indian celt or hatchet found about five miles from Uvalda, Georgia, near the Oconee River.

Indian bowl and grinder found by J. D. Duncan near the Chattahoochee River.

Indian corn grinder found near Opelika, Alabama.

Shell beads from grave D-12 Mound C Tumlin Village Site near Cartersville, Georgia.

Pearl Beads from grave K-12 Mound C Tumlin Village Site near Cartersville, Georgia.

Beads. The Indians of the Etowah Mounds were very fond of ornaments. Both men and women wore strings of pearl and shell beads around their neck, arms, and legs.

Shell pin whose use is not known, although it most certainly was an ornament of some kind. Highly polished and very beautiful.

Other items, including the following: Fine quartzite discoidal, Etowah axes, discoidal stones, fine bone awls, modeled clay leg, worked bone tools, shell gorgets, pearl disk, Etowah pipes, stamped pottery shards, pottery bowl, ornamented pottery, small pot, rubbing stone, tool sharpener, shell drinking cup, stone hoe, stone disk, Indian bowl, and eating bowl.

Selected Items from the Georgia State Museum, Atlanta, Georgia

Prehistoric pottery using many different decorative techniques — incised lines, stamped designs and paint. In some instances they may have served a purpose; however, in the majority of cases they were merely artistic decorations.

"sun circle" stamp

Irene simple check stamp

complicated stamp

pinched rim and brushed body

Swift Creek complicated stamp

Lamar, incised rim and stamped body

plain painted, punctate and incised

punctate rim and stamped body

Etowah, bold incised

Lamar, bold incised

Ceramics

Pottery of the prehistoric peoples of Georgia:

negative incised bottle

tripodal bottle

Southeastern pottery

The first pottery in the Southeast was molded and fiber-tempered. It is believed to have been indigenous, though the idea may have come from the outside area. This was soon replaced by coil pottery made from clay tempered with a variety of grits and shell.

food bowl or dish

food vessel - slab and drag

Potter's implements

trowel - used to smooth vessels as they were being made.

flint scraper - with this, in some cases her fingernail, the Indian incised designed on her pottery.

reproduction of a 'decoration paddle' such as those pressed against the soft clay to produce stamped designs. (Other decorations were made by wrapping the paddles with fabric or cord.)

dish from Heard County

small bowl and ladle - These have been classified as toys by some individuals. However, this is highly improbable, and their exact uses are unknown.

game discs - made from pot shards. These were used in some Indian game, or they may have been "counting" disks.

Pottery Vessels

Women were doubtless responsible for most domestic pottery, and vessels enabled them to better prepare food, easily transport and store liquids, and give them an outlet for creative abilities.

food vessel - Lamar complicated

vessel perforated for repair

Miscellaneous vessels

bird and duck

stems from various type of vessels

dog

engraved vessel

hanging vessels or loop handled

Tools

Hammer stone - used in the makeshift blank, arrow points, knives, etc.

cracking stone

hammer stones

fragment of hammer or maul

paint bowls

weights

colorful stone taken from burial mounds

knife blades used for skinning and scraping hides

chungke stones

Hunting items

Celts-used as scrapers and chisels, etc.

arrowheads-made from gar fish scales

projectile points

Ceremonial Pottery

Commonly referred to as effigy pottery, these were, in numerous instances, made strictly for ceremonial purposes. This is known by the fact that their construction exemplified by the perforated bodies of the Kolomoki bird effigy precludes utilitarian usage.

It is also probable that many effigy pots, pipes, etc., were merely artistic expressions of their makers. Their exact ceremonial functions have, in many cases, been lost in antiquity.

Kolomoki ceremonial bird

frog

Pottery

negative incised bottle

domestic vessels

cooking pot

Arrow flakes, blanks and pottery shards

Atlatl, spear and arrow points

Quartz heads and true arrow points

Hammer stones and axes and celts

Game and chungke stones and drill bits

Miscellaneous:

stemmed stone hoe, plain-edge stone hoe, mouthpiece miscellaneous bits (reamers, borers, and drill), strap drill, flint scrapers, flint knives, Large Mississippian Period handle pipe head, Large soapstone Woodland Period rectangular pipe head, major types of prehistoric smoking pipes, chungke stones, mortar and grinding stone, small chisel and celt, molded earthern spheres, atlatl and spear, atlatle weights, cooking pot.

Miscellaneous States

According to photo credits in the book *Sun Circles and Human Hands: The Southeastern Indians - Art and Industry* (edited by Emma Lila Fundaburk and Mary Douglas Fundaburk Foreman, 1957, published by Emma Lila Fundaburk, Luverne, Alabama.), the following museums have Cherokee artifacts:

The University of Pennsylvania in Philadelphia: Cherokee dance masks, some used in the Booger dance, others made of fur and wood, animal and human effigy pipes from North and South Carolina, a tomahawk effigy and plain elbow pipes, and twilled splint baskets.

The American Indian Museum in New York: Booger type Cherokee masks, one with a carbed rattlesnake.

The Denver Art Museum: Cherokee masks of wood decorated with leather and fur and one representing a deer.

Author Charles Miles has a Cherokee pipe in his personal collection according to his book, *Indian and Eskimo Artifacts of North America* (Henry Regnery Co., Chicago, Illinois, 1963).

RESOURCES FOR STUDY OF CHEROKEE ARTIFACTS

Photographs

I - Georgia State Museum - 5 prints and negatives
KC-8A smoking pipes
KC-9 pottery sherds and bottles
KC-10 "
KC-11A hanging vessels and chunkey stones
KC-12A ceremonial pottery and domestic vessels
II - Georgia State Museum - 9 prints and 12 negatives
KC-1 sherds and bottles
KC-2 engraved vessel and stones
KC-3 sherds
KC-4 hanging vessel
KC-6 ceremonial pottery
KC-7 hanging vessels
KC-8 vessels
KC-11 vessels
KC-12 bowls
III - Georgia State and Emory University Museums - 2 prints and 19 negatives
MC-2 Late Mississippian Food Bowl
MC-3 Type of Civilizations
MC-4 shell beads, bird effigy, Etowah pipe
MC-5 Late Mississippian food bowl
MC-7 Axes
MC-8 Burial urns and food vessels
MC-9 Pipes
MC-10 animal pipes
Emory University
MC-12 gorgets
MC-13 ceremonial pipe
MC-15 chungke stone
MC-16 pipes
MC-17 grinder and bowl
MC-18 effigies
MC-19 javelin points
MC-20 portable paint pot
MC-20A Indian beads
IV - Georgia State and Emory University Museum - 18 prints and 19 negatives. Black and White
Emory University Museum
A-4 fire stick holders
A-5 hide scrapers
A-6 arrowheads
A-7 Indian Ceremonial Pipe
A-8 Shell beads and shell pin
A-9 Beads and Pearl Beads
Georgia State Museum
A-10 Negative incised bottle
A-11 hanging vessel
A-12 hanging vessel or loop-handled
A-13 hanging vessel
A-14 Ceremonial pottery (frog)
A-15 Primitive Art - Irene simple check stamp

A-16 food bowl
A-17 Ceremonial Pottery
A-18 animal effigy pipes
A-19 Chungke stone
A-20 Human effigy bottle
A-21 Spear (detail)
V - Cherokee Museum, Cherokee, N. C. - 12 prints and negatives - Black and White
B-1 Bear Tooth Necklace
B-1A Turtle Bone Necklace
B-2 Hair pins
B-3 Gorgets and ornaments
B-4 Shell Necklaces
B-5 Chunkey stone
B-6 Cherokee pot
B-7 Cherokee water jug
B-8 Duck effigy bowl
B-9 Double wedding vessel
B-10 ear pins and plugs
B-11 ear pins
VI - Cherokee Museum, Cherokee N. C. - 10 prints and 12 negatives - color
C-2 Adzes
C-3 Bone tubes, Turtle Bone necklace, and needles
C-4 Bear Tooth Necklace, fish hook and awls
C-5 Gorgets and ornaments
C-6 Gorgets
C-7 Bannerstones
C-9 Medicine Man item
C-10 Chungke stones
C-11 Chungke stone
C-12 Stone discs
VII - Cherokee Museum, Cherokee, N. C. and Smithsonian Institute (National Museum of Natural History), Washington, D.C. - 9 prints and 20 negatives - color
D-3 Comfrey and Yarrow - Cherokee Botanical Gardens
D-4 Indian Corn Beads - Cherokee Botanical Gardens
D-5 Alleghany Onion - Cherokee Botanical Gardens
D-6 Swamp Pink - Cherokee Botanical Gardens
D-11 Cherokee Eagle Dance Masks - Smithsonian
D-12 Feather Wand - Smithsonian
D-13 Cherokee baskets of cane and splints - Smithsonian
D-14 Cherokee moccasins - Smithsonian
D-15 Cherokee cooking pot - Smithsonian
VIII - Cherokee Museum, Cherokee, N. C. and Smithsonian Institute, Washington, D. C. - 24 prints and 31 negatives - black and white
E-1 Bannerstone - Cherokee Museum
E-2 Boatstone - Cherokee Museum
E-3 Medicine Man Regalia - Cherokee Museum
E-4 Birdstone - Cherokee Museum
E-5 Birdstone - Cherokee Museum
E-6 Plummets - Cherokee Museum
E-7 Shell Beads - Cherokee Museum
E-8 Shell Beads - Cherokee Museum
E-9 Pottery Sherd, Tugalo Incised - Smithsonian
E-10 Pottery Sherd, Tugalo Complicated Stamp - Smithsonian

E-11 Dance Mask -Smithsonian
E-12 Mask - Smithsonian
E-13 Cherokee Moccasins - Smithsonian
E-14 Cherokee Pipe - Smithsonian
E-15 Cane Basket - Smithsonian
E-16 Basket of splints - Smithsonian
E-17 Carrying basket of splints - Smithsonian
E-18 Cherokee earrings - Smithsonian
E-19 Incised paddles - Smithsonian
E-20 Eagle Dance Mask - Smithsonian
E-21 Detail of feather wand - Smithsonian
E-22 Detail of feather wand - Smithsonian
E-23 Cherokee Deer call - Smithsonian
E-24 Cherokee cooking pot - Smithsonian

State of Georgia Archives Picture File, Atlanta, Georgia

Negative File
Portrait of Sequoyah 344
Large Print Collection
Sequoyah 10 by 15 16 22
Small Print Collection - Cherokee Heading
Subject , Item , Box , Number
Ridge, John copy of drawing 5 37B
Ridge, Major " 5 38B
Watie, Stand copy of painting 7 23
Cherokee alphabet copy of photo 3 7B
Cherokee Ball Game copy of newspaper 12 84
Cherokee County - newspaper clipping 16 15
Smith, James Burdine
Cherokee alphabet original photo 3 7
Sequoyah copy of painting 5 48
Cherokee County - copy of photo 12 78
Smith, Joseph Benton
Cherokee County - original photo 4 4
Historian - Marlin, L. G.
Cherokee newspaper - copy of photo 14 38W
Georgia Historical
Profile Series
Vann, David copy of drawing 7 19
Ridge, Major copy of painting 5 38
Vann, James, home of - copy of photo 13 1
Cherokee County - original photo 10 57
Johnson, Joseph E.
Ross, John copy of painting 5 42
Cherokee County - original photo 8 94
Mill, W. D.
Cherokees gathered for removal, Dahlonega, Ga. - copy of photo 13 37D
3 Little Cherokee girls copy of newspaper 6 38B
Cherokee printing office color postcard 5 37C
New Echota
Cherokee women with baskets copy of newspaper 6 38C
Cherokee Removal copy of drawing 6 38B
Ridge, John copy of painting 5 37
The Cherokee Phoenix copy of painting 15 98

Boudinot, Elias

Cherokee Phoenix   postcard   5   37D

The Archives will reproduce prints for $3 for a single item.

Newspaper Clippings
The Georgia Archives, Indian Heading

"Cherokee Hope Talks with George Fruitful" Muskogee Daily Phoenix 4/25/70

"Cherokees Settle the Final Claim" A 7/9/72

"First Will was Linked with Cherokees" *The Forsyth County News,* Cumming, Georgia 3/18/71

"Calhoun Cherokee Site is Explored" C 11/28/69

"Where Civilized Georgia Indians Lived" (Major Ridge) A 10/19/69

"Indians Built this Amazing Georgia House" (Vann House) A 7/20/58

"Cherokee Dreams" No author or date given

"Homes of Distinguished Cherokee Indians - III - The House of John Martin, Treasurer of the Cherokee Nation" J 12/5/33

"Story of how the Indians Gradually Yielded all of Georgia to the White Man" C 5/27/34

"Ten Greatest Events in Georgia History - #7 - The Removal of the Cherokees" J 5/10/36

"Pot of Gold at Toccoa" J 8/23/31

"Georgia's Capital of the Cherokees Being Rebuilt" (New Echota) A 1/13/57

"Indian Village Comes to Life Again" (New Echota) A 9/4/60

"New Echota to Open in '60'" A 11/26/59

"Capital of the Cherokee" (New Echota) J 2/4/60

Chief White Path (No title) J 10/4/67

"Was Burning at the Stake to be Her Fate?" (Nancy Ward) C 4/20/58

"Risked Life for Clay" J 2/16/60

"Sequoyah's Alphabet was a Literary Miracle" J 11/24/57

"Cherokee Feast Features Fatback, Ribs, Creases" J 11/23/73

"Indian Names Enshrined in Georgia" J 10/9/67

"Cherokee Bride Shocked New England" (The Ridges) C 9/22/63

"Who Lived on the Tugaloo Near Toccoa About 5,000 B.C.?" A 7/31/60

"Woes of an Indian Editor" J 5/7/59

"Cherokee Capital in 1827" J 2/5/60

"Grandma Knew the Cherokees" C 9/22/63

"Cherokees still Split Over 'Trail'" J 3/12/71

"Education Needs Cited" C 4/15/70

"Dixie's Indians Need Health, Housing Help" C 4/17/70

"Crime and Drinking Only Part of the Problem" C 41/6/70

"Most Indians still Don't Trust the White Man" C 4/13/70

"Gwinnett, DeKalb Need Indians to Find Lost County Border" J 1/1/58

J - *Atlanta Journal*

C - *Atlanta Constitution*

A - *Atlanta Journal and Constitution Magazine* (Sunday Edition)

"Three States Honor Chief Sequoia" C 6/23/61

"Decatur Man is Chief of Indian Tribe" C 2/23/61

"Indian Powwow Brings Honor to Decatur Woman" J 9/5/58

"Chewani Keeping Indian Lore Alive" C 5/1/57

"Indian Lore Atlantan's Joy" J 1/30/62

"Decatur's Cherokee Princess" J 5/22/63

"Pastor's Open Grave, Take Remains of 'Indian Chief'" C 8/29/62

"Indians Get Paid After 70 Years" J 6/7/63

"U.S. Returns Some Loot to Injuns" C 9/21/63

"Where Indians Came Back to Georgia" A 7/21/63

"Indians on the Rampage Dedicate Rossville House" J 5/30/63

"Everyone a Cherokee for Day as Rossville Honors its Chief" C 5/30/63

"Trail of Tears Paid for Land of Cherokees" A 9/3/61

"State Asks Indians Back Home" C 2/25/62

"Cherokees May Finally Get Justice" C 2/11/62

"Cherokees to Return to New Echota" C 5/6/62

"Trail of Tears Forgiven: Cherokee City Lives Anew" A 5/13/62

"Etowah Cherokees Dated to 600 A.D." C 11/26/59

"Ancient Indian Mound Found Near Toccoa" *Independent* 2/17/57

Bibliography

ADAIR, JAMES
    1930   *History of the American Indians*, edited by Samuel Cole Williams, Johnson City, Tennessee.

ALDER
    1761   Letter from Williams Fyffe to John Fyffe, dated February 1, "The 18th Century Cherokee Archives," 5 *American Archivist*, 240, 1942., Tulsa, Oklahoma, Gilcrease Institute.

ALLEN, PENELOPE J.
    1935   "History of the Cherokee Indians," manuscript, Knoxville, University of Tennessee and University of Tennessee Library.

ALLEY, FELIX E.
    1941   *Random Thoughts and the Musings of a Mountaineer*, Salisbury, North Carolina.

ALVORD, CLARENCE WALWORTH, AND LEE BIDGOOD
    1890a   "Cherokees Ball Play," *American Anthropologist*, Vol. III.
    1890b   "The Booger Bottom Mound: A Forsyth Period Site in Hall County, Georgia," *American Antiquity*, Vol. 17, No. 4, pp. 318-328.
    1912   *The First Explorations of the Trans-Allegheny Region by the Virginians, 1650-1671*, 81.

ANONYMOUS
    1762   "An Equiry into the Origin of the Cherokees in a Letter to a Member of Parliament," 20.

    1818   "Reflections on the Institutions of the Cherokee Indians," *The Analectic Magazine*, 36, 45, July.

ATKIN, EDMOND
    1967   *The Appalachian Indian Frontier*, edited by Wilbur R. Jacobs, Lincoln, University of Nebraska Press.

BALDWIN, J. D.
    1872   "Ancient America," *Notes on Ancient American Archeology*.

BARTON, BENJAMIN S.
    1798   *New Views on the Origin of the Tribes and Nations of America*, Philadelphia.

BARTRAM, WILLIAM
    1780   "Observations on the Creek and Cherokee Indians," *American Ethnological Society Transactions*, Vol. IV, Part 1, pp. 1-81, published 1853.
    1791   *Travels through North and South Carolina, Georgia, East and West Florida, the Cherokee Country, etc.*, Philadelphia. New edition Facsimile Library, Barnes & Noble, Inc., 1940.

BASS, ALTHEA
    1939   *Cherokee Messenger*, Norman, University of Oklahoma Press.

BAUER, FRED B.
    The Land of the North Carolina Cherokees.

BIRD, TRAVELLER
    1971   *Tell Them They Lie*, Los Angeles, Westernlore Publishers.

BJORKLUND, KARNA L.
    1969   *The Indians of Northeastern America*, New York, Dodd, Mead and Company.

BLACKBURN, GIDEON
    1807   Letter dated December 14, Maryville, Tennessee, as cited by Skelton, *A History of the Educational System of the Cherokee Nation, 1801-1910.*

BLOOM
    1942   "The Acculturation of the Eastern Cherokee: Historical Aspects," *North Carolina Historical Review*, Vol. 19, No. 323.

BROWN, JOHN P.
    1938   *Old Frontiers*, Kingsport, Tennessee, Southern Publishers, Inc.

BUSHELL, DAVID I.
    1919   "Native Villages and Village Sites East of the Mississippi," *Bureau of American Ethnology*, Report No. 69.

CALDWELL, JOSEPH R.
    1956   "Progress Report on Excavation at Tugalo River Surveys," *Bureau of American Ethnology*, Smithsonian Institution.
    N.d.   "Cherokee Pottery from Northern Georgia," *American Antiquity*, Vol. 20, No. 3, pp.277-280.
    N.d.   "Trend and Tradition in the Prehistory of the Eastern United States," *Memoirs of the American Anthropological Association*, No. 88.

CAMPBELL, O. B.
    1972   *Vinita, I. T.*, Oklahoma City, Metro Press, Inc.
    1973   *Mission to the Cherokees*, Oklahoma City, Metro Press, Inc.

CARR, LLOYD G.
    1947   "Native Drinks in the Southeast and their Values, with Special Emphasis on Persimmon Beer," *Proceedings of the Delaware County Institute of Science*, Vol. 10, pp. 29-43.

CARTER, SAMUEL III
    1976   *Cherokee Sunset*, Garden City, New York, Doubleday & Company.

CHEVES, LANGDON
    1894   "A Letter from Caroline in 1715 and Journal of the Carolinians into the Cherokee Mountains in the Yamasee Indian War, 1715-16," appendix to *Year Book, City of Charleston, S. C.*

CLARK, MARY WHATLEY
1971   *Chief Bowles and the Texas Cherokees*, Norman, University of Oklahoma Press.

COBLENTZ, CATHERINE C.
1946   *Sequoya*, New York, David McKay Company, Inc.

CORKRAN
1957   "Cherokee Pre-History," *North Carolina Historical Review*, Vol. 34, No. 455, pp. 458-459.

COTTERILL, ROBERT SPENCER
1954   *The Southern Indians: The Story of the Civilized Tribes Before Removal*, Norman, University of Oklahoma Press.

COVARRUBIAS, MIQUEL
1954   *The Eagle, the Jaguar, and the Serpent: Indian Art of the Americas*, New York.

CRANE, VERNER, W.
1964   *The Southern Frontier*, Ann Arbor, Univerity of Michigan Press.

CULIN, STEWART
1902-03   "American Indian Games," *Bureau of American Ethnology*, Report No. 24.

CUSHING, FRANK II
1894   "Primitive Copper Working," *American Anthropologist*, Vol. VII, pp. 93-117.

DALE, EDWARD EVERETT, AND GASTON LITTON
1939   *Cherokee Cavaliers*, Norman, University of Oklahoma Press.

DEBO, ANGIE
1972   *And Still the Waters Run*, Princeton University Press.

DICKENS, ROY S. JR.
1976   *Cherokee Prehistory*, Knoxville, University of Tennessee Press.

DOCKSTADER, FREDERICK J.
1957   *The American Indian in Graduate Studies: A Bibliography of Theses and Dissertations*, New York, Museum of the American Indian, Heye Foundation.

DOUGLAS F. H., ed.
1950   *Indian Culture Areas in the United States*, Denver Art Museum.

DUNNING, E. O.
1872   "Explorations in Tennessee," *Fifth Annual Report of the Trustees of the Peabody Museum of American Archaeology and Ethnology*, Boston, Harvard College, pp. 11-22.

EATON, RACHEL C.
1914   *John Ross and the Cherokee Indians*, Menasha, Wisconsin, George Banta Publishing Company.

EGGAN, FRED, ed.
1972   *Social Anthropology of North American Tribes*, University of Chicago Press.

EVANS, J. P.
N.d.   "Sketches of Cherokee Character, Customs and Manners," John Howard Payne Papers, Vol. 6, No. 202.

FENTON, W. N., AND LESTER HARGETT
1940   Interview with Will West Long, Cherokee, North Carolina, December 4-5.

FEWKES, VLADIMIR J.
1944   "Catawba Pottery-Making with Notes on Pamunkey Pottery-Making, Cherokee Pottery-Making and Coiling," *American Philosophical Society Proceedings*, Vol. 8, No. 2, pp. 69-124.

FIELD, THOMAS W.
1873   *An Essay Towards an Indian Bibliography Being a Catalogue of Books Relating to the History, Antiquities, Languages, Customs, Religion, Wars, Literature, and Origin of the American Indians*, New York, Scribner, Armstrong and Co. Republished by Gale Research Co., Detroit, 1967.

FORD, JAMES A.
N.d.   "Measurements of Some Prehistoric Design Developments in the Eastern United States," *Anthropological Papers of the American Museum of Natural History*.

FOREMAN, GRANT
1930   *Indian and Pioneers*, Yale University Press.
1934   *The Five Civilized Tribes*, Norman, University of Oklahoma Press.
1937   *Sequoyah*, Norman, University of Oklahoma Press.
1939   *Indian Removal*, Norman, University of Oklahoma Press.

FOREMAN, CAROLYN THOMAS
1948   *Park Hill*, Muskogee, Oklahoma.

FOSTER, GEORGE EVERETT
1885   *Sequoyah — A Complete Bibliography of the Greatest of Redmen*, Philadelphia Office of the Indian Rights Association, Tahlequah, Cherokee Nation.

FREEL, MARGARET WALKER
1956   *Our Heritage: The People of Cherokee County, North Carolina, 1540-1955*, Asheville, North Carolina, Miller Printing Company. Reprinted, *Andrews Journal*, Andrews, North Carolina, 1973.

FRIES, ADELAIDE L.
1941, 1942   *Records of the Moravians in North Carolina*, Vols. 5,6, North Carolina Historial Commission.

FROME, MICHAEL
1966   *Strangers in High Places*, Garden City, New York, Doubleday & Company.

FUNDABURK, EMMA LILA
1958   *Southeastern Indians: Life Portraits, A Catalogue of Pictures, 1564-1860*, Birmingham, Alabama, Birmingham Printing Company.

FUNDABURK, EMMA LILA , AND MARY DOUGLASS FOREMAN
1957 *Sun Circles and Human Hands*, Luverne, Alabama.

GABRIEL, RALPH HENRY
1941 *Elias Boudinot, Cherokee, and His America*, Norman, University of Oklahoma Press.

GEARING, FRED
1958 "The Structural Poses of the 18th Century Cherokee Villages," *American Anthropologist*, Vol. 60, 1148, 1149.
1962 *Priests and Warriors: Social Structures for Cherokee Politics in the 18th Century*, 85.

GILBERT, WILLIAM H.
1937 "Eastern Cherokee Social Organization," *Social Anthropology of North American Tribes*, Fred Eggan, ed., University of Chicago Press, (1970), pp. 285-338.

GILBERT, WILLIAM HARLEN JR.
1943 "The Eastern Cherokees," *Bureau of American Ethnology*, Bulletin 133, Anthropological Papers, No. 23, pp. 169-414.

GOVAN, GILBERT E., AND JAMES W. LIVINGOOD
1952 *The Chattanooga Country: 1540-1951*, New York, E. P. Dutton and Company, Inc.

GREGORY, JACK, AND RENNARD STRICKLAND
1967a *Sam Houston with the Cherokees, 1829-1833*, Austin and London, University of Texas Press.
1967b *Starr's History of the Cherokee Indian*, Indian Heritage Edition, Indian Heritage Association, Fayetteville, University of Arkansas.

GRIFFIN, J. B.
1935 "Aboriginal Methods of Pottery Manufacture in the Eastern United States," *Pennsylvania Archaeologist*, Vol. 5, pp. 19-24.

GROSSCUP, B. S., AND WILBUR G. SEIGLER
1883 *Heart of the Alleghenies*, Raleigh, North Carolina.

GULICK, JOHN
N.d. Cherokees at the Crossroads, Chapel Hill, North Carolina, Institute of Research in Social Science.

HALE, HORATIO
1883 "Indian Migrations as Evidenced by Language," *American Antiquities*, Vol. 5, pp. 18-28.

HARRINGTON, M. R.
1922 "Cherokee and Earlier Remains on Upper Tennessee River," *Indian Notes and Monographs*, 24, New York, Museum of the American Indian, Heye Foundation.

HAYWOOD, JOHN
1823 *Natural and Aboriginal History of Tennessee*, Nashville.

HERBERT, JOHN
1936 *Journal of Colonel John Herbert, Commissioner of Indian Affairs for the Province of South Carolina*, reprinted for the Historical Commission of South Carolina.

HEYE, GEORGE G., F. W. HODGE, AND GEORGE H. PEPPER
1918 "The Nacoochee Mound in Georgia," *Museum of the American Indian, Heye Foundation*, Vol. 4, No. 3.

HICKS, CHARLES R.
1826 Letters to John Ross, Fortville, February to July, originals in Ayer Collection, Newberry Library, Chicago, Illinois.

Hodge, F. W.
N.d. *Handbook of American Indians*, Vols. I and II, Bureau of American Ethnology, Bulletin 30.

HUDSON, CHARLES
1976 *The Southeastern Indians*, Knoxville, University of Tennessee Press.
N.d. *Four Centuries of Southern Indians*. Athens, University of Georgia.

HYDE, GEORGE E.
N.d. *Indians of the Woodlands from Prehistoric Times to 1725*.
N.d. *Indians of North Carolina*, U. S. Senate Document No. 677.

JACKSON, HELEN HUNT
1965 *Century of Dishonor*, New York, Evanston, and London, Harper and Row.

JAHODA, GLORIA
1975 *The Trail of Tears*, New York, Holt, Rinehart and Winston.

KEEL, BENNIE C.
1976 *Cherokee Archaeology*, Knoxville, University of Tennessee Press.

KILPATRICK, JACK FREDERICK
N.d. "The Wahnenauhi Manuscript: Historical Sketches of the Cherokees," *Bureau of American Ethnology*, Bulletin 196, Anthropological Papers, No. 77, pp. 175-211.

KILPATRICK, JACK FREDERICK, AND ANNA GRITTS KILPATRICK
1962 "Plains Indian Motifs in Contemporary Cherokee Culture," *Plains Anthropologist*, Vol. 7, No. 16, , pp. 136-137.
1964 "The Foundation of Life: The Cherokee Natural Ritual," *American Anthropologist*, Vol. 66, No. 6, Part I, pp. 1386-1391.
1964 *Friends of Thunder: Folktales of the Oklahoma Cherokees*, Dallas.
1965 *Walk in Your Soul*, Dallas, Southern Methodist University Press.
1966 "The Battle of Wa dho gi Mound, Eastern Cherokee Folktales," *American Bureau of Ethnology*, 196, pp. 434-435.
1967 *Run Toward the Nightland: Magic of the*

Oklahoma Cherokees, Dallas, Southern Methodist University Press.
N.d. "Eastern Cherokee Folktales: Reconstructed from the Field Notes of Frans M. Olbrechts," Smithsonian Institution, *Bureau of American Ethnology*, Bulletin 196, Anthropological Papers, No. 80.
N.d. *Shadow of Sequoyah: Social Documents of the Cherokees, 1862-1964*, Norman, University of Oklahoma Press.

KING, BLANCH BUSEY
1939 *Under Your Feet: The Story of the American Mound Builders*.

KNOWLES
1940 "The Torture of Captives by the Indians of Eastern North America," *Proceedings of the American Philosophical Society*, Vol. 82, No. 151, 177.

KUPFERER, HARRIET JANE
N.d. "The 'Principal People,' 1960: A Study of Cultural and Social Groups of the Eastern Cherokee," Smithsonian Institution, *Bureau of American Ethnology*, Bulletin 196.

LEFTWICH, RODNEY L.
1970 *Arts and Crafts of the Cherokee*, Cullowhee, North Carolina, Land-of-the-Sky Press.

LEWIS, THOMAS M. N.
1953 "The Paleo-Indian Problem in Tennessee," *Tennessee Archeologist*, Knoxville, Tennessee Archeological Society, Vol. 9, No. 2, pp. 38-40.

LEWIS, THOMAS M. N., AND MADELINE KNEBERG
1941 "The Prehistory of the Chicamauga Basin in Tennessee," *Tennessee Anthropology Papers*, No. 1, Knoxville.
1947 "The Archaic Horizon in Western Tennessee," *Tennessee Anthropology Papers*, No. 2, Knoxville, University of Tennessee Record Extension Series, Vol. 23, No. 4.
1954 *Ten Years of the Tennessee Archeologist*, Cattanooga, J. B. Graham.
1958 *Tribes That Slumber*, Knoxville, University of Tennessee Press.
1961 *Eva: An Archaic Site*, Knoxville, University of Tennessee Press.

LONGE, ALEXANDER
1698 "The Ways and Manners of the Nation of Indians Called Charikees," manuscripts 21-22, Tulsa, Oklahoma, Gilcrease Institute.

LURIE
1959 "Indian Cultural Adjustment to European Civilization," *17th Century America: Essays in Colonial History*, Vol. 33, No. 46, edited by James Morton Smith.

MacCURDY, GEORGE GRANT
N.d. "The Wesleyan University Collection of Antiquities from Tennessee," *International Congress of Americanists Proceedings*, Vol. 19, pp. 75-95.

MALONE, HENRY THOMPSON
1949 "Cherokee Civilizations in the Lower Appalachians, Especially in North Georgia Before 1830," unpublished master's thesis, Emory University.
1956 *Cherokees of the Old South: A People in Transition*, Athens, University of Georgia Press.

MALLERY, GARRICK
1886 "Pictographs of the North American Indians," *Bureau of American Ethnology Annual*, Report No. 4, pp. 3-256, 88 plates.

MASON, OTIS L.
1901-1902 "Aboriginal American Basketry," *Report of the U. S. National Museum for 1897*, pp. 171-548.

McCALL, WILLIAM ANDERSON
Cherokees and Pioneers, Asheville, North Carolina, Stephens Press, 1952.

McClary, Ben Harris, "Nancy Ward: The Last Beloved Woman of the Cherokees," *Tennessee Historical Quarterly*, December 1962, pp. 352-364.

McKENNEY, THOMAS L., AND JAMES HALL
1933 *The Indian Tribes of North America with Biographical Sketches and Anecdotes of the Principal Chiefs*. New edition edited by Frederick Webb Hodge, Edinburgh, John Grant.

MENZIES, DAVID
1761 "A True Relation of the Unheard-of Sufferings of David Menzies, Surgeon Among the Cherokees," *The Royal Magazine*, July, pp. 27-28.

MILLER, CARL F.
N.d. "Early Cultural Horizons in the Southeastern United States," *American Antiquity*, Vol. 15, pp. 273-288.

MILLING, CHAPMAN J.
1940 *Red Carolinians*, Chapel Hill, University of North Carolina Press.

MOONEY, JAMES
1891 "Sacred Formulas of the Cherokees," *Bureau of American Ethnology*, Seventh Annual Report.
1900a "Myths of the Cherokee," *Bureau of American Ethnology*, 19th Annual Report.
1900b "The Cherokee River Cult," *American Folklore*, 1, 3.

MOONEY, JAMES, AND FRANS M. OLBRECHTS
N.d. "The Swimmer Manuscript: Cherokee Sacred Formulas and Medicinal Prescriptions," *Bureau of American Ethnology*, Bulletin 99.

MOORE, CLARENCE B.
1915 "Aboriginal Sites on Tennessee River," *Journal of the Academy of Natural Sciences of Philadelphia*, Vol. 16, Part 3, pp. 431-487.

MOOREHEAD, WARREN K.
1917 *Stone Ornaments of the American Indians*, Andover, Massacusetts, Andover Press.

NEELY, CHARLOTTE
1970 *Acculturation and Persistence among North Carolina's Eastern Band of Cherokee Indians, Southeastern Indians Since the Removal Era*, edited by Walter L. Williams, Athens, University of Georgia Press.

PARKER, THOMAS VALENTINE
1907 *The Cherokee Indians*, New York, Grafton Press.

PAYNE, JOHN HOWARD
N.d. Papers, fourteen volumes of manuscripts, Newberry Library, Chicago, Ayer MS 689 (Vols. 1, 3, 4, and 6 deal with ethnology).

PERDUE, THEDA
1979 *Slavery and the Evolution of Cherokee Society, 1540-1866*, Knoxville, University of Tennessee Press.

PRIEGER, H. W.
1929 "American Indian Costumes in the U. S. National Museum," *Annual Report of the Smithsonian Institute for 1928*, pp. 623-61.

PUTNAM, FREDERICK W.
N.d. "Archeological Explorations in Tennessee," *11th Annual Report of the Trustees of the Peabody Museum of American Archeology and Ethnology*, Cambridge, Vol. 2, No. 2, pp. 305-360.

REID, JOHN PHILLIP
1970 *The Law of Blood*, New York University Press.

RICKARD, T. A.
1934 "The Use of Native Copper by the Indigenes of North America," *Journal of the Royal Anthropological Institute of Great Britian and Ireland*, Vol. 64, pp. 265-287.

RIGHTS, DOUGLAS
1950 *Indian in North Carolina*, Durham, Duke University Press.

ROTHROCK, MARY V.
1929 "Carolina Traders Among the Overhill Cherokees," *Eastern Tennessee Historical Society Publications*, No. 1, pp. 3-18.

SCHOOLCRAFT, HENRY R., L.L.D.
1852 *History, Conditions and Prospects of the Indian Tribes of the United States*, collected and prepared under the direction of the Bureau of Indian Affairs, Philadelphia, Lippincott, Grambo and Co., six parts.

SCHWAZE, EDMUND
1923 *History of the Moravian Missions Among Southern Indian Tribes of the United States*, Bethlehem, Pennsylvania, Times Publishing Company, Moravian Historical Society Transactions, Special Series, Vol. 1.

SEARS, WILLIAM
1955 *Creek and Cherokee Culture in the 16th Century*.

N.d. "Ceramic Development in the South Appalachian Province," *American Antiquity*, Vol. 18, pp. 101-109.
N.d. "Prehistoric Pottery of the Eastern United States," *Tennessee Anthropological Papers*, No. 1.

SEEVER, W. J.
1897 "A Cache of Idols and Chipped Flint Instruments in Tennessee," *Antiquarian*, Vol. 1, No. 6, pp. 142-143.

SETZLER, FRANK M., AND JESSE D. JENNINGS
1941 "Peachtree Mound and Village Site, Cherokee County, North Carolina," *Bureau of American Ethnology*, Bulletin No. 131, pp. 4-57.

SKELTON, ROBERT H.
1970 "A History of the Educational System of the Cherokee Nation, 1801-1910," doctor of education thesis, University of Arkansas.

SMITH, DE COST
1949 *Red Indian Experiences*, London, George Allen and Unwin Ltd.

SMITH, W. R. L.
1928 *The Story of the Cherokees*, Cleveland, Tennessee, Church of God Publishing House.

SPECK, FRANK GOULDSMITH
1920 "Decorative Art and Basketry of the Cherokee," Public Museum of the City of Milwaukee, Vol. 2, No. 2, pp. 53-86.
1950 "Concerning Iconology and the Masking Complex in Eastern North America," *University of Pennsylvania Bulletin*, Vol. 15.
1965 *The Iroquois*, Bloomfield Hills, Michigan, Cranbrook Institute of Science.

SPECK, FRANK GOULDSMITH, AND L. BROOM
1950 *Cherokee Dance and Drama*.

SPENCE
1922 "Cherokees," *Encyclopedia of Religion and Ethics*, No. 3, 502.

SPOERHR, ALEXANDER
1947 "Changing Kinship Systems: A Study in the Acculturation of the Creeks, Cherokee and Choctaw," 202, *Anthropological Series: Field Museum of Natural History*, Pub. 583, Vol. 33, No. 4.

STARKEY, MARION
1946 *The Cherokee Nation*, New York, Alfred A. Knopf.

STARR, EMMETT
1921 *History of the Cherokee Nation*, Oklahoma City, the Warden Company.

STEELE, PHILLIP
1974 *The Last Cherokee Warriors*, Pelican Publishing Company, Gretna.

STEWARD, JULIAN H.
1936 "Petroglyphs of the United States," *Smithsonian Institute Annual Report*, pp. 405-426.

SWANTON, JOHN R.
1946 "Indians of Southeastern United States," *Bureau of American Ethnology*, Bulletin 137.
1952 "The Indian Tribes of North America," *Bureau of American Ethnology*, Bulletin 145.

THOMAS, ROBERT K.
1954 "The Origin and Development of the Redbird Smith Movement," master of arts thesis, Tucscon, University of Arizona.

THOBURN, JOSEPH B.
1938 Pamphlet, March, "The Tropical and Subtropical Origin of Mound Builders Culture," *The Chronicles of Oklahoma*, Vol. 16, Series 1, No. 97.

THRUSTON, GATES P.
1892 *The Antiquities of Tennessee and of Adjacent Areas*, Cincinnati, Robert Clark and Company, and "New Discoveries in Tennessee," *American Antiquarian and Oriental Journal*, 14, Chicago.
1898 "Ancient Stone Images in Tennessee," *The American Archeologist*, Vol. 2, No. 9, pp. 225-227.

TIMBERLAKE, LIEUTENANT HENRY
1927 *Memoirs, 1756-1765*, edited by Samuel Cole Williams, L. L. D., Johnson City, Tennessee, Watauga Press.

TOOKER, W. W.
1898 "Paper on the Rechahecrian Indians of Early Colonial Virginia."

TYNER, HOWARD Q.
1949 "The Keetoowah Society in Cherokee History," master of arts thesis, the University of Tulsa.

UNDERWOOD, TOM
N.d. *Legends of the Cherokees*. (Possibly printed by the Cherokee Press, Cherokee, North Carolina).

VAN DOREN, MARK, ed.
N.d. *List of the Towns and Villages in the Cherokee Nation Inhabited at This Date: Travels of William Bartram*, New York, Dover Publications.

WAHNENAUHI, LUCY
N.d. "Historical Sketches of the Cherokees," edited by Jack Frederick Kilpatrick, *Bureau of American Ethnology*, Bulletin 196.

WAHRHAFTIG, ALBERT L.
1970 "Social and Economic Characteristics of the Cherokee Population of Eastern Oklahoma, 1964-65," *Anthropological Studies*, Ward H. Goodenough, editor, Washington, D. C., American Anthropological Association.

WALKER, ROBERT SPARKS
1931 *Torchlight to the Cherokees*, New York, Macmillan and Company.

WARING, ANTONIO J. JR., AND PRESTON HOLDER
1945 "A Prehistoric Ceremonial Complex in the Southeast," *U. S. American Anthropologist*, American Anthropological Association, Menasha and Beloit, vol. 47, No. 1, pp. 1-34.

WASHBURN, CEPHAS
1955 *Reminiscences of the Indians*, edited by Hugh Park, Van Buren, Arkansas, the Press Argus.

WAUCHOPE, ROBERT
1948 "Ceramic Sequence," *American Antiquity*, Vol. 12, No. 3.

WELLMAN, PAUL I.
1959 *Indian Wars and Warriors: East*, Boston, Houghton Mifflin Company.

WEBB
1936 "The Prehistory of Eastern Tennessee," 8, *Eastern Tennessee Historical Society*, Pub. 3, pp. 6-7.

WEST, GEORGIA A.
1934 "Tobacco Pipes and Smoking Customs of the American Indians," *Milwaukee Public Museum Bulletin*, Vol. 17, No. 17.

WICKE, CHARLES R.
1965 "Pyramids and Temple Mounds," *American Antiquity*, Vol. 30, No. 4, April.

WILKINS, THURMA
1970 *Cherokee Tragedy*, London, the Macmillan Company, Collier Macmillan Ltd.

WILLIAMS, SAMUEL C.
1937 *Dawn of Tennessee Valley and Tennessee History*, Johnson City, Tennessee, Watauga Press.

WILLIAMS, STEPHEN
N.d. "An Outline of Southeastern U. S. Prehistory with Particular Emphasis on the Paleo-Indian Era," *The Quaternary of the United States*, 6, H. E. Wright and David G. Grey, editors, Princeton, pp. 69-83.

WINN, BILL
1968 *The First Georgians*, from series of articles published in the *Atlanta Journal*, April.

WITTHOFT, JOHN
1946 "The Cherokee Green Corn Medicine and the Green Corn Festival," *Journal of the Washington Academy of Sciences*, Vol. 36, No. 7, July 15, pp. 213-219.
1949 "Stone Pipes of the Historic Cherokees," *Southern Indian Studies*, Vol. 1, No. 2 (1952), Chapel Hill, University of North Carolina, pp. 43-62.

WOODWARD, GRACE STEELE
1963 *The Cherokees*, Norman, University of Oklahoma Press.

WRIGHT, MURIEL H.
1951 *A Guide to the Indian Tribes of Oklahoma*, Norman, University of Oklahoma Press.

Index

Index of Illustrations